The Stuart Age

A History of England in eleven volumes

General Editor: W. N. Medlicott

The Stuart Age

A history of England 1603–1714

Barry Coward

Longman
London and New York

Longman Group UK Limited
Longman House, Burnt Mill, Harlow
Essex CM20 2JE, England
and Associated Companies throughout the world.

*Published in the United States of America
by Longman Inc., New York*

First published 1980
. *Ninth impression 1990*

British Library Cataloguing in Publication Data

Coward, Barry
    The Stuart Age. – (A history of England)
    1. Great Britain – History – Stuarts,
    1603–1714
    I. Title   II. Series
    942.06   DA375   79–42887

ISBN 0-582-48833-8

Printed in Malaysia
by Vinlin Press Sdn. Bhd.,
Sri Petaling, Kuala Lumpur

Introductory note

One of the effects of two world wars and of fifty years of ever-accelerating industrial and social revolution has been the growing interest of the citizen in the story of his land. From this story he seeks to learn the secret of his country's greatness and a way to better living in the future.

There seems, therefore, to be room for a rewriting of the history of England which will hold the interest of the general reader while it appeals at the same time to the student. This new presentation takes account of the recent discoveries of the archaeologist and the historian, without losing sight of the claims of history to take its place among the mental recreations of intelligent people for whom it has no professional concern.

The history will be completed in a series of eleven volumes. The volumes are of medium length, and are intended to provide a readable narrative of the whole course of the history of England and give proper weight to the different strands which form the pattern of the story. No attempt has been made to secure general uniformity of style or treatment. Each period has its special problems, each author his individual technique and mental approach; each volume is meant to stand by itself not only as an expression of the author's methods, tastes, and experience, but as a coherent picture of a phase in the history of the country.

There is, nevertheless, a unity of purpose in the series; the authors have been asked, while avoiding excessive detail, to give particular attention to the interaction of the various aspects of national life and achievement, so that each volume may present a convincing integration of those developments – political, constitutional, economic, social, religious, military, foreign, or cultural – which happen to be dominant at each period. Although considerations of space prevent minute investigation it should still be possible in a series of this length to deal fully with the essential themes.

A short bibliographical note is attached to each volume. This is not intended to supersede existing lists, but rather to call attention to recent works and to the standard bibliographies.

W. N. Medlicott

Contents

Maps and diagrams

Preface

The structure of this book is simple: it begins and ends with analytical sections on early and later Stuart England respectively, and has four narrative sections in the middle. Throughout I have tried to ensure that the detailed story of events does not overwhelm the themes and problems which I discuss. English history during the reigns of the Stuarts is (and always has been) the subject of intense controversy among historians. Therefore there is a need for a guide to those views of this period which some historians now consider to be invalid and to those which have replaced them. I make no claim that the interpretations I have suggested here are the ones accepted by most historians or even that they are the 'correct' interpretations. It cannot be emphasized too many times that there are few 'correct' interpretations in the study of history. In reaching conclusions about the past historians rely on primary sources for evidence. One of the first things that students of history ought to learn is that there are many questions to which historical evidence simply does not provide clear cut answers. Many historians may use the same primary sources but reach different conclusions about the past.

I have also tried to see the Stuart age as a whole, something which not all historians attempt to do. The year 1660 is a popular date at which many historians either end or begin their periods of study. The list of historians who have written on the history of the period before 1660 differs markedly from that of authorities on the later period. In writing this book I have had to wrench myself free from that tradition and to try to cut through the artificial, unnecessary barrier which has been erected in the middle of the seventeenth century. In doing so my knowledge and view of the whole period from 1603 to 1714 have vastly changed and improved. I hope that this book will have a similar effect on others.

My main regret is that I have not had time or space to include more about the history of Ireland, Scotland and Wales, other than when events in those countries had an important impact on the course of English history. This is not the result of any misplaced English nationalism. This book is part of a History of England series, and those Irish, Scottish and Welsh people whose national sensibilities are offended will, I am afraid, have to be content with that justification for what otherwise might seem a display of blinkered Anglocentric history.

Finally, I would like to record my thanks to all those who have helped me to write this book, including those historians whose books and articles I have plundered. I hope I have fully acknowledged my debt to them in the footnotes to the book. I am deeply grateful to Mr Anthony Fletcher, Mr Graham Gibbs, Professor K. H. D. Haley, Dr Ian Roy and Mr Conrad Russell, who read drafts of various sections of the book. They, and Professor W. N. Medlicott who read the typescript of the whole book, have prevented me from making countless terrible blunders. For those that doubtless remain I am of course solely responsible. My greatest debt is to my children and, above all, to my wife. Without Anthony, Nicholas, and Lynne's distractions I might have produced the book sooner, but I would have been a far less happy person than I am. Without Shirley's encouragement the book would never have been completed. She not only typed all the drafts, coping with my shocking handwriting, but she and the children had to put up with my bouts of (I hope uncharacteristic) grumpiness as I struggled to find a way through the controversial history of Stuart England.

B.C.
August 1979

Acknowledgements

We are grateful to the following for permission to reproduce copyright material: The Economic History Society for data of the output of iron, 1550–1650 from the article by G. Hammersley in *Economic History Review* 2nd Series XXVI 1973; Macmillan & Co. Ltd., London and Basingstoke for a table of figures p. 10 from *Inflation in Tudor and Early Stuart England* by R. B. Outhwaite; Oxford University Press for extracts and a table by Gregory King from *Seventeenth Century Economic Documents* edited by J. Thirsk and J. P. Cooper, and extracts and a table of figures from *English Public Revenue 1660–1688* by C. D. Chandaman.

Abbreviations and short titles

The following abbreviations have been used in the notes:

Agric. H. R.	*Agricultural History Review*
American H. R.	*American Historical Review*
B.I.H.R.	*Bulletin of the Institute of Historical Research*
E.H.R.	*English Historical Review*
Econ. H.R.	*Economic History Review*
H.J.	*Historical Journal*
H.M.C.	*Historical Manuscripts Commission Reports*
J. Eccl. H.	*Journal of Ecclesiastical History*
J.M.H.	*Journal of Modern History*
P. & P.	*Past and Present*
T.R.H.S.	*Transactions of the Royal Historical Society*

In each of the five Parts the first time reference is made to a book or article the title is given in full in the first chapter, thereafter a shortened title is used. For books which are frequently cited I have used the following abbreviated titles:

Clarendon, *History*
W. D. Macray, ed., *The History of the Rebellion and Civil Wars in England* (6 vols. 1888)
Gardiner, *History*
S. R. Gardiner, *History of England from the Accession of James 1 to the Outbreak of the Civil War 1603–1642* (1883)
Kenyon, *Stuart Constitution*
J. P. Kenyon, ed., *The Stuart Constitution: Documents and Commentary* (1966)
Tanner, *Constitutional Documents*
J. R. Tanner, ed., *Constitutional Documents of the Reign of James I 1603–1625* (1960)
Thirsk and Cooper
J. Thirsk and J. P. Cooper, eds., *Seventeenth-Century Economic Documents* (1972)

Part one

Early Stuart England, 1603–1640

This book is largely concerned with political-constitutional and religious-ecclesiastical developments in Stuart England. Throughout, though, I have been anxious not to segregate these from their wider social, economic, and intellectual context. It is not always easy, however, to integrate the separate branches into which the study of history has become fragmented. There are several reasons for this. The divorce between economic history and political history is institutionalized in distinct historical journals, examination papers, and even in some cases, regrettably, in independent university departments of history and economic history. An even greater gulf separates the history of ideas and other branches of history; few historians have attempted to bridge it, and hardly any have succeeded. As will be seen, neither the 'scientific revolution' of this period nor the Protestant Reformation has been proved to be a major engine of political change in Stuart England. Nor have the more numerous attempts to marry social history and political history been any more productive. Historians seeking to explain England's political crisis of the mid-seventeenth century in terms of the social changes that were taking place in the century before 1640 have failed as totally as did sixteenth- and seventeenth-century alchemists in their search for the philosopher's stone.

These failures ought not to deter attempts to bring together different branches of history. As Dr Peter Thomas has recently reminded historians, 'art and politics, literature and history, do not exist in separate compartments of the mind'.[1] This is most forcibly illustrated in early seventeenth-century England by the development of a court culture under the patronage of Charles I, which most articulate English people found alien and abhorrent, and which is inextricably interwoven into the process by which the crown in the 1630s became politically isolated from the majority of its subjects. Nor can it be denied that there was an often close connection between economic and political developments in early Stuart England. The fortunes of England's major industry, the manufacture of woollen cloth, cannot be explained solely by the impact on it of political changes. However, the ending of the long war with Spain in 1604 contributed to the temporary boom in cloth exports in the early years of the reign of James I, while the Cockayne Project of 1614–17, which was essentially a product of the political world of the Jacobean court, was a severe blow to the cloth industry and trade. Economic developments generally in the early seventeenth century make little sense without a consideration of the impact of government intervention. The early Stuart state both indirectly, through its expenditure on armaments and dockyards, and directly, in its attempts to intervene in economic affairs, played a major role in influencing economic development, though not always in the direction it intended. Conversely many aspects of early Stuart politics are inexplicable without a knowledge of economic developments. One major feature of economic life, the rise in prices, contributed both to the financial problems of James I and Charles I, which seriously weakened their political position, and to the creation of an expanding country electorate as inflation brought more people into the ranks of the 40 shilling freeholders. One of the best examples in the early seventeenth century of the way economic and political developments combined is the case of industrial and commercial patents of monopoly issued by both early Stuart kings, which became a major source of political contention in every parliament from 1597 to 1640.

It is hoped that these and other connections between political, religious, economic, social, and intellectual developments will become clear in the narrative sections of the book. The aim of this first section is to analyse separately some of the major characteristics of the economy, society, Church, and government of early Stuart England.

Chapter 1
The economy of early Stuart England

The population and the economy

In approaching the pre-industrial economy of seventeenth-century England it is tempting to follow the lead of some economists who regard it as being very similar to the economies of presentday developing countries in the Third World, in Africa, Asia, and Latin America. If it could be demonstrated that the economy of seventeenth-century England was 'underdeveloped', then it would be possible to use this historical example as a case study from which to draw conclusions to aid a better understanding of the process of economic change in modern developing countries. After a superficial glance at the economy of Stuart England such a comparison seems possible. There are striking similarities between it and some presentday underdeveloped economies. All are predominantly based on agriculture, chronically unstable, and extremely vulnerable to short-term disasters, such as a wet summer and a consequent bad harvest or an outbreak of plague. Professor W. G. Hoskins has demonstrated the large extent to which the stability of the economy of pre-industrial England depended on good harvests. One bad harvest could dislocate the whole economy, especially since even the non-agricultural sectors of it were very dependent on agriculture. As Professor Hoskins has shown, bad harvests were a familiar feature of life in pre-industrial England. He calculated that from 1480 to 1759 25 per cent of the harvests were deficient and over 16 per cent very bad. The late sixteenth and early seventeenth centuries had an even worse record than that, since in those years bad harvests were bunched together, in the 1590s, the early 1620s, the 1630s and the later 1640s.[2] Not surprisingly people in the early seventeenth century, even when judged by the standards of England's presentday reputation as a weather-conscious nation, were preoccupied with the weather to the point of obsession. The diary of Ralph Josselin, the vicar of Earl's Colne in Essex in the middle of the seventeenth century, bristles with weather notes. 'Among all the several judgements on this nation', he wrote in May 1648, 'God this spring, in the latter end of April, when rye was earing and eared, sent such terrible frosts that the ear was frozen and so died.' A month later he recorded, 'The Lord goeth out against us in the season, which was wonderful wet, floods every week, hay rotted abroad. Much was carried away with the floods, much inned but very dirty and dangerous for cattle. Corn laid, pulled down with weeds. We never had the like in my memory, and that for the greatest part of the summer.'[3] Such comments were ominous for the economy of England and for the standard of living of most of its inhabitants.

As in many Third World countries underemployment was also a feature of the early seventeenth-century economy.[4] By its very nature changes in the weather and seasons ensure that agricultural employment is not constant throughout the year. In underdeveloped countries the dependence on good weather and the possibility of long periods of enforced inactivity is increased by the lack of agricultural machinery. In seventeenth-century England domestic part-time employment, in textile manufacturing or wood crafts, compensated to a certain extent for underemployment on the land. But often such by-employment was irregular and there was no certainty that it could be fitted into the pattern of agricultural employment. There are also many demographic similarities between pre-industrial England and Third World countries. The age structure of England's population in the 1690s (based on the statistics of Gregory King) was about the same as that of India in 1951; just over 38 per cent of the population was under fifteen years, in contrast to the relatively old populations of modern industrialized nations (only about 24 per cent of the population of the United Kingdom today is under fifteen years). Similarly the average expectation of life at birth in seventeenth-century England, which has been estimated to be about thirty-two years, is vastly different from presentday figures (sixty-nine for men and seventy-five years for women). These demographic features inevitably helped to lower the productive capacity of the seventeenth-century English economy. Quite simply, the majority of England's population was too young or too old to work as efficiently as mature adults.

Unfortunately, though, for those who want to make the study of history 'relevant' to presentday problems, it is difficult to sustain a comparison between the English economy in the seventeenth century and modern underdeveloped economies. It is likely that there are as many differences as similarities between them. Not only are there the obvious contrasts, like the vastly different speed of changes that are possible in modern underdeveloped economies using technical 'know-how' and cash (limited though it may be) from developed nations, but the social and economic structure of early modern England also differs in several less obvious ways from that in many modern underdeveloped countries. For example, the former never saw the development of the extended family so common in Third World countries. Instead the nuclear family, consisting only of parents and unmarried children, was a common feature of seventeenth-century England. When a son married he set up his own separate household. Since, as a result, households in this period were small (an average of four–five people), so too was the typical economic unit, the family farm or workshop, the family workforce being supplemented only by a few living-in apprentices, labourers or servants. Though small, the nuclear family is much more likely to produce more than it needs for its own subsistence.

Whatever the social benefits of the extended family, it tends to prevent the accumulation of surpluses for the market and inhibits the accumulation of capital since all the family's resources go on supporting an army of relations, many of whom contribute nothing to production. The restricted family was able to produce marketable surpluses.[5]

This accords well with a major feature of the English pre-industrial economy that differs markedly from those in the Third World. Unlike the latter, the English economy of earlier periods was not predominantly a subsistence one. Undoubtedly there must have been many people in seventeenth-century England who produced only enough to feed and clothe themselves (and those who fell short even of doing this), but many sectors of the contemporary economy were organized for production for the market, as they had been since at least the thirteenth century.

Moreover, when one stops looking for modern comparisons and begins to look at the seventeenth-century economy in its proper historical context, one finds that in comparison with other contemporary European economies it was not outstandingly backward. Indeed in comparison with the Scottish economy England's was rich and buoyant. Contemporary glowing accounts of the English economy are not just those written by blinkered, patriotic Englishmen. In England, wrote Paul Hentzner, a visitor from Brandenburg in 1598,

the soil is fruitful and abounds with cattle, which inclines the inhabitants rather to feeding than ploughing, so that near a third part of the land is left uncultivated for grazing. . . . There are many hills without one tree or any spring, which produce a very short and tender grass, and supply plenty of food to sheep, upon these wander numerous flocks extremely white, and whether from the temperature of the air or goodness of the earth, bearing softer and finer fleeces than any other country.[6]

However, in shifting the standpoint away from the model of 'underdevelopment', one is in danger of presenting too optimistic a generalized description of the seventeenth-century English economy. The emphasis on its predominant non-subsistence sectors and its high contemporary reputation is a useful corrective to the stress on its instability, its inbuilt high level of underemployment, and its low productivity. Yet in the last resort conclusions about the performance of the early seventeenth-century English economy depend on the extent to which it coped successfully with the rapid population expansion which had been under way since the early sixteenth century and which came to an end around the middle of the seventeenth.

Despite the massive amount of human and financial resources that have recently been poured into demographic history only a few definitive conclusions have emerged about the population of early modern England. This is largely because of the nature of the primary sources available for this purpose. Parish registers, the most important source, do not survive in England in sufficiently large numbers and are not as comprehensive as those in France where demographic studies have been much more fruitful (see below p. 36). Historical demographers are on firmer ground in explaining short-term fluctuations in English population levels – in terms of bad harvests and delayed marriages, outbreaks of famine and disease – than in explaining long-term changes. Was the long rise in the population of England from the early sixteenth century to the mid-seventeenth caused by the fact that after the Black Death of 1348–9 plague became an urban phenomenon and therefore was no longer a major threat to a predominantly rural population? Was it caused by women marrying at a younger age than in the later seventeenth century when the population level remained stable? Despite these and other uncertainties the broad demographic pattern is fairly well established, though the total figures are no more than well-informed guesses. It is generally considered that the population of England and Wales rose from about 2.5 million in the 1520s to over 3 million in 1545, about 4 million by 1603 and just over 5 million in 1650.

Such a rise, which was especially rapid in the later sixteenth and early seventeenth centuries, made possible alternative economic consequences. On the one hand it presented the potential for economic growth. A growing population could be the source of more and cheaper labour, as well as the basis of an expanding market. On the other hand it could pose serious problems of economic adjustment. Was the English economy capable of both absorbing a large additional supply of labour and feeding a growing population?

Agriculture and inland trade

It has become commonplace to begin descriptions of the English economy of this period by emphasizing that it was predominantly agrarian. This generalization is undeniably true, but it does obscure the variety of the English economic and social scene. A famous occupational census of Gloucestershire in 1608, discovered by R. H. Tawney, makes clear that only half that county's population was directly employed in farming; the rest were engaged in other occupations, the manufacture of cloth and leather goods, and the processing of food and drink.[7] One in seven of the Shropshire community of Myddle in the mid-seventeenth century were craftsmen.[8] It has to be admitted, though, that occupational classifications in this period are notoriously difficult, largely because craftsmen might also be part-time farmers, as were some of the craftsmen in Myddle, and it was very common for farmers to engage in part-time industrial employment. Most crafts in pre-industrial England were dependant on agriculture both for labour and for raw materials (cloth-making for wool, leather crafts for hides, brewing for barley, and so on). Even if not all English people were directly engaged in agriculture, there is no denying that it was the most important sector of the economy. It is therefore crucial to an assessment of the performance of that economy to consider how well English agriculture responded to the challenge posed by a population which more than doubled in the century and a half before 1650.

Not least of the difficulties in answering that question is the great diversity of English farming in this period which has been revealed by recent work on the local farming regions of England.[9] Consequently, one is faced with a series of different regional reactions to the challenge of a rising population, if only because some areas were less able than others to adapt farming methods to new circumstances. It proved, for example, much easier to convert the lighter soil regions of eastern England to mixed animal–arable husbandry than it did the heavy Midland clay vales where the options open to farmers were much more limited. Yet the fact that English agriculture in this period was so diverse was not due solely to differences in prevailing soil and climatic conditions; it also testifies to the willingness of some English farmers to attempt to improve their farming methods and to specialize in the production of certain commodities. The rapidly emerging picture of increasing regional specialization by English agriculture in the sixteenth and early seventeenth centuries ought to displace commonly held assumptions about the subsistence and conservative nature of farming in this period. It is, of course, difficult to know how typical were the innovating farmers who responded to the climate of rising prices and demand for food. In one respect Robert Loder was not a typical early seventeenth-century farmer in that he left a diary of his farming activities in Berkshire, which is one of the most important primary sources for English agrarian history of this period. But perhaps his willingness to consider alternative crops and methods was not untypical. Loder concluded his farming accounts for 1611 with the following observation:

Memorandum that the wheat lands being xxxvj (as abovesaid) bore me xx qtrs. vij b(ushels) i p(eck); and the lxxv barley lands xlvj qtrs. iij b. ij p.(being let to halves), so that the barley lands did not bear so much upon a land one with another as the wheat by about vj qtrs.; and yet the wheat was worth xxxs. the quarter; and the barley but xxiij s. the quarter (as afore is said) wherefore here is to (be) seen great reason for sowing more wheat and less barley.[10]

Dr Thirsk, using the example of the adoption of tobacco as a field crop in many areas of England in the early seventeenth century, rightly concludes 'how adventurous English farmers could be once they had been persuaded of the success of a new farm enterprise'.[11]

The impression of innovation and of the growing commercialization of English agriculture in the late sixteenth and early seventeenth centuries is supported by what is known about the development of the

London food market, provincial market towns, and the expansion of inland trade before 1650. Professor F. J. Fisher long ago described the development of sophisticated marketing facilities for food in London which served the needs of farmers as far afield as Durham, as well as, more obviously, those in the home counties.[12] More recently Professor Alan Everitt has identified about 800 market towns in England and Wales in the reign of Charles I, of which over 300 specialized in the marketing of one commodity. He has also shown the growing importance in the period before 1640 of private marketing, conducted outside the open markets, often in inns and alehouses.[13] All this presupposes the existence of considerable inter-regional trade, as well as of trade between London and the provinces, which until recently has escaped the attention of historians who have been preoccupied with England's overseas trade.

Paradoxically, one of the factors which facilitated the growth of internal trade in England, namely its lack of tolls and customs, has prevented the historian from knowing much about it; there are few official records of the activities of merchants trading within England. Recently, however, historians have rediscovered the network of inland trades in grain, cattle, wool, and dairy products that existed in late sixteenth and early seventeenth-century England. Coastal routes and improved navigable rivers were the most important arteries of these trades, but road transport was not perhaps as poor as it has often been described. It is true that a major breakthrough in road transport did not come until the turnpike revolution and the improvements in road construction associated with Telford and Macadam in the eighteenth century. But earlier progress in methods of transport – the introduction of the stagecoach in the late sixteenth century, the long wheelbase wagon in 1564, and the swivelling front axle – do presuppose some improvements in the conditions of roads at the same time. Perhaps the picture of universally poor roads in seventeenth-century England is another aspect of this period that is about to be shown to be a myth.[14]

Whether or not this is the case, there is enough evidence to suggest that English farmers before 1650 were not insulated from market forces. This ensured that the agricultural textbooks which appeared in this period, urging the adoption of new crops and farming methods, were not written in vain. It would obviously be unwise to credit any textbook with too much influence. In the case of agricultural treatises in this period it is impossible to know how widely they were read, let alone whether they influenced farmers. Some treatises, though, did go through many (if limited) editions, like Walter Blith's *English Improver* (1649) which appeared three years later as *The English Improver Improved*. Moreover, some had clearly learned popularization techniques which have been rediscovered by the modern advertising industry. Thomas Tusser's *Hundred Good Points of Husbandry* (later *Five Hundred Good Points*) reads like the prototype for presentday television commercial jingles:[15]

All these doo enclosure bring,
Experience teacheth no lesse,
I speake not to boast of the thing,
But onely a troth to expresse.
Example (if doubt ye doo make):
By Suffolke and Essex go take.
More plentie of mutton and biefe,
Corn, butter, and cheese of the best,
More wealth any where (to be briefe)
More people, more handsome and prest,
Where find ye (go search any coast)
Than there, where enclosure is most?'

The textbooks, though, did also contain serious information. Their most important function was to serve as a link between English farmers and the more advanced farming methods of the Low Countries. As will be seen, most of the farming innovations of this period originated there, and the agricultural writers undoubtedly contributed to their diffusion in England.

There is little doubt that under the combined pressure of a rising population, the development of food markets and the example of the Low Countries, English farming made rapid strides forward before 1650 by adopting new crops and techniques and by extending the area under cultivation. The first development that automatically springs to mind as an example of agricultural progress is the enclosure of the allegedly inefficient medieval/open fields. Since the days of Lord Ernle, H. L. Gray, and R. H. Tawney, who wrote at the beginning of this century, the historiography of English agrarian history has been dominated by enclosures.[16] One wonders, however, if all this attention has been warranted. Certainly in the process many myths have developed round the subject. Judging by contemporary anti-enclosure literature one might think that enclosure was a new phenomenon from the mid-sixteenth century onwards, and that it was accompanied inevitably by depopulation as inefficient labour-intensive arable farms were converted into efficient labour-saving sheep and cattle estates. But enclosure has a long and continuous history; the most concentrated period of enclosures before the later eighteenth century was the later fifteenth century as wool prices in England soared. Nor was most enclosure carried out by landlords at the expense of their tenants; enclosure agreements were often made between landlords and tenants, and in the early seventeenth century such agreements were registered in chancery. There is no denying that the traditional picture of enclosures contains elements of truth. Enclosure could have the beneficial results trumpeted by people like Tusser. It could cause tremendous social distress: the enclosure of arable land for pasture farming in Leicestershire sparked off a popular uprising in 1607, the Midland Revolt, and in the early 1640s newly erected fences were torn down in many places.[17] But how much enclosure had taken place by 1650 is an open question; Dr Eric

Kerridge's estimate that in 1700 only 'about one-quarter of the enclosure of England and Wales remained to be undertaken'[18] is surely an exaggeration, given the massive amount of land enclosed during the period of parliamentary enclosure in the later eighteenth century. Even more questionable is the assumption that all open fields were inefficient and all enclosed farms efficient. Agricultural improvements were undertaken on open-field farms in the seventeenth century. Robert Loder farmed in the open fields of Harwell in Berkshire. M. A. Havinden has shown how Oxfordshire open-field farmers experimented with new techniques and crops.[19] Many of the reflex assumptions about enclosure need guarding against. Enclosures *could* be a precondition of farming improvement; they were not, though, a *necessary* accompaniment of it.[20]

Enclosure by itself provided no solution to the biggest obstacle limiting agricultural productivity in this period: the shortage of fertilizers. One effect of this was that large amounts of land had to be left fallow each year to allow it to recover its fertility. One obvious solution was to increase the size of the animal population since animals were (and were to remain before the chemical revolution of the late nineteenth century) the main source of fertilizers. 'If they have no sheep to help fat the ground, they shall have but bare corn and thin.' One suspects that often the enigmatic nature of many rural adages disguises their emptiness, but this one is an exception. As in the Middle Ages, sheep were valued only slightly less for their dung than for their wool and undoubtedly more for their dung than their meat. The problem, though, was that the size of the animal population, and therefore the supply of fertilizer, was restricted by the limited ability to produce winter fodder. The picture of the medieval farmer being forced by a shortage of winter fodder to slaughter nearly all his livestock at Michaelmas has been grossly overdrawn, but the only winter fodder available to medieval farmers was the limited amount that could be obtained from natural grasses. In these circumstances, because of the interdependence of animal and arable husbandry, it was imperative that new sources of fodder were found. As with many other innovations, these had long been established in the Low Countries, whence in the last decades of the sixteenth century and the first decades of the seventeenth century came to England, first coleseed, a crop which was crushed to provide oil for lighting and cooking and whose residue was used as winter fodder, and then the turnip. This was for a long time considered by historians to have been introduced in Norfolk in the early eighteenth century by Lord Townshend, but it is now known (thanks largely to the work of Eric Kerridge) that it was grown as a field crop in Suffolk in the early seventeenth century and that its use was popularized in many other parts of East Anglia by immigrants from the Low Countries. As will be seen, other new fodder crops were to be introduced to England in the later seventeenth century, but already before 1650 there was a dramatic increase in the sheep population of the brecklands of Suffolk and

Norfolk, transforming them into rich barley-growing areas, supplying London with grain (including barley for brewing) as well as meat.

The same problem, the need for more fertilizer and therefore for a larger animal population, was tackled at the same time in a different way in western England, in parts of Herefordshire and Wiltshire. In the 1590s a Herefordshire farmer, Rowland Vaughan, began experimental flooding of his sheep pastures in order to protect them against frost and to stimulate earlier-than-usual growth of grass in the spring, earlier lambing and the maintenance of larger flocks. Vaughan and others developed intricate, and therefore expensive, engineering techniques to carry water to upland meadows, and from the 1590s these methods were adopted in other counties, in Berkshire, Dorset, Hampshire, and some Midlands counties, where soil conditions allowed the adoption of combined animal and arable husbandry. But it was not just soil conditions that dictated where the new fodder crops and farming techniques were adopted. Significantly, the improvements were carried out in areas affected by urban demand. Above all, it was London's expansion which fuelled the improvements in East Anglia and stimulated the development in the late sixteenth and early seventeenth centuries of specialized, intensive fruit and market gardening industries in Kent, Hertfordshire, and the Thames Valley. Again the role of immigrants from the Low Countries in this branch of English agriculture underlines the powerful impact that region had on developments in England.

Alternate or 'up and down' husbandry was another attack on the basic problem of improving the fertility of the soil which seems to have spread among farmers in the late sixteenth and early seventeenth centuries. This was a system of cultivating the same period of ground by punctuating long periods of pasture farming (seven to twelve years) with shorter periods of arable farming (two to five years). It was claimed that this allowed an increase in the amount of grazing land without depressing the level of arable production. This was made possible by producing more and better animals on land which was periodically converted to arable, thereby destroying the pests and diseases which flourish on permanent grassland. On reconversion to pasture the new grass was not only pest-free, but it was more nutritious and therefore sustained more and better animals. At the same time alternate husbandry produced higher grain yields, since periodic conversion of the ground improved the soil structure, fixed nitrogen in it and gave it a thorough manuring from the animals on it. Certainly contemporaries (followed by Dr Kerridge) made great claims for alternate husbandry. 'Such a method would please me gallantly, advance the Commonwealth exceedingly, and prejudice whom, I fain would know?', wrote Walter Blith in 1652.

Abundance of poor set on work; abundance of corn raised; abundance of straw which spent and fed upon the land shall make that up again whatever the ploughing fetched out. Doubles rent and more, four or five years in one and twenty. And so every age near fetcheth in the purchase.[21]

New techniques ('floating' the watermeadows, alternate husbandry) and new crops (especially fodder crops) represented an attempt to increase agricultural productivity before 1650 by producing more from existing cultivated land. A second line of advance was made by those who attempted to bring more land into cultivation. The history of English farming since the Romans can be seen in terms of a moving frontier of cultivation, expanding and contracting in response to fluctuating population pressure. The thirteenth and early fourteenth centuries had seen a great expansion in the area under cultivation, and the succeeding 150 years a corresponding withdrawal from marginal areas as the population level slumped after the Black Death. Significantly, in the sixteenth and early seventeenth centuries many of these areas were reoccupied. Many moorland pastures and lowland forest areas of Cumberland and Westmorland, for example, were settled by squatters, many of whom fought, not all of them successfully, a grim battle for survival in poor conditions. Forest areas, the Sussex and Kentish Weald for example, were especially prone to this type of exploitation by migrants from other parts of the country. David Hey shows how the forest areas of Myddle in Shropshire were cleared and settled in the sixteenth and early seventeenth centuries by immigrant squatters. The cumulative impression is of waste and marginal land, including waterlogged land near rivers and coasts, being taken in for cultivation. This is the context for the most spectacular example of land redevelopment in this period, the attempt to reclaim large expanses of marshland in eastern England, which had been largely abandoned since the days of Roman drainage schemes. Here in 1634, taking over earlier schemes developed by the commissioners of sewers, the earl of Bedford, backed by a joint stock company, employed Cornelius Vermuyden and other Dutch engineers to try to prevent the flooding of large areas of the fenland of Cambridgeshire and adjoining counties. The task was immense and therefore a long one; the drainers faced difficult engineering problems and local opposition and fell far short of their target. But some land was reclaimed and on it were established farms, growing the new fodder crops to support large sheep flocks and employing the new methods of combined animal and arable husbandry.

There is no denying that all this – the adoption of new crops and techniques, and the extension of the area under cultivation – by 1650 amounted to a spirited response by English farmers to the pressures of a rising population. The crucial question, however, is how many farmers adopted the new methods. Not all areas were suitable for the adoption of the new husbandry. The fodder crops were restricted to the lighter, sandier soils of parts of East Anglia and western England, and not the heavy, clay Midland vales. Nor could many farmers afford some expensive improvements, like the floating of water-meadows; moreover, many of the drainage schemes failed because of severe technical problems, as well as the hostility of local inhabitants who broke down the sluices and dykes; in this respect the disruption of the 1640s was a great setback to the reclamation schemes.

Unfortunately statistics provide little guide to the achievement of English agriculture before 1650; there are no reliable figures of the output of English farms in this period. Estimates that have been made of the increased yield of wheat – 11 bushels per acre in 1650 as against $8\frac{1}{2}$ bushels per acre at the end of the fifteenth century – are based on too many suppositions to be taken seriously.[22] Consequently, because of the ambiguous evidence recent historians have come to alarmingly different conclusions about the performance of English agriculture before 1650. Dr Kerridge argues dramatically that the rapid progress made in the seventeenth century amounted to an 'agricultural revolution', until one begins to wonder what was left for later generations of farmers to achieve. Dr Thirsk, though arguing that between 1500 and 1640 'farm production made rapid strides', adopts a more moderate position. While Professor E. L. Jones takes his stance at the other extreme from Dr Kerridge: 'Agricultural profit inflation in the late sixteenth and early seventeenth centuries seems to have induced an extension of the cultivated area but by comparison little in the way of change in the mode of farming.'[23] This is carrying the reaction against Kerridge too far. But there are reasons to doubt whether, despite the major advances that were made before 1650, English agriculture kept pace with the food requirements of an expanding population. The decisive evidence is the movement of food prices in the century and a half before 1650.

Like demographic history, the history of prices is bedevilled by intractable primary sources and by regional variations. The Phelps Brown price index is the one most commonly used, but it is based on material from southern England and on wholesale prices, and therefore is not an accurate guide to retail price movements in the country as a whole. With all its many defects, however, there is no better alternative as a *rough* guide to price movements. The index indicates a general price inflation of the order of about five times from 1501–10 to 1641–50, but a rise in the price of food in the same period of nearly seven times.

The rise in prices 1501–1650[24]
(Food prices with industrial prices in brackets. 1471–75 = 100)

1501–10	106 (98)	1581–90	389 (230)
1511–20	116 (102)	1591–1600	530 (238)
1521–30	159 (110)	1601–10	527 (256)
1531–40	161 (110)	1611–20	583 (274)
1541–50	217 (127)	1621–30	585 (264)
1551–60	315 (186)	1631–40	687 (281)
1561–70	298 (218)	1641–50	723 (306)
1571–80	341 (223)		

The table indicates that the biggest leap upwards in food prices before 1650 was in the 1590s (coinciding with a series of disastrous harvests), followed by a slower rise in the first thirty years of the seventeenth century. But any attempt to conclude that this reflects the permanent success of English agriculture in meeting demand must explain the further rapid rise in food prices in the next two decades, which brought the long upward movement of prices to an end. The reasons for this 'price revolution' have been the subject of heated controversy.[25] Most historians, however, now generally recognize that, though monetary factors like debasement may have contributed to it, the major force behind inflation was population pressure which outstripped the resources of English agriculture. The best that can be said for English agriculture before 1650 is that it did not fail to increase its output and efficiency. But the price evidence suggests that the demand for food continually outran the supply that English agriculture was able to provide.

Mining and manufacture

Did English industry expand in this period? To what extent did it provide sufficient employment and generate enough wealth to counter-balance the partial failure of English agriculture before 1650? The first thing to make clear is that 'industry' is a misleading umbrella definition under which to encompass a diverse range of occupations in early seventeenth-century England. Not only was there no sharp division between farming and manufacturing – the two were often done by the same people – but 'industry' has too many post-Industrial Revolution associations to describe adequately the manufacturing structure of pre-industrial England. Manufacturing since the Industrial Revolution has been based on large units, with the workforce employed in large factories or workshops and therefore utilizing a large percentage of fixed capital (plant and machinery), and with a tendency to use mechanized labour-saving methods of production. In contrast, manufacturing units before the Industrial Revolution were labour intensive and small, usually consisting of the nuclear family with a few journeymen and apprentices, employing a large percentage of circulating capital (mainly raw materials) and relying greatly on underemployed rural labour.

For this reason the main criticism of the thesis that was developed in the 1930s and afterwards by Professor J. U. Nef is that it concentrates on peripheral aspects of late sixteenth- and early seventeenth-century economic development. Nef argued that the late sixteenth and seventeenth centuries witnessed an industrial revolution only less important than that which began towards the end of the eighteenth century. There is little doubt that economic historians of early modern England use the word 'revolution' too freely (perhaps it ought to be banned from their vocabulary!), but at first glance Nef's thesis does look convincing. In his two-volumed work, *The Rise of the British Coal Industry* (1932) he argues that between the mid-sixteenth and the late seventeenth century the output of English mines increased fourteen times, and that the output of individual coalfields, especially in Northumberland and Durham, expanded at an even greater rate. This became the first major plank of his 'industrial revolution' thesis, which he developed in later articles and books.[26] He argued that the ample supply of domestic fuel facilitated the growth of towns, especially London. This, in turn, produced an expanding urban demand for consumption goods, and the industries which developed in consequence – soap-boiling, brewing, glass-making, salt production, paper-making – relied doubly on coal, because they used it as fuel. To this list of new consumption industries Nef added those which developed to meet the needs of the state: cannon manufacture, the production of saltpetre and of lead and copper (by the Mineral and Battery Company and the Company of Mines Royal, both established by the state in 1568). Coal also, because of the extensive coastal trade in coal from the north-east to London, encouraged the development of a native shipbuilding industry. The second major argument used by Nef to support his 'industrial revolution' thesis was that there was a national shortage of timber, which alarmed contemporaries, and which he believed was caused by rapid industrial development, and especially by the growth of the one major industry which failed to adapt to the use of coal, the smelting of iron, which was totally dependent on charcoal for its fuel. Finally, all the growth industries of the period Nef described as examples of 'large-scale' production, employing large units of fixed capital and new technical methods.

Nef's work is still of great value and interest, but all its underlying assumptions outlined above are open to serious doubt. Firstly Professor Coleman and others have shown the weaknesses of the statistical work which is the basis of Nef's conclusions about a fantastic rise in the output of coal in the sixteenth and early seventeenth centuries.[27] There are no continuous series of output figures even for the major Northumberland–Durham coalfield, and Nef's conclusions, which are based on a comparison between the few annual output figures which survive for isolated years, do not stand up to any serious statistical examination. While the output of coal did rise, it did so from a very low base and the quantities which were produced were not necessarily large. Moreover, it is likely that the rate of increase slowed down quickly in the early seventeenth century. By the mid-seventeenth century all the main English coalfields were being exploited, but the main use of coal as yet was as a domestic fuel. Its industrial use was important, but only in relatively minor industries. The history of its application to the manufacture of glass is typical. The invention of a coal-fired reverbatory furnace in glass-making in 1612 was a major breakthrough, and Sir Robert Mansell, who secured a patent of monopoly of glass-making in 1615, proved to be more efficient and successful than many other patentees. Yet, although English glass improved in quality and quantity, by the mid-seventeenth century England was still an importer of fine quality glass, and the native industry was hardly a major one.

Secondly, it is now clear that the traditional assumption that the iron industry was held back by a shortage of timber is not correct. In the sixteenth century the smelting of iron underwent a major transformation as a result of the replacement of the 'bloomery' process by the water-powered blast furnace. Although the latter produced a brittle product with a high carbon content, which had to be reheated and beaten in forges, often using water-powered tilt hammers, it has been estimated that the blast furnaces could produce from five to ten times more iron than the 'bloomery' process, and in the early seventeenth century blast furnaces undoubtedly became more efficient. This technical innovation was accompanied by a shift in the centre of the iron industry from the Sussex and Kent Weald to the Forest of Dean, the West Midlands and South Yorkshire, largely because of the comparative inefficiency and lower grade ores of the Wealden industry, not because of shortage of timber in that area. The research of Dr Hammersley has demonstrated that, though there were local shortages of timber in this period, there was no national exhaustion of timber supplies. The price of timber did not rise any faster or higher than other industrial raw materials. Forestry management prevented any danger of wholesale deforestation. Consequently, the iron industry was not held back by fuel supplies and in the sixteenth century, largely as a result of the introduction of the blast furnace, its output rose rapidly, but (as in the case of the coal industry) from a very low base. Then (also as in the case of the coal industry) the output of iron slackened off in the early seventeenth century:

Output of iron, 1550 to the 1650s

1550s	5,000 tons p.a.
1580s	15,000 tons p.a.
1600–10	17–18,000 tons p.a.
1620s	19,000 tons p.a.
1630s	20,000 tons p.a.
1650s	23–24,000 tons p.a.

By the mid-seventeenth century the iron industry was not held back by a shortage of timber, but its output was rising only slowly. England continued to import large quantities of high-grade Swedish bar iron which was cheaper than the English product. The English iron industry by 1650 was by no means a major one.[28]

Thirdly, Nef's frequent use of 'large-scale' to describe manufacturing units in this period is highly misleading. Undoubtedly there were some mines and blast furnaces which employed a great deal of equipment and labour. A survey of Newcastle upon Tyne in 1649 described how many thousand people are employed in this trade of coals; many live by the working of them in the pits, many live by conveying them in wagons and wains to the river Tyne; many men are employed in conveying the coals in keels, from the staithes [coal-wharves], aboard the ships: one coal merchant employeth five hundred, or a thousand, in his works of coal . . .[29]

Disregarding the alarmingly cavalier use of statistics, these were *exceptionally* large employers of labour. Many mines, shipyards, iron and glass works employed only a handful of people. Of more importance, even these small centralized units of production were untypical of the majority. Nef's stress on 'large-scale' centralized production obscures the primacy in pre-industrial England of the domestic system of production. Major manufactures, like the production of leather and leather goods, small iron articles (axes, hammers, nails etc.), stockings, and pottery, were all organized on domestic lines, the workers (often part-time farmers) selling their products to entrepreneurs, who in turn marketed (and sometimes finished) them. Above all, this was the way in which England's major commercial industry in this period was organized: the manufacture of woollen cloth. So important was it, that it is largely on its record that the achievement of English manufacturing in this period ought to be assessed.

Woollen cloth was manufactured in all parts of the country and in a bewildering variety of types and quality. It is, writes Professor Coleman, 'the supreme example of the pre-industrial revolution multiproduct industry'.[30] English cloth ranged from the low-quality product of small farmers for their own use and for sale in the immediate locality to medium and high quality cloth for the wider domestic and international market. What all the various branches had in common, however, was the domestic system of production. On the face of it this is surprising, since the domestic system in many respects compares unfavourably with the factory system of production: the workers are unsupervised and therefore control of the quality of cloth is difficult (complaints about defective cloth were very common in this period); transport and organizational problems are inevitable; and distribution costs are high. Yet the domestic system spread in the English textile industry (and indeed in other industries in England and throughout Europe) because it fitted in well with other aspects of the pre-industrial economy. Although a rising population ensured increased demand, it did not guarantee a sufficiently regular demand for an entrepreneur to risk tying up capital in expensive plant; it was much cheaper and easier to lay off labour when demand slackened. Also, as has been seen, there was ample under-employed rural labour available, and this was especially so in those wood–pasture areas where holdings were small, either because of the type of farming practised or because of the existence of partible inheritance customs which encouraged the splitting up of farms and therefore enforced dependence on by-employment. Cloth-making was especially suited to domestic production because it was simply an adaption of traditional peasant skills and could easily be divided into separate processes by a merchant-entrepreneur. All this ensured that cloth manufacture became largely a domestic and a rural-based industry, though not totally so: it did develop in some towns, in Norwich and Worcester for example. Significantly, these were towns in which manufacturers were not hampered by guild restrictions which pushed up costs in older cloth towns, like Beverley and Lincoln, and which contributed to their decline.

From the fifteenth century onwards England had developed a native cloth industry of major European importance. From being the major supplier of wool to medieval Europe, by the late fifteenth century England had become the predominant European producer of cloth and had left behind its Flemish and Italian rivals. English cloth production for the European market came to be concentrated in three main areas. The first two were far and away the most important: the West Country, Gloucestershire, Wiltshire, Somerset, and Devon, became famous for its heavy, unfinished broadcloths, which were exported to be dyed and finished in the Low Countries; and East Anglia, in Norfolk and on the Essex–Suffolk border, where coloured broadcloth was produced. The cloth made in the third area, the West Riding of Yorkshire, was an unfinished cloth of much lower quality than that produced in the West Country. Despite the differences, though, all three areas produced a cloth made from fine, short-staple wool fibres, which gained their strength and their heaviness from being matted together in the fulling process. All three areas also shared in a significant expansion in the first half of the sixteenth century; the domestic system proliferated, and both output and exports rose.

However, in 1550–1 there was the first of a series of major crises which hit the traditional woollen broadcloth industry during the next century. The opening of the Stuart Age is deceptive in this respect, because exports of English broadcloths rose for a decade after 1604, largely because the end of the war with Spain in that year, followed by the truce between Spain and her rebellious colony in the Netherlands in 1609, reopened the Spanish and Flemish markets for English cloths. But the recovery was temporary; from 1614 onwards sales of English broadcloths in Europe fell, with especially severe recessions from 1614 to 1616, from 1621 to 1623, and from 1640 to 1642. It has been estimated that total exports of English broadcloths fell from a value of £1,193,333 early in the seventeenth century to £846,667 in 1640.[31] As is usual in this period the statistics are probably far from accurate, but they indicate the likely scale of the overall trend. There are various possible reasons for the collapse of the broadcloth industry: the nature of the wool produced in England may have changed, as a result of agrarian improvements, from a short-fibre, fine wool to a long-fibre, coarse wool which was unsuitable for broadcloth manufacture;[32] a Dutch woollen industry developed at Leiden in direct competition to the English industry; and the English industry suffered from unwise state intervention, as the Cockayne Project of 1614–16 illustrates (see below, pp. 24–5). All these factors are important, but often in explaining fluctuations in the fortunes of the textile industry too little emphasis is given to changes in fashion. Quite simply, in the late sixteenth and early seventeenth centuries Europeans seem to have grown tired of heavy broadcloth-type materials and to have demanded instead a lighter, more highly coloured product.

English cloth manufacturers, however, were no less sensitive to market forces than English farmers, and in the late sixteenth and early seventeenth centuries there was a remarkable, sustained effort by the English woollen textile industry to respond to changing fashions in European markets, and especially to demands from southern Europe for a new type of cloth. Manufacturers in the West Country, who were the most heavily committed to broadcloth manufacture, found it more difficult to adapt than others, though there were notable successes in this region. In Wiltshire and Somerset a small thriving industry was established, using fine Spanish wool to produce the so-called Spanish medley cloth associated with the enterprise of Benedict Webb, who was not slow to advertise his activities.[33] At the same time the development of the Somerset serge industry was also a response from within the old broadcloth-producing area to the changes in demand. Manufacturers elsewhere, especially in eastern England had a bigger success in producing what contemporaries called 'the new draperies', varieties of lighter, more highly coloured and cheaper cloths than the old broadcloths, and produced from longer-staple, coarse wool. Their success must be attributed largely to the influx of Protestant refugees who settled in southern and eastern England after fleeing from the Spanish armies in the Low Countries in the last decades of the sixteenth century.[34]

A major theme of English economic history could be written round the impact of immigrants on English economic development. The Protestant immigrants brought with them the technical expertise to produce 'new draperies' and in the late sixteenth and early seventeenth centuries they succeeded in establishing a thriving branch of the English cloth industry, especially in and around Norwich, probably because in that area there were the remnants of a native worsted industry and therefore a reservoir of local skill suitable for 'new drapery' manu-facture. In the Suffolk–Essex border area the integration of the immigrants was more difficult, and there were outbreaks of racial violence between the native broadcloth workers and immigrants employed in the new industry. The key question is whether the 'new draperies' had developed enough by the mid-seventeenth century to compensate for the decline of the 'old draperies'. There are no accurate output figures to answer this properly. J. D. Gould's estimates (they are no more) of the relative values of cloth exports in the early seventeenth century suggest that the new draperies were well on the way to filling the gap left by the old. He estimates a rise in the value of the exports of new draperies from £347,000 at the beginning of the century to £605,000 by 1640.[35]

It is likely, then, that the new draperies made rapid progress in the early seventeenth century. Yet the cloth industry as a whole was severely dislocated as it adjusted to changing circumstances. Severe unemployment and distress in the cloth-producing villages of the West Country during the crises of 1614–16, 1621–3 and 1640–2 is sufficient evidence of this. Nor, despite the undoubted proliferation of new consumption industries and the growth of industries like coal and iron-smelting, is there much evidence to substantiate a belief that there was a *per capita* increase in industrial production in England before 1650. The best that can be concluded is that industrial developments before 1650 were important for the future. It would be wrong to exaggerate their contemporary significance.

Overseas trade and colonization

There seems to be a stronger case for a more optimistic assessment of the performance of English overseas trade and colonization than of English agriculture and manufacturing by the middle of the seventeenth century. On the face of it English merchants in the century before 1650 had responded well to the severe trade crisis of 1550–1, which had made apparent the narrow foundation on which English overseas trade was based. By the middle of the sixteenth century the late-medieval English penetration of the Mediterranean and Baltic trades had ended, and most of English (and indeed European) trade was concentrated on Antwerp, a major entrepôt with sophisticated marketing and credit institutions. Moreover, most of English trade went to Antwerp from London, and many English provincial ports (King's Lynn, Boston, Southampton, Bristol) declined. More seriously, this dominating London–Antwerp trade relied almost totally on the export of English cloth, mainly the broadcloths of the West Country and East Anglia, which were exchanged for a variety of goods, including raw materials for the cloth industry (oil, madder, woad, alum), non-woollen textiles (high quality silks, velvets, taffetas) and exotic foods and spices brought overland from the East. Much of the trade was regulated by the English Company of Merchant Adventurers, but a large share of English trade was in the hands of alien merchants, especially the Hansards of North Germany, or was carried in foreign-built ships. For much of the early sixteenth century all this had not mattered as English overseas trade boomed. But in 1550–1 cloth sales in Antwerp slumped dramatically, and the effect was to jolt English merchants into an effort to end their dangerous reliance on one trade route, one trade organization, and one export commodity.

During the next hundred years it can be argued that English merchants responded energetically to this crisis, and in the process established a new diversified pattern of English overseas trade with new trade routes and new trading companies. English trade to Antwerp never recovered fully after the crisis of the early 1550s, largely because of growing hostility between England and Spain. In 1564 the Merchant Adventurers left Antwerp in the Spanish Netherlands and began to search for new bases in north-west Europe. In the next century Hamburg, Emden, and Stade all became, with varying success, alternative outlets for English cloth to the markets of northern Europe. Gradually also English merchants increased their share of the country's trade – in 1597 the Hansards were expelled from London – and the size of England's mercantile marine increased. English merchants, more-over, began to reappear in parts of the world with which they had abandoned direct trade in the fifteenth century. The Baltic countries, which were the major suppliers of corn to Europe as well as sources of naval stores and a potential market for English cloth, drew English merchants through the Sound between Denmark and Sweden. In 1555 the first joint-stock trading company, the Muscovy Company, received its charter, and in 1579 the Eastland Company was formed to trade in the Baltic. English merchants also began to reappear in the Mediter-ranean from which they had withdrawn in the fifteenth century. In 1581 the Levant Company and in 1585 the Barbary Company were established to conduct the carrying trade in fish, grain, and cloth to the Mediterranean from northern Europe. English merchants also captured a large share of the intra-Mediterranean trade which had previously gone through the Sicilian entrepôt which collapsed in the early 1590s.

In the early seventeenth century English merchants penetrated even further afield than the Baltic and Mediterranean. In 1600 exploratory expeditions to the Far East were consolidated by the foundation of the joint-stock English East India Company, which set up trading posts in Indonesia ('the Spice Islands') and in India. Shortly afterwards the search for new trade routes, notably a north-west passage to the East, and colonies across the Atlantic culminated in the establishment of the first English colony at Jamestown in Virginia in 1607. During the next forty years the English Empire in the New World expanded in three areas: Virginia, with the Bermuda islands from 1615 and Maryland from 1633, became the centre of the tobacco colonies of mainland America; Barbados, St Christopher, Nevis, and Antigua in the Lesser Antilles in the Caribbean from the late 1620s, after a false start as tobacco islands, developed sugar-based economies; and thirdly, the colonies of New England (Plymouth 1621, Massachusetts 1629, and its offshoots) emerged as farming, fishing, and trading communities. It is true that not all these colonies were developed only as a response to England's economic problems. Dislike of the religious trends in Caroline England was a prime motive for the establishment of the New England colonies and of Maryland. But a desire to cure England's overpopulation problem and open up new trades and new markets was a persistent motive behind most of the colonization schemes.

Do all these developments in the century after 1550, however, support the widely held view that this was a period of 'expansion' in

English overseas trade? There are many reasons to doubt such an optimistic conclusion. Despite all the developments mentioned so far, it will be suggested here that English overseas trade by the middle of the seventeenth century was just as insecurely based as it was a hundred years before. It needs to be stressed, though, that, as with many other problems discussed in this book, there is plenty of room for alternative hypotheses. This is generally true of overseas trade in the early seventeenth century because of the lack of customs accounts. From 1604 English customs were collected, not by government officials, but by customs farmers, who paid a lump sum to the crown for the privilege of running the customs on a private enterprise basis. It was not until 1696, when an Inspector-General of Imports and Exports was appointed, that a continuous series of customs accounts recommences. It is therefore difficult to assess trends in overseas trade in terms of the value of the goods traded or to quantify changes in the direction of English overseas trade. Yet, taking together the few scattered figures that survive with the qualitative evidence, it seems probable that in the early seventeenth century there was no increase in the total volume of English overseas trade, and that the bulk of trade was still the export of cloth to Europe from London. It is true that now for the first time most of the trade was in the hands of English merchants, and that a growing proportion of the exported cloth was made up of new draperies which were sent to southern Europe, Spain, north Africa, and the Mediterranean. Also some provincial ports (notably Exeter and Bristol) slightly increased their share of the trade, especially after the reopening of the Spanish and Mediterranean trades. But the bulk of English overseas trade still went through London, and provincial port resentment at the dominance of London continued unabated. In 1604 this exploded in the misleadingly named 'free trade' debate in parliament; those who represented the views of the outports protested *against* the trade monopoly of London merchants and the Merchant Adventurers, *not* in favour of a free trade ideology.

Moreover, all the 'new' trades were subjected to immense difficulties in the late sixteenth and early seventeenth centuries. Before 1650 in the Baltic, Mediterranean, and Far East English merchants faced and were outbid by Dutch mercantile competition. The one possible exception is the Mediterranean, where the Dutch with their unarmed, large and cumbersome *fluits* were less able than the English to withstand the attacks of pirates based in North African ports. Elsewhere, though, the *fluits* gave the Dutch a tremendous advantage over their competitors in lower freight costs: in the Baltic they captured the biggest share of the trade in grain and naval stores; in the Far East it was the Dutch who were there first and who inherited most of the trade which the Portuguese were in the process of relinquishing. Although the English East India Company made profits on its early voyages, by the 1620s its fortunes were at a low ebb. The Company not only had to overcome the risks of long voyages to the East and Dutch hostility, which in 1623 flared into a skirmish between representatives of the rival companies, the 'massacre of Amboyna', but also opposition at home, directed at the export of silver bullion with which the East India Company paid for its spices and silks. This criticism was misguided in that some of the East India Company's imports were re-exported, making up for the loss of silver. But in the early seventeenth century a contemporary could be forgiven for not seeing the Far Eastern trade as an area of rapid growth. Of course, this pessimistic conclusion was to be disproved later, but at the time the impact of East Indian trade on England's total trade was slight.

The same is true of the trade generated by the American colonies. By the 1620s much of the euphoric expectation raised in the hope of the advantages that colonies would bring had been dissipated. By this time the Virginia Company was split by internal divisions, it had paid no dividends to its investors, and in 1624 it collapsed, forcing the crown to take on temporarily the administration of the Jamestown colony. The colonists were hampered by attacks from hostile Indians – in March 1623 the colony was nearly wiped out by an Indian attack – and by opposition in England to their attempts to establish tobacco as the staple export crop. Respectable opinion in England could not tolerate the foundation of a colony which relied on such a morally dubious crop as tobacco, which in the early seventeenth century had the status and the radical, subversive associations of cannibis in the late twentieth century. Virginia also faced a severe labour shortage, partly because prospective emigrants found Ireland a more attractive destination.[36] These problems were eventually overcome: tobacco was established as a profitable crop, and immigrants were attracted to the colony by the indentured labour system, which gave the new settler the prospect of owning his own land after a period of 'temporary servitude'. Before 1650, however, imports of tobacco from mainland America to England were no more than a trickle. This is true also of sugar, which was to be the key commodity in the later prosperity of the new Caribbean colonies. There the labour shortage problem was not overcome before the mid-seventeenth century, because in the small island colonies there was no reservoir of land to attract indentured servants as in the mainland colonies. Although the trade in African slaves was eventually to provide a solution, there was little hint of this before 1650. Nor were the new colonies either the suppliers of raw materials or the markets for English goods which the enthusiastic propagandists had promised; the total colonial population was only about 48,000 in 1650. Moreover the New England colonies had developed an economic structure which, far from complementing that of the mother country, clearly promised to be its competitor in the colonial trade.

Recurrent trade crises, especially in 1614–17, 1621–4, and 1640–2, underline the argument that English overseas trade in the early seventeenth century was no more stable than it had been in the mid-sixteenth century. The crisis of 1614–17 was a direct result of the misguided intervention of the crown in the cloth trade.[37] In fairness to James I and his advisers the scheme put to them in 1614 by Alderman Cockayne and a syndicate of London merchants for a reorganization of the cloth industry and trade was not without some commercial sense. Most of the profit on cloth was from the finishing and dyeing processes. Therefore, since most English cloth was exported unfinished and the Dutch finishing manufacturers took the cream of the profits, Cockayne proposed that the export of unfinished cloth should be banned, the monopoly of the Merchant Adventurers be rescinded, and that he and his syndicate should establish a new company to take over the profitable dyeing process and control the export of the cloth. The crown, through increased customs duties, would gain from the enhanced value of the trade, and Cockayne also offered James a substantial cash payment. In James's financial predicament it was probably the latter consideration that encouraged him to accept Cockayne's project, rather than its alleged commercial advantages. The latter, in fact, never materialized; the new company lacked the Merchant Adventurers' marketing contacts in Europe and the craftsmen with sufficient skill in the difficult art of dyeing cloth. As with many other manufacturing processes – mining, metal smelting, silk-weaving, clock-making – the English were technologically backward compared to others on the continent. Consequently, the Cockayne Project failed badly, and in 1617 the old Company was reinstated and the slide in overseas sales of cloth temporarily reversed.

The crisis of 1621–4 was more serious and its causes more deep-rooted. As long as the English cloth trade was directed to and through one market it was vulnerable to changes, beyond the control of English merchants, that affected that market. In the early 1620s this northern European market was disrupted, not by the Thirty Years' War (this may have generated sufficient demand to offset the dislocation it caused), but by a series of currency debasements undertaken by many north German and east European princes, which had the effect of raising the prices of imported goods, including English cloth. The repercussions in the major cloth-producing areas were serious. The threat to order was made clear by a clothiers' petition in May 1622: 'the livelihood of so many thousands being taken from them, we leave it to your honourable discretions to consider how difficult a thing will be like to be to contain them from mutiny and rebellion.'[38] Consequently, as at other times of economic crisis, the government as well as merchants were jolted into an awareness of the unstable nature of English trade. Government commissions were appointed, and a great public debate took place to identify the causes of the crisis. There is no reason to see this debate as part of a continuous thread of economic policy or economic thought. Once the crisis was over the debate ended. Moreover, it had little impact on the future development of English trade. Contemporary analyses and remedies for the trade depression of 1640–2 are significantly similar to those current in the early 1620s and early 1550s.[39]

The achievements of English merchants in the century before 1650 were not negligible: the capture of English trade from the hands of alien merchants, the export of a greater variety of woollen textiles, the reopening of the south European trade. But it is unlikely that a perceptive observer in 1650 would have been able to forecast the later important shift in the focus of English trade from Europe and the Mediterranean to the Atlantic and the Far East. More obvious to him would have been the recurrent trade crises, and the inferiority complex of early seventeenth-century Englishmen in regarding Dutch merchants. Despite the renewed Spanish–Dutch war from 1621 to 1648 Dutch merchants reigned supreme in Europe. Amsterdam not London was the major European commercial entrepôt.

Towns

Urban studies are at present in a muddle.[40] Despite the current boom in the study of urban history, there is still much that is uncertain about the development of English towns before 1650. Urban historians are not agreed on such fundamental matters as the definition of a town, how many towns there were, or whether towns were growing in size and importance in sixteenth and seventeenth-century England. This being the case, it seems premature for urban historians to attempt answers to the wider problem of assessing the contribution of early modern towns to the country's economic development. Did they stimulate the growth of the economy or were they parasites on it?

Amid the uncertainties, two aspects of the history of English towns before 1650 are clear: London grew at an exceptionally rapid rate; and the proportion of the total population who lived in towns was very small indeed. By 1650 the economic and social importance of London in relation to other towns was greater than ever before or since. From 1500 to 1650 its population quadrupled from 50,000 to 200,000 at a time when the national population only doubled; in the next fifty years its population expanded to 400,000. By 1650 it was about twenty times bigger than the largest English provincial town and was the biggest city in western Europe (Constantinople in Eastern Europe was bigger); it had just overhauled its nearest rival, Paris, and had left other European cities far behind in size: Naples (250,000–300,000), Amsterdam (150,000), Palermo, Venice, Rome, Lisbon (100–125,000).[41] London had spilled beyond the boundaries of the medieval City so that the familiar pattern was already established of poorer housing to the east and on the south bank of the Thames in Southwark, and superior property development to the west, at first following the river frontage along the Strand towards Westminster, and later expanding northwards to Holborn and westwards to St Martin's Lane. John Evelyn's explanation for this is an attractive one. The better classes built or bought houses to the west of the city 'because the Windes blowing near $\frac{3}{4}$ of the year from the west, the dwellings of the West End are so much free from the fumes, steams & stinks of the whole Easterly Pyle; which when Sea Coal is burnt is a great matter'.[42] But, while this illustrates London's great dependence on coal from the mines of the north-east, a more accurate – if more prosaic – explanation is probably that the royal court and the law courts attracted the superior houses and shops to the Westminster area. This embryonic West End produced some examples of enlightened urban development, especially the Covent Garden piazza erected on his Long Acre site by the fourth earl of Bedford and the architects, Inigo Jones and Isaac de Caux. Most landowners, however, were more interested in the profits of property speculation than the aesthetics of town planning. Most of them gave long thirty-one year leases of their London estates to builders, allowing them to develop them as they wished.[43] The result was that many tenements were built in the West End that were as squalid as – and in some cases perhaps even more so than – those in the East End.

Why did London grow at such a rapid rate in the century and a half before 1650? London's growth was sustained by continuous, massive immigration from the provinces (and to a much lesser extent from abroad) and not by a superior birth rate; on the contrary, the death rate in London far outstripped the birth rate because of the above-average incidence of plague and other diseases in the insanitary conditions of the capital. Part of the explanation for London's growth therefore lies in the reasons why people came to live there. As at all times, these, of course, varied. Poor 'subsistence migrants' came to the capital because of its superior official system for the relief of poverty, its private poor relief schemes, and the greater opportunities for survival in London by means of part-time employment, begging and crime. The better-off 'betterment migrants' of the Dick Whittington type came to London to serve as apprentices of London merchants and craftsmen, while London's mercantile community expanded because of the capital's role as the centre of England's overseas and internal trade. Aliens sought refuge in London from political and religious persecution in their own countries. Nor was it economic motivation that drew those from higher up the social scale. Typically, the mysogenic James I thought that 'one of the greatest causes of all Gentlemens desire, that have no calling or errand, to dwell in London, is apparently the pride of women: For if they bee wives, then their fathers, must bring them up to London . . .'. Landed gentlemen, though, probably did not need nagging into visiting London or into buying a house there. London was the residence of the royal court, where attendance by the politically or socially ambitious was a necessity. The main law courts, to the grievance not only of the radicals of the mid-seventeenth century, were all in London, drawing the members of the litigious propertied classes to them. In the capital, too, there were fine schools, Westminster and St Paul's, and the Inns of Court, the 'third university' of the English landed gentry in this period. In addition, London developed unrivalled social facilities for all tastes, shops, entertainment parks like Paris Gardens in Southwark, and the theatre. Professor F. J. Fisher has argued that to the late sixteenth and early seventeenth centuries can be traced the origins of the London social 'season'.[44] Many people, then, came to London for different reasons, but all (with the possible exception of the numerically insignificant foreign immigrants) have one thing in common: they came to London because it was already a big city with developing facilities of all kinds. In other words, the major reason why London grew bigger at such a rapid rate in the sixteenth and early seventeenth centuries is that it was already big by 1500.

To many contemporaries this was something to condemn. 'It is the fashion of Italy', wrote James I, 'that all the Gentry dwell in the principal towns, and so the whole country is empty. Even so now in England all the country is gotten into London, so as with time England will only be London and the whole country be left waste . . .'. Later, in 1641, Sir Thomas Roe wrote dramatically that 'it is no good state of a body to have a fat head, thin guts, and lean members'.[45] It is not easy to judge how justified those fears were. Different conclusions can be drawn from the fact that London's growth was sustained by immigration on a massive scale. Since London was a 'demographic drain', it can be argued that the provinces were thereby stripped of a valuable supply of labour as their able-bodied men and women moved away to London. On the other hand, one could argue that London fulfilled a valuable function in relieving many provincial economies of the excessive pressure put on them by an expanding population. Is it not possible that the growth of London could have had both a beneficial *and* a parasitical effect on the country's economy, depending on different circumstances? Professor F. J. Fisher has shown how the market for food and the development of industries in London stimulated agricultural improvements, regional specialization and commercialization, and internal trade in grain, cattle, other agricultural products, and coal in many provincial economies. In its role in the organization of English overseas trade and the provision of credit London became an 'engine of growth'.[46] Significantly, for example, it was a group of London merchants who successfully established a colony in Virginia in 1607, not their West Country-based rivals who did not have the London money market behind them. On the other hand, in different circumstances London clearly inhibited economic growth. The capital's dominance of English overseas trade was not the sole reason for the decay of provincial ports, like Southampton, but it undoubtedly contributed to it. The London food market, too, was a powerful competitor for sparse food resources in some areas, so depressing the standard of living there. For example, London brewers successfully outbid local rivals for the supply of barley in some Home Counties and diverted precious grain supplies to the capital. Surely London had a multiple impact on the economy of the provinces.

Surprisingly, despite its overwhelming predominance, little research has recently been done on the economic and social history of London in the period. In contrast, a thriving and growing research industry has grown up round the history of early modern provincial towns, which were much less important than London before 1650. Even at the end of the seventeenth century only about 5 per cent of the population lived in towns of over 5,000 inhabitants outside London. Before 1650 there were only a handful of provincial towns in this category, including Norwich and Bristol, which had between 10,000 and 20,000 inhabitants, and Exeter, Plymouth, Worcester, Coventry, Ipswich, Colchester, York, and Newcastle upon Tyne with between 5,000 and 10,000.[47] Did the populations and importance of this group of provincial towns with over 5,000 inhabitants increase in the period before 1650? Unfortunately, urban historians have not yet produced a clear cut answer to that question. Rather they have revealed a vast variety of urban fortunes. Some towns, like Southampton and other provincial ports, were adversely affected as London gobbled up their trade; though clearly not all ports suffered, as those like Bristol and Exeter developed independent trades to southern Europe, and in the case of Newcastle London's demand for coal was the major factor in the rapid rise of that port in the late sixteenth and seventeenth centuries. Some towns, like Coventry, Leicester, Beverley, and Lincoln, suffered in the general movement of industry, especially cloth manufacturing, to the country-side; others, however, emerged in the same period as manufacturing and marketing centres of the cloth industry, like Norwich, Exeter, and Worcester; and others, like Canterbury and Sandwich developed crafts brought by foreign immigrants. The economies of some towns, especially those in the hotly contested Severn Valley, like Gloucester and Bristol, were dislocated during the Civil War in the early 1640s;[48] while others, like those in the south-eastern counties which saw less fighting, were able to carry on their trade and industry with less (if not without) disruption. Some expanded as administrative centres, like York which was until 1641 the seat of the council of the north, or as the meeting places of quarter sessions and assizes; these 'provincial capitals' with their professional services, social and shopping facilities developed as mini-Londons, expanding, of course, in this respect at the expense of neighbouring towns.

The varying ways in which provincial towns developed before 1650 ought to warn against attempts to maintain generalizations about provincial towns being in a state of 'crisis' in this period, and against seeing the period from 1500 to 1700 compared with the Middle Ages as 'a period of substantial and sustained urbanization'.[49] This should not, though, serve to obscure the facts that, beside the growth of London, the development of provincial towns before 1650 was snail-like, and that, seen in the context of the national economy, their significance was slight. English agriculture had not yet become efficient enough to feed a large urban population. The manufacturing sector of the English economy was not diversified enough to enable many towns to develop as industrial centres. Overseas trade had not yet broken sufficiently away from its London – Europe axis to promote the development of the trade of provincial ports. The English economy needed to expand faster and diversify considerably more before towns other than London could grow. This, as will be seen, like a lot of other economic and social developments, was a phenomenon whose beginnings can be traced more clearly to the later seventeenth century than to the period before 1650.

Conclusion

Unfortunately none of the statistical guidelines, especially estimates of the gross national product, which economists use to judge the performance of modern economies, are available to use as a yardstick of the early seventeenth-century English economy. As has been seen, there is evidence that attempts were made to solve major economic problems before 1650: agricultural innovations were introduced and more land was brought into cultivation; a wider range of manufactured goods was produced; and efforts were made to diversify overseas trade, to explore new markets and export new products. Yet it is difficult to avoid the conclusion that all these were more important for the future than for early Stuart England. Agricultural productivity barely kept pace with increasing demand for food; English manufacturing was still largely concentrated on the production of woollen cloth, an industry which was in the process of major readjustment and dislocation; and overseas trade was still dangerously reliant on selling cloth in Europe.

Why did the English economy fail to expand at a greater rate before 1650? Some possible explanations are, at best, only secondary ones. It is doubtful if, as is sometimes suggested, lack of capital held up economic progress. Studies of the landowning classes reveal neither a shortage of surplus capital, nor an unwillingness to invest in industry or commerce. What held back investment on a large scale was the obvious unprofitibility of mining, manufacturing, and colonial ventures. 'Instead of dreining the water', wrote a contemporary about those who invested in mining, 'their pockets are dreined.'[50] In any case, was there a need for large-scale capital investment? When more industrial progress was made in the eighteenth century, manufacturing units were still small, and most of the necessary capital was provided fairly easily from ploughed-back profits and from loans from members of the entrepreneur's family. More serious in holding back economic progress in the early seventeenth century was technological backwardness, which prevented, for example, deep mining. However, the importance of this can be exaggerated, as can be seen by the lack of enthusiasm which greeted major technological discoveries, like the atmospheric engine and coke-smelting of iron, in the later seventeenth and early eighteenth centuries. Moreover, although the imperfect state of many roads and rivers hindered economic growth, this was less of a problem in England than elsewhere because of its many navigable rivers and coastal trade.

More important probably were the adverse effects of government intervention in economic affairs, which was often motivated by the financial necessity of the crown rather than by consideration of the national interest.

It may be that more crucial than any of these factors in holding back economic growth was the lack of a mass market for anything other than agricultural products. There was as yet no expanding colonial market for English manufactures, the European market was unstable, and the Far Eastern market non-existent: in these conditions the state of the domestic market was crucial. This opens up a large chasm of ignorance in early seventeenth-century economic and social history, but it may be that the majority of most peoples' incomes was spent on food with little or nothing to spare for other consumer goods. The key to this, and therefore to the failure of the English economy to transform itself by an industrial revolution of the early seventeenth century, is the poor performance of English agriculture. Not only did its failure to increase its output greatly mean that surplus labour could not be released from non-agricultural occupations or that sufficient industrial raw materials were produced, but also that food prices remained high, inhibiting the development of a mass domestic market for manufactured goods. If this is the case, then England's economic problems before 1650 are closely connected with the condition and standard of living of English people in the early seventeenth century, which is dealt with in the next chapter.

Notes

For abbreviations used throughout see p. xiv.
1. P. W. Thomas, 'Two cultures? Court and country under Charles I', in Conrad Russell, ed., *The Origins of the English Civil War* (1973), p. 193.
2. W. G. Hoskins, 'Harvest fluctuations and English economic history, 1480–1619', *Agric. H.R.*, XII (1964), pp. 28–46; and 'Harvest fluctuations and English economic history, 1620–1759', *ibid.*, XVI (1968), pp. 13–31.
3. Thirsk and Cooper, p. 49.
4. D. C. Coleman, 'Labour in the English economy in the seventeenth century', *Econ. H. R.*, 2nd ser., VIII (1956), pp. 280–95, repr. in E. Carus-Wilson, ed., *Essays in Economic History*, II (1962), pp. 291–308.
5. L. A. Clarkson, *The Pre-industrial Economy in England 1500–1750* (1971), p. 41.
6. W. B. Rye, ed., *England as seen by Foreigners in the Days of Elizabeth and James I* (1865), pp. 109–110.
7. R. H. Tawney, 'An occupational census of the seventeenth century', *Econ. H.R.*, 1st ser., V (1934–5), pp. 25–64.
8. David Hey, *An English Rural Community: Myddle under the Tudors and Stuarts* (1974), p. 142. See Dr Clarkson's occupational classification, *Pre-industrial Economy*, pp. 88–9.
9. Joan Thirsk, 'The farming regions of England', in J. Thirsk, ed., *The Agrarian History of England and Wales, IV, 1500–1640* (1967); Eric Kerridge, *The Agricultural Revolution* (1967), ch. 2.

10. Thirsk and Cooper, p. 116.
11. Thirsk, ed., *Agrarian History*, p. 176.
12. F. J. Fisher, 'The development of the London food market 1540–1640', *Econ. H. R.*, 1st ser., V (1935), repr. in Carus-Wilson, ed., *Essays*, I, pp. 135–51.
13. Alan Everitt, 'The marketing of agricultural produce' in Thirsk, ed., *Agrarian History*, pp. 466–592, especially p. 495.
14. J. A. Chartres, *Internal Trade in England 1500–1700* (Macmillan Studies in Economic History, 1977); *ibid.*, 'Road carrying in England in the seventeenth century: myth and reality', *Econ. H.R.*, 2nd ser., XXX (1977), pp. 73–94. See also T. S. Willan, *River Navigation in England, 1600–1750* (1936), *The English Coasting Trade, 1600–1750* (1938), *The Inland Trade: Studies in English Internal Trade in the Sixteenth and Seventeenth Centuries* (1976).
15. E. Power and R. H. Tawney, eds., *Tudor Economic Documents* (3 vols., 1924), III, p. 64.
16. Lord Ernle, *English Farming Past and Present* (1912; and see the 1961 edition for a useful introduction by G. E. Fussell); R. H. Tawney, *The Agrarian Problem in the Sixteenth Century* (1912; see the New York 1967 reprint edn. with an introduction by L. Stone); H. L. Gray, *English Field Systems* (1915) – see A. R. H. Baker, 'H. L. Gray and the English field systems: an evaluation', *Agricultural History*, XXXIX (1965), pp. 86–91. For recent views of enclosures see Joan Thirsk, 'Enclosing and engrossing', in Thirsk, ed., *Agrarian History*, pp. 200–55; and J. A. Yelling, *Common Field and Enclosure in England 1450–1850* (1977).
17. L. A. Parker, 'The agrarian revolution of Cotesbach', *Trans. Leicestershire Archaeological Society*, XXIV (1949), repr. in W. G. Hoskins, ed., *Studies in Leicestershire Agrarian History* (1949), pp. 41–76.
18. Kerridge, *Agricultural Revolution*, p. 24.
19. M. A. Havinden, 'Agricultural progress in open-field Oxfordshire', *Agric. H.R.*, IX (1961), pp. 73–83.
20. For a refreshing new look at enclosures see D. N. McCloskey, 'The persistence of English common fields', in W. N. Parker and E. L. Jones, eds., *European Peasants and Their Markets: essays in agrarian economic history* (Princeton, 1976).
21. Thirsk and Cooper, p. 134, and see Kerridge, *Agricultural Revolution*, ch. 3.
22. M. K. Bennett, 'British wheat yield per acre for seven centuries', *Economic Journal Economic History Supplement*, III (1935), pp. 23–6, repr. in W. E. Minchinton, ed., *Essays in Agrarian History* I (1968), pp. 53–72; P. Bowden, 'Agricultural prices, farm profits, and rents', in Thirsk, ed., *Agrarian History*, pp. 606, 651–2.
23. Kerridge, *Agricultural Revolution, passim*; Thirsk, 'Farming techniques', in Thirsk, *Agrarian History*, p. 199; E. L. Jones, 'The condition of English agriculture 1500–1640', *Econ. H.R.*, 2nd ser., XXI (1968), p. 618.
24. R. B. Outhwaite, *Inflation in Tudor and Early Stuart England* (Macmillan Studies in Economic History, 1968), based on E. H. Phelps Brown and Sheila V. Hopkins, 'Wage-rates and prices: evidence for population pressure in the sixteenth century', *Economica*, XXIV (1957), p. 306.
25. Outhwaite, *Inflation*, is the best summary of this controversy.
26. *The Rise of the British Coal Industry* (2 vols., 1932). His most important later articles are 'The progress of technology and the growth of large-scale

industry in Great Britain 1540–1640', *Econ. H.R.*, 1st ser., V (1934); and 'Prices and industrial capitalism in France and England 1540–1640', *ibid.*, 1st ser., VII (1937); both repr. in Carus-Wilson, ed., *Essays*, I, pp. 88–107, 108–34.

27. D. C. Coleman, *Industry in Tudor and Stuart England* (Macmillan Studies in Economic History, 1975), *passim*. See Eric Kerridge's quixotic attempt to defend Nef's statistical method and D. C. Coleman's reply in *Econ. H.R.*, 2nd ser., XXX (1977), pp. 340–5.
28. Hammersley, 'The charcoal iron industry and its fuel 1540–1750', *Econ. H.R.*, 2nd ser., XXVI (1973), pp. 593–613, on which this paragraph and the table are based.
29. Thirsk and Cooper, pp. 363–4.
30. D. C. Coleman, 'Textile growth' in N. B. Harte and K. G. Ponting, eds., *Textile History and Economic History: Essays in Honour of Miss Julia de Lacy Mann* (1973), p. 9.
31. J. D. Gould, 'Cloth exports 1600–40', *Econ. H.R.*, 2nd ser., XXIV (1971), p. 251.
32. This is the suggestion of P. Bowden, 'Wool supply and the woollen industry', *Econ. H.R.*, 2nd ser., IX (1956).
33. Thirsk and Cooper, pp. 206–8; E. A. L. Moir, 'Benedict Webb, clothier', *Econ. H.R.*, 2nd ser., X (1957), pp. 256–64.
34. D. C. Coleman, 'An innovation and its diffusion: the New Draperies', *Econ. H.R.*, 2nd ser., XXII (1969), pp. 417–29.
35. Gould, 'Cloth exports 1600–40', p. 251.
36. See pp. 108–9, 147–8 for a discussion of early seventeenth-century Ireland.
37. For the Cockayne Project and the trade crisis of the early 1620s see A. Friis, *Alderman Cockayne's Project: the commercial policy of England in its main aspects* (Copenhagen, 1927) and B. E. Supple, *Commercial Crisis and Change in England 1600–42: a study in the instability of a mercantile economy* (1959).
38. Thirsk and Cooper, p. 15.
39. Compare the documents in Thirsk and Cooper, pp. 1–15 and pp. 39–46.
40. For a good recent attempt to clarify urban studies see P. Corfield, 'Urban development in England and Wales in the sixteenth and seventeenth centuries', in A. H. John and D. C. Coleman, eds., *Trade, Government and Society* (1976), pp. 214–47. See also three Open University publications: *Towns and Townspeople 1550–1780, The Fabric of the Traditional Community*, and *The Traditional Community Under Stress* (Milton Keynes, 1977).
41. E. A. Wrigley, 'A simple model of London's importance in changing England's society and economy 1650–1750', *P.&P.*, XXXVII (1967), pp. 44–5.
42. Quoted in C. Wilson, *England's Apprenticeship 1603–1763* (1965), p. 47.
43. L. Stone, *The Crisis of the Aristocracy 1558–1641* (1965), pp. 357–63.
44. F. J. Fisher, 'The development of London as a centre of conspicuous consumption in the sixteenth and seventeenth centuries', *T.R.H.S.*, XXX (1948), pp. 37–50; repr. in Carus-Wilson, ed., *Essays*, II, pp. 197–207.
45. Thirsk and Cooper, p. 45.
46. Fisher, 'The development of the London food market', *passim*; F. J. Fisher, 'London as an "engine of economic growth"', in J. S. Bromley and E. H. Kossman, eds., *Britain and the Netherlands*, IV (The Hague, 1971), pp. 3–16.

47. For recent work on the history of London see Valerie Pearl, 'Change and stability in seventeenth-century London', *The London Journal*, V (1979). The exact populations of few provincial towns in the seventeenth century are known. Corfield, 'Urban development' is the best guide to recent estimates.

48. Ian Roy, 'England turned Germany? The aftermath of the civil war in its European context', *T.R.H.S.* XXVIII (1978), pp. 127–44.

49. P. Clark and P. Slack, *English Towns in Transition 1500–1700* (1976), p. 12.

50. Quoted in Stone, *Crisis*, p. 340.

Chapter 2

Society in early Stuart England

The 'history of society'

Social history has until recently held an inferior position among English historians. For a long time its reputation was tarnished by G. M. Trevelyan's description of it as 'history with the politics left out', which was often used to dismiss it as a study unworthy of the interest of professional academic historians. Such was social history's subordinate status that it was not until 1971 that the *Economic History Review* altered the title of its annual 'List of publications in the Economic History of Great Britain and Ireland' to 'Economic *and Social History*'.[1] This change reflected a marked improvement in the academic reputation of social history first discernible in the late 1960s, and which was partly inspired by the influence of the French *Annales* school of historians, notably Lucien Febvre, Marc Bloch, and Fernand Braudel, whose work had until then been largely ignored by English historians. The approach of the *Annales* historians to social history is the complete antithesis of that of G. M. Trevelyan. They advocated 'total history', not a fragmentation of history; furthermore, they urged historians to look beyond the limits of the traditional discipline and to apply to their work the concepts, terminology, and methods used in the social sciences.[2] This approach Professor Eric Hobsbawm called 'a history of society' not 'social history'.[3] From sociology and anthropology the historian would learn to ask new questions about the history of society. Professor Hobsbawm was writing with reference to post-Industrial Revolution history, but the approach he reflects has influenced recent historians of pre-industrial England to ask new questions suggested by the experience of social scientists, to exploit a vast range of source material, to use statistical techniques, computers and mechanical aids, and, if necessary, to establish cooperative research ventures.

Historians who approach the history of society in these ways are rightly excited at the prospects of revealing aspects of the lives of people in the past which it was once thought would always remain hidden.[4] Their enthusiasm, however, needs to be moderated by a proper realization of the problems they face.[5] Since not all sociologists and anthropologists agree amongst themselves about many of the concepts and conclusions drawn from their own areas of study, it is not always wise to use these for comparative historical purposes. In any case, even generalizations that seem true of one society might not be applicable to another. E. P. Thompson is surely right to wonder whether 'studies of Napse Religion and the Sherpas of Bengal [can] serve as a "model" for understanding funeral rites in seventeenth-century Essex'.[6] Anthropological studies have prompted some historians to ask interesting questions about seventeenth-century English society, especially about beliefs in magic and witchcraft, as will be seen, but there is a danger of assuming that there are more similarities between different societies at different periods than is the case. Nor is the use of statistics, any more than the social sciences, a magic wand that will necessarily make the view we have of the past any clearer. Few statistics, official or otherwise, survive from before the mid-nineteenth century, a fact which not even the use of sophisticated statistical techniques and computers can alter. This is not to say that statistics are of no use for the study of this period of history; what needs to be stressed, however, is that statistical tables designed to illustrate aspects of seventeenth-century history can give the impression of certainty and conclusiveness which is not warranted by the sparse data on which they are based.[7]

Historical demography – the history of population – is especially vulnerable to the charge that its practitioners pay too little regard to the limitations of the primary sources, especially parish registers, which they use. Not only do most English parishes in the seventeenth century have registers which suffer from serious under-recording and have large gaps when there are no surviving registers, but the reliability of parish registers as a historical primary source depends on the existence of an immobile population. Since, as will be seen, this is an assumption on which one cannot rely, 'aggregative analysis' of parish register data (the counting of baptismal, marriage, and death rates and of fluctuations in the size of parish populations) is not always accurate. In order to try to overcome the problem of short distance migration English historical demographers have adopted a historical method long used by French historians: 'family reconstitution', which involves compiling as much biographical information about as many people as possible in one parish or group of adjacent parishes. Since the survival of early parish registers is nowhere near as complete as in France, where 'family reconstitution' has been used successfully, English historians attempting this method, even with the aid of the massive resources of the Cambridge Group for the History of Population and Social Structure, have had only a few successes, such as Dr E. A. Wrigley's study of Colyton in Devon.[8] Even Dr R. S. Schofield, a leading exponent of 'family reconstitution', admits that 'it is rare to find a group of adjacent parishes all of whose registers are suitable for family reconstruction'.[9] Moreover, of those individuals whose biographies are 'reconstituted' the suspicion remains that they may be an immobile sample, who cannot therefore be considered typical of the mass of seventeenth-century English people.

A similar criticism – that the sources used reflect a minority and possibly an untypical minority – can be made of some attempts to trace the history of the family, another area of the history of society which is growing in popularity.[10] Generalizations about relationships between members of individual families and changes in those relationships in the seventeenth century which are based on diaries, correspondence, memoirs, didactic books, and plays are likely to reflect only what was happening in some upper-class families, and not by any means in all of them. What one certainly cannot assume is that those lower down the social scale aped the customs and attitudes of their social superiors.[11]

Finally, there is a practical consideration that historians of society have to take into account: the need for large-scale investments of time and labour. While one is bound to applaud the aim of 'reconstructing historical communities', one's enthusiasm for it is accompanied by the sobering thought that to follow the advice of its latest exponent one would need the support of a large research team and a considerable financial grant.[12]

Given these problems and more, it is not surprising that few conclusions about the history of society have received the widespread approval of historians. Recent research, however, has produced at least two major discoveries which have caused long-held concepts about social mobility and family patterns to be abandoned. Perhaps the most startling discovery is that pre-industrial villages were not insular communities from which most of the inhabitants rarely moved. Dr Cornwall's study of 206 people who acted as witnesses in two ecclesiastical courts in Sussex between 1580 and 1640 shows that over 75 per cent of them no longer lived in the place of their birth; most had moved only once and over a short distance of up to twenty miles. These witnesses, however, were 'gentry, farmers, and respectable tradesmen',[13] and it is highly likely that those lower down the social scale were forced to move more frequently and over longer distances, tramping from village to village in search of work. Between 1580 and 1640 migrants arrived in three Kentish towns who had travelled from every part of England and Wales.[14] The second success of historians of society has been to establish certain features about family structure and behaviour in this period. The nuclear family, not the extended family, was common, with important economic implications as has been seen. The age of marriage of both sexes and at most social levels was fairly late, often in the late twenties. As a result the size of most families was small. This was brought about also by two other features which recur in demographic studies of pre-industrial England: high infant mortality and the practice of adolescents leaving home to work elsewhere. Furthermore, because of the late age of marriage and the low expectation of life, most marriages did not last very long and remarriage was very common.

All these are important conclusions, but it is difficult to extend the list. The study of many other areas of the history of society is, at best, only in its infancy. It is more remarkable that research on topics such as sexual behaviour, illegitimacy rates, prenuptial pregnancy, and the practice of infanticide has actually begun than that no definitive conclusions about them have been reached yet.[15] There seems to be some circumstantial support for Joan Thirsk's view that family ties were strongest in upland areas, where the competing claims of village community ties were weaker than in the nucleated villages of arable regions.[16] But Professor Stone's monumental hypothesis of changes in the family, of the growth in the seventeenth century of love and affection between husbands and wives and between parents and children, replacing the allegedly callous, cool attitudes which prevailed in the sixteenth century, is well described by Keith Thomas as

reminiscent of one of those pioneering maps for the age of discovery. Some of its outlines are clear, a few perhaps deceptively so. Others are blurred and incomplete. . . . In the course of time such maps are inevitably superseded. But they are not discarded altogether. Instead they are preserved by later generations to hang on the study wall as an eloquent and valued memorial of how much and how little was once known.[17]

The same might be said of other areas of society now being studied – the history of children and the role and status of women, for example. What we have at the moment are, at best, 'pioneering maps'. There is a long way to go before anyone will be able to provide an Ordnance Survey guide to these subjects.

There are two major areas of the history of society in the early seventeenth century which have not been mentioned above, and which have been the subject of intensive research: conditions and standards of living of people in the early seventeenth century, and their attitudes and beliefs. About both these topics there is no broad measure of agreement among historians. Nor is generalization made any easier by the diversity of material conditions and intellectual and religious beliefs in early seventeenth-century England. In the two following sections, therefore, perhaps more than in any other in this book, one enters a minefield of historical controversy and uncertainty.

Social groups and standards of living

There is no commonly accepted way of describing English society in the early seventeenth century. It is easier to reject terminology for this purpose than it is to find acceptable categories. 'Middle classes' still appears in some examination answers to questions on sixteenth- and seventeenth-century English history, but most examiners after reading J. H. Hexter's demolition of it, find it difficult to take seriously a term better suited to an industrialized and urbanized society.[18] It is more common to find historians distinguishing between those at the top of seventeenth- century society in terms of 'aristocracy' and 'gentry'.

However, although it is true that peers did have a superior social status and some privileges which were of economic value, like the right of self-assessment for taxation and protection in law against creditors, the distinction between peers and gentry is primarily a legal, not an economic, one. Both peers and gentry were rentier landowners; peers could be poorer than gentry. Too few historians have heeded R. H. Tawney's wise words, written in 1954: 'The groups described by the words "aristocracy" and "gentry" melt at their edges into each other, and the terms themselves contain an element of opinion as well as of fact.'[19] 'Gentry' itself is not a precise term: the most usual definition is those who had the right to bear coats of arms, but it is clear that contemporaries considered others also to be 'gentlemen'. Of the 398 'gentlemen' in Cheshire Grand Jury lists from 1625 to 1642 only five had been given the right to bear coats of arms by the College of Heralds; and of the 770 freeholders in the Lancashire freeholders' book of 1600 only seven are not styled 'gentlemen'.[20] Similar confusion surrounds the terminology used to describe those lower down the social scale; of these 'yeoman' and 'freeholder' are perhaps the most ambiguous.[21] Contemporaries themselves clearly had difficulties in describing the social order, especially since it was constantly changing. It was not uncommon for men to style themselves as 'gentlemen' in their wills, only to be described as 'yeomen' by the neighbours who drew up their probate inventories. The most comprehensive contemporary attempt to describe early seventeenth-century English society is by Thomas Wilson in 1600.[22]

Thomas Wilson's analysis of English society in 1600

	Average annual income
61 lay nobles (1 marquis, 19 earls, 2 viscounts and 39 barons)	£3,607
500 knights	£1,000–2,000
16,000 gentlemen	£500–1,000

Although Wilson's estimates of the sizes of social groups and incomes are probably far from accurate, his description is a good indication of the variety of conditions and the unequal distribution of wealth in English society at the beginning of the seventeenth century. However, Wilson's social groups are not distinct ones. As he himself wrote, 'many [knights] equall the best Barons [in wealth] and come not much behind many Erles . . .'.[23]

The following description of the structure of early seventeenth-century society is as artificial in its categorization as many others. Society in the early seventeenth century, as at any other time, did not consist of homogeneous, self-contained groups. However, an attempt has been made here to group together people whose economic fortunes and standards of living in this period were *broadly* similar.

The landowning classes

The landowning classes dominated early seventeenth-century society: they form a social group which it is notoriously hard to define. There were great variations in sources of income, wealth, and status among early seventeenth-century landowners. Although it was not a clear one, there was a division in the society of every county between the greater 'country gentry' and the lesser 'middling and parochial gentry'. The county magnates got a much greater proportion of their incomes from rent and less from direct farming than their less wealthy neighbours. They were also set apart by their greater influence and different social relationships. The great rentier landowners had estates scattered throughout the county (and in some cases beyond also); the lesser landowners had estates only in a few adjacent parishes at the most. The former dined and hunted together with their fellow county magnates, they governed together as sheriffs, JPs, and deputy lieutenants, and from this group were chosen the senior MPs for the county seats, the knights of the shire. The influence of lesser landowners, however, extended only in the small part of the county where their estates were: they might become JPs or MPs for a borough seat, but in normal times they were more likely to hold lesser posts in the county or parochial administration, as undersheriffs of the county or head constables of the hundred, and to serve on county Grand Juries. (In the abnormal conditions of the 1640s some lesser gentlemen came to hold important places in the county administration, excluding gentlemen of higher rank from places on parliamentary county committees; see p. 193 below.) Contemporaries were very careful in the use of terminology to describe the social stratification within the landowning classes: nobles, knights, esquires, and gentlemen. However, it must be emphasized that these distinctions were overshadowed by the divisions between those who were landed gentlemen and those who were not. In the late sixteenth century Sir Thomas Smith described gentlemen as those who could

live without manual labour, and thereto is able and will bear the port, charge and countenance of a gentleman, he shall for money have a coat and arms bestowed upon him by the heralds, and thereunto, being made so good cheap, be called master, which is the title that men give to esquires and gentlemen, and reputed for a gentleman ever after.

The borderline between Smith's gentlemen and non-gentlemen was the most important one in early seventeenth-century society.

The economic fortunes of this landowning gentleman class have been the centre of one of the fiercest debates between historians since the 1940s.[24] In a controversy aptly known as 'the storm over the gentry', a generation of historians tore each other apart in print and produced a bewildering variety of hypotheses about the century before 1640, 'the rise of the gentry', the decline of a class of 'mere gentry', and 'the crisis of the aristocracy'. Why this should have happened is largely explained by the conviction (so far unfounded) of many of the participants in the debate that in the changing fortunes of the great landowners before 1640 would be found a major cause of the English Revolution of the mid-seventeenth century. Less obviously, the debate originated in the ambiguity of the primary sources for assessing the wealth of landowners. Estate accounts of this period were designed to record the financial liability of bailiffs, receivers, and other officials to their lord, not to show (what the historian seeks) the profits and losses made by estate owners annually. It is very difficult to discover the income of any early seventeenth-century landowner; he probably had only an hazy idea himself. It is also possible for different historians to put forward conflicting theories of social change because in the period before 1640 it is easy to find examples of great landowners whose wealth declined *and* of those who prospered. With the dust now settled on 'the storm over the gentry' one is left with the unspectacular conclusion that there were great variations of wealth, standards of living, and economic fortunes among landowners before the middle of the century. This is no doubt true of any period: there always have been improvident, as well as enterprising, landowners. Is it possible that there were features of the period before 1640 that ensured that landowning fortunes were more unstable than at most other times? This may be so, but if it is, the opportunities for landowners to increase their wealth far outweighed the difficulties that might cause a landowner's wealth to be drastically reduced.

One of the dangers threatening great landed fortunes in   : late sixteenth and early seventeenth centuries was that the social pressures on those who had attained the ranks of the county élite to spend were perhaps greater than at any other time. Those who had wealth were expected to display it in every possible way: by building grand houses, providing lavish hospitality, and by making generous provisions for their children.[25] These pressures were naturally more intense in London, and, once established in the capital, some landed families found that London absorbed more and more of their time and money. In the 1640s the Sussex gentleman, Sir Thomas Pelham, and his family stayed in London for six months a year at enormous expense. 'They spent the decade' writes Anthony Fletcher, 'buying their way into fashionable London society.'[26] The obsession of the landed classes with expensive displays of wealth and status is illustrated also by their interest in genealogy (which was frequently carried to the lengths of fabricating long family trees, claiming ancient gentility) and in coats of arms. As Sir Thomas Smith admitted in the middle of the sixteenth century, gentlemen could buy from the King of Heralds coats of arms 'newly made and invented, the title whereof shall pretend to have been found by the said herald in perusing and viewing of old registers'. 'To purchase arms (if he emulates gentry)', wrote John Stephens in 1615, poking fun at aspiring gentlemen, 'sets upon him like an ague: it breaks his sleep, takes away his stomach, and he can never be quiet till the herald hath given him the harrows, the cuckoo, or some ridiculous emblem for his armoury.'[27] But, despite satirical comments, the expensive scramble for coats of arms and purchases of titles went on increasingly in the early seventeenth century (see below, pp. 123–4).

One other form of expenditure – on litigation – was probably heavier in this period than at other times. Landowners are always inevitably involved in litigation over property, but in the late sixteenth and early seventeenth centuries this could be especially time-consuming and expensive, because the land law regarding the descent of property was peculiarly ambiguous. So uncertain was the land law that Sir Francis Bacon in 1600 believed that 'the inheritances of this realm are tossed at this day, as upon a sea, in such sort that it is hard to say which bark will sink, and which will get to the haven: that is to say, what assurances will stand good, and what will not'.[28] So unsure were lawyers what the land law was regarding the inheritance of property that it became difficult for landowners to devise settlements which ensured the descent of their property intact for more than one generation. On the death of a landowner in cases where there was no direct male heir, therefore, inheritance disputes between competing claimants often occurred. At best the uncertain state of the land law caused landlords to spend vast sums on litigation, and at worst it could lead to the division of the estates among the claimants in extra-legal settlements.[29] The law regarding credit was also peculiarly hostile to landowners in the late sixteenth and early seventeenth centuries. Borrowing was a normal part of the economic life of large landowners; it did not indicate that they were in permanent financial difficulties (as was assumed by some of the participants in 'the storm over the gentry') but simply that they needed cash temporarily, because of fluctuations in the level of their incomes or for an unusually expensive project (for example, housebuilding). Unfortunately for borrowers the law courts in the late sixteenth and early seventeenth centuries interpreted the law regarding repayment of loans, especially redemption of mortgages, very strictly. Judgement was given against defaulters, who were given no extra time to redeem mortgages, and creditors were allowed to enter the debtor's property immediately. In the reign of James I the Howards found that even royal favour did not keep them out of the grasp of London moneylenders like Thomas Sutton and Lionel Cranfield.[30] Both the land law and the law regarding credit were to be later corrected in the landowners' favour by the evolution of the strict settlement and the principle of equity of redemption, but neither of these legal devices was common before the mid-seventeenth century.

'Peace and the law have beggared us all', wrote Sir Thomas Oglander in about 1625.[31] There was some truth in his exaggerated comment, but for most landowners there were more opportunities to increase their wealth than to lose it in this period: firstly from the profits from land, and secondly because of favourable political developments. Land was naturally the main form of investment by landowners, but it is worth noting that English landowners in this period were willing to invest in trade and industry. It is true that they felt themselves to be superior to merchants and tradesmen. 'Gentlemen of worth', said an anonymous tract in 1598, 'wayed no wealth, but held Coyne in utter contempt, not vouchsafing to touch, handle, or dispose of it.'[32] A 1629 pamphlet was concerned enough to ask *Whether Apprenticeship Extinguisheth Gentry?*[33] But these scruples did not prevent English landowners (unlike the French nobility) from exploiting coal and iron resources on their estates, investing in trade and colonization companies, and taking a leading part in property development in London. Some *nouveaux riches* landowners with mercantile origins in Northamptonshire, ironmasters in Sussex, and coalmasters in Durham, owed their new wealth to trade and industry. But they were exceptions; not many landlords made fortunes from industrial and commercial investment or from office holding.[34] Given the state of the English economy, which has already been described, and the English crown's lack of a large bureaucracy, which will be seen later, this is not surprising.

Despite this, there seems little doubt that in the century before 1640 great landowners overcame the problems of the price revolution. By forcing them to pay more for food and by eroding their rental income inflation *could* have ruined them. One way that they could have prevented this would have been to revert to direct farming, and so benefit from soaring food prices, as their predecessors did in similar circumstances in the thirteenth century.[35] However, in the early seventeenth century only minor landowners engaged in commercial farming to any great extent. The only form of large-scale farming engaged in by a few large landowners was sheep farming, and even these landowners, for example the Spencers of Althorp, soon reverted to leasing their estates as wool prices fell.[36] A plausible explanation for their failure to become farmers is that they found other ways of protecting their income from inflation. Most landowners were unaffected to any great extent by rising food prices, since most had a demesne farm to supply their households. It was also common for large landowners to demand that tenants who farmed in the neighbourhood of their houses should pay rents in the form of food or fuel. Great tithes, which were often paid to secular landowners, were also sometimes paid in kind. Moreover, not only did landowners insulate themselves from the worst effects of the price revolution in these ways, but most managed to raise their rental incomes by at least as much as the rise in prices. There were, of course, those landowners, who did not, either because of incompetent management or because their estates were let out on conditions which secured their tenants against change. As will be seen, many copyhold tenants possessed a greater degree of security of tenure than was once thought (see p. 46 below). But there were tenants whose tenure was too insecure to resist landlord pressure. Perhaps, though, it is a mistake to describe landlord-tenant relations in this period in terms of conflict: landlords trying with varying degrees of success to squeeze greater rents and entry fines from unwilling tenants. It may be that nearer the truth is the fact that rising demand for tenancies (a result of the expanding population and profits to be made from farming in this period) was more responsible for pushing up the level of rents than the machinations of 'covetous' landlords. 'I have seene and observed among them [tenants] a kind of madnesse,' said John Norden's surveyor in 1607. When

the Lord hath beene at liberty to dispose thereof [i.e. let some estates] at his will, for best advantage by choyse of a new Tennant, Proclamation to that effect hath beene made in open Court, where I have seene, and it is daily in use, that one will out-bid another, in so much as I have wondred at their emulation.[37]

For whatever reason, most estates in the later sixteenth and early seventeenth centuries that have been studied show evidence of a marked rise in rents, at least in line with the rise in land values and the fall in the value of money.[38]

The landowning classes were also helped in overcoming the problems of the price revolution by developments that had as much to do with politics as with economics. In the early seventeenth century the English landed classes were the lightest taxed in the whole of Europe. With the exception of increasing wardship payments and fines to be paid by Catholics, all attempts to change this in this period failed. The peerage assessed their own incomes for taxation purposes, and those landlords who were not peers were assessed by commissions made up of their fellow members of the county élites. Consequently landowners paid taxes on incomes that bore no resemblance to reality. Dr Cliffe discovered that Yorkshire gentlemen in the early seventeenth century returned incomes for contributions to parliamentary subsidies that were usually fifty times less than the real value of their estates. Sir Timothy Hutton of Marske's real income was £1,077 in 1606 and £1,096 in 1625, yet between 1605 and 1625 he was always assessed on an income of £20 p.a. and during that time his total subsidy payments were only £64.[39]

Moreover, landowners were the major beneficiaries of the massive sales of crown and Church lands which went on from the Dissolution in the 1530s to 1640. Many myths about those sales have now been exposed.[40] The lands were not sold cheaply; nor did the bulk go to speculators who founded new landed families in the process. Local studies show that the purchasers were of diverse types, but many were established land-owners. Local variations ought not to obscure the fact that the prevailing trend of landownership was from the crown and the Church to secular landowners. Varied and diverse may have been the fortunes of individual landowners in late sixteenth- and early seventeenth-century England, but there are many reasons to believe that the problems preventing them from increasing their wealth and standards of living were not so important as is sometimes suggested.

Farmers

This is a group which, like the previous one, cuts across legal classifications. Some farmers were owner-occupiers and freeholders; others were tenants: leaseholders, copyholders, or tenants-at-will. Although some supplemented their incomes from other sources – the lesser gentlemen by letting out parcels of their estates, yeomen and husbandmen by working as craftsmen – all the individuals considered here got the bulk of their income from direct farming. As in the case of the landowning classes, there were great variations in wealth and standards of living among farmers in early seventeenth-century England. Moreover, even the size of farms held by farmers of equivalent status differed from area to area. For example, to be a substantial farmer on the Lincolnshire claylands necessitated a smaller holding (30–80 acres) than on the adjacent Lincolnshire wolds (80–100 acres).[41] A study of one community, then, will not be typical of the whole country, but it will illustrate the diversity of farmers and farms that existed in early seventeenth-century England. Myddle in Shropshire was dominated by six large farms, ranging from 250 to 650 acres, consisting of rented and freehold land.[42] They were held by farmers who called themselves, and were called by their neighbours, 'gentlemen', and who aspired to become undersheriffs and constables of the hundred. Only slightly inferior to these 'resident minor gentry' were farmers holding 100–200 acres, who were usually called 'yeomen', but sometimes 'gentlemen'; one of them, John Downton of Alderton Hall was granted the right by the Heralds' Visitation in 1623 to bear a coat of arms. Below these were a group of farmers with farms ranging from under 10 acres to 88 acres. They were often described as 'husbandmen', but the richer ones were sometimes called by the superior title of 'yeomen'.

By the middle of the eighteenth century English farming was not characterized by the same diversity in the size of farms. By that time there were more large farms, and many middling and small farmers had disappeared. In this, the evolution of English society differed from that in many other parts of Europe, where a class of independent peasantry survived into the eighteenth century and beyond. Therefore, it is important to ask when and why the large class of small, independent English farmers disappeared.[43] This is a question which has attracted the attention of fewer historians than those interested in the fate of English landlords in this period. However, it apparently rouses in some historians the same kind of vitriolic reaction which caused Professor R. H. Tawney to complain during 'the storm over the gentry' that 'an erring colleague is not an Amalekite to be smitten hip and thigh'.[44] One wonders what, if he had been alive, Tawney's reaction would have been to the invective which Dr Eric Kerridge directed against his great book, *The Agrarian Problem in the Sixteenth Century* (1912). In 1969 Kerridge pilloried Tawney for allowing his political activities to prejudice his historical judgement.

Hence [wrote Kerridge] his wholly untrue picture of early capitalism as cruel and greedy, destructive alike of social welfare and true spiritual values. No one would wish to deny that Tawney was a great man, but this greatness caused him to lead whole generations of history students into grievous error.[45]

This is not the place to begin a detailed defence of Tawney's influence on historical studies of the sixteenth and seventeenth centuries, but it is to be hoped that Kerridge's words will not cause Tawney's books to be neglected. One does not have to agree with the interpretations put forward by historians to be inspired by them; progress in historical understanding is frequently the product of disagreement between historians. Although Kerridge exaggerates Tawney's general argument,[46] it is true that Tawney in *The Agrarian Problem* argued that landlords met the problem of inflation by striving to force tenants to accept leases with commercial annual rents or higher occasional entry fines. In the process, argued Tawney, customary tenants were given little protection by the law, and the traditional paternal relationship between landlord and tenant was undermined. Although Tawney did not see this as the end of the class of small, independent English farmers, he did consider that it was a major step towards its eventual elimination. With all this, Kerridge disagrees. In his view landlord–tenant relations in the sixteenth and early seventeenth centuries were characterized more by cooperation than by conflict. In any case, he argues, even when landlords wanted to raise rents and entry fines to excessive levels, they were prevented from doing so by the custom of the manor, which interpreted what were and what were not 'reasonable' fines and rents. Above all, Kerridge emphasizes that many tenants, especially copyholders for one life or more, whom Tawney considered to be customary tenants, were in fact recognized in the early seventeenth century to be, technically and legally, freeholders. In the words of the great early seventeenth-century lawyer, Sir Edward Coke, 'In respect of the state of the land, so copyholders may be freeholders; for any that hath any estate in any land, whatsoever, may in this sense be termed a freeholder.'[47] Therefore, argued Kerridge forcibly, this group of tenants, whom Tawney calculated made up 42 per cent of his sample of occupiers of the land, enjoyed complete security of tenure at this time.

This 'storm over the peasantry', like 'the storm over the gentry', presents the student with diametrically opposing hypotheses. Was the period before 1650 a vital one in the disappearance of the class of small, independent farmers in England? The question will not be dodged, but it is important to recognize that the diversity of conditions and fortunes enjoyed by farmers in the early seventeenth century makes this a difficult question to answer. There were both farmers who prospered *and* farmers who struggled and failed to survive. What were the principal determinants of success or failure for farmers in the early seventeenth century?

In approaching this question historians have often emphasized the importance of the type of tenure by which farmers held their lands. In this respect owner-occupiers and freeholders (which now, after Kerridge's work, must also include all those holding tenures for life) had virtually complete security of tenure. Freeholders paid only a fixed 'chief' rent which was only a nominal sum: in Myddle, 'chief' rents of 1*d* a year were common, and in one case a freeholder paid 'a pair of gilt spurs or 1*d*'.[48] Therefore, owner-occupiers and freeholders were able to take for themselves all the increased profits from farming in an age of rising food prices. Customary tenants, especially tenants-at-will, who had no copies of their conditions of tenure, were in a less enviable position when faced with landlords who wanted to raise rents and fines. Kerridge is correct in pointing out that the custom of the manor protected tenants against 'unreasonable' rent increases, but one wonders whether customary tenants were able in practice to take advantage of the theoretical protection which the law gave them. Did they have the time, money, and expertise to take their powerful landlords to court? Customary tenants in Cumberland and Westmorland in the early seventeenth century were not protected by the law or the crown. After 1603 and the union of the crowns of England and Scotland they were no longer able, as they had done in the sixteenth century, to claim 'tenant right' against excessive entry fines because of their military obligations to serve in the Borders against the Scots. As a result, landlords, including the crown on its estates, forced tenants to accept greatly increased entry fines or leases at commercial rates.[49]

However, in concentrating on legal aspects, it may be that historians have focused on matters which were only of secondary importance in affecting the standards of living of farmers. Economic resources possessed by farmers and economic pressures on them were perhaps more important. The larger the farm, the larger the amount of food to be sold, and the larger the profits, is no doubt a truism, but one of great importance in an age of rising food prices. The size of farms was often determined by prevailing inheritance customs. Primogeniture (the descent of all property to the eldest son) was by no means the rule everywhere in England in the early seventeenth century. Partible inheritance (the division of the property among all the deceased's sons) was common in some parts of the country, and in these areas it could mean that tenancies were split into smaller and smaller parcels, therefore making it increasingly likely that farms would no longer be viable commercial units.

Perhaps more important than size of farms and inheritance customs in determining a farmer's standard of living was the type of economy he practised. Local studies show that farmers in arable, fielden, grain-growing areas, described by contemporaries as 'champion countries' (such as Sherington in Buckinghamshire, and Chippenham and Orwell in Cambridgeshire)[50] faced more problems than those in upland, forest, and moorland regions with a predominantly pastoral economy (such as Myddle in Shropshire, the Lincolnshire Fens, the Northamptonshire Forest, and Willingham in Cambridgeshire).[51] Pastoral farms required less labour and capital outlay than arable farms; only the richer arable farmers were able to spend large sums on improvements like 'floating' the watermeadows and the introduction of mixed husbandry. Moreover, in upland areas there were more opportunities for farmers to earn income from other sources than farming to carry them through periods of temporary disaster. By-employment was more common in these areas, as was access to waste and forest land, which was a valuable communal asset as a source of fuel, food, and pasture not available in the more highly enclosed 'champion' areas.[52] This distinction is naturally too clearcut. The moorland areas of Cumberland and Westmorland, where squatters settled in such great numbers in the early seventeenth century that the area became overpopulated, causing extreme poverty, obviously do not fit the pattern of prosperous upland areas.[53] Nor do the thriving market gardeners in the Thames Valley conform to the picture of struggling small farms in arable regions. But it may be that these were exceptions that do not invalidate the underlying generalization.

A combination of legal and economic pressures, then, produced varied conditions and standards of living for farmers in the early seventeenth century. However, can one offer a more positive answer to the important question asked earlier: was the period before 1650 a vital one in the history of the disappearance of the small, independent farmer in England? There is little doubt that some small farmers, especially those in arable areas with not enough capital to withstand a series of bad harvests, disappeared in the late sixteenth and early seventeenth centuries. In some areas the bad harvest years of the 1590s and early 1620s caused intense distress. In both periods in Cumberland and Westmorland people died of starvation; they may also have done so in Ashton-under-Lyne in Lancashire in 1623–4, when burials reached a level three times above the normal, the number of births fell by half, and infant mortality greatly increased.[54] The crisis of the early 1620s was especially serious because bad harvests coincided with the collapse of the cloth trade, which slashed by-employment in the cloth industry. However, very few cases of severe distress, like those in the north-west, have been uncovered elsewhere for this period. Certainly rural England suffered nothing like the recurrent crises of subsistence which hit seventeenth-century France. The economic climate favoured most farmers. Even small arable farmers were helped by the fact that grain prices generally kept up in the early seventeenth century. The small farmers of Myddle and of Wigston Magna in Leicestershire survived; 'monumental stability' is how Professor W. G. Hoskins described society at this level in the Leicestershire villages.[55] Large farmers probably did more than survive. The 'great rebuilding' of the late sixteenth and early seventeenth centuries, the proliferation of lesser manor houses and solid farmhouses and farm buildings in all parts of the country, indicates that there is substance in contemporary comments about a growing class of yeoman farmers in this period.[56] All this is, of course, not conclusive evidence, but it does suggest that before 1650 many English farmers survived and that some of them prospered. It was not until the late seventeenth and early eighteenth centuries that small farmers were severely hit by falling agricultural prices, precipitating a major transformation in English landed society.

Farm labourers and vagrants

Professor W. G. Hoskins wrote in 1952 that 'the history of the farm labourer is almost unknown. Perhaps we can never know much about it before the days of the reports to the Board of Agriculture, beginning with Fraser's report in 1794. It is not that he has no history, but that it is unrecorded until comparatively recent times'.[57] There are obviously formidable difficulties in studying a social group which has left few written records. Historians, however, are trained to extract from documents information which the records were not originally designed to show. Professor Alan Everitt's work on farm labourers before 1640 is a brilliant example of this aspect of the historian's craft.[58] By using subsidy assessments, manorial surveys, lawsuits, wills and probate inventories he has advanced our knowledge of a social group about whom previously very little was known. The difficulties presented by these sources, though, ought not to be minimized. Taxation and legal documents record only those with money or property. For example, probate inventories, which are lists of peoples' possessions made when they died, are full of information about housing and living conditions, employment, and even diet. They are the principal primary source for reconstructing the lives of farm labourers, but, because only the wealthiest of labourers had any property worth recording when they died, probate inventories give an exaggerated impression of the wealth and standards of living of farm labourers.

As with other social groups, the term 'farm labourers' encompasses a great variety of economic and social conditions; from those who had a smallholding of a few acres and sometimes some animals to those who were solely dependent either on wages from casual employment at harvest time or on private charity or poor relief. Although those labourers who had some land and animals could be self-sufficient in basic commodities, like peas, beans, milk, and dairy products, supplemented occasionally by pork, only the wealthiest labourers could grow grain, the basic item of their diet. Of Everitt's sample, drawn from thirteen counties, of 650 labourers who held land only 7 per cent held over four acres, which was the legal minimum which all cottages were supposed to have according to an Act of 1598. The rest fell well below that minimum: 67 per cent held only 1 acre or less. These 650 labourers represented the fortunate few; Everitt's estimate is that only one quarter of labourers in the period before 1640 held any land. Nevertheless some labourers might be able to graze animals on common land or waste, which was also a source of fuel and food in the form of wild animals, fruits and herbs. They might also be able to combine farm work with some form of industrial by-employment. Perhaps the best form of cushion against inflation for farm labourers in this period was by living and eating in the house of their employer, as many of them did. These fortunate labourers might prosper and perhaps move into the ranks of husbandmen or skilled craftsmen, while others faced the prospect of a stable or declining standard of living.

It is important that the diversity of conditions is recognized, but this ought not to obscure the general trends affecting the lives of agricultural labourers before 1640. The first of these is that the standard of living of many of them was falling, especially if they were principally reliant on wages for their incomes. There is no doubt that in the century and a half before 1650 the real wages of labourers fell. Wage-rates, of course, varied from area to area and from job to job; in the mid-seventeenth century a thatcher might be paid 2s 6d a day when the normal day labourer's wage was one shilling. But these rates represented something approaching a 50 per cent fall in real terms compared with those paid in 1500.[59] The machinery for regulating wages under the Statute of Artificers of 1563 seems largely to have been inoperative, and when JPs did enforce wage assessments they seem to have done so in order to keep wages down in times of temporary labour shortage.[60] But in the early seventeenth century these times were rare. The fifteenth century, a time of population stability and high demand for labour, had been 'the golden age of the English labourer';[61] in the succeeding 150 years, a time of rising population and a plentiful supply of labour, the farm labourers were the principal sufferers of the Price Revolution.

Secondly, the size of the labouring population grew rapidly in the period before the mid-seventeenth century. Professor Everitt's rough estimate (it can be no more exact than that in precensal days) is that in the early seventeenth century labourers composed about one quarter or one third of the total rural population. Moreover, this percentage was growing, as the labouring class was swelled by a rising population, dispossessed small farmers, and propertyless younger sons who, in regions where partible inheritance was uncommon, were bequeathed by their fathers only 'that which the catt left on the malt heape'.[62] Thirdly, labourers were a highly mobile group, forced to travel in search of work. Many moved to forest areas, attracted by the hopes of settling on newly cleared or unenclosed land and working in rural industries. The woodland community of Myddle was a frontier settlement in the late sixteenth and early seventeenth centuries. Landless migrants flocked there, living in scattered settlements of squatters, who eventually paid rent to the lord or his steward. Employment in the bigger farms, extensive common rights, and demand for rural craft labour made Myddle a haven for wandering labourers. From 7 per cent in 1541–70 the percentage of labourers among Myddle's population grew to 23.4 per cent by 1600 and 31.2 per cent by 1660.[63] Once established in these types of areas labourers did not necessarily settle permanently. Some areas became too populous, like the moorland areas of Cumberland and Westmorland, which became 'overpopulated in a Malthusian sense' in the early seventeenth century.[64] Others became a base from which labourers migrated temporarily to be employed at hiring fairs as labourers on arable farms at harvest time.

Inevitably some labourers became migrant workers with no permanent base. It is difficult to distinguish these from the vagrants who tramped the roads of early Stuart England. Vagrants are even more difficult to study than farm labourers. 'His (the vagrant's) history is inevitably written by his enemies', wrote Tawney.[65] Contemporary opinion, horrified by the threat it was felt that vagrants posed to respectable society, is reflected in hundreds of lurid descriptions of the country swarming with wandering groups of professional thieves and beggars. There is little doubt, though, that these descriptions were overdrawn. It is true that there were vagrants who were professional thieves, fortune-tellers, entertainers, and gypsies, who travelled in bands. A gang of 'wandering people', whose leader was known as Black James, terrorized the Horsham area of Sussex in 1614.[66] However, from the records of vagrants who were arrested, and from vagrants' passports issued to enable vagrants to return to their place of birth, emerges a sadder and perhaps more typical side of the life of the early Stuart vagrant.[67] Clearly labourers were often forced to take to the road by unemployment on the land, sometimes then suffering personal tragedies which condemned them to permanent vagrancy. Richard Walker, who arrived in Salisbury in 1600, when interrogated, said 'he lost his leg in Plymouth, had a passport from the mayor there to be conveyed to where he was born and lost his passport by the way'. Many vagrants were young, often unmarried, travelling alone for long periods. Ann Standley was arrested as a vagabond in Salisbury in 1600, 'and she confesses she has been a wanderer for the last year, has been punished three times before, and had passports accordingly'.[68] Some vagrants also travelled very long distances. The constable of Hastings rape in Sussex in 1638 and 1639 arrested vagrants from Yorkshire, Northamptonshire, Norfolk, Wiltshire, Glamorgan, and Devon.[69] Some of the 666 vagrants in Salisbury who were whipped and then given passports in the early seventeenth century had come from Ireland and the north of England; over 20 per cent had travelled more than a hundred miles to Salisbury.[70] Towns like Salisbury became the goal of many poor 'subsistence migrants', as has been seen, and the latter provide one of the many links between rural and urban society in the early seventeenth century.

Townspeople

Like other social categories this is an artificial one. The links between town and countryside were not confined to the migrant rural poor. The better-off classes on the land sent their sons to be apprenticed to urban craftsmen and merchants. Landed gentlemen bought or rented houses in London and the provincial capitals. Merchants bought landed estates and founded landowning families. The gentry 'invaded' towns to secure the election of their nominees to parliament. E. A. Wrigley estimates that one in every six English men and women visited London at least once in his or her lifetime.[71] Nevertheless there are significant distinguishing features of early seventeenth-century urban society to justify treating it separately from landed society: firstly, inequality in the distribution of wealth was more marked in towns than in the countryside; and, secondly, in the late sixteenth and early seventeenth centuries there emerged groups of professional people rarely found outside the towns.

Much of the evidence about the social structure of towns in the early modern period comes from the early sixteenth century, because the subsidy assessments of 1523–7 were unique among sixteenth- and early seventeenth-century taxation records in the effective way they reflected the real ownership of wealth in the country. There seems little doubt that conclusions based on these assessments are applicable also to seventeenth-century towns. Direct comparisons between the 1520s assessments and the Hearth Tax returns of Restoration England are not possible, but work on the latter suggests that 'the rough shape of the social pyramid in towns had altered relatively little since the early sixteenth century'.[72] If anything, inequality in the distribution of urban wealth became more marked with the passage of time. Already, in the early sixteenth century, urban poverty was extensive. One-third of the population of many towns was excluded from the subsidies of the 1520s because they earned less than £1 p.a., the lowest point on the taxation scale; in Coventry 48.5 per cent of the population were too poor to pay the tax. Of those who were assessed for the tax, moreover, the great majority received only the minimum £1 p.a., which led W. G. Hoskins to conclude that 'two-thirds of the urban population of the 1520s lived below or very near the poverty line'.[73] Studies of towns in the late sixteenth and early seventeenth centuries suggest that this group of poverty-stricken townspeople may have been getting bigger. The growing population that could not be absorbed by the agrarian economy spilled over into the towns. All urban studies note that the numbers of migrants from the countryside were rising; and a systematic study of a group of Kentish towns between 1580 and 1640 argues that this created 'an immigration crisis of severe proportions'.[74]

Most towns in the early 1520s were dominated by a handful of rich families; one-third of Leicester's wealth was held by six families and one-quarter of Coventry's by three men. In many towns nearly two-thirds of the wealth was held by 6–7 per cent of the population. During the next hundred years this class of very wealthy merchants and manufacturers became even more easy to isolate from the mass of townspeople, especially in London. Of the 140 men who became aldermen in London between 1600 and 1624 fifty-five were worth over £20,000 p.a. in goods when they died, and one, Sir John Spencer, probably owned nearly £400,000; most of the remaining seventy-eight left personal estates (excluding landed wealth) of £10–20,000. London was outstanding in the channels of profit open to merchants: overseas and domestic trades – over one-half of the 140 Jacobean aldermen made their fortunes from the latter – and government loans and customs administration.[75] Lionel Cranfield (later James I's lord treasurer) amassed a huge fortune as overseas merchant, lessee of government concessions, moneylender, and speculator in the customs administration.[76]

Although outside London urban élites were not so wealthy or large, yet in most towns there was a clear trend towards the control of urban economies and government by fewer and fewer people. This is reflected in the growing exclusiveness of town guilds. Often a small élite tightened its grip on one dominant guild (or, in the case of London, the major group of guilds, the Twelve Livery Companies) by raising the entry fees, effectively barring the less wealthy from guild membership. At the same time town governments became restricted to the small groups who controlled the guilds. The majority of borough charters issued in the sixteenth and early seventeenth centuries drastically reduced the democratic element in town governments. Moreover, the oligarchic aspirations of town élites were supported by the crown, which felt, rightly, that its control was enhanced when urban power was in the hands of a few people. As a result of these developments the classification of urban society in the late sixteenth and early seventeenth centuries is not fraught with the same uncertainties as analyses of landed society. The economic, social, and political gulf between the few rich families and the mass of urban power was rarely bridged. Newcomers to urban élites came from outside the towns, not from the lower classes in the towns. The gap between rich and poor in late sixteenth- and early seventeenth-century towns was even often visible in a residential pattern which was the opposite of that in many modern towns: well-to-do merchants built big houses in the town centres, while the urban poor lived in ghettos in the suburbs.

It has been estimated that between 1611 and 1640 the percentage of the wealth of Northampton held by the professional classes increased from 'virtually nil' to 10 per cent.[77] The only lay profession in medieval England was the law, but in late sixteenth- and early seventeenth-century towns other lay professional groups emerged in significant numbers, especially doctors and teachers. This is partly reflected in the development of professional institutions. For the medical profession the key steps were the establishment of the Royal College of Physicians in 1518, the College of Barber-Surgeons in 1540, and the Society of Apothecaries in 1617. In addition, within the medical profession efforts were made to ensure that separate functions were practised by physicians, surgeons, and apothecaries. In the early seventeenth century there were many battles in the law courts, in which physicians brought actions against apothecaries for diagnosing illnesses and prescribing drugs as well as supplying them. In the legal profession, also, separate functions were envisaged for attorneys, who were to represent litigants in court, and solicitors, who were to act as their clients' representatives in legal transactions outside courts. Moreover, in the early seventeenth century barristers, the élite of the profession who practised in the great central law courts in London, attempted to establish their seniority. In 1637 Lord Keeper Finch told a gathering of sergeants-at-law that they must not 'hugg an attorney, nor make an attorneys' feast and soe drawe them by those meanes to bringe them clyents'.[78]

Important as these developments are in the history of the professions, they do not adequately reflect the provision of professional services in early seventeenth-century England. Rarely in practice was there a distinction between attorneys and solicitors. William Pownell in Monmouth was no legal specialist. He represented clients in the courts of assize and quarter sessions, conveyed land from one client to another, as well as acting as a moneylender and estate agent. Like his fellow country lawyers, he might also have been retained by a great landowner as bailiff, auditor or attorney-general, by a town corporation as town clerk or recorder, or by a commission of the peace as clerk of the peace. The omnipresence of lawyers is better known than the impressive size of the medical profession in early seventeenth-century England. The monopoly claimed by the Royal College of Physicians was ineffective outside London. Whereas before 1640 there were less than forty licentiates of the College, one recent estimate (probably an under-estimate) is that there were 814 physicians outside London between 1603 and 1643.[79] There were undoubtedly many more apothecaries and surgeons, who, despite the opposition of physicians, acted as general practitioners. William White of Midhurst in Sussex, like William Pownell, was no specialist. In his will, in 1632 he called himself a surgeon, but 'he owned books on both physick and surgery, mortars, stills and "urinalls and other glasses" as well as an incision knife, spatula, stitching quill, bodkin, lancets and syringes'.[80] The clearest division among those who practised medicine in this period is between those academic doctors mentioned so far and the legion of people, 'wise' and· 'cunning' men and women, who prescribed magical or herbal remedies, which often must have seemed infinitely preferable to the savage prescriptions of purging and bleeding recommended by licensed doctors. Not surprisingly, many contemporaries like John Aubrey considered 'that if the world knew the villainy and knavery (besides ignorance) of the physicians and apothecaries, the people would throw stones at 'em as they walked in the streets'.[81] This sentiment must have fuelled the attacks on official medicine in the 1640s and 1650s, which was part of a general opposition to the monopoly which all professional groups attempted to establish in early Stuart England.[82]

Social mobility: affluence and poverty

Though there are serious disagreements among historians about the changes that were taking place in English society and in the varying fortunes of different social groups before 1650, no one challenges the view that inflationary and demographic pressures made the period one of great social mobility. Late sixteenth- and early seventeenth-century England in no way accorded with the stable, ordered society that many contemporaries would have liked it to be. The prosperous people of the period left monuments to their rising standards of living which still survive: 'prodigy houses', the stately homes of rentier landlords; manor houses built by lesser gentry with profits made from rents and farming; substantial farmhouses of thriving yeomen farmers; funeral monuments and educational endowments of successful merchants and clothiers; and, though less obvious, tucked away as they are in county record offices, probate inventories of well-to-do husbandmen, labourers, and craftsmen. William Harrison, writing in the later sixteenth century, noted improved standards in housing and living conditions:

There are old men yet dwelling in the village where I remaine, which have noted three things to be marvellouslie altred in England within their said remembrance. . . . One is, the multitude of chimnies latelie erected. . . . The second is the great (although not generall) amendment of lodging. . . . The third they tell of, is the exchange of Vessell, as of treene platters into pewter, and wooden spoones into silver or tin.[83]

Yet Harrison also observed that these improvements were not to be seen 'further off from our southern parts'. The geographical inequality in the distribution of wealth is best illustrated by county subsidy assessments. An analysis of those from 1515 produced the unsurprising conclusion that all but four of the counties with wealth higher than the average lay south of a line drawn from the Severn to the Wash. More startling is the scale of the disparity in the distribution of wealth; in 1515 Lancashire was assessed at £3.8 per 1,000 acres, while Middlesex's assessment was fixed at £238.1 per 1,000 acres.[84] Though the 1515 situation changed during the next century — for example the West Country and East Anglia declined, reflecting the fortunes of their textile industries — it is likely that the major change was that the rich southern counties pulled even further ahead of the poor north, especially as London grew rapidly. The unequal distribution of wealth among social groups is as striking as the regional differences. Those who became poorer in this period, improvident landlords, small farmers hit by bad harvests or rising rents, unemployed labourers and vagrants, and the urban poor, have left as many enduring (if not as obvious) signs of their presence as their more fortunate contemporaries: almshouses, workhouses, poor law statutes, and contemporary comments. Robert Gray in 1609 got right to the heart of the cause of poverty in this period. 'Our multitudes', he wrote, 'like too much blood in the body, do infect our country with plague and poverty. Our land hath brought forth but it hath not milk sufficient in the breast thereof to nourish all those children which it hath brought forth.'[85]

Not the least important indication of the size of the poverty problem in England in the late sixteenth- early seventeenth century is the combined effort of officialdom and private individuals to deal with it. Since poverty was more extensive in towns, it was naturally urban authorities which led the way in doing so. During the sixteenth century London and the provincial capitals, which were the main goals of streams of poor migrants, began to make censuses of the poor and build houses of correction in which to provide workhouses and outdoor relief for the young, old, and sick. In 1547 London was the first authority to authorize a compulsory poor rate to finance these schemes, and the capital's lead was soon followed by Norwich, Ipswich, Colchester, York, and other towns. In most towns expenditure on poor relief rose; the tiny community of Tiverton in Devon more than doubled its financial provision for the poor between 1612 (£120) and 1656 (£300).[86] At times of severe economic crisis, especially during the early 1620s when trade dislocation combined with plague and bad harvests, the threat of being overwhelmed by hoards of desperate, poor people encouraged some towns to formulate imaginative schemes. The best known is the establishment of a municipally run brewery at Salisbury in the early 1620s, the profits of which were intended to be used to finance poor relief in the town. In addition, no doubt to prevent the poor squandering their dole on municipal ale, the Salisbury authorities issued poor relief tokens which could only be exchanged for goods at a town storehouse.[87]

In all this English towns responded to the poverty problem in ways similar to those of many continental towns. Where England differed is that the state adopted some of the urban poverty relief schemes to establish a national poor relief system. The first major step was an Act of 1572 which established a compulsory poor rate in every parish. The economic crisis of the 1590s prompted parliament in 1598 to produce two statutes which drew on urban experience in coping with the poor, and which were to be the basis of the national poor relief system in England until 1834. The two statutes reflected the way contemporary opinion divided the poor. The first dealt with the able-bodied poor, who were considered to be poor because they were idle and who were therefore undeserving of poor relief; all such 'sturdy beggars' over the age of seven were to be whipped and returned to the parish of their birth if it was known, or, if it was not, to the place where they had last lived for at least a year. A statute of 1610 made further provision for 'sturdy beggars' by ordering each parish to establish a house of correction to employ and punish them. The second Act of 1598 was concerned with the impotent poor, who were poor because of no fault of their own; these old or sick deserving poor were either to be given outdoor relief in the form of pensions, food or clothing, or they were to be put into workhouses. Poor children where possible were to be found apprenticeships. These Acts and a codifying statute of 1601 placed the responsibility for organizing poor relief on the parishes, who were to appoint overseers to administer poor relief and to collect the compulsory poor rate.

Legislation reflects intention not achievement. How successfully did the parish authorities in the early seventeenth century administer the national system of poor relief? Unfortunately the establishment and operation of it was too piecemeal to allow a clear answer. Not all parishes established a compulsory poor rate after the passage of the 1572, 1598, and 1601 legislation, and those that did administered it with varying degrees of efficiency and zeal. Often more energy seems to have been directed by parish authorities into the punishment and resettlement outside their parish of the vagrant poor and into outdoor relief for the deserving poor, rather than into the more complicated business of establishing workhouses and employment schemes. Few parishes in the West and North Riding of Yorkshire had stocks of material on which the poor could work until the reign of Charles I.[88] The control of alehouses was also a common concern of both county and parish authorities, partly on moral grounds and because alehouses were seen to be the breeding ground of crime and disorder, but also because alehouses were considered to be a major cause of poverty, as well as providing shelter for wandering beggars. The predominant emphasis of poor law administration in individual parishes was on restricting the numbers of paupers within their jurisdiction and therefore in keeping down the escalating cost of poor relief. Concern at the latter undoubtedly grew; parishioners grumbled at too high assessments, and quarter sessions had to sort out numerous rating disputes. Though there are few instances of blatant inefficiency and corruption in early seventeenth-century poor law administration, this is no doubt a reflection of the available primary sources rather than of reality; overseers' and churchwardens' accounts are hardly likely to record instances of maladministration and corruption. It would be dangerous to argue that none occurred. But perhaps one can be too sceptical. At times of severe distress most poor law authorities acted zealously, although once the immediate crisis was over the authorities probably relaxed their administrative vigilance. This is probably true of the administration of poor relief in the 1630s through the Books of Orders, as will be seen later. With varying results the poor relief system was established in most English parishes in the early seventeenth century, especially from the 1620s onwards. 'When the civil war broke out, the poor rate had become a fact of life': Anthony Fletcher's conclusion about Sussex was probably true of most areas of England.[89]

It is a mistake to assume from the patchy quality of poor law administration in the early seventeenth century that the major role in the relief of poverty was filled, not by the official poor law, but by the philanthropy of individuals. This is Professor W. K. Jordan's contention, which he supports by massive research into all charitable endowments and bequests made between 1480 and 1660.[90] Landed gentlemen considered it their duty to look after the poor by distributing largesse. 'Twice a week', wrote Sir Hugh Cholmondley, a Yorkshire landowner, looking back to the 1630s, 'a certain number of people, widows and indigent persons were served at my gates with bread and good pottage made of beef, which I mention that those which succeed may follow the example.'[91] Even more important was the money poured into poor relief by merchants. Jordan has shown that private charity was important before 1660; he has not, however, proved that it was growing in value nor that it was more important than official charity. Indeed, when the fall in the value of money in the sixteenth and early seventeenth centuries is taken into account (which Jordan does not do) the *real* value of private philanthropy did not grow at all. Moreover, the charities established by individuals were probably no more efficiently administered than those set up by the poor law authorities. Some municipal authorities found irresistible the temptation to dip into charitable funds and use the money for other purposes.

There seems no doubt that the poor law was more important than the erratic contribution of private charity in the relief of poverty in the early seventeenth century. Both, however, were at best palliatives, and had no success in significantly reducing the size of the pauper population. As Robert Gray recognized at the time, poverty was deep-rooted in the economic structure of early Stuart England, in which unemployment and underemployment were common. When such an economy was hit by a run of bad harvests, then the condition of life for many people could become very bad indeed. The harvest failures of the 1620s, 1630s, and 1640s led Bowden to conclude that these decades 'witnessed extreme hardship in England, and were probably the most terrible years through which the country has ever passed.'[92]

Intellectual developments and popular beliefs

There are many aspects of the period before 1650 that seem to be progressive forerunners of future developments: educational opportunities increased; more people became literate, modern scientific principles were discovered; and Protestantism, a rational and anti-magical religion, was the prevalent ideology. However, it would be misleading to describe these developments in education, science, and religion in the early seventeenth century as 'modern' or 'progressive'. Even if more people were becoming literate, it does not necessarily follow that they read or were taught new, 'modern' ideas. Though the scientific discoveries of this period were important for the future development of science, before 1650 few of them were known outside a narrow group of English and European scientists. Furthermore, these men easily combined their work on the new discoveries with equal interest in matters that are nowadays considered to be irrational and superstitious. Nor is it clear that Protestantism, any more than science, was a catalyst of change, a solvent of old attitudes and beliefs.

Historians looking back to the period before 1650 are too prone to characterize it as one which makes a clear break with the Middle Ages, in the history of ideas no less than in the history of government. In both cases this approach can produce a distorted picture: what is unusual is highlighted as the norm and the most common ideas and beliefs of the period are obscured.

Education and literacy: an 'educational revolution'?

Educational opportunities for boys were plentiful in England in the late sixteenth and early seventeenth centuries. For the sons of landed gentlemen education often began at home or in the household of a neighbouring magnate. Some gentlemen employed tutors, though education in large households was not confined to academic subjects. Boys learned how to run households and estates by service as household officials, which was seen as

a gentlemanly profession. ... [It] was in no sort servile, nor the paynes belonging it any pennance, but they ioyed as much in their libertie, and florished as freshe in their profession as any other; their fare was always of the best, their apparell fine, neate, handsome and comely, their credite and esteeme always equall with their birth and calling in good regarde.[93]

For other boys also education often began outside a school. Promising youngsters might be singled out to be taught to read and write by local clergymen or curates. Others who were able attended village 'petty' schools, which attempted to teach basic reading and writing. Naturally, the quality of such schools varied. In the Shropshire village of Myddle there can be little doubt which was the better school: Mr Osmary Hill ran a school at Bilmarsh Farm, which had a good local reputation and 'many gentlemen's sons of good quality were his schollers', while Mr Twyford merely 'taught neighbours' children to read and his wife taught women to sew, and make needle workes'.[94] Only after learning to read was a boy supposed to enter a grammar school to be taught to read and write Latin. Both petty and grammar schools were abundant in the early seventeenth century in all parts of the country that have been studied. Between 1574 and 1628 most Cambridgeshire villages had a schoolmaster; in early seventeenth-century West Sussex there was a petty or grammar school in at least twenty towns and villages; seventy schoolmasters were licensed to teach in Leicestershire between 1600 and 1640; in the same period there were thirty eight teachers in Canterbury, twelve schools in Faversham, and twenty eight in Maidstone in Kent. It has been estimated that between 1560 and 1640 over £293,000 were given by individuals for the establishment of grammar schools, and that 142 new grammar schools were established between 1603 and 1649. These statistics probably underestimate the scale of educational provision because many unendowed schools and unlicensed teachers are hidden from the records. There is also some indication that schoolteachers were becoming better qualified; from the 1580s to the 1630s the percentage of teachers with degrees, licensed to teach in the diocese of London, more than doubled.[95]

Numerous contemporary treatises reflect the high value placed by many on education to produce an educated magistracy and to promote Protestantism by increasing the ability to read and interpret the Bible. Higher education, as well as elementary and secondary education, consequently flourished. New colleges were founded at Oxford and Cambridge: Jesus and Wadham at Oxford in 1571 and 1612, Emmanuel and Sidney Sussex at Cambridge in 1584 and 1596. Even more striking is the apparent increase in the numbers admitted to the universities in the same period, rising from under 800 a year in 1560 to a peak of over 1,200 a year in the 1630s. Professor Lawrence Stone concludes that this represented a proportion of the seventeen- to eighteen-year-old age group at university that was not exceeded until three centuries later.[96] Many of the undergraduates did not stay to take a degree. After a year many sons of landed gentlemen went to one of the Inns of Court to gain a smattering of legal knowledge to help them in the administration of their estates. In the early seventeenth century, especially after the establishment of European peace in 1604 and 1609, it was becoming customary for them to complete their education by foreign travel. The Grand Tour was established as a normal part of a gentleman's education, despite great parental concern, due not only to its expense and the opportunities it gave young men to enjoy pleasures forbidden them at home. It was also felt unfortunate that the major European centres of culture were also hotbeds of Catholicism, and in any case early seventeenth-century gentlemen were no less distrustful of foreigners than their descendants in the reigns of William III and Queen Anne. Sir Henry Slingsby of Scriven in Yorkshire told his son in 1610 to 'take heed what companie he keepes in too familiar a fashion for the frenche are of an ill conversacon and full of many loathsome deseases'.[97]

Stone believes that not only were educational opportunities abundant in this period, but that there was an increase in the provision of and an improvement in the quality of education between 1560 and 1640 that amounted to 'an educational revolution'. This raises two associated questions: how extensive were educational opportunities and how high were educational standards before 1560, and how can one measure changes in educational standards after 1560? Too often the argument that there was a marked improvement in education after 1560 minimizes the later medieval expansion of English education. Between 1350 and 1529 six Oxford colleges and nine Cambridge colleges were founded. Although there are few statistics, many grammar schools were also founded in this period. The historian of education in the later Middle Ages cannot be more exact because of the scarcity of primary sources. Licensing of schoolteachers and diocesan visitation recording of schools did not begin until the 1550s. Matriculation registers were not regularly kept at Cambridge until 1544 and at Oxford until 1571. The historian of English education from the mid-sixteenth century onwards is consequently faced with an abundance of sources. What he or she must guard against is assuming that this by itself is proof of anything other than an improvement in educational administration and record-keeping.[98]

The difficulties of measuring educational changes in the late sixteenth and early seventeenth centuries are illustrated by the research on the extent of literacy in this period. Some of the evidence used for this purpose is of dubious value. Clearly it would be wrong to assume that those convicted criminals who recited 'the neck verse' to prove that they were beneficed clergymen and so exempted from corporal punishment, were actually reading the passage. A more probable indicator of literacy is the ability to write one's name instead of signing documents with a cross mark, especially since it was common in the early seventeenth century to learn to read before learning to write. (One wonders, though, how many people simply learned to write their name and nothing else.) Using a sample of nearly 6,000 signatures to depositions in ecclesiastical courts from 1530 to 1750 as evidence of literacy, David Cressy concludes that there was a marked increase in literacy in the last decades of the sixteenth century until by 1600 one-third of the male population could read and write. But he does concede that over the whole period there was 'no steady cumulative progress', only 'irregular fluctuation'. Moreover, illiteracy persisted among the labouring poor, farmers, skilled crafts-men, and most women. Literacy was confined to the landed élite, wealthy merchants, shopkeepers and professional men.[99] In some Kentish towns more people owned books in 1640 than in 1580, but the ownership of books was restricted to propertied males. When Bartholomew Dann of Faversham found his wife 'reading and leaving her book in some place . . . he would catch the book out of her hands and tear it in pieces or otherwise fling it away'.[100] Significantly those who had the temerity to suggest that women should be educated had to assure their readers that the male dominance of society would not be thereby disrupted.

We are not advising that women be educated in such a way that their tendency to curiosity shall be developed, but so that their sincerity and contentedness may be increased, and this chiefly in those things which it becomes a woman to know and to do; that is to say, all that enables her to look after her husband and to promote the welfare of her husband and her family.[101]

So in 1657 wrote Jacob Comenius, one of the most liberal men produced by the seventeenth century. The same fears that his words were designed to calm were also felt about the consequences of popular education. Too many schools, felt Sir Francis Bacon in 1611, caused on the one hand a lack

both of servants for husbandry and apprentices for trade; and on the other side, there being more scholars bred than the state can prefer and employ, and the active part of that life not bearing a proportion to the preparative, it must needs fall out that many persons will be bred unfit for other vocations and unprofitable for that in which they are brought up, which fills the realm full of indigent, idle and wanton people, which are but *materia rerum novarum*.[102]

It is likely that his fears were unfounded. For the mass of English people at that time the task of gaining enough to eat left no spare time for education. If there was an 'educational revolution' before the middle of the century, it did not extend to women or to the poor.

How 'modern' were the subjects taught in the schools and universities of early seventeenth-century England? This ought to be an easy question, since the curricula they were to adopt were laid down in school regulations and university statutes. However, these were not necessarily adhered to, especially by the universities. One can be more certain about what was taught in grammar schools, in which the curriculum was dominated by religious and classical subjects, especially the teaching of Latin grammar. The same set books recur in early seventeenth-century grammar school syllabuses: the Catechism, Psalter, Book of Common Prayer, the Bible, a Latin grammar textbook (usually William Lily's written in the early sixteenth century) and various selected classical authors with 'lewd or superstitious books or ballads' weeded out, and 'all filthy places in the poets' quickly passed over.[103] In vain, some writers urged schools to adopt a more practical and vocation-orientated syllabus. In 1570 Humphrey Gilbert proposed the establishment of a school which would teach mathematics, horse-riding, map-making, navigation, biology, and other subjects.[104] Significantly, reformers in the revolutionary decades of the mid-seventeenth century were still recommending similar things.

What was taught in early seventeenth-century universities is the subject of debate which is difficult to resolve because different types of source material produce conflicting accounts. University statutes and examination requirements indicate that the formal curriculum of universities was dominated by scholasticism, and that new ideas, like those in science, made little headway. It is true that in 1619 Oxford established the Savilian professorship in geometry and astronomy, the Sadlerian chair of natural philosophy, and the Tolmins lecture in anatomy. But by and large the formal university institutions ignored the new science. What is less certain is the extent to which individual tutors taught new ideas which were outside the official syllabus. By its very nature such teaching is ill-recorded, but it is known that there were some lecturers who propounded new ideas, such as the mathematicians, William Oughtred at King's Hall, Cambridge, and Thomas Allen at Gloucester Hall, Oxford.[105] Many of these had connections with London and with Gresham College. The most famous is Henry Briggs, who in 1620 left Gresham to take the Savilian chair in geometry at Oxford. What one would like to know is how typical such teachers were. The surviving evidence is inconclusive, but if students' notebooks are a guide to what was taught (not always a totally safe assumption!) then the syllabus at Oxford and Cambridge at that time was very conservative and narrow. 'Vera et sana philosophica est vera Aristotelica' jotted down Lawrence Bretton of Queen's College, Cambridge, in his student notebook in the 1630s.[106] Aristotelian philosophy seems to have reigned supreme at the universities before the English Revolution.

The scientific revolution

The concept of 'the scientific revolution' to describe changes in the intellectual climate of the sixteenth and seventeenth centuries is more acceptable than the idea of 'an educational revolution'. It is true that there were medieval scientists, like the thirteenth-century Oxford scholars, Robert Grosseteste and Roger Bacon, who emphasized the importance of observation and experimentation. But it was not until three centuries later that more than a handful of scientists began to question long-held conclusions about man and his environment which were based on traditional methodology. Medieval science was rooted in the works of Greek philosophers, Galen and Ptolemy who lived in the second century AD, and Aristotle who lived in the fourth century BC. Medical principles were based on the Galenic concepts of anatomy and physiology: the body was composed of four basic 'humours', phlegm, blood, black bile, and yellow bile, and, since both physical and psychological disorders were caused by a superfluity of one of these humours, conventional medical remedies consisted of ways of purging the body of it. Galen had done some dissection, but mainly on apes not humans, and throughout the Middle Ages his conclusions were accepted and not tested by experiments and dissections of the human body. The Ptolemaic view of a finite, earth-centred universe, in which the moon, sun, and planets revolved round a stationary earth, was as ancient as Galen's anatomy and as deeply rooted in medieval thought. Both derived heavily from Aristotle's theories about physics and the universe, especially his views that matter consisted of only four elements, fire, earth, water, and air, and that bodies moved only in two ways, in straight lines and in circles. The validity of these fundamental principles was tested, not by experiment, but by reason, and on the basis of these principles broad theories were built by logical deduction. By the sixteenth century the 'ancients' and their ideas were so revered that the intellectual climate was against discovery; it was believed that was little left to be discovered about natural phenomena. Any change was likely to be a change for the worse: old ways and old books were the best. This is, of course, the antithesis of the equally unfounded belief in Progress and the modern tendency to regard new books as better than old books.

During the sixteenth and seventeenth centuries scientists began to question the deductive method of Aristotelian philosophy and in so doing they discovered some of the fundamental principles of modern science. The first major developments were in the fields of anatomy and astronomy, which were marked by the publication in 1543 of two treatises, the Italian Vesalius's *De Humanis Corporis Fabrica* and the

Pole Copernicus's *De Revolutionibus Orbium Coelestium*. Both were implicit attacks on Greek science. Vesalius's description of human anatomy was based on dissections of the human body, and Copernicus's theory that the sun, not the earth, was the centre of the universe was the result of observation. Copernicus's work was developed by other astronomers, Tycho Brahe, a Dane, Johannes Kepler, a German, and Galileo Gaililei, an Italian. It is clear, then, that the emerging scientific movement was a European one, and a notable feature of it is the way scholars of different nationalities freely communicated their research conclusions to each other. The reasons for the timing of these remarkable developments remain controversial, but that they were a European phenomenon suggests that they had more powerful impulses behind them than English Puritanism.

This is not to say that Englishmen did not participate in the European scientific movement. Already by the early seventeenth century much had been achieved in England, notably by mathematicians and astronomers like Robert Recorde, John Dee, Thomas Digges, Thomas Harriot (who carried on his work into the seventeenth century before he died in 1621), and by William Gilbert, whose work on magnetism was published in 1600. One of the most important contributions of Elizabeth's reign to English science in the seventeenth century was the foundation of Gresham College in 1597 under the terms of the will of the financier, Sir Thomas Gresham. He stipulated that this London College should have seven professorships, in law, rhetoric, divinity, music, physics, geometry, and astronomy, and that lectures should be in both Latin and English. Gresham College was a research and a teaching institution, and many of the notable developments in early seventeenth-century English science were connected with it because of the wide contacts of Henry Briggs, Gresham's Professor of Anatomy, whom Christopher Hill calls a 'contact and public relations man'.[107] The specific English contributions to European science in the early seventeenth century were in the spheres of mathematics and medicine. A crucial feature of the new science was its reliance on statistics and mathematical logic as the vital proof of truths rather than by deductive logic. Therefore John Napier's invention of logarithms (his *Descriptio* was published in 1614) and its subsequent development and popularization by Henry Briggs were important aids to the new experimental science. Arguably of even greater importance in the history of mathematics is William Oughtred, the clergyman, who invented trigonometry and who had an extensive reputation as a great teacher. William Harvey's discovery of the circulation of the blood (his *De Motu Cordis et Sanguinis* was published in 1628) is the most important English contribution to the new science before the middle of the century. Significantly it demonstrates the close links of English science with the continent, since Harvey developed his idea after studying at Padua University where the tradition established by Vesalius was maintained by Hieronymus Fabricius. Unlike all the scientists mentioned so far there is no agreement about the role and significance of Sir Francis Bacon in the scientific movement in the early years of the century. However, one does not have to believe that he was the creator of the new experimental science or that he was very influential before 1640 (the first proposition is certainly wrong and the second very doubtful) to suggest that his views are typical of the new science. He rejected the ideas of 'the ancients' and recommended a search for new scientific explanations by experiments, observation, and induction. The results of experiments were to be collected by a 'College of Natural History' with the aim of using scientific knowledge for the progress of mankind. 'The true and lawful goal of the sciences', he wrote, 'is none other than this: that human life be endowed with new discoveries and power.'[108]

The philosophical implications of the new science as illustrated in the writings of Bacon are without doubt one of the greatest developments in modern European thought: the replacement of the passive acceptance of traditional, unchallenged truths, which were revered because they were ancient, by the Idea of Progress, that man can change his condition and environment for the better. However, important as this is, it would be wrong to exaggerate the modernity of the 'natural philosophers' of the early seventeenth century and the break they represented with the past. In the late sixteenth and early seventeenth centuries the modern borderline between rational science and irrational, occult, and esoteric investigations did not exist. Scientists sought explanations in mystical tradition and experience as much as in the mechanical world. John Dee combined his mathematical work with astrology and spiritualism. John Napier used his mathematical talents to unravel prophecies in the Book of Revelations, forecasting the struggle against Antichrist and the end of the world, and to calculate the chronology of their fulfilment. William Gilbert, the first person to demonstrate the magneticism of the earth by careful experiments, believed that the earth was alive. 'We consider', he wrote, 'that the whole universe is animated, and that all the globes, all the stars, and also the noble earth, have been governed, since the beginning by their own appointed souls and have motives of self-conservation.'[109] Like many other contemporary European scientists, Gilbert was swept along by a current of belief in magic, the revival of Neoplatonism, 'the last school of ancient pagan philosophy'.[110] Hermes Trismegistus, who was (wrongly) thought to have been a pre-Christian sage, became a cult figure among intellectuals. Hermeticists considered the universe to be animated by spirits and matter to be possessed of sympathetic and antipathetic influences, and their aim was to discover these by scientific enquiry in order to control natural phenomena. So influential were the magical beliefs of Renaissance Hermeticism that some historians of science have argued that it played the key role in the attack on Greek science.[111] The most notable illustration is the work of the Swiss Paracelsus on chemical remedies for diseases, which owed much to the Hermetic tradition and was a major attack on Galenic medicine. Paracelsian iatro-chemistry was very influential among scientists in the late sixteenth and early seventeenth centuries. Clearly there was a great intellectual gulf between them and the modern professional scientist.

How great was the impact of the new science on early seventeenth-century England? Its significance for the future development of science can tempt one to exaggerate its contemporary importance. After reading Bacon's *Advancement of Learning* James I is alleged to have remarked that 'it is like the peace of God, that surpasseth all understanding'.[112] There is point to James's witticism. Many of the new ideas were too difficult to follow. It was not until the later years of the century that Harvey's discovery gained wide acceptance, after the Italian Marcello Malpighi, using an improved microscope, confirmed the existence of the capillaries which Harvey had suggested carried blood from the arteries to the veins. Other discoveries, like that of Copernicus, were too revolutionary to gain widespread acceptance. The Ptolemaic view of the universe, in any case, provided satisfactory explanations of visible astronomical features.[113] Even Tycho Brahe did not fully accept the implications of Copernican astronomy. Defenders of the 'moderns' like George Hakewill, whose *An Apologie or Declaration of the Power and Providence of God* was published in 1627, were in a minority, and it is difficult to avoid the conclusion that the 'ancients' had the better of the literary debate.[114] Charles Webster has recently shown how Gresham College 'was extremely variable in its effectiveness, in both its research and teaching capacities'. Many Gresham professors spent a lot of time on other business. Samuel Hartlib thought that most of them were 'very idle'. John Greaves, the professor of astronomy, went to the Middle East in 1633 and did not return to London until 1640.[115] It is true that some members of the landed élite took a fashionable interest in the new science, and these *virtuosi* began to conduct experiments and collect curiosities. But their activities bore only a superficial resemblance to Bacon's hopes of a massive coordinated research programme. On the contrary, as Professor Stone argues, 'the quest [by the aristocratic *virtuosi*] for rareties, mechanical, natural, or antiquarian, was the very antithesis of the Baconian ideal. . . . So far from conforming to a rational programme of controlled research, it encouraged the mentality of the fair-ground peep-show.'[116] Before 1640 the impact of the new science was slight. Its practical application was confined to improvements in navigation, map-making, and surveying.

Popular beliefs: magic and witchcraft

The beliefs of ordinary men and women in England in the sixteenth and seventeenth centuries are one of the most fascinating areas of recent research. There is, though, no point in minimizing the obstacles in the way of such investigation. The major type of evidence available is printed material, which is hardly a perfect source for discovering the beliefs of people, many of whom were illiterate. In any case, at any time common beliefs are not recorded, simply because they are well-known. After the work of Keith Thomas and Alan Macfarlane, however, there is little doubt that belief in magic was prevalent in early seventeenth-century society, and that it formed part of a popular subculture, separate and distinct from the Hermeticism and mystical beliefs which it has been seen were current in intellectual circles at this time.[117] In its most striking forms popular belief in magic in the late six-teenth and early seventeenth centuries manifested itself in two major ways.

The first is evident in the witchcraft accusations brought before the assize courts in this period. In the early seventeenth century the numbers were fewer than in the 1580s and 1590s, which were the peak years in this respect, but there were more cases than in the later seventeenth century. The accusations reveal a belief in witchcraft of a different type than that prevalent in contemporary Scottish and Continental witchcraft trials. Very few people in England were alleged to be witches who had made covenants with the Devil or who wore distinctive clothes. Most of those accused of witchcraft in England were women, who were usually older than their accusers and who often lived alone. They were charged with having worked maleficent magic, causing harm to the person of the accuser or death or illness to the accuser's children, relatives, or animals. With the exception of the case of Matthew Hopkins, the professional witchfinder who was active in East Anglia in 1645, the initiative in the prosecution of English witches in this period came from their neighbours, not from the magistrates or the ecclesiastical authorities. The second manifestation of popular belief in magic in this period is the existence of people variously called 'cunning' or 'wise' men and women, 'white witches', and 'wizards', who it was believed had powers to work beneficial magic. Healing, recovering stolen goods, and discovering those responsible for thefts recur in the few surviving casebooks of cunning men. Many appear to have operated rather like modern psychiatrists, listening to problems brought to them and sometimes succeeding in providing acceptable solutions simply by confirming what their clients already suspected. Others had some success as faith healers and by prescribing herbal medicines. By such means local men and women gained reputations as wise people who had magical powers. Unlike witches, those believed to possess white magic were largely tolerated and rarely brought before the courts in this period.

There is little doubt that many people in the late sixteenth and early seventeenth centuries believed in magic. However, it is slightly disconcerting that much of the evidence is drawn from a county, Essex, where witchcraft prosecutions were numerous and perhaps exception-ally high. Between 1560 and 1700 299 people were indicted for witchcraft before the assizes in Essex, but only 91 in Kent, 52 in Hertfordshire, 54 in Surrey, and 17 in Sussex appeared before the assizes for the same offence.[118]

This discrepancy does raise doubts about the value of witchcraft prosecutions as a gauge by which to measure witchcraft beliefs. At best, they represent only the cases which got to court, and they were dependent on the willingness of the authorities to let them proceed. One cannot, therefore, assume that they are a record of all witchcraft cases, nor that when prosecutions became less frequent (from the mid-seventeenth century onwards) popular belief in witchcraft died. Belief in magic was prevalent in the late sixteenth and early seventeenth centuries, but it is not certain that it was more widespread and intense than in earlier or later periods.

Some uncertainty also surrounds attempts to explain the persistent belief in magic. These have been of two major types. Firstly, those which attempt to link it to the economic instability of this period. Since population and pressure on resources were increasing in the late sixteenth and early seventeenth centuries, it is argued that people had less and less to give away in the form of charity. Consequently, the medieval tradition of neighbourliness in villages was weakened. Witchcraft cases appear to support this thesis. Many witchcraft accusations arose out of incidents when individuals turned down requests for charity from poor neighbours. As a result, it is argued, the former felt guilty about their callous attitude and, after suffering a misfortune, turned their guilt against those who had been refused charity, by accusing them of witchcraft and of being the cause of their misfortune.[119] A major doubt about this line of argument is whether neighbourliness was a reality in medieval villages and whether it was being eroded in villages in this period.

The second type of explanation is more convincing.[120] The starting-point is the fact that in the sixteenth and seventeenth centuries tragedies for which there were no rational explanations happened frequently; conventional medicine was unable to diagnose most human and animal diseases, infant mortality was high, and bad harvests frequent. In the absence of mechanical explanations people felt that the cause lay in the occult. In pre-Reformation England the Catholic Church – by means of the confessional role of priests, and belief in the healing capacity of saints and the power of holy water and relics – had provided explanations of and remedies for tragedies. But the Reformation 'denied the value of the church's rituals and referred the believer back to the unpredictable mercies of God. If religion continued to be regarded by its adherents as a source of power, then it was a power which was patently much diminished.'[121] With the protective magic of the Catholic Church removed, it is argued that individuals had to attack the agents of maleficent magic, witches, and so began the rash of witchcraft accusations and trials from the mid-sixteenth to the mid-seventeenth centuries. Speculative though this explanation remains, it is an attractive one. Clearly the work of Thomas and Macfarlane has created a new dimension to social history by establishing the central role of magic in peoples' lives.

Religious beliefs

Since most people are themselves genuinely uncertain about their religious faith, it is difficult at any time to discover peoples' attitudes to religion. In the early seventeenth century this is doubly difficult because religious uniformity was imposed by the state. Given the severe statutory penalties for nonconformity it is hardly surprising that nonconformists often hid their real faith by occasional attendance at a parish church, or that sympathetic magistrates sometimes did not enforce the penal laws. The recusant Catholic who refused to attend a parish church and was proceeded against by the authorities is relatively easy to identify, but this is not true of those who practised Catholicism in the privacy of their own homes and who also attended a parish church. The problem facing the historian as far as non-Catholics are concerned is one of categorization as well as of identification. Did Protestantism outside the state Church exist, either in its Presbyterian form of a national Church without bishops, or its separatist form of independent congregations following their own forms of worship and liturgy? Among those who were committed to the state Church was there a clear distinction between 'Anglicans' and 'Puritans'? Finally, were there people in the early seventeenth century who were totally indifferent to religion?

Indifference

The last question may seem irrelevant to those accustomed to seeing this as a period in which religion played a central role in everyone's life. Keith Thomas believes that this is a false assumption. 'It can be confidently said that not all Tudor and Stuart Englishmen went to some kind of church, that many of those who did went with considerable reluctance, and that a certain proportion remained throughout their lives utterly ignorant of the elementary tenets of Christian dogma.'[122] There is considerable circumstantial evidence for this view. In many parishes the churches were not large enough to seat all the members of the community. The authorities often tried to impose religious uniformity on 'the better sort' not on the poorer classes. Moreover, it is likely that enforcement of religious legislation was laxer in areas where parishes were large, communities scattered, and the power of the Church weak, as in the forest areas of Sussex and Kent and the pastoral regions of the north-west. In 1607 John Norden found that in areas of

great and spacious wastes, mountains and heaths . . . the people [are] given to little or no kind of labour, living very hardly with oaten bread, sour whey, and goats' milk, dwelling far from any church or chapel, and are as ignorant of God or of any civil course of life as the very savages amongst the infidels.[123]

Of those who attended church some misbehaved, 'nudged their neighbours, hawked and spat, knitted, made coarse remarks, told jokes, fell asleep, and even let off guns'.[124] 'Some sleep from the beginning to the end [of sermons]', noted John Angier, a Lancashire preacher, 'as if they come for no other purpose but to sleep, as if the sabbath were made only to recover the sleep they have lost in the week.'[125] However, it is sometimes difficult to tell whether such behaviour is evidence of religious indifference or of hostility to the established Church. Without denying the existence of the former, it will be seen that Protestantism and, to a lesser extent, Catholicism played a great part in the lives of men and women in this period.

Catholicism
Among ordinary people in the late sixteenth and early seventeenth centuries Catholicism was strongest in the areas contemporaries called 'the dark corners of the land',[126] where there were few Protestant preachers and existing clergymen were poorly paid and educated. In Lancashire there was 'widespread popular Catholicism', and in Wales 'half-understood relics of the missal and breviary survived in the home for generations after they had been banished from the church'.[127] These remnants of unreformed Catholicism in areas where the Reformation had made little impact are often difficult to distinguish from magical beliefs. In 1628 Benjamin Rudyerd talked in the House of Commons about 'the utmost skirts of the North, where the prayers of the common people are more like spells and charms than devotions'.[128] An assault was made on popular Catholicism by a Protestant campaign of evangelization by preachers and lecturers and by endowment of schools in 'the dark corners of the land'. The appointment by some London merchants in the 1620s of trustees, the Feoffees for Impropriations, to buy tithes from landowners to augment church salaries, and the passage of the Act for the Propagation of the Gospel in Wales in 1650 illustrate that the campaign was maintained in the early seventeenth century, and that it was not totally successful.

Nevertheless, it is likely that the hold of unreformed Catholicism on ordinary people was gradually becoming weaker in the early seventeenth century. This is not true of reformed, Counter-Reformation Catholicism, whose adherents among the landowning classes probably grew in numbers in this period. Clearly the total number of Catholics was tiny: they made up $1\frac{1}{2}$ per cent of the population of Yorkshire in 1604, and probably amounted to only 35,000 in the whole country. However, by 1640 the total Catholic population had risen to 60,000.[129] Why did reformed Catholicism not only survive, but make 'modest progress' in a country where it was outlawed? The explanation lies mainly in the protection it received from landed gentlemen. Counter-Reformation Catholicism in England was a seigneurial religion, which survived within the shelter of the households of great magnates, some of whom were too powerful to be proceeded against by local magistrates.[130] In some cases the local magistrate was a Catholic: a Sussex Catholic landowner, Sir Henry Compton of Brambletye, was a JP and deputy lieutenant from the 1620s to 1642 in a county where Catholicism had received strong gentry support in the reign of Elizabeth I.[131] In other cases the heads of households conformed while their wives did not, which may account for the comparatively large number of devoted women Catholics in the early seventeenth century. Credit for the survival of Catholicism must also be given to the work of Jesuit, Benedictine, and secular priests. In the early seventeenth century the in-fighting between Jesuits and secular priests, which had absorbed much of their energies in the 1580s and 1590s, was temporarily ended. Moreover, they dropped the role of political activism which some of them had adopted in the reign of Elizabeth I. Professor Bossy calls the Gunpowder Plot of 1605 'the last fling of the Elizabethan tradition of a politically engaged Catholicism'.[132] More typical of Catholicism at this time was the introvert, 'quasi-monastic' life styles followed in Catholic households of great magnates.

Protestantism

The word 'Puritanism' causes so much confusion among students of the history of the period from 1558 to 1660 that it is tempting to abandon it. It was used in the late sixteenth and early seventeenth centuries as a term of abuse: 'that odious and factious name of Puritans', John Pym called it. Consequently, it was not used at the time with any great precision, and some historians, with less excuse, have followed suit in using it to describe individuals and groups with widely varying views. Christopher Hill rightly calls 'Puritanism' 'an admirable refuge from clarity of thought'.[133] Many of the characteristics often described as 'Puritan' were shared by many (perhaps the vast majority of) English Protestants, including the hierarchy of the English state and Church until at least 1625. What were the beliefs which were common to most Protestants in early seventeenth-century England?

Predominant among them was the belief in predestination: that an individual's fate after death is preordained, since the Elect are already chosen. Predestinarianism is based on the doctrine of justification by faith: an individual's salvation after death owes nothing to his or her good works on earth but to the grace of Jesus Christ. Its core is expressed by St Paul in Ephesians ii:8 'For it is by his grace that you are saved, through trusting him; it is not your own doing. It is God's gift, not a reward for work done.' Secondly, all Protestants emphasized that it was essential that everyone should read the Bible, and that the central point of church services should be the sermon, and exposition of the Bible's teaching. The Gospel should be spread by preaching. Therefore, it was important that everyone should be able to read, and that the clergy should be educated enough to preach eloquent and intelligent sermons and be effective in propagating the Gospel in 'the dark corners of the land'. This stress on predestinarian theology, preaching, an educated clergy, literate congregations, and sermon-orientated church services was the essence of late sixteenth and early seventeenth-century Protestantism, and was directly opposed to the Catholic theology of free will and the sacramental and ceremonial aspects of the church service.

Anti-Catholicism was a central aspect of Protestantism in this period. All Protestants were fearful for the future of their faith because they saw the world, in the past, present, and future, in terms of a continuing and escalating struggle with Catholicism. This war between the forces of Christ and Antichrist, it was believed, would soon culminate in a final battle in which Antichrist would be vanquished and the Millennium would be established: King Jesus would return again to rule on earth. As will be seen, this world view, popularized in influential books like John Foxe's *Acts and Monuments* and reiterated in sermon after sermon, seemed to be confirmed by contemporary events, as from 1618 onwards European Protestantism seemed threatened by the rising tide of Counter-Reformation Catholicism in the Thirty Years' War. Such a view was by no means confined to fanatics. Millenarianism was in the mainstream of English Protestantism in the early seventeenth century; it flowered in the 1640s and 1650s (see below, pp. 206–11); and was still a very potent influence in the later seventeenth century.

A natural consequence of the Protestant emphasis on Bible reading, sermons, preaching, and the need for vigilance against the machinations of Antichrist was that the Sabbath should be set aside for worship and religious education.[134] In 1604 the House of Commons refused to have a conference with the Upper House on a Sunday. There was a growing campaign in the early seventeenth century against Sunday sports and pastimes. It is true that this had undertones of concern about law and order. Churchales – festivities held in churchyards after Sunday evening prayers – sometimes led to disorder, drunkenness, and (it was alleged) crime and illegitimacy.[135] Similarly the desire to control alehouses, as has been seen, was strengthened by a variety of motives, besides that of moral reformation. However, what certainly did not contribute to Sabbatarianism was opposition to enjoyment *per se*. Early seventeenth-century Protestantism seems to have been remarkably free from any 'kill-joy' spirit.

Lastly, there was a broad measure of agreement among most Protestants in the early seventeenth century about the form of Church government they wanted. Most were by now reconciled to the hybrid nature of the English Church: a reformed Church but a Church with bishops. The Presbyterian movement of the 1570s and 1580s had been shattered by Elizabeth I and Archbishop Whitgift. Most English Protestants, moreover, were passionately in favour of one national Church. There was no discernible support for toleration of congregations outside the state Church; all attempts to establish separate congregations in the 1590s had been brutally crushed by the beginning of James I's reign. Support for Presbyterianism – a state Church without bishops – and Independency – independent congregations outside the state Church – is not very obvious before 1640.

Is it then possible, or even useful, to distinguish between Protestant supporters of the established Church and 'Puritans'? Were there real difference between 'Anglicans' and 'Puritans'? As has been emphasized above, a distinction between Anglicans and other Protestants is difficult to draw, and this remained true until at least 1625. However, the main reason for retaining 'Puritanism' is that it is useful in identifying individuals in early seventeenth-century England whose attitudes to life and death were shaped much more strongly than those of other Anglicans by the Protestant principles outlined above. The differences were 'of degree, of theological temperature so to speak, rather than of fundamental principle'. What were the characteristics of these Puritans, 'the hotter type of protestants'?[136]

Puritans had a distinctive lifestyle. In 1653 Thomas Taylor instructed all Protestants as follows:

Let every master of a family see to what he is called, namely to make his house a little church, to instruct every one of his family in the fear of God, to contain every one of them under holy discipline, to pray with them and for them.'

Unlike other Protestants, Puritan heads of households carried out this instruction to the letter. In William Gouge's house 'there were prayers twice daily, three times on Sunday: there was Bible-reading, and children and servants were catechized'.[137] Lady Margaret Hoby of Hackness in Yorkshire meditated privately every day, conducted household prayers, and attended church several times a week. Her diary for Friday 21 December 1599 reads:

After privat praier I ded a litle, and so went to church: after the sermon I praied, then dined, and, in the after none, was busy tell 5 a clock: then I returned to privat praier and examenation: after supped, then hard publeck praers and, after that, praied privatly, havinge reed a Chapter of the bible, and so went to bed.[138]

On Sundays naturally the routine of prayer, meditation, and worship in Puritan households was much more rigorous. It was common to attend three sermons, take notes, and meet afterwards with other 'godly' people to discuss the content of the sermons. When a minister's views were not approved, these private meetings could become especially important and serve as alternative services to those offered in the parish church. Some Puritans might travel outside their own parish to hear a minister whose views were more agreeable. In the 1630s Lawrence Clarkson felt that the minister of his home town, Preston in Lancashire, was 'a pitiful superstitious fellow'. Only occasionally did 'true laborious ministers of Christ' visit Preston, 'who when they came, would thunder against Superstition, and sharply reprove Sin, and prophaning the Lords-day; which to hear, tears would run down my cheeks for joy'. So he would often travel to Standish and other places 'where we could hear of a Godly minister, as several times I have gone ten miles, more or less, fasting all the day when my Parents never knew of it, and though I have been weary and hungry, yet I came home rejoycing'.[139] Such godly men and women lived their daily lives at a high level of spiritual intensity. They spent long periods in introspection and self-examination in order to convince themselves that they were chosen as one of the Elect. They considered the coursé of their lives, misfortunes as well as successes, to be dictated by Providence, by the working of God's will. Robert Loder, the Berkshire farmer, wrote in 1616: 'This year in sowing too early I lost (the Lord being the cause thereof, but that the instrument wherewith it pleased him to work) . . . the sume of £10 at least, so exceeding full was my barley with charlock.'[140] The deaths of Puritans, like their lives, were marked by a distinctive ethos. Even the funerals of wealthy Puritan landowners were simple, and they abandoned the ostentatious funeral monuments of their peers.

The 'godly' Puritan household had much in common with devout Catholic households in the early seventeenth century. Unlike Catholics, however, Puritans were not content to practise their religion within the family circle: Puritans were evangelizers. They wanted to spread their views and to reform the Church and society in accordance with them. Puritans led the demand for an educated clergy: Puritan landlords appointed able preachers to parishes to which they owned the right of presentment; they cooperated with Puritan town corporations in appointing lecturers to preach sermons in addition to those delivered by the appointed minister. Puritans were also zealous reformers, they wanted to rid the Church of what they considered to be popish ceremonies. In the early seventeenth century, then, Puritans were militant Protestants with a distinctive lifestyle, who urged reform of the Church. However, the changes they wanted were *within* the existing Church. They showed no desire to destroy the framework of the established Church or to get rid of bishops. It was not until the Arminians began to have a real impact on the liturgy and practice of the Church of England in the 1630s that Puritans found themselves in serious conflict with the diocesan authorities.

Were there Protestants in England before 1640 who did not accept the established Church? If there were they have left few traces. No doubt some of the godly individuals who met together after church services in private religious 'exercises' formed the basis for the independent 'gathered churches' which were established after 1640, (see pp. 193–4). But between the 1590s and 1640 there is little evidence that independent churches existed. The exception is in London, where in 1616 Henry Jacob established an independent church, from which before 1640 developed various offshoots in the City. However, the total membership of those independent churches was never more than 1,000.[141] Perhaps also in the 1630s there began a popular anti-episcopalian movement in response to the Arminian policies of the Laudian bishops; in Cheshire there is some evidence of this.[142] But, although these groups are inevitably obscure, there is little doubt that Independency and anti-episcopalianism in terms of numbers and influence were negligible elements in English Protestantism before 1640.

Moreover, even 'the hotter type of Protestants', the Puritans, dissociated themselves from the implication that they intended to change the fundamental structure of the Church or break away from it.

It is nowadays fashionable to point to the revolutionary implications in Puritan ideology: it is argued that the stress on the individual's duty to interpret God's word created a questioning mentality that, when extended beyond religious topics, became a radical challenge to the established political and social structure. However, before 1640 the Puritans who can be identified as such were conservative upholders of the *status quo*. They wanted Church reform, but not at the expense of political and social upheavals. When in the early 1640s it appeared that this might be the consequence of reform, many of them drew back even from that. Most Protestants accepted unquestioningly that religious diversity was a sure recipe for anarchy in society. 'If a toleration were granted', wrote Thomas Edwardes in 1646, 'men should never have peace in their families more, or ever after have command of wives, children, servants.'[143] This belief effectively bridled in Puritans any tendency towards radicalism.

Notes

For abbreviations used throughout see p. xiv.

1. N. B. Harte, 'Trends in publications on the economic and social history of Great Britain and Ireland 1925–74', *Econ. H.R.*, 2nd ser., XXX (1977), p. 21. The first issue of the journal *Social History* appeared in January 1976.
2. P. Burke, ed., *The Economy and Society in Early Modern Europe: essays from Annales* (1972), pp. 1–10; P. Burke, ed., *A New Kind of History from the Writings of Febvre* (1973).
3. E. J. Hobsbawm, 'From social history to the history of society', *Daedalus*, C (1971), pp. 20–43; repr. in M. W. Flinn and T. C. Smout, eds, *Essays in Social History* (Oxford, 1974), pp. 1–22.
4. See the optimism of P. Laslett, *The World We Have Lost* (2nd edn., 1971).
5. See the review of Laslett's book by Christopher Hill, 'A one-class society?', in C. Hill, ed., *Change and Continuity in Seventeenth-Century England* (1974), pp. 205–18.
6. E. P. Thompson, 'Anthropology and the discipline of the historical context', *Midland History*, I (1972), p. 43.
7. See, for example, the criticisms of Stone's *Crisis* by D. C. Coleman in *History*, LI (1966), pp. 165–78, and by Conrad Russell and Christopher Thompson in *Econ. H.R.*, 2nd ser., XXV, 1972, pp. 117–21, 124–31.
8. For the methodology advocated by historical demographers see E. A. Wrigley, ed., *An Introduction to Historical Demography* (1966), and *ibid.*, *Population and History* (1969). For Colyton see *ibid.*, 'Family limitation in pre-industrial England', *Econ. H.R.*, 2nd ser., XIX (1966), pp. 82–109, and 'Mortality in pre-industrial England: the example of Colyton, Devon, over three centuries', *Daedalus*, XCVII (1968), pp. 246–80.
9. *Local Population Studies*, VIII (1972), p. 15. There is little doubt that in the 1980s the work of the Cambridge Group will be more fruitful than it has been to date. See especially, R. S. Schofield and E. A. Wrigley, *The Population History of England 1541–1871. A Reconstruction* (forthcoming).

10. L. Stone, *The Family, Sex, and Marriage in England 1500–1500* (1977) is the most recent comprehensive study.
11. This is the assumption of Professor Stone.
12. A. Macfarlane, *Reconstructing Historical Communities* (1977).
13. J. Cornwall, 'Evidence of population mobility in the seventeenth century', *B.I.H.R.*, XL (1967), pp. 143–52.
14. P. Clark, 'The migrant in Kentish towns 1580–1640' in P. Clark and Slack, eds, *Crisis and Order in English Towns 1500–1700* (1972), pp. 117–63.
15. See, for example, P. Laslett, *Family Life and Illicit Love in Earlier Generations* (1977) and K. Wrightson, 'Infanticide in early seventeenth-century England, *Local Population Studies*, XV (1975), pp. 10–22.
16. Joan Thirsk, 'The family', *P.&P.*, XXVII (1964), pp. 116–22.
17. *Times Literary Supplement*, 21 October 1977, p. 277.
18. J. H. Hexter, 'The myth of the middle class in Tudor England' in his *Reappraisals in History* (1961), pp. 71–116.
19. R. H. Tawney, 'The rise of the gentry 1558–1640: postscript', *Econ. H.R.*, 2nd ser., VII (1954), repr. in Carus-Wilson, ed., *Essays*, I, p. 214.
20. J. S. Morrill, *Cheshire 1630–60: county government and society during the 'English Revolution'* (1974), p. 14; J. P. Cooper, 'The social distribution of lands and men in England 1436–1700', *Econ. H.R.*, 2nd ser., XX (1967), p. 426.
21. D. M. Hirst, 'The seventeenth-century freeholder and the statistician: a case of terminological confusion', *Econ. H.R.*, 2nd ser., XXIX (1976), pp. 306–10.
22. F. J. Fisher, ed., *The State of England, Anno Dom. 1600, by Thomas Wilson* (Camden Soc., 3rd ser., LII, 1936), pp. 1–47. Wilson's 16,000 'gentlemen' includes 'esquires', *ibid.*, p. 23.
23. *Ibid.*, p. 23.
24. See the Bibliographical note, pp. 465–7.
25. Stone, *Crisis*, pp. 547–86.
26. Anthony Fletcher, *A County Community in Peace and War: Sussex 1600–60* (1975), p. 43.
27. *Essayes and Characters* (1615), quoted in J. Dover Wilson, ed., *Life in Shakespeare's England* (Pelican, 1944), p. 31.
28. J. Spedding, *et al.*, eds, *The Works of Sir Francis Bacon*, VII (1859), p. 395.
29. Barry Coward, 'Disputed inheritances: some difficulties of the nobility in the late sixteenth and early seventeenth centuries', *B.I.H.R.*, XLIV (1971), pp. 194–215.
30. M. Prestwich, *Cranfield: politics and profits under the early Stuarts* (1966), pp. 73–4.
31. Quoted in Christopher Hill, *Change and Continuity*, p. 150.
32. *A Health to the Gentlemanly Profession of Serving Men by I.M., 1598* (Shakespeare Association Facsimiles no. 3, 1931), sigs. G2–G3.
33. Clark and Slack, *English Towns in Transition*, p. 120.
34. For investment, see Stone, *Crisis*, pp. 335–84; J. T. Cliffe, *The Yorkshire Gentry from the Reformation to the Civil War* (1969), pp. 57–66; Everitt, *Change in the Provinces*, pp. 13–14; Fletcher, *Sussex*, p. 26; Mervyn James, *Family, Lineage and Civil Society: a study of society, politics, and mentality in the Durham region 1500–1640* (1974), esp. pp. 68–74; for office-holding see G. E. Aylmer, 'Office-holding as a factor in English history', *History* XLIV (1959), for a cogent critique of H. R. Trevor-Roper's argument that office-holding in the royal administration was an important source of

wealth for landowners, *The Gentry 1540–1640* (*Econ. H.R.*, supplement 1953).

35. J. Z. Titow, *English Rural Society 1200–1350* (1969), pp. 43–54.
36. Bowden, 'Agricultural prices', pp. 639–40.
37. John Norden, *The Surveyor's Dialogue* (1607), p. 15.
38. See Bowden, 'Agricultural prices', pp. 190–1, for a summary of the evidence.
39. Cliffe, *Yorkshire Gentry*, pp. 139–40.
40. J. Youings, *The Dissolution of the Monasteries* (1971), *passim*.
41. Cooper, 'Social distribution of lands and men', p. 426, where he also gives other examples of sizes of farms in the sixteenth and seventeenth centuries.
42. The rest of this paragraph is based on Hey, *Myddle*, pp. 88ff.
43. Since this section was written I have read Alan Macfarlane's *The Origins of English Individualism: The Family, Property and Social Transition* (Oxford 1978) which has convinced me of the need to avoid describing small farmers in England as 'peasants'. However, even though a peasantry as defined by Macfarlane never existed in England, the problems posed here still need explaining: when and why did small farmers become less important in the social structure of England in the seventeenth century.
44. Tawney, 'Gentry: postscript', in Carus-Wilson, ed., *Essays*, I, p. 214.
45. Eric Kerridge, *Agrarian Problems in the Sixteenth Century and After* (1969), p. 15.
46. See the review of Kerridge's book by M. A. Havinden in *Agric. H. R.*, XIX (1971), pp. 180–2.
47. Quoted in Kerridge, *Agrarian Problems*, p. 33.
48. Hey, *Myddle*, pp. 71–2.
49. A. B. Appleby, 'Agrarian capitalism or seigneurial reaction? The northwest of England 1550–1700', *American H.R.*, LXXX (1975), pp. 574–94.
50. A. C. Chibnall, *Sherington: fiefs and fields of a Buckinghamshire village* (1965); M. Spufford, *Contrasting Communities: English villagers in the sixteenth and seventeenth centuries* (1974).
51. Hey, *Myddle*; J. Thirsk, *English Peasant Farming* (1957); Spufford *Contrasting Communities*.
52. J. Thirsk, 'Seventeenth-century agriculture and social change', in J. Thirsk, ed., *Land, Church and People: essays presented to H.P.R. Finberg* (1970), pp. 148–77.
53. A. B. Appleby, 'Disease or famine? Mortality in Cumberland and Westmorland 1580–1640', *Econ. H.R.*, 2nd ser., XXVI (1973), pp. 403–32. See also his *Famine in Tudor and Stuart England* (Liverpool 1979).
54. Laslett, *The World*, pp. 114, 123.
55. W. G. Hoskins, *The Midland Peasant* (1957), p. xvi.
56. W. G. Hoskins, 'The rebuilding of rural England 1570–1640', *P.&P.*, IV (1953), pp. 44–59.
57. W. G. Hoskins and H. P. R. Finberg, eds, *Devonshire Studies* (1952), p. 419.
58. Alan Everitt, 'Farm labourers', in Thirsk, *Agrarian History*, pp. 396–465. The following paragraphs are based on this essay.
59. Everitt, 'Farm labourers', pp. 435–6; Bowden, 'Agricultural prices', pp. 599–600.
60. G. C. F. Forster, 'The English local community and local government 1603–25', in A. G. R. Smith, ed., *The Reign of James VI and I* (1973) p. 204.
61. According to J. T. Thorold Rogers, quoted in Bowden, 'Agricultural prices', p. 594.

62. This bitter comment, not surprisingly, was written by a younger son, Thomas Wilson, *The State of England*, p. 24.
63. Hey, *Myddle*, p. 169.
64. Appleby, 'Agrarian capitalism', p. 579.
65. Quoted in A. L. Beier, 'Vagrants and the social order in Elizabethan England', *P.&P.*, LXIV (1974), p. 3.
66. Fletcher, *Sussex*, pp. 116–17.
67. Beier, 'Vagrants and the social order'; Paul A. Slack, 'Vagrants and vagrancy in England 1598–1664', *Econ. H.R.*, 2nd ser., XXVII (1974), pp. 360–79.
68. Paul Slack, ed., *Poverty in Early-Stuart Salisbury* (Wiltshire Record Society, XXXI (1975)), pp. 26–7.
69. Fletcher, *Sussex*, pp. 165–6.
70. Slack, *Poverty in Early-Stuart Salisbury*, p. 3.
71. Wrigley, 'A simple model', p. 49.
72. Clark and Slack, *English Towns in Transition*, p. 113.
73. W. G. Hoskins, 'English provincial towns in the early sixteenth century', *T.R.H.S.*, VI (1956), p. 18.
74. Clark, 'The migrant in Kentish towns 1580–1640', p. 150.
75. R. C. Lang, 'Social origins and social aspirations of Jacobean London merchants', *Econ. H.R.*, 2nd ser., XXVII (1974), p. 30.
76. Prestwich, *Cranfield, passim*; R. H. Tawney, *Business and Politics under James I. Lionel Cranfield as Merchant and Minister* (1958).
77. Everitt, *Change in the Provinces*, p. 44.
78. Quoted in J. H. Baker, 'Counsellors and barristers: an historical study', *Cambridge Law Journal*, XXVII (1969), p. 224.
79. Keith Thomas, *Religion and the Decline of Magic* (1971), p. 10; J. H. Raach, *A Directory of English Country Physicians 1603–43* (1962).
80. Fletcher, *Sussex*, p. 41.
81. Quoted in Thomas, *Religion and the Decline of Magic*, p. 14.
82. Christopher Hill, *Change and Continuity,* pp. 127–78.
83. *Tudor Economic Documents*, III, pp. 69–70.
84. R. S. Schofield, 'The geographical distribution of wealth in England 1334–1649', *Econ. H.R.*, 2nd ser., XVIII, 1965, pp. 505–7.
85. Thirsk and Cooper, p. 758.
86. Clark and Slack, eds, *Crisis and Order*, p. 20.
87. Paul Slack, 'Poverty and politics in Salisbury 1597–1666' in Clark and Slack, eds, *Crisis and Order*, pp. 164–203.
88. Forster, 'The English local community', p. 203.
89. Fletcher, *Sussex*, p. 156.
90. W. K. Jordan, *Philanthropy in England: a study of the changing pattern of English social aspirations 1480–1660* (1959).
91. Cliffe, *Yorkshire Gentry*, p. 114.
92. Bowden, 'Agricultural prices', p. 621.
93. *A Health to the Gentlemanly Profession of Serving Men*, sig. C3.
94. Quoted in Hey, *Myddle*, p. 189.
95. M. Spufford, 'The schooling of the peasantry in Cambridgeshire 1575–1700', in Thirsk, *Land, Church and People*, pp. 112–47; Fletcher, *Sussex*, pp. 34–5; B. Simon, ed., *Education in Leicestershire 1540–1940* (1968), p. 41; Peter Clark, 'The ownership of books in England 1560–1640: the example of some Kentish townsfolk', in L. Stone, ed., *Schooling and Society: studies in the history of education* (1976), p. 106; Jordan,

Philanthropy, p. 283; David Cressy, ed., *Education in Tudor and Stuart England* (1975), p. 10.

96. L. Stone, 'The educational revolution in England 1560–1640', *P.&P.* XXVIII (1964), p. 53.

97. Cliffe, *Yorkshire Gentry*, p. 78.

98. Elizabeth Russell, 'The influx of commoners into the university of Oxford before 1581: an optical illusion?', *E.H.R.*, XCII (1977), pp. 721–45.

99. David Cressy, 'Levels of illiteracy in England 1530–1730', *Historical Journal*, XX (1977), pp. 1–23; *ibid.*, 'Literacy in seventeenth-century England: more evidence', *Journal of Interdisciplinary History*, VIII (1977), pp. 141–50.

100. Clark, 'Ownership of books', p. 97.

101. Cressy, ed., *Education in Tudor and Stuart England*, p. 111.

102. *Ibid.*, pp. 24–5.

103. John Brinsley, in 1612, quoted in *ibid.*, pp. 84, 88.

104. *The Erection of an Academy in London for Education of Her Majesties Wardes, and Others the Youth of Nobility and Gentlemen*, printed in *Archaeologia*, XXI (1827), pp. 508–20.

105. Charles Webster, *The Great Instauration: Science, Medicine and Reform 1626–60* (1975), p. 126.

106. H. Kearney, *Scholars and Gentlemen: universities and society in pre-industrial Britain 1500–1700* (1970), p. 84.

107. Christopher Hill, *The Intellectual Origins of the English Revolution* (1965), p. 38.

108. Quoted in A. R. Hall, *The Scientific Revolution 1500–1800. The Formation of Modern Scientific Attitudes* (2nd ed., 1962), p. 165.

109. Quoted in Antonia McLean, *Humanism and the Rise of Science in Tudor England* (1972), p. 158.

110. Thomas, *Religion and the Decline of Magic*, p. 223.

111. See especially the works of Frances Yates.

112. Quoted in P. M. Rattansi, 'The social interpretation of science in the seventeenth century', in P. Mathias, ed., *Science and Society 1600–1900* (1972), p. 18.

113. McLean, *Humanism and the Rise of Science*, p. 108.

114. R. F. Jones, *Ancients and Moderns: a study of the rise of the scientific movement in seventeenth-century England* (2nd ed., 1961), esp pp. 29–35.

115. Webster, *Great Instauration*, pp. 51ff.

116. Stone, *Crisis*, p. 717.

117. Thomas, *Religion and the Decline of Magic*; A. Macfarlane, *Witchcraft in Tudor and Stuart England* (1970).

118. C. L. Ewen, *Witch Hunting and Witch Trials* (1929), p. 99.

119. This is the hypothesis of Macfarlane, *Witchcraft*, pp. 200–206; Keith Thomas presents a slightly modified version of it in *Religion and the Decline of Magic*, pp. 560–9.

120. Thomas places more emphasis on this second hypothesis in *Religion and the Decline of Magic*. In his recent book, *The Origins of English Individualism*, p. 59, Dr Macfarlane concedes that his earlier stress in *Witchcraft* on the transition from neighbourliness to individualism in sixteenth-century communities may have been wrong.

121. Thomas, *Religion and the Decline of Magic*, p. 77.

122. Thomas, *Religion and the Decline of Magic*, p. 159. See also Christopher

Hill, *Society and Puritanism in Pre-revolutionary England* (Panther ed., 1969), pp. 457–8.

123. Quoted in Thirsk, *Agrarian History*, p. 411.
124. Thomas, *Religion and the Decline of Magic*, p. 161.
125. Quoted in Christopher Haigh, 'Puritan evangelism in the reign of Elizabeth I', *E.H.R.*, XCII, 1977, pp. 47–8.
126. Christopher Hill, 'Puritans and "the dark corners" of the land', in his *Change and Continuity*, pp. 3–47.
127. Haigh, 'Puritan evangelism', p. 30; A. H. Dodd, *Studies in Stuart Wales* (1952), p. 53.
128. Quoted in James, *Family, Lineage and Civil Society*, p. 125.
129. A. G. Dickens, 'The extent and character of recusancy in Yorkshire, 1604', *Yorks. Archaeological Journal*, XXXVII (1948), p. 33; H. Aveling, 'Some aspects of Yorkshire Catholic recusant history 1558–1791', in G. J. Cuming ed., *Studies in Church History*, IV (1967), p. 110; J. Bossy, *The English Catholic Community 1570–1850* (1975), p. 188.
130. J. Bossy, 'The character of Elizabethan Catholicism', *P.&P.*, XXI (1962), pp. 39–57; Stone, *Crisis*, pp. 729–33.
131. Fletcher, *Sussex*, p. 97; R. B. Manning, *Religion and Society in Elizabethan Sussex* (1969).
132. J. Bossy, 'The English Catholic Community 1603–25', in Smith ed., *Reign of James VI and I*, p. 95.
133. Hill, *Society and Puritanism*, pp. 1–2.
134. Hill, *Society and Puritanism*, pp. 141–211.
135. T. G. Barnes, 'County politics and a puritan cause celèbre: Somerset churchales 1633', *T.R.H.S.*, 5th ser., IX, 1959, pp. 103–22.
136. P. Collinson, *The Elizabethan Puritan Movement* (1967), pp. 26–7.
137. Hill, *Society and Puritanism*, pp. 440–1.
138. Quoted in Cliffe, *Yorkshire Gentry*, p. 273.
139. Lawrence Clarkson, *The Lost Sheep Found* (1660, published by *The Rota* at the University of Exeter, 1974) p. 4.
140. Quoted in Thomas, *Religion and the Decline of Magic*, p. 81.
141. M. Tolmie, *The Triumph of the Saints: the separate churches of London 1616–49* (1977), p. 37. Unlike other London separatists Jacob maintained contacts with those within the Church. There is evidence of a separatist congregation in Yarmouth and Baptist congregations in London, Lincoln, Coventry, Salisbury, and Tiverton from the 1620s onwards, M. R. Watts, *The Dissenters From the Reformation to the French Revolution* (1978), pp. 52–3, 159, 166.
142. Morrill, *Cheshire*, p. 20.
143. Thomas Edwards, *Gangraena*, part 3 (1646), p. 156.

Chapter 3

The Elizabethan constitution

The knowledge that the Tudor and early Stuart constitution collapsed in 1640–1 inevitably colours any analysis of early seventeenth-century political, constitutional, and religious history. Therefore, historians need to guard against assuming that contemporaries knew of the impending constitutional crisis and that they were preparing for it for many years beforehand. Of course, this is not true. For a large part of the period from 1603 to 1640 both the crown and the political nation worked together to ensure that the ancient constitution functioned, and they were by and large successful. The first part of this chapter points to the most important features of this constitution and emphasizes that it was generally accepted by the political nation and the wider population of the country. There were no large-scale popular rebellions in early seventeenth-century England. The ancient constitution may have been 'a clumsy political machine'[1] and as inefficient as many other European governments at this time, but it continued to work until 1640, a fact often masked by those primarily interested in the early seventeenth century in order to discover the origins of the English Revolution.

The framework of government

The king's government

Constitutional history written in terms of institutions rather than of individuals can give the impression that central government in the early seventeenth century was more formalized than it could have been when its focal point was the monarch. The character of government, as well as its efficiency, depended very much on the personality of the monarch. In one respect James I and Charles I were medieval monarchs: they ruled as well as reigned. Neither claimed absolute power; both acted within the common law and respected the inviolability and superiority of parliamentary statute. Yet their powers were theoretically and practically very wide; they appointed their own advisers and officials; they could obstruct parliamentary legislation by veto or by dissolution of parliament; they could dispense individuals from the law; and they took part directly and personally in the initiation of all government decisions. 'Government' is an imprecise word at any time. But the monarch was more synonymous with early seventeenth-century English government than is a prime minister or president with governments in modern democratic states, where governmental power is more widely shared.

This is not to deny that James I and Charles I were open to many influences, voiced by different individuals and pressure groups, when they made decisions. The ultimate responsibility for authorizing the Cockayne Project was the king's, but James I was persuaded to do so by his advisers, who believed that the project would be very profitable to the crown, and by Cockayne and his fellow merchants, who argued that it would be of commercial benefit to the nation. Early Stuart kings had formal institutions which had developed in the sixteenth century, to help them make decisions. The first was the office of principal secretary, which had been held by Thomas Cromwell in the reign of Henry VIII and by William Cecil Lord Burghley in the reign of Elizabeth I. By the early seventeenth century it had become usual for the office to be called secretary of state, and for it to be held by two people, who were theoretically equal in status though in practice there was a senior and junior secretary; when in 1600 John Herbert was appointed as 'second secretary' to William Cecil's son, Sir Robert Cecil, he was popularly and scornfully known as 'Mr Secondary Herbert'. Under the Cecils the office of secretary developed a sophisticated bureaucracy and a wide degree of influence; they were the closest advisers of Elizabeth I and James I and the main channels by which the monarchs communicated with their subjects and with foreign powers. Secondly, the early Stuarts inherited the privy council as an advisory, administrative, and judicial body, which had developed in the previous century from the royal council of medieval kings.

However, institutional history can hide the realities of where power lay; this is true of the history of the secretaryship of state and of the privy council. The former was important when the Cecils were secretaries, because William and Robert were men of outstanding abilities. It became less important from the death of Robert Cecil in 1612 to 1642, when it was held by lesser men than the Cecils. Too much significance can also be attached to the privy council. The fact that it grew in size, from thirteen in 1601 to forty by 1625, increased the likelihood that important decisions would be taken outside meetings of the full council, as was probably also the case in the previous reign. Some matters came to be discussed by small standing committees – on trade, Ireland, the militia, and the colonies under Charles I – or by *ad hoc* committees of privy councillors. One of these meetings of a selected group of councillors met officially to discuss foreign affairs, but in practice it dealt with many other matters. Contemporaries called it 'the cabinet council' though it is doubtful if one could trace (as some historians have hoped to do) a continuous development from it to the later Cabinet. As far as early seventeenth-century government is concerned 'the cabinet council' was only one (and probably not the most important) of many private semi-official meetings between the king and men chosen by him, which are unfortunately not recorded, but which were at the core of decision-taking in central government in early Stuart England.

'Policy', like 'government', is also a word that needs using with great care in an early seventeenth-century context. It is often assumed that James I and Charles I and their advisers had long-term, coherent plans to initiate changes in contemporary institutions and society. However, it is unlikely that they had such 'policies'. Rather one is inclined to think that early Stuart kings met each situation as it arose and reacted accordingly. Later commentators have sometimes interpreted what were often a series of panic reactions to short-term crises as a long-term strategy. The outstanding example of this is the common belief that sixteenth- and seventeenth-century governments had a 'mercantilist' economic policy. 'Mercantilism', however, was the invention of Adam Smith in the late eighteenth century, who used it to support his belief that state intervention in the economy was harmful. It was later taken up by a protectionist school of historians in Germany and in England in the late nineteenth and early twentieth centuries to support their case in favour of state intervention. 'Mercantilism' is intelligible with reference to the later ideological debate between free trade and protection. It has little to do with the attitudes of early seventeenth-century governments.[2] When James I established committees of merchants and politicians, during the severe trade crisis of the early 1620s, he did so in order that they should recommend ways of ending the crisis, not that they should draw up any economic policy document on the future of the English economy.

If the king was the focus of early seventeenth-century government, the royal court was the main arena of politics. The 'court' was therefore seldom united, but was the scene of unending competition between factions for the patronage of the king and frequent debates between groups recommending different courses of action on the king. The two often merged. The bitter quarrel at court between Buckingham and Cranfield in the early 1620s, for example, was a personal battle for political survival, as well as an argument about the desirability of declaring war against Spain. Political in-fighting at the early Stuart court often spilled over into parliament. As will be seen, many conflicts in early seventeenth-century parliaments were primarily caused by disagreements between the king's advisers, not by opposition to royal policies.

The formal royal administrative and financial bureaucracy at the disposal of early Stuart kings is an apparent striking contrast with the informal way in which decisions were reached. Professor Aylmer has examined the administrative machinery through which early Stuart kings communicated with their subjects and foreign powers – using the sign manual and signet in the secretaries' office, the privy seal held by the lord privy seal, and the great seal held by the lord chancellor – and the formal financial departments – the exchequer, the court of wards, and the duchy of Lancaster.[3] The importance and growth in size of this bureaucracy ought not to be minimized; it formed the basis of a powerful civil service which developed under the last two Stuart kings. But it may be misleading to talk in terms of an early Stuart 'administrative system'. Certainly there was no administrative system in the modern sense of a non-political civil service, made up of departments, each with its own separate and jealously guarded areas of jurisdiction. The court was the centre of the king's administration, as well as of politics. There was no division between politicians and administrators in the early seventeenth century. The secretaries of state and privy councillors were the king's political advisers as well as his chief administrators. The concept of government 'departments' also is anachronistic. Administration and financial institutions were called 'courts' or 'councils' and each had overlapping functions and jurisdictions. The exchequer, the major financial 'department', and chancery, part of the machinery of administration, were both also courts of law. It is true that the machinery for collecting and spending royal revenue was more rigidly organized than the administrative bureaucracy. The exchequer consisted of the upper exchequer responsible for auditing accounts and the lower exchequer for the receipt and expenditure of revenue, and was headed by the lord treasurer and his junior, the chancellor of the exchequer. It dealt with all crown income except royal feudal income, which was administered by the court of wards, and receipts from the duchy of Lancaster. However, the bureaucracy that dealt with the latter ought to be a reminder of the major differences between early seventeenth-century central administration and a modern departmentalized civil service. The duchy of Lancaster was responsible for managing those estates which had come to the crown in 1399, it collected some royal revenues, it was a court of law, and it exercised palatinate jurisdiction in Lancashire by means of a system of courts which duplicated those at Westminster.

Finally, the most striking difference between early seventeenth-century administration and its modern counterpart is that official salaries were very low, ranging from £100 p.a. for secretaries of state to clerks of the signet who received no annual salary.[4] Although official salaries also included pensions, annuities, and subsistence allowances, officials were expected to get the bulk of their income from fees and gratuities paid to them by clients. Such payments were an accepted part of the administrative procedure, but clearly these could (and sometimes did) go over the narrow borderline which separated them from corrupt payments made to bribe officials.

Local government

For most ordinary people in early seventeenth-century England the king's government was remote. Much more familiar would have been the major officials of local government: lord-lieutenants, sheriffs, undersheriffs, and justices of the peace in the counties; high constables of the hundreds (or wapentakes or rapes); petty constables (or headboroughs), overseers of the poor, surveyors of highways, and churchwardens in the parishes; officers of town coporations; and officials of the council of the north, the council in the marches of Wales and the Church courts. Indeed, although the major offices were dominated by the landed gentry, men of humbler origins – farmers, tradesmen, and craftsmen – were expected to serve in lesser local government posts, especially in parishes and towns. In that sense local government in the early seventeenth century represented a wide segment of the local community. Therefore, tension between the local community and central government was perhaps inevitable in this period, especially when the latter attempted to interfere in local affairs. Not surprisingly, this has been the major theme highlighted by the many local and regional studies on the early seventeenth century which have appeared in the last twenty years.[5] Inevitably there was a conflict of interests between the government's desire to impose its decisions on the country and county communities which resented interference in their affairs by outsiders.

The king's government had means at its disposal to counter localism. The council of the north, based at York and with a jurisdiction covering Yorkshire, Durham, Northumberland, Cumberland, and Westmorland, and the council in the marches of Wales, which governed Wales, Shropshire, Glamorgan, Worcestershire, and Herefordshire from its headquarters at Ludlow, were staffed by professional lawyers and local men who were directly responsible to the privy council. The justices of assize, who travelled on their legal circuits hearing cases too serious to be dealt with at the quarter sessions, were also used to communicate privy council orders to the localities, to lecture justices of the peace on their duties, and to provide the crown with the names of reliable men to be appointed to local government offices. Lord Keeper Finch told a gathering of justices that they were 'the great surveyors of the kingdom on whom lesser officers should wait as on the king himself'.[6] The Church, too, played an important role in buttressing the authority of the state, which was very natural at a time when it was believed that religious uniformity was inseparable from political order. Not only could the crown rely on the votes of the twenty-six archbishops and bishops in the House of Lords, but the Church was also the main organ of censorship: all printed books and pamphlets, as well as schoolmasters, had to be approved by it. Not only did the Church control, it also moulded, public opinion. The pulpit was the most important means of disseminating government propaganda in the days before other means of mass communication. Bishops, too, were agents of the central government in the localities, another means by which the privy council attempted to get objective assessments of the state of affairs in the county communities.

There is mounting evidence that in the late sixteenth and early seventeenth centuries the crown came to rely more and more on two other officials to overcome local particularism, the lord-lieutenant, and the administrative patentee.[7] The Tudor origins and development of the office of lord lieutenant are paralleled by the declining power and status of sheriffs. By the early seventeenth century the only major responsibility of the sheriff was to preside over the county court. Since this court's only important function was to organize the election of knights of the shire, the sheriff's power only became significant at election times. His other duties were routine: summoning people to attend quarter sessions, collecting fines, and executing writs. Moreover, the office of sheriff was an expensive one to hold. Sheriffs paid the fees of their under-officers, provided hospitality for visiting assize judges, and were personally accountable for the money they were charged to collect. During 1637–8 the arrears on the ship money tax in Yorkshire were £1,237, and Sir Thomas Danby, the unfortunate sheriff who was responsible for collecting the tax, was ordered to pay the arrears 'to his great damage'.[8] Not surprisingly, when the time came for the monarch to 'prick' the names of sheriffs from lists prepared by the privy council, the latter was snowed under with letters from those who had no wish to be chosen.

During the reign of Elizabeth I lord-lieutenants had been appointed to organize the military defence of groups of counties in times of crisis. When emergencies were over the commissions of lieutenancy lapsed. Paradoxically, it was during the reign of the *rex pacificus*, James I, that the lord-lieutenant, whose duties remained principally the organisation of the militia, became a permanent part of English local government. By 1626 there were lieutenants in all counties, although some lieutenants were responsible for more than one county.[9] Naturally, their effectiveness varied. The notebook of a Jacobean deputy-lieutenant in Northamptonshire, Sir Edward Montagu, indicates that he carried out his duties efficiently, but there is little doubt that not all militias were as well organized as that in Northamptonshire. It needs little imagination to realize what must have been the defects of a militia which was starved of money, was reliant on people, who were mainly farmers, to maintain their own arms and to bring them to the musters, and in which most of the training was done by deputy-lieutenants who had no professional military experience. This is why during the early seventeenth century there were sporadic efforts to reform the militia, including the introduction of muster masters, men who were familiar with modern techniques in drilling soldiers, new tactics, and armaments, which were being introduced on the continent under the inspiration of Gustavus Adolphus. These efforts at reform culminated in Charles I's scheme for an 'exact militia'. But, as will be seen, these schemes were resisted by the localities (see below, pp. 146–7). In 1604 the Marian statutes, which laid down the types of arms to be borne by various income groups, were repealed. Thereafter, the powers of lieutenants were based solely on the royal prerogative, and innovations in the militia came to be interpreted as unwarranted interventions by the king's government in local affairs. These fears that lord-lieutenants were agents of a centralizing regime extended to the appointment by the crown in the late sixteenth and early seventeenth centuries of patentees, who bought the rights to carry out specific administrative functions. As will be seen, the most notorious example was the monopoly of alehouse licensing which was given to Giles Mompesson. Administrative patentees, like lord-lieutenants, came to be seen as major threats to the traditional machinery of local government by justices of the peace and quarter sessions (see pp. 133–4).

However, in its efforts to impose its wishes on the localities there is little doubt that the crown was fighting a losing battle. Many of the officials, including lord-lieutenants, deputy-lieutenants, and members of regional councils, were local men, and even if, like bishops, they were outsiders, they soon became drawn into the social and political power structure of the local communities. This is an illustration of perhaps the most important development in sixteenth- and seventeenth-century historical studies in the last twenty years: the realization that for most people in this period provincial attachments were more important than national loyalty. What happened in their county communities – in Lancashire or in Kent – was more important to most people than events elsewhere. When they wrote or spoke of their 'country' they meant their county. Strong ties held together individual county communities. Of these, no doubt kinship was very important, especially since it was common for gentlemen to choose their wives from within their own county and social group. In counties, like Kent, where 'virtually all the county families could have been incorporated into a single family tree',[10] kinship perhaps was a cohesive force behind county unity and insularity. However, common experiences of divisions and hatreds within families ought to be a warning that family connections are not necessarily as solid a basis for political and social alliances as bonds based on patronage and clientage.[11] The relationship between patron and client in the fifteenth century K. B. McFarlane described as 'one of mutual convenience and profit'; writing on the sixteenth century J. E. Neale felt it was 'an association of self-interest, a mutual benefit society. Members expected their patron to sponsor their interests at court and cast his mantle over them whenever the prestige of his name or the cogency of his recommendatory letters might help'.[12] At the time the phrase most commonly used to describe this relationship was 'good lordship'. In the same way as the crown distributed patronage to its greater subjects, so the latter granted offices, leases of land, protection and help in court cases, and so on, to lesser magnates. McFarlane's colourful description of the system in operation in fifteenth-century society applies equally to the early seventeenth century. 'These busy letter-writers', he wrote of late medieval gentlemen, 'cover their crisp sheets of paper, one after another, ladling butter, rolling logs and scratching backs.'[13] Provincial insularity was deep rooted and persistent in English society. This fact makes statements that 'during the sixteenth century Tudor rulers transformed a feudal land into a national state' look slightly odd.[14] Although early Stuart England was more united than many other contemporary European countries, it was nevertheless 'a union of partially independent county states, each with its own ethos and loyalty'.[15]

The major institutional expression of the county community was the commission of the peace. Its members, justices of the peace, bore the main burden of local government in the seventeenth century, as in the previous century. The administrative and judicial duties of JPs defy brief description. These duties grew greatly during this period, as did the size of the commissions. Moreover, in some counties meetings of groups of JPs between quarter sessions, which had often been held informally, received institutional recognition with the development of petty sessions, which was encouraged by a privy council order of 1605. Given that the duties of JPs were burdensome and that they were unpaid, it is slightly puzzling why a place on the commissions of the peace was such a prized one. The answer lies in the fact that gentlemen were taught from birth that it was their duty to serve the community, and in the more practical consideration that a JP held high social status and local power. Although the crown (and later the parliamentary and Cromwellian regimes) attempted to control JPs by means of the assize judges, by the fear of dismissal, and by sporadic purges of men considered to be unreliable, it largely failed. Commissions of the peace were captured by the local gentry, and this meant that early Stuart local government was controlled by the local county community.

However, it would be wrong to assume that, since local gentlemen were jealous both of their spheres of influence as magistrates and of the independence of their 'countries', they were by any means necessarily 'opponents' of the crown. As has been suggested, tension was an inherent part of the framework of government in the early seventeenth century, but for much of the period local magistrates found no difficulty in reconciling their dual loyalties to the crown and to their 'countries'.

Parliament

A few years ago it would have been fairly easy to describe the role and the development of parliament in the framework of government in the early seventeenth century. The thesis developed by Professor J. E. Neale in his books on sixteenth-century parliaments, and by Professor Wallace Notestein in his work on parliaments in the early seventeenth century, was widely recognized as the 'correct' one.[16] The Reformation Parliament of the 1530s, so went the orthodox view, marked a turning point in the history of parliament's place in the constitution. Henry VIII's decision to carry out the Dissolution of the Monasteries and the break with Rome by parliamentary statutes awakened among members of the House of Commons a demand that they should have a more important place in the government of the country. So it was natural that during the reign of Elizabeth I this 'rise of parliament' should continue, and Neale described the way in which it seemed to do so as the House of Commons continually demanded in the later sixteenth century the right to express itself on matters which hitherto had been regarded as the concern solely of the monarch: religion, the queen's marriage, and the succession. Moreover, Neale showed how the later parliaments of Elizabeth's reign saw important procedural innovations (the introduction of rules to facilitate orderly debates, voting by formal divisions instead of by acclamation, and the practice of sending Bills to committees) and the establishment of special parliamentary privileges (freedom from arrest and freedom of speech for MPs). All this, Neale believed, reflected the attainment by parliament of 'institutional maturity'; by 1597, he wrote, parliament's adolescence was over. Neale's view of Elizabethan parliaments neatly complemented that already current about early seventeenth-century parliaments. In 1924 Notestein had delivered the Raleigh Lecture on *The Winning of the Initiative by the House of Commons*. Although he was careful not to press his argument too far,[17] later writers assumed that he meant that by continuing procedural development, especially the establishment of the Committee of the Whole House, the House of Commons aimed to free itself from royal control and to claim the right to be consulted in the initiation of government policy. This the House of Commons persevered in during the early seventeenth century in the face of determined resistance from James I and Charles I, who would, if they had been given a free hand, have dispensed with parliaments altogether.

As a result of recent studies, however, many of the assumptions on which the Neale-Notestein thesis is based are questionable.[18] First, the concept of the 'rise of parliament', of a parliament growing from early sixteenth-century infancy to later sixteenth-century adolescence and early seventeenth-century maturity, is called in question by Professor Roskell's studies of the reigns of Richard II and Henry IV, when parliament played an active political role, claiming to control the crown's finances and ministers.[19] Some historians are too eager to anthropomorphize institutions. Some are also too ready to equate an abundance of records with institutional importance and vice versa. In the case of parliament and its records this is not necessarily true. Late fourteenth and early fifteenth-century parliaments left few records, but they were called more frequently and sat for longer periods than two centuries later. Nor are procedural developments or the assertion of privileges indications of enhanced parliamentary power. MPs were not protected by privileges of free speech or freedom from arrest. After many of the parliaments of the reigns of Elizabeth I, James I, and Charles I the crown had no compunction in arresting and imprisoning those MPs with whom it was displeased.

Did MPs in the early seventeenth century want to be consulted in the formulation of government policy, and were they aiming to enhance the constitutional powers of parliament? Since it has already been suggested that the concept of 'government policy' is anachronistic at this time, it is likely that the answer is 'no'. What then, did MPs consider to be the role of parliament in the early seventeenth century? For most MPs parliament represented the correct, traditional way of securing legislation and the resolution of grievances. They wanted legislation, however, not to bring about fundamental changes in government or society, but to remedy local grievances. Most parliamentary business in the late sixteenth and early seventeenth centuries was concerned with local, private Bills. Most MPs also came to parliament to pursue political ambitions at court, to secure office or favours for themselves or for their dependents at home. MPs in the early seventeenth century were continually considering the needs and interests of their constituents. After the research of Dr Derek Hirst it can no longer be safely assumed that early seventeenth-century MPs represented a tiny minority in the country. The county franchise, the forty shilling freehold, had been increased greatly by inflation and the practice of treating some customary tenants as freeholders. Many borough franchises were even wider and Derek Hirst calculates that the total electorate may have been as high as 300,000, which was at least 27 per cent and maybe as much as 40 per cent of the adult male population of the country.[20] The demands made on MPs, then, came from a wide section of the local communities. This is why it is often difficult to identify one particular House of Commons' point of view on any issue. On the contrary, the Commons was no more united than was the court, which is one important reason why (as will be seen later) it is too simplistic to interpret early seventeenth-century politics in terms of 'Court *versus* Commons', 'King *versus* Parliament', or 'Government *versus* Opposition' (see below, pp. 132–41).

There are two more assumptions about parliament in the early sixteenth century that are dubious. First of all, it may be that previous historical studies have placed too much emphasis on the House of Commons. The Upper House played a far from subordinate role in the politics of the late sixteenth and early seventeenth centuries. Its size grew from 81 in 1603 to 128 in 1625, reflecting its enhanced importance. It will be seen how often political rivalries at court spilled over into the House of Lords. Certainly contemporaries considered the Upper House to be at least as important as the House of Commons in the early seventeenth century. Finally, it can be too readily assumed that early Stuart kings wanted to get rid of parliaments. There is no evidence for this. For the crown, as for MPs, parliament had important functions. Parliament was necessary to vote taxation, 'extraordinary' supply without which by the early seventeenth century the crown found it very difficult to manage. Above all, however, parliament was, as Professor Elton has recently called it, 'a point of contact', a place not only where MPs could pursue their political ambitions, but also where the court could gauge opinion in the local communities, and where it could explain the reasons behind its decisions.[21] In 1629, it is true, Charles I decided that the disadvantages of parliamentary government temporarily outweighed its advantages. He did not relish the prospect of meeting parliament again very soon and, not surprisingly after the stormy parliaments of 1626 and 1628–9, he wanted to rule without it for as long as possible. But there is no evidence that Charles I wanted to rule permanently without parliament.

Order and obedience

The large area of common ground between early Stuart kings and their most important subjects is often ignored. The latter were far from being the factious, embryonic rebels they are sometimes portrayed as being. The above description of the framework of early Stuart governments illustrates that the members of the political nation had strong motives of self-interest in the maintenance of the existing system of government. The central government, the court, absorbed their political ambitions and was a lavish source of patronage. The system of local government allowed them to retain power and to benefit from very low taxation. Moreover, existing social and political order was supported by a formidable political ideology, which both early Stuart kings and the majority of their subjects accepted.

The basis of this ideology was the theory of the Divine Right of Kings. James I's exposition of this is often seen as provocative and controversial. On 21 March 1610 he told parliament that

The state of monarchy is the supremest thing upon earth; for kings are not only God's lieutenants upon earth, and sit upon God's throne, but even by God himself they are called gods. . . . Kings are justly called gods for that they exercise a manner or resemblance of divine power upon earth, for if you will consider the attributes to God you shall see how they agree in the person of a king. God hath power to create or destroy, make or unmake, at his pleasure; to give life or send death, to judge all and to be judged not accountable to none; to raise low things and to make high things low at his pleasure; and to God are both soul and body due. And the like power have kings.[22]

This statement may grate on modern ears, but it is unlikely that it did on any of those listening in the parliament of 1610; they held similar views. Sir John Eliot, a leading parliamentarian, wrote a treatise, *De Iure Maiestatis* which exalted the power of kings in even more sweeping terms.[23] In any case James I in his speech in 1610 made important qualifications to his theoretical position. 'But yet is all this power ordained by God', he went on to say, '*ad aedificationem, non ad destructionem.*' Kings should rule justly, not like tyrants. Furthermore, God gave wide powers to kings before the establishment of laws and the settlement of 'civility and policy'. Thereafter, James argued, kings were bound to rule under the law, by the 'observation of the fundamental laws of the kingdom'. This was the view established in the fifteenth century by Sir John Fortescue: the constitution was a balanced one;

kings ought not to rule alone (*dominium regale*), but with parliament (*dominium politicum et regale*). In the early seventeenth century it was believed that this was a constitution whose origins were rooted in antiquity. Early Stuart kings and subjects adhered to this 'ancient constitution', which required kings to rule in accordance with 'the fundamental law', which was as ancient and as sacred as 'the ancient constitution'.

Everyone accepted the king as 'the head' of the 'body politic' or as 'the key' of 'the arch of government'. Another common metaphor to express the same thing was The Great Chain of Being, which bound everyone in a relationship of inferiority to the person above him in the chain, and of superiority to the person immediately below him. Everyone owed obedience to his superior and protection to his inferior. It was a doctrine well-expressed by Sir John Fortescue, who was widely read in the early seventeenth century:

God created as many different kinds of things as he did creatures, so that there is no creature which does not differ in some respect superior or inferior to all the rest. So that from the highest angel down to the lowest of his kind there is absolutely not found an angel that has not a superior and an inferior; nor from man down to the meanest worm is there any creature which is not in some respect superior to one creature and inferior to another. So that there is nothing which the bond of order does not embrace.[24]

There were sound, practical arguments for not breaking the chain; if this happened the inevitable consequence would be anarchy. Already there was a foretaste of what could happen in the presence in early Stuart England of migrant labourers, masterless men and women, who could not be integrated into the 'great chain' of order and dependence. The need for obedience was reinforced by the teaching of the Church in its role as a mouthpiece of government propaganda. Since 'the powers that be are ordained of God', the Church taught that disobedience to politically constituted authority was not only treason but also sinful. Even rebellion against a tyrant was unjustified. 'Let him [the monarch] rage, kill, massacre, hee is but a storm, sent of God to chastise his children', said William Goodwin in 1614. 'We may not *conspire* against them; our *hands bound* we may not so much as *lift up* our little *finger against them.*'[25] The doctrine of obedience was extended to relations between husbands and wives, parents and children, employers and employees, landlords and tenants. Propertied people, therefore, had strong motives for obeying the old constitution. The inevitable consequences of political change were felt to be escalating disorder.

It is easier to understand why the upper classes accepted the old constitution than it is to explain why the lower orders in early Stuart society did not pose a great threat to it. Despite the enormous inequality in the distribution of wealth, there was no large-scale popular challenge in the early seventeenth century to the established social and political order. It is true that the times were punctuated by riots and popular disturbances: the Midland rising of 1607 and revolts in Wiltshire in the early 1630s against enclosures; grain riots in many southern counties in 1630–1, popular protests against fen drainage, enclosure, and forest laws in the 1630s and early 1640s. But most riots in this period tended to be small scale; in Kent between 1558 and 1640 there was no popular disturbance involving over 100 people.[26] Most also were very limited in aim; it was common, for example, for grain rioters, having prevented grain from leaving their locality, to return it to the authorities. There are as yet only a few tentative answers to explain why there was no great popular rebellion in sixteenth- and early seventeenth-century England against the established political order.[27] It may be that poverty and dearth were such common features of the lives of ordinary men and women in this period that they were accepted stoically. In case they were not, the Church and government offered persuasive explanations – bad harvests were punishments for people's sins or high food prices were caused by the activities of middlemen – which, in explaining the reasons for poverty, perhaps made it easier to bear. Another possibility is that public and private poor relief, although it did not cure poverty, at least helped to alleviate its worst effects. The authorities did act in times of economic crisis to relieve extreme distress, by controlling grain prices, distributing grain to famine areas, and by ordering JPs to administer existing poor relief regulations. The Books of Order in 1630–1 are an example of this (see below pp. 145–6). The paternal role of early seventeenth-century magistrates may have contributed to the apparent political quiescence of the masses in this period. Yet it is striking that, even when the relief machinery did not work and local people resorted to violence, the main aim of rioters appears to have been to get the authorities to act and to enforce existing regulations. Riots in the early seventeenth century were not directed against the existing social and political order, but on the contrary, were aimed at its maintenance. There is no more striking illustration of the extent to which the doctrine of deference and obedience permeated early Stuart society.

Stresses within the Elizabethan constitution

Historical revision which emphasizes the large measure of agreement between the early Stuart monarchy and its subjects is necessary. It can of course, be carried too far. The Elizabethan constitution did collapse in 1640–1, and among the major problems for the historian of the early seventeenth century are to explain why this occurred and to discover when it became inevitable. Because these problems will be dealt with fully in Part II, only a brief indication of the weak points in the Elizabethan constitution is necessary here.

It has been seen that in the early seventeenth century the concepts of 'the fundamental law' and 'the ancient constitution' were part of the common political vocabulary of James I, Charles I, their advisers, and the majority of their subjects. Paradoxically, in both these concepts lay the seeds of political conflict. When Edmund Waller asked for a definition of 'the fundamental law' in the House of Commons in 1641, he was told that if he did not know the answer he had no right to sit in parliament.[28] Significantly, though, no one attempted a specific answer to his question; nor did anyone else in the early seventeenth century. Clearly there was ample room for different interpretations of what was meant by 'the fundamental law'.

The problem with the concept of 'the ancient constitution' is that it led most people to assume that the existing constitutional framework was perfect. This clearly was not the case; there were glaring inadequacies in the early seventeenth-century Church and state. However, anyone who attempted to remedy these was in danger of being smeared as a dangerous 'innovator' who was undermining the framework of 'the ancient constitution' and therefore threatening traditional values. By proposing changes in the methods of government and in the Church in the early seventeenth century the crown found itself open to these charges. In a reversal of the roles normally ascribed to them by later historians contemporaries came to see the crown and the court, not the parliamentary classes, as revolutionaries.

The unreformed state: centralization versus the local community

Many of the inadequacies inherent in early Stuart government have already been hinted at. James I and Charles I lacked a professional bureaucracy to execute their decisions. The fact that the king's officials were poorly paid (or unpaid) meant that bribery could become a normal part of the administrative machinery. Local government was in the hands of the rulers of the county communities and was therefore not always responsive to the wishes of the monarch. Moreover, both James I and Charles I, like the Tudors, possessed no professional army or police force. All these inadequacies were the consequences of the poor financial situation which the Stuarts inherited from Elizabeth I. The roots of their financial troubles are not unfamiliar to presentday governments or individuals. The sixteenth and early seventeenth centuries were periods of inflation, and the royal revenue system was incapable of meeting the growing demands on it. The crown had three major sources of ordinary revenue. The first of these – the crown estates – had been greatly enlarged from 1399 to the 1530s, but successive monarchs from Henry VIII onwards, including the early Stuart kings, sold many of them. When the fall in the value of money is taken into account, the decline in income from the crown estates is even more alarming than is apparent from the following figures: the average annual income dropped from £200,000 in the 1530s, to £72,000 in 1619, and to only £10,000 in the 1630s.[29] Even the denuded crown estate did not produce its full potential; many crown tenants held long leases at low rents. The crown similarly found it difficult to increase its income from its two other main sources of revenue, customs and feudal incidents. To collect customs duties efficiently would have necessitated a large bureaucracy, and therefore instead the crown, sporadically in the later sixteenth century and systematically after 1604, farmed customs duties out to private syndicates of merchants, who paid an annual rent to the crown. This meant that it was the customs farmers, not the crown, who took the cream of the revenue from overseas trade. Finally, as both James I and Charles I found, income from feudal incident, especially wardships, could only be increased at the expense of raising political opposition. In this situation the early Stuarts, like Elizabeth I, came to rely on parliamentary taxation, which in theory was meant to provide money only for extraordinary needs, as a normal part of their income. However, as has been seen, assessments for parliamentary taxation bore little relation to the true wealth of the country and yields were comparatively small. More and more, James I and Charles I were driven to rely on loans from the City of London for ordinary government expenditure. Leaving aside the question of James I's extravagance, the crown's finances were not geared to meeting the cost of government, even in peacetime, in the early seventeenth century.

It is often assumed that these inadequacies made the collapse of the early Stuart monarchy inevitable. This is not necessarily so. Other contemporary monarchies suffered from similar weaknesses, and, far from collapsing, grew in strength.[30] Moreover, as has been seen, the deficiencies of the early Stuart monarchy were a source of political unity between it and its leading subjects, who had a vested interest in maintaining the constitutional *status quo*. In normal circumstances neither the crown nor its subjects showed any real desire to reform the king's administration; significantly, the major attempts at reform in peacetime in the early seventeenth century, by Sir Robert Cecil and Lionel Cranfield, met with a distinct lack of enthusiasm both at court and in parliament (see pp. 119–23, 126–8).

However, during wartime, and at times when war seemed a distinct possibility the crown was forced to contemplate changes in its financial and administrative procedures. Royal income was barely adequate to meet peacetime requirements; it certainly fell far short of meeting the escalating cost of warfare in the early seventeenth century. Therefore the crown in the 1590s and in the 1620s was driven to resort to extraordinary financial measures – forced loans and other forms of extra-parliamentary taxation – and to assert its power more forcibly than in peacetime (see pp. 136–40). As at other times in the seventeenth and early eighteenth centuries, war and the needs produced by war became important catalysts of political change. Like the regimes of the 1640s and 1650s and the governments of William III and Queen Anne in the 1690s and 1700s, the crown in the early seventeenth century discovered that war necessitated the establishment of a strong and efficient central executive.

Inevitably such changes in the royal revenue system in the early seventeenth century were interpreted as threats to the independence of county communities, especially when they were combined with efforts both to make local government more responsive to the wishes of central government and to reform the militia. Given the strength of provincial loyalties any centralizing measures were bound to be resisted. This was made even more certain by events that were taking place on the continent and which heightened contemporary fears for the future of county independence and of parliament. Just as later in the century European events helped to fuel opposition to James II (see pp. 295–6), so in the early seventeenth century the contemporary trend in Europe towards powerful absolutist monarchies and the elimination of representative assemblies had an important impact on English political opinion: fears about the future of the English parliament were apparent in every parliamentary session. Far from wanting to secure more powers for parliament, the limits of the ambitions of most MPs for parliament was to ensure its survival. In these circumstances sensitive local opinion, fearful of the absolutist designs of central government, was, especially in wartime, a major threat to constitutional harmony.

The unreformed Church: Arminianism versus Puritanism

The English Church was far from perfect in the early seventeenth century. As has been seen, Puritan demands for reform highlighted its major shortcomings: many clergymen were ill-educated, some held more than one living and did not live in their parishes. Moreover, the ecclesiastical hierarchy was accused of gross worldliness. Cathedrals were considered to be 'dens of loitering lubbers', who were fonder of enjoying the comforts offered by wealthy cathedral foundations than of pastoral work.[31] From the 1570s onwards a principal aim of many Protestants was to bring about 'a godly and learned ministry', and this concern, if anything, intensified in the early seventeenth century.[32] As with the defects of early Stuart government, so the root cause of the Church's problems was financial.[33] The wealth of the Church was very unequally distributed. Most of its estates were held by bishops and by deans and chapters of cathedrals; the only land remaining in the hands of parish churches was glebe land, which rarely amounted to a substantial amount. Moreover, a large part of the income which ought to have gone to the parish clergy was received by laymen. The history of tithes lay at the heart of the economic problems of the Church in the early seventeenth century. Tithes, 10 per cent of the income of every parishioner, were originally paid to parish clergy for their maintenance. But even before the Reformation many tithes had been impropriated by laymen, and after the Reformation many more fell into the hands of lay rectors, who, as well as having the right (the advowson) to present nominees to church livings, were obliged to provide for the vicar's support. In practice, many lay rectors took the great tithes of corn and hay for themselves, treating it as an important part of their rental income, leaving only the small tithes of animal produce for the vicar.

Small tithes were difficult to assess and collect; moreover, since they had often been commuted to a fixed money payment, their value declined greatly in a period of inflation.

This situation was considered to be scandalous by many sections of opinion in early seventeenth-century England. Puritans were the most vociferous in condemning it, but their concern was shared by many bishops and by both James I and Charles I. One of James I's first decisions on his accession was to promise to restore royal impropriated tithes to their proper use, and he was very sympathetic to many of the aims of Protestant reformers during his reign (see below pp. 112–14). Under Charles I, too, the crown and bishops were intent on improving the quality of the clergy. Nor were they without some success. By the 1630s most clergymen were graduates;[34] lay patrons, including town corporations, often appointed able preachers to livings and lectureships; and many of the worst manifestations of the plunder of the Church by the crown, which had been common in Elizabeth I's reign, had ended. Yet, as the many complaints about non-preaching clergy in the early months of the Long Parliament illustrate, the achievement fell far short of what the reformers wanted.[35] The reform movement within the Church in the early seventeenth century failed almost as totally as did attempts at administrative and financial reform of the government. The central problem of the early Stuart Church – lay impropriated tithes – remained untouched. Too many people, propertied gentlemen and institutions, had a vested interest in the maintenance of impropriated tithes to allow schemes to restore them for the good of the Church to be successful. The Feoffees for Impropriations in the 1620s and Archbishop Laud's plans in the 1630s to buy back tithes failed as completely as did Cecil's and Cranfield's administrative reforms (see below, p. 150).

The Church, then, remained largely unreformed. This, though, by itself was not dangerous to constitutional harmony in the early seventeenth century. Although many were not willing to give up their property rights which would have ensured its success, the crown, bishops, and many laymen were agreed that reform of the Church was necessary. However, this concensus was a fragile one. In the early seventeenth century many were as fearful about the future of Protestantism in England as they were about the continuance of the English parliament. Again the events in Europe were responsible for exciting those fears. The lesson of the outbreak of war in Germany in 1618, the invasion and annexation of the Protestant Palatinate by Catholic forces, and the ensuing war between Protestant and Catholic countries in Europe was not lost on Protestant Englishmen. As a result, although many Protestants wanted some changes in the English Church, few were willing to contemplate any major alterations to the form of worship and theology in the English church as it had been established since 1559. On the contrary, anyone who suggested such changes was in danger of being charged with being sympathetic to Catholicism which was rampant on the continent. As has been seen, the essence of English

Protestantism in the early seventeenth century lay in a predestinarian theology, in preaching, and in a sermon-orientated church service. In the first decade of the seventeenth century a Dutch theologian, Arminius, challenged this. He criticized the belief in the Elect, and instead emphasized God's universal grace and the free will of all men to obtain salvation. Moreover, his followers demoted the sermon and highlighted the ceremonial and sacramental role of ministers in church services. When Arminianism was imported into England it was rightly seen by English Protestants as a direct attack on the English Church as it had existed for two generations. Although they made little impact on the English Church or opinion in England until the 1620s, Arminians were seen, not surprisingly, as revolutionary innovators. For this reason the rise of Arminianism was the greatest potential threat to constitutional harmony in the early seventeenth century. It was not inevitable that this threat should have become a reality; that it did so was ensured by Charles I's adoption of Arminianism and his promotion of Arminians in the Church in the late 1620s and 1630s. By doing this Charles I alienated the crown from the religious mainstream of the country. Part II will illustrate how Arminianism played a vital role in bringing about the collapse of the Elizabethan constitution.

Notes

For abbreviations used throughout see p. xiv.

1. F. J. Fisher, 'The growth of London', in E. W. Ives, ed., *The English Revolution 1600–60* (1968), p. 86.
2. D. C. Coleman, ed., *Revisions in Mercantilism* (1969), *passim*.
3. G. E. Aylmer, *The King's Servants: the civil service of Charles I* (1961).
4. *Ibid.*, pp. 203–4.
5. See the Bibliographical Note, pp. 464–5, 468–9.
6. Quoted by Ivan Roots, 'The central government and the local community', in Ives, *English Revolution*, p. 41.
7. The only systematic work that has been done on this theme is by A. H. Hassell Smith, *County and Court: government and politics in Norfolk 1558–1603* (1974).
8. Cliffe, *Yorkshire Gentry*, p. 253.
9. L. Boynton, *The Elizabethan Militia 1558–1638* (1967); J. C. Sainty, *Lieutenants of Counties 1585–1642* (*B.I.H.R.* supplement, 1970), pp. 1–9.
10. Alan Everitt, 'The county community' in Ives, *English Revolution*, p. 54.
11. The danger of assuming that family relationships are the basis of political alliances has been well illustrated by recent work on the politics of the reigns of William III and Queen Anne, see pp. 308–9.
12. K. B. McFarlane, *The Nobility in the Later Middle Ages* (1973), p. 113; J. E. Neale, 'The Elizabethan political scene', *Proceedings of the British Academy* (1948), p. 106.
13. McFarlane, *Nobility*, p. 114.
14. M. Judson, *The Crisis of the Constitution* (1949), p. 1.

15. Alan Everitt, 'Social mobility in early modern England', *P.&P.*, XXXIII (1966), p. 59. See J. E. Neale, *The Elizabethan House of Commons* (1949), for a similar observation about late sixteenth-century England.
16. Neale, *Elizabethan House of Commons*; *Elizabeth I and her parliaments* (2 vols., 1953, 1957); W. Notestein, *The Winning of the Initiative by the House of Commons* (1924).
17. Conrad Russell, 'Perspectives in parliamentary history 1604–29', *History*, LI (1976), pp. 3–4.
18. Russell, 'Perspectives', pp. 1–27. I have been helped enormously here by being able to read Conrad Russell's *Parliament and English Politics 1621–29* (1979) in typescript. While writing this section my views were also confirmed by hearing Professor G. R. Elton's Neale lecture in English history on 7 December 1978, 'Parliament under the Tudors: its functions and fortunes'. (This is printed in *H.J.*, XXII, 1979, pp. 255–78.)
19. J. S. Roskell, 'Perspectives in English parliamentary history' in E. B. Fryde and Edward Miller, eds, *Historical Studies of the English Parliament* (Cambridge 1971), II, pp. 296–323.
20. D. Hirst, *The Representative of the People? Voters and voting in England under the early Stuarts* (1975), p. 105.
21. G. R. Elton, 'Tudor government: points of contact: Parliament', *T.R.H.S.*, 5th ser., XXIV (1974), pp. 183–200.
22. Kenyon, *Stuart Constitution*, pp. 12–13.
23. Robert Ashton, *The English Civil War: conservatism and revolution 1603–49* (1978), p. 14.
24. Quoted in Anthony Fletcher, *Tudor Rebellions* (2nd ed., 1973), p. 5.
25. William Goodwin, *A Sermon . . . 1614*, quoted in Judson, *Crisis of the Constitution*, p. 181.
26. Peter Clark, 'Popular protest and disturbance in Kent 1558–1640', *Econ. H.R.*, 2nd ser., XXIX (1976), p. 379.
27. Clark, 'Popular protest'; John Walter and Keith Wrightson, 'Dearth and the social order in early modern England', *P.&P.*, LXXI (1976), pp. 22–42.
28. J. A. Pocock, *The Fundamental Law and the Ancient Constitution* (1959), p. 48, n 2.
29. G. R. Batho, 'Landlords in England: the crown', in Thirsk, *Agrarian History*, pp. 256–76.
30. H. G. Koenigsberger, 'Revolutionary conclusions', *History*, LVII (1972), pp. 394–98.
31. C. Cross, 'Dens of loitering lubbers: Protestant protest against cathedral foundations 1540–1640', *Studies in Church History*, IX (1972), pp. 231–7.
32. Collinson, *Elizabethan Puritan Movement*, pp. 280–2.
33. C. Hill, *The Economic Problems of the Church* (1959). This and many other aspects of the Church in this period are dealt with in two collections of essays: R. O'Day and F. Heal, eds, *Continuity and Change: personnel and administration of the Church in England 1500–1642* (Leicester 1976); and F. Heal and R. O'Day, eds, *Church and Society in England: Henry VIII to James I* (1977).
34. R. O'Day, 'The reformation of the ministry 1558–1642' in O'Day and Heal, eds, *Continuity and Change*, pp. 55–75.
35. Anthony Fletcher, 'Concern for renewal in the Root and Branch debates of 1641', *Studies in Church History*, XIV (1977), pp. 279–86.

Part two

The reigns of the early Stuarts, 1603–1640

The meeting of the Long Parliament in November 1640 marked the collapse of the Elizabethan constitution. At that time Charles I had only a handful of supporters, Laudians, customs farmers, monopolists, and a few Catholics.[1] He was alienated from the bulk of the political nation. When and why Charles I found himself in such a weak and vulnerable situation are among the major historical problems of the early seventeenth century. It is tempting to frame one's answer to those problems in metaphorical terms: for example, by arguing that 1640 was the end of 'the high road to civil war' which began in 1529 or 1558 or 1603, and that progress along the road was even and inevitable. This is a temptation to be resisted. Although the history of the late sixteenth and early seventeenth centuries is full of political tension, it is arguable that there was no fundamental break between the English crown and the political nation at least before 1621 and probably much later. During the first thirty years of the seventeenth century political life in England was not divided into two camps, 'court' and 'country'; on the contrary there was a great deal of contact between the parliamentary classes and the court, as the careers of most political leaders of the period testify. If this is true, then the oft-repeated belief that James I, by his stupidity, opened up an unbridgeable rift between crown and parliament on constitutional issues must be rejected.

When, then, did the breach which culminated in the constitutional crisis of 1640–1 occur? Much more serious strains were put on the traditional constitutional framework by Charles I after his accession in 1625 than by his father, resulting in the fierce antagonism to royal policies seen in the parliaments of the late 1620s. Was the breach, then, irrevocable by 1629? To such hypothetical questions there can, of course, be no one 'correct' answer. Not everyone became alienated from the Caroline regime at the same time. Nevertheless the physical separation of Charles I from his natural supporters, which was the result of his failure to summon a parliament for eleven years after 1629, allowed the issues and suspicions dividing them to have full rein. As each of these eleven years went by the lack of a political forum in which king, royal councillors and parliamentary leaders could meet and discuss current issues increasingly made constitutional deadlock a more distinct possibility than it had been at any time before 1629 and certainly during the reign of James I.

The Stuart family tree

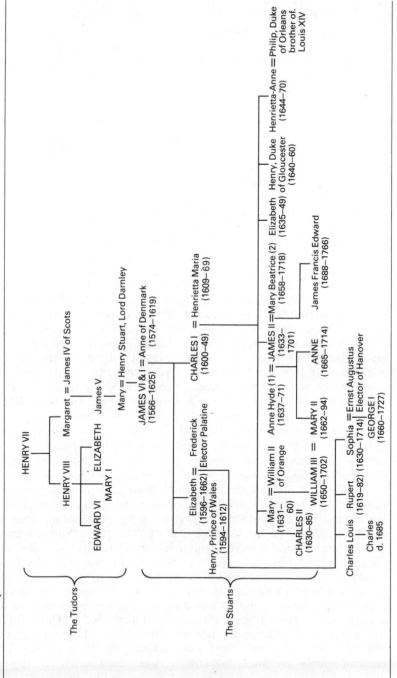

Chapter 4

The survival of the Elizabethan constitution, 1603–1621

James I and the succession

At the end of the first session of parliament in the summer of 1604 some MPs recounted for the benefit of the new king how they felt on the day Elizabeth I died and James I was proclaimed king of England. On 24 March 1603, they wrote, 'a general hope was raised in the minds of all your people that under your Majesty's reign religion, peace, justice, and all virtue should renew again and flourish; that the better sort should be cherished, the bad reformed or repressed, and some moderate ease should be given us of those burdens and sore oppressions under which the whole land did groan'.[2] It was only the passing of time which lent enchantment to the reign of Elizabeth I and allowed the tradition of 'the reign of our late queen of blessed memory' to pass into popular mythology. In 1603 there were few who mourned her passing and fewer who did not welcome the peaceful accession of the new king. J. E. Neale's study of Elizabeth's later parliaments reveals the extent of the disaffection at many aspects of Elizabethan government felt by those represented in parliament. Nor had Elizabethan government been a guarantee of political stability, which might have compensated for its defects. Elizabeth's refusal to marry or to name a successor, even on her deathbed, ensured that her reign was dominated by uncertainty, which increased yearly and became the principal domestic issue of her reign. James VI of Scotland was Elizabeth's most obvious successor, but no one in the late sixteenth century could have been certain that his succession would go unchallenged. In 1600 Thomas Wilson tried to console himself with the conviction that James VI would be accepted as king of England, but, looking at the vast range of competing claimants, he wryly commented that 'this Crowne is not like to fall to the ground for want of heads that claime to weare it, but upon whose head it will fall is by many doubted'.[3] James was an alien and a member of a nation hated by the English. Legally his claim was weakened by Henry VIII's will, which debarred from the succession the heirs of Margaret Tudor. A peaceful succession was thus not guaranteed. That the fears of contemporaries did not materialize was due partly to James's diplomatic negotiations with European powers in Elizabeth's last years, and, possibly to a greater extent, to the political skill of Robert Cecil in England. Not the least of James's attributes in the eyes of Englishmen was that he already had two sons and that his accession promised an end to the uncertainty over the succession to the English throne which had threatened political stability in England since at least the 1450s.

The new king had a long and successful record of kingship behind him in 1603. Recent research confirms what historians of Scotland long suspected: that James VI was the most competent king Scotland ever had. In great contrast to his Scottish reputation James has been one of the most maligned rulers of England.[4] Without doubt some of the criticisms that have been levelled against him are unfair. Contemporary accounts of the deterioration in his physical appearance and habits as an old and sick man in the last five or six years of his life have been used, wrongly, out of chronological context. James's appealing characteristics have been consistently overlooked. His scepticism both about the alleged royal power of curing those afflicted with scrofula, 'the king's evil', and, in later life, about witchcraft we can applaud as healthy signs of a mind suspicious of superstitious nonsense. His views on the health hazards of tobacco (he published a powerful *Counterblast against Tobacco* in 1604) and his hatred of duelling seem eminently sensible. His love of peace may have been a symptom of his alleged personal cowardice, but both characteristics now seem more appealing than they did to Sir John Oglander, who sneered that

King James was the most cowardly man that I ever knew. He could not endure a soldier or to see men drilled, to hear of war was death to him, and how he tormented himself with fear of some sudden mischief may be proved by his great quilted doublets, pistol-proof, as also his strange eyeing of strangers with continual fearful observation.[5]

Perhaps also historians in the second half of the twentieth century can be more tolerant than some of their predecessors of James's undoubted homosexual tendencies, if not of his misogynic leanings. Women, James advised his son, 'are no other thing else but *irritamenta libidinis*'.[6]

But as an early seventeenth-century king James I is difficult to defend. He could not afford to be 'a man ahead of his time'; he had to be a man with whom his contemporaries could identify. As will be seen, many of James's deeply held beliefs – his willingness to extend a measure of toleration to Catholics and his pacific approach to foreign affairs, for example – struck a discordant note in the ears of the political nation. Nor did James pay much attention to cultivating his personal popularity, unlike Elizabeth I who mastered the technique of image projection long before the days of the public relations industry. In great contrast to his predecessor, when large crowds came to see him James is said to have shown his resentment, and on one occasion at least, on being told that the people had come to express their love for him, he cried out (fortunately perhaps in Scottish), 'God's wounds! I will pull down my breeches and they shall also see my arse.'[7] James's irritation at popular adulation was matched by his dislike of attending to matters of routine administration. His preference for hunting, while leaving day-to-day government business to others need not, as has often been assumed, have led to administrative inefficiency. The personal application to routine matters of a Philip II of Spain or a Henry VII of England was not necessary in a king so long as he delegated administrative business to capable subordinates. In Robert Cecil, until he died in 1612, James had such a minister. Unfortunately James also placed his trust in other men, like the Howards, Robert Carr, and George Villiers, who were not as politically talented or as administratively capable as Cecil. What was worse the Scottish favourites with whom James surrounded himself in England (although never in the large numbers suggested by some of his critics) were hated by the English. A flavour of the pent-up hatred of the Scots which often amounted in seventeenth-century Englishmen to racial hostility can be seen in Lady Anne Clifford's comment on the Jacobean court: 'We all saw a great change', she wrote in her diary, 'between the fashion of the court as it is now and of that in the Queen's time, for we were all lousy by sitting in the chamber of Sir Thomas Erskine.'[8] Most seriously of all, James probably underestimated the problems that awaited him in his new kingdom. Compared with Scotland England might seem to be 'the promised land', but James's extravagance, as will be seen, was disastrous given the antiquated system of public finance he inherited from the Tudors.

James, then, was far from being an ideal king, but he was equally far from being the 'wisest fool in Christendom' of the school textbooks. Elizabeth's legacy to the new king in 1603 was not a good one: a country at war, dissatisfaction in many quarters with the condition of the Church, a royal revenue system in need of fundamental reform, and grievances about which the late queen had failed to satisfy the last turbulent parliament of her reign in 1601. James's record in dealing with these problems was much better than he has often been given credit for.

Peace with Spain and the settlement in Ireland

Financial considerations alone would have been enough to cause a revaluation of English foreign policy in 1603. With military expenditure escalating, could the country afford to continue the long-drawn-out Spanish war? In James's mind, however, there was more to it than this. In his view of the relationships between nation states war was to be used only in the very last resort. James's vision of himself as *rex pacificus* and international peacemaker dominated his conduct of English foreign policy. One of his first acts as king of England was to issue a proclamation forbidding the capture of Spanish ships, and in his speech to his first parliament in March 1604 he outlined his pacific philosophy.

The first . . . of these blessings which God hath, jointly with my person, sent unto you is outward peace, . . . which is no small blessing to a Christian

Commonwealth, for by peace abroad with their neighbours the towns flourish, the merchants become rich, the trade doth increase, and the people of all sorts of the land enjoy free liberty to exercise themselves in their several vocations without peril or disturbance. Not that I think this outward peace so unseparably tied to my person as I dare assuredly promise to myself and to you the certain continuance thereof; but thus far can I well assure you . . . that I shall never give the first occasion of the breach thereof, neither shall I ever be moved for any particular or private passion of mind to interrupt your public peace except I be forced thereunto, either for reparation of the honour of the kingdom or else by necessity for the weal and preservation of the same; in which case a secure and honourable war must be preferred to an unsecure and dishonourable peace.[9]

James's pacificism, it is often forgotten, had very definite limits.

Peace with Spain in 1604 was not inevitable. English Protestant hatred of Catholic Spain was still intense, and the generation-long war had developed strong vested interests for its continuance among privateers and merchant-profiteers who supplied the navy. Strategically, too, could the prime purpose of the war, the defence of the Dutch against Spanish invasion, be abandoned? James did not allow his desire for peace to blind him to England's true interests. He eagerly responded to Archduke Albert's peace initiative – with the collapse of Spanish intervention in Ireland in 1601 many on the Spanish side saw little point in continuing the war. But in the peace negotiations James made sure that his commissioners resisted Spanish efforts to prevent continued English unofficial military and commercial help for the Dutch rebels. The Treaty of London in August 1604 extricated England from a costly war without repudiating the interests of her Dutch allies. Even a modern critic of James's conduct of foreign affairs concedes the result as 'a victory for English diplomacy'.[10] While the major reasons for the twelve-year Spanish–Dutch truce of March 1609 lay elsewhere, English mediation played a small part in the conclusion of the Truce of Antwerp, the next step in the establishment of a general European peace.

Immediately it was made this peace was threatened. Four days before the truce was finally sealed the death of William duke of Cleves resulted in a disputed succession to his dukedom which threatened to divide Europe in a line-up which presaged the outbreak of the Thirty Years' War nine years later: France against Spain, each supporting respectively the Protestant Evangelical Union and the Catholic Union of German states. James supported Henry IV of France in a frenzy of diplomatic and military preparations designed to prevent Hapsburg control of the vital strategic Cleves–Jülich provinces on the Lower Rhine. That the outcome was a peaceful one was largely due to the assassination of Henry IV in May 1610, but in reaching the eventual compromise settlement in 1614 James played the role of international mediator. There is no doubt either that James enjoyed this chosen role or that he ever questioned the feasibility of making permanent peace between France and Spain, Catholic and Protestant Germany, by maintaining his contacts with both power blocs. In this scheme dynastic marriages played a large part.

.... Western limit of Cromwellian conquest at end of 1650

The Ulster plantation

Other areas settled or re-settled by English and
Scottish settlers, 1603–40

Map 1   Ireland

The marriage in February 1613 of his daughter, Elizabeth, to one of the
leading members of the Protestant Evangelical Union, Frederick the
Elector Palatine, was balanced by the soundings made by the English
ambassador in Madrid on the possibility of a Spanish bride for the

Prince of Wales. James's pacific policy, his efforts to remain uncommitted unreservedly to any European alignment, eventually failed. But its failure was not inevitable and for more than a decade it was carried on very successfully.

James's reputation as a peacemaker was enhanced by his record in Ireland. In 1607 the dominance of the powerful Irish chieftains, which Elizabeth's Irish wars had failed to break, came to an end when the earls of Tyrone and Tyrconnell fled to the continent. Their flight signalled the end, temporarily at least, of Irish resistance to English rule, and a renewal of the Elizabethan policy in Ireland of consolidating military gains by colonization. James, who showed little interest in the colonizing ventures in the New World, took an active part in the plantation of Ulster, and in the work of the commissioners he appointed in 1608 to supervise the project. The principles for the settlement worked out by the commissioners were almost totally dictated by strategic motives. The native Irish inhabitants were to be forcibly removed from the land and settled separately in the west of Ireland in order to clear the land for English and Scottish settlers. As always in their dealings with the Irish in the seventeenth century the English considered the Irish to be a barbaric, uncivilized, sub-human species. In order that the settlers would be capable of holding down the country stringent military conditions were attached to the grants of land. Depending on the amount granted each proprietor was to build on his estate a military fortification. They were not to alienate their land to Irishmen or even to allow natives to hold land on their estates. In addition a strict plan was laid down for the establishment of twenty-three towns in Ulster (Londonderry, Belfast and Enniskillen were the main ones) and in 1615 a Highways Act provided for the building of roads to facilitate military control. Within this framework the actual process of colonization was left to private enterprise. The most famous is the City of London joint stock company which acquired the proprietorship of Coleraine and took in hand the settlement of the town and county of Londonderry. But there were other privately-organized ventures in Antrim and County Down, the proprietors in turn granting the land to English and Scottish settlers. Between 1610 and 1640 40,000 Scots are estimated to have settled in Ulster: the beginning of the Presbyterian domination of that province. The Jacobean Ulster plantation scheme and the injustices it did to the native Irish, of course, contributed directly to the rebellion of 1641. But until then the plantation went on apace peacefully, and was one of the most successful colonization schemes of the reign of James I.

Puritans and Catholics

Of all the political problems of his reign James I undoubtedly dealt most successfully with the dangers of religious nonconformity. One cannot exaggerate just how seriously contemporaries considered the threat which refusal to accept the legally established Church posed to the state.

When the head of the state, the monarch, was also head of the Church religious nonconformity was not only heresy; it was treason. 'Although many religious men of moderate spirits must be borne with', wrote Sir Robert Cecil, 'yet such are the turbulent humours of some that dream of nothing but a new hierarchy directly opposite to the state of monarchy, as the dispensation with such men were the highway to break all the bonds of unity, to nourish schism in the Church and Commonwealth.'[11] By 1603, despite the efforts of Archbishop Whitgift since 1583 to enforce religious orthodoxy, there were many of the new king's subjects who were far from happy with the Church to which they were forced to belong.

Most English Catholics since the Reformation had been loyal subjects of the English crown. Especially in the 1570s and 1580s, however, a minority led by the more militant Catholic exiles, Allen and Parsons, had been active in organizing propaganda and, occasionally, armed force against the English crown. But the decade of the 1590s, with its feuding among English Catholics and the death of William Allen, marks the end of 'the heroic age' of English Catholicism. 'What was most obviously new about the English Catholic body after 1603', writes John Bossy, the best recent historian of Elizabethan and Jacobean Catholicism, 'was its retreat from the political engagement which had marked the Elizabethan period.'[12] In the first decade of James's reign there were few defenders of the papal deposing power among English Catholics; even Robert Parsons (who died in 1610) no longer urged his co-religionists to support it. In 1603 there were even high hopes among Catholics, fostered by James before his accession, that they would be allowed some relief from the penal laws. Not all were as misguided as one Oxfordshire Catholic lady who rejoiced on Elizabeth's death, 'now we have a Kinge who ys of our religion and will restore us to our rightes'.[13] But James was prepared to make a distinction between Catholics who were 'quiet and well-minded men, peaceable subjects' and those who were 'factious stirrers of sedition and perturbers of the commonwealth'; as to the former, he 'would be sorry to punish their bodies for the error of their minds'.[14] Not all Protestant Englishmen, however, would go this far in extending toleration to Catholics; anti-Catholicism was as deeprooted and widespread in seventeenth-century England as was anti-Communism in Macarthyite America in the 1950s. As with other issues the policy dictated by James's personal leanings ran counter to that dictated by political commonsense.

This is probably why James's public attitude to English Catholics in the first decade of his reign fluctuated from tolerance to severity, which, however, must not obscure his success in allowing a measure of toleration to Catholics without offending too much the anti-papist prejudices of his subjects. There is ample evidence that James saw the political dangers of a 'soft' policy towards Catholics. One of his earliest proclamations, in May 1603, ordered the collection of recusancy fines. In the 1604 session of parliament he encouraged the progress of legislation against Jesuit priests. Probably to counter suspicions raised by an unofficial embassy to the pope led by Sir James Lindsay, and by Catholic involvement in the Main and Bye Plots, in February 1605 James inaugurated a purge against recusants. Gardiner estimated that 5,560 in all were convicted of recusancy as a result. And in November 1605 came the Gunpowder Plot. Considerable doubt still surrounds the episode. What were the motives of the conspirators? What was the role of Cecil and the government in the conspiracy? The extant historical evidence does not support conclusive answers. However, evidence that Cecil supported the conspiracy in order to implicate prominent Catholics in it, as some Catholic historians have suggested, is slight. The most probable explanation of the conspirators' motives is that they were Catholics, desperate because Spain had recently made peace with England and possibly because of renewed persecution of Catholics. Amid the speculation what is certain is that the Plot confirmed the suspicions of most Englishmen that all Catholics were potential traitors, a point which both the trials of the conspirators and of Henry Garnet, the Superior of the English Jesuits, and the earl of Northumberland hammered home.[15] When parliament reassembled in January 1606 two severe penal laws against Catholics were passed. Yet it seems that the anti-Catholic measures were not rigorously enforced. Here James's lack of administrative drive coincided with his own personal inclination and also with the desirè not to upset Spain. The result may have been fortuitous, but it took much of the political sting out of the Catholic issue for the time being. While the Catholic minority was allowed to worship in private in peace, and indeed to increase slightly in numbers (see above, pp. 70–1), the anti-Catholic prejudices of Englishmen were appeased, partially at any rate, by the harsh legislation of 1606.

A more potentially explosive issue than Catholicism lay in the existence in early Jacobean England of those who wanted to reform the English Church in a Protestant direction. The problems that arise when using the term 'Puritan' to describe such people have already been discussed. Before 1640 the differences between 'Puritans' and other Protestants were not major ones. Puritans were those whose life-styles were more influenced than others by Protestant principles and who were more concerned than others to reform the Church (see above, pp. 71–5). In 1603 it is highly unlikely that there were many Puritans who wanted a disestablished Church, or even a state Church without bishops. Those who had advocated radical measures like these in the later years of Elizabeth's reign had been severely punished. It is not surprising, therefore, that the Puritans who publicized themselves in 1603 held fairly moderate reforming ideas, typified by the so-called Millenary Petition presented to James I on his journey to London from Scotland in 1603. There may, of course, have been Puritans in 1603 who adopted a radical stance, but one has to be satisfied with the conclusion that, if they existed, they were too prudent to show themselves to the authorities – or to the historian. If some of their reforms were open to a radical interpretation, there were few reforms suggested by the petitioners of 1603 or those put forward in the 1604 parliament that posed a fundamental threat to the doctrine or organization of the English Church. There is no reason to challenge the disclaimer of the petitioners that they were 'neither as factious men affecting a popular parity in the Church, nor as schismatics aiming at the dissolution of the state ecclesiastical'.[16] Their requests were moderate: for modifications in the church service (the abolition of the sign of the cross in baptism and the use of the ring in the marriage ceremony, and so on) for the freedom of ministers not to wear church vestments, for an educated, preaching clergy, for the abolition of non-residency, and for the reform of the ecclesiastical courts and church discipline.

It is always difficult to determine the exact nature of anyone's personal faith, even of one's contemporaries, let alone of people long dead. How one envies the certainty of examination candidates who 'know' the religious beliefs of Elizabeth I or James I. Whatever his private beliefs, outwardly at any rate James I appeared to be a Calvinist, a firm believer in predestination, as were most of his subjects. Nor was he unsympathetic to most of the requests of the Puritans at the beginning of his reign. James soon made clear that he wanted to stop one of the great abuses suffered by the Church, the 'plunder' of Church property and income by the crown and secular landowners. In July 1603 he announced that all income from impropriated tithes would in future be devoted to paying better salaries to Church ministers, and he encouraged the enactment of a statute in 1604 which forbad archbishops and bishops to alienate ecclesiastical property even to the crown.

James was, therefore, fairly well disposed towards the Puritan reformers, and he relished the prospect of presiding over an academic, theological debate when he summoned representatives of the Church hierarchy and the reformers to a conference at Hampton Court in 1604 to discuss the Millenary Petition. Unfortunately, William Barlow's account of the conference, which is the major primary historical source, probably misrepresents the true nature of what happened at Hampton Court. Barlow represented the extreme wing of the Church establishment and his account of the conference is naturally biased against the reformers with whom he had few sympathies. Barlow's propaganda version has misled generations of historians into thinking that James was hostile to the Puritan demands and that the conference ended in a series of bitter clashes between the king and the Puritan representatives. In an important revisionist article[17] Professor Mark Curtis argued that James was willing to listen to the Puritan demands; that the only serious clash at the conference (the famous 'no bishop, no king' episode) came when the king mistakenly thought that Dr Reynolds, one of the Puritan delegates, advocated the abolition of episcopacy, not a modified form of episcopacy; and that at the end of the conference the king agreed to execute some of the Puritans' key demands, including the reform of the court of high commission, the abolition of the powers of chancellors and lay officials to excommunicate, and the introduction of measures to ensure a well-paid, educated ministry, and to promote preaching missions in Ireland, Wales, and the northern borders, 'the dark corners of the land'. Yet it is true that the only permanent achievement of the conference was the beginning of a new English translation of the Bible, the Authorised Version, completed in 1611. James, perhaps because of his administrative laziness, failed to carry out the reforms agreed on at Hampton Court and a major opportunity to reform the Church was lost. But the failure was not the king's alone. Behind the clerical Puritan demands in 1603–4 was the support of powerful secular opinion among the landed gentry, and it was they who had it in their power to bring about a Church staffed by well-paid, learned men. Of the 9,244 Church livings in England 3,849 were impropriated in lay hands, which meant that the majority of the tithes in these cases were paid to the landowners, who also nominated ministers to the Church benefices. Too few English landowners were willing to surrender part of their incomes for the good of the Church. In this situation was ecclesiastical reform possible?

When discussions between members of the Commons and the bishops about Church reform came to nothing the victory of orthodox opinion in the Church seemed complete.[18] This was emphasized when the canons passed by convocation in 1604 were published, because they upheld the orthodox view of the Church on doctrine and liturgy, as well as on many practices, like the insistence on clerical dress, the use of the sign of the cross in baptism and the practice of bowing at the name of Jesus, which had been condemned by Puritans in the Millenary Petition, at Hampton Court, and in the parliament of 1604. James, in a proclamation on 16 July 1604, gave the canons his full support and ordered anyone who did not subscribe to them by the end of November to be deprived. The appointment of Richard Bancroft as Whitgift's successor at Canterbury – he was consecrated archbishop on 4 December 1604 – meant that this proclamation, at least, would be put into effect, since the new archbishop's hatred of Puritanism was extreme. Within three weeks of his consecration he ordered that all beneficed clergy who refused to conform to the canons of 1604 should be expelled from their livings.

Was James, then, guilty of alienating Puritan opinion in England by failure to carry out reforms in the Church and by his support of Bancroft's campaign to enforce uniformity? Certainly the deprivation of ministers by Bancroft caused a great outcry. In the spring of 1605 petitions of complaint flooded in from Northamptonshire, Essex, London, Warwickshire, Leicestershire, Lincolnshire and Lancashire. Sir Francis Hastings, the instigator of the Northamptonshire petition, was placed under house arrest and deprived of the deputy-lieutenancy and place on the county Bench. Yet Bancroft and James can hardly be said to have created a narrowly based Church by exluding many Puritan ministers and harassing nonconformist opinion. Probably not more than ninety ministers (less than 1 per cent of the total benificed clergy) were deprived by Bancroft.[19] There was no wholesale purge of Puritan lecturers in London, and Archbishop Tobie Matthew (appointed in 1606) in the province of York was generally tolerant of nonconformist opinion.[20]

Nor did James ever make the mistake of identifying himself with the new theological reaction against Calvinism among a few Anglican divines like William Barlow, Lancelot Andrewes, and Richard Bancroft. James had no sympathy for divines who, like Bancroft, were beginning to believe that the authority of bishops depended not on the king but existed by divine right. Nor had he any time for the few theologians who questioned the doctrine of predestination and stressed the contrary doctrine of free will. Most of the bishops appointed by James were orthodox Calvinists; in this sense the appointment of Bancroft as archbishop of Canterbury was 'a Jacobean anomaly'.[21] When the novel theological doctrines, which were associated with the views of a Dutch professor, Jacobus Arminius, were discussed at the Synod of Dort in 1619 James enthusiastically joined in the Synod's condemnation of 'Arminianism'. In 1611 James emphasized where he stood by his rejection of Lancelot Andrewes, an Arminian, as Bancroft's successor. Instead he appointed George Abbot, an orthodox Calvinist, as archibishop of Canterbury. Apart from his refusal to countenance parliamentary initiative in ecclesiastical reform James only occasionally offended Puritan opinion. In this respect James's Declaration of Sports, which he issued in 1618, was an exceptional episode in his reign. The Declaration, which condoned selected Sunday amusements, 'such as dancing, either for men or women, archery for men, leaping, vaulting, or any other such harmless recreation',[22] but not bear- and bull-baiting or bowling, alarmed Puritan opinion. But James eventually withdrew his order that it should be read in the churches, and it is significant that, as Gardiner noted, 'during the first ten or twelve years of Abbot's primacy the ecclesiastical history of the country was almost totally barren of events'.[23] James's religious conservatism, his attachment to the Calvinist ideals of the Elizabethan Church, thus defused what could have been a Puritan explosion. Religion was never a major divisive issue between James I and his parliaments.

James's first parliament, 1604–1610

The case of the Buckinghamshire election 1604

It has already been stressed that there was no fundamental divergence of constitutional views between James I and his leading subjects. Yet there was a great deal of ambiguity about the early seventeenth-century constitution, which allowed scope for disagreement on specific topics. In addition, many English MPs were determined that the English parliament should not suffer the fate of other European representative institutions whose powers were being taken away by absolute monarchs (see above, pp. 95–6). In at least one county, Norfolk, Elizabeth's attempts to bypass the usual channels of local government by imposing 'prerogative' government had raised a political storm in her last parliament.[24] Fears about the continuing existence of parliament go a long way to explain why the mood of the House of Commons which assembled on 19 March 1604 resembled that of its immediate predecessor in the last parliament of Elizabeth's reign in 1601: resentment at outstanding grievances, like wardship, purveyance, and monopolies, combined with an ultra-sensitivity about its institutional status and privileges. However, James's handling of the House of Commons, which differed markedly from that of Elizabeth I, contributed to the discord of the session. Cecil, James's principal secretary in the early years (created Lord Cecil of Essendon, 13 May 1603, Viscount Cranbourne, 20 August 1604, and earl of Salisbury, 4 May 1605) sat in the Lords, which, as yet, was in need of little management. The failure to ensure that experienced privy councillors sat in the Commons meant that there was no one there to take the initiative in raising non-controversial topics or to lead debates away from politically sensitive areas such as the extent and scope of the royal prerogative. A minor illustration of what could result from lack of royal parliamentary preparation was the chaotic start to the first session, when the king began his opening speech to parliament before the members of the Commons assembled, and the speech had to be repeated a few days later. Also, ominously and unusually, there was a ripple of opposition to the official candidate as speaker of the Commons, Sir Edward Phelips, proposed by Secretary Herbert.

More importantly, James blundered in allowing debates on specific topics to broaden out into discussions on fundamental constitutional principles. Indeed he seemed to revel in the ensuing theoretical discussion. In so doing James gave an opportunity for the submerged fears about the future of parliament to surface. This is why the disputed Buckinghamshire election became the major political topic of the first session of James I's first parliament.[25] On the first day of parliamentary business the Commons learned that the election of Francis Goodwin as one of the MPs for Buckinghamshire had been annulled by the court of chancery on the grounds that Goodwin was an outlaw; and that at a second election Sir John Fortescue, a privy councillor, had been returned in Goodwin's place. With European and recent Elizabethan precedents in mind many English MPs needed little persuading that this was a clear case of undue royal interference with parliamentary business. After hearing Goodwin at the bar of the House, the Commons voted to reinstate him as an MP, and refused to discuss the matter any further with the Lords. Yet given careful handling perhaps Goodwin's case could have been settled without controversy. James's tactics made the incident into a much more serious one than it need have been.

James's first move was irreproachable. Because he felt that the Commons had acted illegally in allowing an outlaw to sit as an MP he asked them to confer with the Lords and to get legal advice. But instead of restricting the debate within narrow legal limits he chose to raise wider constitutional issues, when he told the Commons that 'they derived all matters of privilege from him and by his grant'[26] and that all disputed elections ought to be decided by the court of chancery not the Commons. 'Now the case of Sir John Fortescue and Sir Francis Goodwin has become the case of the whole kingdom,' said one MP in the excitement of the ensuing debate. Not quite. But James's intervention raised a major political storm, and in the end James had to give way. In an apparent compromise on 11 April the king 'did meet us half way' and suggested that both Goodwin and Fortescue should be unseated and a writ be issued for a new election. But in fact James conceded the principle at issue: the Commons had established its right to decide disputed elections, which, to emphasize the point, it immediately proceeded to do in two outstanding cases.

Historical hindsight gives greater significance to the Goodwin case than it perhaps deserves. While it illustrates the Commons' sensitivity about status and privileges and the fears that lay behind that sensitivity, which were exacerbated by heavyhanded dealings with the Commons,[27] it does not mean that from the outset of the reign parliamentary government was impossible. Listing the points of disagreement between James and some MPs in this first session might appear to support the opposite conclusion. The king's refusal to allow the Commons to introduce ecclesiastical reforms irritated some MPs, as has already been seen, although James was merely continuing the Elizabethan precedent of maintaining the royal prerogative right to decide religious questions. There were also rumblings of discontent on wardship and purveyance, and deep suspicions were voiced when the question of union between England and Scotland was suggested; all became major constitutional issues in later sessions, as will be seen. But it is significant that near the end of the first session many MPs voted against presenting *The Form of Apology and Satisfaction* to the king; it cannot be claimed that this radical document represented the opinion of the Commons.[28] Indeed too much of the history of James's first parliament has been written as though there was one 'Commons' view' on every political issue. It is likely that most MPs' recollections of the first session as they dispersed after the prorogation of parliament in July 1604 was of deep divisions amongst themselves on issues like 'free trade', rather than of a united Commons in opposition to the king. Unfortunately for James in later sessions of the first parliament it became clear that there were two royal proposals which, if they were debated long enough, would produce something like a united opposition to them: the proposal for a union of England and Scotland, and that for a reform of the king's finances.

Union of England and Scotland

In the early sessions of James's first parliament the Commons clearly took the procedural initiative. It did not win (nor probably were few members seeking) initiative in the making of policy.[29] Yet opinion in the House of Commons was very influential in shaping and, sometimes, in negating royal policy, as is illustrated by the fate of James's hope that he might make England and Scotland one country. This plan was part of his grand design for his new kingdom: internal peace, as well as peace abroad, an end to civil war and an end to Anglo-Scottish wars. And were there not strong strategic arguments for a union of England and Scotland: 'if 20,000 men be a strong army, is not the double thereof, 40,000, a double the stronger army?'[30] Unfortunately, most Englishmen did not see a union with Scotland in the terms outlined by James's statistics, a union of equals. 'This Kingdom the more glorious the more honourable',[31] jotted down the clerk of the Commons in the *Commons' Journal* in an attempt to summarize the reaction of MPs in April 1604 to James's proposal to unite the two kingdoms under one name, Great Britain. It did not augur well for James's hopes that merely the suggested name of the new united kingdom encountered intense opposition; by May 1604, according to Bacon, the name 'Great Britain' became 'a thing left, and no more to be spoken of'. But at least parliament agreed in June 1604 to an Act appointing commissioners, including Bacon, who were to discuss with Scottish delegates the means to 'perform and accomplish that real and effectual Union already inherent in his Majesty's Royal Blood and Person'. After the prorogation James took every step he could to further the union. By a proclamation of 20 October 1604 he declared himself 'King of Great Britain, France, and Ireland, Defender of the Faith, etc.' On 16 November he announced the issue of a union currency, beginning with a 20 shilling gold piece to be called, prophetically he hoped, a 'unite'. On 12 April 1606 all British ships were ordered to carry a new union flag devised by the college of Arms.

The union commissioners had their report ready for the third session of parliament in November 1606. The debates on the union dominated the whole session, during which it became crystal clear that few English MPs were enthusiastic about uniting with a long-established enemy and one many Englishmen considered to be a nation of barbarians. 'They have not suffered above two Kings to die in their Beds, these two hundred Years. Our King hath hardly escaped them', sneered Christopher Piggot, MP for Buckinghamshire.[32] As in other cases of racial hostility irrational intolerance had some economic logic, which in this case was expressed in Nicholas Fuller's parable in the full-scale Commons' debate of February 1607:

one Man is owner of two Pastures, with one Hedge to divide them; the one Pasture bare, the other fertile and good: A wise Owner will not pull down the Hedge quite, but make Gates, and let them in and out etc. If he do, the Cattle will rush in in Multitudes, and much against their Will return'.[33]

In this mood the Commons would only confirm a minor proposal of the union commissioners: the repeal of mutually hostile legislation.

There was bitter opposition to the commissioners' plans for a commercial union and for the naturalization of Scotsmen in England and *vice versa*. The Commons heeded Sir Edwin Sandys's advice to 'proceed with a leaden foot'. It was Sandys who was instrumental in bringing about the collapse of the proposals when he introduced a scheme for a 'perfect union' which was idealistic and impractical. When Sir William Maurice tried to revive the union proposals at the beginning of the fourth parliamentary session in February 1610 he was greeted with whistles of derision.[34] All that was salvaged from James's dream was the repeal of some mutually hostile laws in 1607, an extradition agreement binding the English authorities to hand over to Scotland criminals who sought refuge in the English border counties, and, finally, a union flag which was flown by English ships until 1634.

Financial reform and the Great Contract

James regretfully had to withdraw his proposals for union. Much more serious for him was the cool parliamentary reception for his requests for help with his financial difficulties. The failure to reach a parliamentary solution to them was the prime reason for the temporary breakdown of parliamentary government in 1610.

If James, thought S. R. Gardiner, 'had consented to regulate his expenditure . . . in such a way as a man of ordinary business habits would have been certain to approve of, he might, in the course of a few years, have found himself independent of Parliament, excepting in time of extraordinary emergency'.[35] James, of course, was not 'a man of ordinary business habits', but it is an open question whether even such a man would have made the English crown solvent in the early seventeenth century. Only by extreme parsimony, which strained the patience and loyalties of some of her courtiers and officials, and by massive land sales, did Elizabeth I keep the royal debt down to manageable proportions. In 1603, although £300,000 of the subsidy of 1601 had still to be collected, the crown debt was £400,000. The fundamental reasons for the insufficiencies of English public finance in the early seventeenth century have already been considered: a royal revenue system badly in need of reform, allied to escalating government costs. As a married man James had additional financial burdens; Lord Treasurer Dorset estimated that because James had a wife and family his ordinary expenses were £80,000 p.a. greater than Elizabeth's.[36]

All this, though, is not an adequate defence of James's extravagance in the face of the crown's financial problems. Only a mere eighteen months after James's accession the aged Matthew Hutton, archbishop of York, was writing reproachfully to the king about popular fears 'that his excellent and heroical nature is too much inclined to giving, which in short time will exhaust the treasure of this kingdom and bring many inconveniences'.[37] In the first five years of his reign James's wardrobe expenditure increased fourfold compared with the previous four years.

The treasurer of the chamber spent 40 per cent more in the same period. Some increase in royal largesse to ministers and courtiers was perhaps inevitable, but the scale of gifts (£68,153) and pensions (nearly £30,000 p.a.) in the first four years of his reign was excessive.[38] Moreover, James compounded a financial fault by the political folly of making many gifts to Scottish favourites, notably to successive masters of the wardrobe, George Home earl of Dunbar, and James Hay (later viscount Doncaster and earl of Carlisle). But, although parliamentary critics singled these out, James was lavish in his gifts to English courtiers as well, especially the Howards (the earls of Northampton, Suffolk, and Nottingham). Office-holders were expected to exploit their privileged position for their own private pockets, but James put no limit on this practice. Sarcastic commentators nicknamed Thomas Sackville earl of Dorset, the lord treasurer, 'Lord Fill-Sack'. The great Jacobean palaces built by courtiers, Hatfield, Knole, Audley End, Northumberland House, are monuments to private greed and to James's failure to curb public expenditure.

On the death of Dorset in 1608 Cecil was appointed lord treasurer, combining the office with his duties as principal secretary. Cecil's administrative ability has never been in doubt. What is less clear is whether a man with Cecil's vested interests in the existing royal revenue system, especially in the customs farms, could possibly succeed in reforming it. Nevertheless his tenure of the treasurership saw the first systematic attempt to curb expenditure and increase royal income for over half a century. By 1608 the crown debt had risen to £597,337, and in November Salisbury succeeded in extracting a public declaration from the king that he would curtail his gifts of land. Six months later James made a more sweeping promise not to alienate any crown land without the consent of the principal privy councillors, nor to grant any sources of revenue as gifts or pensions. Promises, promises. James realized what the remedies were, but he failed to carry them out. This was hardly Cecil's fault; nor was the fact that his attempt to raise an economic rent from the crown estates met with only limited success. In 1608 he ordered a survey to be made of all crown lands, with the ultimate aim of revising the crown's leasing policy. This was clearly a task beyond the capability of the bureaucratic machinery of the early Stuart state. The survey was not completed; those surveys which were produced were inaccurate. Cecil had to resort instead to short-term expedients of raising money, continuing the Elizabethan sales of crown estates, and the established practice of deficit borrowing: a system of financial juggling, by which old debts were repaid by taking on new ones.[39] In the early part of the reign, until the City fathers discovered the worthlessness of royal credit, the biggest source of crown loans was the City of London; in 1608 a loan made by the City in 1604 was repaid largely because a new loan of £69,000 was being negotiated from the same source.

In this situation the prospect of a new source of income for the crown was very welcome, and this seemed to be at hand as a result of a decision in the court of exchequer in 1606. John Bate, apparently with the support of his fellow merchants trading to the east Mediterranean, refused to pay the import duty – the 'imposition' – of 5s 6d on each hundredweight of currants. Since this was in direct contravention of the crown's long-established right to levy impositions, the decision of the judges against Bate was not surprising, and raised little contemporary controversy outside that portion of the mercantile community whose pockets were hit. What made the Bate Case of political importance was that Cecil considered that the judges' decision gave the crown the right to levy impositions as a source of revenue, as well as a means of regulating trade. In July 1608, in the first major revision of English customs duties since the marquis of Winchester's reforms in the 1550s, Cecil issued a new Book of Rates which levied impositions on 1,400 items, with a projected income for the exchequer of between £60,000 and £70,000 p.a. What had been something which in 1606 affected a few merchants' profits, in 1608 became a constitutional issue affecting the liberties of parliament. Impositions contravened the 'old fundamental right' of parliament that 'no such charges should ever be laid upon the people without their common consent'.[40] 'If this power of imposing were quietly settled in our Kings', commented James Whitelocke in parliament in 1610, 'considering what the greatest use they make of assembling of Parliaments, which is the supply of money, I do not see any likelihood to hope for often meetings in that kind because they would provide themselves by that other means'.[41] It is doubtful, though, whether many people appreciated the finer constitutional issues involved. Significantly the Commons' petition of 1610 against impositions placed equal emphasis on the commercial damage they caused: 'the overthrow of merchants and shipping, the causing of a general dearth and decay of wealth among your people'.[42] Yet the furore stirred up by the Bate Case and the Book of Rates illustrates a central theme of importance in James's reign: that finance, unlike religion, was a major political issue. A permanent solution to the crown's financial problems had to be one approved of by parliament. This Cecil realized and it accounts for his efforts to conclude the Great Contract in the fifth parliamentary session of James's reign in 1610.

At the beginning of the 1610 session Cecil spelled out to a conference of both Houses the seriousness of the king's financial position. Despite massive land sales since 1608 the crown debt was £280,000, with current annual expenditure running at £511,000. If Cecil hoped to shock the Commons into agreeing to his request for a subsidy of £600,000 he was disappointed. Instead the House proceeded to debate possible sources of revenue other than a subsidy. One suggestion, that of collecting more fines from Catholic recusants, satisfied anti-Catholic prejudices as well as fears of higher taxation. Another, that of curbing royal expenditure, had already been tried by Cecil. He realized, just as much as radical parliamentary critics like Mr Thomas Wentworth, that by itself increased revenue was not enough, except it would please the King to resume his pencions granted to cortiers out of the exchecquer, and to diminish his charges and expences. For (sayes he) to what purpose it is for as to drawe a silver streame out of the country into the royall cisterne, if it shall dayly runne out thence by private cocks.[43]

The proposal which found most favour in the Commons was for the abolition of wardships and purveyance, in return for an annual composition to the king in compensation. This had been suggested in the 1604 and 1606 sessions and had a lot to recommend it both to the king and to parliament. Although under Cecil's mastership the revenue from the court of wards increased substantially, the king's actual profit was small, because of the leakage of revenue into the pockets of officials. Certainly the profits did not compensate for the opposition raised by wardships. In the parliament of 1604 Sir Edwin Sandys voiced a general feeling that the abolition of wardships was 'but a restitution unto the original right of all men, by the Law of God and Nature, which is that children should be brought up by their parents and next of kin and by them be directed in their marriages'.[44] In previous parliamentary sessions James had forbidden discussions of the topic on the Elizabethan grounds that his feudal revenue was a prerogative matter and no concern of the Commons. But on 12 March 1610 he gave way and for the next three months there was intense haggling between the Commons and the king's representatives about the amount of compensation to be allowed the king in return for the abolition of wardships: by early May £200,000 was being considered as a possible annual payment.

Negotiations for the Great Contract seemed to be going quite smoothly. James's concession on the discussion of wardships pleased the Commons. The king, with considerable political adroitness, also dealt with some other grievances. He agreed to suppress Dr Cowell's book, *The Interpreter*. More significantly he listened favourably to many of the Commons' long-standing demands for ecclesiastical reform: better execution of the recusancy laws, the reinstatement of deprived ministers, the end of pluralities, non-residency, excommunication for trivial offences and prohibitions. However, the real obstacle to the successful conclusion of the Contract was the opposition to impositions levied by Cecil's Book of Rates. When the Commons' committee of grievances considered the matter James, on 11 May, announced that all discussion of the matter was to end, and ten days later he addressed the Commons personally, defending his right to levy impositions. Not surprisingly, given the precedents of Elizabeth's later parliaments, the Commons considered this an attack on the 'ancient, generall, and undoubted right of parliament to debate freely all things properly concerning the subjects, and theyre rights and interests'. The negotiations over the Contract were thus jeopardized. But James smoothed the path by removing his ban on discussion of impositions and by making it clear that any MP was welcome to approach him privately, 'without using ceremonies and compliments', to thrash out any grievances. Moreover, in late June and early July he promised to agree to an Act which would prevent him from levying impositions in future without parliamentary consent. Since this left untouched those impositions already in existence James's concessions could hardly have satisfied the Commons completely. But perhaps they had done enough to divide the House and gain some support for the Contract. By the time parliament was prorogued on 23 July the prospects for a successful conclusion of the Contract seemed good. A subsidy was agreed, a Bill prohibiting impositions passed the Commons, and agreement was reached on £200,000 as an acceptable compensation for the abolition of feudal tenures and wardships.

Why, then, did the Great Contract fail? When parliament reassembled in October most MPs were quite clearly dragging their feet. A week after the appointed starting date of the session only one hundred MPs were present and penalties were proposed for non-attendance. One explanation for the change of mood is that it was a reflection of opinion in the constituencies. Could James be trusted to redress the Commons' grievances as he had promised he would do in July? 'If we should now return into our country', said one MP, 'with nothing for the good of the commonwealth, they would say we have been all the while like children in ketching butterflies.'[45] In any case how would the £200,000 p.a. be raised? By a permanent land tax? 'It is impossible to rayse 200,000 *li* out of the land onely', said another MP, 'the rest out of merchandise and a running subsidy from the monied men.' 'If we go forward,' said Sir Thomas Beaumont, 'wee are undone, charging the land so deeply as is desyred.'[46] More seriously, would not a permanent addition to the royal revenue make the king independent of parliament at a time when other representative assemblies in Europe were losing any power they had to absolutist monarchs?

But it was not only MPs who had had second thoughts during the recess. Sir Julius Caesar, the chancellor of the exchequer, questioned whether the financial gains to the king from the abolition of feudal tenures would be very great. Since the king would lose an estimated £115,000 p.a. which he got from his feudal rights, the actual increase in revenue would only be £85,000 p.a., which was hardly sufficient to meet a total debt of £600,000 and high current expenditure. The Great Contract, concluded Caesar, 'wilbee the most unprofitable bargaine that ever King made, to part with most of the greatest prerogatives of gaine and honor which he hathe, and not to relieve that want which was the onelie motive of that resoluccion'.[47] There were others on the king's side who had more selfish motives than Caesar to poison the king's mind against the Contract; many had much to lose if the sale of wardships was abandoned. Robert Carr, James's Scottish favourite, who was the butt of much of the anti-Scottish feeling in the Commons, aligned himself against the Contract and the continuation of parliament. Not for the last time division among James's courtiers was reflected in events in parliament. In addition, by the autumn James, with a newly negotiated

City loan of £100,000 in his pocket, felt more financially secure. As a result when the negotiations on the Contract were resumed in November both sides raised their terms and the Contract quickly collapsed. Parliament was prorogued until February 1611, but before that James dissolved his first parliament.

How serious was this failure of parliamentary government? How deep and wide was the gulf between James and the parliamentary classes in 1610? James had failed either to satisfy many grievances or to calm the widespread fears about the future of parliament in the constitution. But there were large areas of agreement between him and his leading subjects: the king's foreign policy had been successful; on religious questions the king generally took an uncontroversial stance; and he had shown that even on the issues of impositions and parliamentary freedom of speech he was willing to listen to reason. The attachment of the political nation to the monarchy and the old constitution was still strong in 1610. The events of the next eleven years strained but did not break that attachment. Though only one parliament met briefly in 1614, the events which took place from 1610 to 1621 did not erect an insurmountable barrier between 'court' and 'country'.

Rule without parliament, 1610–1621

The Howards and the ruin of the royal finances, 1610–1618

Despite the City loan of 1610 the failure of the Great Contract left James desperately short of money. More than ever in the following years he was ready to listen to anyone who had a scheme to raise extra-parliamentary revenue. The result was a succession of financial expedients which did not raise enough money either to meet the king's escalating costs or to compensate for the injury they did to the crown's reputation. Some of the money-raising ventures were well-used ones, such as continuing the sale of crown estates and monopolies, increasing the price of wardships, and levying a forced loan (in 1611), but the fact that they were not new (indeed all of them had been used by Elizabeth I) did not make them any more popular.

Perhaps the most damaging to the crown, was a scheme certainly not resorted to by the late queen, the sale of honours. Elizabeth I exercised just as much tight-fisted control on the creation of new titles of honour as she did on royal expenditure. In his wholesale creation of knights on his accession James I was therefore simply giving way to the pent-up demands of many gentry for outstanding recognition of their social status. James, however, went too far. By permitting courtiers to sell knighthoods he allowed the rank to fall into popular disrepute. 'Two walking espyed one a far off', began a popular joke; 'the one demanded what he should be, the other answered he seemed to be a gentleman; no, I warrant you, says the other, I think he is but a knight.' The devaluation of the knightage provided the opportunity for James to take up one of the many ideas being mooted for the creation of a new hereditary dignity. In 1611 the order of baronets was established, to consist of 200 members, and, although James promised that only those from worthy, ancient families would be chosen, little care was taken in this regard. Baronetcies were sold to anyone who could afford the £1,095 purchase price, bringing in a revenue to the crown by March 1614 of £90,885.[48] Thereafter the income to the crown from the sale of baronetcies fell rapidly, as James allowed courtiers and others to sell them for services rendered. The baronetcy, like the knightage before it, became devalued, which struck at the roots of a society which valued the stability brought by respect for order, 'degree' and precedence. Nor were these financial expedients sufficiently successful in their primary aim. In August 1612 James established a special commission, headed by Sir Thomas Roe, whose terms of reference were to devise yet more money-making projects.

In the years after 1610 as damaging to the crown as the 'inflation of honours' and the other schemes was the growing influence at court of the Howards. Cecil's failure to secure the Great Contract marked the end of his special relationship with the king. Before and after his death in May 1612 his enemies at court lost no opportunity to attack him and his reputation. Yet with all his faults and limitations Cecil's death in 1612 was a great loss to the crown. There was no one of equal administrative ability to replace him, which perhaps James, to his credit, recognized. He put the treasury into commission and made no appointment to Cecil's other office of secretary, which must have been a great blow to the Howards, who hoped to benefit from Cecil's death. Their setback was shortlived, however. In 1613 the divorce of Lady Frances Howard, the earl of Suffolk's daughter, and the earl of Essex enabled Lady Frances to marry the king's youthful favourite, Robert Carr, now earl of Somerset. James intervened personally to secure the divorce against the opinion of Archbishop Abbot. The marriage signalled the triumph of the Howards' political ambitions. It is difficult to see any benefits whatsoever from their period of dominance at court.

Certainly with the success of the Howards at court all hope of curbing James's extravagance was gone, and without retrenchment the plans for financial reforms produced by a treasury commission in 1613 inevitably remained paper schemes. James was reduced to the plight of borrowing from courtiers (in 1613 he borrowed £25,000 from Somerset) and selling more crown lands. So, despite Howard opposition, the pressure for calling another parliament became intense, and James gave way in February 1614. But the Howards were more successful in blocking concessions on grievances, such as impositions and monopolies, urged on the king by Sir Henry Neville and Francis Bacon. Nor, as ten years earlier, were provisions made to provide official leadership in the Commons. James appointed Ralph Winwood as secretary only seven days before parliament met in April 1614. While it is not surprising that in these circumstances the Commons proved intractable, it is ironic that the fiercest opposition developed because of suspicions that there had been too much royal influence before parliament met. Hard on the heels of the grievances about the activities of royal 'undertakers' (seen in the Commons' attacks on Parry and Bacon) came the more predictable stormy debate on impositions, which, as in 1610, developed into a debate on the Commons' freedom of speech (personalized in the case of Bishop Niele). The 1614 parliament well deserves its nickname 'the Addled Parliament'. It was dissolved on 7 June, having passed no legislation and, more seriously for James, no subsidy. Why did it fail? Was it due entirely to lack of royal management and the failure to remove outstanding grievances before Parliament met? It may be that some royal advisers, notably the earl of Northampton, did not want the parliament to succeed and worked hard behind the scenes for its failure, perhaps by encouraging rumours of the activities of royal 'undertakers'. The Piedmontese ambassador thought that 'the dissolution of Parliament is not displeasing to many of the more important councillors, since it appears that there was to be an investigation of some of them, which would have caused them much trouble and embarrassment'.[49] The failure of the Addled Parliament may be one of the more tragic legacies of the Howards to James's reign.

James's celebrated outburst to Gondomar, venting his frustration at parliament in 1614, is often used as evidence of James's ultimate ambition never to call parliament again. There is little corroboratory support for this. In the following years serious consideration was frequently given to summoning parliament, as the search for ways to pay the mounting royal debts became more desperate. Because royal credit was so bad the City dried up (temporarily) as a source of loans; in June 1614 it made James a free gift of £10,000 rather than lend him £100,000. The king, however, had not lost everyone's goodwill. When he appealed for a voluntary loan or 'benevolence' there was some resistance, but it was far from universal. Thomas Wentworth in Yorkshire, for example, spoke in its favour and there is evidence that some MPs towards the end of the Addled Parliament had been willing to vote a subsidy to prevent the dissolution.[50]

But other financial expedients after 1614 did have more serious consequences. The Cockayne Project for the reorganization of the cloth trade, which has already been mentioned, is not the only example of this (see p. 25). The real aim of the commission set up in May 1615, despite its overt town-planning motives and James's protestations, was not to prevent further building in London but to raise money by collecting fines for evading the ban on building. The irritation felt at this, though, was a pinprick compared with the sale of peerages which began in 1615. The gains were lucrative (earldoms went for £10,000 each) but a lot of the profit was syphoned off by intermediaries, and the sales were naturally resented by the established aristocracy. Nor was the increase in crown revenue sufficient to meet the crown's expenditure. By

1617 the royal debt was £726,000 and James had great difficulty in paying for his visit to Scotland in that year. One man had even been willing to bet that it (and Raleigh's trip to Guiana, and the Spanish marriage) would never take place.[51] So suspicious was the City of the soundness of royal credit that it would lend James £100,000 for one year only; it surrounded the loan with unprecedented guarantees and still the City authorities had great difficulties in forcing merchants to contribute to it.

Not only the royal credit (in the financial sense) was brought low during the supremacy of the Howards; so too was its general 'credit', its reputation. The revelations and allegations in 1615 of the earl and countess of Somerset's role in the murder in 1613 of Sir Thomas Overbury, who had opposed Lady Frances's divorce, and the subsequent investigation and trial formed one of the seamier scandals of Jacobean England. The Howards were also the centre of another *cause célèbre* in 1618 when the earl of Suffolk (lord treasurer since 1614) and his wife were tried for financial corruption, and their fall brought the disgrace of many important Howard clients, including William Lord Knollys and Sir Thomas Lake. By this time the Howards could be forgiven for feeling they were the subject of a witch-hunt, because in a sense they were. The attack on them was pressed home by an anti-Howard faction at court (including Archbishop Abbot, Lord Ellesmere who died in 1617, Sir Edward Coke, and the earls of Southampton and Pembroke). It was they who promoted George Villiers in his attempt to replace Somerset in the king's affections. Their (and his) success is charted in Villiers's rapidly rising fortunes: cupbearer, 1614; gentleman of the bedchamber, 1615; master of the horse and viscount Buckingham, 1616; earl of Buckingham, 1617; marquis of Buckingham, 1618; and duke of Buckingham, 1623. It remains to be seen whether Buckingham was an able champion of the cause of reform against the financial and moral corruption of the Howards.

Buckingham, Cranfield, and reform, 1618–1621

Able men round James, like Sir Francis Bacon who became lord chancellor in January 1618, saw that reform was necessary in order to restore royal credit, financially and otherwise, from the low point to which it had been reduced by the Howards. Buckingham rose to a powerful position as a protégé of this reforming, anti-Howard faction; and soon he was secure in James's favour. 'Christ had his John', James is alleged to have said, 'and I have my George.' Buckingham, however, had little reason to desert those who were working for financial reform, especially since reform was a useful stick with which to beat the Howards. As a reformer Buckingham found an ally not only in the lord chancellor but also in Lionel Cranfield.

Despite snobbish jibes at his mercantile 'apprentice-boy' background Cranfield had carved out a useful career for himself at court: in 1613 he became surveyor-general of the customs and in 1616 master of the court of requests. An astute, careful businessman in the running of his own personal and business affairs, he was ideally suited to cutting out wasteful and needless public expenditure. This was the aim of what turned out to be a series of investigatory commissions into the running of royal departments of state. The first, concerned with the royal household, was intended to be 'the beginning for the Reformation of all the heads of his Majesty's expense'. Cranfield and Sir Richard Weston, together with officials from the exchequer, painstakingly examined the household consumption of food, drink, fuel, and clothes. No detail was beneath them; Cranfield even investigated the waste of unburnt candle ends. At the end of their investigation the commissioners issued a new book of orders for the running of the household which effected an estimated saving of £10,000 p.a. In June 1618 another commission with Cranfield prominent in its membership, began to investigate the administration of the navy, revealing similar waste and corruption to that in the household. Buckingham also took a first-hand interest in the work of this sub-commission, and with his support (in autumn 1619 he replaced Nottingham as lord admiral) the programme of retrenchment met with a great deal of success. In the treasury the blatant peculation, which resulted in the disgrace of the Suffolks and their colleagues, was uncovered by yet another team of investigators led by Cranfield. The reform of two other departments was Cranfield's own personal triumph. As master of the wardrobe from September 1618 he halved royal expenditure; and he increased the revenue of the court of wards by one quarter after he became master of the court in January 1619.

Impressive as was Cranfield's work in its thoroughness in rationalizing the existing administrative system, it was not a permanent solution to James's shortage of money. Why could even an administrator of the proven ability of Cranfield (and Cecil before him) not achieve the reform that James needed? The Stuarts' lack of a large and experienced bureaucracy is only part of the answer. Even if there had been the necessary administrative machinery was fundamental reform of the crown's finance and administration possible? It is significant that there was a great deal of powerful opinion against reform; too many people had a vested interest in the existing system. Buckingham's very presence at court meant that royal largesse, in the form of grants of offices, pensions, and monopolies, went on unabated. Despite his adopted role, Buckingham's powerful position (and that of his mother and brothers) depended far too much on the court system for the duke to be a serious reformer. It is difficult to escape the conclusion that for Buckingham reform was valued as a political weapon against the Howards rather than a desirable end in itself. The influence of Buckingham's mother, Lady Compton, was all-pervasive, building up a Villiers connection so impressive that Gondomar, the Spanish ambassador, wrote home ironically to his masters in Madrid that he had more hope than ever of the conversion of England, since he found that there were more prayers and oblations offered to the mother than to the son.[52] The Villiers, like the Howards before them, were a serious obstacle to reform. So too was Cranfield himself. How serious depends on whether or not one considers the private fortune he made as a royal servant justified as a reward for his administrative ability and technical expertise in dealing with customs farmers and other financiers. One is left with the impression that both inside and outside the court circle there was a general unwillingness to countenance radical and administrative reform. It is easy to understand why courtiers resented the imposition of irksome economy measures and the pruning of valuable sinecures and pensions by a man they considered to be a social upstart. Yet the same is true of the man making his career at court and the man living on his country estates in the early seventeenth century: both saw the court as the fount of honour and advancement. Courtier and parliamentarian, royal administrator and country gentleman must have had an ambivalent attitude to reform. Was it only James's extravagance, aided and abetted by the Howards, Villiers, and others at court, that frustrated the reforming efforts of the two men with most administrative ability in James's reign, Cecil and Cranfield? Or is it justifiable to place part of the blame, at least, at the door of the whole political nation? It is possible that some of those who demanded reform, administrative as well as ecclesiastical, in the early seventeenth century had in their own hands the means to carry it out.

It was inevitable, therefore, that at some stage James would have to recall parliament. What finally ensured that it was called were international developments which threatened the European peace established in 1604 and 1609. As has been seen, James believed that he could play a vital role in maintaining this peace by not aligning himself solely either with France or with Spain, either with the Protestant or with the Catholic sides in Germany. He hoped that his daughter's marriage to the Protestant Elector Palatine would be balanced by a Spanish Catholic marriage for his son. This is why James's negotiations with Spain became the keystone of his foreign policy in his later years. As he saw it, Spain must not be allowed to feel isolated in Europe; by keeping diplomatic channels open James could use his influence to defuse international crises. His attachment to this policy, contrary to the traditional view, owed little to the influence of the Spanish ambassador, Gondomar – James's foreign policy was his own – and even less to the Spanish pensions paid to Somerset, the Howards, Buckingham, and others. James was not alone in his financial difficulties; quite often the Spanish pensions were never paid. And as Professor C. H. Carter notes, 'Spain, far from being in control of its hirelings, was rather in the position of a hapless diner who must "bribe" a surly waiter with tips to avoid soup getting spilled on him.'[53]

Even after his son-in-law's rebellion – in September 1618 Elector Palatine Frederick accepted the rebels' offer of the Bohemian crown – James tried to maintain an uncommitted position. Despite the pressure of some of his advisers, led by Archbishop Abbot, for stronger action, James continued to rely on a diplomatic solution. The marriage negotiations in Madrid continued, and in Brussels Sir Richard Weston and Sir Edward Conway were sent to argue against the invasion of the Palatinate. Even after this happened at the end of August 1620 James did not abandon his diplomatic contacts with Spain. But the invasion of the Palatinate did force him to consider the possibility, at least, that he might have to go to war against Spain; as he had made clear in 1604 James's pacific philosophy did not rule out the use of war as the last resort when diplomacy failed. War preparations meant the need for parliamentary finance and writs for parliamentary elections inevitably followed Spinola's invasion of the Lower Palatinate. The always close connection between foreign policy and domestic history is nowhere better illustrated. It is no coincidence that England's temporary involvement in the Thirty Years' War in the 1620s was a crucial period in England's domestic political history.

Notes

For abreviations used throughout see p. xiv.

1. Most Catholics were uncommitted in 1640, K. J. Lindley, 'The lay Catholics of England in the reign of Charles I' *J. Eccl. H.*, XXII (1971), pp. 199–222; *idem.*, 'The part played by Catholics', in B. Manning, ed., *Politics, Religion and the English Civil War* (1973) pp. 126–76.
2. Tanner, *Constitutional Documents*, p. 220.
3. F. J. Fisher, ed., *The State of England Anno Dom. 1600 by Thomas Wilson*, Camden Society, 3rd ser., LII (1936), p. 5.
4. D. H. Willson, *King James VI and I* (Cape paperback edn 1963) is the best biography, but many of its unsympathetic judgements on James stand in need of substantial revision. The following go some way towards this, but a new biography of James is needed: A. G. R. Smith, 'Introduction', in A. G. R. Smith, ed., *The Reign of James VI and I* (1973), pp. 1–21; M. L. Schwarz, 'James I and the historians: towards a reconsideration', *J.B.S.*, XIII no. 2 (1973), pp. 114–34,; R. C. Munden, 'James I and "the growth of mutual distrust": King, Commons, and Reform, 1603–40', in Kevin Sharpe, ed., *Faction and Parliament: essays on early Stuart history* (1978), pp. 43–72.
5. Quoted in Willson, *James VI and I*, p. 274.
6. Quoted in *ibid.*, p. 135.
7. Quoted in *ibid.*, p. 165.
8. Quoted in *ibid.*, p. 191.
9. Tanner, *Constitutional Documents*, p. 25.
10. Maurice Lee, *James and Henri IV: an essay in English foreign policy 1603–10* (1970), p. 37.
11. Quoted in Gardiner, *History*, I, p. 199.
12. John Bossy, 'The English Catholic community 1603–25', in A. G. R. Smith, ed., *The Reign of James VI and I*, p. 92.
13. Quoted in P. McGrath, *Papists and Puritans in the Reign of Elizabeth I* (1967) p. 339.
14. Tanner, *Constitutional Documents*, p. 29.

15. A. J. Loomie, *Guy Fawkes in Spain: the 'Spanish Treason' in Spanish documents*, (*B.I.H.R.* supplement 1971) is a corrective to the view of those Catholic historians who see the plot as being engineered by Cecil.

16. Kenyon, *Stuart Constitution*, p. 132.

17. M. Curtis, 'The Hampton Court Conference and its aftermath', *History*, XLVI (1961), pp. 1–16.

18. R. C. Munden, 'James I and "the growth of mutual distrust"', pp. 66–8 argues that Bancroft ordered the bishops to withdraw from these discussions. This is part of Dr Munden's wider argument that it was the king's advisers rather than James who were responsible for the failures of the 1604 parliamentary session.

19. S. B. Babbage, *Puritanism and Bancroft* (1962), pp. 147–219.

20. Paul S. Seaver, *The Puritan Lectureships: the politics of religious dissent 1560–1662* (Stanford California, 1970) pp. 201–39; R. A. Marchant, *The Puritans and the Church Courts in the Diocese of York 1560–1642* (1960), p. 29.

21. N. Tyacke, 'Puritanism, Arminianism and counter revolution', in Conrad Russell, ed., *The Origins of the English Civil War* (1973), p. 126.

22. Tanner, *Constitutional Documents*, p. 56.

23. Gardiner, *History*, III, p. 252.

24. A. Hassell Smith, *County and Court: government and politics in Norfolk 1558–1603* (1974), *passim*.

25. On the attitude of the Commons to their privileges in this and other cases in the early seventeenth century, see Derek Hirst, 'Elections and the privileges of the House of Commons in the early seventeenth century: confrontation or compromise?', *H.J.*, XVIII (1974), pp. 851–62.

26. Tanner, *Constitutional Documents*, p. 204.

27. For a different view of James's handling of the case, see R. C. Munden, 'The defeat of Sir John Fortescue: Court *vs* Country at the hustings?', *E.H.R.*, XCIII (1978), pp. 811–16.

28. G. R. Elton, 'A high road to civil war?', in C. H. Carter, ed., *Essays in honour of Garrett Mattingley* (1966), pp. 315ff.

29. Conrad Russell, 'Parliamentary history in perspective 1604–29', *History*, XLI (1976), pp. 1–27. See pp. 88–91.

30. Tanner, *Constitutional Documents*, p. 26.

31. Quoted in S. T. Bindoff, 'The Stuarts and their style', *E.H.R.*, IX, 1945, p. 194. Brian P. Levack, 'The proposed union of English law and Scots law in the seventeenth century', *Juridical Review*, 1975, part ii, pp. 97–115 is the best discussion of the proposed union.

32. *The Parliamentary or Constitutional History of England* V (1763), p. 178.

33. *Commons Journals*, I, p. 334.

34. W. Notestein, ed., *The House of Commons 1604–10* (1971), p. 256.

35. Gardiner, *History*, I, p. 294.

36. J. P. Cooper, 'The fall of the Stuart monarchy', in *The New Cambridge Modern History*, IV (1970), p. 544.

37. *H. M. C. Salisbury*, XVI, pp. 220–21.

38. M. Prestwich, *Cranfield: Politics and Profits under the Early Stuarts* (1966), pp. 12–14. Mrs Prestwich amends the figures of James I's expenditure in F. C. Dietz, *English Public Finance 1558–1642* (1932).

39. R. Ashton, 'Deficit finance in the reign of James I', *Econ. H.R.*, 2nd ser., X (1957), pp. 15–29.

40. Kenyon, *Stuart Constitution*, p. 72.
41. Tanner, *Constitutional Documents*, p. 262.
42. Kenyon, *Stuart Constitution*, p. 73.
43. S. R. Gardiner, ed., *Parliamentary Debates in 1610*, (Camden Soc., 1st ser., LXXXI 1862), p. 11.
44. Quoted in Notestein, *The House of Commons 1604–10*, p. 92.
45. Quoted in Prestwich, *Cranfield*, p. 29.
46. *Parliamentary Debates in 1610*, p. 129.
47. *Ibid.*, p. 176.
48. L. Stone, *The Crisis of the Aristocracy 1558–1641* (1965), p. 85.
49. Quoted in Clayton Roberts, *The Growth of Representative Government in Stuart England* (1976), p. 22.
50. J. P. Cooper, ed., *The Wentworth Papers 1597–1628*, Camden Society, 4th ser., XII (1973), pp. 79–80 and 80 n. 1.
51. Gardiner, *History*, III, p. 82.
52. Gardiner, *History*, III, pp. 207–8.
53. C. H. Carter, *The Secret Diplomacy of the Hapsburgs 1598–1625* (1964), pp. 126–7.

Chapter 5

The breakdown of the Elizabethan constitution 1621–1640

1621–1624: 'court' versus 'country'?

It is not easy to analyse the politics of the 1620s, largely because political groupings were very fluid, changing rapidly in response to different issues and circumstances. What is certain is that analyses in terms of 'court' and 'country', 'king and parliament', 'crown and opposition' are too simple, too cut-and-dried to take account of the numerous political alliances of courtiers, privy councillors, and parliamentary leaders in the 1620s. MPs could ill afford lightly to cut themselves off from the prospects of court office or court patronage, without which their local prestige would suffer. When and why most of them did break with the court are, of course, the crucial questions in explaining the collapse of the old constitution and the crisis of 1640–1. It does not seem, though, that many were forced into taking this drastic course in the last years of James I's reign.

In 1621 there was, of course, a lot which the leaders of English landed society found distasteful in the events since the dissolution of the Addled Parliament: the increasing use again of patents and monopolies, which were associated with the rapidly worsening economic crisis; the 'inflation of honours' which was partially responsible for the new, more critical, role of the House of Lords in the constitutional conflicts of the 1620s; the policy of continued negotiations with Spain, which was seen by many as as indefensible – indeed as wicked – as some later felt Chamberlain's policy of 'appeasement' with Hitler to be after the invasion of Austria in 1938; and the corruption of the Jacobean court. No doubt William Davenport in Cheshire was not the only country gentleman to note disapprovingly in his commonplace book court scandals like the Essex divorce and Overbury murder.[1] Yet the reasons behind the political battles in James's last two parliaments of 1621 and 1624 lie as much in differences between royal councillors as in 'country' distrust of 'court' policies.[2]

The parliament of 1621 began fairly well for the crown. In February, in only the third week of the opening session, James was offered a grant of two subsidies (about £140,000), which, though not enough to pay for an army, did not preclude the possibility of a further grant. Unfortunately, though, the privy council, although much better represented in the Commons than in any previous Jacobean parliament, was deeply divided. The crown's leading advisers, Bacon, Coke, and Cranfield, treated each other with mutual wariness. Already the royal preparations for the parliamentary session (which were much more thorough than in 1614) had been hindered by opposition in the privy council, led by the Villiers connection and by Coke, to Bacon's proposal to withdraw some patents of monopoly before parliament met and so remove this source of grievance. Sir Edward Coke's antipathy to Bacon was due to a mixture of long-standing professional rivalry, personal incompatibility, and differing views on the independence of the judiciary, for his defence of which Coke had been dismissed in 1616 as chief justice of the King's Bench. In 1617 he was restored to the privy council and was hopeful of preferment as lord treasurer. In these circumstances the appointment in December 1620 to the treasurership of Sir Henry Montague, who had replaced Coke as chief justice in 1616, was, to say the least, ill-timed, and partly accounts for Coke's criticism of royal policies later. If Coke hated Bacon, Cranfield's mercantile origins and his continuing reform programme left him isolated at court. It is a tragedy that he was unable to find any common personal ground with Bacon, who also had plans for reform.

Members of parliament were treated to the unusual[3] sight of privy councillors, Coke and Cranfield, encouraging them from the start of the parliamentary session to enquire into royal grants of patents of monopoly. They found willing support among MPs in making this the dominant issue of the session (30 January to 4 June 1621) for two main reasons. First, parliament met at a time of grave economic crisis and MPs did not need convincing that monopolies had been injurious to trade. The patent of the monopoly of gold and silver thread, for example, it was said in the Commons on 26 February, 'did waste 20,000 *l* of our coin, and stayed the importation of 20,000 *l* more in bullion brought in from Venice in that commodity', thus contributing to the 'want of money' which contemporaries believed to be at the root of the crisis.[4] Moreover, many monopolies seemed to have been granted to courtiers who could pay for a patent, regardless of good commercial sense. The Cockayne Project was still fresh in people's memories. Second, not all patents were grants of a commercial monopoly; James I, like Elizabeth before him, entrusted specific administrative functions of government to patentees, a system which bypassed the normal local government process and which was open to the charge of being 'government by patentees'. Two such grants, giving the right to commissioners to license inns and alehouses respectively, had caused special annoyance to local magistrates and the Commons began proceedings against Giles Mompesson and Sir Francis Michell, the chief patentees. Mompesson was especially singled out for attack, because he was both a multiple monopolist (as well as the patent for inns, he was also involved in the patent for the manufacture of gold and silver thread and for the concealment of crown lands) and an MP and therefore vulnerable to the process of existing parliamentary judicature. Ominously for the crown a subcommittee of the Commons began systematically investigating any royal patent or monopoly which was referred to it, questioning the patentee and deciding on its validity.

Not only were these novel incursions into judicial spheres by the Commons directly encouraged by privy councillors, but Coke and Cranfield were also involved in promoting an attack on their rival, Bacon, which was of even greater constitutional significance. The lord chancellor had been one of the referees who had sanctioned the grants of patents, and, with vocal support from Coke and Cranfield, the demand grew for punishment of the referees as well as the patentees, so that 'the Saddle [may be] set on the right Horse'.[5] The willingness of the House of Lords to cooperate with the Lower House in the proceedings against Bacon was crucial. Hitherto in previous Jacobean parliaments, opposition in the Lords had been fairly unimportant, but in 1621 the leadership of the earls of Southampton and Oxford, who were in close contact with the Commons' campaign against Bacon, swayed the Lords, many of whom were dismayed by Buckingham's domination of the king. Nor did James do anything to protect his lord chancellor. In addition to making it known, as he did on 10 March, that he would listen favourably to a Bill against monopolies, he also allowed Bacon to be sacrificed. Lacking the king's support, Bacon submitted to the Lords on a charge of having accepted bribes in his position as a judge, and he was fined, imprisoned, and excluded from office.

These events clearly threatened Buckingham and his brothers, who were involved in many patents. Therefore, soon after the parliamentary recess Sir Edwin Sandys and the earls of Southampton and Oxford were arrested in an attempt to frighten the parliamentary leaders. There was also a concerted attempt to conciliate them. On 10 July a royal proclamation cancelled eighteen monopolies and promised to review seventeen others; a privy council standing committee began an investigation into the causes of the economic crisis; and the outports were allowed to trade in the new draperies, despite the monopoly of the Company of Merchant Adventurers.

Unfortunately, although the arrested MPs and other political prisoners (including the ninth earl of Northumberland, who had been in prison since 1605) were released in a general amnesty suggested by the new lord keeper John Williams, the damage to parliamentary liberties had been done. What is more James again seemed to threaten these liberties in the second session of parliament, when he refused (as had Elizabeth I) to allow the Commons to discuss foreign policy. It is probable that this by itself would have raised the Commons to a strong protest. James made this inevitable by foolishly accompanying his ban on discussion with a theoretical statement claiming that parliament's privileges originated in a royal grant and that they had not held them for ever. Historically he was right; politically he was foolish, especially since he made clear that he 'never meant to deny them (the Commons) any lawful privileges that ever that House enjoyed in our predecessors' times'.[6] This gloss failed to allay MPs' fears. On 18 December they passed a Protestation that their privileges were 'the ancient and undoubted birthright and inheritance of the subjects of England'.[7] The adjournment followed on the next day and the dissolution soon after. Coke was quickly arrested and imprisoned; Sir Robert Phelips and William Mallory followed him; John Pym was placed under house arrest. Other 'ill-tempered spirits' from the Commons arguably fared even worse; they were sent as royal commissioners to Ireland.

For James's finances dissolution without further supply was a blow. Cranfield's campaign of economy measures was continuing (in 1621 he became lord treasurer and earl of Middlesex) but by now was suffering from the law of diminishing returns. Some minor increases in impositions were made and a benevolence levied after the dissolution brought in only the equivalent of one subsidy. Parliamentary finance was needed, but what determined the calling of parliament at the end of 1623 was Buckingham's and Charles's changed view of the Spanish marriage. In the spring of 1623 prince and favourite visited Madrid, spurning the advice of both career diplomats in Spain like Cottington and Digby and of the king.[8] Inevitably they found themselves at a disadvantage in dealing with the Spaniards, who humiliated Buckingham and foisted a disadvantageous marriage treaty on Charles. Their return to England in the autumn met with popular rejoicing; 'When Israel came out of Egypt and the house of Jacob from among the barbarous people', sang the choir in St Paul's in celebration. Within the space of seven or eight months Buckingham and Charles had been converted to a war policy against Spain. They overcame the objections of James and those in the privy council like Cranfield, who pointed out the financially ruinous consequences of a war, and at the end of the year writs went out for a new parliament.

Ill and old, James found the control of events slipping out of his hands. At the opening of the 1624 parliament on 19 February he went against Elizabethan precedent by asking for parliament's 'good and sound advice'[9] on foreign policy. Meanwhile Buckingham and Charles had been formulating a parliamentary alliance with Sandys, Digges, Phelips, and Eliot in the Commons and with the earl of Pembroke in the Lords, coordinating tactics for the new session. As proof of their good faith Buckingham and Charles brought to prominence at court (like producing a trump card from their sleeve) the Puritan divine, John Preston, who had been Charles's chaplain since 1621 and Buckingham's client since October 1622. It was a parliamentary alliance based on a common hatred of Spain and of popery. In the 1621 parliament the Lords had set aside a Commons' sentence of £1,000 fine and the pillory on a Roman Catholic barrister who had made offensive references to the elector palatine and his wife and replaced it with one of branding and whipping, a fine of £5,000 and life imprisonment. In 1624 the Commons was alive with rumours of a second gunpowder plot, and elated with the long-awaited opportunity to join the Protestant crusade in defence of the usurped elector palatine. In the foreign policy debate in March in the Commons Buckingham's and Charles's parliamentary allies called for an end to the Spanish negotiations and for a declaration of war against Spain. Ominously though for the alliance, the Commons only granted £300,000. When John Glanville, the lawyer, suggested a higher grant he was sharply reminded by Thomas Belasyse, the landowner, that 'subsidies come not in so easily as fees'.[10] Others, like Eliot, believed that a naval war against Spain would bring its own profits. And for the moment Buckingham as lord admiral was tempted by this war strategy. The fall of Cranfield, who had maintained a consistent anti-war line, was an inevitable consequence. Once again court and parliament cooperated in legal proceedings against a king's official and, isolated and marked out as a victim by Buckingham as he was, Cranfield was lost.

Parliamentary support had to be paid for. The importance of the device of appropriating the subsidy to treasurers appointed by parliament and for specific uses laid down by parliament can be exaggerated. It was not used again until the 1660s, and in 1621 James made it clear that for security reasons strategic military decisions 'must be in the council of mine own heart'.[11] James might have lost some control, but not all. He prevaricated about ending the Spanish negotiations, and, while he lived, diplomatic relations with Spain were never cut nor war with Spain officially declared. Under pressure from Buckingham and Charles, though, James did concede a Monopoly Act, forbidding grants of monopolies to individuals. Also the Commons' committee on trade and the privy council's commission on trade worked together to combat the economic crisis, and the crown made some concessions to the outports' demands for free trade in non-white clothes. Perhaps the price paid was a high one, but James's last parliament produced some promising signs of cooperation with the crown.

The prerogative 'extended . . . beyond its just symmetry', 1625–1629

The accession of Charles I marks a definite turning point in the history of the 1620s. After 1625, although many people in parliament retained contacts with the court, ever hopeful of court office and patronage, it is clear that the parliamentary leaders were finding it harder than ever both to cooperate with royal ministers and to keep their local prestige. Why were the prospects of parliamentary cooperation with the crown more bleak after 1625 than before? The most obvious reason, though not the most important, was the personality of the new king. A great contrast to his father, Charles was a shy man of few words, possibly as a result of a speech defect. 'I mean to show what I should speak in actions', he told his second parliament. Consequently, his contemporaries (like historians)[12] found that he was unapproachable and, what was worst, uncommunicative, especially in parliament, where his intentions and his actions often went unexplained, leaving others free to interpret them to his disadvantage. Moreover, when Charles became king the duke of Buckingham's position at court was more dominant than ever before. Disliked by the old nobility as a parvenu who had encouraged the sales of honours, the duke increasingly from 1625 until his assassination in 1628, prevented other councillors from getting close to the king. Buckingham thereby not only blocked a valuable channel of patronage but also a means by which royal decisions could be influenced at court. Consequently in the later 1620s the tendency for disagreements between courtiers to be carried on in parliament, which has already been noted in previous parliamentary sessions, was accelerated.[13] Of equal importance Charles's accession signalled the involvement of England in war, first against Spain, and later against Spain and France. Financial and military necessities caused the crown to wield its emergency 'prerogative' powers on a scale and with an intensity unparalleled since the last years of Elizabeth's war against Spain.[14] As a result, during wartime the inherent tension that existed between central and local government became more pronounced than in normal times. Finally, though its impact was delayed, Charles's accession also signalled an important religious change. The new king's support for 'Arminianism' in the English Church was at odds with the most deeply held beliefs of practically the whole of the political nation.

Even before the death of the old king in March 1625 the parliamentary alliance of 1624 was breaking up. In November 1624 a French alliance, providing for the marriage of Prince Charles and Henrietta Maria, was concluded at a high price: the suspension of the recusancy laws in England and English help for the French against the Protestant Huguenot rebels at La Rochelle. Moreover, the money granted in 1624 appeared to have been wasted. A force of pressed Englishmen under the German mercenary Mansfeld, which set off for the Palatinate in January 1625, was reduced by poor supplies, bad weather, and French lack of cooperation from 12,000 to 3,000 men only a few days after crossing the Channel. By May 1625 Charles was committed to spending £20,000 a month supporting Danish involvement in the war, as well as a similar sum pledged to Mansfeld. The war promised in 1624 had not yet been declared; instead a costly fleet and army of 10,000 men was being assembled at Plymouth. A cheap, but profitable, naval war envisaged by the Commons in 1624 hardly seemed to be in prospect.

With a planned expenditure of £1m Charles needed cooperation from his first parliament which met on 18 June 1625. Given the waste of money on a continental war strategy, the broken promises, and the pro-Catholic nature of the French alliance, he was not likely to get it, especially when he refused to explain his position to parliament or even to ask for a specific subsidy. A measure of the Commons' distrust was the grant of a paltry two subsidies (about £140,000) and tonnage and poundage for one year only instead of for the king's life. As far as the Commons were concerned Buckingham's foreign policy was misdirected and mishandled.

In addition, the serious implications of Charles's conversion to theological beliefs which his father and most of the political nation found abhorrent became apparent in the case of Richard Montague. Montague was an Arminian divine who in 1624 published a tract, *A New Gag for an Old Goose*, which rejected the predestinarian Calvinism which had been accepted by the English Church since the Elizabethan Settlement.[15] Charles signalled his support for Montague's radical beliefs by making Montague his chaplain in 1625, when the Commons began proceedings against him. This, together with the appearance at court of William Laud, foreshadowed the Arminian supremacy in the Church which became a reality in the 1630s. When in August the parliament of 1625 met in Oxford after an adjournment there may have been an attempt at conciliation with Buckingham by the duke's ex-parliamentary allies, led by Sir Nathaniel Rich and the earl of Warwick in the Lords.[16] But Charles would make no concessions, and personal criticisms of Buckingham in the Commons by more extreme MPs like Seymour and Phelips made the dissolution inevitable.

Unfortunately for the court the events of the autumn and winter of 1625 illustrated Buckingham's incompetence. After the fleet finally sailed in September it failed even to take the poorly-manned town of Cadiz, let alone capture the Spanish treasure fleet. More English troops were lost from lack of food and too much local wine than from enemy gunfire. To this disaster Buckingham seemed to be adding the prospect of a French war as well, as he tried to please his parliamentary critics by ordering punishment of recusants and threatening to return the English ships being used against La Rochelle. Even with the prominent parliamentary critics of 1625 removed by the ingenious device of pricking as sheriff men like Seymour, Phelips, Coke, and Wentworth, the parliament planned for February 1626 would be stormy. Yet all hope of cooperation was not gone on the parliamentary side. At the request of the earl of Warwick Buckingham chaired a theological debate at York House on 11 and 17 February 1626 on the writings of Richard Montague, hoping to wean Charles away from Arminianism. The task was hopeless; in order to retain the king's favour John Preston was discarded and William Laud adopted. Buckingham rarely allowed attachment to principle to get in the way of his political ambitions. He now had few supporters in the Commons; his former parliamentary clients and allies, Eliot, Digges, Sandys, and Phelips, encouraged by Buckingham's enemies in the Lords, began impeachment proceedings against him. In vain, Charles tried to stop the impeachment by a thinly veiled threat in which he described the fate of European countries where kings ruled without parliaments, whose subjects are 'like so many ghosts, and not men, being nothing but skin and bones, with some thin cover to their nakedness, and wearing only wooden shoes on their feet, so that they cannot eat meat or wear good clothes, but they must pay and be taxed unto the King for it'.[17] The only way he could protect his favourite was by dissolving parliament.

With the country at war and in severe financial difficulties Charles began to exercise the crown's emergency powers. To many they were seen as dangerous innovations, threatening the traditional government process and the right of the propertied classes. It is arguable that between the dissolution of the 1626 parliament and the end of 1627 opposition to the Caroline court reached a peak it was not to reach again until the late 1630s. The refusal of the City to lend more than £20,000 and the 'colossal failure'[18] of a free gift immediately after the dissolution prompted the crown to order a forced loan equivalent to five subsidies. This clear attempt to levy taxation without consent of parliament was very successful, perhaps because, as in Sussex, the counties were allowed to use the money locally for billeting and other charges.[19] Within ten months £240,000 had been collected, but collected in the face of widespread opposition. The judges refused to endorse its legality, for which Chief Justice Carew was dismissed. Archbishop Abbot was suspended for refusing to licence Robert Sibthorpe's sermon defending the loan. The fears of the parliamentary classes were intensified by the judges' decision in a test case in the King's bench – the 'Five Knights' Case' – upholding the king's prerogative right to imprison without trial those who refused to pay the forced loan.

In the counties the activities of Charles's government were seen as a concerted attack on their liberties. The maritime counties not only had to pay the forced loan but also ship money, which the Yorkshire commissioners refused to collect because 'haveing noe legall power to Levie the same upon the subiect wee dare not presume to doe itt'.[20] In addition the mustering of troops for the war against France and the billeting of the army after its failure at the island of Rhé off La Rochelle in October brought to a head (especially in the southern and western counties) the opposition to the powers of the deputy lieutenants who had since 1625 been trying to make the militia more effective. To the burden of increased militia payment was added the imposition of martial law and the enforced billeting of troops. 'Every man knowes there is no law for this,' complained the recorder of Taunton. 'We know our houses are our castles.'[21]

For all the success of the forced loan Charles eventually had to fall back on parliamentary taxation. Sources of extra-parliamentary revenue were drying up. A new City loan of £120,000, being negotiated at the end of 1627, was only secured in return for the transfer of extensive crown estates to the City. Soon after parliament met in March 1628 a grant of five subsidies was resolved on but was not even recorded until the king should satisfy their grievances. The extension of prerogative government 'beyond its just symmetry' since the last parliament moved the emphasis in the Commons away from attacks on Buckingham to a united demand that the king recognize the illegality of extra-parliamentary taxation, billeting, martial law, and imprisonment without trial. However there were differences among the parliamentary leaders about how this should be done. The course proposed by more extreme MPs like Selden, Coke, and Eliot, a statutory Bill of Rights, would have led to a head-on clash with the king and would probably have been rejected by the Lords. The device of proceeding by petition, supported by Rich and Digges, though not welcomed by Charles, was more traditional and conciliatory, and Lord Saye and Sele was able to persuade the Lords that the petition was not a revolutionary limitation on the royal prerogative. Under the threat of further proceedings against Buckingham on 7 June 1628 Charles gave his formal assent to the Petition of Right, and the Commons passed the subsidy Bill.

The Petition of Right is one of the great landmarks in England's constitutional development. Yet it had little immediate significance. Despite the king's acknowledgement of the illegality of his recent activities and the removal of Buckingham by the assassin Felton in August, when parliament reassembled for a second session in January 1629 the political crisis continued. Why did the Petition of Right fail? It left unresolved two fundamental points of disagreement between Charles and the parliamentary leaders. First, since the Petition did not explicitly mention impositions or tonnage and poundage, Charles was able to claim that he had not surrendered his rights to levy these customs duties without parliamentary consent. During the recess in the summer and autumn of 1628 merchants who refused to pay the duties were imprisoned. Second, the Petition made no attempt to express the Commons' distaste at the growing influence of the Arminians in the Church and at court, especially those divines like Robert Mainwaring, who was impeached by parliament in June 1628 for supporting the forced loan. In these circumstances Charles's favour to Arminians in the summer of 1628 was inflammatory. Noted Arminians were appointed to bishoprics, including Laud as bishop of London and Montague as bishop of Chichester. Another divine, Mainwaring (like Montague condemned by parliament) was pardoned and given a lucrative benefice in Essex.

Even so, the disquiet aroused by Arminianism *at this stage* can be exaggerated. It is noteworthy that those moderate parliamentary leaders led by Rich in the Commons and by Saye and Sele and Warwick in the Lords, who had worked for conciliation with the court in recent previous parliaments, were still anxious not to force a breach with the king. They failed because of the intransigence of, on the one hand, MPs like Eliot and Selden who persisted in pressing opposition to extra-parliamentary tonnage and poundage as well as to Arminianism, and, on the other, of the king. On 25 February parliament was adjourned for a week, during which the king in private negotiations with the parliamentary leaders refused to make any concessions on his interpretation of the Petition of Right. He thereby played into the hands of Eliot and his allies who organized the famous demonstration in the chamber of the House of Commons on 2 March. Speaker Finch was forcibly prevented by Denzil Holles and Benjamin Valentine from reading the royal order to adjourn until the Commons had passed three resolutions, expressing opposition to extra-parliamentary tonnage and poundage and to innovations in religion. The dissolution followed two days later.

One of the great mistakes in analysing any historical development is to assume that events proceed evenly along an unbroken line. That there is abundant evidence of widespread opposition to the crown in 1626 and 1627 does not necessarily mean that this opposition was maintained in the years immediately following. There is some evidence of a royalist 'backlash' in reaction to the attacks on the crown by Eliot and his allies in 1628 and 1629. Even in the debate on 2 March some MPs expressed doubts about the wisdom of Eliot's criticism of the new lord treasurer, Sir Richard Weston. Sir Simonds D'Ewes felt that 'the cause of the breach and dissolution was immaterial and frivolous, in the carriage whereof divers fiery spirits in the House of Commons were very faulty and cannot be excused'.[22] After 1629 many critics of the crown in the parliaments of the 1620s were willing to work in central and local government. Wentworth was already reconciled to the court after the Petition of Right had been accepted; in December 1628 he became lord president of the council of the north. Others followed him later. William Noy became attorney-general in 1631. Phelips found that in the early 1630s there was not the same conflict between cooperating with royal government and retaining his local prestige in Somerset which had driven him into opposition in the parliaments of the late 1620s. This is true also of future anti-royalists of the 1640s like William Brereton of Handforth, who worked loyally in Cheshire local government in the 1630s. The allegations by the prosecution at the trial of Eliot, Holles, and Valentine in 1630 that 'there was a conspiracy between the defendants. . . . to raise sedition and discord between the King, his peers and people'[23] was exaggerated, but many contemporaries undoubtedly felt that it contained a germ of truth.

In the period immediately after the dissolution of parliament in 1629 it was not yet clear that Charles's unapproachability, his financial policies, and especially his religious beliefs, would eventually make it impossible for people to be loyal both to the court and their 'countries'. The date when this sank in differed, of course, from individual to individual. However, it may be that for the majority of the political nation this did not happen in the 1630s. Most MPs who went to Westminster in April and in November 1640 probably assumed that they would still be able to preserve their double loyalty to court and 'country'. Many did not face the choice between the two until 1641 and 1642, and some, even then, sought to postpone the decision.

The personal rule, 1629–1640

The differing historical interpretations of Charles I's government in the 1630s are bewildering in their variety; cases have been made out for the personal rule both as a benevolent paternal government and as an '11 Years Tyranny'.[24] There is no single 'correct' interpretation of the 1630s (or indeed of any period). Yet in order to be plausible historical interpretations of one period ought not to rely excessively on hindsight, on a biased identification with the 'winners' in history, or on an uncritical acceptance of the opinion of contemporary observers. Too often historians, knowing that revolutionary events in the 1640s followed the 1630s, believing that the views of the opponents of the king triumphed in the long-term development of the English constitution, and after reading Laud and Wentworth's critical views of their colleagues in the regime, have been blinded to the positive aims of Charles's government and have pre-dated the development of serious opposition to the crown. Nevertheless, having accepted that there was a genuine attempt by the crown to produce some effective, reformative policies in the 1630s, one has to recognize that the achievement fell far short of the aim. More seriously, because Charles and his court became increasingly isolated from the mainstream of contemporary religious, intellectual, and cultural life, the policies pursued by Charles and his ministers went unexplained and were consequently often misunderstood. As often in history, what people believed to be true was more important than the truth itself in influencing the course of events.

Financial expedients, 1629–1637

The immediate effect of the failure to secure parliamentary subsidies in 1628 and 1629 was to bring home to the king and his advisers, lord treasurer Weston and chancellor of the exchequer Cottington, the serious financial situation. Historical judgements of the financial administration of Weston and Cottington have too often been coloured by the disparaging way in which Laud and Wentworth referred to them in their correspondence as 'Lady Mora and her waiting-maid'. In fact, before Weston's death in March 1635, the pair fared no better and no worse than Cecil or Cranfield before them in meeting the perennial problems faced by all early Stuart administrators: the need to cut expenditure and increase revenue. When Laud initiated an enquiry into Weston's treasurership in 1635 he may have been disappointed to find little evidence of financial mismanagement. The crown's debt was still large, but the current annual deficit had been reduced to only £18,000. How was this achieved? Even with parliamentary subsidies in the 1620s England could not afford an active foreign policy; without parliamentary supply withdrawal from the Thirty Years' War was inevitable, and peace treaties were made with France (1629) and Spain (1630). In an attempt to reduce expenditure even further Weston inaugurated the first concerted attempt since Cranfield's fall to reform the royal spending departments. From 1629 to 1632 the navy, ordnance, and royal household departments were investigated, revealing that much of the earlier economies had been undone. Short-term savings were therefore possible in the household, which soaked up over 40 per cent of the royal revenues. Expenditure on food and drink and expensive entertainment fell significantly in 1629–30, but in the following year had doubled.[25] Once again administrative reformers in the early seventeenth century came up against a fundamental obstacle: that inevitably a permanent reduction in the size of the household, in pensions or in offices curtailed the extent of crown patronage and therefore hit the vested interests of both patron and clients. This attempt at administrative reform failed; but Weston and Cottington were more successful in increasing royal revenue and it can be argued that they did so without causing too much resentment. Resistance to tonnage and poundage collapsed in 1629 and customs duties became an important part of the royal revenue in the 1630s. The increase in income from recusancy fines from an average of £5,300 p.a. in the late 1620s to £26,866 in 1634 could hardly offend violent anti-Catholic contemporary opinion.[26] Even the levying of ship money by the sheriffs in maritime counties in October 1634 was successful and almost the full amount was collected.[27] In Yorkshire, for example, Sir John Hotham, who had been imprisoned in 1627 for his opposition to the forced loan, cooperated as sheriff in the collection of the tax. Elsewhere also there seemed no reason to oppose a tax which was based on precedent, and was apparently an expedient to deal with the menace of pirates off the south and west coast of England.

More resentment was caused in the early 1630s by the activities of commissioners appointed in 1630, who were to fine anyone holding land worth £40 p.a. or more who had not received a knighthood. In August 1630 the exchequer barons confirmed that the crown was legally entitled to do this, although the precedents for it were hardly recent and dated back to the mid-sixteenth century. The tax was a heavy one; most fines were of £10, but they could be as high as £70. It also involved the local commissioners in a lot of hard and distasteful work; though often they probably were able to shift the tax on to minor gentry, sometimes they had to squeeze it from their fellow JPs, and the privy council, supported by the court of exchequer, inflicted heavy fines on dilatory com-missioners. That the exchequer court had to proceed against such offenders is evidence of some resentment at distraint of knighthood, but not of serious opposition. Sir David Foulis's attempt to rally gentry opinion in Yorkshire against the tax fell flat. Foulis, an expatriate Scot, scolded his Yorkshire neighbours for no longer being 'stout-spirited men' who 'stood for their rights and liberties . . . but now in these days Yorkshiremen were becoming degenerate, more dastardly and more cowardly than the men of other countries'. Elsewhere too – across the Pennines in Cheshire for example – those liable for the tax grumbled but paid up.[28] Weston also offended sections of mercantile opinion, especially by reviving grants of industrial and commercial monopolies to corporations, exploiting a loophole in the Monopoly Act which had only forbidden grants to individuals. That the only consistent element behind such grants was to gather revenue was revealed by the restoration in 1634 of the Merchant Adventurers' monopoly, partially lost in 1624, and the incursion into the East India Company monopoly by a grant in 1635 to the courtier, Endymion Porter, and the merchant, Sir William Courteen, to trade in the Indian Ocean. Not only did the grants seem arbitrary to those merchants involved, but one, the grant in 1632 of a monopoly in soap manufacture to a syndicate with strong Roman Catholic affiliations, roused popular opposition, at least in London, as well as the opposition of those soap manufacturers who had been left out of the monopoly. Even an officially sponsored demonstration in December 1633 by two washerwomen (using an advertising technique beloved by the modern detergent industry) failed to convince anyone that clothes washed in 'Papist soap' 'were as white and sweeter than' those washed by the washerwoman using an unnamed brand.[29]

More annoyance was given to landowners and merchants by revenue raising schemes after Weston's death than in the early 1630s. The crown's claim that in all of them it was acting within the letter of the law was no doubt true, but this was scant compensation to those who were told that not only had they transgressed against long-forgotten obligations to be knights, but also against enclosure laws; that their estates were within the royal forest; that wardship fines were to be drastically increased, and on top of all this, that ship money was to become a permanent land tax. From 1635 the long-dormant forest courts were revived patently for fiscal purposes. Landowners, great and small alike, who had estates within their jurisdiction were deemed to have encroached illegally on the royal forest and were subsequently fined. Nor was there any pretence that the commission on depopulation set up in the same year was anything other than a device to sell licences confirming enclosures. What is more, the government proved efficient in collecting revenue; fines were exacted, enclosures were sought out and Cottington as master of the court of wards raised the revenue from wardships to £61,900 by 1637, nearly treble the level in 1613.[30]

It is not surprising that the decision to extend the demand for ship money to inland counties from June 1635 met with more disapproval than meets most new tax demands. It now appeared to be a permanent land tax; in December 1635 the judges declared that the king was acting legally, and successive new ship money writs were issued in each year from 1636 to 1639. Moreover opposition to ship money may have extended below the substantial freeholder classes. Although there was some confusion about the basis on which the sheriffs were to make the assessment for the tax, most sheriffs seem to have taken personal, as well as real, property into account (in Cheshire the sheriff used the mise roll used for levying the local poor rate);[31] the result was that the new tax directly affected more people than a parliamentary subsidy. To the taxpayers also the new tax seemed difficult to justify on the grounds of dire necessity; there seemed to be no immediate threat of invasion in the mid-1630s. This was perhaps the strongest argument used by Oliver St John in 1637 at the trial of John Hampden for refusing to pay ship money, and five out of the twelve judges gave their verdict against the crown, which stiffened the resolve of many to oppose the tax. Yet certainly down to the end of 1637 and possibly later one can exaggerate the seriousness of the opposition to ship money. Between 1634 and the end of 1638 90 per cent of the tax was paid.[32] Large-scale opposition to ship money did not become evident until Charles and Laud's religious policy brought England and Scotland to the verge of war in 1638.

The Books of Orders, the 'Exact Militia', and Ireland

It is tempting to treat the administrative activities of the king's government during the personal rule as a coherent policy of 'thorough'. It may be that Laud and Wentworth would have liked to have achieved effective paternalistic government, not by any radical departure from, but by a stricter enforcement of existing legislation and methods. However, there is little evidence that they were able to put such policies into effect in the 1630s. Rarely does it seem that Caroline government succeeded in breaking free from the normal pattern of *ad hoc* decision-making. Most of the efforts of Charles I's government to increase administrative efficiency in local government were made in response to immediate crises, and, once these were over, the privy council relaxed its pressure on the localities and programmes of reform were not sustained. Moreover, it is likely that even these limited aims of Caroline government were misunderstood and widely seen as excessive inter-ference by central government in local affairs.

The decision to issue Books of Orders in 1630 and 1631 is a good illustration of these generalizations. Successive harvest failures in 1629 and 1630 prompted the privy council to undertake what Professor Barnes considers to be 'the most concerted effort, almost until our own times, to make the statute book an effective reality'.[33] Soaring corn prices and unemployment in the cloth manufacturing areas, exacerbated by the politically motivated refusal of merchants to export cloth in 1629 and by outbreaks of plague, threatened law and order. There were food riots in the worst affected areas in the West Country. As a direct result on 5 January 1631 most of the members of the privy council were appointed commissioners to see that the laws concerning poor relief were put into force and that 'other public services for God, the King and the Commonwealth, are put into practice and executed'.[34] On 31 January steps were taken to give teeth to the conciliar commission: 314 printed Books of Orders were sent to the sheriffs for distribution to JPs and municipal authorities, setting out the scope of the authority and duties of local officials in executing existing legislation on all subjects, not just on poor relief. Similar Books had been issued in the 1570s and 1580s, but what was novel about the Books of 1631 was the procedural machinery laid down in them: JPs were to meet monthly in each hundred to supervise the work of the hundred and petty constables, churchwardens, and overseers of the poor; the JPs were to send reports to the sheriffs, who in turn reported to the assize judges on circuit, who were the direct agents of the conciliar commission. It is often difficult to unravel the process by which Stuart governments made decisions, but in this case it seems fairly certain that the earl of Manchester was an influential voice in the privy council in favour of the Books of Orders. He was closely in touch with his brother, Lord Montague, a Northamptonshire JP, and they discussed the practicability of the scheme.[35] The Books of Orders, then, originated in a time of economic crisis, and they were the blueprint for a permanent reform of local government, reinvigorated by centralized conciliar direction.

How successful were the Books of Orders in practice? A simple answer cannot be given. Historians are divided. Professor Barnes feels that 'throughout the 1630s the contents of the Books was effectively translated into reality': while Professor Jordan reaches the opposite conclusion.[36] Firm generalizations about the success of the Books are difficult to make because few private papers of JPs active in the 1630s survive, and therefore detailed knowledge of the working of the Books of Orders is often lacking. Undoubtedly the Books made a significant impact in alleviating the worst effects of the 1629–30 economic crisis in those places which have been studied. They also helped to regularize meetings of petty sessions, and procedures for licensing alehouses and apprenticing poor children.[37] However, once the worst of the crisis was over, it is hard to imagine, even given the maintenance of its supervisory powers, that the privy council could have kept JPs up to the mark. It was not that local magistrates objected to the aims of the Books of Orders – on the contrary JPs like the Caroline council realized the need to maintain social harmony and order – but most disliked the dictatorial tone of the Books. As they had shown in their reaction to administrative patentees earlier, JPs resented central government intrusion in what they considered to be their own spheres of influence. In fact, after its brief exertions in the early 1630s, the privy council seems to have relaxed its efforts, and local magistrates reasserted their rights to control local affairs.

This same kind of tension between central and local government is also evident in the efforts made by the Caroline government to reform the militia.[38] The defects of the militia were patent, and during the last fifteen years of James I's reign the privy council had initiated sporadic attempts to remedy the militia's lack of professional training and its chronic shortage of money. From 1624 to 1627 these efforts were stepped up as the country became involved in wars against France and Spain. Charles and his advisers began to talk about producing an 'exact militia', and, like the Books of Orders, this scheme had a lot to recommend it. Why, then, did it meet with a hostile reception in many counties? In 1604 the parliamentary statutes passed in the reign of Mary Tudor regulating the militia were repealed. Consequently from now on lords-lieutenant and their deputies derived their authority directly from the crown, and this enabled people to question the legality of their activities. As early as 1620 John Bishe of Brighton refused to attend the militia musters on the grounds that 'there was no law to enforce him'.[39] During the war years of the later 1620s such opposition became more pronounced. When the officers of the lieutenancy began administering unpopular policies like forcible billeting gentlemen curried popular favour, as did Sir Robert Phelips, by denouncing 'the oppression of the deputy lieutenants'.[40] Opposition to the exact militia was focused especially on muster-masters, professional soldiers appointed to train the local militia.[41] Not only were these men appointed by the lieutenants, but (unlike during the reign of Elizabeth) they were paid out of rates levied locally on no authority other than that of the royal prerogative. Opposition to muster-masters (as to many other things in the early seventeenth century) was fed by depleted purses, as well as by injured principles and local independence. How effective such opposition was in preventing the foundation of an exact militia is not clear. In Cheshire and Sussex more reforms were achieved than in Somerset.[42] Yet, as in the case of the Books of Orders, the vigilance of the privy council was shortlived. Its energy aimed at producing an exact militia was at its height in the late 1620s; after 1630 when peace was concluded its pressure was relaxed. It is true that Charles's exact militia was never given a test like a patriotic war against a universally hated enemy; by the late 1630s the Scots were far from being that. However, there is little doubt that by that time many county militias fell far short of their exact ideal.

Wentworth, as lord-deputy of Ireland from 1633, was more consistently successful in imposing administrative efficiency in Ireland than was the privy council in England in the 1630s.[43] His first task was to impose his own authority on the Dublin council. Whereas previous lord-deputies had been parties to faction rivalries in Ireland, Wentworth stood outside them. When the Irish parliament met in 1634 therefore Wentworth was able to play the time-honoured political game of divide and rule. Having granted three subsidies in the first session they learned that Wentworth refused to remedy their grievances. The 'graces' which had been promised were not conceded. Having secured control and money Wentworth proceeded to press ahead successfully with the colonization of Ireland at the expense not only of the native 'mere' Irish whose interests had never been considered, but also of the Catholic 'old English', the descendants of the pre-Elizabethan planters. Wentworth's plantation of Connacht involved the confiscation of the estates of the most eminent 'Old English' aristocrat, the earl of Clanricarde.

The 'New English' also stood in the way of Wentworth's plans. This protestant landlord-undertaker class who spearheaded late sixteenth- and early seventeenth-century colonization of Ulster and Munster had become very rich, as well as very powerful in the Dublin administration. In trying to reform both the financial administration and the Church in Ireland Wentworth could not fail to attack this class who had benefited at the expense of both. The crown's income was augmented considerably by a revivified court of wards and liveries; the Statute of Uses which Wentworth guided through the Irish Parliament in 1634 prevented Irish landlords from evading their feudal obligations, something which Henry VIII had failed fully to do in England by a similar statute a century earlier. What really offended the 'new English', though, was Wentworth's ecclesiastical reforms. Even the powerful Richard Boyle earl of Cork was forced to disgorge his ex-ecclesiastical property to its former owner. Moreover the high commission in Ireland began to impose on the Protestant landlord class, as well as on Presbyterian settlers, a Laudian uniformity, which seemed to them indistinguishable from Catholicism. By the late 1630s Wentworth had doubled the revenues of the Irish administration and rid the Irish Church of many abuses, but only at the expense of uniting in an unnatural alliance 'Old' and 'New' English, Catholics and Protestants.

Arminianism and isolation

There were, of course, many reasons for the growing dissatisfaction with Charles's personal government, but it is likely that the king's attachment to Arminianism made the greatest contribution to it. Like a lot of other 'isms' there is no simple definition of Arminianism. The best one is by a contemporary who, when he was asked what the Arminians held, replied 'all the best bishoprics and deaneries in England'. It is easier and perhaps more important to stress what many contemporaries *thought* it was. What it was and what it appeared to be were not the same. Arminianism, in the sense of a group of people all holding the same set of beliefs in common, did not exist. There was no doctrinal unity among those divines whom contemporaries called 'Arminians' in the 1620s and 1630s. Students of the beliefs of these divines have even argued that the doctrinal gap between them and their opponents on questions like predestination and the importance of the scriptures was not as wide as it seemed. It is not hard to find 'puritanical' traits in the arch-Arminian, William Laud. When William Cavendish (later duke of Newcastle) broke his horse's neck in a fall on a Good Friday, Laud noted in his diary, 'should not this day have other employment?'[44] Moreover, was not Laud's concern to reform the Church by recovering ecclesiastical endowments from lay hands in order to finance an educated clergy similar to that of many 'Puritan' reformers since the reign of Elizabeth?

Yet contemporaries were not wrong in seeing in the views of Laud and other divines promoted in the Church under Charles I an attack on a set of assumptions about the Church and religion that were widely held in late sixteenth- and early seventeenth-century England. Undoubtedly the most fundamental of these was the belief in the Calvinist doctrine that individuals had no control over their destinies which were arbitrarily predetermined by God. Men and women were members of the elect, or of the damned. In this sense most members of the Elizabethan–Jacobean Church were Calvinist in theology. In the late sixteenth century in England only a very few divines questioned this chilling doctrine, as did independently in the United Provinces a Leyden divine, Jacobus Arminius. Arminius elaborated the contrary, less awesome, doctrine of free will, that God's grace was open to all and that an 'individual' could attain salvation by good works. This new theology found favour with a minority of Jacobean bishops (Richard Neile, Lancelot Andrewes, and John Buckeridge) and with a younger generation of clerics led by William Laud. Secondly, Arminians posed a challenge to the emphasis placed by most clerics and laymen in the late sixteenth and seventeenth century on the scriptures and on their dissemination by preaching. To most people it followed that the function of the parson was limited to interpreting the Bible to the congregation; the sermon was the centrepiece of the church service. Arminianism placed less emphasis on the scriptures, preaching, and sermons. Instead their belief in the indiscriminate granting of God's grace led Arminians to highlight the sacramental and ceremonial aspects of the church service and of the vicar's role in it. Some, though not all, Arminians even went so far as to claim that the existence of bishops depended not on the king's grant, but on divine right. Thirdly, to most people Arminians seemed to be out of sympathy with the increasingly widespread practice of setting the Sabbath aside for religious meditation and education. The fairly general agreement among people in the early seventeenth century on fundamentals such as predestination, preaching, and sabbatarianism perhaps helps to explain why (as has already been noted), despite Bancroft, the Jacobean Church was reasonably tolerant of nonconformist opinion. The accession of Charles and the ascendancy of Arminianism in the English Church challenged these fundamentals. By attempting to impose a new, more restrictive, uniformity on the Church, Arminians were seen, as Dr Tyacke points out, as revolutionaries threatening the *status quo* in Church and society.[45] Arminians, then, came to be seen as a group with a coherent doctrinal position and aims which were completely opposite to those held by most of their fellow Englishmen. Laud, as archbishop of Canterbury from 1633, became the most hated archbishop in English history. It is not difficult to see why. He carried into practice the theoretical attack on predestination, preaching, and the sanctity of the sabbath with a good deal of success, and attacked vested property interests as well.

What convinced most people that Laud was a dangerous innovator was his attempt to move the communion table from its accustomed position in the nave of most parish churches to the east end of the church, where (as in most cathedral churches) it was to be surrounded by rails. Why did this, apparently slight, internal reorganization of churches cause great contemporary furore? For one thing the change, by emphasizing the sacrament of the altar, was a sign of the Laudian attack on the doctrine of predestination that everyone could recognize. By reviving the annual archepiscopal metropolitan visitations Laud attempted to enforce uniformity in this respect. Moreover no one seeing the change needed an understanding of doctrinal niceties to see it as an innovation. Indeed to most people the railing off of the communion table must have seemed, as it did to the Root and Branch petitioners of 1640, 'a plain device to usher in the Mass'.[46] What is more, the removal of family pews, which was sometimes necessary to accommodate the communion table in its new 'altar-wise' position and to enable the congregation to see the communion being celebrated, was a clear instance of how Laudian innovations could upset the social *status quo*. Nor was any effort made to convert people to the wisdom of the changes. On the contrary, the published reason for the change appeared to be to bring about uniformity for its own sake. The canons of 1640 reiterated Laud's opinion that the repositioned communion table 'doth not imply that it is or ought to be esteemed a true and proper altar whereon Christ is again really sacrificed'. A high price was paid in renewed opposition and distrust for something which was 'in its own nature indifferent'.[47]

Laud's accession as archbishop coincided with the re-publication of James I's *Declaration of Sports*, permitting secular activities on the sabbath, and with an intensification of the campaign against unlicensed preaching which had begun in December 1629. Significantly the fact was forgotten that bishops were also told to live in their dioceses and not alienate their episcopal estates. Instead the measures that caused offence were those which attempted to deter the appointment of nonconformist lecturers, by ordering that only those who read the prayer book in a surplice and hood could deliver the sermon. In 1633 Laud succeeded in abolishing (via star chamber) the Feoffees of Impropriations, a group of Puritan London merchants and landowners founded in 1625, which was beginning to buy livings and appoint Puritan preachers to them. The episode reveals the Arminian dilemma: Laud abolished a reforming organization, whose aim, the recovery from lay ownership, for the Church, of tithes and livings was identical to his own.

One did not need to be a sophisticated theologian or ardent Puritan to recognize Laud as a threat. Landowners could see their possession of tithes and control over advowsons in danger. Nor did the court of high commission, its powers strengthened, make any social distinctions when prosecuting defendants under Laud's guidance. Great and small, men and women alike, were hauled before the ecclesiastical courts which in the early seventeenth century had a wide jurisidictional sphere. The ownership of tithes, probate of wills, the payment of alimony, 'adultery, whoredom, incest, drunkenness, swearing, ribaldry and usury', activities not confined to any particular social group, were all matters for the ecclesiastical courts. The growing interference of clerics in secular affairs was resented, whether it was Laud's influence on financial expedients like the commission for depopulation, Bishop Juxon's appointment in 1635 as the first ecclesiastical lord treasurer since the fifteenth century, or clerical nominations to county benches.

A significant result was to weaken the attachment of contemporaries to episcopacy, which had never been seriously questioned since the 1580s. It may be that the anti-episcopal movement found most support among the ranks below that of gentleman (given the lack of sources on these groups before the 1640s it is impossible to be certain). Certainly the revival of radical sects in the late 1630s suggests that this was the case. Propertied men, after all, had a vested interest in the maintenance of episcopacy – 'no bishop, no magistrate'. But the activities of Laud and those Laudian bishops in key positions (Neile at York, Wren at Ely, Pierce at Bath and Wells, for example) undermined that attachment. The savage star chamber punishment in 1637 of three authors of anti-episcopal pamphlets, Prynne, Burton, and Bastwicke, aroused fairly universal horror (in contrast to Prynne's earlier ear-cropping in 1632). It mattered little that some felt horror at the physical punishment of gentlemen by branding and ear-cropping, rather than sympathy for their anti-episcopal views. Prynne especially won popular acclaim for himself and hatred for Laud: his brandmark S.L., he wrote, stood not for 'seditious libeller' but for '*stigmata Laudis*'. By the late 1630s Calvinist episcopalianism no longer had the almost universal support it had had even a decade earlier.[48]

So the contemporary caricature of Arminianism was formed. Although Laud himself might claim otherwise, his attempts to reform the Church came to be seen as signs of encroaching Catholicism. Even in the eyes of a future Cheshire royalist, Arminianism was 'a plotting, undermining and dangerous sect'.[49] In the eyes of its critics it was, paradoxically, at the same time a means by which an independent Church would dominate the secular state and lay magistracy, and a source of theoretical support for the claims of royal absolutism. Might it have been otherwise? If the contacts between the court and the parliamentary classes which had been maintained in the 1620s had not been cut in the 1630s, might one side have appreciated the common ground it had with the other? Fortunately, might-have-beens are not the primary concern of the historian. Anyway the fact is that the Caroline court, instead of being a forum in which royal policies could be explained and the views of the political nation listened to, became increasingly alien. The 'popery, painting and playacting' of the court[50] emphasized its exclusion from the religious, intellectual, and cultural, as well as the political, temper of the country. Ironically even Laud himself was unrepresented at court and powerless to prevent the open favour shown to Catholics by Henrietta Maria. A court which could receive papal agents, as it did Gregorio Panzani in 1634 and George Con in 1636, only increased the distrust felt by most Englishmen for royal policies and threatened to make the gap between 'court' and 'country' a reality for the first time.

England and the Scottish revolution, 1637–1640

Despite the growing opposition in England to Charles's financial and religious policies, in 1637 the king had no reason to contemplate the end of his personal rule without parliament. It was the outbreak of rebellion in Scotland, for which Charles was largely responsible, that precipitated the collapse of the personal rule. In many respects Charles's handling of Scottish affairs mirrors the mistakes he made in England. Just as he cut himself off from powerful English opinion, so Charles remained ignorant of Scottish opinion. His advisers were anglicized Scots and his policies were consequently misdirected and misunderstood. This is illustrated by his precipitate announcement, without explanation, in November 1625 that he intended to revoke all crown gifts of royal and kirk property made since 1540. In fact his intentions were not so radical as this announcement implied. Although landowners were to lose their tithes (which were to be commuted) and the feudal dues attached to the land, Charles intended to confirm the grants in return for compensation to the crown.

As in England, though, Charles's greatest blunder was in promoting Arminianism in Scotland, thereby upsetting the ecclesiastical *modus vivendi* developed by his father. One of James's most significant achievements was to make episcopacy acceptable to the majority of Scots people, by erecting a system of Church government which combined elements of episcopacy and Presbyterianism. By identifying Scottish bishops with Arminian policies Charles succeeded, as in England, in forcing into more radical opposition those who previously had been willing to accept episcopacy. By increasing the secular power of bishops in government Charles and Laud strengthened the anti-episcopal movement in Scotland as well as in England.

Laud urged Charles to introduce the English prayer book into Scotland as early as 1629, but it was not until after the king's visit to Scotland in 1633 that the fatal decision seems to have been taken. All protests from Scotland against introducing the prayer book were ignored or suppressed; Lord Balmerino was sentenced to death in 1634 for possessing a copy of a petition concerning the religious grievances. No attempt was made to consult Scottish opinion, apart from the bishops, thus infusing a strong nationalist anti-English element into the opposition. Charles did not deviate from his plan. In 1635 he issued a new book of canons, based on the English canons of 1604, and the Scottish privy council were ordered to command the use of the new prayer book when it was ready early in 1637. In the face of the king's uncompromising attitude Scottish moderates were forced into allying with radical elements like Archibald Johnston Laird of Wariston, heirs of a long apocalyptic tradition in Scotland which professed 'a verie near paralel betwixt Izrael and this Churche (of Scotland), the only two suorne nationes of the Lord'.[51] This powerful nationalist and radical religious opposition stirred up by Charles culminated in prearranged demonstrations against the prayer book when it was first used in July 1637. The furious violent scene in St Giles Church in Edinburgh on 23 July was characterized by the leadership of formidable Edinburgh 'matrons'. As in some riots in early seventeenth-century England women played a prominent part in these Scottish demonstrations. Robert Baillie, fortunately for him, turned down the bishop of Glasgow's request that he conduct a service in the city using the new prayer book. He later reported that 'at the outgoing of the church about 30 or 40 of our honestest women, in one voice, before the Bishop and Magistrates, did fall in railing, cursing, scolding with clamours on Mr. William Annan [his replacement]' and that night 'some hundreds of enraged women, of all qualities, are about him, with fists, and staves, and peats, [but] no stones: they beat him sore'.[52]

Defiance always made Charles more uncompromising and he made clear his decision to continue with a policy which was clearly impractical. The reaction from Scotland was an organized petitioning movement and in November the petitioners elected a permanent representative body, which in February 1638 drew up the National Covenant. Even now there were still supporters of limited episcopacy in Scotland; the Covenant, though denouncing the canons and the prayer book, did not mention bishops. Charles's stubbornness and insincerity in the next ten months cut the ground from beneath the feet of the moderates. When the Glasgow Assembly met in November 1638 episcopacy was abolished. In effect the king's power had been directly challenged and undermined. The 'Scottish revolution' had begun. Both sides began to prepare for war.

The lack of enthusiasm in England for war against the Scots is a measure of the opposition Charles faced at home. Laud had achieved the impossible: to make himself more hated in English eyes than the Scots. Charles's command to call out the trained bands released a flood of complaints about the cost and legality of the militia. The king also found that his financial position, though improved by increased rents from the customs farmers after the renegotiation of the great and petty farm of the customs in the winter of 1637–8, was not adequate for wartime needs. Appeals to the City, its Irish estates confiscated by the crown, brought no offers of a loan. By now too the yield of ship money fell dramatically; only 20 per cent of the expected receipts from the 1639 writ was actually paid to Sir William Russell, the treasurer of the navy.[53] The incidence of violent assaults on the tax collectors increased; George Vernon of Whatcroft in Cheshire 'drew out his knife and threatened the constable to whett it in his guts'.[54] Charles had little choice but to negotiate with the Scots army and conclude a truce at Berwick on 18 June, agreeing to a meeting of the Scottish assembly and parliament and the disbandment of both armies.

But the truce settled nothing. The covenanters did not disband their army and the Edinburgh assembly and parliament which met in the autumn completed the ecclesiastical and constitutional revolution and repudiation of royal control. When Wentworth returned from Ireland in September realizing that the projected cost of the war of £300,000 could not be met by loans from privy councillors and customers alone, he advised the king to call an English parliament, which eventually met on 13 April. Was the failure of the Short Parliament inevitable? Undoubtedly, as Derek Hirst and others have shown,[55] some candidates in 1640 were elected on a popular anti-court platform, which presupposes widespread opposition to Caroline government among the electorate. The flood of local petitions to parliament, cataloguing the grievances of the 1630s, indicates some degree of organization behind the opposition. Yet the picture of a united opposition developing in the 1630s, using colonizing and trading organizations, such as the Providence Island Company, as a front for its political activities, is too simplistic. Not all elections in 1640, by any means, were dominated by national issues; nor were MPs united on the tactics needed to secure a redress of grievances; nor was Charles entirely devoid of support. On the contrary, in the Short Parliament the king could count on a majority in the Lords in favour of voting him subsidies. And his announcement of the illegality of ship money must have won him support in the Commons, despite John Pym's long tirade against the record of Caroline government since the 1620s. The issue which in the end seems to have turned the Commons against granting the king subsidies was that of military charges for the Scottish war. These were to continue and were much heavier than ship money. The Yorkshire MP, John Hotham, pointed out that, whereas Yorkshire's ship money assessment was £12,000, coat and conduct money levied on the county was £40,000.[56]

By 1640 the old constitution was still intact. Nor was it inevitable that it would break down as it did in 1641 and 1642. The causes of this lay largely in events which took place after (not before) 1640, as will be seen. However after the dissolution of the Short Parliament in May 1640 it is difficult to see any possibility of Charles securing enough support to avoid a serious constitutional crisis. What little chance of cooperation remained he threw away by arresting Warwick, Brook, and Say and Sele, and the leading parliamentary spokesmen in the Commons, and, despite Laud's conciliatory advice, ordering the continuation of Convocation, which proceeded to adopt new canons, embodying the Laudian innovations of the 1630s. A vain attempt was made by Cottington to salvage Charles's financial position by an ingenious commercial deal involving the purchase and resale of over 600,000 pounds of pepper, which raised over £50,000. But the City again refused to lend the crown any money until a parliament was called. The militia in many countries was undisciplined and more inclined to pull down communion table rails and enclosure fences than march against the Scots. In Yorkshire the gentry petitioned the king against the expense of billeting the troops there. The Scots, therefore, met little resistance when they crossed the Tweed on 20 August 1640, and within ten days, after a minor skirmish at Newburn, they occupied Newcastle. If Charles's military standing was weak, his diplomatic and political position was worse. The Council of Peers which met at York on 24 September refused to cooperate until Charles called a new parliament. So did the authorities and the moneylenders of London, Charles had little choice but to issue writs for a new parliament and to accept humiliating conditions as the basis for a truce with the Scots. His commissioners agreed at Ripon on 21 October 1640 to pay the Scots army £850 a day while they occupied English soil. This alone ensured that the second parliament of 1640 would not be got rid of as easily as the first.

Notes

For abbreviations used throughout see p. xiv.

1. J. S. Morrill, *Cheshire 1603–60: county government during the 'English Revolution'* (1974), pp. 21–2.
2. Derek Hirst, 'Court, country, and politics before 1629', in Kevin Sharpe, ed., *Faction and Parliament*, pp. 105–38, and Conrad Russell, *Parliament and English Politics 1621–29* (1979) for a more detailed exposition of this argument than is possible here. Both were published too late for me to use as extensively as I would have liked. However, I am grateful to Conrad Russell for allowing me to read his book in typescript. My debt to it in writing the following paragraphs is very great.
3. Elizabethan privy councillors had sometimes encouraged parliamentary opposition to royal policies but never as blatantly as in 1621.
4. Thirsk and Cooper, p. 3. See p. 25.
5. Quoted in C. Tite, *Impeachment and Parliamentary Judicature in Early Stuart England* (1974), p. 89.
6. Tanner, *Constitutional Documents*, p. 287.
7. *Ibid.*, p. 289.
8. The accounts of their escapades *en route* and in Spain read like the synopsis of a comic opera.
9. Kenyon, *Stuart Constitution*, p. 49.
10. Quoted in R. E. Ruigh, *The Parliament of 1624: politics and foreign policy* (1971), p. 222.
11. Quoted in Ruigh, p. 231.
12. Significantly there is no good biography of Charles I.
13. Derek Hirst, 'Court, country and politics', in Sharpe, ed., *Faction and Parliament*, pp. 111–12, 133.
14. For suggestive parallels between politics in the late 1620s and the 1580s and 1590s see Hassell Smith, *County and Court, passim*.
15. Given James I's consistent commitment to Calvinist predestinarianism his failure to suppress *A New Gag* is one of the minor unexplained mysteries of his last years.
16. Christopher Thompson, 'The origins of the politics of the parliamentary middle group 1625–29', *T.R.H.S.*, 5th ser., XXII (1972), p. 76.
17. Kenyon, *Stuart Constitution*, pp. 50–1.

18. T. G. Barnes, *Somerset 1625–40: a county's government during the 'Personal Rule'* (1961), p. 163.
19. I owe this suggestion to Mr Anthony Fletcher.
20. J. T. Cliffe, *The Yorkshire Gentry from the Reformation to the Civil War* (1967), p. 292.
21. Barnes, *Somerset*, p. 218.
22. J. O. Halliwell, ed., *The Autobiography and Correspondence of Sir Simonds D'Ewes* (2 vols, 1845), I, p. 402.
23. Kenyon, *Stuart Constitution*, p. 52.
24. For a good, brief discussion of different views about the 1630s see H. F. Kearney, *The Eleven Years' Tyranny of Charles I* (Historical Association Aids for Teachers Series, no. 9, 1962).
25. G. E. Aylmer, 'Attempts at administrative reform 1625–40', *E.H.R.*, LXXI (1957), p. 252.
26. M. J. Havran, *Caroline Courtier: the life of Lord Cottington* (1973), p. 121.
27. £79,000 out of £80,609. M. D. Gordon, 'The collection of ship money in the reign of Charles I', *T.R.H.S.*, 3rd ser., IV (1910), p. 143.
28. Cliffe, *Yorkshire Gentry*, p. 300; Morrill, *Cheshire*, p. 27.
29. Gardiner, *History*, VIII, p. 73.
30. Havran, *Cottington*, p. 138.
31. Morrill, *Cheshire*, p. 28.
32. Gordon, 'The collection of ship money', p. 143.
33. Barnes, *Somerset*, p. 178.
34. Kenyon, *Stuart Constitution*, p. 498.
35. P. A. Slack, 'Books of Orders: the making of English social policy, 1577–1631', *T.R.H.S.* (forthcoming: paper read at the Royal Historical Society, 2 February 1979). Barnes, *Somerset*, p. 173, considers that Laud was the primary influence behind the Books of Orders.
36. Barnes, *Somerset*, p. 196; W. K. Jordan, *Philanthropy in England 1480–1660* (1959), pp. 133–6.
37. See especially Anthony Fletcher, *A County Community at Peace and War: Sussex 1600–1660* (1975), p. 224.
38. L. Boynton, *The Elizabethan Militia 1558–1638* (1967), pp. 244–97, for the 'exact militia'.
39. Fletcher, *Sussex*, p. 187.
40. Barnes, *Somerset*, p. 257. Phelips's stance loses its force as an alleged illustration of a 'court versus country' episode by the fact that a few months later Phelips accepted the post of deputy lieutenant, *ibid.*, p. 266.
41. Opposition to muster masters was not new. See the controversy in Wiltshire in 1603–6, W. P. D. Murphy, ed., *The Earl of Hertford's Lieutenancy Papers 1603–12*, (Wiltshire Record Society, XXIII, 1969) p. 11–13.
42. Morrill, *Cheshire*, p. 26; Fletcher, *Sussex*, p. 184; Barnes, *Somerset*, pp. 258–71.
43. H. F. Kearney, *Strafford in Ireland 1633–41: a study in absolutism* (Manchester 1959): T. W. Moody, F. X. Martin, F. J. Byrne, eds, *A New History of Ireland*, III: *Early Modern Ireland 1534–1691* (1976), pp. 243–69.
44. Quoted in H. R. Trevor-Roper, *Archbishop Laud* (2nd edn, 1962), p. 159. William Lamont, *Godly Rule: politics and religion 1603–60* (1969), p. 69, calls Laud's diary 'an authentic puritan document'.
45. N. Tyacke, 'Puritanism, Arminianism and counter-revolution', *passim*. See pp. 71–5, 98.

46. Kenyon, *Stuart Constitution*, p. 174.
47. *Ibid.*, p. 171.
48. The extent of anti-episcopal sentiment among propertied people before 1640 can be exaggerated, see p. 74. Sir Robert Phelips in 1637 wrote to Laud congratulating him in dealing with those 'lunatics', Burton, Bastwick, and Prynne. I am grateful to Conrad Russell for this information.
49. Morrill, *Cheshire*, p. 28.
50. For this cultural divide between the Caroline court and the country see P. W. Thomas, 'Court and Country under Charles I', in Conrad Russell, ed., *Origins*, pp. 168–93.
51. Quoted in S. A. Burrell, 'The apocalyptic vision of the early covenanters', *Scottish H.R.*, XLIII (1964), p. 17.
52. Quoted in J. McCoy, *Robert Baillie and the Second Scots Reformation* (Berkeley, California, 1974), pp. 29–30.
53. Gordon, 'The collection of ship money', pp. 143–4.
54. Morrill, *Cheshire*, p. 29.
55. Derek Hirst, *The Representative of the People? Voters and Voting in England under the Early Stuarts* (1975), *passim*.
56. Cliffe, *Yorkshire Gentry*, p. 518.

The English Revolution, 1640–1660

Chapter 6

The making of the English Revolution, 1640–49

The 'causes of the English Revolution'

The debate on the causes of the English Revolution, one of the great historical controversies, has gone on since the mid seventeenth century, and has engaged the attention of seventeenth-century commentators (Harrington, Hobbes, Baxter, Clarendon) and some of the best twentieth-century historians.[1] It is not difficult to see why. Whether or not one agrees with the term 'revolution' to describe what happened in the 1640s in England, the dramatic and unique nature of those events is incontrovertible. Within less than a decade the power of the monarchy was first drastically reduced, and then extinguished, the king executed and monarchy abolished, along with the other pillars of traditional society, bishops and the House of Lords. The downfall of the crown and the established Church meant the collapse of effective censorship of the press, and the emergence of radical ideas about religious toleration, political democracy, economic reform, fundamental restructuring of education and the law, and the imposition of new social values. What is more, these ideas were often voiced by men and women of low social status, whose views were only rarely heard in England before 1640 and after 1660.

In searching for an explanation of these phenomena the views of historians have inevitably been coloured by the prejudices and preoccupations of their own time. Unfortunately, the hypotheses of most historians tell more about the intellectual climate of the age in which they lived than about the causes of the English Revolution. Historians living in Victorian and Edwardian England thought that the most perfect constitutional system was the Victorian and Edwardian British constitution, which was the culmination of a long and inexorable historical development. S. R. Gardiner was the greatest of these Whig historians; his multi-volume work on early seventeenth-century England is breathtaking in the range of sources used and the technical brilliance employed: it is indispensable as a work of reference for any seventeenth-century historian. But even Gardiner regarded the defeat of Charles I as necessary and inevitable, so that parliamentary sovereignty could eventually triumph in his own day. Lesser Whig historians than

Gardiner based on this assumption the belief that the parliamentary leaders in the 1640s were consciously aiming at something like the nineteenth-century British constitution.

Marxist historians of the twentieth century share the belief of the Whig historians in the inevitability of the historical process. Where they differ is not so much in seeing people as pawns in the historical process, as in emphasizing that the effects of peoples' activities are often directly counter to their initial intentions. This is easier to swallow than the other conviction of some Marxist-influenced historians that the events of the 1640s were the direct result of social and economic changes in the preceding century. The efforts of historians, from R. H. Tawney onwards, to establish a connection between social and political changes is one of the most fascinating episodes in postwar English historiography, and one of the most fruitful in terms of stimulating research into sixteenth and seventeenth-century history.[2] None of the detailed studies inspired by 'the storm over the gentry', however, provides any support for any of the major theories of social change produced by the participants in the debate. Even if one accepts that one of the theories is correct, it is difficult to correlate it with what happened in the 1640s. The allegiances of individuals do not appear to have been determined by their social status or wealth. There were prosperous and declining landed gentry, merchants, and lawyers on both sides. Also, as will be seen, it is not clear what is the relevance of social and economic motivation to individuals who changed sides or, what was more common, remained neutral in the 1640s.

Two major charges can be levelled against the participants in the 'causes of the English Revolution' debate. The first is that too many broad hypotheses have been made without sufficient factual basis. The second is that historians have not always been clear what they are trying to explain, and have confused two essentially different questions: (1) Why was there a constitutional crisis and why was Charles I in such a weak position in 1640? The answer to this has been attempted in Part II. (2) Why did the crisis continue once the parliamentary leadership had secured a speedy redress of their grievances in the first session of the Long Parliament? Why, as no one in the Long Parliament when it met in 1640 gave any indication that they had radical aims, did succeeding regimes adopt increasingly more and more radical policies? Long-term social and economic changes have not yet been shown to provide the answer. A much duller, but perhaps more historically sound, solution may lie in the pressure of events from 1640 to 1649: simply that the king's opponents were forced to become more radical because of the fear and distrust of counter-revolution, rather than by social, economic, or ideological forces. The novel means proposed by the parliamentary leaders to ensure the permanence of the constitutional gains made in the first session of the Long Parliament provoked a conservative reaction which culminated in civil war; the radicalism produced by the war caused a second conservative reaction which, in turn, forced the army to make its drastic intervention into the political arena, and so on. The radical decisions were taken each time by a minority, causing a conservative or apathetic reaction from the majority. With each turn of the revolutionary/counter-revolutionary spiral, the radical minority became smaller, until only a handful of people committed themselves finally to the revolutionary events of December 1648 to January 1649. In this respect the pressure of events from 1640 to 1649 provides an explanation for the radical escalation which began with a constitutional crisis led by men with moderate reforming aims, and ended with the creation of the English republic.

The constitutional crisis, November 1640–September 1641

Unity

It is often said with a great deal of truth that when the Long Parliament first met on 3 November 1640 the political nation was united. Derek Hirst, however, has convincingly shown that the political nation was in reality bigger than was once thought, and that the electorate had grown in numbers and in independence since the late sixteenth century.[3] Inevitably among such a wide electorate and those elected to the Long Parliament there were people with vastly differing aims and expectations. Wildly optimistic, millenarian aspirations were voiced in some quarters in 1640. Anna Temple, a Warwickshire lady, wrote excitedly to her daughter, 'Wee shall see idolatory and superstition rooted out and God's ordinances set up in the puritie and power of them.' Thomas Knyvett made the same point more prosaically; 'Now reformation goes on again as hot as toast.'[4] England became a mecca for European radicals, reformers, and idealists who hoped that they would now have an opportunity to try out their ideas in practice. That both parliamentary leaders and some rank-and-file MPs were affected by this exciting atmosphere is not in doubt. Reformers like Samuel Hartlib, John Comenius, and John Drury were patronized by important political leaders like the earl of Bedford in 1640; a 'godly reformation' was prayed for by preachers of some of the fast sermons to parliament which were given the seal of official approval and were ordered to be printed.[5] It is difficult, though, to know whether some MPs shared in the euphoria of 1640 out of conviction or for cynical, political motives. Sir Edward Dering, MP for Kent, certainly seems to have led his constituents to believe that he would support the abolition of episcopacy, something he did not consistently do once at Westminster, as will be seen. There was a huge gulf between those who resented the royal policies of the 1630s because of their disruptive effect on law and order in the localities and those who objected to those policies on grounds of principle and wanted their removal to be merely the first step towards a radical constitutional and ecclesiastical reformation. But in most cases these divisions were hidden in 1640. All factions and shades of opinion were united on an immediate programme of dismantling the worst features of Caroline government. It was not until the question arose of what to put in their place that serious divisions emerged.

The same is true of those men who seem to have been at the forefront of parliament in 1640 and 1641, rich and powerful aristocrats, notably the earls of Bedford and Warwick, and lords Saye and Sele and Brook, with John Pym, Oliver St John, and John Hampden among their dependants and subordinates in the Commons. Though these men shared in the excitement and anticipation of the time and were willing to use popular pressure for their own immediate political advantage, their aims were essentially moderate and pragmatic. They faced practical day-to-day problems, notably the need for money to carry on government and pay the Scots, which was partly and temporarily met by the negotiation of a City loan in November and a parliamentary grant of two subsidies in December. Undoubtedly, however, a more pressing and more serious problem was their own security, which is why in the first week of the Long Parliament Strafford was arrested and the drafting of charges against him became the main business of parliament during the whole of November 1640. True, the other leading ministers in Charles's government were proceeded against; the ship money judges impeached, and Laud imprisoned and his impeachment voted. But the haste behind Strafford's prosecution is unique and testifies to the separate category of fear and hatred in which he was held. Was it not he who might advise Charles to bring over the Irish army to use against the English parliament? And was it not Strafford who might reveal the treasonable negotiations of some of the parliamentary leaders with the Scottish covenanters? There were difficulties (as will be seen) but by May 1641 Strafford was abandoned by Charles I, who gave his assent to a Bill of Attainder on 10 May, and on 12 May Strafford was executed.

By this stage the alleged perpetrators of the 'abuses' of the 1630s were dead, in prison, or in exile; the next step was to get rid of the abuses themselves. Judging by the volume of petitions to parliament and parliamentary speeches, support for this course was unanimous. Gardiner called the great debate on grievances at the beginning of the parliament on 7 November 'one long outburst of suppressed complaint'.[6] The comprehensiveness of the legislation of the first session of the Long Parliament and the speed with which it was enacted (the last major measures were passed in August 1641) testify to the strength and unity of agreement among MPs in favour of abolishing the royal financial expedients of the 1630s (tonnage and poundage without parliamentary consent, ship money, forest fines, distraint of knighthood, monopolies) and the prerogative courts (star chamber, council of the north, the ecclesiastical court of high commission). In addition two Acts were passed to try to ensure that the crown should not be able in future to rule for long without parliament. The Triennial Act (15 February) set a maximum gap of three years between parliaments. More drastically a brief Act on 10 May declared that the present parliament should only be dissolved when it, and not the king, saw fit.[7] Momentous as this legislation was for the future (only the last two Acts were repealed at the Restoration in 1660), the immediate significance of the legislation of the spring and summer of 1641 can be exaggerated, simply because, although Charles I gave his assent to each measure, there was no guarantee that he would not repudiate them when the crisis ended, on the grounds that he had been forced to acept them under duress. The legislation of 1641 left unsolved a central problem of the 1640s: how could the parliamentary leaders ensure that the constitutional gains of 1641 would be made permanent? Apart from providing for the continued sitting of the present parliament and for regular meetings of parliament in the future, the parliamentary leaders were not yet prepared to commit themselves to a radical and effective solution to that problem.

On the contrary, it is highly likely that Bedford had in mind a very conservative solution: that the guarantee of 'good government' in the future was for Charles to give him and his dependants important state offices, enabling him to wield influence in the privy council and with the king. This is certainly in line with the activities of some members of Bedford's circle in the parliaments of the 1620s (see above, pp. 135–40). There is little reason to doubt the accuracy of Clarendon's account of Bedford's suggestion in April 1641 that in return for his support in parliament for merely removing Strafford from office the earl should be made lord treasurer, Saye and Sele master of the court of wards, Pym chancellor of the exchequer, and Denzil Holles secretary of state.[8] Charles appears to have seriously considered this proposition to end the crisis (as he saw it) by buying off the opposition; already he had offered St John the solicitorship, and later Saye and Sele became master of the court of wards. The Bedford group had a detailed programme of financial reforms worked out to give the crown an adequate extra-parliamentary revenue. With this, and with themselves in power, they hoped to ensure that royal government would once again work as they wanted it to do.[9] The practicality of the scheme is open to question; neither Laud in the 1630s nor Digby in the 1640s were able to use their positions in office to control Charles's activities. In any case with Bedford's death (9 May 1641) and with Charles's hopes that he could defeat the opposition by other means, the scheme collapsed.

As yet all groups within parliament were united. Future royalists, like Sir Edward Hyde (later earl of Clarendon) and Viscount Falkland, supported the legislative programme of 1641, and in some cases took a leading part in it, as did Hyde in securing the abolition of the council of the north. The unity was in part a function of the universal agreement on what was wrong with royal government as it had developed in the 1630s; it was also partly a result of the skilful political tactics of the Bedford group and especially of Pym in the Commons. By careful planning and coordination of tactics, by securing the control of key Commons' committees, Pym and his lieutenants were able to give the Commons something like 'front-bench' leadership to steer the business of the House as they wished and certainly to avoid potentially divisive issues whenever possible.[10] Nor did the parliamentary leaders shrink from encouraging popular participation in politics. Petitions and mass demonstrations in favour of parliament were actively solicited. On key occasions, for example when in May 1641 Commons' approval was being sought for the Protestation and the Bill for the attainder of Strafford, Pym used his contacts with radical groups in the City to organize marches of apprentices and others to Westminster,[11] and he maintained an artificial atmosphere of danger by theatrically revealing details of a plot within the army against the leading parliamentarians. In this Pym was undoubtedly helped by the activities of Charles and his wife. Henrietta Maria's contacts with Catholic foreign powers and elements in the army were fruitless and did little but enable Pym to feed the details into his propaganda machine to help him persuade moderate opinion to swallow the incursions that had been made so far into the royal prerogative, and to maintain parliamentary unity.

Disagreements

The political skill of Pym and his parliamentary allies, however, could not avoid controversial issues being discussed even in the first session of the Long Parliament. The first signs of a breach in parliamentary unity came paradoxically in the discussions on the method to be used to get rid of Strafford. Soon after Strafford's trial began on 22 March 1641 it became obvious that it would not be a straightforward affair. For one thing, it was clearly difficult to make stick a charge of treason against a man who still had the king's confidence. 'Almost every article set forth a new treason that I never heard of before,' mocked Strafford at his trial.[12] And, on the principal count against him, his alleged intention to bring over an Irish army to 'reduce' England, the evidence of the only witness, Sir Henry Vane senior, was ambiguous. As a result the Commons voted, against Pym's advice, to proceed against Strafford by a parliamentary Bill of Attainder.[13] Many wanted to get rid of Strafford without delay. The earl of Essex rejected Bedford's proposal that Strafford should be removed by imprisonment rather than by execution, with a cryptic 'Stone dead hath no fellow'. 'We give law to hares and deer, because they be beasts of chase,' St John is reported to have said when he defended the legality of the Bill of Attainder, 'it was never accounted either cruelty or foul play to knock foxes and wolves on the head as they can be found, because they be beasts of prey.' A significant minority had qualms, not surprisingly given arguments like St John's, that the execution of Strafford had been justified as an act of necessity rather than an act of law. Perhaps the division, noticed by contemporaries, between a large body of 'anti-Straffordians' and a few 'Straffordians' was not serious, but it was the first real breach in parliamentary unity and provided the king with his first significant convert from the opposition, Lord George Digby.

It was the issue of Church reform, however, that revealed much more serious disagreements within the parliamentary ranks. After Laud and Laudianism were swept away there was little agreement on what to put in their place. Some radical groups hoped that there could now be a 'godly reformation' and an end to all bishops. Popular anti-episcopalianism has been noted in Cheshire, Kent, London, and elsewhere in 1640–1; but Laudian bishops had done little to endear themselves to gentlemen either. Certainly in the elections of 1640 some MPs had given radical religious views their tacit blessing either to gain electoral support or because the radical social implications of 'root and branch' abolition had not yet sunk in. The former rather than the latter (despite his later pleas) seems to have been the explanation for Sir Edward Dering's otherwise surprising support for the London Root and Branch Petition (11 December 1640) which catalogued the alleged evils of bishops and demanded that 'the said government [of bishops] with all its dependencies, root and branches, may be abolished'. In January 1641 Dering also presented a Kent petition against bishops, and in May 1641 actually moved a Root and Branch Bill in parliament. Later, in 1642, he claimed that the radical intentions of the Root and Branchers had not been clear in 1640 and 1641, and that he did not realize that their aim was not a modified form of episcopacy, but a wholesale reconstruction of the Church, involving popular participation by congregations in church affairs, especially in the nomination of their ministers.[14]

That there was strong opposition to the abolition of bishops among MPs became clear in the Commons' debates in early February 1641 on the London Root and Branch Petition, despite strong pleas on its behalf by religious radicals like Nathaniel Fiennes, younger son of lord Saye and Sele. In parliamentary debates and printed pamphlets a multitude of different plans for Church reform were canvassed, but few envisaged the abolition of bishops.[15] During 1641 pro-bishops petitions flooded into parliament to stiffen the resistance of MPs to root and branch reform. Why was there such strong support for bishops, despite their close association with the hated Church policies of the 1630s? In the early 1640s it was feared by many that James I's maxim of 'no bishop, no king', would be extended quite validly to 'no bishop, no king, no magistrate'. The political and social implications of the *de facto* collapse of ecclesiastical hierarchical discipline and relaxation of censorship laws could already be seen. Reports of altar rails and 'images' being ripped down and of interruptions to services using the Book of Common Prayer were common. The violent actions and language of religious radicals (a Cheshire Puritan minister was reported to have said that the Book of Common Prayer 'doth stink in the nostrils of God and hath been the means of sending many souls into hell'[16] produced an inevitable reaction in favour of bishops. In Cheshire this was led by Sir Thomas Aston whose *Remonstrance against Presbytery*, the printed version of his petition presented to parliament on 27 February 1641, expressed the social and political fears of conservatives. 'Freedom of their consciences and persons is not enough, but they must have their purses and estates free too. . . . Nay they go higher, even to the denial of the right to proprietie in our estates.' The aim of the reformers, the *Remonstrance* alleged, was to 'pull down 26 bishops and set up 9324 potential Popes' (one in each parish).[17]

The equation that religious freedom equalled social disorder also received confirmation (quite wrongly) from the rash of outbreaks of riots which were not directly concerned with religious matters. Protests against enclosures, the destruction of drainage sluices by fen-dwellers in Lincolnshire, and disorder among the inhabitants of Windsor Forest had more to do with a recurrence of economic crisis as bad as that in the early 1620s than with the collapse of ecclesiastical discipline. But this was not a distinction made by those who, like Dering, were dissuaded from supporting anti-bishop factions at Westminster and in the constituencies in the summer and autumn of 1641. As a result the debates on Church reform in 1641 were barren. All that the Commons could agree was that the secular powers of bishops should be curtailed and an Exclusion Bill to this effect was sent up to the Lords in March 1641. But the Lords would not even go this far; they objected especially to the Bill's proposal to exclude bishops from the Lords and rejected it on 8 June 1641. The religious issue was shunted off the parliamentary stage by the decision to set up an assembly of divines to discuss it. This was announced in the Grand Remonstrance in November 1641, but the Westminster Assembly of Divines did not begin work until July 1643. In this way the clash was postponed, not resolved.

By the summer of 1641 Charles must have seen these disagreements among his opponents as promising signs that the end of the crisis was in sight. Where he had had few supporters a year ago, moderate opinion was now moving in his favour. With the major grievances legislated away attendance in the Commons became thin; the euphoria of the previous winter was evaporating. An accommodation between king and parliament, though, was not a practical possibility. Charles's announcement in June that he intended to go to Scotland to ratify the treaty between the two countries made clear that the gulf of distrust between king and parliament was much wider than that opening up between factions among the king's opponents. In Scotland Charles hoped to appeal to a body of potential royalists who objected to the course the Scottish revolution had taken since 1637. So great was the distrust of Charles in England that he might attempt to mobilize an army in Scotland, that when the king left for Scotland in August a parliamentary committee of defence was appointed and commissioners selected to accompany the king to keep a watch on his activities. Yet much more than the fears generated by the Scottish visit prevented an end to the crisis. The Ten Propositions, accepted by both Lords and Commons on 24 June 1641, would have been parliament's negotiating position in any discussions on a settlement. Charles would not have found it easy to control his wife and her Catholic connections, the issue which loomed largest in the Propositions (clauses IV, V, VI, and X). But he would have found it even harder to accept the proposed limitation on the king's hitherto unrestrained choice of advisers and control of the army, which were hinted at in clauses III and VII[18] Also, although this contentious issue was omitted from the Ten Propositions, Charles would undoubtedly have had to accept religious changes that would, at the very least, have placed limitations on episcopal authority and admitted a parliamentary voice in the making of an ecclesiastical settlement. These incursions into the royal prerogative would have been an obnoxious dose for any seventeenth-century king to accept, let alone anyone as stubborn and as unwilling to compromise as Charles I.

The crisis becomes a civil war, September 1641—July 1642

Recent studies, especially of the reactions of local communities to national events immediately before and during the civil war in 1642 and 1643, have highlighted the danger of exaggerating the degree to which opinion in the country polarized for and against king and parliament. Certainly, as we will see, there was much confusion about allegiances and determination not to be involved in the war was common. But it was perhaps easier to take sides *before* the war; taking up a debating position did not require the commitment demanded by a call to arms. During the early months of the second session of the Long Parliament political opinion divided much more clearly than before, and it is difficult to believe that political opinion outside Westminster (which was so closely in touch by means of MPs and others who sent home letters full of political news) was insulated from the events taking place in London, Scotland, and Ireland.[19] Two major questions present themselves about the period immediately before the outbreak of the civil war: firstly, why were the supporters of parliament, who in 1640 and early 1641 had wanted only moderate constitutional and ecclesiastical reforms, now pushed into accepting more radical measures and finally into the drastic step of taking up arms against the king? Secondly, why did the king get a party, when by the summer of 1641 there had only been a few signs that opinion had begun to swing in his favour? Clues to the answers to both these questions lie in events in Scotland and Ireland at the end of 1641. As in 1639 and 1640, the impact of events in those two countries did much to precipitate the worsening of the crisis in England.

In 1641 conditions in Scotland were ripe for a counter-revolution. The unity of the Scots covenanters, like that of the English parliamentarians, was fragile. For many Scotsmen radical lay covenanters, like Johnston of Wariston, had gone too far too quickly in abolishing episcopacy and in proceeding unconstitutionally in defiance of royal authority. Although the covenanters acquired a moderate leader in the earl of Argyll, opposition to them began to crystallize when in August 1640 the earl of Montrose and seventeen other Scottish nobles signed the Cumbernauld Bond, protesting at the 'particular and indirect practising of a few'.[20] The allegation was not quite true: the covenanters had fairly widespread support, but it was not total. The opposition, however, was hindered by Charles's failure to give it support at the right time. 'It was ever his [Charles's] constant unhappiness to give nothing in time,' said Robert Baillie.[21] This was borne out when Charles arrived in Scotland in August 1641. His concessions were granted too late and with such apparent reluctance that his sincerity was doubted. On 16 September Charles agreed in principle that his nominations of officers of state in Scotland should be confirmed by the Scottish parliament; he then indicated that he had no intention of keeping to the spirit of this declaration by appointing the royalist earl of Morton as his chancellor. What, however, really destroyed Charles's chances of gaining much support in Scotland was the revelation of a plot, 'the Incident', by some of the more extreme Scottish royalists led by the earl of Crawford, to seize the covenanters leaders, Argyll, Hamilton, and Lanark. The extent of Charles's complicity is not known; what is, is that most people believed he was deeply implicated, a feeling which he hardly dispelled by attending parliament in Edinburgh on 12 October to proclaim his innocence, accompanied by a force of armed royalists. The 'Incident' destroyed any hopes Charles might have had of gaining support in Scotland; before he returned south on 17 November 1641 he had to appoint all the leading covenanters to key offices in Scotland. In England the 'Incident' intensified the mistrust of the king in the eyes of many parliamentarians: might not Charles attempt a similar coup in England? When the English parliament reassembled after the recess on 21 October, one of its first acts was to appoint a hundred men to stand guard in the Palace Yard at Westminster.

The repercussions of events taking place in Ireland at the same time were even more disastrous than those in Scotland for the hopes of a settlement between king and parliament. The fall of Strafford had resulted in the collapse of the unnatural coalition between the Catholic 'Old English' and the Protestant 'New English' which had developed in Ireland by 1640. Hatred of Strafford had been the only thing that had kept the alliance together, and the grievances of the 'Old English' were intensified by the negotiations of the 'new English' lords justices in Ireland, Sir William Parsons and Sir John Borlase, with the English parliamentary leaders for measures to be taken against Irish Catholicism. Irish Catholics were also encouraged to rebel by Charles's negotiations with the 'old English' leaders, the earls of Ormonde and Antrim, in order to recruit a royalist army in Ireland. The negotiations were not pursued, but when the Irish rebellion began in October 1641, many who joined it felt they did so in the name and in the defence of King Charles.

It is very difficult indeed to discover what happened in Ireland in the winter of 1641 largely because English propaganda culminating in Sir John Temple's *The Irish Rebellion* (1646) painted a horrific picture of the massacre of English settlers. Clarendon thought that at least 40,000 were killed, a figure S. R. Gardiner reduced to 4,000. In England, though, appearances were of more importance than reality. The emotional, irrational fear of popery was diffused throughout seventeenth-century society. Dr Robin Clifton describes it as 'a latent force; buried beneath the day-to-day business of living until a crisis burst upon the country'. In England at the end of 1641 there were panic-laden rumours of imminent invasion by the Irish rebels; recusants were arrested and night-watches organized. At Pudsey (Yorkshire) the church service was interrupted by someone who 'came and stood up in the chapel door and cried out with a lamentable voice "Friends," said he, "we are all as good as dead men, for the Irish rebels are coming; they are come as far as Rochdale . . . and will be at Halifax and Bradford shortly".' Joseph Lister, a Bradford clothier, who was in the church, was naturally alarmed, 'for we must needs go to Bradford, and knew not but Incarnate Devils and Death would be there before us'.[22] The 'Irish rebels' in this case were probably Protestant refugees from Ireland, but it needed little to trigger off anti-Catholic scares whether in Pudsey or in Westminster.

In this rumour-laden atmosphere for many Charles's credibility was now destroyed, and it is not surprising that, when he proposed to raise an army against the Irish, many feared he would use it instead against parliament. So just as fear forced the attainder of Strafford through parliament, so the pressure of events forced the parliamentary leadership to take radical steps they would not have even considered twelve months before. On 8 November, after a fierce political struggle against moderate opinion led by Hyde and supported by Sir Simonds D'Ewes, Pym secured majority support (151/110 votes) for an 'additional instruction' to be sent to the parliamentary commissioners in Scotland. As a condition of helping Charles raise an army against the Irish, the king must employ 'only such councillors as should be approved of by Parliament'; otherwise parliament 'should take such a course for the securing of Ireland as might likewise secure our selves'. This looked forward to a second radical step: parliamentary control of the army. At the same time as the 'additional instruction' was being discussed parliament appointed the earl of Essex to the command of the trained bands south of the Trent, and an Impressment Bill was introduced which proposed to take away the king's power to order men to serve outside their own counties. More radically, on 7 December, Sir Arthur Hazelrige introduced a Bill which would take the command of the trained bands out of the king's hands altogether: army commanders were to be appointed by parliament.[23]

This was a move which was temporarily resisted by the Lords. But it was not only the members of the Upper House who were worried by Pym's tactics. The polarization of opinion that was taking place in the Commons can be seen in the debates late in November on the Grand

Remonstrance, a statement of the grievances of parliament. Though they disliked its violent language, it was not just the contents of the Remonstrance that the moderates objected to. What also was alarming to them about it was its intention to be a direct appeal to the people. The chaotic scenes in the Commons on the night of 22 November took place *after* the Grand Remonstrance had been approved by the narrow margin of 159/148, on the question of whether or not the Remonstrance should be printed. 'When I first heard of a Remonstrance,' said Dering, 'I presently imagined that like faithful councillors we should hold up a glass to His Majesty. . . . I did not dream that we should remonstrate downwards and tell stories to the people.'[24] No matter that Dering and others had been 'remonstrating downwards' since the 1640 elections. By now he and others backed away from the constitutional and religious radicalism that the popular participation in politics encouraged by the parliamentary leadership seemed to entail.

Consequently, when Charles returned to London from Scotland at the end of November 1641 he found he had more supporters in England than when he left. On 25 November the City aldermen gave him a lavish welcome, to which Charles responded by promising to return the City's Londonderry estates he had confiscated in the 1630s. In his public pronouncements in December Charles was able to pose convincingly as the defender of the 'fundamental law' against the parliamentary revolutionaries. He it was, he said, who stood between the Church and 'the irreverence of those many schismatics and separatists, wherewith of late this kingdom and this city [London] abounds, to the great dishonour and hazard both of Church and State, for the suppression of whom we require your timely aid and active assistance'.[25] This was a tempting appeal to which 'constitutional royalists' like Hyde, Falkland, and Colepeper responded, especially when their fears seemed to become reality. On 21 December 1641 the ruling oligarchic clique in the City of London was defeated in City elections by a faction which had close ties with the parliamentary leadership, and which had not scrupled to organize mass demonstrations in support of the policies of Pym.[26]

The growing support for him at Westminster and the county petitions in favour of episcopacy perhaps persuaded Charles that the time was ripe for a coup against the parliamentary leaders. Obviously the timing was crucial; and in late December 1641 there were signs that the royalist 'backlash' was on the wane. Certainly Charles's misguided choice as lieutenant of the Tower on 23 December of Sir Thomas Lunsford, a man outlawed by respectable gentry society in his native Sussex,[27] rebounded against the king. Most seriously of all, dramatically, the breach between the Lords and Commons on the Impressment and Militia Bills was temporarily healed. After a popular demonstration had prevented the bishops from attending the House of Lords, they returned on 29 December and moved that all the Lords' proceedings during their absence should be declared null and void. The majority in the Lords interpreted this as a breach of their privileges and accepted from the

Commons a vote of impeachment against the bishops. Before events moved further out of control Charles decided to act. On 3 January he announced the impeachment of Pym, John Hampden, William Strode, Hazelrige, Denzil Holles, and Lord Kimbolton, and on the following day, disastrously his attempt to arrest them in the chamber of the Commons failed. A Commons' committee sitting in the Guildhall declared these events a violation of parliamentary privileges, and Philip Skippon was appointed Sergeant Major-General of the City trained bands as a defensive measure. On 10 January Charles, possibly physically frightened by the popular outburst against him and alarmed for his own and his wife's safety, retreated to Hampton Court; and on the following day the five MPs returned in triumph to Westminster. For many MPs the incident was the final confirmation of the king's untrustworthiness, and it hastened the slide to civil war. It is difficult to see that, even if the coup had succeeded, there could have been any other result. If Pym had been removed would the parliamentary cause have collapsed?

The immediate aftermath of the attempted coup was to strengthen the parliamentary leadership in its determination to carry out the radical programme which had emerged during the last few months: press for the removal of 'evil councillors' round the king, secure parliamentary approval of the commanders of the militia, forts, and the Tower, and force an Exclusion Bill preventing bishops from sitting in the House of Lords through the Upper House. Popular support for this programme was actively encouraged. In January and February 1642 there is every sign of an organized petitioning movement in the counties, coordinated by the parliamentary leadership, again reinforcing the point that there was no artificial divide between Westminster and local politics in the 1640s. Often the presentation of these petitions was made the occasion for mass demonstrations. When, on 11 January 1642, one of the first county petitions was presented, 4,000–5,000 supporters are said to have accompanied it from Buckinghamshire to Westminster. In the following weeks other county petitions followed, blaming every evil, from the violation of parliamentary privileges to the 'decay of trade' on evil councillors, bishops, and popish lords. At one huge demonstration on 31 January in Moor Fields, London, these petitioners threatened that unless bishops were removed 'your petitioners shall not rest in quietness'.[28]

Under this kind of pressure the opposition in the Lords collapsed: on 5 February they accepted the Exclusion Bill and on 15 February approved the Commons' Militia Ordinance. The actual Ordinance was not finally issued until 5 March, significantly without the king's approval. The situation also demanded novel financial measures to supplement City loans and parliamentary subsidies. A poll tax levied in the summer of 1641 had produced only £169,000, because potential taxpayers desperately, and successfully, tried to pay less than the amounts demanded. As a result in March 1642 parliament approved a proposal to raise £400,000, ironically on the ship money principle of fixed assessments from each county. Also like the majority of ship money assessments the so-called Act of £400,000 was very effective: Sussex, Anthony Fletcher calculates, contributed over half as much as a result of that Act in 1642 as it had done to all kinds of taxation in the war years of the 1620s.[29]

Given the almost total unanimity of opposition to the king in 1640 and the cumulating evidence since then of Charles's intention not to accept the constitutional legislation of 1641, it is easier to understand the reasons for the adoption of radical measures by parliament than why the king gained supporters from parliament in 1641 and 1642. Yet for the growing numbers of 'constitutional royalists' like Hyde, attacks on bishops and novel parliamentary claims to choose the king's advisers, control the army, and enact legislation without the king were unacceptable constitutional innovations and their consequences more to be feared than the events of 4 January 1642. Others had more than constitutional qualms about the directions of events. Not only did the parliamentary financial measures seem indistinguishable from the centralized government of the 1620s and 1630s, but the political crisis was associated more and more with the breakdown of order, with huge political demonstrations, with enclosure riots, and disturbances in churches. These fears were skilfully exploited by the king's reply (drafted by Colepeper and Falkland) to the parliamentary Nineteen Propositions in June 1642. Not only would the parliamentary proposals be 'a total subversion of the fundamental laws', but eventually they would encourage the common people

to set up for themselves, call parity and independence liberty, devour that estate which had devoured the rest, destroy all rights and proprieties, all distinctions of families and merit, and by this means this splendid and excellently distinguished form of government end in a dark, equal chaos of confusion, and the long line of our many noble ancestors in a Jack Cade or Wat Tyler.[30]

Gardiner believed that, after parliament rejected a petition from Kent in favour of bishops and against the Militia Ordinance at the end of March 1642, civil war was inevitable. Within a few weeks, well before the official declarations of war in August, it had in fact begun. Mostly it was a war of words as royal declarations were met with parliamentary replies in an unprecedented public political debate. The central issue was the legality of the Militia Ordinance, and this was a question which could not be confined to the realms of debate. Local gentlemen had to choose whether or not to obey the orders sent to them to secure the local militia for parliament. From June the decision was sharpened when the king began to send out Commissions of Array appointing his own local army commanders. Not surprisingly armed conflict resulted as both sides tried to get control of local stores of ammunition. Inevitably the attention of historians has focused on the king's attempt in April to seize control of the garrison at Hull (so important as a store of ammunition for the Scottish war and as a strategic post for supplying armies in the North) and the successful defence of the town by Sir John Hotham. But this was only one of many other similar skirmishes in the spring and summer of 1642: the most serious were the marquis of Hertford's confrontation with Alexander Popham in Somerset, and Lord Strange's failure to secure the Manchester magazine, a skirmish in July 1642 which parliamentary propagandists claimed was 'the start of the civil war'. As will be seen, enthusiasm for the war was rare. The language of politics for so long had been couched in terms of king *and* parliament, that it took an enormous mental adjustment to come to grips with the concept of a parliament in arms against a king. But Charles's declaration of war by raising his standard at Nottingham on 22 August 1642 only made official the slide into civil war which had been apparent for months.

The first civil war, 1642—1646

Commitment and neutralism, 1642–3

In trying to make sense of the line-up at the beginning of the civil war, historians have commonly tried to analyse the division of royalist against parliamentarian in social and economic terms. In this they are following some contemporary commentators (both royalist and parliamentarian) who took it for granted that the royalist cause appealed much more to rich landowners and merchants, while parliament drew its strength from the lower ranks of society, craftsmen, small merchants, lesser gentry, farmers. Lucy Hutchinson's analysis is typical: 'most of the Gentry of the country [i.e. the county of Nottingham] were disaffected to the Parliament. Most of the middle sort, the able substantial free holders, and the other Commons, who had not their dependence upon the malignant nobility and gentry, adhered to the Parliament.'[31] This has received support from modern local studies. In his study of Somerset Professor Underdown ascribes part of the reason for the initial parliamentary control of that county in August 1642 to popular opposition to the royalist commander there, the marquis of Hertford. Nor can one lightly discount the class hostility sometimes seen in the war. In August 1642 in the Stour valley in Essex mobs attacked the persons and property of unpopular large landowners, like Sir John Lucas.[32] It was not uncommon, either, for tenants to join armies led by oppressive landlords or to use the war as an excuse to destroy legal documents concerning their tenancies. The correlation between cloth-making areas (like north-east Somerset and the clothing towns of Lancashire and Yorkshire) and strong parliamentary support also suggests that social and economic factors were important in determining the line-up in 1642. 'On the parliament's side', wrote Richard Baxter, 'were ... the smaller part (as some thought) of the gentry in most of the counties, and the greatest part of the tradesmen and freeholders and the middle sort of men, especially in those corporations and countries which depended on clothing and such manufactures'.[33]

Interesting as is this approach to the way the country divided at the beginning of the civil war, it is of limited historical value. One does not have to look very hard to find instances of great landowners fighting for parliament. Those who have made detailed studies of the members of the Long Parliament have found no evidence that the way MPs divided in 1642 depended in any way on social status or wealth.[34] Members of the same families fought on different sides. Nor did people remain constant in their loyalties of 1642. One might think that Sir Edward Dering's oft-quoted career was exceptional in its inconstancy. Yet there are many more examples of men who changed sides: Sir John Hotham, the parliamentary hero of the siege of Hull, the earl of Holland, and, one is tempted to add, all the leading gentry of Somerset who were members of the parliamentary county committee in Somerset in late 1642 and early 1643 and who ran the county for the king when it was taken over by royalist forces in the summer of 1643. Professor Underdown's comment on these men points the way to what is the most serious limitation on attempts to analyse the divisions of 1642 in social and economic terms. 'We might think of them [the Somerset gentry]', he writes, 'as having changed sides, but they had not: they were Somerset men first, partisans second.'[35] It is probable that the commonest reaction in most counties to the coming of the war and the war itself was non-commitment, neutralism, and that the activists for the royalists and parliamentary causes were few.

Neutralism just before and in the early stages of the war took many forms. In some places individuals grouped together and made neutrality pacts, agreeing not to support either side. Cheshire is the best-studied example of this type of organized neutralism, which culminated in an agreement on 23 December 1642 at Bunbury (Cheshire) between royalist and parliamentarian gentry who agreed to disarm and disband their troops. Similarly at the Staffordshire Quarter Sessions on 15 November 1642 a group of gentry committed themselves to the demilitarization of the county. Probably, however, the commonest response to the coming of the war was passive neutralism. Significantly in some counties neither the Militia Ordinance nor the Commission of Array was put into operation until the local gentry were forced to do so. Often the choice of sides was determined, not on grounds of principle, but by whether the region was controlled by royal or parliamentary troops. In some cases individuals made clear their non-commitment by supporting with men and money both sides at the same time. In part, the lack of enthusiasm for the war can be explained by the fact that literate Englishmen had at hand in the well-reported war in northern Europe evidence as to what disruptive effects war could have. 'Oh lett the miserable spectacle of a German devestation', said a Norfolk petition of January 1643, 'persuade you to decline those perilous casualties which may result from a civil war.'[36]

The current economic crisis was linked in many people's minds with the breakdown of political order. Petitioners agreed that the restoration of political and economic order would go hand in hand. Similarly many believed that the breakdown of political order was responsible for social and religious radicalism. Sir John Hotham, for example, argued that, if an agreement with the king was not reached, then 'the necessitous people of the whole kingdom will presently rise in mighty numbers and whatsoever they pretend for at first, within a while they will set up for themselves to the utter ruin of all the nobility and gentry of the kingdom'.[37] 'They would take advantage of these times', some anti-enclosure demonstrators were alleged to have said, 'lest they have not the like again'.[38] Very often the anti-war sentiments of 1642–3 sound like crypto-royalism, echoing the sentiments already quoted in the king's answer to the Nineteen Propositions. But the peace petitions of the summer and autumn of 1642 and the winter of 1642–3 reflected not committed royalism, but conservative localism, the unanimous desire of the traditional ruling élites in the counties and boroughs of England to maintain what they called 'the peace of my country'.

Historians of sixteenth- and seventeenth-century England have learned not to see Westminster politics in isolation. What happened at Westminster is often explicable in terms of opinions in the localities. In the second half of 1642, therefore, the desire for peace was as strong at Westminster as in the country at large. Denzil Holles later explained that he became the leading spokesman in parliament in favour of a speedy settlement with the king, because he was afraid that in the train of political instability would come a social revolution, when 'Servants should ride on Horses' and 'the meanest of men, the basest and vilest of the nation, the lowest of the people, have got the power into their hands; trampled upon the Crown; baffled and misused the Parliament; violated the Laws; destroyed, or suppressed the Nobility and Gentry of the kingdom'.[39] Holles, however, wrote that comment when in exile in 1646–7, when he had more reason than in 1642 to connect war with the appearance of popular radicalism. In 1642 shocked reaction at the horror of war probably played a greater part in the desire of Holles (and others) for peace. Holles was present at the siege of Sherborne castle in September 1642, when, as soon as the royalist cannons were fired, the frightened untrained parliamentary soldiers ran, or so said the earl of Bedford, 'as if the devil had been in them'.[40]

Not surprisingly in these circumstances the early military engagements of the war (like the battle of Edgehill, 23 October 1642) were indecisive. The rank and file, as well as most of the generals on both sides, were fairly inexperienced. The failure of either side to win a decisive battle gave force to the growing peace movement, especially in the House of Lords among people like the earls of Pembroke, Holland, and Northumberland. On 29 October 1642 the Lords proposed that negotiations be opened with the king, and, under pressure from opinion in the City and country, on 2 November the Commons agreed. Even

Charles's continued march along the Thames Valley towards London, despite his agreement to open peace negotiations, did not stop the pressure for peace on the parliamentary side. After the king's march had been halted by the London trained bands at Turnham Green (13 November 1642) peace petitions were received sympathetically at Westminster. In December parliament agreed on peace proposals and negotiations on them between commissioners from both sides began at Oxford on 1 February 1643 and lasted until 14 April. With hindsight one can see that the Oxford 'treaty' negotiations, the peace petitions and neutrality pacts of 1642 and early 1643 were the culmination of a great effort to end the war. Their collapse marks the definite end of the first phase in the war.

The collapse of neutrality pacts and of the Oxford 'treaty', 1643

Neutralism was never totally extinguished during the civil war. In 1643, though, it temporarily lost its political force and it became increasingly difficult to be neutral or to be in favour of peace negotiations without appearing to be a royalist 'delinquent'. Charles as usual did not help his own cause; he did little to dispel either the suspicions raised by his attempted coup in January 1642 or the impression that Henrietta Maria's Catholic circle had more influence with the king than Hyde. The king's march on Brentford and Turnham Green in November 1642 was used to great propaganda effect against him, as evidence that he was not serious in wanting peace. This was supported by the prevarication of the royal commissioners at Oxford, and confirmed later in the year when it became known that Charles was negotiating with the Irish rebels, negotiations which culminated in the Cessation Treaty between the king and the Irish in September 1643.

What really destroyed the peace hopes of the early part of the war, however, was not Charles's duplicity, which, after all, was not revealed for the first time in 1643. The changed political climate was primarily caused by a new military situation: in the spring and summer the royalist armies threatened both to carry all before them and to enable the king to set aside the reforms of the Long Parliament. It is not often before 1645 that one can talk in terms of either side as having and carrying out a nationwide war stategy. But in 1643 Charles *seemed* to have achieved just that. His three armies appeared to be acting in accordance with a preconceived strategic scheme: the northern army under the earl of Newcastle would occupy Yorkshire and march south through East Anglia to Essex; Sir Ralph Hopton and the king's western army would march through the south-western counties towards London, both armies acting out a kind of pincer movement on the capital, while the king's forces kept the main parliamentary army under the earl of Essex occupied in the Thames Valley. In fact, as will be seen, both sides were so reliant on local commanders that overall strategies never got beyond the discussion stage. However, in the spring and summer of 1643 it must have seemed to many (albeit wrongly) as if the king did have a three-pronged strategy that was succeeding beyond all expectations. In February 1643 Henrietta Maria landed at Bridlington with arms and money which she had collected during her year's absence on the continent. She joined Newcastle's army at York and the royalist army proceeded to conquer the whole of Yorkshire apart from Hull, where the Fairfaxes held out. By the end of July Newcastle had taken Gainsborough (Lincolnshire) and was threatening to push southwards · into East Anglia. Meanwhile Hopton overran Cornwall and Devon (except Exeter and Plymouth) and in Somerset he joined forces with the marquis of Hertford and Prince Maurice. This combined force decisively defeated the parliamentary commander in the west, Sir William Waller, at Roundway Down near Devizes (Wiltshire) on 13 July 1643, a battle which delivered nearly all of south-west England into royalist hands and made Prince Rupert's siege of Bristol an easier task than it might otherwise have been. The parliamentarians were understandably shattered by the surrender of Bristol on 26 July 1643, and subsequently court-martialled the governor of Bristol, Nathaniel Fiennes. Fiennes, however, had had little support. Waller by this time had abandoned Bath and was retreating westwards slowly towards London. Nor did the earl of Essex help Fiennes or parliamentary morale. His only success was the capture of Reading in April 1643 (resulting in the royalists' court-martialling of the governor, Colonel Fielding), but Essex made little further progress. Tied down in the Thames Valley, he was so disillusioned that by July 1643 he suggested reopening peace talks with the king.

Such a course, however, was not now practical. The possibilities now arose of an unconditional royalist military victory, the consequent return of the king to the power and position he had in 1639, and the loss of the constitutional gains of 1640–1. Significantly, to support the polarization which was taking place, political ideologies began to be formulated on both sides.[41] The ablest exponents of the royalist brand of political theory were Henry Ferne and Dudley Digges who erected a theory of constitutional royalism which had first been outlined in Falkland and Colepeper's Answer to the Nineteen Propositions: that the king rules not by arbitrary power but under the law and limited by parliament, but still retains necessary prerogative powers over foreign affairs, sole control of the militia, the right to appoint his own advisers and officers, and to call and dismiss parliament. The theory allowed that the crown was but one of three estates, but it was the supreme one, and in challenging it, parliament was guilty of treason and rebellion. Parliamentary political theorists had therefore to formulate a justification for taking up arms against the king. This, as elaborated by Henry Parker and others, came to be that government rests on popular consent and that, since Charles had betrayed the trust given him by his people, rebellion was justified. The obvious charge against this theory of parliamentary sovereignty (and the royalists were not slow to make it) was that parliamentary rule would be as arbitrary and unchecked as that of an individual tyrant. Parker in perhaps his most important work, *Observations*, argued that the safeguard against arbitrary rule by parliament was its representative nature. Parliament, wrote Parker, is 'so equally and geometrically proportionable' that it took 'away all jealousies'.[42] Derek Hirst has shown that this was a claim that had some substance in reality, and that the 'claim to be representative of the people was central to Parliament's stand in the war':[43] a justification for rebellion, an ideology to stiffen the resistance of those who baulked at the necessary step of fighting the king if all that had been gained was not now to be lost.

Parliamentary factions and the management of the war, 1643–1644

Faced with the possibility of a long-drawn-out civil war, from 1643 onwards opinion on the parliamentary side on how the war should be conducted was divided. The divergences of opinion among parliamentarians have been matched by the division of opinion among historians in describing them. Parliamentarians were not agreed on short-term objectives (should peace negotiations be carried on during the war or should a total military victory be secured first?), let alone on what should be their long-term objectives regarding a political and religious settlement. The problem for the historian is to put these divergences of opinion into an analytical framework. The belief that the parliamentarians during the war divided into two groups along religious lines (religious presbyterians who were moderate in politics and 'doves' and religious independents who were political radicals and 'hawks') was first brilliantly and persuasively exploded by Professor J. H. Hexter in an article in 1938–9. However, it proved more difficult to get agreement on what new analysis to put in its place.[44] The dust has now settled on the 'Presbyterian–Independent' controversy; as a result certain features of the parliamentary political scene in the early 1640s now seem clear. Firstly, political groupings in the 1640s (as in the 1620s) were ephemeral and their composition changed as political issues changed. In addition, even within as loose a political framework as this, there was a mass of independent, floating opinion in the middle whose views it would be difficult to categorize on any issue. Secondly, political alliances in the early 1640s cut across religious opinions. During the major part of the war the nature of the future religious settlement was secondary, as a political issue, to the more immediate problem of pursuing the war. Thirdly, although of course not embracing all MPs, at least three political groups can be identified in the war years, the 'peace', 'war', and 'middle' groups, each of which had distinctive views about the conduct of the war, and, to a lesser extent, about the political and religious settlement to be made when the war was over.[45]

As in 1642, Denzil Holles was the most vocal advocate of a settlement with the king at any price, except perhaps that of agreeing to a return to

Laudianism in the Church. So fearful were Holles and the 'peace group' of the social and religious radicalism brought by the war that they were willing to trust Charles to maintain the legislation of 1641 without any safeguards. Until such a settlement was negotiated, they advocated a purely defensive war policy, as was being followed by Essex in the Thames Valley. It is impossible to be precise about the long-term religious and political aims of 'war group' MPs such as Sir Henry Vane jnr, Henry Marten, and Arthur Hazelrige. Their enemy, Clarendon, alleged that they aimed to 'change the whole frame of the government in State as well as Church'.[46] What is certain is that the 'war group' advocated an offensive strategy, aimed at a total military victory and carried out, if necessary, by new generals. Until this was achieved there should be no negotiations with the king at all. Between these two extremes a 'middle group' led by John Pym until his death in December 1643 and thereafter by Oliver St John, maintained a balance. Unlike the 'peace group' MPs, Pym and St John were not willing to trust the king until he had been defeated militarily and forced to accept limitations on his power. Consequently, they allied with the 'war group' in securing parliamentary approval for measures for an effective prosecution of the war. Yet, unlike the 'war group', Pym and St John wanted an eventual constitutional settlement that was of the traditional sort with the novel features introduced in 1641 grafted on to it. They were therefore loath to break completely with conservative MPs like Holles, and consequently often are difficult to identify as a separate group. Yet whenever Pym, St John, and their allies can be seen to be acting independently it was as mediators, trying to shunt off controversial religious issues to the Westminster Assembly and to get support for reforms designed to win the war against the king.

Right from the beginning of the war some MPs had battled against the desire for a settlement with the king. But they had few successes: new fiscal measures were bogged down in Commons' committees and the only progress towards a Scottish alliance was parliament's approval of a letter to be sent to the Scots agreeing to the abolition of episcopacy, as a bait for a military alliance. It was not until February 1643 that the political climate at Westminster and in the country changed and that Pym's political leadership was able to push through reforms and overcome what Professor Hexter called the '"heartburnings" and the symptoms of a slightly dyspeptic conservatism' of most MPs. The 'heartburnings' are not surprising. It is one of the great paradoxes of the 1640s that the parliamentary leadership adopted a programme of centralized government and high taxation, in many respects identical to that which in 1640 they had been determined to abolish.

The first priority for an effective war strategy was money. Already parliament had departed from traditional channels of public finance in the so-called Act of £400,000 of March 1642. But more radical measures were needed and resulted in a remarkable series of financial Ordinances in 1643 instituting weekly assessments (February), sequestrations

(March), compulsory loans (May), and the excise (July). The weekly assessments (later monthly assessments) became the backbone of parliamentary finances both during and after the civil war. The irony was probably not lost on some that the new tax continued the ship money principle of fixed county assessment: a connection that was very clear when (as in Cheshire) ship money assessments were used as the basis for collecting 'the weekly pay'. The advantage to the government was that the new tax, again like ship money, hit a much wider section of society than did parliamentary subsidies. It was more geared to tapping the true wealth of the country: the more prosperous south and east counties were more heavily assessed than poorer ones. Despite some complex technical provisions in the Ordinance which hindered its administration, the weekly assessment was a major improvement in public finance and the contrast in receipts from it and from parliamentary subsidies was staggering. The second plank of the new parliamentary financial system was the sequestration of the property of the king's supporters. The Ordinance was enacted on 27 March 1643 at a time when it was clear that the Oxford 'treaty' was on the brink of collapse. Only then would a majority in parliament accept a measure which could force a deep rift in county society. These 'delinquents', whose estates were to be taken over by local commissioners and the profit forwarded to a central committee in Guildhall, would in all probability be the friends, relatives or dependents of those who had voted for, or who would have to administer, the sequestrations. Compulsory loans introduced by Ordinance in May 1643 were equally distasteful, reminiscent as they were of the earlier hated forced loans. All those worth £10 p.a. in land or £100 p.a. in goods were to lend a maximum of one-fifth of the annual revenue of their estates or half the value of their goods, repayable 'upon the public faith'. Already the worthlessness of that promise had become apparent through the workings of an Ordinance of November 1642, which allowed commissioners for provisions to requisition food, fuel, and horses for parliamentary garrisons in return for chits promising repayment. Easily the most hated of the new financial expedients was the excise tax, a purchase tax on a very wide range of consumption goods and therefore one which affected everyone. To collect the new taxes (apart from the excise) local committees were appointed, often staffed (at least at first) by the old local government officials, deputy lieutenants, sheriffs, justices of the peace. The extent of the powers of the parliamentary county committees varied, but generally their administrative and judicial functions were wide and efforts were made to see that they were made up of 'well-affected' men. As will be seen, the financial and administrative reconstruction in 1643 did not fulfil all the hopes of its creators, but undeniably that it was created at all was a major achievement.

If the war was to be won there had also to be some military reorganization. The defects of the militia were plain. Organized on a county basis, it suffered from entrenched localism, and prevented the execution of a national war strategy. Looking at the military history of Staffordshire, Pennington and Roots could see no strategic pattern: 'its military history is largely one of sporadic and gentlemanly conflicts between garrisons and leaguers, and between the small companies that often seem to be moving about the county with as little co-ordinated purpose as ducks on a pond.'[47] The same was true of the country as a whole: Hopton, for example, found that his Cornish levies fought keenly in Cornwall, but were very reluctant to cross the Tamar into Devon. Both sides attempted to overcome this obstacle by organizing counties into regional groups. But even those considered local defence rather than cooperation in a national strategic plan to be their main function. The parliamentary Eastern Association of Norfolk, Suffolk, Essex, Cambridgeshire, and Hertfordshire established on 20 December 1642 under lord Grey of Warke refused to support the earl of Essex in the Thames Valley, and Oliver Cromwell's regiment in the Association was depleted because of the 'eronious opinion . . . of our unexperienced country soldiers that they ought not to be drawn or ledd . . . beyond the bounds of the five counties'.[48] Faced with these frustrations some on the parliamentary side (though not Pym) began to campaign for the replacement of Essex by Waller as the chief parliamentary general, in the belief that Essex was only concerned to reach a negotiated peace with the king. Pym instead, in an effort to develop an army responsive to central commands, supported two important Ordinances which were passed on 10 August 1643: an impressment Ordinance ending the reliance of the parliamentary armies on volunteers; and an Ordinance reorganizing the Eastern Association under the earl of Manchester who was empowered to impress 20,000 men. For the first time the army was given effective finance: the collection and spending of the assessment raised in the counties of the Eastern Association was to be organised by a central committee based at Cambridge under Manchester's control. Manchester also began to choose his officers more for their previous military experience than for their local affiliations and social origins. Significantly, though, he was not interested in mercenaries: immoral, though efficient, officers were expelled; 'godly' soldiers were promoted. All were welcomed, said Manchester, who 'love Christ in sincerity', though 'differing in judgement to what I profess'. With its new leader, a reorganized financial and administrative structure, and a high ratio of committed and professional officers the army of the Eastern Association was the most effective army to take the field so far in the civil war.

Pym's last contribution to the parliamentary cause was to secure a military alliance with the Scots. The difficulty was not in getting Scottish agreement: the Scots covenanters knew that the permanence of the 'Scottish Revolution' depended on the victory of the English parliament over the king. Within ten days of their arrival in Scotland on 7 August 1643 the English commissioners had reached agreement with the Scots and signed the Solemn League and Covenant. When the Covenant was brought before the English parliament for ratification, however, it met intense hostility, not only from ' peace group' MPs. English contempt for Scots and all things Scottish was not new; it was now reinforced by detestation of Scottish Presbyterianism which the Scots, with missionary zeal, hoped to bring to England. The ecclesiastical supremacy of the kirk in secular affairs was too reminiscent of Laudianism for most Englishmen of whatever religious persuasion. Significantly, before the alliance was ratified on 7 September, the English parliament deleted the description of the Scottish Church as being established 'according to the word of God'. Robert Baillie, one of the Scottish commissioners who came to England as a result of the alliance, was quite right: 'The English were for a civill League, we for a religious Covenant.' The differences were ominous, but temporarily were consigned to the Westminster Assembly. More importantly, they were overshadowed by confirmation of the king's Cessation Treaty made with the Irish rebels on 15 September 1643, and the acceptance of the committee of both kingdoms by parliament (the Lords finally approved it on 16 February 1644) cemented the Anglo-Scottish alliance.

The immediate fruit of the fiscal, administrative, and military innovations of 1643 was the crushing victory at Marston Moor on 2 July 1644 of the combined armies of the Scots, the Yorkshire troops of Sir Thomas Fairfax, and the army of the Eastern Association under Manchester and Cromwell over Prince Rupert and the earl of Newcastle. The royalist threat from the north east, which had been there since the beginning of 1643, was ended; Newcastle went into exile. But the battle was far from being the turning point in the war it is often said to have been. The royalists were still strong in the south-west where Prince Maurice and Hopton were assembling an army. The king was having no difficulty in holding out in Oxford against Essex. And the parliamentary euphoria after Marston Moor was soon dissipated by subsequent military failures.

Military deadlock, 1644

Why had a state of military deadlock been reached by the end of 1644 despite the parliamentary victory at Marston Moor? Part of the answer lies in the fact that neither side was able to maintain adequate communications with its army commanders in the field. Beset by conflicting advice the king gave his generals no clear directives. The committee of both kingdoms also proved ineffective in organizing coordinated military action. The members of the committee were split on the conduct of the war, and the command chain from the committee to the armies was too long; local army commanders were often left following a course dictated by local and personal considerations rather than the orders of the Westminster strategists.

In many ways, too, the parliamentary programme of 1643 proved inadequate. Though not totally effective (this varied naturally from area to area depending on the efficiency and incorruptibility of local officials) the yield from the new taxes compared favourably with that from traditional methods of taxation. What must have been a disappointment to the parliamentary leaders, however, was that the bulk of the receipts from taxation (apart from excise) never reached London, but was used locally. Sometimes the taxation revenue was not even seen by the local county treasurers but was requisitioned by garrisons and troop commanders in the areas it was collected. Dr Morrill calculates that only 2 per cent of the money raised before March 1645 in Cheshire left the county.[49] As a result money was not always channelled where it was needed most. Army pay in some regiments got into arrears and in 1644 and 1645 there were outbreaks of mutinies and disorders in the parliamentary armies, as well as cases of plundering and desertion, the first signs of army discontent that increased in scale and in political importance at the end of the civil war.

Nor did the military measures adopted in 1643 fully live up to the expectations their backers had of them. The programme of 1643 – impressment, the Scots alliance, reliance on the armies of Essex and the Eastern Association – proved to have serious drawbacks. Impressment was not designed to produce willing or manageable soldiers, a situation which was not improved by the poor rates of pay in the parliamentary armies. Foot soldiers were still only paid at the Elizabethan rates of 8*d* a day (against 1*s* 6*d* a day for dragoons and 2*s* a day for cavalry troopers). Desertion was therefore probably highest in the infantry regiments, and sometimes took place on a large scale. The earl of Bedford calculated that over half of his force deserted during the Sherborne campaign of September 1643.[50] One-tenth of five infantry regiments in the army of the Eastern Association ran away between 7 June and 1 October 1644.[51] Disease, especially typhus and other infectious diseases, probably accounted for even more losses than desertion, a generalization supported by evidence from European armies in the Thirty Years' War.[52]

Cromwell's claims that his regiments, not the Scottish army, won the battle of Marston Moor are naturally biased. However, there is some evidence to suggest that the Scottish army may have been a paper tiger in 1644. It was badly supplied; so much so that in January 1644 its general, Alexander Leslie earl of Leven, ordered it to march south into England to prevent it disintegrating in the Border counties. Nor did the army have a united nation behind it. Royalist support in Scotland, centred on the marquis of Montrose, was fostered (belatedly, as usual) by Charles, who in February 1644 appointed Montrose lieutenant-general of the king's forces in Scotland. In April Montrose's invasion failed, but Leven could never commit himself totally to an English campaign without looking back over his shoulder towards Scotland. In the autumn of 1644 his fears were realized when Montrose returned, joined a Scottish force which had returned from Ireland led by the earl of Antrim, and won a battle at Tippermuir on 1 September 1644. From now on the Scottish covenanters were fighting the war on two fronts: in the Highlands as well as in England. Equally seriously, the Anglo-Scottish alliance was shot through with distrust because of the religious differences between the two countries. The Scots made no secret of their disgust at the slowness of the Westminster Assembly in recommending the introduction in England of 'rigid' Scottish Presbyterianism. Meanwhile the English parliamentarians began to suspect that the Scots' military backwardness grew out of a desire to negotiate a peace with Charles in return for his acceptance of Scottish Presbyterianism. The alliance was soured, and the committee of both kingdoms rendered ineffective.

The events of the summer of 1644 also gave good reason for St John and his allies to doubt the wisdom of continuing Pym's policy of shielding Essex from the efforts of the 'war group' to get rid of him. Essex's remarkable decision, taken against the advice of the committee of both kingdoms and without the support of any other parliamentary force, to march westwards against Prince Maurice and Hopton, was fatal. As he marched further and further into enemy territory, with his supply lines stretched behind him, he found himself isolated in Cornwall. At Lostwithiel at the end of August his army was decimated and Essex forced to escape ignominiously in disguise, his military reputation in shreds. Equally ominously for the parliamentary cause the autumn of 1644 proved that the military effectiveness of the army of the Eastern Association was being undermined by politico-religious rifts within its ranks. Cromwell's firsthand experience on the Marston Moor campaign of the determination of the Scots to export their brand of Presbyterianism to England seems to have been at the root of his public quarrel with the Scottish major-general in the Eastern Association army, Lawrence Crawford, who accused Cromwell of purging his regiments of Presbyterians and packing them with 'such as were of the Independent judgement'. Cromwell's conversion to more militant religious radicalism undoubtedly frightened the earl of Manchester, which probably accounts for the earl's transformation by the autumn of 1644 from the dynamic, win-the-war general of the summer into the indecisive leader at the second battle of Newbury (27 October 1644). It would be wrong to swallow whole the charges of Manchester's ineptitude in failing to cash in on the parliamentary army's superiority in numbers at the battle. His enemies from the right (Essex) and left (Cromwell) wanted a scapegoat. Lack of finance, poor morale among the troops, a high level of desertion, and a divided strategy contributed to the military failure. But Manchester did not hide his conversion to a defensive military strategy and peace negotiations. 'If we beate the King 99 times', he said at the post mortem on the Newbury campaign, 'he would be King still, and his posterity, and we subjects still; but if he beate us but once we should be hang'd, and our posterity be undonne.'[53] By the end of 1644 the policies pursued by Pym and his political heirs lay in ruins. All semblance of unity among parliamentary supporters was gone: the quarrel between Cromwell and Manchester was bitterly fought out at Westminster. The victory hoped for by the 'middle' and 'war' groups seemed further away than ever.

The impact of the war

It is fairly commonly believed that, as long as they had the good fortune not to be recruited into one of the numerous armies, the civil war passed most people in England by. This is a view that historical research is bringing increasingly into doubt.[54] Of course, the extent to which individuals were affected by the war varied, depending for one thing on the proximity of their home to the fighting. Those, for example, who lived in East Sussex, out of the war zone, suffered much less than those in West Sussex where the bulk of the fighting was concentrated.[55] Yet as the war dragged on it became increasingly difficult for anyone, even those not directly affected by the fighting, to insulate their lives from the effects of the war.

Vastly increased taxation demands were one obvious offshoot of the war which hit everyone. As has been seen parliamentary war taxation represented a far heavier financial burden for all classes than any other previous taxation. Royalist administration was perhaps not quite so effective, but 'step by step the King kept pace with Parliament, introducing the same measures, overriding property rights without Parliamentary assent'.[56] The 'contribution' agreements (the royalist equivalent of weekly assessments) made with royalist-controlled areas represented a massive increase on earlier taxation levels. The £61,000 annual 'contribution' levied on royalist Oxfordshire was ten times bigger than the county's assessment for the parliamentary subsidy of 1641.

Great as was the impact of direct taxation it is highly likely that it was surpassed (as in those areas of northern Europe ravaged by the Thirty Years' War) by the cost of providing armies with free quarter and supplies, and by making good the damage to property done by ill-disciplined, ill-paid, plundering soldiers. Both sides freely billeted soldiers on civilians and requisitioned food, fuel, and horses in areas under their control. Constables of each village were supposed to record the cost of providing lodgings and meals to soldiers according to scales of compensation. From these records it is clear that the sums involved were very large and that, except in cases where they had caused severe hardship, they were seldom repaid. In Cheshire Dr Morrill estimates the cost to the county of providing free quarter may have been £120,000 as against a total of £100,000 raised in direct taxation during the war.[57] The cost of plunder by the armies of both sides is impossible to quantify. Both military and civilian authorities vainly tried to maintain discipline in their armies. Largely because the soldiers of both sides were ill-paid, petty thefts by passing bands of soldiers were common. More serious, if not as widespread, are the recorded instances of large-scale pillaging, carried out by troops usually after they had won a victory, when the generals proved unable to prevent their junior officers and rank-and-file taking their share of the spoils. Essex's army after the siege of Reading in April 1643, and Rupert's army after the siege of Bristol three months later, went on the rampage for days before normal military discipline was reimposed. Even this was overshadowed by the plunder and indiscipline of the royalist troops of Lord Goring – 'Goring's Crew' – in the south-western counties.

Apart from the effects on village economies of the loss of small husbandmen, craftsmen, and labourers by impressment, other economic effects of the war are less identifiable. To what extent can the war be blamed for the 'decay of trade' complained of in the 1640s? Certainly the fact that roads from London to Bristol and the West, and from London to the north-east, were controlled in places by royalist garrisons must have hit metropolitan trade, as well as disrupting more localized markets and trade. The economies of towns and villages in the war zones must have been hit, especially when a town was besieged and the suburbs demolished as the garrison retreated into a more defensible position inside the town.

It is not surprising that quite soon popular enthusiasm for the war, even where it existed, was converted to at best sullen apathy, or at worst open opposition to the manifestations of the war. The passive neutralism of 1642 (noted above) persisted: people 'swimming with the tide', obeying the power that happened to be stronger and then, apparently, 'changing sides' when the control of the locality changed from one side to the other. What are more interesting are the more militant expressions of anti-war opinions, in the early 1640s. It is only recently that the significance of this before 1645 has been recognized. But civilian protests at the war were a major factor both armies had to contend with even before the more well-known manifestation of anti-war opinion in 1645, the Clubman movement. Dr Ian Roy, for example, has documented the remarkable way in which armed groups of dairy farmers in Gloucestershire protected themselves against Prince Rupert's ill-disciplined troops after the fall of Bristol in the autumn of 1643. In September they even ambushed an eighty-strong royalist troop of 'crack cavalry', killing six of them.[58] Also in 1643 moderate gentry in Kent led a rebellion against the imposition of the Presbyterian covenant and high war taxation. There is no evidence that either the Gloucestershire farmers or the Kent gentry rebelled respectively for parliament or for the king. Their activities were essentially negative, neutralist, anti-war in character.

The impression that incidents like these were not uncommon even in the early part of the war must await confirmation. It is not until 1645 that there is strong evidence of widespread concerted civilian resistance to the armies of both sides by the Clubmen of central-southern and south-western counties of England and in South Wales, significantly areas with long histories of riots and disorder. Despite recent work on the Clubmen movement, there are a lot of questions still to be answered about it.[59] To what extent was it 'a movement' in terms of contacts between different groups? Were the Clubmen used and infiltrated by the politically-committed for their own ends? Fairly certainly most Clubman groups grew out of incidents of spontaneous civilian resistance to pillaging or outrages committed by soldiers of both sides. Thereafter the leadership passed often to men of gentry origins, who organized their followers, called mass meetings, and drew up resolutions to protect themselves from 'plunder and all other unlawful violence'. Both parliamentary and royalist armies were attacked by Clubmen in an effort to protect 'the peace of my country'. In fact, what is emerging from recent research is a vindication of the Clubmen's neutralist protestations: unlike the Clubmen of Dorset and Wiltshire, the Clubmen of Somerset allied with Fairfax and the New Model Army, but they did so because of the havoc and terror caused by 'Goring's Crew', not because they were parliamentarians. The Clubmen movement makes more sense, not as a crypto-parliament or crypto-royalist movement, but as a cry of resentment against the disruptive effects of war.

The end of the war, 1645–1646

Given the deadlocked military situation and parliamentary disunity at the end of 1644, the parliamentary victory in the civil war came remarkably quickly. In the summer of 1645 the New Model Army won what proved to be decisive battles at Naseby and Langport, and in the following spring Charles gave up the military struggle. The reorganiz-ation of the parliamentary armies in 1645 undoubtedly helped to bring about this transformation. But it is not the sole – or even perhaps the major – cause of the royalist defeat in the civil war.

Until the end of 1644 St John and the 'middle group' had held out against drastic reorganization of the parliamentary armies. But in November, when it became known that the Scots were offering to make peace with Charles on the basis of Scottish Presbyterianism, their growing disillusionment with the Scots alliance was complete. In December, too, there were indications that Essex and some of the leading 'peace group' MPs were willing to sink their religious differences with the Scots and accept the prospect of the unconditional return of the king in order to halt the religious radicalism of the Scots, and especially the influence of 'that darling of the sectaries', Cromwell. From now on, St John and his political allies had little alternative but to combine much more closely than hitherto with the 'war group' to advocate new measures to win the war: the removal of the discredited military leaders and the reorganization of the army. For a time it is difficult to identify specific 'middle group' policies, and the political activists at Westminster do seem (temporarily at least) to polarize into two groups, political 'Presbyterians' and political 'Independents'.

The completion of the military reorganization, however, did not take place until after the failure of another attempt to reach a settlement with the king. Many parliamentarians were no doubt sincere in their desire for peace, but it is difficult to see how the Uxbridge 'treaty' negotiations, which began at the end of January 1645, could have succeeded. The programme for a settlement offered by the parliamentary commissioners was an uncompromising one, and Charles was never the person to make compromises at the right time. The failure of the Uxbridge 'treaty' weakened the Lords' opposition and paved the way for the acceptance of the New Model Army Ordinance on 17 February and the Self-Denying Ordinance on 3 April. Many moderate MPs supported the latter in the belief that it would force the resignation from their military commands, not only of Manchester and Essex, but also of Cromwell. They were disappointed; but Cromwell owed his eventual promotion in June to the rank of Lieutenant General in the New Model Army to the military needs of the moment and not to his own Machiavellian guile. The New Model Army Ordinance merged the armies of Manchester, Essex, and Waller into an army of ten cavalry regiments (later another was added) of 600 men each, twelve foot regiments of 1,200 men, and one regiment of 1,000 dragoons. Fairfax was appointed its commander-in-chief and Philip Skippon its major-general.

There was not a great deal that was new about the New Model Army.[60] Manchester in the army of the Eastern Association, like Fairfax and Cromwell in the New Model, tried to use volunteers rather than conscripts wherever possible, on the grounds that pressed men make poor soldiers. Manchester also had promoted his officers for their military merit rather than their social rank. He would have agreed with Cromwell's often-quoted declaration that 'I had rather have a plain russett-coated captain that knows what he fights for, and loves what he knows, than that which you call a gentleman and nothing else'. There were, though, many pressed men in the New Model Army and many officers who owed their rank to social status rather than military ability. Nor were its creators totally successful in creating a 'new' army that was free of local ties and responsible solely to a centralized high command in the Derby House committee in London (as the successor of the committee of both kingdoms was known). The New Model Army was limited, like all the other parliamentary armies, by an uncertain division of control between the civilians at Derby House and Fairfax in the field, and by the difficulty of communicating orders from one to the other. What made the New Model Army distinctive was that it was better paid, and therefore better disciplined, than some other contemporary armies, largely because from March 1645 royalist composition fines were paid direct to Goldsmiths' Hall and not, as in the case of royalist sequestrations, swallowed up locally. Payments did get into arrears (with tremendous political results as will be seen), but the New Model Army was more regularly paid than other armies, and it is significant that when it went to the south-west in 1645 it attracted some Clubman support, because (in stark contrast to the royalist forces) it paid for its quarters. In the last resort the military success of the New Model Army may not lie in any distinctive ideological commitment, training, or discipline its soldiers may have had, but in the mundane fact that its commanders were careful never to enter a major engagement with the enemy unless their own forces were much greater in numbers. When the New Model Army won its famous victory at Naseby (near Leicester) on 14 June 1645 its forces were nearly double (14,000 against 7,500) those of the royalist army.

The concentration of historians on the New Model Army obscures the fact that there were other parliamentary armies in the field (Poyntz's army in the north and Massey's in the west, about which little is known) and that there were other important reasons for parliament's victory. What the formation of the New Model Army does not explain is why the victories at Naseby and Langport were a turning point in the civil war, while Marston Moor was not. The answer need not necessarily lie in the control by parliament of more wealthy parts of the country than the royalists, including especially the south-east and London; parliament had held these areas and resources since the beginning of the war. Ultimately it was not the possession of resources by each side that was crucial, but the uses to which they were put. In only one respect did the royalists employ their resources more efficiently than the parliamentarians: the use of propaganda, which was directed from Oxford by John Berkenhead. The royalist newspaper he edited weekly from January 1643 to September 1645, *Mercurius Aulicus*, was the envy of its parliamentary rivals. One of these, *Mercurius Britannicus*, in 1643 claimed that *Aulicus* 'had as exact intelligence from some of the close committee and both Houses as can be wished', and the Commons initiated an enquiry into how *Aulicus* knew 'some Things privately passed in the House?'[61] But propaganda – even brilliant, well-informed propaganda – was not enough to win the war. The decisive difference between the two sides was parliament's superior administrative and financial organization created by Pym. With all its defects this system extracted more money to be used as the parliamentary leadership wished than was sent to Oxford from 'contributions', sequestrations, loans, and the excise. Disunited as it was, the parliamentary committee of both kingdoms (and later the Derby House committee) was much more effective than the Oxford royalist council at war, to whose advice Charles did not always pay much attention, and which from October 1644 was split by violent differences between Digby and Prince Rupert over policy.

Consequently in the post-Naseby campaign the royalist army was at a grave disadvantage, short of money and supplies and beset by conflicting advice. The defeat of Goring at the battle of Langport (10 July) opened up the south-west to the New Model Army which was able to consolidate the victory in a way that had not been possible after Marston Moor. After the surrender of Bridgewater (23 July) and Bristol (11 September) Charles ordered the Prince of Wales, who was in nominal command in the south-west, to leave for France. Hopton still held out, but in March 1646 surrendered. In the north the crucial battle was at Rowton Heath (near Chester) on 24 September 1645; it prevented Charles from linking up with the Scots. In any case Montrose's defeat at Philiphaugh (13 September) had already weakened the chances of Scottish royalist support, and Charles fell back on Oxford, which finally fell to parliamentary forces on 24 June 1646. Before that Charles had recognized the inevitability of defeat: on 27 April he left Oxford in disguise. But the fact that he chose to surrender to the Scottish army in Nottinghamshire rather than to the parliamentary army indicated that, for Charles, the struggle with parliament was far from over.

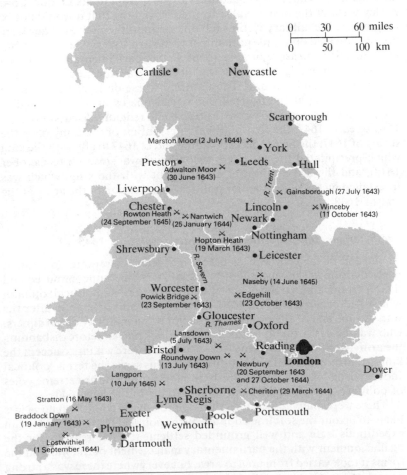

Map 2 The English Civil War 1642–1646: principal battles and garrison towns

The search for a settlement: king, parliament, the army, and the Scots, 1645–1649

Naseby and Langport marked decisive turning points in the first civil war. From the autumn of 1645 to December 1648 the attention of all the king's former military adversaries was centred on the constitutional and religious settlement to be made with the king. In explaining the failure of the search for such a settlement historians have rightly emphasized the important roles of Charles's continual refusal to negotiate seriously and the deep divisions among his opponents. But Charles's 'wait-and-see' political strategy, which is often condemned as foolish, did have a fair chance of success. The violence and radicalism produced by the war initiated an inevitable strong conservative reaction in his favour. Lord Astley was not the only royalist to predict, rightly, that it would not be long before the military victors fell out amongst themselves. They were not only divided on simple parliament *versus* army *versus* Scots lines, but there was little measure of agreement among parliamentarians, among soldiers or among Scotsmen on the means of transforming the military victory into a political one. The nature of these disagreements can be seen by looking at the four chronological phases of postwar English politics: the parliamentary constitutional and religious discussions from 1645 to early 1647; the first political intervention of the army from the spring of 1647; the Scots' decision at the end of 1647 to ally with the king which precipitated the so-called 'second civil war' (March to October 1648); and the last attempt at a settlement with the king, which was forestalled by the second major political intervention of the army at the end of 1648.

Presbyterians, Independents, and counter-revolution, 1645–47

At the end of the civil war (as before and later) there were no clearcut party divisions. The vast majority of MPs remained uncommitted and therefore uncataloguable. Yet the polarization of political opinion which had occurred in late 1644 to early 1645 still held good after the war. At one end of the political spectrum was a minority of hardliners, who wanted cast-iron limitations on Charles's power before disbanding the army; at the other extreme were those who were willing to accept the king's return with minimal conditions. In this sense the terms 'political Independents' and 'political Presbyterians' represent the extreme poles of political opinion among parliamentarians in the late 1640s.

There were many indications that opinion in the country at large was likely to favour the soft line adopted by the political Presbyterians for an expeditious 'safe and well grounded settlement'. The reasons for the disillusionment with the parliamentary management of the war and the forms it took varied from area to area, but everywhere there was a strong conservative reaction to the violence, high taxation, and disruption caused by the war which had already provoked the Clubmen movement, as has already been seen. The serious harvest failures and consequent high prices after the wet summers of 1646 and 1647 also resurrected fears of food and enclosure riots and an eagerness among the propertied classes for the restoration of political order. The assorted strands of anti-war sentiment came to be focused on the parliamentary county committees and the army. The county committees were the agents of the 'arbitrary' policies of parliament (the intrusion of central government into local affairs, high taxation, imprisonment without trial) which to many seemed identical with those adopted by Charles in the 1620s and 1630s. In addition, the county committees came to be infiltrated by men from outside the traditional ruling borough and county élites. The Isle of Wight county committee, sneered the snobbish royalist, Sir John Oglander, was dominated by 'Ringwood of Newport, the pedlar; Maynard, the apothecary; Matthews, the baker; Wavell and Legge, farmers, and poor Baxter of Hurst Castle'.[62] Too much, however, can be made of the low social origins and radicalism of the 'new men' (John Pyne in Somerset, Sir John Gell in Derbyshire, Anthony Weldon in Kent, Herbert Morley in Sussex, Sir William Brereton in Cheshire and Staffordshire, for example). They were not often members of the major magnate families, but nevertheless they were prosperous propertied gentry. And often their radicalism consisted only of subordinating local interests in favour of a more effective prosecution of the war. Sometimes, though, they were set apart from most of the traditional rulers of the country by their radical religious beliefs, their commitment to a 'godly reformation'. They and the county committees came to be an embattled minority in the face of (sometimes organized) county opinion for a return to the running of society as it was in prewar days. The army was an equally obvious target of the peace movement of 1645–7, especially when unrest in the army grew in scale towards and immediately after the end of the war. Dr Morrill found that by late summer 1646 twenty-two counties had reported cases of army mutinies, in addition to organized plundering by unpaid regiments who were now unemployed but still not disbanded.[63] By the end of the war the best-paid parliamentary army, the New Model, was owed £601,000 in arrears of pay. A conservative estimate of the total arrears due to all the parliamentary forces from 1642 to 1647 is around £2.8 m.[64] Not surprisingly, indiscipline in the army was rife. In July 1646 the Nantwich garrison threw members of the local sequestration committee into gaol until the county committee promised to do something about the garrison's arrears of pay. Incidents like this were frightening to the gentry, especially when the mutinies appeared to be led and organized from within the ranks and in defiance of the officers.

Two factors, however, frustrated the overwhelming desire for a return to the traditional political order. First, the split in the parliamentary ranks deepened, as from 1645 onwards, for the first time since 1640–1, the religious issue moved to the centre of the political stage at Westminster. Ever since 1640 any religious agreement among parliamentarians had been on the negative grounds of what to abolish, rather than on any constructive proposals. On the whole the divisions had been relegated to the Westminster Assembly of Divines, where a vocal minority, the Dissenting Brethren, had upheld the cause of religious toleration and Independency against majority support for Presbyterian uniformity. In January 1645 parliamentary approval was given for the abolition of the Book of Common Prayer and its substitution by the Presbyterian Directory of Worship. With the encouragement of the Scottish representatives, however, the Westminster divines also came out in favour of the Scottish system of appointing elders and ministers by the Church authorities not the state. This was obviously anathema to most English MPs who considered that its logical outcome was that 'the whole nobility, gentry, and Commons must be brought under the power of the clergy'.[65] As a result the Ordinance establishing Presbyterianism in England (finally approved by the Lords in March 1646) gave parliament the supreme voice in Church affairs. 'A lame Erastian Presbytery' the Scot, Robert Baillie called it. But the unity of most English MPs extended only as far as a hatred of Scottish Presbyterianism and support for a parliamentary controlled state Church. The key controversial issue was how extensive should be the interference of state control in the doctrinal and liturgical practices of individual congregations. Support for some measure of toleration was not confined to the Dissenting Brethren and those sects who were already establishing their independent gathered churches. Fast-day sermons to parliament proposing limited toleration in 1646 and 1647 were received sympathetically.[66] Former 'middle group' men like St John were in contact with Cromwell who made no secret of his pro-toleration views. 'He that ventures his life for the liberty of his country, I wish he trust God for the liberty of his conscience, and you for the liberty he fights for,' he wrote to the Speaker of the Commons after Naseby.[67] St John and other middle group men were perhaps not willing to go as far as Cromwell, but, as St John's commonplace book shows, he was in favour of some measure of toleration.[68] Parliament's failure to present a united front on its proposals for a religious settlement seriously hindered the prospects of agreement with the king. More seriously, so too did the mistrust of Charles's sincerity which was confirmed by the publication of the Naseby and Digby 'cabinets', the captured correspondence of the king and Digby, which revealed the king's treacherous negotiations with the Irish and other foreign powers during the Oxford and Uxbridge 'treaties'. This was enough to enable the political Independents to ensure that the Propositions of Newcastle, which were sent to the king in July 1646, represented no 'sell-out', and that they would be unacceptable to Charles.

The growing chorus of demands in 1646 from all parts of the country for the reduction of high taxation, the demobilization of much of the army, and the abolition of the county committees, however, ensured that the political initiative was held by the political Presbyterians.

During the winter of 1646–7 they began, under Holles's guidance, to advocate a consistent programme: demobilize the army, keeping only a smaller force for service in Ireland; create an alternative 'safe' army, based on the London trained bands purged of Independents; and reach a settlement with the king on the basis of a revised version of the Newcastle Propositions. It was this attempted 'counter-revolution' that provoked the political intervention of the army.

The army and the Levellers, 1647

As has been seen, the parliamentary armies had a lot to complain about at the end of the civil war. Their wage arrears amounted to nearly £3 m; it was likely that most regiments would be disbanded before these arrears were settled; and for some officers there was the prospect of being found guilty of treasonable acts committed during the war. These material grievances were the dominant motive behind the army mutinies of 1646 and 1647. But at some stage in 1647 radical ideological religious and political demands became inextricably bound up with the army's professional grievances. Both the timing and significance of this process are unclear.[69] Baxter was horrified to find in Cromwell's army after Naseby 'a new face of things which I never dreamt of. I heard the plotting heads very hot upon that which intimated their intention to subvert both Church and State.' Even though there were 'but a few proud, self-conceited, hot-headed sectaries', they were 'Cromwell's chief favourites, and by their very heat and activity bore down the rest . . . and were the soul of the army'.[70] Yet probably for most soldiers bread-and-butter issues continued throughout to be the most important reason for their determination to resist parliament. The sophistication of the political and religious ideas discussed, in any case, was probably beyond the majority of rank and file soldiers, who were probably as anxious as their social betters for a return to prewar order in politics and society. Nevertheless in the face of the growing conservatism of parliament the army began in the spring of 1647 to put forward ideological, as well as material, demands, and to establish links with the radical movement in London.

The capital was a hothouse for the growth of radical ideas in the 1640s. Hierarchical social discipline was much laxer than in many rural areas (especially arable); and the economic dislocation caused by the war was felt very severely in London. During the war years the radical movement was probably not as well organized as it was later, but it had thrown up a trio of influential pamphleteers, John Lilburne, Richard Overton, and William Walwyn, who, despite differences in temperament and religious beliefs, had in common a disillusionment with the failure of the Long Parliament and the Westminster Assembly to bring about 'a godly reformation'. The titles of some of their pamphlets alone express this; Lilburne's *London's Liberty in Chains* (November 1646), Overton's *An Arrow against all Tyrants* (October 1646), and Walwyn's

England's Lamentable Slaverie (October 1645). Inevitably their demands for greater political and religious liberty were not popular with the parliamentary and City authorities, but repressions and imprisonments only stimulated the Levellers to organize themselves and to demand economic, legal, educational, as well as political and religious reforms. 'Wee still find the Nation oppressed with grievances of the same destructive nature as formerly though under other notions', said the Leveller Large Petition (March 1647). Arbitrary judicial power was exercised, not by star chamber, but by parliament; religious nonconformists were oppressed, not by bishops, but by Presbyterian clergy. The law and penal system were unreformed; tithes and monopolies still in existence; and 'thousands of men and women are permitted to live in beggery and wickednesse all their life long'. Not surprisingly, the Commons ordered the petition to be burned.

The timing and the extent of the link between the London radicals and the discontented elements in the army is uncertain. A pamphlet of 26 March 1647, *An Apollogie of the Soldiers*, protested at the imprisonment of 'those honest people [Lilburne and Overton] who have shown themselves with us'.[71] But the Leveller infiltration of the army does not seem to have been significant before May, and before then the army was forced by the intransigence of parliament to adopt more extreme demands. On 18 February the Commons decided to reduce the army to only 5,400 horses and 1,000 dragoons, and on 8 March voted that only Presbyterians and non-MPs should be officers in the new army. Despite negotiations between parliamentary commissioners and army officers at Saffron Walden in March and April, the army petition of 21 March was condemned as treasonable, unpopular Presbyterian generals (Skippon and Massey, not Cromwell and Fairfax) were appointed to lead the army to Ireland, and the City authorities were allowed to purge the London trained bands of Independents. In the face of this provocation eight militant cavalry regiments at the end of April elected 'agitators' to represent their views. The final breach between the mutinous army and parliament came in May. On 18 May the Commons accepted the king's third reply to the Propositions of Newcastle, in which Charles conceded Presbyterianism for three years and parliamentary control of the militia for ten years, as the basis for reopening negotiations. With the prospect of a settlement before them, the Presbyterian leaders decided to break with the army. On 25 May the Commons voted to disband the New Model infantry regiments with only eight weeks' arrears of wages paid. Four days later Fairfax ordered a general rendezvous of the army at Newmarket, and on 2 June Cornet Joyce seized the king from his parliamentary guards at Holmby House (Northamptonshire) and took him to Newmarket.

The army had now committed itself to political action, and all the indications are that it was done on rank-and-file initiative and that the officers had to choose between following or resigning their posts. Joyce's capture of the king is a case in point. As Christopher Hill points out, Cromwell, who had now thrown in his lot with the army again, knew of Joyce's plans, but there is no evidence that he initiated them.[72] The army's *Humble Remonstrance* (4 June) agreed that the army should not disband until its grievances were met. In the meantime an army council was to sit, consisting of two commissioned officers and two 'agitator' privates from each regiment. Slowly the army began to march towards London, rejecting parliament's minor concessions. In a development unique among sixteenth- and seventeenth-century European armies the New Model Army now became politicized. Although in continental armies mutinies about wage arrears and poor conditions were common, none developed into a political movement. On 5 June the New Model Army announced in *A Solemn Engagement* that it refused to disband until its grievances were met. Nine days later in *A Representation of the Army*, drafted by Ireton, Cromwell, and Lambert at St Albans, the army announced that it was 'not a mere mercenary Army', but a political force with a political programme: a purge of the present parliament; future parliaments of fixed duration; guaranteed right of the people to petition parliament; liberty of tender consciences. They were an army dedicated to 'the defence of our own and the people's just rights and liberties'.[73]

Despite these ringing declarations, it soon became clear that the army (like the parliamentarians) was not united in its aims. The differences between senior army officers such as Cromwell, Ireton, and Lambert, and NCO and rank-and-file opinion became clear in the debates (in the army council at Reading) on a draft of *The Heads of the Proposals*, which it was intended to present to the king. *The Heads* did bow to Leveller-agitator opinion in promising reforms to the excise, monopolies, tithes, and the law. The proposed checks on the king were severe: permanent parliamentary approval of the king's ministers, and parliamentary control of the militia for ten years. And, dramatically, the *Heads* advocated religious toleration for all except Catholics. However, biennial parliaments and a redistribution of seats according to taxation assessments were not sweeping enough for the agitators, who wanted to ensure popular control of future parliaments. Agitator suspicions were also alerted by Cromwell's negotiations with Charles at Caversham (near Reading), and they called for an immediate march on London.

Events in London soon forced the army leaders to agree. Although London was the main centre of radical Levellerism, the extent of the support for Leveller ideas in the capital can be exaggerated. The conservative reaction which swept the country after the civil war also made a deep impression on many in London who were as anxious as anyone for a return to political normality. Many believed that this was the major remedy for 'the decay of trade'. Conservative popular sentiment, as well as fear, since the army singled out him and ten other political Presbyterians ('the Eleven Members') for impeachment, encouraged Holles and his colleagues to step up their plans for a Presbyterian counter-revolution. At the end of July their plans culminated in a series of organized popular demonstrations in favour of peace and settlement, and against a Militia Bill designed to restore Independents to the London militia. On 26 July, apparently with the connivance of Holles, Waller, and Sir John Clotworthy,[74] a mob invaded the chamber of the Commons and forced the House to pass a resolution inviting the king to come to London. Eight days later the army assembled on Hounslow Heath. Significantly, the political Independent MPs joined it, rather than support the Presbyterian sell-out to the king. On 6 August the army, without any resistance, occupied Westminster, and on 8 August the City.

With parliament under their control and sole political power in their hands, the army leaders found the search for a settlement no easier than had parliament. The rifts in the army ranks, which had been apparent at Reading, opened up again in London, as radical opinion quickly became disillusioned with the results of the occupation of the capital. The 'grandees', senior army officers, began to negotiate with the king, despite his rejection of the *Heads*. The expulsion of the Eleven Members was confirmed, but the radicals' demand for a purge of all those MPs who had continued to sit after 26 July was ignored. The Leveller heroes, Lilburne and Overton, remained in prison and nothing was done to meet any of the Leveller demands. To add fuel to the radicals' sense of grievance, food prices rocketed after another disastrous wet summer. *The Case of the Army Truly Stated* (18 October), said to have been drafted by newly elected, more militant agitators, was a swingeing indictment of the 'grandees' for their backsliding, urging them to adopt the radical religious and constitutional programme of the Levellers. These proposals were set out in the *Agreement of the People*, probably written by the civilian Leveller leaders in the names of the army agitators, and was ready for discussion by the Army Council at Putney at the end of October.

The view of the famous Putney debates (28, 29 October and 1 November) as a head-on confrontation between the conservative 'grandees' and the radical Levellers and agitators has been blurred by recent studies. What has emerged from the protracted controversy among historians as to the extent of the Leveller commitment to complete democracy is that individual Levellers differed: some were more prepared than others to accept the exclusion from the franchise of certain social groups.[75] What is more important is that few Levellers had probably ever bothered to work out exactly the technical details of an extended, reformed franchise. Even the existing franchise was too complex for many to master, so that, as Dr Hirst says, the 'speakers at Putney did not always know what they were talking about'.[76] All this, though, must not obscure the huge gulf between the 'grandees' and agitators that was revealed at Putney. In the long, involved discussions on the nature of the 'engagements' entered into by the army in May and June the 'grandee' representative indicated that they were not interested in the wide-ranging constitutional changes which some Levellers hoped for. The exchange between the army Leveller, Colonel Thomas Rainsborough, and Ireton has lost none of its significance in illustrating this point:[77]

Rainsborough: For really I think that the poorest he that is in England hath a life to live as the greatest he; and therefore truly, sir, I think it's clear, that every man that is to live under a government ought first by his own consent to put himself under that government; and I do think that the poorest man in England is not at all bound in a strict sense to that government that he hath not had a voice to put himself under . . .

Ireton: . . . I think that no person hath a right to an interest or share in the disposing of the affairs of the kingdom, and in determining or choosing those that shall determine what laws we shall be ruled by here – no person hath a right to this, that hath not a permanent fixed interest in this kingdom.

Clearly some Levellers had moved into areas where 'grandees' would never follow.

Whether or not Cromwell engineered the escape of Charles I from Hampton Court on 11 November is uncertain: it certainly suited his and his fellow officers' purposes. In the face of the renewed threat posed by the king, the army closed ranks. Leveller dissatisfaction at the failure to get the support of the 'grandees' for the *Agreement of the People* at Putney produced only a ripple of opposition in the army. At Corkbush Field near Ware (Hertfordshire) on 15 November a Leveller-inspired mutiny in two regiments was crushed efficiently and brutally, but also easily. Discussions on religious and constitutional issues were temporarily abandoned. The army was united behind the 'grandees' on a programme of securing a settlement of their wage arrears and the defeat of another wave of counter-revolution.

Charles, the Scots, and the second civil war

After his escape Charles deliberately chose to ally with the Scots in preference to resuming negotiations with the English parliament: at the end of December he rejected the Four Bills sent to him by parliament before his escape, and he concluded an 'Engagement' with the Scots, promising to establish Scottish Presbyterianism in England for three years. The Engagement represented a victory for a conservative faction in Scotland led by the marquis of Hamilton, who from the beginning had questioned the wisdom of allying with the English parliament. Now these doubts were confirmed by the victory of the anti-Presbyterian army in England, and radical Covenanters, like Argyll and Johnston of Wariston, who had supported the alliance, consequently lost a great deal of influence in Scotland. In England Charles's rebuff to parliament enabled the radicals in January 1648 to push through a parliamentary vote that 'the Lords and Commons do declare that they will make no further addresses or applications to the King'.

The finality of this vote was blunted by the continuing evidence that the prevailing sentiment of the majority in England was in favour of a settlement, a return to prewar order in society and government. The reasons had been apparent since 1645, as has been seen, and were reinforced by the events of 1647. Dislike of high taxation, centralization, arbitrary rule by low-born county committeemen, disorders provoked by the army, recurred in the county petitions received by parliament in the first part of 1648. In south Wales and in the heavily taxed south-eastern counties of Essex and Kent this desire for a return to traditional forms of government exploded in April, May, and June into a series of rebellions against parliament and its county committees. Off the Kentish coast the parliamentary navy revolted against its Leveller admiral, Rainsborough, and reinstated its old Presbyterian com-manders. In the north the major garrisons were taken over by pro-royalist forces. Generally, though, there is little evidence of ardent royalist fervour among the rebels of 1648. Like the Clubmen of 1645 they were more concerned to demonstrate their dislike of outside interference in local affairs. This series of uncoordinated risings hardly deserves being called a war. The superior coordinated forces of the New Model Army (Hardress Waller in Cornwall, Cromwell in south Wales, and John Lambert in the north) soon restored army control. The Scottish invasion, too, when it came early in July proved a minor threat. The weakness of the Scottish army reflected the internal divisions in Scotland; it was badly led by Hamilton and ill-supplied. Cromwell's victory at a series of battles round Preston (Lancashire) from 17 to 19 August paved the way for Hamilton's surrender on 25 August, and Cromwell's expedition to Scotland, where he allied with the enemies of the 'Engagers', Argyll and Johnston of Wariston. Pontefract in Yorkshire held out until March 1649, but by October 1648 the 'war' was over.

The 1648 risings and the Scottish invasion reunited the army, but widened the gap between it and most parliamentarians. Whereas to many in the army (though not yet all) Charles was a 'man of blood' and therefore a settlement with him inconceivable, the longing of most people outside the army for a treaty with the king had increased. Even the former 'middle group' MPs who had supported the army in 1647 (Professor Pearl calls them the 'royal Independents')[78] now broke with the army and supported the movement in parliament for a reconciliation with the king in the summer and autumn of 1648: the revocation of the Vote of No Addresses, the readmittance of the Eleven Members, and the preparation of proposals to be put to the king at Newport on the Isle of Wight in September.

1648–1649: the English Revolution

The English Revolution – the purge of parliament in December 1648 and the trial and execution of the king in January 1649 – was carried out by a tiny clique against the wishes of the vast majority in the country. By October 1648 this clique included Ireton among the 'grandees' (though not yet Cromwell, who was in the north), rank-and-file supporters of the agitators in the army, civilian republicans, like Henry Marten and Edmund Ludlow, in parliament, and their militant supporters in the counties, like John Pyne the 'boss' of the Somerset county committee. On 18 November Ireton persuaded the army council (now shorn of the agitators) to accept his *Remonstrance of the Army*, calling for a purge of parliament and the king's trial, under the threat that the Newport negotiations were going to succeed: indeed on 15 November the Commons had voted to accept Charles's request to come to London. Also early in November Ireton began negotiations with the civilian Leveller leaders, which culminated in the so-called Whitehall Debates early in December. The Debates revealed grave differences between Levellers and 'grandees' on the extent of religious toleration desirable, as well as on constitutional issues as seen at Putney earlier. But they did ensure, temporarily, Leveller support for the army's slow march on London. Ironically, the Newport proposals were finally rejected by Charles at the same time as the army entered Whitehall for the second time on 2 December.

Obstinately the Commons continued to discuss the Newport treaty, and on 5 December actually voted, by 129 to 83 votes, to continue the negotiations with the king. Army retaliation was inevitable; the only hesitation appears to have been on the question of a purge or a dissolution of parliament. Wisely, Ludlow advised Ireton against a dissolution and new elections, which would only have ensured the return of another set of MPs hostile to the army. In the Purge, which began on the morning of 6 December when colonel Pride and lord Grey of Groby stood at the door of the Commons, about 110 MPs were forcibly excluded and about 260 other MPs voluntarily withdrew (of the latter about a hundred returned after February 1649). The next major step, the trial of the king, was only decided on after a fierce rearguard debate by Cromwell, who returned to London on 6 December, but by the end of December he was converted to the view that negotiations with Charles could not succeed. From then on the execution of the king (30 January 1649), despite the weak legal arguments used by the prosecution at his trial, was inevitable.

The fact that the events of December 1648 to January 1649 were carried out by a minority drawn largely from outside the traditional ruling élite in England and against the wishes of that élite goes a long way towards explaining the eventual failure of the new English Republic. Yet, paradoxically, the history of the Republic confirms that only a limited political revolution had taken place in 1648–9, and one that was reversed in 1660. The basic structure of society remained unaffected. Yet it is surely semantic quibbling to deny the unique revolutionary nature of the abolition of episcopacy, monarchy, and the House of Lords, the involvement in politics of masses of people from outside the normal political sphere, and the ventilation of radical ideas of universal importance in the late 1640s. What was done was not as wide-ranging as the Russian Revolution or as permanent as the French Revolution, but if there ever has been an English Revolution it surely took place from December 1648 to January 1649.

Notes

For abbreviations used throughout see p. xiv.

1. See R. C. Richardson, *The Debate on the English Revolution* (1977), for an excellent survey from the seventeenth century to the present day. See also L. Stone, *The Causes of the English Revolution, 1529–1642* (1972), chs 1 and 2.
2. See pp. 40–1 and the Bibliographical Note, pp. 465–7, 468–9.
3. Derek Hirst, *The Representative of the People? Voters and voting in England under the early Stuarts* (1975), *passim*.
4. Quoted in Anthony Fletcher, *A County Community at Peace and War: Sussex 1600–1650* (1975), p. 251; and Anthony Fletcher, *The Outbreak of the English Civil War 1640–43* (forthcoming). I am grateful to Anthony Fletcher for allowing me to read sections of this book in typescript.
5. H. R. Trevor-Roper, 'Three foreigners: the philosophers of the Puritan Revolution' in his *Religion, the Reformation and Social Change* (1967), pp. 237–93 and 'The fast sermons of the Long Parliament' in his *Essays in British History* (1964), pp. 85–138; P. Christianson, 'From expectation to militance: reformers and Babylon in the first two years of the Long Parliament', *J. Eccl. H.*, XXIV (1973), pp. 225–44; J. F. Wilson, *Pulpit in Parliament* (1969); E. W. Kirby, 'Sermons before the Commons', *American H.R.*, XLIV (1938–9), pp. 528–48. From its first meeting the Long Parliament ordered that occasional days should be set aside as fast days. Beginning on 23 February 1642 regular fasts were held on the last Wednesday of every month, when two preachers invited by the Commons delivered sermons, one in the morning and one in the afternoon.
6. Gardiner, *History*, IX, p. 224.
7. Only two major grievances were not dealt with in the first session of the Long Parliament. Purveyance was declared illegal in December 1642, and the court of wards and liveries and all feudal tenures were formally abolished in February 1646.
8. Clarendon, *History*, I, pp. 280–2. See Clayton Roberts, 'The earl of Bedford and the coming of the English Revolution', *J.M.H.*, XLIX (1977) pp. 59–76.
9. Conrad Russell, 'Parliament and the king's finances', in Conrad Russell, ed., *The Origins of the English Civil War* (1973), pp. 111–13.
10. See J. H. Hexter's brilliant exposition of the work of Pym in his *The Reign of King Pym* (1941).
11. Naturally the evidence for this is not very clear: if the demonstrations were organized, those responsible were hardly likely to do so openly. Therefore, it is possible to argue that the marches of apprentices and others at this time were spontaneous.
12. Quoted in Fletcher, *The Outbreak* (forthcoming).
13. If anyone was in control of the direction of affairs in the Commons at this time it was Pym, but it is possible to exaggerate the size of his following and the extent of his influence in the House.
14. Derek Hirst, 'The defection of Sir Edward Dering 1640–41', *H.J.*, XV

(1972), pp. 193–208; W. Lamont, *Godly Rule: politics and religion 1603–60* (1969), pp. 83–93.

15. J. P. Cooper, 'The fall of the Stuart monarchy' in *The New Cambridge Modern History*, IV; *1609–48/59* (1970), pp. 571–2; Gardiner, *Constitutional Documents*, p. 167; Anthony Fletcher, 'Concern for renewal in the Root and Branch debates of 1641', in D. Baker, ed., *Studies in Church History*, XIV (1977), pp. 279–86.

16. Quoted in J. S. Morrill, *Cheshire 1603–60. County Government during the 'English Revolution'* (1974), p. 35.

17. Quoted in *ibid.*, *Cheshire*, p. 50.

18. The Propositions are printed in Gardiner, *Constitutional Documents*, pp. 163–6.

19. For a slightly different view see J. S. Morrill, *The Revolt of the Provinces: conservatives and radicals in the English Civil War 1630–50* (1976), pp. 34–5.

20. Quoted in G. Donaldson, *Scotland: James V to James VII* (1965), p. 328.

21. R. Baillie, *The Letters and Journal of Robert Baillie* (3 vols, 1841), II, p. 373.

22. Robin Clifton, 'The fear of popery' in Conrad Russell, ed., *The Origins of the English Civil War* (1973), pp. 165–6; J. T. Cliffe, *The Yorkshire Gentry from the Reformation to the Civil War* (1969), p. 329.

23. W. H. Coates, ed., *The Journal of Sir Simonds D'Ewes* (1942), pp. 104, 244–5.

24. John Rushworth, *Historical Collections* (1659–1701), IV, p. 425.

25. The king's answer to the petition accompanying the Grand Remonstrance, 23 December 1641, in Gardiner, *Constitutional Documents*, p. 235.

26. V. Pearl, *London and the Outbreak of the Puritan Revolution: city government and national politics 1625–43* (1961), especially, pp. 132–45.

27. Fletcher, *Sussex*, pp. 54–5.

28. Quoted in B. Manning, 'The outbreak of the English civil war' in R. H. Parry, ed., *The English Civil War and After 1642–58* (1970), p. 11.

29. Fletcher, *Sussex*, p. 210.

30. Kenyon, *Stuart Constitution*, p. 23.

31. Lucy Hutchinson, *The Life of Colonel Hutchinson* (1973 ed), p. 54.

32. D. Underdown, *Somerset in the Civil War and Interregnum* (Newton Abbott 1973), pp. 31–41; C. Holmes, *The Army of the Eastern Association in the English Civil War* (1974), pp. 35–6.

33. Richard Baxter, *Autobiography* (1974 ed), p. 34. For the apparently strong connection in the seventeenth century between regions of forest and pastoral economies and dissent and radicalism see pp. 69, 424.

34. E.g. D. Brunton and D. H. Pennington, *Members of the Long Parliament* (1954).

35. Underdown, *Somerset in the Civil War and Interrregnum*, p. 39.

36. Quoted in Holmes, *Eastern Association*, p. 44.

37. Quoted in Cliffe, *Yorkshire Gentry*, p. 341.

38. Quoted in Holmes, *Eastern Association*, p. 44.

39. Denzil Holles, *Memoirs* in F. Maseres, ed., *Select Tracts Relating to the Civil Wars in England* (1815), p. 191.

40. Quoted in Underdown, *Somerset in the Civil War and Interrregnum*, p. 41.

41. M. Judson, *The Crisis of the Constitution* (1949), chs 9 and 10.

42. Quoted in Judson, *Crisis*, p. 431.

43. Hirst, *The Representative*, p. 157.

44. See the Bibliographical note for the major contributions to this debate.

45. Among recent historians only L. Mulligan (née Glow) and J. R. MacCormack deny the existence of a 'middle group'.
46. Clarendon, *History*, III, p. 492.
47. D. H. Pennington and I. Roots, eds, *The Committee at Stafford 1643–5* (1957), p. lxi.
48. Quoted in Holmes, *Eastern Association*, p. 85.
49. Morrill, *Cheshire*, p. 100.
50. Underdown, *Somerset in the Civil War and Interregnum*, pp. 41–2.
51. Holmes, *Eastern Association*, p. 168.
52. L. A. Clarkson, *Death, Disease and Famine in Pre-Industrial England* (1975), pp. 222–4.
53. J. Bruce, ed., *The Quarrel between the Earl of Manchester and Oliver Cromwell*, Camden Society, new series, XII (1875), p. 93.
54. For a statement of the view that the economic effects of the war were slight see A. M. Everitt, *The Local Community and the Great Rebellion* (H. A. pamphlet 1969), pp. 24–6. For a different view which I have followed here see Ian Roy, 'The English civil war and English society', in Brian Bond and Ian Roy, eds, *War and Society: a Yearbook of Military History* (1975), pp. 24–43; and Ian Roy, 'England turned Germany? The aftermath of the civil war in its European context', *T.R.H.S.*, 5th ser., XXVIII (1978), pp. 127–44.
55. Fletcher, *Sussex*, p. 270.
56. Ian Roy, 'The English civil war and English society', p. 29.
57. Morrill, *Cheshire*, p. 108.
58. Ian Roy, 'The English civil war and English society', pp. 35–42.
59. There is no detailed published study of the Clubmen. A good starting point is Morrill, *Revolt*, pp. 98–111 and 222–3 note 23.
60. Mark Kishlansky, 'The case of the army truly stated: the creation of the New Model Army', *P.&P.*, LXXXI (1978), pp. 51–74, and his forthcoming book *The Rise of the New Model Army*.
61. P. W. Thomas, *Sir John Berkenhead 1617–79: a Royalist career in politics and polemics* (1969), pp. 41–4.
62. F. Bamford, ed., *A Royalist's Notebook* (1936), pp. 110–11.
63. J. S. Morrill, 'Mutiny and discontent in English provincial armies 1645–7', *P. & P.*, LVI (1972), p. 53.
64. Ian Gentles, 'The arrears of pay of the parliamentary army at the end of the 1st civil war', *B.I.H.R.*, XLVIII (1975), p. 55.
65. Quoted in V. Pearl, 'The "Royal Independents" in the English civil war', *T.R.H.S.*, 5th ser., XVIII (1968), p. 92.
66. W. Haller, *Liberty and Reformation in the Puritan Revolution* (1955), pp. 247–9.
67. W. Abbott, ed., *Writings and Speeches of Oliver Cromwell* (4 vols, 1937–47), I, p. 360.
68. V. Pearl, 'Oliver St John and the "middle group" in the Long Parliament', *E.H.R.*, LXXXI (1966), pp. 500–1.
69. The best modern account is Ian Gentles, 'Arrears of pay and ideology in the army revolts of 1647', in Bond and Roy, eds, *War and Society*.
70. Baxter, *Autobiography*, p. 49.
71. G. E. Aylmer, ed., *The Levellers in the English Revolution* (1975), pp. 75–81 (the Large Petition), pp. 22–3.
72. C. Hill, *God's Englishman: Oliver Cromwell and the English Revolution* (1970), pp. 88–9.

73. A. S. P. Woodhouse, ed., *Puritanism and Liberty, Being the Army Debates, 1647–9* (2nd ed, 1974), pp. 401–3 (A Solemn Engagement), 403–9 (A Representation of the Army).
74. V. Pearl, 'London's counter-revolution' in G. E. Aylmer, ed., *The Interregnum: the quest for settlement 1646–60* (1973), p. 52.
75. See Keith Thomas, 'The Levellers and the franchise' in Aylmer, ed., *Interregnum*, pp. 57–78 for a survey and judicious conclusion to this debate.
76. Hirst, *The Representative*, p. 22.
77. Woodhouse, pp. 55–6.
78. V. Pearl, 'The "Royal Independents"', *T.R.H.S.*, XVIII (1968), pp. 69–96.

Chapter 7

The retreat from revolution, 1649–1660

Conservative, propertied opinion in England was horrified by the events of the last weeks of 1648 and the first weeks of 1649. But a radical minority, especially those in the army and among the religious sects, wanted to follow up the limited political revolution of 1648–9 with sweeping legal, social, and religious changes. The great need, therefore, of the republican regimes of the 1650s was to find policies that would both satisfy the demands of the army and the sects for further reform and the desire of the pre-civil war rulers of the counties and boroughs of England for a return to stability. Major efforts were made to find such policies from 1649 to 1658: by the Commonwealth governments of the Rump parliament from 1649 to April 1653; by the Barebones Parliament which met from July to December 1653; and during the Cromwellian Protectorate from December 1653 until Cromwell's death in September 1658. In this 'quest for settlement' Oliver Cromwell played a dominating part, not least because his character embraced both divergent trends of the Revolution, the radical and conservative. Each attempt failed: few others had Cromwell's capacity to be sympathetic both to those wanting reform and those wanting a return to normality. Yet the regimes of the 1650s ruled more successfully and came nearer than is often realized to achieving a permanent political-constitutional framework which would comprehend revolutionary radicalism and conservative traditionalism. It is important to try to understand the reasons for the eventual failure of the Commonwealth and Protectorate regimes; but it is equally important that their achievements should not be overlooked.

The search for a 'godly reformation'

The civil war and its aftermath released radical demands that were far removed from the moderate, constitutional aims of many parliament-arians of 1640–2. In the beginning conservatives and 'middle group' politicians had been willing to use popular radicalism for their own immediate political purposes. But soon most of the parliamentary leaders at Westminster, and the gentry rulers in the localities, shied away in horror from the extreme ideas which had been allowed to flourish by their initial tolerance and by the collapse of the old political order. From 1640 until the early 1650s parliamentary ordinances attempting to suppress pamphlets and books were largely ineffective; the state as well as the Church was in no position to clamp down on the free expression of opinion as it had done before 1640 and as Cromwell was to do after 1655. The collection of pamphlets made in the 1640s and 1650s by a London bookseller, George Thomason, is a good indicator of the quantity of material printed in those two decades. Although he did not get his hands on everything published, Thomason, a fanatically keen bibliophile, collected over 18,000 items between 1640 and 1655, after which the flow diminished; between 1655 and 1660 he collected over 3,000 printed works. The Thomason Collection, which is still intact in the British Library, is a monument to the intellectual activity released by the English Revolution, from the lively, scurrilous, and libellous, to the serious, highminded, and academic. It also gives a unique insight into the normally unrecorded beliefs and aspirations of ordinary men and women.

The reforming and radical ideas which flourished in the ideal climate of the 1640s and early 1650s do not fall easily into separate neatly labelled categories, 'economic', 'social', 'religious', 'political'. Individual thinkers and writers moved easily from one topic to another. Samuel Hartlib, for example, appears in the catalogue of the Thomason Collection as the author of tracts on many subjects including Church reform, agriculture, medicine, and the creation of a Utopia called Macaria.[1] Even the Levellers, who in the winter of 1647–8, developed an unusually elaborate internal organization, included people with different views on a wide range of topics. Individual Levellers differed not only on the exact nature of the franchise (as has been seen), but also on religious doctrine: Lilburne for most of his life was an orthodox Calvinist predestinarian: Walwyn propounded the doctrine, often known as antinomianism, that God's grace and salvation were potentially available to all believers. Nor did Leveller pamphlets concentrate solely on demands for political and religious liberty for the individual, but covered a wide range of topics from proposals for prison reform to the evils of monopolists and patentees. Despite the disparate nature of radical individuals and groups in the 1640s and 1650s, the frequent recurrence of ideas common to them all is as striking as the differences among them. What undoubtedly bound them all together was the popular mid-seventeenth-century belief that the establishment of the perfect society was imminent. Defined in this broad, general sense there is now little doubt that millenarianism, far from being the creed of a few cranks, was part of the mainstream of English intellectual life in the first half of the seventeenth century, and was widely diffused throughout society at all levels.[2] The belief in the Second Coming, the reign of King Jesus, was widespread among the people at large, as well as among those intellectuals who read the works of influential millenarian writers like Thomas Brightman. Because historians in the past have failed to appreciate this, groups like the Fifth Monarchists have commonly been dismissed as fanatical eccentrics.[3] In a sense this is not surprising; the views of the Fifth Monarchists, who flourished in the early 1650s and especially among the clothworkers of London, are hard nowadays to take seriously. Central to their philosophy were the biblical prophecies in the Books of Revelations and Daniel, which had been the subject of ingenious speculation for centuries. Like many others before them, the Fifth Monarachists interpreted the prophecy in Daniel VII, that after the rise and fall of four great empires a kingdom would be established that would last for ever, to mean that Christ's kingdom – the Fifth Monarchy – would follow the collapse of the four great empires of Babylon, Persia, Greece, and Rome. Using this and other imaginative interpretations of key Old Testament prophecies (King Charles was the 'little horn' of Revelations, and so on) John Rogers and his followers proclaimed that the execution of Charles was the sign for the establishment of the reign of King Jesus. Ludicrous as these ideas seem, they were well in line with those held by many people in the mid-seventeenth century. Cromwell (as will be seen) was for a time closely connected with the Fifth Monarchists. It is difficult to escape the conclusion that the uniqueness of the Fifth Monarchists lies only in the detailed way they elaborated the structure of the new kingdom of Christ (in their plans for an interim government controlled by a minority, based on the Jewish Sanhedrin, until King Jesus should return to rule in person; in their determination to abolish the legal profession and establish the Mosaic Law, and so on), and in their resolve to bring about the millennium by force and to establish the reign of King Jesus over all the world. Other individuals and groups were less precise about the shape that the millennium should take and the way in which it should be brought about, but were no less sincere that a new age was at hand.

The millenarian ideal of a 'godly reformation' was most commonly expressed in religious terms. The astounding proliferation of religious sects in the 1640s and 1650s can be confusing to the student who is confronted with an array of apparently exotic sects – Particular Baptists and General Baptists, Grindletonians and Muggletonians, Quakers and Ranters – with widely differing theological standpoints – adult or infant baptism, predestinarianism or free will. The differences between them are important, but all were united in the belief that God worked through the individual. The Protestant Reformation had challenged the notion that the interpretation of the word of God in the Bible was the preserve of the priesthood. The radical sects of the mid-seventeenth century took this a step further and claimed that 'a poor plain countryman by the spirit which he hath received, is better able to judge of truth and error touching the things of God than the greatest philosopher, scholar or doctor in the world that is destitute of it'.[4] Since this conviction was common to most religious sects of the period, each developed a very similar programme of religious reforms. The belief in the primacy of the inner spirit of every individual precluded any concept of a national, uniform Church imposed on the individual by the state, and also meant a drastic reduction in the power of the clergy over the individual. It was also compatible with a wide extension of religious toleration, at least for all Protestants, although most sects qualified this by maintaining that individuals in each congregation must abide by the interpretations decided on by that congregation. Since there was to be no state Church and individual congregations were to be autonomous, ministers were to be elected by congregations and (to emphasize their rejection of a clerical élite) were to be one *of* the congregation. As if all this (the abolition of the state Church, religious toleration, congregationalism) were not radical enough, most radical sects also demanded the abolition of tithes (so attacking the property rights of landowners who received the most valuable tithes in the form of rent) and advocated the rights of women to take part in Church government and sometimes to preach (so striking at the roots of the traditional, hierarchical, and patriarchical society).[5]

It is arguable that the subversive implications of this programme would not have become apparent or abhorrent to conservative opinion, but for the activities of those associated with the Ranters and Quakers, who developed that programme in a very extreme way indeed. For those familiar with Quakerism as it developed from the later seventeenth century onwards, it may appear strange to identify Quakers with extreme and subversive views of any kind. George Fox and the early Quakers of the 1650s, however, were very different from their respectable, pacific successors. It needs to be emphasized, though, that the history of the early Quakers is bedevilled by the historical evidence, which is largely drawn from hostile sources (this is also true of the Ranters) which tend to lump Quakers and Ranters indiscriminately together. At times though, especially in the early 1650s, it is likely that the line between them is a very hazy one indeed. Both seem to have carried the emphasis on the inner spirit much further than any other sect, and sought to perceive that inner spirit by use of alcohol and tobacco, which in the mid-seventeenth century were considered to possess the same powers claimed for cannabis and other 'soft' drugs in the second half of the twentieth century. For many Ranters and Quakers what their inner spirit led them to do overrode all considerations of law, conventional morality or religion. One Ranter was alleged to have said, 'those are most perfect which commit the greatest sins with the least remorse'. 'There is no such act as drunkeness, adultery and theft in God . . .', wrote Lawrence Clarkson.

Sin hath its conception only in the imagination. . . . What act soever is done by thee in light and love, is light and lovely, though it be that act called adultery. . . . No matter what Scripture, saints or churches say, if that within thee do not condemn thee, thou shalt not be condemned.[6]

This, as Christopher Hill has shown, is the philosophy of the hippy-like counterculture of the 1650s which flew in the face of law and morality and which was considered with horror by respectable society. What is more, Quakers were especially singled out for hatred (as later in the seventeenth century) for their refusal to take off their hats in the presence of their social superiors, and (unlike later in the century) for their close involvement with political radicalism (see below, pp. 250, 424). Given all this, the savage treatment meted out by Cromwell's parliament in 1656 to one of the principal Quaker leaders, James Nayler (see below, p. 233), is hardly surprising.

Often interwoven with, and gaining its force from the same millenarian aspirations as religious radicalism in the 1640s and 1650s was a strand of secular radicalism, which was also as bewilderingly diverse in the range of ideas it dealt with and the number of thinkers it threw up. It is hardly an exaggeration to say that every institution and aspect of life was subjected to minute and often drastic criticism. Apart from the political reforms proposed by the Levellers, however, two major spheres absorbed a large part of the energies of the radicals: reform of the law and of education. Many of the radicals' complaints about the law – its slowness, expense, and unintelligibility – might well have been written in the early nineteenth century. Throughout their writings two principal proposals for reform recur: (1) decentralization of the law courts and abolition of unwieldy and inefficient central courts like chancery, to make justice available locally and cheaply; and (2) codification of the law in English, so that it might be freely and intelligibly available to all. Professional groups, like lawyers and clerics, were prime targets for the radicals; so too were university teachers 'which occasions all the trouble in the world'. There exists a vast corpus of writings pilloring universities and university teachers (like lawyers) for hindering rather than serving the cause for which they were established. 'The secrets of the creation', wrote Gerrard Winstanley, 'have been locked up under the traditional, parrot-like speaking from the universities and colleges for scholars.'[7] Universities were to be reformed as part of a fundamental restructuring of education, establishing universal education for both sexes to the age of eighteen years, and university training for those suitable. But in this educational utopia the university curriculum was to be stripped of its emphasis on the classics and divinity, and was to concentrate on vocational and scientific subjects.

Often, of course, reform of the law and education was only part of much wider schemes for reforming society as a whole. Many moderate social reformers were simply concerned to attack the symptoms of the acute economic crisis of 1649 by providing labour exchanges, which was one of the functions of Hartlib's proposed 'Office for Addresses'.[8] Other radicals, however, were not content with reform within the existing structure of society. Gerrard Winstanley is important as a political theorist of the stature of contemporaries like James Harrington and Thomas Hobbes.[9] But what makes Winstanley interesting is that, not only does he provide a complete formula for the restructuring of society, government, law, and education, but that he also tried to put that formula to the practical test. Developing the 'Norman Yoke' idea common to other contemporary radical thinkers – the idea that before the Norman Conquest there existed a golden age, when men lived freely and equally under the law and the earth was 'a common treasury of all mankind' – Winstanley argued that the Conquest established the existing social and political structure which he wanted to overthrow and, in its place, establish a state of pure communism, in which the land would be owned communally, in which there would be no need for law or the state, and in which there would be universal education. Later he compromised by envisaging a transitional stage in which magistrates would temporarily be necessary,[10] but he went further than any other thinker towards a total reappraisal and subversion of the traditional society. For a year from April 1649 Winstanley and his followers (their enemies called them the Diggers, they called themselves 'True Levellers') attempted to set up a commune on the commonland of St George's Hill at Walton, and later at Cobham Heath, Surrey.[11] Their efforts were tragic and pathetic and stood no chance of success in the face of violent opposition from local landowners and tenant farmers. It remains to be seen to what extent and why, not only the True Levellers, but the hopes of many radicals for the creation of a new society, a 'godly reformation', were disappointed following the execution of the king.

The Rump Parliament, 1649–1653

Conservatism and the Rump

In the weeks following the execution of the king radical expectations were at fever pitch. 'Me thinks I see the kingdom of Jesus Christ begin to flourish, while the wicked . . . do now perish and fade like a blowne-off-blossom', wrote William Rowse to Speaker Lenthall. When the rule of the saints had been established in England, believed John Owen, God would 'sooner or later shake all the Monarchies of the Earth'. 'Beware of Nol Crumwel's Army', John Spittlehouse warned Rome, 'lest Hugh Peter come to preach in Peter's Chaire.'[12] Disillusionment came less rapidly for some than others. In 1650 Winstanley the Digger still advocated supporting the Rump as a lesser evil than the restoration of the monarchy,[13] as did many other radicals. It was the Levellers who led the way in denouncing the new regime, undoubtedly because the Rump's extremely narrow representative nature offended their democratic aspirations. John Lilburne's two-part pamphlet, *Englands New Chains Discovered* (February and March 1649), sneered at 'this new kind of liberty' offered by the Rump, which was no liberty at all:

A Councel of State is hastily erected for Guardians thereof, who to that end are possessed with power to order and dispose all the forces appertaining to England by Sea or Land, to dispose of the publicke Treasure, to command any person whatsoever before them, to give oath for the discovering of Truth, to imprison any that shall dis-obey their commands, and such as they shall judge contumatious. What now is become of that liberty that no mans person shall be attached or imprisoned, or otherwise dis-eased of his Free-hold, or free Customs but by lawful judgement of his equals?[14]

By 1653 radical disillusionment was complete. It is a measure of Cromwell's ability to straddle conservative and radical opinion that in 1649 he was denounced by the Levellers, and in 1653 was a mouthpiece of the radicals' disappointment at the Rump. According to Whitelocke's account of the dissolution of the Rump on 20 April 1653, Cromwell 'told the House, that they had sat long enough . . . that some of them were whoremasters . . . that others of them were drunkards, and some corrupt and unjust men and scandalous to the profession of the gospel, and it was not fit that they should sit as a parliament any longer'.[15]

This kind of exaggerated language is explained by the Rump's failure to bring about the hoped-for 'godly reformation'. It is true that the political changes introduced by the Rump were dramatic enough. Immediately after the execution of the king the Rump ordered the seclusion of any MP who had voted on 5 December for continuing negotiations with the king. On successive days (6 and 7 February) the House of Lords and the monarchy were abolished, and with them disappeared the apparatus of monarchical government: the privy council and the prerogative courts. The administrative departments (the exchequer, the admiralty) were replaced by a council of state and a whole host of subcommittees with wide executive powers. But these changes were effected with a great show of reluctance. The legislation enacting the abolition of the monarchy and the House of Lords did not appear until over a month after the votes of early February. The Act declaring England to be a Commonwealth was not passed until the middle of May. Even the Engagement (2 January 1650) which the Rump ordered to be taken by all males over eighteen years of age, promising obedience to 'the Commonwealth, as it is now established, without a King or House of Lords', owed little to ideological enthusiasm. Indeed Blair Worden considers that 'the engagement was imposed on the nation chiefly out of panic'.[16]

The council of state and the Rump soon signalled their conservative disposition by their repression of Levellerism. The alliance between the Leveller leaders and senior army officers in late 1648 had collapsed before the execution of the king. The Whitehall Debates produced no consensus version of the *Agreement of the People*: the Levellers' second *Agreement* (15 December) and the officers' *Agreement* (20 January) differed fundamentally, especially on the extent of religious freedom to be allowed. By February and March 1649 the breach was public; and on 28 March Lilburne, Walwyn, Overton, and the Levellers' treasurer, Thomas Prince, were arrested. This did not prevent the spread of Leveller pamphleteering (especially a marvellous piece of political polemic, *The Hunting of the Foxes*, and the third *Agreement*, smuggled out of the Tower), and Leveller-inspired mutinies in the army. As in 1646–7 these were triggered off by a threat to send the army to Ireland. But there were major differences between the army disorders of 1646–7 and 1649. The 1649 mutinies were smaller (in Whalley's regiment in London led by Robert Lockyer, and in two regiments in Salisbury and north Oxfordshire led by Robert Thompson); they were not connived at or encouraged by senior army officers; and they were efficiently suppressed. Lockyer was executed at the end of April; Cromwell and Fairfax pursued the Salisbury mutineers to Burford (Oxfordshire) and shot the ringleaders on 14 May; and Thompson was killed later in Northamptonshire. The vital difference was that the Rump, unlike the parliamentary leaders of 1646–7, was willing and able to satisfy the wage grievances of the army rank-and-file. In 1649 the soldiers were paid in debentures, entitling them to ex-crown land, which they sold (often regiments acting collectively) and the cash was distributed.[17] The coincidence of the demise of Levellerism and the payment of army wage arrears reinforces the view that political and religious radicalism as well as having only limited support in London, had very shallow roots in the army. Lilburne gloriously survived his trial in September and was acquitted; but by then Levellerism in the army was dead. 'Posterity', said Lilburne, 'shall reap the benefit of our endeavours what ever shall become of us.'[18] That is as good an epitaph for the Levellers as any.

If confirmation were needed of the Levellers' views of the new regime, it was received in the autumn. After the last Leveller outbreak in the army (at Oxford in early September) had been crushed, the Rump passed an Act on 20 September severely restricting the liberty of the press. A formidable pair, Thomas Scott and Elizabeth Atkin, 'Parliament Joan', searched out and suppressed all unauthorized printing presses. From December 1649 until January 1653 when his blindness forced him to resign, John Milton inspected all printed matter and acted as 'a kind of propaganda minister and censorship minister combined'. A few pamphlets got through the net; it was not until 1655 that Cromwell made government censorship completely efficient. But there was now no rival to the government newspaper, *Mercurius Politicus*, launched on 6 June 1650 and edited by Marchamont Needham, who only a year before had been arrested for editing a royalist newspaper, *Mercurius Pragmaticus*. Needham's journalistic talents transformed what could have been a dull official newspaper into a brilliant exercise in successful propaganda and a landmark in English literature.[19]

For many radicals, though, especially anti-democratic religious groups, like the Fifth Monarchists, the suppression of the Levellers and the re-imposition of censorship would have been unimportant if the Rump had made any serious steps towards the 'godly reformation' they hoped for. Unfortunately, reform came no easier to the immediate heir of the revolution than it did to early seventeenth-century pre-revolutionary governments. The Rump's major reform achievements were carried out under strong army pressure after the army's victory at

Dunbar (3 September 1650) and were pitifully few in number. On 27 September 1650 the Rump repealed all statutes compelling church attendance. Later in 1650 the Rump, by converting all proceedings in law courts into English from Latin and into ordinary handwriting from court hand, went some way towards making the law more intelligible to laymen and breaking through the mumbo-jumbo thrown around the law by lawyers. Yet, despite a lot of discussion, little further religious or ecclesiastical reform was achieved. The Presbyterian system set up from 1646 to 1648 remained unrepealed, and moves to abolish tithes received little support. Although there was general concern that the clergy should be well-paid and educated, the Acts for the Propagation of the Gospel passed by the Rump to effect this applied only to Wales, Ireland, and selected parts of England. There was no national Act and even the Act for Wales was not renewed when it expired in 1652. To add to the radicals' fury the Rump passed severe measures in the summer of 1650 against religious nonconformity, and revealed its obsessive fear and hatred of the excesses of the Ranters by enforcing observance of the sabbath, suppressing 'the detestable sin of prophane swearing and cursing', and prescribing the death penalty for those guilty of adultery, fornication, and incest. Sweeping reforms of the law progressed no further than the discussion stage. Significantly, the Hale Commission on law reform, which from January to July produced a string of radical law reform proposals, was only appointed by the Rump after Colonel Pride 'attended at the door while this was in debate';[20] equally significantly not one of Hale's recommendations was put into effect.

It was the Rump's dilatory record on constitutional reform that led directly to its dissolution. As with other matters, the Rump talked a lot but did little. It considered a multitude of schemes for redistribution of parliamentary seats and decided in principle to alter the qualification for the franchise in county elections from possession of a forty shilling freehold to £200 in real or personal property. But little was done to put any proposal into effect. Like other measures considered by the Rump, what was known as 'a Bill for a new representative' was committed and recommitted, amended and revised, but in this case the Rump appears to have been on the brink of passing a Bill which provided for its immediate adjournment until elections were held in November, when the Rump would reassemble, vet the new MPs and then hand over power to the new assembly. This was the Bill killed by Cromwell's dissolution of the Rump on 20 April. After four and a half years the hoped-for millennium seemed further away than ever. Monopolies were unchecked; the grievances of the depressed rural classes not even considered. Again, as in 1647 and 1648, the army was provoked by civilian conservatism into entering the centre of the political arena.

Reasons for the Rump's conservatism

Before the autumn of 1651 the Rump had sound reasons to explain its failure to act quickly and effectively to remedy the grievances of the soldiers and saints. The new regime was launched during what was arguably the worst economic crisis of the seventeenth century. Nor was the security situation conducive to a period of social experimentation. The most immediate danger came from Ireland, which had been in revolt since 1641 and was a potential launching-pad for an invasion of England. Hyde, at the exiled court of Charles Stuart, believed that Ireland rather than Presbyterian Scotland was the more favourable starting point for a Stuart restoration. In January 1649 Ormonde, the king's lieutenant in Ireland, concluded an agreement with the Confederate Catholics of Ulster, who were to provide the men for an expeditionary force to England under naval cover provided by Prince Rupert. Not only was this a serious military threat to the new regime; it also added to the Rump's already large financial problems. Despite an assessment of £90,000 per month from March 1649, the continuation of the excise, and the sale of crown and dean and chapter lands from April 1649, the Rump was never free of crushing financial demands.

Throughout the rebellion the Irish cause was held back by divisions among the confederate rebels: the pro-royalist Old English had only their Catholicism in common with the Ulster Catholics led by Owen O'Neill. The leadership of the Protestant Ormonde was not likely to smooth over these divisions. It was ominous for Charles that in May 1649 George Monck, at the head of the parliamentary army in Ireland, induced O'Neill to sign a secret armistice, which, although later denounced by the Rump, gave Cromwell in England a much-needed breathing-space to organize his army for Ireland. The fate of earlier English armies in the bogs of Ireland meant that Cromwell's success was not assured. His victories in Ireland were not simply due to the disunity of his opponents; Cromwell was careful to make painstaking preparations before he left. By appointing Lord Broghill, the son of Richard Boyle earl of Cork, to a command in his army he won over some English Protestant settlers in Ireland to his cause. He also ensured that before he left for Ireland the wage arrears of his army were paid, and that he was guaranteed sufficient financial provision by the Rump. Cromwell and his well-paid and disciplined army were also encouraged by a racial contempt and hatred for the Irish. 'I had rather be overrun with a Cavalierish interest, than a Scotch interest; I had rather be overrun with a Scotch interest, than an Irish interest; and I think of all this is the most dangerous . . . all the world knows their barbarism', said Cromwell, who had swallowed whole the horror stories of Irish atrocities against English settlers in 1641.[21] Only this can explain Cromwell's justly infamous behaviour in Ireland, especially when he condoned the massacre of the civilian populations of Drogheda (September 1649) and Wexford (October 1649). Otherwise his intolerance and bigotry on his Irish campaign stands out starkly from his record of tolerance of the opinions of others in England and in Scotland.

Hardly had the Irish expedition been organized and financed than the infant English republic was faced with another major crisis, in Scotland.

There Charles Stuart, the dead king's eldest son, who had been on the continent since 1646, was preparing to regain his throne. Cromwell's victories in Ireland in the autumn of 1649 forced Charles into a very irksome course of action: negotiations with the dominant Presbyterian party in Scotland, who were in the process of defeating the Scottish royalists and hanging his chief supporters, Hamilton, Montrose, and Huntly. Even early in his career Charles never let principle stand in his way. In June 1650 he arrived in Scotland, swore an oath of loyalty to the Covenant and denounced his parents. So only a month after returning from Ireland in May 1650, Cromwell (Fairfax having turned down the command) headed north with Fleetwood, Lambert, and an expeditionary force against the Scots. As in Ireland, success was due to Cromwell's political and organizational, as well as military, talents. He followed up his victory at Dunbar (3 September 1650) against heavy numerical odds (3,000 English against 11,000 Scots) by skilfully widening the political and religious divisions among the Scots. Cromwell, said Whitelocke, 'sought to win them by fair means rather than to punish them'. In contrast to his intolerance of Catholics in Ireland, he won over moderate Scots opinion by his willingness to listen to the Presbyterian case. It was a divided enemy that Cromwell fought after Dunbar and decisively defeated at Worcester, exactly a year after Dunbar.

Before Worcester the Rump was faced by the prospect of invasion and with almost universal international hostility provoked by the execution of Charles I. The pursuit of international respectability and adequate defence were consequently given a higher priority than the creation of a utopia. But it is fairly certain that this alone does not adequately explain the Rump's reactionary record. By 1650 the immediate economic crisis was over, and after Worcester there was no longer the excuse of imminent royalist or foreign invasion. Recent studies of the Rump have emphasized the unrevolutionary nature of its members.[22] Older views of the Rump made two false assumptions: that Pride at the end of 1648 purged all religious Presbyterians from Parliament, and that all religious Independents were political radicals. On the contrary, there were few MPs in the Rump, whether religious Independents or religious Presbyterians, who held revolutionary opinions. Twenty-two of the forty-one members of the council of state, among which might be expected to be found the most committed republicans, refused to swear an oath approving of the execution of the king and the abolition of the House of the Lords and the monarchy. Even the transformation of Ireton from his revolutionary posture of 1648 to his support of the *status quo* in 1649 is more apparent than real. Pragmatic, rather than ideological, considerations induced most people to support (or at least not to oppose) the Rump. Whitelocke's reasoning was typical: although 'a strict formal pursuance of the ordinary rules of the law . . . hath hardly to be discerned in the late proceedings on either side . . . unavoidable necessity hath put us upon these courses, which otherwise perhaps we should not have taken'.[23]

For Whitelocke, who became a commissioner of the great seal, and for many others the Rump was highly preferable to rule by the army. The antipathy between the Rump and the army was possibly the major factor in the Commonwealth's dismal failure to produce far-reaching reform. As a result, religious Independents, as well as Presbyterians, opposed any extension of toleration. The activities of the Quakers and Ranters made many fearful that moderate reform would be the thin end of the wedge: 'If a toleration were granted', believed Thomas Edwardes, 'they shall never have peace in their families, or ever after have command of wives, children, servants.'[24] Similarly, not only lawyers resisted changes in the law. So too did many Rumpers who had no vested interest in the legal *status quo*, but for whom moderate legal reform came to be associated with army rule and extremism. Would not moderate legal reform be the first step towards the eventual overthrow of the common law, when views like those of the Fifth Monarchist, John Rogers, were ventilated? 'It is not easy to change some of these Lawes, and so to reform them', wrote Rogers, 'O no: that will be to poor purpose, and it is not your worke now, which is . . . bringing in the Lawes of God given by Moses for Re-publique Lawes'.[25]

What was the role of Cromwell in the Rump's failure to introduce reforms? As usual, it is not easy to slot Cromwell into any one category. He frequently called on the Rump to adopt radical measures; he also was a notable force behind the moderation of the Rump. In the crucial early weeks of the Republic he worked behind the scenes for the return of the secluded MPs, building political bridges between Presbyterians and political Independents. Cromwell's religious confidant, John Owen, on the day after the king's execution, urged the Commons in a fast sermon to 'labour to recover others, even all that were ever distinguished and called by the name of the Lord, for their late fearful and sinful returning to sinful compliance with the enemies of God and the nation'. So anxious was Cromwell for a rapprochement with the moderates that in April 1649 he even urged that 'the presbyterian [church] government might be settled, promising his endeavours thereto'. Such political tactics might be justified by the dangers of 1649–51. What then, of Cromwell's continued contacts with conservative MPs after the battle of Worcester? Cromwell appears to have been a fairly close political ally of Oliver St John after Worcester, and apparently approved of St John's reforming, but limited, programme. At one meeting after Worcester St John came out clearly in favour of the superiority of monarchical over republican government. Cromwell agreed, against the republican views of Desborough and other army officers: 'I think', he said, 'if it may be done with safety, and preservation of our Rights, both as Englishmen and Christians, that a Settlement with somewhat of Monarchical power in it would be very effectual'.[26] It is highly likely that, despite Cromwell's denunciations of the Rump's conservatism, he was partly responsible for its failure to bring about a 'godly reformation'.

The Rump's achievements

The Rump was not a revolutionary regime: was it a competent one? Historical opinion in the past has been fairly unanimous in condemning the Rump as a dilatory, corrupt regime, which subordinated public concerns to the private interests of its members. Partly this has arisen by confusing the standards by which the Rump is to be judged: by twentieth-century standards of public morality, or in comparison with other seventeenth-century governments? Too often, modern standards have been used to condemn it. If seen in the context of its own time, the Rump achieved international respectability, and its enemies in the local communities at home were forced into a grudging recognition that republican government was not a recipe for social anarchy, but rather a bulwark against it. Partly also the Rump's adverse historical reputation is due to the difficulty of discovering who were the policy-makers. Was policy made by merchants in the interests of merchants? Among the usual fluid political groupings the influence of a group of committed republicans round Henry Marten and Thomas Chaloner appears to have been more successful than most in moulding the foreign and commercial policies of the Rump. But MPs who were active in foreign and commercial matters represented diverse mercantile interests. It is likely that the foreign and commercial policies pursued by the Marten–Chaloner group received *general* support in the Rump, because they gained enormous international prestige for the new regime.

It was a well-known seventeenth-century maxim that 'power and profit are jointly to be considered', national greatness and commercial property go hand in hand. This was the reason for the establishment of the council of trade appointed in August 1650 by the Rump to find remedies for the trade depression. The most notable product of the council, before its demise in December 1651, was the Navigation Act (9 October 1651), by which all imports to England had to be in English ships or in ships of the country where the imported goods originated. Both the authors and the purpose of the Act have been the subject of historical debate,[27] but there seems little doubt that its major aim was to attack the Dutch hegemony of the carrying trade. It was not the sole reason for war with the Dutch which began in 1652; there was a long history of commercial rivalry in the East and West Indies, in North America and in West Africa between the Dutch and English, but the Act hardly helped Anglo–Dutch relations. The war was received enthusiastically in England for a variety of motives: the Fifth Monarchists hated the Dutch for their Presbyterianism, as well as for their dominance of the cloth markets (many Fifth Monarchists were clothmakers and clothworkers); civilian Rumpers saw the war as a test of national republican prestige. Even conservative Presbyterians, who were uneasy about a war against co-religionists, saw the war as an assertion of national power and a means of diverting attention away from domestic reform.

Perhaps the most notable achievement of the Rump was not its glittering foreign and commercial policies, but that, despite high odds against it, it made republican government tolerable to many. There was much that the traditional rulers of England found hateful in the Rump: it was a regicide regime, which continued to exact high taxation and to interfere in local affairs. In some counties prominent opponents were removed from the commission of the peace in the purges of 1650 and 1651, and the powers of a minority of radical activists strengthened. The council of state appointed the commissioners of the new county militias, created in July 1650. Yet significantly the Rump met no serious opposition. Partly this was due to its moderation: the purges of JPs were only partial, and only the most prominent royalists were executed (the earls of Holland and Derby). Partly also, the Rump produced a persuasive theoretical justification for accepting a *de facto* regime in the works of Francis Rous, Marchamont Needham, and John Drury. Mainly, however, most people came to see the Rump as the only practicable government. There was little enthusiasm for the return of the monarchy, and the only alternative to the Rump was the army. The prevalence of 'loyalism' was based on the belief that the Rump was the upholder of law and order and the bulwark against radicalism; it had ridden out a severe economic crisis; and it had enhanced England's international prestige in an immensely successful war.

The dissolution of the Rump

It is commonly said that the major reason for the dissolution of the Rump on 20 April 1653 was that Cromwell was forced to get rid of it when he realized that it meant to perpetuate its own power. The evidence for this hypothesis is slim:[28] it rests on Cromwell's assertion that the Bill being considered by the Rump in the spring of 1653 provided merely for by-elections to fill vacant seats in parliament. But the provisions of the Bill do not survive, and, as has been seen, they may have arranged for elections to a new parliament. If this is so, then Cromwell's motives for dissolving the Rump were not so cut-and-dried as was once thought. Why did he suddenly throw overboard his policy of cultivating moderate opinion, and break his contacts with the St John circle? Part of the answer seems to be that this was another instance of Cromwell's volatile temperament; as will be seen, in 1653 he was gripped by a bout of millenarian enthusiasm. In addition, by the spring of 1653 there were pressing practical considerations: he was no longer able to keep the loyalty of the army *and* maintain his contacts with the parliamentarians of the Rump. The rift between the Rump and the army was now so wide that Cromwell had to take an unequivocal stand on the side of the army and reform. It remains to be seen how permanent this would be.

The Rump was a victim of the republican dilemma: it was too conservative for the army and sects, but not conservative enough to heal the breach which Pride's Purge and the king's execution had opened up between the republic and the political nation. The shallowness of the Rump's achievement is reflected in Cromwell's contemptuous comment. Its passing, he wrote, occasioned 'not so much as the barking of a dog'.[29]

Oliver Cromwell

'Without doubt', wrote Clarendon of Oliver Cromwell,

no man with more wickedness ever attempted any thing, or brought to pass what he desired more wickedly, more in the face and contempt of religion, and moral honesty; yet wickedness as great as his could never have accomplished those trophies, without the assistance of a great spirit, an admirable circumspection and sagacity, and a most magnanimous resolution . . . he will be looked upon by posterity as a brave bad man.[30]

Cromwell is one of the great personalities of the past about whom it is more than usually difficult to be objective or to get a clear idea of his character and his aims. During his lifetime he aroused intense emotions, leaving for historians biased political memoirs, whether from Clarendon on the royalist side or from the civilian republican Edmund Ludlow, and propaganda-laden newspapers and pamphlets. Assessing Cromwell's character can be compared to writing a biography of Harold Wilson using the memoirs of Edward Heath and Richard Crossman and political comment in the *Daily Telegraph* and *Morning Star*. In addition, like many other people, Cromwell never made his own motives clear. The two editors of his *Letters and Speeches* used his papers to depict him as a heroic figure (Thomas Carlyle) and a Hitler-like evil genius (W. C. Abbott). At key points in the 1640s and 1650s, to the frustration of the historian, Cromwell often remained enigmatically silent or away from the centre of events, leaving a host of questions unanswered. Did he encourage the development of the agitating movement in the army in the spring of 1647 or was he swept along by it? Did he engineer Cornet Joyce's seizure of the king from the parliamentarians in July 1647 and Charles's escape in November 1647? What was his attitude in the last months of 1648 to the army's demands for a dissolution or purge of the Long Parliament and the trial of the king? How deeply committed was he to the radicalism of the junior army officers in the early 1650s? Was he the instigator of the coup in December 1653 which led to the collapse of the Barebones Parliament? Did he encourage his second parliament to offer him the throne?

What irritated Cromwell's opponents at the time and made them (and later commentators) suspect him of low political cunning is that so often events went his way: miraculously, it seemed, he overcame body blows like the Self-denying Ordinance and the rifts in the ranks of his supporters at Putney. It is easy to see why he had such a strong belief in Providence, and why both royalist and republican observers condemned him as a hypocritical politician, who only used radical movements for his own ends: in order to seek power for himself (the royalist view) or to prevent a wide-ranging revolution (the republican view). To them he had a consistent conservative aim, clothed in a Machiavellian disguise of radicalism. There are many problems associated with this view, not least the fact that, as has been seen, on many occasions – being exempt from the Self-denying Ordinance and the capture of the king at Holmby House, for example – Cromwell was not the mastermind behind events.

Another explanation of Cromwell's apparently ambivalent attitude to radicalism has been that at some stage he underwent a transformation from youthful idealism to middle-aged pragmaticism; that, like a lot of radicals, he spurned his one-time radical allies and beliefs, when he came face to face with the day-to-day problems of government. This explanation has the merit of reconciling Cromwell, the man who in the early 1640s proclaimed that his goal was to attain 'godly rule', with Cromwell, the man who in the late 1640s negotiated with Charles I until weeks before his execution; who ruthlessly suppressed the Levellers, his former allies; and who in the 1650s nearly accepted the title of king. On this view the only matter of dispute is when the change took place: was it at Putney in 1647 when he realized that some of his fellow saints were intent, not only on establishing 'godly rule' but also on attacking property as well? But Cromwell's career does not fall into the neat progression from radicalism to pragmaticism that this view pre-supposes. At times in the 1650s he appeared more radical than he had been a decade earlier.

How does one harmonize the conflicting facets of Cromwell's undoubtedly ambiguous character: his support of the East Anglian fenmen against the capitalist enclosing syndicate in the 1630s with his ruthless suppression of the Leveller mutineers at Burford in 1649; his anti-aristocratic sentiments (it was alleged that he told the earl of Manchester in 1644 that 'it would not be well till he was Mr Montague') with his apparent love of the courtly trappings of his entourage when Protector? The correct answer may be, not that Cromwell was a hypocrite or a disillusioned idealist, but that he was someone who oscillated with alarming rapidity from revolutionary enthusiasm to cautious temporizing and vice versa. Christopher Hill sees this aspect of Cromwell's character as an indication that he was a manic depressive.[31] At times he appeared to take decisions suddenly, inexplicably, and to be elated with millenarian enthusiasm; at other times he was as tortured by indecision and as careful in building political alliances based on compromise and conciliation as Elizabeth I. Sometimes it is difficult to find reasons for these apparently arbitrary changes of mood, his 'ideological schizophrenia'.[32] Often, though, his moods of political caution coincided with times when the parliamentary or republican regimes were in danger (either from a conservative reaction or from radical extremism), and his outbursts of revolutionary zeal occurred in periods of diminished political danger.

Cromwell never elaborated any theoretical goal for himself. The nearest he came to formulating his constitutional ideal was in 1654, when he laid down four fundamental principles for a constitutional settlement: (1) government by a single person and a parliament; (2) parliaments of limited duration; (3) liberty of conscience; (4) the militia to be jointly controlled by parliament and the head of the state. Clearly he was no democrat. 'Where is there any bound or limit set if . . . men that have no interest but the interest of breathing' shall be given the vote? he asked at Putney. Nor was he against the traditional social structure, as he made clear to his first parliament in 1654: 'a nobleman, a gentleman, a yeoman: that is a good interest of the nation, and a great one'. But within these limits, he was strongly in favour of moderate reform of the law, of education, and of the Church. The one principle on which he was most loath to compromise was his belief in religious toleration: 'I had rather that Mahometanism were permitted amongst us than that one of God's children should be persecuted.'[33] As long as the traditional structure of society was not threatened he wanted moderate reform and an extension of religious toleration. In this he was not alone; this after all was something like the moderate programme supported by the 'middle group' men in the 1640s, and significantly Cromwell was in frequent touch with St John and other members of that group after 1649.

What set him apart, even from people like St John who were willing to countenance moderate political, religious, and legal reforms, was his association with the army. Cromwell was therefore suspected of intending a much more extensive reformation than he did. The tragedy of his political career is that the large measure of common ground he had with the traditional governors of the country was swept aside by his association with the 'wild men', the soldiers and saints. His plans for moderate reform were interpreted as stepping-stones to anarchy; his programme of religious toleration seen as indistinguishable from the extremism of the Ranters and Quakers.

The Barebones Parliament, July–December 1653

Cromwell's public statements after the dissolution of the Rump give the impression that he had thrown all political caution to the winds and surrendered himself to millenarian enthusiasm. 'Truly you are called by God to rule with Him, and for Him,' he told the Barebones Parliament when it assembled on 4 July 1653.

I confess I never looked to see such a day as this . . . when Jesus Christ should be so owned as He is, at this day . . . this may be the door to usher in the things that God has promised; which have been prophesied of . . . we have some of us thought, That it is our duty to endeavour this way; not vainly to look at that prophecy in Daniel.[34]

These were 'Overturning, Overturning, Overturning dayes', some London Fifth Monarchists told the members of the Barebones Parliament, urging them to 'indeavour the erecting of the Kingdom of Jesus Christ to the uttermost parts of the earth'.[35] With some justification the hopes of the Fifth Monarchists were high. Cromwell had turned down John Lambert's proposal that a council of twelve should rule temporarily in the political hiatus created by the dissolution of the Rump, and listened favourably to the Fifth Monarchist Thomas Harrison's idea that a larger assembly of godly men should meet, based on the Jewish Sanhedrin. Not surprisingly, the decision to summon an assembly of 138 men 'of approved fidelity and honesty' (121 for England, 6 from Wales, 5 from Scotland, and 6 from Ireland), to whom were to be transferred supreme authority to make a new constitution, was interpreted by Lambert as a victory for Harrison and extreme radicalism.

Lambert was wrong. There were several down-to-earth considerations behind the decision to call a nominated assembly. Radical demands for new elections were unrealistic in that they were bound to produce an anti-army, anti-reform majority; whereas the composition of a nominated assembly could be controlled. In choosing the members Cromwell and his advisers had to rely heavily on local advice and especially the opinion of gathered churches (this was true, for example, in North Wales where Major-General Harrison was active). But Cromwell ensured that the assembly was not simply a gathering of 'saints', radical idealists inexperienced in government. London Baptists were represented, including Praise-God Barebones, a London leather-seller. So too were the Fifth Monarchists, although Dr Capp could identify only twelve. But Clarendon's jibe – 'much the major part of them consisted of inferior persons, of no quality or name, artificers of the meanest trades, known only by their gifts in praying and preaching . . . they were a pack of weak senseless fellows, fit only to bring the name and reputation of Parliament lower than it was yet' – grossly exaggerated the truth.[36] The majority of members were the usual type of seventeenth-century MPs: university and inn-of-court educated drawing their wealth mainly from the land, and serving on the commission of the peace in their home counties. Some served in future Protectorate and royalist parliaments. In handing over power to such a body Cromwell's aims were partly practical: to secure an interim period of enough moderate reform to satisfy the radicals, and enough well-ordered government to convince the old rulers of the counties that the republic merited support. After that elections could be safely held.

It is not often realized that the Barebones Parliament (one of the first acts of the assembly was to vote itself a parliament) did go some way towards meeting Cromwell's hopes. It spent a lot of its brief life discussing reforms that were uncontroversial and designed to remedy widely recognized imperfections in the machinery of government, the Church, and the law. The abolition of the Church courts had left a huge vacuum, to fill which the Barebones Parliament established machinery for the probate of wills and for registering births, marriages, and deaths. Civil marriages, solemnized by JPs, were legalized. Measures were proposed to rationalize the revenue system, including the abolition of the hated excise. Many of the law reforms proposed by the Barebones Parliament were uncontroversial. It was hardly shocking to suggest that the debtor's law should discriminate between genuine and fraudulent bankrupts, that punishments should match crimes, or that the law should be made intelligible to litigants as well as to lawyers. Enlightened Acts were passed for the relief of creditors and poor prisoners and to regulate conditions under which idiots and lunatics were kept. Even the discussions on finding a more reasonable method than tithes for paying church ministers were not at first unwelcome. After all this was a problem that had concerned people since the Reformation, because poor salaries ensured an ill-educated, inadequate clergy. Better salaries, whether guaranteed by the state or by individual congregations, were seen as a possible remedy for many of the ills of the Church. The Barebones Parliament, too, was just as concerned as the Rump had been with national prestige. Despite Cromwell's peace moves it continued the popular Dutch war and went ahead with proposals for the union of England and Scotland, taking care that Scottish interests would be subordinated to those of England.

Why, then, did the Barebones Parliament fail to persuade the political nation to forget the traumatic events of 1649? Its task was greater than that of the Rump. The dissolution of 20 April 1653 isolated the republican regime even further than before from the mainstream of political opinion. Rumpers could not forgive what they saw as a violation of parliamentary privileges by the army in 1653. From July to October 1653 many JPs who had supported the Rump were ejected from commissions of the peace, leaving fewer greater gentry on them than ever before. Nothing was more symbolic of the alienation of moderate opinion from the republic in 1653. What frightened moderates most of all were the activities in the Barebones Parliament of the Fifth Monarchists and members of other radical sects, who, although only few in number, were very well organized. They planned their political tactics in Arthur Squibb's house in London, and at times were able to push through the parliament very controversial measures: a vote to abolish the court of chancery (5 August), a vote to allow the introduction of a Bill to abolish lay patronage of church livings (17 November), and on 10 December the rejection (by 56 votes to 52) of a committee's report to retain tithes. These were brief, temporary, and narrow victories for the radicals, but they were enough to frighten moderate opinion that property and society as they knew it were in danger. This was no way to heal the wounds of 1649, and Cromwell's conservative instincts for the preservation of the regime were alarmed. He later said that, if the Barebones Parliament had continued, the result would have been 'the subversion of the laws and of all the liberties of this nation, the destruction of the Ministry, of this nation, in a word the confusion of all things'.[37] Cromwell may not have initiated the device on 12 December, by which the moderates in the Barebones Parliament met very early one morning and outvoted the radicals to hand power back to him; but he certainly needed little persuasion to accept it. The civilian radicals by now had little time for Cromwell and the army. Christopher Feake, a Fifth Monarchist, called Cromwell 'the man of sin, the old dragon'; and some suggested that the expenditure on the army be drastically cut and that senior army officers receive no pay for a year. One can imagine the relish with which the radical minority were dispersed by the soldiers from Westminster on 12 December 1653. For Cromwell and the army, though, the end of the Barebones Parliament solved nothing. The dilemma of the revolution remained, and was neatly encapsulated in two questions asked by a contemporary pamphlet: 'whether the old Parliament (the Rump) was not turned out for leaving undone what they ought to have done,' and 'whether the little Parliament [Barebones] was not turned out for doing what the others left undone.'[38]

Cromwellian government, 1653–1658

There are huge gaps in our knowledge of England during the Cromwellian Protectorate. Much more work has been done on the 1640s than on the 1650s. Consequently, opinions about the Protectorate differ greatly. At one extreme the period is seen as one approaching anarchy in which central government all but collapsed; at the other it is considered to have been a repressive, military dictatorship. Both views agree that the 1650s were an irrelevant, unnecessary interruption in the long-term development of the English constitution. That this was so, the argument goes, was recognized by the logic of events in the 1650s: an inevitable reactionary progression from experiments with new forms of government to the adoption by Cromwell in his later years of monarchical government in all but name. This approach ignores important historical questions: why did Charles Stuart receive so little support in England in 1651? Why were the royalist revolts of the mid-1650s such damp squibs? Why as late as August 1659 was Sir George Booth's royalist rebellion such a complete failure? The answer lies only in part in differences among royalists, in the incompetence of their leaders, and in the military strength of the Cromwellian regime. Before the middle of 1659 there is very little evidence of widespread enthusiasm for the return of the Stuarts. It is difficult to know what the masses felt about the Protectorate; though one can speculate with a fair degree of certainty, for example, on what the popular reaction was to the closure of many alehouses in the 1650s. The key problem is to analyse the reactions of the traditional rulers of the counties and boroughs to Cromwellian government. The weakness of the Stuart cause in the 1650s suggests that there were aspects of Cromwellian government that they found attractive. The first of the next two sections isolates some of those aspects. Government during the 1650s did not break down. In some respects it was very efficient and went some way towards satisfying the craving of the political nation for a return to stable, ordered government. At the same time it did not lose touch entirely with the revolutionary ideals of 'godly reformation', of the 'Good Old Cause'. The second section (the history of Cromwell's parliament and the major-generals) shows why, despite its achievements, Cromwellian government secured the loyalty of only a minority, and why Oliver's legacy to his son was, if not hopeless, very insecure.

The achievements of Cromwellian government

The Protectorate was not a revolutionary regime. If the decision to call the Barebones Parliament was a victory for Harrison and the radicals, the Instrument of Government, which Cromwell accepted on 12 December as lord protector for life, was a victory for the conservative wing of the army. Lambert, now back in London, had a decisive role in drafting the Instrument. The council of state, an advisory body akin to the old privy council, consisted not only of generals (Lambert, Skippon, Desborough), but of civilian and aristocratic moderates like Anthony Ashley Cooper, Sir Charles Wolsely, Sir Gilbert Pickering, and Philip Sidney viscount Lisle. As before and later, Cromwell veered away from radical policies and devoted a large part of his time to wooing the political nation and securing peace and stability. One of his earliest acts was to abolish the oath of Engagement which forced men to recognize the abolition of the monarchy and House of Lords. The 'loyalism' which had induced moderates to support the Rump was transferred to Cromwell, who sought to acquire the Rump's mantle as the bulwark against radical change. Cromwell's theme in his speeches to the first Protectorate parliament when it met in September 1654 was the need for 'healing and settling'. Sequestrations, which had opened up deep wounds in county society, were reduced, and there was no wholesale purge of local government officials. Still, the commissioners of the peace consisted far more than before the civil war of men from outside the old county élites, but established gentry began to drift back to act as JPs and assessment commissioners. As will be seen, the major-generals' interlude in 1655–6 slowed down the process, but only temporarily. The Protectorate, writes Professor Underdown, 'was moving in the right direction, towards a reunion of the nation and of the local communities of which it was made'.[39]

Not only did the new regime interfere as little as possible with the personnel of local government, it also (with the outstanding exception of the rule of the major-generals) allowed local officials a large amount of freedom to get on with administering the areas under their control. Nor was this a recipe for the breakdown of local government, which it is often assumed took place in the 1650s. On the contrary, the normal administrative and judicial processes of local government in those counties which have been studied continued with remarkably little interruption. Indeed the administration of the poor law, which was the biggest task of seventeenth-century local authorities, appears to have been carried out in the 1650s more efficiently than ever before. Far from being abandoned, as older historians like E. M. Leonard believed, the poor laws were enforced in the 1650s, outdoor relief granted, pauper children apprenticed and educated, and provisions made in work-houses, hospitals, and almshouses for the aged and infirm. In other spheres, too – road maintenance, criminal jurisdiction, the control of wages and of the prices of consumption goods – the record of local government in the 1650s seems to have been no worse, and in some cases much better, than at other times in the seventeenth century.[40]

It was not the desire for the return of efficient local government that contributed to the downfall of the Protectorate. Nor was it the lack of firm central government. The Cromwellian government satisfied the requirements expected of seventeenth-century governments, whether monarchical or republican: the regulation of the domestic economy and overseas trade and the maintenance of internal law and order, England's defence against invasion and the country's international prestige. In many respects government in the 1650s did this in just as muddled and inconsistent a way as before. This is true of the regulation of the economy, for example; this was no embryonic age of economic *laissez-faire*. The Cromwellian government's interference in the economy was as misdirected and unsuccessful as had been that of earlier govern-ments.[41] In two respects, however, the record of the Cromwellian government seems to have been superior to that of the Stuarts. It was less corrupt and the most obvious administrative wrangles were stamped out.[42] Secondly, its handling of foreign affairs was admired even by its enemies. The hoary examination question often asked about Cromwell's foreign policy, whether it was dominated by commercial or religious motives, is really irrelevant. Not only are the two motives not always incompatible, but the question presupposes that foreign policy is made in a vacuum. In reality foreign policy is made up of a succession of day-to-day decisions, one decision forcing another. In making peace with the Dutch in April 1654 Cromwell had little option but to choose a French alliance not a Spanish alliance, because of the current Franco-Dutch friendship. Motives are often superimposed on foreign policy by historians. What is remarkable about Cromwell's foreign policy is that it was as successful as it was. There were few among Cromwell's entourage who had much expertise in international affairs. In these circumstances failures could be expected. The Western Design, an attempt to break into the Spanish Caribbean Empire, was a fiasco. The combined land and sea expeditionary force lacked Cromwell's usually meticulous attention to detail; it was badly supplied, and led by two men, one from the army and one from the navy, who differed both about the aims and methods of the Design. Its one success, the capture of Jamaica, so highly

prized in the eighteenth-century, was seen in the 1650s as scant reward
for the expenditure on it of men and money. Yet elsewhere much seemed
to have been achieved. English rule was firmly established in Ireland and
Scotland. The Dutch peace was very advantageous to England and rid
Charles Stuart of a Dutch base and support. The Protector signed a
series of commercial treaties with European powers, which were as
important as indicators of England's standing as for their content.
England's reorganized navy under Admiral Robert Blake was busy
sweeping nests of pirates and royalists off the seas, and the Spanish war,
though expensive, was popular as a patriotic war against England's
national and religious enemy. In the second half of the seventeenth
century the 1650s were looked back to as a time when England's
diplomatic standing in the world was very high.

The Protectorate's success in appealing to moderate opinion
inevitably meant that its achievements as a reforming regime were
limited. Its record in this respect, though, is not totally barren. Certainly
it fell far short of the reforming ideals Cromwell had seemed to
champion earlier. The reforming ordinances issued by the Protector and
council of state before the first parliament met in September 1654 were
pale shadows of the sweeping reforms many in the army had wanted.
The difficulties, of course, were immense, as the history of the Rump and
of the Barebones Parliament had demonstrated. Even Cromwell's
ordinance to make the access of litigants to chancery easier and cheaper
– a 'milk-and-water ordinance' compared with the radicals' dream of
abolishing chancery – met with fierce opposition from lawyers in the
first Protectorate parliament.[43] There was also the problem of priorities.
Given the vast financial and constitutional problems of the regime
educational schemes, like the proposed new university at Durham,
inevitably suffered. It is a tribute to Cromwell's sincere desire for reform
that projects like this were considered, and, as in the case of the Durham
college, sometimes completed.

Cromwell's most appealing and successful achievement was in the
organization of religious life in England. During the Protectorate only a
minimum of state control over religion was exercised. In keeping with
Cromwell's strategy of appealing to the pre-civil war rulers of the
counties, most of the state's control was exercised by local commissioners of 'ejectors', set up by an ordinance of August 1654, who had
the power to expel ministers they felt unfit to hold office. An earlier
ordinance of March 1654 set up a general commission of 'triers' in
London who were to approve the appointment of all ministers. No
doubt to the relief of many landowners the 'triers' made no attempt to
question their right to present nominees to livings in their possession.
The only other intervention made by the state was by trustees, set up by
an Ordinance of September 1654, who were to supplement the income of
poorly endowed clergy from the income of ex-ecclesiastical estates.
Within this loose framework of state control a vast diversity of religious
practices was tolerated. For the first time in England the initiative which

determined the form of worship in each parish came from below, from the individual ministers and congregations, and not from above, from the established Church and state. In the majority of parish churches this probably meant that there was no great change: congregations continued to worship with ministers ordained before 1640 as they had in the days before Laud's innovations. The biggest difference was the substitution of the Presbyterian *Directory of Worship* for the *Book of Common Prayer*, but, as Dr Cross explains, the *Directory*

offered a guide to the form of service to be performed by the incumbent but did not prescribe set forms of prayer. Few Calvinists could have disagreed with its theology and probably the majority of English parish ministers who remained in their livings still were under the influence of Calvin and his popularisers.[44]

In some parishes congregations went further towards the establishment of a Presbyterian system with lay elders, and even the development of interparochial classical organizations in some parts of the country. The Cromwellian church also included more radical Protestants than the Presbyterians. At the Restoration well over a hundred Independent ministers were ejected from the parochial livings into which they had been accepted by the Cromwellian general commission of 'triers' in London. Other religious groups, at both ends of the doctrinal spectrum, though not given the official seal of approval by the 'triers', were allowed to worship without any harassment from the government. At the radical end, separatist Protestant churches of every conceivable variety flourished during the Protectorate: gathered churches in which the form of worship and often the ministers were chosen by the individual congregations, and which only sixty years before had been ruthlessly suppressed by Elizabeth I. In these circumstances of diverse doctrines and personalities it was not easy to organize associations of similar churches, but some gathered churches did so, the most outstanding examples being the General Baptists and the Particular Baptists who developed regional organizations in the 1650s.[45] Some even began to work for cooperation among ministers and congregations of different types in a genuine ecumenical spirit. The most famous example, Richard Baxter's Worcestershire Association, included Independents, episcopalians, and 'men of no faction nor siding with any party, but owning that which was good in all as far as they could discuss it'. Baxter later felt that England was on the road 'to have become a land of saints and a pattern of holiness to all the world, and the unmatchable paradise of the earth'.[46]

Even the minority of high-church episcopalians and Catholics in England were given remarkable freedom from persecution by Cromwell's government, as long as they did not threaten public order. For this reason sects, such as the Quakers, Socinians, and Ranters, whose activities were often violent and antisocial, were persecuted more than those Catholic priests and Laudian clerics whose activities were confined to the houses of their landed patrons. It is the tolerance of

Cromwell and his regime that stands out: in Oliver's conversations with the Quaker leader, George Fox, his friendship with the Catholic Sir Kenelm Digby, the readmission of the Jews, and so on. What substance is there in the popular legend of the intolerant, 'kill-joy' aspects of the Protectorate? This seems to be rooted in the hopes of achieving a moral reformation, common to all the regimes of the 1650s, and which resulted in the campaigns to suppress alehouses and Sunday sports, for example. Such aspirations were widely shared, certainly by many gentry, for security, as well as moral, considerations. Too often, they have been used to erect Cromwell into a caricature of an intolerant philistine 'Puritan', against music, dancing, painting, and the arts. Enough is now known of Cromwell's weakness for his long weekends at Hampton Court, his patronage of secular music and dancing, artists and writers, to explode that myth for ever.[47]

As will be seen, Cromwell's excessive tolerance went too far for many contemporaries. But he was always careful not to offend respectable contemporary opinion. His Church settlement respected local interests and property rights. As it evolved in the 1650s it had many elements desired by many moderate parliamentarians of the 1640s: a loose form of state control, retention of lay patronage and tithes, toleration of those Protestant sects which did not disrupt public order.

Had Cromwell lived for a further decade [in the opinion of Dr Cross] perhaps many of the Independent churches and some of the Baptist churches on the periphery of the national church might have been more fully comprehended within it. With the deaths of the remaining Laudian bishops perhaps some modified form of episcopacy, as envisaged by Ussher and Baxter, might possibly have been voluntarily adopted as a means of unity by the national church.[48]

The failures of Cromwellian government

Whatever case can be made out for the Cromwellian government (and it is likely that future research may have yet more to say in its favour), Cromwell, like every regime since 1640, failed to find an acceptable constitution to replace the one overthrown in 1640. Consequently, the achievements outlined in the previous section were shortlived. Professor Trevor-Roper suggested that Cromwell, like James I and unlike Elizabeth I, 'failed through lack of . . . parliamentary management by the executive'.[49] As he must have known, there was more to it than that. Cromwell failed because, despite his genuine desire for 'healing and settling', he was the leader of the army; in Christopher Hill's words, 'in the last resort he was sitting on bayonets and nothing else'.[50] By 1653 the traditional rulers of England were at one in seeing the army as the prime danger to everything they held dear: rule through parliament, their own supremacy in their localities, low taxation, their control of the Church, their wives, children, servants, and tenants. In spite of Cromwell's efforts to woo the parliamentary classes, his only slim chance of getting a cooperative parliament elected on a propertied franchise (as Cromwell made clear at Putney and later he was not willing to consider any other kind of franchise) was to cut his links with the army, risking an army revolt and the reversal of much that had been achieved. In 1657 he apparently came very near to doing that, but, by rejecting the crown offered him, he signalled his inability or unwillingness (or both) to carry it through. This is the fundamental reason for Cromwell's failure. His task was almost impossible: to rule as an army leader and secure the confidence of a political nation which would not tolerate the intervention of the army in politics.

Despite Cromwell's conciliatory speech to parliament when it met in September 1654, in which he emphasized his desire for a settlement, his conservative social prejudices and his achievements in the last ten months, his position as Protector came under strong attack in the first week of the session. This was not simply a result of his failure to manage the House, although the redistribution of seats and new franchise under the Instrument of Government made its management a great deal harder than previously: compared with the Long Parliament there was a massive increase in the numbers of country MPs at the expense of borough MPs. Nor was the opposition to Cromwell simply from hardened civilian republicans like Hazelrige, Thomas Scot, and John Bradshaw, who could never forgive and forget the dissolution of the Rump; many of these withdrew after Cromwell's dramatic intervention in parliament on 12 September, when he forced MPs to sign a 'Recognition', promising not to alter the Government 'as it is settled [by the Instrument of Government] in a single person and a Parliament'. Nevertheless parliamentary opposition continued. Not all features of the Instrument of Government were objectionable to MPs: the executive authority of a single person with constitutional checks, and the guarantees of regular parliaments were welcomed. What few MPs could accept were the powers given by the Instrument to Cromwell and the army, especially the Protector's authority to enact ordinances when parliament was not in session. In the few short weeks of its life parliament voted against these and other rights which the Protector had been granted by the Instrument. Even the Protector's control of the army was questioned; it was proposed that after Cromwell's death the army should be controlled by parliament alone, and in the meantime there should be an immediate reduction in the army establishment. In the first Protectorate parliament the root of the difference between Cromwell and the parliamentary classes was laid bare. The Instrument of Government perpetuated the power of the army and there would be no parliamentary cooperation until the Instrument in that respect was amended. Cromwell impatiently dissolved parliament on 22 January 1655, interpreting the five months minimum parliamentary session as lunar, and not calendar, months.

In March 1655 a royalist rising in Wiltshire led by Penruddock was easily suppressed by Desborough, who was appointed 'Major General of the West' for the purpose. This, and the discovery of paper plots by the royalists in other parts of the country, was made the occasion for the appointment later in 1655 of eleven major-generals, and England and Wales were divided amongst them.[51] By October they had received their instructions and were on their way to their 'cantons'. Like a lot of other things about the major-generals experiment, though, the reasons for it are not clear. Perhaps hindsight puts the royalist threat in 1655 into a perspective not possible at the time; but John Thurloe and his government spies were always one step ahead of the plotters, and Cromwell knew how divided amongst themselves they were. It may be that, as well as royalist insurrections, the major-generals were designed to solve the Protectorate's growing financial problems. To get the support of the landed classes Cromwell had to reduce taxation, which meant reducing expenditure on the army. This may have been the intention behind the local volunteer militias, to be organized by the major-generals and financed by a 'decimation' tax of one-tenth of the estates of known royalists worth over £100 p.a. in lands and £1,500 p.a. in goods. Not only would the new militia be cheaper than the professional army, but it was to be locally run by commissioners appointed to assist the major-generals. Security would be tightened up, and the standing army replaced by a cheaper, locally run militia. Perhaps this was the package for which Cromwell hoped to get support. If so, he was sadly mistaken.

Part of the odious reputation of the rule of the major-generals owes more to the jibes of their enemies than to historical accuracy. Their social backgrounds were different from those of the gentry with whom they came into conflict in the localities, but they were not all low-born nonentities, the 'silly mean fellows' of Mrs Hutchinson's sneer. Although their enemies labelled them as dictatorial 'satraps' and 'bashaws', most acted in strict accordance with the law and their instructions. Their 'kill-joy', 'puritanical' image also is a caricature that has only some truth. Not all the major-generals were concerned with improving the morals of the population under their control; and those who were felt that racehorse meetings, cockfights, and alehouses were as much a threat to security as to morals. Though admittedly those major-generals who were concerned to stamp out immorality were much more efficient at it than any of their sixteenth- and early seventeenth-century predecessors. Major-General Charles Worsley was proud of his record of having closed two hundred alehouses in Blackburn Hundred (Lancashire) alone.[52]

The striking fact that emerges about the major-generals, when some of the myths about them have been stripped away, is the differences among them. This is certainly true about their effectiveness. All faced enormous difficulties: non-cooperation of local people, too-large areas under their control and, often, a central government insensitive to their needs. How they coped with these difficulties depended on their strength of character. William Goffe, the major-general of Sussex, Hampshire, and Berkshire, was 'temperamentally unsuited to the administrative task set him'.[53] Consequently, his constructive impact on local administration was slight. Major-General Worsley, on the other hand, had none of Goffe's timidity and lack of self-confidence. His dynamic administration in Lancashire, Cheshire, and Staffordshire was sometimes embarrassing even for the government, which intervened to moderate his enthusiasm.[54] Their differences apart, however, what united the major-generals was the hatred they roused in the localities. They represented an experiment in direct rule from Westminster. Outsiders were imposed on the localities and provincial resentment, so strong in the sixteenth and seventeenth centuries, was roused. Not only this, but the major-generals began to reopen the wounds in county society inflicted in the 1640s. Operating the decimation tax meant unearthing royalist pasts which many were trying to forget. The local communities closed their ranks, and in the elections to parliament in August 1656 demonstrated their total opposition to the centralization, high taxation, and army rule represented by the major-generals, who failed dismally to persuade the electors to send pro-Cromwellian MPs to the new parliament. Provincial England never forgot the major-generals, and the political nation became even more determined to oppose the political role of the army.

The prospects of cooperation were, therefore, not bright when the second Protectorate parliament met in September 1656, even though Cromwell and the council excluded over a hundred MPs thought likely to be critics of the regime. In the first parliamentary session this was confirmed, when another obstacle to Cromwell's rapprochement with civilian parliamentarians appeared. The case of James Nayler illustrated that few MPs shared Cromwell's commitment to extensive religious toleration, but feared it as a recipe for political and social subversion. Nayler's 'crime' was to re-enact in Bristol in October 1656 Christ's entry into Jerusalem. So innocuous an act became a national issue because it provided a focus for the fears roused by the disruptive activities of the Ranters and Nayler's fellow Quakers. Cromwell could do little to prevent parliament savagely punishing the unfortunate Nayler.

In 1657, however, two events emphasized that Cromwell might still reconcile the political nation to his rule. First, political realist as he was, he gave way to parliament's demand to end the rule of the major-generals. There is little doubt that the Protector connived at the defeat of Desborough's Bill to continue the decimation tax; Oliver's son-in-law, John Claypole, led the attack on the Bill in parliament. Second, Cromwell at last killed the Instrument of Government, the army's constitution, and accepted a parliamentary constitution, the amended Humble Petition and Advice. During 1656 and 1657 Cromwell had been cutting his political links with the army 'grandees' and forging new links with conservative civilian supporters. More and more Lambert, Fleetwood, and Desborough found that they had to compete for the Protector's ear with civilians like Lord Broghill, Sir Charles Worsley, and viscount Fauconberg.[55] Ominously for the 'grandees' the assessment to support the army was drastically cut in 1657 to £35,000 a month from its level of £60,000 a month from 1654 to 1657 and £120,000 a month during 1653 and early 1654.[56] The Humble Petition and Advice was the culmination of these 'civilizing' tendencies. It was an anti-military constitution: it enhanced parliament's power at the expense of the army-dominated council of state. It was also a conservative constitution: it erected a two-chamber parliament, hereditary succession, and set limits to religious toleration. But that was as far as Cromwell would go. He would not accept the crown offered by the backers of the Humble Petition and Advice. He wanted to conciliate the army, while at the same time winning new civilian supporters. Was this possible? The evidence is inconclusive; Cromwell died on 3 September 1658, having failed. But the last part of Cromwell's life does not prove that, given more time, he would not have succeeded. It was the republican MPs excluded in 1656, who returned to parliament in the second session in 1658 and dynamited the new constitution, and forced Cromwell to dissolve his last parliament in February. Despite Lambert's resignation Cromwell still retained the loyalty of the army, as well as of the civilian Cromwellians. Yet there is precious little evidence, either, that Cromwell would have succeeded. By the end of his life the extent of committed civilian support at his court and in the country was small. The most that one can say is that Cromwell was the only man who could possibly have retained the support of the army, while broadening the base of his political party in the country. What happened to a Protector who took an alternative course and cut his links with the army is seen in the brief reign of Oliver's son, Richard.

The end of the Good Old Cause, 1658–1660

The question usually asked about the closing stages of the Interregnum, why was the monarchy restored in 1660, ignores the equally important question, why was the monarchy *not* restored until nearly two years after Oliver Cromwell's death. Amid the confusion and complexities of post-Cromwellian politics one fact shines out: the lack of widespread enthusiasm for the Stuarts. Most Englishmen continued to hope that an alternative constitutional settlement to Stuart monarchy could be found. As in 1651 and 1655, the planned nationwide royalist rising in the summer of 1659 was a total failure. However, by the end of 1659 opinion had swung in favour of the restoration of Charles Stuart. From September 1658 to December 1659 all the major political groups who came to power failed to agree or to produce a workable constitutional settlement, until the country was faced with political and economic anarchy. It is this which accounts for the political conversion of most people in England in the winter of 1659–60. Restoring the monarchy was considered to be the only way of restoring stability.

Most of the contending political groups in the Commonwealth were represented in the parliament called by Richard in November 1658, which met at the end of January 1659: civilian Cromwellians, republicans, army officers, and an uncommitted mass of independent MPs. Richard's lack of connections with the army only partly explains his failure to maintain his father's balance between these factions. While he could have done little to prevent the expected opposition of republicans to the Humble Petition and Advice, Richard does not seem to have made a serious effort to gain army support. Instead he relied heavily for advice on the civilian Cromwellians, and therefore alienated the army grandees, among whom Fleetwood was now prominent. The fears of the 'Wallingford House grandees' (named after Fleetwood's London residence) that they were losing power were confirmed when Richard allowed the civilian Cromwellians in parliament to lead the conservative majority there in support of measures to restrict both the extent of religious toleration and the army's freedom to indulge in political activity. The army responded to parliament's votes of 18–20 April, which would have stripped the army of all political power, by forcing Richard to dissolve parliament on 21 April.

It is not certain that the grandees would have taken such immediate and drastic action if left to themselves. The senior officers, however, were faced with a situation very like that in 1647. Early in 1659 there was a resurgence of radicalism within the junior ranks of the army, calling for many of the reforms demanded in 1647, and fuelled by the same sort of material grievances. As in 1647 the grandees were forced by pressure from below to take more radical action than they really wanted. The most bizzare element in this reincarnation of 1647 was the alliance between the army radicals and the republicans. The hatred between the army and Rump Commonwealth was forgotten, and ironically the army, which had dissolved the Rump in April 1653, now recalled it on 7 May 1659. It is a measure of the diminishing political options left open to the army that the Rump, which had disappointed radical expectations in 1649, was recalled on a wave of renewed radicalism ten years later.

Not surprisingly the Rump failed again to live up to the army's expectations of it. It spent the summer in long, sterile constitutional debates and in demonstrating the antipathy felt by civilian republicans for the army. It only lasted until the autumn, because the army spent August crushing Booth's rebellion.

Inevitably, when that danger was removed, the army on 13 October reacted to the army purges proposed by the Rump and the attempted arrest of Lambert by expelling the Rump for a second time. Both Richard and the Rump had demonstrated their political bankruptcy; it was now the turn of the army.

The committee of safety, headed by Fleetwood, set up by the army grandees on 27 October as an interim government, proved as barren of successful constitutional ideas as its civilian predecessors. More seriously, Fleetwood also failed to maintain even the loyalty of all the army. The army in Scotland under George Monck declared for the

Rump and was followed by Fairfax and his army in Yorkshire, the army in Ireland, and the navy in the Downs. The coincidence of a government which lacked effective support combined with renewed acute trade depression undoubtedly convinced many that the Republic could no longer guarantee law and order. Faced with the growing demands for a 'free' parliament or the return of the secluded members of 1648, and with organized threats to withhold taxes, Fleetwood panicked and on 24 December resigned and handed over his powers to the Rump.

In reality, however, Fleetwood's resignation paved the way for General Monck, who, as the Rump reassembled, began his march south into England. Viewed with the benefit of hindsight Monck appears wiser and more sure of his goal than he probably was. Yet he was enough of a political realist, after being in London for three weeks, to grasp that the Rump was too unpopular, and the army too divided, to rule; that there was no other alternative but the restoration of the Stuarts. On 21 February, under Monck's protection, the return of the secluded MPs of 1648 to parliament made that inevitable. The republicans of the Rump were now easily outvoted, and on 16 March the Long Parliament, which had first met nearly twenty years before, declared itself dissolved. In June 1660 the Republic collapsed because it no longer, unlike the regimes of the Rump and of Oliver, provided stability and security.

Notes

For abbreviations used throughout see p. xiv.

1.   G. Fortescue, *Catalogue of the Pamphlets, Books, etc. Collected by George Thomason 1640–61* (2 vols, 1906), I, p. xxi; II, p. 590.
2.   Lamont, *Godly Rule*, passim.; C. Hill, *Antichrist in Seventeenth-century England* (1971).
3.   For a fundamental revision of this sect see B. S. Capp, *The Fifth Monarchy Men: a study in seventeenth-century millenarianism* (1972).
4.   C. Hill, *The World Turned Upside Down: radical ideas during the English Revolution* (1972), p. 80, quoting William Dell.
5.   For the role of women and contemporary attitudes to them see E. M. Williams, 'Women preachers in the civil war', *J.M.H.*, I (1929), pp. 561–9; K. Thomas, 'Women and the civil war sects', *P.&P.*, XIII 1958, pp. 42–62; Patricia Higgins, 'The reactions of women, with special reference to women petitioners', in Manning, ed., *Politics, Religion and the English Civil War*, pp. 179–222.
6.   Quoted in Hill, *World Turned Upside Down*, pp. 166, 172.
7.   Quoted in *ibid.*, pp. 242, 244.
8.   C. Wilson, 'The other face of mercantilism', *T.R.H.S.*, 5th ser., IX (1959), pp. 81–101, repr. in D. C. Coleman, ed., *Revisions in Mercantilism* (1969), pp. 118–39.
9.   The best introduction to Winstanley is by Christopher Hill in C. Hill, ed., *Winstanley: The Law of Freedom and other writings* (1973).
10.   J. C. Davis, 'Gerrard Winstanley and the Restoration of the True Magistracy', *P.&P.*, LXX (1976), pp. 76–93. Davis qualifies Hill's analysis of Winstanley's writings, as do Lotte Mulligan, John K. Graham and

Judith Richards, 'Winstanley: a case for the man as he said he was', *J. Eccl. H.*, XXVIII (1977), pp. 57–75.

11. Hill, *World Turned Upside Down*, pp. 86–103. Although the evidence is thin, Dr Hill thinks that other Digger colonies were established in Northampton-shire, Kent, Buckinghamshire, Hertfordshire, Middlesex, Bedfordshire, Leicestershire, Gloucestershire, and Nottinghamshire.

12. Quoted in Capp, *Fifth Monarchy Men*, pp. 55, 53.

13. G. E. Aylmer, ed., 'Englands spirit unfoulded', *P.&P.*, XL (1968) pp. 3–15.

14. Aylmer, ed., *Levellers*, pp. 143–4.

15. Quoted in B. Worden, *The Rump Parliament* (1974), p. 1.

16. *Ibid.*, p. 227.

17. H. J. Habakkuk, 'The parliamentary army and the crown lands', *Welsh H.R.*, pp. 403–26; I. Gentles, 'The management of crown lands 1649–60', *Agric. H.R.*, XIX (1971), pp. 25–41.

18. Aylmer, ed., *Levellers*, p. 146.

19. P. W. Thomas, ed., *The English Revolution, iii: Newsbooks 5, I, Mercurius Politicus* (1971), pp. 1–8.

20. Quoted in Worden, *Rump*, p. 271.

21. Abbott, *Writings*, II, pp. 38–9.

22. Worden, *Rump*; D. Underdown, *Pride's Purge: politics in the Puritan Revolution* (1971), especially pp. 208–96.

23. Bulstrode Whitelocke, *Memorials of the English Affairs* (4 vols, 1853), II, p. 523.

24. Quoted in Worden, *Rump*, pp. 13–14.

25. Quoted in Capp, *Fifth Monarchy Men*, pp. 74–5.

26. Quoted in Worden, *Rump*, p. 276; Abbott, *Writings*, II, p. 507.

27. See J. P. Cooper, 'Social and economic policies under the Commonwealth', in Aylmer, ed., *Interregnum*, pp. 134–5 for the debate.

28. See Worden, *Rump*, especially pages 345–8 for a radical revision of the older view.

29. Abbott, ed., *Writings*, III, p. 453.

30. Clarendon, *History*, VI, pp. 91, 97.

31. Hill, *God's Englishman*, pp. 193–4.

32. Worden, *Rump*, p. 69.

33. Abbott, *Writings*, III, p. 435; II, pp. 520–1.

34. *Ibid.*, III, pp. 61, 63–4.

35. Quoted in Capp, *Fifth Monarchy Men*, p. 67.

36. Clarendon, *History*, V, p. 282.

37. Abbott, *Writings*, IV, p. 489.

38. Quoted in G. D. Heath, 'Making the Instrument of Government', *J.B.S.*, VI (1967), p. 17, n. 10.

39. D. Underdown, 'Settlement in the counties 1653–8', in Aylmer, *Inter-regnum*, p. 177.

40. The view of E. M. Leonard, *The Early History of English Poor Relief* (1900) is not upheld by A. L. Beier, 'Poor law in Warwickshire 1630–60', *P.&P.*, XXXV (1966), pp. 77–100; G. E. Aylmer, *The State's Servants: the civil service of the English Republic 1649–60* (1973), pp. 308–11; Morrill, *Cheshire*, ch. 6; and G. C. F. Forster, 'County government in Yorkshire during the Interregnum', *Northern History*, XII (1976), pp. 84–104.

41. G. D. Ramsay, 'Industrial *Laisser Faire* and the policy of Cromwell', *Econ. H.R.*, 1st ser., XVI (1946), pp. 93–110.

42. Aylmer, *State's Servants*, especially pp. 139–67, 328.
43. I. Roots, *The Great Rebellion* (1966), p. 175. See also I. Roots, 'Cromwell's ordinances: the early legislation of the Protectorate', in Aylmer, ed., *Interregnum*, pp. 143–64.
44. C. Cross, 'The Church in England 1646–60', in Aylmer, ed., *Interregnum*, p. 107.
45. B. R. White, 'The organization of the Particular Baptists 1644–60', *J. Eccl. H.*, XVII (1966), pp. 209–25.
46. Baxter, *Autobiography*, p. 84.
47. Hill, *God's Englishman*, pp. 197–9.
48. Cross, 'The Church', in Aylmer, ed., *Interregnum*, pp. 119–20.
49. H. R. Trevor-Roper, 'Cromwell and his parliaments', in *ibid.*, *Religion, the Reformation and Social Change* (1967), p. 388.
50. Hill, *God's Englishman*, p. 154.
51. The best starting point for the major-generals is I. Roots, 'Swordsmen and decimators – Cromwell's major-generals', in Parry, ed., *English Civil War*, pp. 78–92.
52. Aylmer, ed., *State's Servants*, p. 313.
53. Fletcher, *Sussex*, p. 307.
54. Morrill, *Cheshire*, pp. 276–87.
55. Austin Woolrych, 'Last quests for a settlement 1657–60', in Aylmer, ed., *Interregnum*, pp. 183–204.
56. M. Ashley, *Financial and Commercial Policy under the Cromwellian Protectorate* (1934), p. 77.

Part four

The Reigns of Charles II and James II, 1660–1688

'The Great Rebellion willy nilly had permanent consequences', writes Professor Roots. 'Like some kind of many-lived Cheshire cat it left a persistent grin behind.'[1] Undeniably England after 1660, as a result of the English Revolution, was never the same again. Yet the Revolution was a failure. The violent conservative reaction to it at the Restoration helped to produce an English Church, government, and society that was very different from that which many supporters of the 'Good Old Cause' had wanted; moreover, its contribution to England's long-term political, constitutional and ecclesiastical development was inconclusive. Every regime from 1640 to 1660, despite heterogeneous experiments, had failed to reach a pragmatic settlement of two of the most pressing problems of the seventeenth century: first, the constitutional problem of deciding where sovereignty lay, in the executive or legislative, or, if it was to be divided, what the balance of power between executive and legislative was to be; and, secondly, the problem of whether or not religious toleration was compatible with political stability. One of the most persistent and unfounded assumptions about late seventeenth-century English history is that after 1660 the eventual supremacy of parliament over the crown in the constitution was assured. For many the effect of the English Revolution was to strengthen their attachment to the monarchy, not to weaken it. Therefore, one of the central questions about the period from 1660 to 1688 is why did England not become an absolute monarchy on the European pattern? A second major legacy of the English Revolution, despite the evidence of Cromwellian rule that toleration of a wide variety of religious opinions did not endanger the stability of the state, was to confirm many in the belief that religious nonconformity was indistinguishable from political sedition. Therefore another fundamental problem for the historian of late seventeenth-century England is to explain this apparent paradox. Why did schemes for religious toleration for Protestant dissenters after 1660 fail?

The failure to reach a stable constitutional and religious settlement was just as marked between 1660 and 1688 as during the English Revolution. There are no simple explanations for the two broad trends – the failure to establish a settled constitution on the continental pattern and the collapse of plans for religious toleration – which provide the major themes for this section on the history of England from 1660 to 1688. What is clear, though, is that the development of absolutist government before 1688 was principally retarded (as will be seen, it was not stunted completely) by the determination of Charles II and James II to pursue Catholic policies that most Englishmen found abhorrent. For most English Protestants in the late seventeenth century anti-Catholicism proved to be stronger than their fear and hatred of other Protestants. Especially in the 1670s and in the late 1680s anti-Catholicism was a more powerful political force than Protestant disunity. Yet throughout the later seventeenth century the gulf separating Anglicans and Protestants dissenters was never permanently bridged, and it was strong enough to prevent the establishment either of toleration for those excluded from the Church of England or of one comprehensive Protestant Church.

Notes

1. Ivan Roots, *The Great Rebellion 1642–60* (1966), p. 257.

Chapter 8

The failure of 'the Restoration Settlement', 1660–1667

The Convention Parliament, 1660: old wounds reopened and old problems unsolved

The 'Restoration Settlement' is a misnomer. The series of *ad hoc* decisions made in the early 1660s by the Convention and Cavalier Parliaments, which are traditionally called 'the Restoration Settlement', settled very little. The political history of the period 1660–7 is characterized by escalating political instability and by growing conflict between Charles II and parliament, until in 1667 the king only averted a serious constitutional crisis by deserting his principal minister, Clarendon.

The main task facing the Convention Parliament,[1] which met on 25 April 1660, was that which had faced every regime since the 1640s: to continue the search for 'settlement'. Unfortunately, the MPs of 1660 were no more united on what form a settlement should take than the victorious parliamentarians of 1646. Not only was the Convention split on religious lines – Anglicans, Presbyterians and Independents – but political divisions were sharpened by the bitterness of civil war and regicide. There was a wide gulf between those who had remained committed royalists throughout the Revolution and those who had collaborated with the republican regimes of the 1650s and who had only supported the Restoration as a means of ending the political anarchy of the months following Oliver's death. Charles II was only recognizing political realities when he included representatives of both groups in his new privy council: consistent royalists like Hyde (the new lord chancellor, created earl of Clarendon in 1661), Sir Edward Nicholas, and the duke of Ormonde, alongside men who had only recently served the Cromwellian government, notably Monck (now duke of Albemarle), Edward Montague (now earl of Sandwich), and Anthony Ashley Cooper (later earl of Shaftesbury). Seen in this context it is perhaps not surprising that the Convention failed to solve problems which had defeated earlier regimes.

Within a week of its first meeting the Convention resolved that government ought to be in the hands of king, Lords, and Commons, and agreed that a fleet (with the politically agile Ashley Cooper on board) be sent to bring Charles Stuart back to England. Why was Charles II allowed to return unconditionally, with the Nineteen Propositions, the Propositions of Newcastle, and the 'Treaties' of Oxford, Uxbridge, and Newport apparently forgotten and certainly not mentioned publicly?[2] Partly it was a recognition that there was no alternative to the monarchy as a basis for political stability. Partly also it was a result of Charles's Declaration issued from Breda, which was read to the Convention when it first met. The Declaration of Breda was a skilfully assembled package which contained something for every political faction in England. By leaving the problem of confiscated estates to parliament the Declaration raised the hopes of royalists that their lost lands would be restored; by promising 'liberty to tender consciences' the Declaration held out the prospect to Independents, especially the sectaries in the army, of the continuation of the religious toleration of the 1650s; and the fears of those who had collaborated with the regicide regimes of a reign of terror were calmed by the Declaration's promise of a free and general pardon for all except those to be named by parliament. In these ways the Declaration eased the transition to the new regime. What it did not do was provide a blueprint for a constitutional and religious settlement. Nor did the Convention. The divisions within it and the weight of more immediate problems facing it ensured that fundamental questions concerning the respective powers of crown and parliament were not resolved, and that Charles II was restored in 1660 free of limitations such as parliamentary control of the army and of his ministers, without which many MPs in the Long Parliament would have thought the restoration of the monarchy inconceivable.

Since money had been a major source of political friction in the early seventeenth century it was essential for constitutional harmony that crown and parliament agree on a workable financial settlement in 1660. Why did this not happen? Uppermost in the minds of some MPs was the fear that generous financial provision for the crown would make it independent of parliament. But of greater importance was the fact that, as in the case of their predecessors in the 1620s, the intricacies of public finance were unintelligible to most MPs in 1660 and in the following years. (With the notable exception of Professor Chandaman, this stricture applies to many historians as well.[3]) As a result even the parliamentary grant for paying the arrears of the navy and army, which most MPs of course wanted to disband quickly, was £375,000 short of what was needed. In addition Charles never received another £550,000 which he had spent in payment of his own and his father's debts. Nor did the Convention provide a settled income of £1,200,000 p.a., which was calculated as the sum necessary for ordinary royal expenditure and which curiously remained as an unquestioned figure in the subsequent negotiations. In September the Convention's financial committee estimated that, if the crown were compensated by a grant of £100,000 p.a. for the loss of its feudal revenue from wardships which were not renewed in 1660, the crown's annual revenue would fall short by £425,000 p.a. of the agreed £1,200,000 p.a. Two months later, when the matter was discussed again, the Convention decided to grant the Commonwealth liquor exise to Charles for life, assuming that this was adequate compensation both for the abolition of wardships and the deficiency of £425,000 p.a. Clearly, as Professor Chandaman has shown, this was a false assumption, of which both Clarendon and the new lord treasurer, the earl of Southampton, were aware, but which they failed to explain to parliament.

All the parties to the financial negotiations in 1660 can be excused in some measure for their failure to produce a reasonable financial provision for the crown. MPs, apart from lacking the necessary knowledge of public finance, could not have foreseen that an army would be retained and Tangier garrisoned at a minimum cost of £140,000 p.a.[4] Charles's ministers, on the other hand, had good reasons for refraining from asking the Convention for more money. The period before 1660 had been one of unprecedented high taxation. It must have seemed easier to borrow than to risk discontent by imposing further financial burdens. However, in doing this the court allowed MPs to disband in 1660 thinking that the revenue problem had been solved. It had not: by the end of 1660 the crown was saddled with debts of £925,000 and an ordinary revenue that was at least £300,000 short of the magic figure of £1,200,000 p.a.

Of equal significance for later English history was the Convention's failure to provide a religious framework which most English Protestants would accept. On the face of it this did not seem a likely outcome. There was a section of opinion in England in 1660 in favour of erecting a wide comprehensive Church. Some churchmen and moderate Presbyterians resurrected Archbishop Ussher's scheme of the early 1640s for modified episcopacy. Charles appeared to support this move to reconcile opposing Protestant factions and in this he was assisted by Clarendon. Prominent non-Anglicans (Richard Baxter, Edmund Calamy, Simeon Ashe, and Thomas Reynolds) were appointed royal chaplains. Moreover, during the parliamentary recess in September 1660 Charles and Clarendon made a determined effort to get some kind of agreement between Anglicans and Presbyterians. These culminated on 25 October in a meeting between Charles and some Presbyterian leaders at Clarendon's lodgings, Worcester House, after which the king issued a declaration proposing a Church settlement in which the powers of bishops were to be limited by councils of presbyters and in which contentious matters of liturgy and ceremony were to be referred to a committee of divines 'of both persuasions' and a national synod. At the same time bishoprics were offered to leading Presbyterians. Whether or not Charles or Clarendon were sincere in wanting a comprehensive Church is not known. The evidence is inconclusive and has led to divergent interpretations. There is less doubt about Charles's sincerity than Clarendon's.[5] As will be seen the king for much of the first half of his reign inclined to a policy of reconciliation with dissenters. It will be argued later that he did so largely to erect an alternative political alliance to that of the crown and Church (see below, pp. 251–2). Clarendon, too, may have been sincere in 1660 in wanting comprehension. With the army not yet demobilized, the government had good reason to want to avoid antagonizing non-Anglican opinion. Why, then, did schemes for a comprehensive Church come to nothing in 1660, leaving the way clear for the restoration of an intolerant Church? Perhaps the division of religious opinion represented in the Convention is enough to explain why, despite meeting once a week from 6 July until the adjournment of 13 September 1660 as a Grand Committee to discuss religion, nothing was decided. But probably of more importance in explaining the failure of comprehension in 1660 is the influence of the government, which, like the political leaders of the early 1640s, wanted to postpone decisions on this explosive, divisive issue until the new regime was more firmly established. Charles also probably wanted to keep the settlement in his own hands. As will be seen, in this aim he was totally unsuccessful. It very soon became clear that so strong was intolerant Anglican opinion in the country that comprehension of non-Anglicans in the state Church was not a practicable possibility.

It has long been recognized that the Convention was more successful in dealing with immediate problems than with fundamental constitutional, financial, and ecclesiastical issues. Many of its day-to-day decisions were moderate and sensible compromises. It resisted the extreme demands of Cavaliers and passed Acts confirming judicial decisions made during the Interregnum and continuing those already in progress; it approved an Act of Indemnity which pardoned all but a few who had been closely connected with the execution of Charles I; and it worked out a settlement of confiscated estates and forced sales of land that attempted to alienate as few interests as possible. But it has perhaps not been emphasized enough that all this did not mean that the bitterness that had its roots in the 1640s and 1650s had been forgotten. On the contrary the debates on the Indemnity Bill revealed the depths of hatred felt by many (including William Prynne[6]) for those who had been associated with the regicide regimes; hatred which was not appeased by the Act's moderation and which found expression in the grisly exhumation of the bones of Cromwell, Pym, Blake, and others, even those of Cromwell's mother. In many counties royalist vindictiveness was directed against prominent parliamentarians and Cromwellian collaborators under the guise of proceedings against suspected conspirators. As Professor Roots says, 'there was only a smear of blood at the Restoration, but a whole streak of meanness'.[7] The land settlement was a valiant attempt to appease different interests.[8] The confiscated estates of crown and Church were restored (by clauses in the Act of Indemnity and the Act for the Confirmation of Judicial Proceedings), as were those of some royalists (by private Acts of parliament and by separate orders of the House of Lords to sheriffs). But nothing was done to help those royalists who had sold estates to enable them to pay composition fines, even though as one prominent royalist, the eighth earl of Derby, caustically said, such sales were no more voluntary 'than when a man beset with robbers delivered them 9 parts of his goods to save the 10th and perhaps his life'.[9] Consequently, the land settlement was a compromise that failed: it inflamed rather than soothed old wounds. It was, wrote Thomas earl of Ailesbury later,

the source of what was termed in years following 'Whiggism', and it really sprang by degrees from the discontent of noble families and of many good families of the first gentry in the Counties whose ancestors were sequestered, decimated and what not on account of their steadfast loyalties, and so many losing their lives also.

Royalist hopes of receiving reward from a grateful king were not fulfilled. Instead Charles II cynically rewarded 'his enemies to sweeten them, for that his friends were so by a settled principle, and that their loyalty could not be shaken'.[10] The Convention was dissolved on 29 December 1660. Its successor, the Cavalier Parliament, which met first on 8 May 1661, was to show that Anglicans and royalists were determined to get their revenge for the humiliation they felt they had suffered.

The Cavalier Parliament and the restored monarchy, 1661–1664

The elections which followed the dissolution of the Convention reflected the tide of pro-royalist feeling in the country. Gentry memories of the way parliamentary county committees and major-generals had undermined their power combined with continued fears of political instability which appeared to be the only alternative to monarchical rule. Venner's Rising (see below) was contemporary with the elections, and the government had little difficulty in maintaining an atmosphere of panic as it made public its spies' reports of meetings of conventicles and allegedly seditious meetings. It is possible, though, to exaggerate the militant royalism of the Cavalier Parliament even in 1661. One hundred of the new MPs had sat in the Long Parliament, and this legacy of a fund of parliamentary experience alone ensured that the Cavalier Parliament would not be willing to fill the role of rubber stamp for royal authority. Nor, even in the atmosphere of royalist euphoria of 1660–1 were MPs prepared to abandon all the constitutional gains of the early 1640s. Charles I's financial expedients of the 1630s remained illegal, and star chamber, the court of high commission, council of the north, court of wards, and feudal tenures remained abolished. It is often, correctly, said that the monarchy that was restored in 1660 was that of 1641 not 1640.

Yet the powers of the monarchy that the Cavalier Parliament did restore are as significant as those that it did not. The attempt which had been initiated in the winter of 1641–2 to impose two principal limitations on the power of the monarchy was abandoned in the 1660s. The Cavalier

Parliament made no attempt to challenge the king's right to appoint privy councillors and state officials or fill Church and local government posts. And in the Militia Acts of 1661 and 1662 the Cavalier Parliament in effect conceded that the crown (not parliament as claimed by the Militia Ordinance of March 1642) should have sole control of the militia. As further evidence of reaction against the pretensions made by parliament during the Revolution an Act of 1661 laid down the penalty of praemunire[11] for anyone who claimed that parliament had legislative powers without the king. In addition the Triennial Act of 1664 repealed its 1641 predecessor and replaced it with an emasculated version, which simply declared that the maximum period between parliaments ought to be three years: it did not maintain the 1641 machinery for enforcing this if the king ignored it, as in fact Charles II did at the end of his reign, as will be seen. Further Acts against 'tumultuous petitioning' (1661) and in favour of censorship of the press (1662) emphasized the reaction in the crown's favour at this time. The powers of the restored monarchy were still enormous: the power of vetoing legislation, of dispensing individuals from parliamentary statutes or suspending statutes completely, of dissolving and calling parliaments, of making foreign policy. The royalist reaction produced by the recent memories of sequestrations and decimation taxes helped Charles II to inherit a position *potentially* as powerful as that of Louis XIV in France.

In the early 1660s, however, two things prevented Charles II from developing his power as Louis XIV was doing in France: Charles had neither the ability nor the financial resources of his brother monarch across the channel.[12] The views of historians about Charles II differ greatly.[13] He has had his ardent admirers as well as stern critics. Although it is difficult to take seriously the case for Charles as a great king, his detractors have sometimes criticized him for the wrong reasons, judging him on highminded moral grounds rather than in the light of whether or not he was an able and effective ruler. His extramarital adventures are fascinating for the scope and catholicity of the king's sexual appetite and taste which they reveal: in Professor Kenyon's words, in these matters Charles 'was not a gourmet so much as a gourmand'.[14] Although Charles's mistresses were of some political importance, as will be seen, it is possible to place too much emphasis on them in accounts of the political history of this period. Mistresses and effective monarchical rule, as Louis XIV's activities illustrate, were not incompatible in the seventeenth century. None of Charles's mistresses had much political influence on the king. Nor did they cause his public attachment to his wife and family to waver, even when a divorce might have been the way out of the serious succession crises of his reign. Even his habit of seeing ministers in his mistresses' appartments is not *necessarily* evidence that Charles ignored affairs of state, merely that he preferred to conduct government business informally. The tittle-tattle related by that arch-gossipmonger Pepys is too often used to argue that Charles's pursuits of women was the root cause of his neglect of state affairs. Pepys's amusing story about Charles trying to catch a moth in Lady Castlemaine's room while the Dutch fleet sailed up the Medway is guaranteed to appear in a large percentage of examination answers on Charles II, but the story is unsupported and probably apocryphal. Moreover, criticisms of Charles's undoubted cynicism and unprincipled behaviour are often also moral rather than political judgements. His cynical treatment of his friends and enemies alike, his double-dealing, and resort to short-term political expediency were just the amoral qualities required by Machiavelli in a successful ruler. As will be seen, Charles's political sense in knowing when a position could no longer be held, regardless of the principle involved, was his greatest strength.

Yet it cannot be denied that many of Charles's activities and his life-style were detrimental to the efficient running of the king's government and to good political relations with the parliamentary classes. He did prefer the racecourse and associated pleasures of Newmarket and the brothels of Covent Garden to the day-to-day tedium of government. Royal government suffered in consequence because there was no one at Westminster to supervise administrative details for him. Not even Clarendon in the early 1660s had enough of the king's confidence to take his place. Similarly, the one man who might have been able to do this after Clarendon's downfall, Danby, was rarely taken into the king's secret counsels. Indeed Charles and Danby often followed contradictory policies, with each detesting that of the other. Perhaps Charles's greatest defect as a ruler was his financial extravagance. To that extent his profligate life-style was politically important: his mistresses and his bastards (of whom fourteen were acknowledged) had to be paid for. Moreover, his extravagance and dissolute living made it increasingly hard for ministers to persuade MPs to grant the king more money. Above all, Charles's extravagance was not confined to what Professor Chandaman calls his 'harem finance'.[15] Like James I, there was an unbridgeable gulf between Charles's attitude to money and the retrenchment schemes that were dreamed up in the lord treasurer's department. Given the financial resources of the Stuart monarchy this was disastrous, and never more so than in the 1660s.

Even without the king's extravagance the royal financial position would have been poor. Although the Cavalier Parliament recognized soon after it met that the Convention had not provided the king with enough permanent ordinary revenue, it never made good the deficit.[16] The Cavalier Parliament's own addition to the crown's permanent revenue, the hearth tax, in May 1662, was an ingenious device, but raised insufficient for the purpose. Even on the best parliamentary estimate the crown's ordinary revenue barely reached £1 million. It is true that in the short term the crown's total revenue was boosted by grants of massive parliamentary subsidies and did reach an average of £1,200,000 p.a. from 1660 to 1664. But there was no doubt that parliament would not be willing to maintain such levels of taxation, especially after the high tax years of the 1650s, and especially when the bulk of revenue seemed to be spent on Charles's extravagant life-style. More seriously, the feeling grew among MPs that (despite the evidence of financial experts, including their own) the crown now had a sufficient permanent revenue. By 1664, however, Charles's debts had risen to £1.25 million and the likelihood was that the position would get worse. The causes were diverse: from the inadequacies of lord treasurer Southampton to Charles's extravagance. But it is difficult to escape the conclusion that at this stage the major reason was an inadequate parliamentary grant of permanent revenue to the crown, which grew out of the ignorance of most MPs of public finance. This by itself was enough to ensure deteriorating relations between king and parliament. The shape of the restored Church proved to be an even greater divisive issue.

The Cavalier Parliament and the restored Church, 1661–1664

No greater contrast could have been devised than that between the broad, tolerant Cromwellian Church and the narrow, bigoted Anglican Church that was restored in the early 1660s. The hopes of some non-Anglicans that they might be included in the new state Church were kept alive by the Savoy Conference, which took place at the bishop of Lincoln's lodgings in the Strand from 5 April to 23 July 1661, between Anglican and Presbyterian representatives. However, by this stage comprehension was clearly a lost cause. As in 1660 both Charles II and Clarendon wanted to include Presbyterians in the Church of England, but the religious situation was now beyond their control. Already, regardless of official pronouncements the Anglican Church was being restored willy-nilly. During the winter of 1660–1 Anglican ministers who had been ejected in the 1640s returned to their livings under the patronage of Anglican gentry patrons. Anti-Puritanism was not confined to the gentry, but was reflected in harsh, popular satirical plays and broadsheets directed against Presbyterians, Baptists, and Quakers with titles like *The Lecherous Anabaptist or The Dipper Dipped*. Ben Jonson's *Bartholomew Fair* was revived and Samuel Butler produced his popular anti-Puritan diatribe, *Hudibras*, between 1662 and 1678. Nor was violence against Baptists and other nonconformist sects in the early 1660s uncommon. Dissent and republicanism were seen as interchangeable. According to a popular broadsheet ballad:

A Presbyter is such a monstrous thing
That loves democracy and hates a King,
For royal issue never making prayers,
Since kingdoms (as he thinks) should have no heirs,
But stand elective: that the hóly crew
May, when their Zeal transports them, choose a new.[17]

If religious nonconformity and political sedition were not already identified closely enough in the popular mind, then this was the lesson for many of Venner's Rising in January 1661. Thomas Venner was closely associated with the Fifth Monarchy men, some of whom were undoubtedly planning to resist the new regime. But in fact Venner posed no real threat. His active followers were perhaps as few as fifty and certainly no more than three hundred, and he was ignored by the army, which anyway was demobilized completely (apart from one regiment of foot and one troop of horse) by February. However, as so often in politics, the cliché – in this case Dissent equals Sedition – was more important to contemporaries than hard facts.

When the Cavalier Parliament met on 8 May 1661, therefore, despite the presence in the House of Commons of some MPs sympathetic to protestant dissenters,[18] a majority were determined to crush religious and political nonconformity at the same time. Within ten days of its first meeting bishops had been restored to the House of Lords, and the House of Commons voted by 228 to 103 votes that the Solemn League and Covenant should be burned by the public hangman, and that all MPs were to take the sacraments according to the Church of England. Exactly what form this should take still had to be decided. But it was Convocation not the Savoy Conference that completed the revision of the Prayer Book by December 1661, and predictably the revised Prayer Book, which was accepted by parliament in April 1662, was as obnoxious to many dissenters as the Elizabethan Prayer Book. The Cavalier Parliament then proceeded to enact a series of statutes – the so-called Clarendon Code – designed to impose severe penalties on those who refused to conform to the new state Church. Doubts about the chancellor's position there may be (as has been seen) but clearly Clarendon was not the initiator of the Clarendon Code. On the contrary until the end of 1663, most notably in his unsuccessful attempts in the House of Lords in 1661 and 1662 to make the Act of Uniformity less severe on dissenters, Clarendon tried to stem the tide of Anglican reaction. This he failed to do. The Corporation Act (1661) set up commissions empowered to evict all municipal officials who did not swear oaths of allegiance and non-resistance, declare the Solemn League and Covenant invalid, and take the Anglican sacraments. Similarly the Act of Uniformity (1662) was designed to restrict all positions in the Church, schools, and universities to Anglicans. All teachers and holders of ecclesiastical posts who did not make the necessary oaths and declarations by St Bartholomew's Day (24 August) 1662 were to be deprived of their livings. A taste of the pettiness and meanness that lay behind this legislation can be seen in the change to Bartholomew's Day as the final date rather than Michaelmas Day as in the original draft of the Bill, because MPs wanted to prevent nonconforming clergy from receiving their Michaelmas tithes before they were ejected. The exact number of English clergy who left their livings by St Bartholomew's Day 1662 is not known, but was probably 1909.[19] An Act of 1662 singled out the Quakers for especially severe punitive treatment. All nonconformist sects were hit by two further Acts of the Clarendon Code. The

Conventicle Act (1664) prohibited all assemblies not held in accordance with the Book of Common Prayer and attended by five or more adults who were not members of the household in which the service was conducted. The Five Mile Act (1665) forbade all preachers and teachers who did not take the necessary oaths and declarations from coming within five miles of any town or city, and all ejected clergy from travelling within five miles of the parish where they had been incumbents.

After his failure to amend the Uniformity Bill Clarendon must have realized the political wisdom of becoming a 'Clarendonian'. Government support for the Clarendon Code was part of the bargain which produced the grants of parliamentary supplies in the early 1660s (which have already been noted). Probably also Clarendon realized just how valuable a supporter of the restored monarchy the restored Church could be. So enthusiastically royalist was the Restoration Church that it carried the theories of the divine hereditary right of kings and the sinfulness of rebellion to established order to the ultimate absurdity of erecting the executed Charles I into a Holy Martyr. 'The Church of England', sermonized Dr Robert South in November 1661, 'glories in nothing more than that she is the truest friend of kings and kingly government, of any other church in the world; that they were the same hands that took the crown from the king's head and the mitre from the bishops.'[20] The restored Church and the restored monarchy must stand together. Sheldon and Sancroft, archbishops of Canterbury from the Restoration to 1691, as well as Clarendon, recognized the force of this. One of the major puzzles of the Restoration period is why Charles II, until the last years of his reign, did not. Why did he persist in pursuing a policy that effectively undermined the alliance of Church and monarchy?

As will be seen Charles never stood firm on the principle of toleration, but the first twelve years of his reign are peppered with efforts to bring about a general toleration for Protestants and Catholics (1660, 1662, 1663, 1668, 1672). On 26 December 1662, despite the clear evidence of the Cavalier Parliament's fervent Anglicanism which had produced the Corporation and Uniformity Acts, Charles issued a declaration announcing that he intended to honour his Breda promise of 'liberty to tender consciences' by asking parliament to allow him to dispense individuals from the penal laws. It is true that Charles was under some pressure to curb the vindictive nature of the Act of Uniformity. Clarendon continued to advise him that, if the Act was put into effect, it might cause moderate dissenters to consider rebellion. Henrietta Maria, the earl of Bristol, and Sir Henry Bennett urged toleration in favour of Catholics, while the king also received petitions against the Act of Uniformity from Presbyterians and Independents. However, the parliamentary storm which followed Charles's declaration could surely easily have been foreseen. Already, before the new parliamentary session began in February 1663, the bishops began to coordinate opposition to Charles's plans. Although a Bill embodying his December proposals received some support in the more tolerant Lords, the Commons refused to discuss it, and at the beginning of April Charles was forced to withdraw it, issue a new proclamation against priests and Jesuits, and condone the passage in the Commons of Bills against both Protestant and Catholic dissenters. Why did Charles pursue such an obviously unpopular policy instead of taking the easier course of swimming with the Anglican tide? There is no easy answer to this question. It certainly does not seem to be rooted in any strong religious views held by the king. Although he probably did declare himself a Catholic on his death bed, this was probably, as Sir Charles Firth said, 'fire insurance'. Charles seems to have preferred Catholicism as a religion which supported absolute monarchies, but it is difficult to find evidence that he felt strongly enough about Catholicism to cause him to take extremely unpopular measures to promote it. His religious apathy is well captured in a story about Dr Robert South who when he was preaching to Charles II and his court noticed that most of his congregation had gone to sleep.

Stopping and changing the tone of his voice, he called thrice to Lord Lauderdale, who, awakened, stood up: 'My Lord', says South very composedly, 'I am sorry to interrupt your repose, but I must beg that you will not snore quite so loud, lest you should awaken his majesty,' and then as calmly continued his discourse.[21]

A more likely explanation is that Charles had no wish to become dependent on overbearing Anglican clergymen and that (like James II in 1686–7) he toyed with the alternative policy of allying with dissenters and Catholics. Certainly this is well in line with Charles's dislike of being dominated by others in his policy-making, whether it be by Clarendon or Danby. Whatever the explanation, it was a policy that only succeeded in souring his relations with parliament and the Church, as will be seen.

Despite Charles, the Anglican Church which had been reduced to ruins in the early 1640s emerged triumphant in the early 1660s. The Church's lands and revenues were restored, and the Church courts were once again active. It is worth emphasising also that many of the defects of the old Church were also restored, especially the system of lay impropriation of tithes and benefices, and the inequality in the distribution of wealth within the Church, resulting in a badly-paid clergy who too often had been appointed with no reference to their qualifications for their positions. The Church, though, that was restored in the 1660s did not have exactly the same position as in 1639. In great contrast to the days before 1640, the Clarendon Code, scant comfort though it was to those it persecuted, did give legal recognition to Protestant dissent. 'Whereas Laud had always endeavoured to coerce the Puritans into conformity and obedience', writes Professor Kenyon, 'Sheldon simply rejected them.'[22] The persecution of Protestant dissenters, especially of the Quakers and Baptists, after 1660 is well recorded.[23] What is less often emphasized is that Protestant nonconformity, which had flourished and spread in the 1640s and 1650s, survived after 1660 despite the efforts to eradicate it. The way in which it survived has many parallels with the continued existence of Catholicism in very similar circumstances in late sixteenth-century England, when Catholicism, like Protestant dissent later, was very closely associated in the minds of the authorities with political subversion. Restoration Protestant dissent could not have survived without the patronage and support of powerful landowners and merchants. The political and social pressures on the gentry to conform were great and most undoubtedly succumbed. Not all landowners in Restoration England, however, fall into the 'church – and – king' stereotype. The best-studied example of a man who does not is Lord Wharton, whose house at Woburn near High Wycombe (Bucks) became a haven for nonconformist divines after 1660. There were other Puritan gentry who in 1660 became dissenters and who also helped keep the Puritan tradition alive.[24] The Conventicle Act (1670) implicitly admitted that the Clarendon Code had not always been enforced: penalties were enacted against officials who turned a blind eye to the activities of dissenters. JPs, parish and town officials alike often found it difficult to see their inoffensive nonconformist friends and neighbours as the evil, seditious plotters official propaganda portrayed them to be. Even bishops sometimes tried to moderate the persecution of the Clarendon Code.[25] The exact extent of Protestant dissent in Restoration England is impossible to estimate. The religious census ordered by Danby and Sheldon in 1676 calculated that of the adult population over the age of sixteen 2,477,254 were conformists, 108,676 were nonconformists, and 13,656 were papists, and that nonconformists were much stronger in the south and eastern parts of England than in the north and west.[26] Since Danby's purpose was to minimize the numbers of dissenters in order to convince Charles of the futility of relying on their support, it is not unduly critical to question the accuracy of the census. Clearly it underestimated the strength of nonconformity, especially since a lot of nonconformists probably conformed simply for the sake of the census. Occasional conformity was not new even in the 1670s. Whether openly or not what is certain is that the Puritan spirit which had played a major role in late sixteenth- and early seventeenth-century society survived the difficult years immediately after the Restoration in the guise of Protestant dissent, and (as will be seen) later underwent a period of resurgence so that many contemporaries feared (wrongly) that it represented a serious challenge to Anglican dominance of the state and society in later Stuart England.[27]

The second Dutch war and the downfall of Clarendon, 1664–1667

'In 1661 the House of Commons was a house of courtiers; by 1667 it was becoming a house of critics', wrote David Ogg in one of those neat sentences which make his *England in the Reign of Charles II* a pleasure to read.[28] As has been seen, the major reasons for the Cavalier Parliament's increasing opposition to the court were the king's apparent preference for a policy of toleration and his continual demands for money. What made matters worse was that Charles's extravagance gave point to the recurrent complaint of backbench MPs in the seventeenth century of administrative waste and corruption. Moreover, the early years of the Restoration were for most landowners a time of economic difficulties. Not only had some royalist landowners got heavily into debt during the Revolution, but there was now an almost universal belief that rents were falling after a long period of rising rent-roll incomes before 1640 (see below, p. 447). There was a great fear that the subsequent fall in land values would strike at the roots of landed society, which explains why the Cavalier Parliament was obsessed with what seem unimportant campaigns, such as that aimed at banning the import of Irish cattle into England. It is not surprising that in these circumstances many MPs were loath to vote taxes to be squandered on a dissolute court. The importance of the second Dutch war (1665–7) in the politics of the reign of Charles II is the role it had in intensifying the sense of puzzlement and distrust of the court that was developing among many MPs in the 1660s. However, it would be wrong to equate this with the emergence of a 'country opposition' to the crown. Despite their growing uneasiness at court policies, most MPs were nevertheless wholly behind the king.

As far as one can judge the second Anglo-Dutch war, which effectively began in the summer of 1664, but which was not officially declared until 22 February 1665, was not unpopular in England. It represented no radical change of direction in English foreign policy and it appealed to the same mercantile interests in England as did the first war begun by the Rump in 1652. Such was the wealth of commercial grievances between the two countries that, despite an Anglo-Dutch treaty of September 1662, a recurrence of war seemed inevitable. Not only did the expansion of extra-European trade in the second half of the seventeenth century (see pp. 437–41) automatically intensify competition for the carrying trade to and from West Africa, the West Indies, North America, and the East Indies, but also the Convention Parliament in 1660 produced a Navigation Act that was much more effectively directed against the Dutch than its 1651 predecessor. By enforcing the registration of all foreign-built ships owned by English merchants the new Act made it much more difficult for foreign-owned ships to escape its provisions. It was also more specific in that it named the goods that had to be imported from the continent in English ships or in ships of the country from which the goods originated. Similarly certain other 'enumerated' goods could only be carried to England from the colonies in English or colonial ships. In 1663 the Staple Act went further in attempting to drive the Dutch out of the colonial trade, by forcing English colonists to import European goods only from England and only in English ships. Of the pressure groups clamouring for war with the Dutch the most vociferous was the East India Company, which had a history of conflict with its Dutch counterpart going back to the beginning of the century, and incidents like the 'massacre' at Amboyna in the East Indies in 1623 acquired increasing importance in the escalating English propaganda against the Dutch. In March and April 1664 a committee of the House of Commons came out in favour of the war, and its report was endorsed by the whole House. Also in March 1664 Charles added to the likelihood of war by granting the New Netherlands at the mouth of the Hudson river (the site of the present New York) to his brother, James duke of York. As usual, Charles's advisers were not united and their enthusiasm for the war varied. Clarendon, and perhaps Sir William Coventry,[29] realizing the financial implications of war, argued against it, but were overruled by Henry Bennet, Thomas Clifford, the duke of York, and eventually also by Charles himself. In the summer of 1664 the king borrowed £200,000 from the City of London for war preparations, and he endorsed the piratical expedition of Captain Robert Holmes against the trading stations of the Dutch West India Company in West Africa. Possibly the deciding factor for the king was the prospect of huge profits from the capture of Dutch merchant ships, which in the war of 1652–4 had possibly doubled the tonnage of the English merchant fleet.[30]

Although Clarendon was now clearly finding it difficult to maintain his primacy at court, his advice was taken on the tactics to be adopted in the new parliamentary session which began in November 1664. Sir Robert Paston, a Norfolk MP who had not hitherto been associated with the court, agreed to propose a large parliamentary war grant of £2,500,000. It could hardly be expected that agreement on such an unprecedented sum would be easy. Many backbench MPs in Charles II's reign seemed no more aware of the high cost of war than were those in the parliaments of the 1620s. One MP, Edward Vaughan, suggested that £500,000 would be sufficient to finance the war, which eventually cost over ten times that amount. That parliamentary sanction for the grant of £2,500,000, which was to be spent over three years, was delayed, however, was due mainly to the abhorrence MPs had of adopting the method of collecting the sum by means of county assessments, which had proved to be so effective in the 1640s. It was undoubtedly this aspect of it (its effectiveness) as well as its associations with the Revolution that MPs in the 1660s found distasteful. But eventually the superiority of monthly assessments in certainty and predictability of yield over the older parliamentary subsidies determined its acceptance, albeit reluctantly, in February 1665. Parliament met again next in the autumn, in Oxford to escape the plague in London. Within days of the opening of parliament the Commons agreed on a further grant of £1,250,000, again to be raised by monthly assessments. The subsequent adoption of Sir George Downing's proposal that the grant should be appropriated as the Commons directed is often, wrongly, interpreted as an indication of parliamentary distrust of the crown. It is more significant both in the history of public finance and as yet another illustration of Clarendon's growing isolation at court than of parliamentary assertiveness. Downing introduced it with the full backing of Charles, Bennet (now earl of Arlington), and Sir William Coventry, but without consulting Clarendon or Lord Treasurer Southampton. Its aim was to appropriate the new parliamentary grant, which would take two years to collect, in order to repay the crown's debtors in strict rotation. Downing hoped that this would encourage smaller investors to have more confidence in lending money to the crown.[31] In the parliamentary sessions of 1664–5 the relative absence of parliamentary criticism of government policy is striking. A Commons' Bill (October 1665) against the embezzlement of prize goods, aimed at the earl of Sandwich, was one of the rare sour notes in these sessions. With the later grant in the parliamentary session of September 1666 to February 1667 of £1,800,000 and other minor extraordinary sources of income, Professor Chandaman calculates that parliament provided £5,367,000 for the war, which cost the English government £5,250,000.[32] The bargain was not all one-sided – the Five Mile Act was passed in October 1665 – but the court had succeeded in extracting from parliament adequate provision for the war.

How, then, can one account for the great contrast between the 1664–5 parliamentary sessions and the stormy ones of 1666–7? The answer seems to be that instead of the victory many MPs expected their unprecedented grants would bring when they dispersed at the end of October 1665, the next twelve months brought naval disasters, diplomatic isolation, and near financial collapse for the government. At first the war had seemed to go well. The first great naval battle, off Lowestoft on 3 June 1665, was seen by Pepys as 'a greater victory never known in the world',[33] and perhaps his exaggeration is understandable. But soon doubts began to rise, especially when what had seemed a victory was not followed up, and in August 1665 reports came in of a bungled, treacherous attack in the neutral port of Bergen by English ships on a Dutch fleet returning from the East Indies. Early in 1666 France and Denmark joined the war against England and in April England's one ally, the bishop of Münster, defected. The French in fact gave little help to their allies, but it was fear that they might do so that decided Prince Rupert and the duke of Albemarle, the commanders of the English navy, to divide their fleet in anticipation of a French attack and so weaken it considerably in the Four Days' Battle with the Dutch in the Channel (1–4 June 1666). Despite heavy Dutch losses, even English propaganda could not portray the deaths of two admirals, the loss of 8,000 men, and the destruction of twenty ships as a 'victory', although at a later engagement at the mouth of the Thames on 25 July 1666 (the St James' Day Battle) Rupert and Albemarle do seem to have had a more unqualified success.

The government's prospects for renewed supply were, therefore, not good when parliament met again in September 1666, and it is not surprising that the war failures and financial losses were blamed on maladministration in the navy and corruption in the government. It is perhaps a commentary on the divisions at court that little effort seems to have been made to put forward an alternative, more respectable, explanation for the need for more money: that the crown's ordinary revenue, especially its income from customs, had been drastically reduced not only by the dislocation of trade by war but by the Great Plague of 1665 and the Great Fire of 1666. The effects of the Great Plague, which was at its height in the summer and early autumn of 1665, can perhaps be exaggerated. The extent of mortality was, of course, high. (There were perhaps 70,000 deaths in 1665, although the primary source material, especially the London Bills of Mortality, on which this estimate is based, are notoriously limited). But plague, especially in the towns, was a fairly common phenomenon before 1665 and, though familiarity did not lessen its virulence, it is likely that it had its greatest impact on the poor rather than on the trading and governing classes. Without doubt the economic and social effects of the Great Fire were much more serious. The capital still controlled a disproportionate, if decreasing, amount of the nation's trade and disruption of trade in London therefore had wide economic repercussions. Though most of the newly developed areas nearer to Westminster in Holborn and Covent Garden escaped, contemporaries estimated that the five-day fire (3–6 September 1666) gutted most of the City, and destroyed 13,200 houses, 89 churches and goods valued at £3.5m,[34] The fire's long-term importance in allowing the rebuilding of London on radical lines is well known: not only wider streets and buildings made of stone and brick resulted, but also the acceleration of the development of the West End of London.[35] Its immediate impact on the crown's ordinary revenue was equally, if not as excitingly, dramatic. For the three financial years from Michaelmas 1662 to Michaelmas 1665 the crown's permanent ordinary revenue averaged over £824,000 p.a.; during the next two years the average fell to nearly £647,000 p.a.[36] In the absence of this explanation from the court for the king's financial difficulties MPs at the end of 1666 began to look for scapegoats. On 26 September the Commons ordered the officers of the navy, ordnance, and stores to bring in their accounts for inspection, and MPs attacked the maladministration of officials, especially Sir George Carteret, the treasurer to the navy board. As has been seen, the Commons agreed on a grant of £1,800,000, but this time, against the wishes of the court, it was proposed to tack on to the grant a clause setting up a commission to examine the public accounts. Charles's anger appears, though, to have been caused by the attempt to *force* him to appoint a commission. When the Lords on 19 December 1666 petitioned him to do this he gave his assent.[37] But the Supply Bill did not finally pass until January 1667 and not before Charles had addressed the Commons personally and agreed to the passage of a Bill prohibiting the import of Irish cattle.

Charles began to negotiate a peace in January 1667; and in March the Dutch agreed to begin peace discussions at Breda. In the anticipation of an early peace the latest parliamentary grant was diverted from war expenditure to paying off the earlier war deficit. So sure were ministers of an early peace that some ships and crew were paid off and economies were made in repairing ships and shore defences. As a result de Ruyter's daring raid up the Medway in June 1667 and his attack on the naval base at Chatham were devastatingly successful. Despite Clarendon's objections, parliament was recalled in July, earlier than had been intended, in order to pay for an army hastily mobilized after the Medway disaster. The chancellor's attitude is understandable. All that the five-day parliamentary session achieved was to add one more grievance, a standing army, to the parliamentary catalogue against him. The session also gave the chancellor's enemies at court, Arlington, Sir William Coventry, and Buckingham, more ammunition to use against him. Unlike 1663, when the earl of Bristol attempted to impeach him, Clarendon was now isolated both at court and in parliament: his only hope was for a successful conclusion to the war. However, when peace with the Dutch was eventually concluded by the Treaty of Breda, the gains to England were seen to be minimal: in contemporary terms the acquisition of New York and New Jersey was insignificant.

Charles II was never known for his gratitude to those who had given him good service. Moreover, Clarendon had failed to stem the Cavalier Parliament's intolerant Anglicanism, and Charles's dislike of the chancellor's criticism of his personal behaviour was well known. Yet perhaps it was for political, rather than private, reasons that Charles gave way to the pressure to dismiss Clarendon and ask for his resignation on 30 August 1667: might not Clarendon's dismissal end the political crisis? In any case it is difficult to see how Clarendon could have survived politically after the Medway debacle. When parliament assembled again in October 1667 articles of impeachment were brought against him. Yet what was not inevitable was that he should end his life in exile as he did. The House of Lords refused to commit Clarendon to custody as the Commons wished, and it is difficult to see how the charge of treason could have been upheld in any court of law. Why then did Clarendon flee to France? His own explanation was the public-spirited one that by going abroad good relations between Lords and Commons could be restored. However, with the king supporting his enemies, it would have taken a lot of courage for Clarendon to stay. He probably had a clear recollection of the fate of Strafford in 1641. Undoubtedly he was right in that his departure did help to reduce the political temperature. Relations between crown and parliament in the parliamentary sessions of 1670–1 were perhaps the most harmonious of the whole reign. What destroyed the chances of parliamentary cooperation permanently were the activities of Charles and his brother immediately after the fall of Clarendon. The effect of these, when they became widely known, was to revive anti-Catholicism as the dominant issue in politics for the next fifteen years.

Notes

For abbreviations used throughout see p. xiv.

1. In June the Convention passed an Act legitimizing itself as a parliament.
2. The council of state, which ruled the country between the dissolution of the Long Parliament and the meeting of the Convention (17 March to 25 April 1660), believed that Charles would have to accept conditions; it spent a week examining the 'treaties' of the 1640s, D. Ogg, *England in the Reign of Charles II* (2 vols, 1955), I, p. 27.
3. The figures in the rest of this paragraph are from C. D. Chandaman, *The English Public Revenue 1660–88* (1975), pp. 196–202.
4. John Childs, *The Army of Charles II* (1976), p. 47. I am grateful to Professor K. H. D. Haley for bringing this reference to my attention.
5. R. S. Bosher, *The Making of the Restoration Settlement: the influence of the Laudians 1649–62* (1951) argues that Clarendon was a consistent intolerant Anglican. G. R. Abernathy, *English Presbyterians and the Stuart Restoration* (Trans. American Philosophical Society, LV, part 2 (Philadelphia 1965), attacks this view of Clarendon. See also Anne Whiteman, 'The re-establishment of the Church of England, 1660–63', *T.R.H.S.*, 5th ser., V (1955); *Idem*, 'The restoration of the Church of England, in G. F. Nuttall and O. Chadwick, eds, *From Uniformity to Unity* (1962); and Ian Green, *The Re-establishment of the Church of England 1660–63* (1978).
6. W. Lamont, *Marginal Prynne 1600–69* (1963) pp. 206–7.
7. Roots, *Great Rebellion*, p. 261.
8. Joan Thirsk, 'The restoration land settlement', *J.M.H.*, XXVI (1954); H. J. Habakkuk, 'The land settlement at the Restoration of Charles II', *T.R.H.S.*, 5th ser., XXVIII (1978), pp. 201–21.
9. Lancashire Record Office DDK 1602/9.
10. *Memoirs of Thomas Earl of Ailesbury, Written by Himself* (2 vols, Roxburgh Club, 1890), I, pp. 6–7.
11. Forfeiture of lands and goods, life imprisonment, and inability to sue for one's rights at law.
12. A third, equally important, reason – Charles's religious policies – will be dealt with on pp. 251–2.
13. For a brief survey see K. H. D. Haley, *Charles II*, Historical Association pamphlet, general series no. 63 (1966).
14. J. P. Kenyon, *The Stuarts* (Fontana ed, 1970), p. 105.
15. Chandaman, *English Public Revenue*, p. 271.
16. *Ibid.*, pp. 203–9.
17. C. E. Whiting, *Studies in English Puritanism from the Restoration to the Revolution, 1660–88* (1931), pp. 111, 425–8.
18. D. R. Lacey, *Dissent and Parliamentary Politics in England, 1661–89* (New Jersey, 1969), p. 30 and appendix 2.
19. Including 149 ejected from universities and schools, A. G. Matthews, *Calamy Revised. Being a Revision of Edmund Calamy's account of the Ministers and others ejected and silenced, 1660–62* (1934), pp. xiii–xiv.
20. Quoted in G. V. Bennett, *The Tory Crisis in Church and State 1688–1730: the career of Francis Atterbury Bishop of Rochester* (1975) p. 5, and see pp. 419–21 below.
21. Quoted in *The Times Literary Supplement*, 28 January 1977, review of Irene

Simon, ed., *Three Restoration Divines: Barrow, South, Tillotson. Selected Sermons* (2 vols, Paris, 1977).

22. Kenyon, *Stuart Constitution*, p. 364.
23. See e.g. Whiting, *Studies*, especially pp. 54ff, 98ff; M. R. Watts, *The Dissenters from the Reformation to the French Revolution* (1978), pp. 221–62.
24. R. A. Beddard, 'Vincent Alsop and the emancipation of Restoration Dissent', *J. Eccl. H.*, XXIV (1973), p. 169; G. F. Trevallyn Jones, *Saw Pit Wharton: the political career from 1640 to 1691 of Philip, fourth Lord Wharton (Sidney, 1967)*; Whiting, *Studies*, pp. 415ff and 432ff; Anthony Fletcher, *A County Community in Peace and War: Sussex 1600–60* (1975), pp. 123–4.
25. Whiting, *Studies*, pp. 18–19.
26. The census is printed in A. Browning ed., *English Historical Documents*, VIII: 1660—1714 (1953), pp. 413–16.
27. The questions of the state of the Church of England and the survival and role of dissent in later Stuart England are discussed in more detail on pp. 419–26.
28. Ogg, *Reign of Charles II*, p. 321.
29. D. T. Witcombe, *Charles II and the Cavalier House of Commons, 1663–74* (1976), pp. 26–7, n. 6, presents the evidence for Coventry's doubts about the war. I have drawn heavily upon this admirable book in my account of the Cavalier Parliament before the rise of Danby.
30. Chandaman, *English Public Revenue*, p. 223 note.
31. See p. 415 for the significance of the 1665 appropriation in the history of English public finance and the development of the British constitution.
32. Chandaman, *English Public Revenue*, p. 211.
33. Quoted in Ogg, *Reign of Charles II*, p. 288.
34. *Ibid.*, p. 305.
35. T. F. Reddaway, *The Rebuilding of London after the Great Fire* (1940).
36. Chandaman, *English Public Revenue*, p. 332.
37. Extracts from the Act establishing the commission are printed in Kenyon, *Stuart Constitution*, pp. 392–5.

Chapter 9

'Catholic' or 'Cavalier' policies, 1668–1674

With hindsight one can see at various times in the past certain alternative courses of action which, if followed, might have changed the course of events dramatically and thereby obviated the consequences of decisions that were in fact taken. The six years after 1667 fall into this category. After the downfall of Clarendon two distinct courses of action were open to Charles II, which can be labelled 'Cavalier' and 'Catholic'. The former entailed unqualified support for the restored Anglican Church, the suppression of all nonconformity as seditious by the enforcement of the Clarendon Code, and (though less important at the beginning) a Protestant foreign policy. 'Catholic' policies, on the other hand, combined toleration for Protestant and Catholic nonconformists at home with alliance with France abroad. It would be simplifying things too much to suggest that the choice between 'Cavalier' and 'Catholic' policies was clearcut. Charles and his ministers sometimes followed both policies simultaneously. Yet, as will be seen, by making the treaties with France in 1670, and by issuing the Declaration of Indulgence and declaring war on the Dutch in 1672, Charles committed himself to 'Catholic' policies at a time when it was suspected (and in 1673 confirmed) that the heir to the throne, James duke of York, was a Catholic. Charles thus aligned the English monarchy in the eyes of many Englishmen with popery and absolutism, and so ensured that it would be much harder to gain parliamentary cooperation in the 1670s than in the 1660s. It therefore becomes of prime importance to try to understand why Charles chose a set of policies that could be smeared as papist and absolutist and rejected policies that might have produced a cooperative parliament.

It is important to stress that Charles himself was responsible for policy-making. After the fall of Clarendon there was no 'cabal' of ministers – an embryonic prime-ministerial cabinet – advising Charles, as was often thought in the past. Even the use of 'cabal' as a mnemonic (the initial letters of five of Charles's ministers after 1667, Clifford, Arlington, Buckingham, Ashley Cooper, and Lauderdale, spell 'cabal') can be misleading, since it omits other influential men who were also around the king at this time, including Sir William Coventry until 1669, Sir George Downing, and Heneage Finch. It also wrongly suggests that the five men were of equal political importance and were agreed on public policy. Nothing could be further from the truth. The two principal characters at court from 1667 to 1673, Arlington and Buckingham, hated each other, and politics at court and in parliament were often expressed in terms of this rivalry, which was sharpened by striking personal differences between the two men. Arlington's correct behaviour reflected his diplomatic and administrative background; he was the type of royal servant who is often willing to subordinate his own ideas in order to carry out his master's policy. On the other hand, in Ogg's words, Buckingham 'set a standard of ducal independence and vagary never since approached'.[1] He was always a law to himself and, as with his father (the favourite of James I and Charles I), it is difficult to see any consistent principles in his political career. Arlington, with Clifford, was taken into the king's confidence in the making of the secret Treaty of Dover; the king's other ministers, like everyone else, knew nothing of it. If anyone was in control of policy in England after 1667 it was the king himself.

Immediately after the departure of Clarendon there was as yet no overt sign of Charles's preference for pro-French policies. On the contrary in January 1668 England joined the United Provinces and Sweden in a formal anti-French treaty. The Triple Alliance had its origins in the situation on the Continent and especially in the Dutch republic, which, under the leadership of Johan de Witt as Grand Pensionary, was still very powerful, especially at sea. The English had failed in the second Dutch War to make any impression on Dutch commercial supremacy. But Dutch naval and mercantile strength contrasted with the country's military weakness. Earlier this had not mattered because of the Franco-Dutch alliance of 1662, but just when the war with England was being concluded this situation changed. Louis XIV began to claim the neighbouring Spanish Netherlands by the so-called right of 'devolution' which, it was claimed, was vested in his wife, daughter of Philip IV of Spain. In May 1667 the French general, Turenne, invaded and soon overran the Spanish Netherlands. It was this threat to the United Provinces posed by French expansion which forced de Witt to abandon the French alliance and look to England. Arlington seems to have welcomed the prospect of the Dutch alliance, which was concluded by Sir William Temple. Charles's motives and attitude are, as usual, less obvious. Did he agree to the Triple Alliance as a step on the road to a French alliance, as a means of forcing on Louis XIV the need to detach England from the United Provinces? Certainly the Triple Alliance seems to have had this effect, since in August 1668 Louis sent Charles Albert de Croissy (the brother of his famous minister, Colbert) as ambassador to London with instructions to propose an alliance with England.

If Charles was not yet definitely commited to alliance, he was ready to press for a measure of religious toleration. The events of the next two parliamentary sessions again drove home to the king the unacceptability of this to the parliamentary classes. When parliament met in February 1668 Charles (as in 1660 and 1662) spoke in favour of toleration. The House of Commons responded by refusing to make the customary vote of thanks for the king's speech at the opening of the session, and by pointedly beginning work on another Bill against conventicles to replace the 1664 Act, which had lapsed. This, together with accusations of maladministration of the Dutch war, was revived in the next parliamentary session of October – December 1669. The two sessions produced supply totalling only £300,000 at a time when the crown's financial situation was extremely serious. Despite the work of the treasury commission, which had taken over after the death of Southampton in May 1667, in instituting a new credit order system and a retrenchment scheme, Charles's extravagance prevented an overall improvement.[2] Consequently, in the parliamentary recess (December 1669 to February 1670) the decision was taken to revert to the Cavalier policies which had been so successful in gaining supply from 1661 to 1665. The details are necessarily difficult to discover (behind-the-scenes political compacts are never very well-documented) but in discussions with some parliamentary leaders Charles appears to have agreed to a new Conventicle Bill in return for supply.[3] In addition, contemporaries believed that during the next session Arlington, with Clifford as 'bribe master general', anticipated the methods later used by Danby to manage the House of Commons.[4] As a result the two parliamentary sessions of February to April 1670 and February to April 1671 produced 'the most generous additional supplies of the reign', a massive increase in indirect taxation with new duties on wines, legal proceedings, and an additional excise.[5] However, despite this clear evidence of the gains that came with Cavalier policies, Charles had already begun to commit himself to alternative 'Catholic' policies.

Ever since de Croissy's arrival in England in August 1668 negotiations had been proceeding in secret for an alliance with France. Charles had also been promoting a French alliance by means of his correspondence with his sister, Henrietta, the wife of the duke of Orleans, Louis XIV's brother. By October 1669 the main lines of an agreement had been worked out, and at Dover on 22 May 1670, under the cover of Charles's meeting with his sister, Arlington, Clifford, and de Croissy signed the secret Treaty of Dover. Both kings agreed 'their joint resolution to humble the pride of the States General, and to destroy the power of a people which has . . . shown ingratitude to those who have helped it to create its republic'; and Louis was to pay Charles £225,000 p.a. during the ensuing war against the Dutch. More surprisingly, the treaty declared that Charles, 'being convinced of the truth of the Roman Catholic religion is resolved to declare it, and to reconcile himself with the Church of Rome as soon as his country's affairs permit'; and, in order to meet the opposition which, not surprisingly, such a declaration was expected to raise, Louis agreed to pay Charles £150,000 and to provide and pay 6,000 troops 'for the execution of this design'. 'The time for this declaration of Catholicism', asserted the Treaty, 'is left entirely to the discretion of the King of England.'[6] A version of this treaty, omitting this Catholic clause, was signed by all the members of the so-called 'cabal' on 21 December 1670.

Given the secrecy of these negotiations and their controversial nature, Charles and his closest advisers naturally did not make clear their thoughts and motives in 1670. Consequently it is impossible to know certainly what his intentions were, and historians have put forward various alternative hypotheses. One is forced to suggest motives for the making of the Dover policy on the basis of very little direct evidence. The easiest part of this difficult task is to try to explain Charles's motives in allying with France. Even Charles was probably not so foolish as to think that the promised French subsidy offered a way out of his financial predicament, as some historians have argued in the past. Professor Kenyon's comment on the later subsidies Charles received from Louis applies equally to this first one: 'It is only a strange persistance in thinking of *livres tournois* as directly equivalent to pounds sterling that has led so many historians to brand Charles II as a remittance man of France.'[7] Charles may have had a financial motive in making the French alliance: he got total subsidies of £375,000 and there was the prospect of profits from prizes on the same scale as those taken in the previous two Dutch wars. Probably far more important, however, in Charles's mind were two other factors. First, the prospect of allying with a country Charles had always admired and whose king seemed to have found a way of getting rid of a representative assembly, whose English counterpart had become extremely troublesome to a man who liked a quiet life. Secondly, Charles responded to that part of public opinion in England that wanted revenge for the Medway disgrace. Moreover the war of 1665–7 had done nothing to resolve the commercial rivalry between the two countries. With hindsight, especially with the knowledge that France was to be a major threat to English security and the English Empire, the wisdom of Charles's French alliance can be called into question.[8] As early as 1670 some perceptive observers did see the dangers to England of French conquests in the Low Countries and of French commercial expansion. But in fairness to Charles few people saw this, and it is highly likely that, if it had not become bound up with Protestant fears, the third Dutch war and the French alliance would not have been unpopular.

The real problems surrounding the Dover policy are to explain why Charles insisted on associating with it the Catholic clause in the secret treaty, and why he later (in March 1672) published the Declaration of Indulgence two days before declaring war on the Dutch. It was these, and especially the latter (since the secret clauses of 1670 were never officially made public) that helped to make the new trend in policy so unpopular. There is no really satisfactory explanation why Charles insisted, despite Louis's reservations, on including the Catholic clause in the secret treaty. It is fairly certain that the answer is not that he was a sincere convert; nor, as has been suggested, need he have included the clause to get Arlington's support for the French alliance; Charles was not the man to let a minister stand in his way. A subsidiary motive may have been that Charles saw the Catholic clause as a means of forcing Louis to raise the French subsidy by £150,000, as did in fact happen. However, this was not his main motive. It is more likely that he considered the major purpose of the Catholic clause as providing a personal link between the two kings – a kind of 'special relationship'.[9]

Even this, though, seems insufficient reason for taking such a grave political risk. Yet the Catholic clause in the Dover treaty is, if anything, easier to explain than Charles's Declaration of Indulgence of March 1672, which suspended all the penal laws, allowed Roman Catholics to worship in their own homes, and offered licences to Protestant dissenters to hold public worship. Given the more tolerant attitude to Protestant dissenters in the last parliamentary session, by itself the latter part of the Declaration might have been acceptable. But it is difficult to imagine how Charles could have expected that parliament would swallow any measure of toleration for Catholics. Charles's motives (as usual) are clouded in doubt. One possibly is that the Declaration was intended to persuade Louis XIV to push ahead more quickly with preparations for war against the Dutch; the French king was using Charles's failure to declare himself a Catholic as an excuse for delaying a war declaration.[10] Probably the most telling consideration from the king's point of view as far as domestic policies is concerned, is that Charles was again gambling on an alliance of Catholics and dissenters against Anglican opinion. Arlington thought that the aim of the Declaration was to conciliate dissenters 'that we might keep all quiet at home whilst we are busy abroad'. Even without the benefit of hindsight that must have been a very vain hope. As will be seen, the Declaration of Indulgence united most of the political nation, not against the Dutch, but against Charles and his ministers.

It is easier to defend Charles's Dover policy against the charge that he ought instead to have persevered with Cavalier policies because the financial prospects for the crown were now much better than in the 1660s. It is certainly true that the trend of the crown's permanent ordinary revenue from 1668 onwards was upwards, and with the addition of parliamentary supplies the situation was, of course, even healthier (see below pp. 275–6). In the 1670s, even without parliamentary supplies, financial solvency for the crown became a possibility. Yet it is perhaps not surprising that Charles was not attracted by this improving financial situation. Even if he understood it, which is doubtful (the permanence of the increase in revenue was not, after all, immediately obvious in 1670) he would still have had to curtail his expenditure severely. 'A long-term programme of recovery involving undeviating effort and frugality'[11] was hardly one to attract someone of Charles II's temperament. Moreover, in the early 1670s the *immediate* financial situation was very serious indeed. The total royal debt, which had been rising since the Restoration because of Charles's prodigality, now escalated because of the expense of war preparations. In addition, the credit order system begun in 1667 put too great a burden on the exchequer. So serious was the short-term position that on 7 January 1672 Charles and his advisers were forced to suspend for a year most repayments of the capital of loans to government creditors. After this 'Stop of the Exchequer' the way was cleared for the full implementation of the Dover policy, the Declaration of Indulgence (15 March 1672), and the formal declaration of war on the Dutch (17 March 1672).

Charles's gamble that the combination of the Stop, toleration, and war against the Dutch would be a way out of his difficulties was doomed to disappointment. For one thing the third Dutch war, like the second, went badly for England. The English navy's attack on the returning Dutch Smyrna fleet in March 1672 was bungled, and the naval battle off Southwold Bay on 28 May 1672 was indecisive. Although English propaganda could persuasively argue that the English and French navies had 'won' the battle of Southwold Bay, it could not hide the fact that the victors of the war appeared to be, not the English, but their allies the French. In the early part of June 1672 Turenne and Condé crossed the Rhine and occupied Utrecht. The effect in the United Provinces was to precipitate the bloody downfall of Johan de Witt and his brother, and the appointment of William of Orange as Stadhouder. In England the effect of the French victories was to turn public opinion for the first time against the French alliance. The potential threat to English national security from French expansion in the Low Countries, which only a few had seen in 1670–1, now became apparent to all. But, as yet, the greatest criticism in England was reserved for the Declaration of Indulgence. It is striking that, when parliament met in February 1673 for the first time since April 1671, even with the evidence of French expansion in the Low Countries nine months old, Charles's foreign policy was not yet directly challenged. On the contrary, within two weeks of its first meeting the Commons voted in principle to grant a supply of £1,126,000 by means of eighteen monthly assessments. The main parliamentary attack was directed against the Declaration of Indulgence, which most speakers in the Commons saw as being designed to encourage the growth of popery, and as a major threat to parliament because of Charles's intention arbitrarily to suspend parliamentary legislation. On 14 February the Commons voted *nem. con.*, that 'penal statutes in matters ecclesiastical cannot be suspended but by an Act of parliament'.[12] In the counties, too, anti-Catholicism again reared its head and resulted in the most determined effort to enforce the recusancy laws since the Restoration. In some counties the numbers of convicted recusants increased dramatically: in Wiltshire more papists were convicted in 1673 than in the previous twelve years since the Restoration.[13]

The hysterical anti-Catholicism seen in the parliamentary debates of February and March 1673 is not surprising. What perhaps is, is the first signs that the divisions within the Protestant ranks were begining to close in face of the alleged Catholic menace. Even some Protestant dissenting MPs spoke against the Declaration of Indulgence, and on 14 February a Bill for the relief of Protestant dissenters, which was on roughly the same lines as the Toleration Bill enacted in 1689, was introduced into the House of Commons. Arguments for the toleration of Protestant dissenters were voiced in parliament that would have been unthinkable in the 1660s.[14] Ominously for Charles and for James the spring parliamentary session of 1673 showed that in the face of the common fear of Catholicism and absolutism Anglicans and Protestant dissenters could sink their differences. This was to be the lesson of 1688, as will be seen. Unlike his brother later, however, Charles recognized the strength of this alliance, and on 8 March 1673 despite contrary pressure in the privy council from James, Clifford, and Shaftesbury, Charles announced the cancellation of the Declaration of Indulgence, and a few days later he gave his assent to a Test Act, which excluded all non-Anglicans from holding public offices.

Charles tried to gain every political advantage he could from his apparent reversion to cavalier policies in England. His attempt to dissociate the French alliance from its damaging Catholic and absolutist associations was, however, foiled by two factors in the summer of 1673: the spread of effective Dutch propaganda and the public admission of James's conversion to Catholicism. William of Orange's rise to power in the United Provinces in the revolution of 1672 not only strengthened Dutch resistance in the war, but also resulted in the emergence of what Professor Haley calls 'political warfare',[15] directed by William, with the aim of undermining English support for the French alliance. Soon after his appointment William and Gaspar Fagel, the new Grand Pensionary of Holland, began to encourage the dissemination of Dutch propaganda in England, alleging that the principal aim of the Anglo-French alliance was to spread Catholicism in England. This was the theme of the most effective pamphlet published in 1673, *England's Appeal from the Private Cabal at Whitehall to the Great Council of the Nation*, probably written by Peter du Moulin, a close associate of William of Orange. *England's Appeal* was published in England in the late February 1673, too late to have much impact on the spring parliamentary session. But it was widely circulated and read in the late spring and summer of 1673. Its effect was to make 'France, Popery and Absolutism' as inseperable and as powerful a political cliché in the 1670s as 'Dissent and Sedition' had been in the 1660s. If the Dutch propagandists had known of the secret Catholic clause in the Treaty of Dover, their allegations would have been even more telling. As it was, soon after the appearance of du Moulin's pamphlet, they received what was arguably as big a boost as the revelations of the Dover Catholic clause would have been. In June 1673 the suspicions raised by Dutch propagandists were amply confirmed, when under the terms of the Test Act Clifford and James resigned their respective offices of lord high treasurer and lord high admiral. James had been a secret Catholic since at least the beginning of 1669, but the first public affirmation of his conversion was his failure to take the Anglican sacraments at Easter 1673. After James's resignation in June his Catholicism was not in doubt, especially when in September 1673 he married a Catholic princess, Mary of Modena. (His first wife Anne Hyde had died in 1671.) The Catholicism of the heir to the throne was to be the prime political issue of the next fifteen years.

The immediate effect of Dutch propaganda and James's conversion was to make the parliamentary sessions of October–November 1673 and January–February 1674 the stormiest of Charles's reign to date. Whereas in the spring sessions of 1673 opposition had been confined in the main to the Declaration of Indulgence, it now widened to encompass a vast range of issues, many of which had not been raised before: the French alliance was now directly criticized; so was James's marriage (in October 1673 the Commons voted belatedly against the marriage taking place); a new Test Act was proposed, designed to prevent Catholics from sitting in both Houses of parliament; in January and February 1674 a long list of bills was drafted to limit the power of future Catholic monarchs, including provision for the Protestant education of the king's children; and, finally, the king's principal ministers were attacked as popish and dangerous. It was resolved that Lauderdale and Buckingham be removed from the king's council, and articles of impeachment were brought in against Arlington. Ashley Cooper (since 1672 earl of Shaftesbury and lord chancellor) no longer supported government policy. Although in February 1673 in his famous *Delendo est Carthago* speech he had defended the government's record, the events of the following summer convinced him that Charles did intend to promote Catholicism and of the need to guard against a Catholic successor. Shaftesbury's first reaction was to press Charles to divorce Catherine of Braganza and remarry with the hope of producing a Protestant heir, a project which seems to have first been discussed at court in 1669 when Catherine had a miscarriage.[16] Then and later Charles would have nothing to do with the divorce plan; on this, unlike many other issues, he refused to make any concessions. Instead on 9 November 1673 he dismissed Shaftesbury from his office of lord chancellor, and in the following May expelled him from the privy council and the lord-lieutenancy of Dorset. From this date Shaftesbury's efforts to secure the dissolution of the Cavalier Parliament and the exclusion of James from the throne began.

In this, though, Shaftesbury was out on a limb; until the Popish Plot 'revelations' few MPs supported his extreme tactics. Not exclusion but the securing of limitations on a Catholic monarch, on the lines laid down in the parliamentary session of January–February 1674, was the programme of most MPs from 1673–4 to 1678. This was enough of a coherent programme to make historians suspect a more than usual degree of coordination behind parliamentary tactics in the sessions of late 1673 and early 1674. Had a 'country party' emerged by this time? As in the 1620s and 1640s, so in the reign of Charles II the question of the development of party organization is bedevilled by anachronistic nineteenth- and twentieth-century concepts of organized political parties. Although, as will be seen, for a brief period from 1679 to 1681 and for a longer period in the reign of Queen Anne political parties did become highly organized, these were exceptions in the seventeenth-century context. For most of the seventeenth century political groupings lacked any systematic organization in the constituencies or at Westminster. Indeed the majority of MPs considered themselves to be 'independent', and felt that party organization was factious and abhorrent. Yet political friendships had inevitably been forged in the frequent parliamentary sessions since 1660, which had also given many MPs a greater wealth of parliamentary experience even than MPs in the 1620s and 1640s. Although the evidence is slight, there are brief glimpses of MPs in the early 1670s meeting to coordinate tactics before and during parliamentary sessions. Inevitably those who did this were usually those who were critical of government policy. By 1674 there was a hard core of such 'opposition' MPs, including Sir William Coventry, Lord Cavendish, William Russell, Sir Thomas Meres, and William Sacheverell; in addition, from the summer of 1673 there was a strong political issue – James's Catholicism – round which opposition groups could coalesce. To that extent by 1673–4 a 'country party' had emerged.[17]

In February 1674 in the face of this hardening opposition Charles, as in the previous year, withdrew by making peace with the Dutch with the Treaty of Westminster (9 February 1674), which made no major changes in the prewar situation. The 'country party' had thus won two major victories: Charles had torn up the Declaration of Indulgence and abandoned the Dutch war. But the events after the prorogation of parliament on 24 February 1674 showed just how insubstantial as yet was the 'country party'.

This sudden prorogation [reported a correspondent of du Moulin] caused many of the guilty Commons (Lord St John, Sir Thomas Lee, Sir Robert Thomas, Sir N. Carew, Sir Elias Harvey, Sacheverell, and many others) who had bespoken a large dinner for that day at the Swan Tavern in King Street, to leave . . . and to haste away (some by coach, some by water) into the city, suspecting themselves . . . unsecure in the suburbs.[18]

As after the dissolutions of the parliaments of 1621 and 1624 the king still held the whip-hand. And at this stage Charles acquired a minister, Sir Thomas Osborne (later earl of Danby), who had the necessary qualities to enable the crown to recover the political initiative. It remains to be seen whether Charles's choice of 'Catholic' policies in the crucial preceding six years had made Danby's eventual failure inevitable.

Notes

For abbreviations used throughout see p. xiv.

1.   Ogg, *Reign of Charles II*, p. 329.
2.   Chandaman, *English Public Revenue*, pp. 212–19.
3.   Witcombe, *Cavalier House of Commons*, p. 98.
4.   A. Browning, *Thomas Osborne Earl of Danby and Duke of Leeds 1632–1712* (3 vols, 1944–51), I, p. 83, n. 4.
5.   Chandaman, *English Public Revenue*, p. 221.
6.   Browning, *English Historical Documents*, pp. 863–7.
7.   Kenyon, *The Stuarts*, p. 135.
8.   See Haley, *Charles II*, pp. 18–19, for a forthright condemnation of the French alliance.
9.   See Haley, *ibid.*, p. 17 for the view, which seems to me the most plausible. See John Miller, *James II; a study in kingship* (Hove, Sussex, 1978), p. 61, for the view that Charles's promise to declare himself a Catholic was a bargaining device in the negotiation with Louis XIV.
10. John Miller, *Popery and Politics in England 1660–88* (1973), p. 115.
11. This is Professor Chandaman's assessment of what Charles needed to do to attain financial solvency for the crown, *English Public Revenue*, p. 274.
12. Quoted in Witcombe, *Cavalier House of Commons*, p. 133.
13. Miller, *Popery and Politics*, p. 132.
14. Witcombe, *Cavalier House of Commons*, p. 134.
15. K. H. D. Haley, *William of Orange and the English Opposition 1672–4* (1953), p. 10.
16. K. H. D. Haley, *The First Earl of Shaftesbury* (1968), pp. 276–80.
17. See Haley, *Shaftesbury*, pp. 351–2 and Witcombe, *Cavalier House of Commons*, pp. 58–60 for discussions of this 'country party'.
18. Quoted in Haley, *William of Orange*, p. 191.

Chapter 10

Anti-Catholicism and exclusion, 1674–1681

Anti-Catholicism

One of the most striking features of seventeenth-century England is the strength and persistence at all levels and among all classes of society of anti-Catholicism, which from the early 1670s came to play an increasingly important part in politics. Dr Clifton has shown that in the early seventeenth century there were frequent local outbreaks of panic that Catholics were about to murder and pillage the community, (notably in 1605 and 1641–2.)[1] Despite the growing strength of the intellectual case for toleration, there is very little sign that popular hatred of popery diminished in the second half of the century. William Prynne believed that the New Model Army in 1647–8 had been infiltrated by Catholics and that Pride's Purge and the execution of Charles I were 'nothing else but the designs and projects of Jesuits, Popish priests and recusants'.[2] If Prynne and sober respectable people like Richard Baxter could believe nonsense like this, then the common, uncritical assumption that Catholics were behind the Great Fire of 1666 and the widespread belief in Titus Oates' 'revelation' in 1678 of a Catholic conspiracy to kill the king are more easily understandable. Henry Care's lurid description of an imaginary Catholic England reflects many of the elements in the seventeenth-century anti-Catholic tradition: the men

forced to fly destitute of bread and harbour, your wives prostituted to the lust of every savage bog-trotter, your daughters ravished by goatish monks, your smaller children tossed upon pikes, or torn limb from limb, whilst you have your own bowels ripped up . . . or else murdered with some other exquisite tortures and holy candles made of your grease (which was done within our memory in Ireland), your dearest friends flaming in Smithfield, foreigners rendering your poor babes that can escape everlasting slaves, never more to see a Bible, nor hear again the joyful sounds of Liberty and Property. This gentlemen is Popery.[3]

The paradox of English anti-Catholicism is that it grew at a time when there were very few Catholics in England. Given the outlawed position of Catholics, it is not surprising that estimates of the size of the Catholic community in late seventeenth-century England vary wildly.

Dr Miller's estimate of 66,000 (just over one per cent of the total population) based on the Danby ecclesiastical census of 1676, is probably nearest the truth. Even if this is an underestimate, Catholics almost certainly made up no more than 5 per cent of the population. Not only was the size of the Catholic lay community small, but its political activism was a myth (as it had been in the early part of the century). Nor was there much substance behind the often-hysterical fears of the subversive activities of the Catholic clergy. One can be no more certain about their numbers than one can about the Catholic population as a whole; the most widely accepted estimate, that of Claudius Agrette, a papal agent, in 1669, of 230 secular clergy and about 255 regular clergy (mainly Jesuits, Benedictines, and Carmelites) hardly substantiates contemporary allegations of thousands of Catholic priests in the English mission.[4] Nor were those Catholic priests who were at work very well organized. They were split by a long-standing antagonism between seculars and regulars, and lacked any clear leadership from the papacy. So distrustful was the papal curia of the efforts of some Catholic secular clergy (especially the so-called Blackloites) to secure a rapproachment with Cromwell and, later, Charles II, that it failed to appoint a bishop in England after 1655. The political indecisiveness of the Jesuits and the papal curia in the later seventeenth century, which amounted at times to ineptitude, contrasts sharply with the Protestant caricature of Jesuit and papal guile and political sophistication. For example, at a time when most Englishmen saw James Duke of York's marriage to Mary of Modena as part of a cunning papal-inspired design to convert England to Catholicism, the papal curia could not make up its mind about the marriage and its bureaucratic incompetence nearly prevented the marriage from taking place. What makes English anti-Catholicism even more inexplicable is that, for the most part, there was little tension between Protestants and Catholics in the local community. This is most easily demonstrated among the landowning classes. Catholic and Protestant gentry shared the same life styles, met each other socially and sometimes their families intermarried. Catholic neighbours were not considered to be dangerous papal agents and this (as much as administrative inertia) accounts for the lax enforcement of penal legislation against Catholics in the late sixteenth and seventeenth centuries. Seventeenth-century Englishmen had a schizophrenic attitude to Catholics. While the earl of Anglesey was preparing a book against the Jesuits in the 1670s he spent his spare time dining with and calling on his Catholic neighbours. How can one, then, account for the hatred and fear of Catholics in seventeenth-century England?

By 1660 Englishmen had been subjected to over a century of Protestant propaganda that the Catholic religion was abhorrent and more evil than the worst type of heresy. 'In pamphlet and sermon, popery was presented as essentially the *debasement* of Christ's teaching, a total and blasphemous perversion of Apostolic practice.'[5] Easily the most important literary contribution to this view and one of the most popular books of the late sixteenth and seventeenth centuries was John Foxe's *Acts and Monuments*, first published in 1563. Foxe not only recounted the martyrdom of about 300 people during the reign of Mary Tudor, he also portrayed the burnings at Smithfield as one episode in a developing struggle between true Christianity and the forces of evil represented by Rome. Later writers interested in eschatology followed Foxe and used the prophecies in the Book of Revelations to identify Rome as the Antichrist and England as the 'Elect Nation' chosen by God to fight and defeat the 'Whore of Babylon'. As with all general theories of historical development it was then possible to find events that 'supported' this interpretation. Were not the St Bartholomew's Day Massacre of French Huguenots in 1572, the Gunpowder Plot in 1605, the Irish Rebellion in the 1640s, and the Great Fire in 1666 simply further episodes in the struggle between Christ and Antichrist?

Protestant propagandists also had answers to Catholic apologists who rightly argued that English Catholics had always been demonstrably loyal during times of national crisis, from the Armada onwards, and that Catholics during the seventeenth century had withdrawn from the political arena. William Blundell, a Lancashire Catholic, argued that 'all Catholic subjects of a lawful Protestant king (such as king Charles the 2nd) are obliged faithfully to adhere to that king in all invasions, whatsoever, though made by Catholic princes or even by the pope himself'.[6] Many Protestants, however, found more convincing the standard anti-Catholic jibe that Catholicism 'draweth with it an unavoidable dependency upon foreign princes'.[7] After all, were there not Catholic conspiracies against the state, from the Rudolfi Plot to the Great Fire, to support this? Especially serious was the refusal of many Catholics to take the Oath of Allegiance of 1606. Their refusal to swear that their faith was 'impious', 'heretical', and a 'damnable doctrine' is understandable, but those who did so laid all English Catholics wide open to the charge of sedition. Nor did English Protestants have much time for those who argued that Catholics could not be a threat because there were not many of them. On the contrary, their enemies countered, were not Catholics, though numerically insignificant, very well represented among powerful groups like the aristocracy and gentry? The most damning charge of all (one which James II believed just as much as the Protestant polemicists) was that thousands of Catholics conformed to the Church of England and were only waiting for the right moment to declare their true allegiance. By its very nature this was a charge that was difficult to refute, and was not shown to be groundless until James II's reign when the hoped-for rally of Catholics to the 'true faith' failed to materialize.

Catholicism, maintained a Commons' petition of December 1621, 'hath a restless spirit, and will strive by these gradations: if it once get but a connivancy, it will press for a toleration: if that should be obtained, they must have an equality: from thence they will aspire to superiority, and will never rest till they get a subversion of the true religion'.[8] This point was often made in the seventeenth century, and from the 1660s onwards it received added emphasis from events taking place in Europe. The effect on European Protestant opinion of Louis XIV's often savage persecution of his Protestant Huguenot subjects cannot be exaggerated. The Revocation of the Edict of Nantes in October 1685, which took away the limited toleration enjoyed by French Huguenots, reinforced anti-Catholic propaganda. Without the Revocation, it will be argued later, the successful intervention of William of Orange in England in 1688 (and therefore the 'Glorious Revolution') would have been impossible. As Huguenot refugees came to England, first in a trickle and then, after 1685, in a flood, they brought concrete proof, in Louis XIV's *dragonnades*, of the truth of Protestant allegations of the cruelty and intolerance of rampant Catholicism. It was this powerful hatred of popery that Charles II's decision to ally with France and the announcement of James's conversion to Catholicism brought to the centre of the English political stage for much of the 1670s and 1680s and with which Charles II and Danby, and, later, James II, would have to contend.

Danby, 1674–1678

The immediate aftermath of the dramatic revelation of James's Catholicism was a political vacuum at court. Shaftesbury and Buckingham joined the ranks of the government's critics, Lauderdale spent most of his time in Scotland, Arlington lost most of his political influence, and Clifford resigned and died (probably by committing suicide). Clifford was replaced as lord treasurer by a Yorkshireman, Sir Thomas Osborne (created earl of Danby in June 1674, marquis of Carmarthen in 1689, and duke of Leeds in 1694). Although Danby (like everyone else) could never be certain of Charles's continued support, for at least three years from the end of 1674 his power as leading minister of the crown was fairly secure. During that time he followed distinct policies aimed at restoring the crown's financial position after the debacle of the Stop of the Exchequer, and at establishing permanently good relations between crown and parliament by returning to 'Cavalier' policies: unqualified support for the Church of England, persecution of Protestant and Catholic dissenters, and hostility to France. As will be seen, he was not wholly unsuccessful in either of these aims. During his tenure of the treasurership the total revenue of the crown increased dramatically. Moreover, the crown's critics in the four parliamentary sessions held in 1675, 1677, and 1678 did not have any impact on government policy to match their success in forcing Charles to cancel the Declaration of Indulgence in 1673 and to end the Dutch war in 1674.

Yet Danby did not improve the overall financial position of the crown; nor did he reduce parliamentary distrust of the crown and its policies. Could he have succeeded more completely than he did? Like so many historical questions this one is capable of different answers. Yet an analysis of the reasons for Danby's failure suggests that his task was hopeless from the start. After 1670–3 the political situation changed dramatically and permanently. Danby had to accept the consequences of the fact that the heir to the throne was now a Catholic. Nor could he detach the king from his preference for an alliance with France. Indeed, given Louis XIV's ability to reveal the Catholic clause in the secret Treaty of Dover, it is difficult to see how Charles, even if he had wanted to, could have permanently abandoned the French alliance. It is ironic that Charles's choice of policies that were (in part at least) aimed at strengthening the monarchy arguably delayed the creation of a strong monarchy for at least a decade. A Catholic heir and a pro-French foreign policy raised a barrier of mistrust between crown and parliament that even Danby's 'Cavalier' policies could not breach.

Danby and the royal finances

When he became lord treasurer in 1673 Danby inherited what appears to have been a hopeless financial situation. The suspension of the repayment of the capital on loans decided on by the Stop of the Exchequer, which had been intended as a temporary measure, was extended. In addition, parliamentary supplies (£1,800,000) for the Dutch war fell short by £443,000 of total war expenditure.[9] Yet Danby's chances of improving the crown's finances were considerably greater than the possibility of his securing a cooperative parliament. The late 1660s and early 1670s were a turning point in the development of public finance as well as in political history. Danby was fortunate in that his period at the treasury coincided with an improvement in the collection of three major branches of the revenue, the hearth tax, the excise, and the customs. Undoubtedly the most important of these, from the long-term point of view, was the last. From the late 1660s England entered a period of commercial prosperity, which continued (though with periodic interruptions) for most of the century. Customs revenue increased in proportion, and, moreover, the benefit to the crown was greater than it might have been, because in September 1671 the crown had taken over the direct administration of the customs as in the sixteenth century, so that the full benefit of the trade boom accrued, not to customs farmers but to the exchequer. Nor did the third Dutch war dislocate trade to the same extent as the second Dutch war. Danby's contribution to the improvement in the revenue was to bring his considerable financial experience to the treasury. As a protégé of Buckingham he first came to the forefront in politics as joint treasurer of the navy in 1668, and in 1671 he was promoted sole treasurer. The effect of the fortuitous combination of Danby's financial expertise and the rise in customs revenue can be seen in the following table.

Net government income 1668–79[10]

Financial year	Permanent ordinary revenue	Total revenue with parliamentary and non-parliamentary additions
	£	£
1663–9	873,174	883,605
1669–70	953,813	990,323
1670–71	840,170	1,165,554
1671–2	1,000,432	1,902,180
1672–3	1,006,860	1,363,395
1673–4	1,027,653	1,342,417
1674–5	1,138,010	1,430,183
1675–6	1,027,427	1,420,963
1676–7	1,042,815	1,409,508
1677–8	1,026,020	1,360,060
1678–9	1,063,723	1,325,894

Unfortunately for the crown and for Danby, as revenue increased so did royal expenditure, and at an even greater rate. When Danby left the treasury in March 1679 he bequeathed a floating debt of about £750,000 greater than he had faced in 1674, with the result that the overall financial position of the crown in the 1670s was, if anything, slightly worse than in the 1660s. Yet the similarity ends there. Whereas the crown's financial difficulties in the 1660s were largely due to the failure of the Convention and Cavalier Parliaments to provide the monarchy with an adequate permanent ordinary revenue, in the 1670s the major cause was Charles's extravagance: 'the simple Caroline law that the extravagance of the king tended to increase in proportion to his resources.'[11] In 1675 and 1677 Danby initiated drastic retrenchment schemes with the privy council's and Charles's approval. But Charles, like his grandfather in similar circumstances, ignored his promises. It seems hard to blame Danby for his failure to cut his master's spending. He depended totally on Charles for his political position, and, like Cecil and Cranfield in the reign of James I, was in no position to enforce rigid economy on the king. His failure, however, was a major factor in retarding the growth of strong monarchy in England in the late seventeenth century. It made the crown more than ever financially dependent on parliament, and increased the importance of Danby's task of securing a cooperative parliament.

Danby and parliament

To overcome parliamentary distrust of royal intentions, caused by the French alliance and a Catholic heir, Danby had two major parliamentary strategies: first to develop the art of parliamentary management, and second, to persuade Charles to adopt Cavalier policies which would appeal to the intolerant prejudices of Anglican MPs. Although the importance of Danby's 'party organization' has been exaggerated in the past, it is important for the insight it gives into the working of politics in the reign of Charles II.[12] Both Clarendon and Clifford had previously made rudimentary and haphazard efforts to coordinate support for government policies in parliament. Danby was much more systematic. His first attempt to influence MPs in favour of his policies grew out of his success in improving the collection of the excise. A by-product of this was that he, and not the excise farmers, secured control of the payment of pensions drawn on the excise revenue, and he began to distribute these pensions to MPs in the hope of consolidating support for the crown in parliament. By the autumn of 1675 pensions on the excise totalling £10,000 p.a. were being paid to between twenty-three and thirty-four MPs. Other MPs were appointed customs commissioners or officials of the Irish revenue. Danby also placed a lot of emphasis on approaching MPs directly to ask for their support. He extended the system of sending letters to potential supporters just before a session, reminding them of the necessity of attending. His agent, Sir Richard Wiseman, tirelessly canvassed opinion, drew up endless lists of MPs who might be persuaded to support the government if approached personally, and organized dinners to woo supporters. The extent of Danby's activities in organizing parliamentary support for the court is reflected in his surviving letters and papers.[13] But did he succeed in organizing a 'Court party'? There are many reasons for doubting that he did. Payment of 'bribes' in the seventeenth century, whether paid by Gondomar, the Spanish ambassador in the reign of James I, Danby, or Barrillon, the French ambassador in the 1670s and 1680s, rarely seem to have persuaded anyone to change their opinions or influenced anyone's activities. Moreover, what could be achieved by the distribution of offices was limited, because Danby had nothing like the government resources of patronage, not to mention electoral connections, that were at the disposal of Walpole or Newcastle in the eighteenth century. Most important of all, the effectiveness of Danby's 'party organization' was limited because it tended to be resented. For example, his attempt to suppress coffee-houses, which were considered to be places where government critics met and read anti-government pamphlets, roused great opposition. Danby was well in line with the suspicious attitude of all sixteenth- and seventeenth-century governments to social gatherings, even when only apparently innocuous drinks like coffee, chocolate, sherbert, and tea were being sold. Yet his intervention was resented and in the end he was forced to withdraw the ban. Danby's organization never produced a solid block of supporters in either House on whom he could rely, and his activities tended to help his opponents, who portrayed them, as did Shaftesbury, as a 'conspiracy' to raise the power of the monarchy and Church, and abolish Magna Carta and 'the rights and liberties of the people'.[14]

Danby's greatest political quality was that he was thoroughly acquainted with the mood of the mass of country MPs, and he sympathized with their desire for a return to the policies of the Clarendon Code and for the court to cut its ties with Louis XIV. The clearest exposition of his Cavalier philosophy is in a memorandum he drafted for Charles II at the end of 1674 or the beginning of 1675. He proposed that the crown ought to align itself firmly alongside the Church of England in penalizing dissent by enforcing the Corporation and Five-mile Acts. The king should also reward Anglican Cavaliers by promoting them to the commission of the peace and lieutenancy, so that 'preference in all counties may be given to those . . . who have actually been in armes or sufferers for your majestic or royall father, and to the sons of such'. He even proposed that recusancy fines should be used to pay salaries to sheriffs, JPs, and 'officers of the militia'.[15]

In the autumn of 1674 Danby began a series of conferences with bishops, which resulted in the following February in a privy council order that all the measures designed to preserve the monopoly of the Anglican Church should be rigorously enforced. To publicize this policy he released plans for the rebuilding of St Paul's, for the erection of a brass statue of Charles I at Charing Cross, and for a ceremony to re-inter the 'Martyr King'. At the opening of the parliamentary session in April 1675 Charles's speech pushed home the point further: 'I' said Charles, who never minded lying for the sake of political expediency, 'will leave nothing undone that may show any zeal to the Protestant religion, as it is established in the Church of England, from which I will never depart.'[16] Two days later Danby introduced into the Lords a Test Bill, which proposed that all MPs and officeholders make a declaration of non-resistance and swear never to try to alter the established government in Church and state.

Yet the two parliamentary sessions of 1675 were not a success. In the first session (April–June) the Commons attempted to remove Lauderdale and articles of impeachment were brought against Danby. Although both were unsuccessful they were hardly the responses Danby had hoped for. Even after the vigorous effort to mobilize support in the summer, the second session (October–November) produced only a grudging supply of £300,000 for the navy, far short of what the court wanted to pay off all anticipations on the revenue. A motion that all the money should be paid into and administered by the Chamber of the City of London, and not the exchequer, was only defeated by a narrow majority of eleven. When a clause was tacked on to the Supply Bill appropriating all the customs revenue to the navy parliament was prorogued for fifteen months. Partly the explanation for the failure of Danby's parliamentary policies in 1675 lies in the fact that the extreme Anglican measures proposed roused the resistance of MPs who were beginning to find the persecution of Dissent distasteful. According to Burnet, the Test Bill was vigorously opposed from 15 April to 2 June by Shaftesbury, Buckingham, and Halifax, and produced the greatest and longest debate in the House of Lords 'that he could remember'.[17] It was even rumoured that Danby's Anglicanism forced Shaftesbury and the duke of York to consider a political alliance to defend the dissenters and Catholics. Partly also many MPs opposed Danby because they considered his efforts to build up a court party to be a threat to parliamentary independence. At the end of April 1675 there was an unsuccessful move in the Commons to prevent placemen sitting in parliament or at least to force them to seek re-election. Danby's failure, however, is largely to be accounted for by the fact that he had failed to overcome the suspicions of most MPs of Charles's pro-French and Catholic leanings. In the 1675 parliamentary sessions this can be seen especially in the great opposition to Charles's apparent reluctance to recall English soldiers still serving in the French army. In fact, parliament's suspicions of Charles were well grounded. Charles's negotiations with Louis XIV culminated in two secret agreements in August 1675 and February 1676, by which Louis agreed to pay Charles a subsidy of £112,000. Danby disapproved of the continuation of the French alliance, but his failure to persuade Charles to abandon Louis and make an alliance with the Dutch undermined all the good done by his pursuit of Cavalier policies at home.

Despite Danby's failure in 1675 it is difficult to accept the views of older historians that by this date parliamentary politics had already polarized 'into two fairly well-defined parties with a voting strength of rather more than 150 each'.[18] It has already been suggested that Danby's attempts to produce a 'court party' were largely unsuccessful; there is very little sign yet of a 'country party' either. Certainly there was no generally recognized opposition leader. Shaftesbury, who was to fill this role during the exclusion crisis, was as yet too extreme for most MPs. His attempt in 1675 to force Charles to dissolve parliament by exploiting the inter-House dispute, *Shirley* v. *Fagg*, received little support in the Commons. Few MPs were anxious to face the electorate and perhaps lose their seats. 'I am afraid of a dissolution, because God is my witness, I am afraid the next will be worse.' Sir John Birkenhead's comment in parliament was laughed at, but it expressed what a lot of MPs feared. Indeed when parliament reassembled after fifteen months' prorogation (November 1675 to February 1677) and Shaftesbury, Buckingham, Salisbury, and Lord Wharton claimed that parliament was dissolved on the grounds that a statute of Edward III declared a prorogation of more than twelve months illegal, they were sent to the Tower by the Lords, and received little sympathetic support in the Commons. Danby was able to seize the initiative and secure promises of large parliamentary supplies: a seventeen months' assessment calculated to yield £585,000, renewal of the expiring additional excise, and approval of the government's plan to borrow £200,000 on the security of the excise. Moreover, an attempt to attach an appropriation clause to the Supply Bill was heavily defeated. In return Danby gave government support for a programme of limitations on a Catholic successor, which government critics had been proposing since 1673. Danby and the Cavalier majority in the Commons were closer than at any other time since his rise to power.

This accord was disrupted by Charles's continued attachment to the French alliance. Danby's failure to alter this proved to be as decisive as his inability to curb the king's extravagance in determining the shape of England's future political development. The ignorance of many MPs about foreign affairs in the reign of Charles II matched their misunderstanding of public finance. On hearing of the fall of Ghent to French troops in February 1678 Colonel Birch said in the Commons, 'I know not this Ghent, but 'tis said to be a great place'.[19] Yet, even if some MPs were hazy about the details, they were clear by 1677 both that they wanted a Dutch alliance and that they feared and detested the spread of French power. These fears increased in the spring of 1677 as the French army swept into Flanders. The Commons, consequently, with Danby's support, demanded that Charles take action to defend the Spanish Netherlands against France. Charles responded by adjourning parliament on 28 May and it did not meet again until January 1678.

Yet, as Danby knew, the adjournment did not change anything. 'Till hee [the king] can fall into the humour of the people hee can never bee great nor rich', noted Danby in a memorandum just after the adjournment.[20] Danby now also had personal reasons which made it more urgent than ever to persuade Charles to abandon France and secure a cooperative parliament. In the summer of 1677 the treasurer's position at court, which had been supreme since early 1675, was being slowly undermined as a result of a reconciliation between Charles and Buckingham, who was now released from the Tower. It was this which forced Danby's conversion to the project of a marriage between William of Orange and James's elder daughter, Mary; this would, Danby hoped, be a preliminary to a military alliance with the Dutch; it would also have the advantage of proclaiming to suspicious MPs the court's commitment to Protestantism abroad as well as at home. Mary was in no position to refuse to agree, although so distressed was she at the prospect of marrying the tiny, hunchbacked William that she is said to have wept for one and a half days. What is not clear is why Charles agreed to the betrothal in October 1677. There are various explanations. He undoubtedly saw the political advantages of the marriage at home; the announcement of the marriage was greeted with public rejoicing and bonfires. David Ogg thought that Charles also agreed to spite his brother, whom he disliked, by imposing 'a brusque and ambitious son-in-law on him'.[21] Yet, although military preparations were made in the winter of 1677–8 for war against France, and Laurence Hyde was sent to the United Provinces to negotiate a Dutch alliance, it is difficult to believe that Charles ever seriously considered the marriage as the first step to such an alliance. It is doubtful, in any case, given the 1670 Catholic clause, whether Charles *could* have abandoned Louis; in the spring of 1678 he was negotiating another secret agreement with the French king.

The most likely explanation is that Charles intended to use the marriage as a means of persuading Louis to make peace, in the hope that this would defuse parliamentary opposition to the government's foreign policy.[22] If this was Charles's scheme, it failed totally: Louis refused to make peace, and when parliament reassembled in January 1678 it became clear that Charles's apparent change of foreign policy had done nothing to remove parliamentary suspicions.

The parliamentary session of January to July 1678 was marked by intensified distrust of the court. The Commons voted (by a poll tax of March 1678) inadequate war supplies that would produce nowhere near the £1 million promised by an earlier vote on 18 February. Not surprisingly many MPs were sceptical of the sincerity of Charles's about-turn in foreign affairs, a view they would certainly have held even without the campaign of propaganda and bribery conducted by the French ambassador, Barrillon, aimed at undermining Danby's position. There was widespread fear that the army being raised supposedly to fight the French would be used instead against parliament. All these doubts and fears were crystallized in Andrew Marvell's *An Account of the Growth of Popery and Arbitrary Government* which was written late in 1677 and was now published. Its opening sentence put into words what many felt: 'There has now for divers years a design been carried on to change the lawful government of England into an absolute tyranny, and to convert the established Protestant religion into downright Popery.' Consequently after news of an armistice between the French and Dutch reached London the Commons early in June voted £200,000 for the disbandment of the army. Yet the army was not disbanded, because, according to the official explanation, European peace was not formally concluded (this was not done until the Treaty of Nijmegen, 31 July 1678). Many MPs however, feared that the real reason was that the court was planning a military *coup d'état*. When parliament was prorogued on 15 July 1678, therefore, many feared the imminent establishment of popery and absolutism backed by an army of around 30,000 men. There is no better demonstration of the failure of Danby's parliamentary policies; but it is arguable that, until Charles dissolved parliament at the end of the year, the opposition to the court was as powerless as in February 1674. How important was the 'Popish Plot' in transforming the fortunes of the 'country party'?

The Popish Plot

There was no Popish Plot. Most of the details of a conspiracy masterminded by the Jesuits to assassinate the king had their origins in the twisted minds of Titus Oates and Israel Tonge. Their allegations were first made known to the king on 13 August 1678 and were passed to Danby for further investigation. In the following days Oates and Tonge added more details of the 'plot', and on 6 September Oates swore to a deposition, forty-three articles long, before a justice of the peace, Sir Edmund Berry Godfrey. Partly at the instigation of James duke of York the matter was then brought before the privy council at the end of September, when Oates and Tonge produced a new version of their allegations, now eighty-one articles long. The plot, they said, had been finalized at a Jesuit 'consult' at the White Horse Tavern on 24 April 1678, when plans had been made to shoot the king, and, if that failed, for the queen's physician, Sir George Wakeman, to poison him. Though the details were vague, the sequel to Charles's death was intended to be a Catholic uprising in Ireland and in England, and possibly an invasion from France. Not only later commentators have been sceptical about Oates's and Tonge's story. During the privy council's investigations Charles exposed Oates as a liar on points of detail and the Tory propagandist, Roger L'Estrange, later made fun of the internal inconsistencies and absurdities of the 'revelations'. Yet within ten days of its reassembling on 21 October 1678 the Cavalier Parliament recorded its unanimous conviction 'that there hath been and still is a damnable and hellish plot contrived and carried on by the popish recusants for the assasinating and murdering the King, and for subverting the government, and rooting out and destroying the Protestant religion',[23] and anyone who dared to cast doubts on the plot's authenticity was in danger of his life. The first important question, therefore, about the Popish Plot is, why were allegations that were patently false so universally believed?

The most important explanation lies in the anti-Catholic tradition which it has been seen was so strong in seventeenth-century England. Many people found the Popish Plot story convincing because it was unoriginal and incorporated much English anti-Catholic mythology. To Oates's and Tonge's audience the present 'plot' was an obvious sequel to the Catholic conspiracies in the seventeenth century, including the Gunpowder Plot, the outbreak of the Civil War, the 'murder' of Charles I, and the Great Fire. In the summer of 1678 political events had intensified people's fears of Catholicism; Oates and Tonge could not have produced their story confirming those fears at a more propitious moment. In the early stages also Titus Oates convinced many sceptics by his confident performance before the privy council and at the bar of the House of Commons. (This was less true later on, when at some of the trials of alleged conspirators he seemed to lose his nerve.) It was difficult to disbelieve someone who 'remembered' dates and places of conspiratorial meetings in such an authoritative way. This helps to explain why the privy council was so impressed when Oates at the council meeting on 28 September identified the Jesuit authors of five incriminating letters received by Thomas Bedingfield, James's confessor, even though he was only shown a line or two of each letter. The obvious explanation – that Oates or Tonge had forged the letters – was ignored. The privy council was 'amazed' and from then on 'this very thing took like fire, so that what he said afterwards had credit.'[24] Oates was also fortunate that among those he implicated in the 'plot' was an ex-secretary to James and his wife, Edward Coleman, who for many years since 1673 had corresponded with Jesuits and French agents discussing wild schemes to help the Catholic cause in England. When Coleman was arrested and his correspondence seized the fact that Oates failed to recognize Coleman when they first met was forgotten. The Coleman papers appeared to substantiate the Popish Plot story. What finally dispelled all doubts was the news of the disappearance on 12 October of Sir Edmund Berry Godfrey, the JP who had taken Oates's original depositions, and the discovery five days later of his body, which had been strangled and stabbed with his own sword. Later investigators have spent a lot of time speculating about the unknown cause of Godfrey's death; was it suicide, or murder by strangulation or by a sword, or a suicide made to look like murder?[25] What is more important than discovering how Godfrey died is that at the time most people believed he had been killed by Catholics to silence a man who might make more damaging revelations against them.

For a few months at the end of 1678 and the beginning of 1679 there is a lot of evidence that the country was gripped by a wave of anti-Catholic hysteria and panic like that of 1640–2. Letters of the time are full of rumours that the French and Spanish had landed, that 'night riders' had been seen, that Catholics were arming themselves secretly, that bombs had been placed under churches. Poor communications and the lack of official pronouncements (the details of the 'Plot' were not released until April 1679) allowed the spread of wild rumours that had not even occurred to Oates's fertile imagination. Panic was greatest and lasted longest in London where fear of another fire was endemic. Everywhere the authorities searched the houses of known Catholics for arms, and called the militia out. In London chains were put across the major streets and the trained bands kept on the alert day and night. The panic was reflected in parliament, where various committees heard more witnesses and added more allegations and names to the already long list of Catholic 'crimes' and 'conspirators'. In November and December 1678 Coleman and three others were tried and executed for their alleged part in the 'Plot' and articles of impeachment were brought against five Catholic peers named by Oates as deeply implicated in the 'conspiracy'. From the end of 1678 until the beginning of 1681 about thirty-five people were tried and executed for their alleged part in it.[26]

Yet it is clear that the effects of the 'Popish Plot' can be exaggerated. The wave of anti-Catholic hysteria it produced was shortlived; even in London it is difficult to find evidence of it after the spring of 1679, especially as the cumulative effects of one unfounded rumour after another became apparent. Also during the winter of 1678–9 the appearance of new informers with further allegations produced a diminishing impact. Indeed the attempt of William Bedloe (closely followed by Oates who did not relish being upstaged) to implicate the queen in the planning of Godfrey's murder produced a 'backlash' in favour of the court and did much to weaken both Oates's credibility and people's belief in the imminence of a Catholic uprising. Too much can perhaps be made also of the political effects of the 'Popish Plot'. Although Danby at first encouraged the investigation into Oates's allegations in the hope that they might unite Protestants and monarchy against the Popish menace, the 'Plot' undoubtedly harmed the court. Oates had at first been careful not to attack James directly, but Coleman's letters did implicate his ex-master in his plans and emphasized the Catholic danger at court. But even without the 'Popish Plot' Danby and the court would have met a storm of opposition in parliament, since the army was still in being, despite the grant of parliamentary supplies for its demobilization in June. Nor were the demands for limitations on a Catholic successor or for anti-Catholic legislation new or unexpected. Moreover, despite the Plot, Charles had a great deal of success in taking the sting out of the parliamentary opposition by a policy of limited concessions.

I am come to assure you [he told parliament on 9 November], that whatsoever reasonable bills you shall present to be passed into laws, to make you safe in the reign of my successor, so as they tend not to impeach the right of succession, nor the descent of the crown in the true line, and so as they restrain not my power, nor the just rights of any Protestant successor, shall find from me a ready concurrence.[27]

To prove his point Charles reissued anti-Catholic proclamations, encouraged local officials to carry them out (convictions of recusants in some counties rose sharply),[28] and gave his assent to a Test Act excluding Catholics from parliament. His strategy worked and gained him enough support to get a narrow majority (158 to 156) in favour of a proviso excluding James from the Test Act. The opposition in parliament had so far been contained. The prime targets were still Danby and the standing army, and the extremists, Shaftesbury in the Lords and Russell in the Commons, had not succeeded in weaning the majority away from pressing for limitations on a Catholic successor to the more explosive issue of exclusion.

The revelations of Ralph Montagu changed the political scene much more fundamentally than did those of Titus Oates. They led directly to the dissolution of the Cavalier Parliament. Montagu had little reason to like Danby, who early in 1678 had vetoed his appointment as one of the secretaries of state and who had been instrumental in ending his appointment as the English ambassador at Paris in June. With the encouragement of Barrillon and Shaftesbury, Montagu returned to England determined to secure Danby's downfall by revealing letters written by Danby in January and March 1678 and containing details of the secret subsidy negotiations with Louis XIV. Before he could be stopped Montagu produced the letters in the House of Commons on 19 December 1678. The effect was dramatic. Two days later the House agreed to draw up articles of impeachment against Danby and all other parliamentary business came to a standstill. On 30 December Charles prorogued the session, and on 24 January 1679, to prevent further damaging revelations of his French treaties, he declared the Cavalier Parliament dissolved. Montagu had brought about what the extreme opposition had been trying to do since 1673.

It is tempting to emphasize the contrast between the new parliament – the First Exclusion Parliament which met from 6 March to 27 May 1679 – and the last sessions of the Cavalier Parliament. Shaftesbury estimated that there were about 302 'worthy' and 'honest' MPs as against only 158 courtiers in the new parliament, a much higher anti-court majority than in the old parliament.[29] The new House of Commons voted for two readings of a Bill to exclude a Catholic from the English throne, something which had never even been discussed in the Cavalier Parliament. Yet for the first two months of its session the new parliament followed very closely the pattern of the old, concentrating on getting rid of the army, securing the impeachment of Danby, and imposing limitations on a Catholic monarch. And like its predecessor it had only limited success in all three aims: the army was not disbanded until the summer; Danby, unlike Clarendon, stayed to face the proceedings against him and both articles of impeachment and a Bill of Attainder directed at him failed (though he spent the next five years in the Tower); and the opposition's only success in protecting personal liberties against arbitrary government was the Habeas Corpus Amendment Act. Although in retrospect this Act, requiring judges to bring a prisoner to trial within a specific period, was a great step forward in the progress of human rights, at the time it was of negligible significance in the opposition's aim of tying the hands of a Catholic monarch. The slow progress made in this direction may have contributed to the growing support among MPs for exclusion at the end of April 1679. Many also may have been at last convinced by the arguments of the extremists that, if they were put in the statute book, limitations would be ignored by a Catholic king. They would be, as one MP had said in 1677, 'like empty casks for whales to play with, and rattles for children to keep them quiet'.[30] The immediate reason, though, for the conversion of many hitherto moderate MPs to exclusion was the public disclosure in April 1679 of part of Coleman's correspondence which seemed to implicate James in negotiations with Rome, and therefore, most people assumed, in the 'Popish Plot' as well. On 11 May Thomas Pilkington moved that James be impeached of high treason and on 15 May the first Exclusion Bill was read, providing that on Charles's death the crown should not pass to James, but to the next in succession. On its second reading the Bill passed by a majority of 207 to 128. Two weeks later Charles prorogued (and later dissolved) the parliament.

The exclusion crisis, May 1679–March 1681

For two years from the spring of 1679 the political nation was split on the question of exclusion. Whig supporters and Tory opponents of exclusion became better organized than any other political groups hitherto. At times (in August 1679 and March 1681 for example) the growing gulf between the Whigs and the Tories seemed to make the possibility of a second civil war a reality. Yet to compare 1679–81 with 1641–2 is to exaggerate the seriousness of the later crisis. As will be seen, the English monarchy was in a much stronger position in 1679 than in 1641 and the opposition to it was much weaker. Charles's eventual victory was not a foregone conclusion, but it was easier to achieve than is often recognized.

From 1679 to 1681 the opposition to the crown appeared to be very strong, and in the parliaments of October 1680 to January 1681 and March 1681 the Whigs secured majorities in the House of Commons for Bills excluding James from the throne. Some of the credit for this is due to the earl of Shaftesbury, who for the first time since he had left the court in 1673 emerged at the forefront of the opposition. Dryden's description of Shaftesbury in his *Absalom and Achitophel* as an unprincipled, power-grasping man, is, as one might expect from such a piece of propaganda, a caricature. As has been seen, many of his class had, like Shaftesbury, changed sides since the 1640s, supporting parliamentary, royalist, and Cromwellian regimes alike and welcoming the Restoration. Throughout his career he remained true to certain principles: toleration for Protestant dissenters, but not for Catholics; and government by king in parliament, but not by the masses. Neither Shaftesbury nor the Whigs were the forerunners of the nineteenth- and twentieth-century concept of liberal democracy. 'There is no prince' wrote Shaftesbury, 'that ever governed without nobility or an army; if you will not have one, you must have the other, or the monarchy cannot long support, or keep itself from tumbling into a democratical republic.'[31] Shaftesbury considered that James's accession would end all hopes of toleration and herald the imposition of arbitrary rule. To prevent this he was willing to use unscrupulous methods. It is fairly clear that Shaftesbury did not instigate Oates's and Tonge's (and later Bedloes's) allegations, but he did patronize these and other inventors of plot stories, and encouraged people to believe them.

Not all the Whigs' tactics, though, were crude. In the two general elections of August–September 1679 and the early months of 1681 Shaftesbury and his supporters developed a political organization that became increasingly sophisticated and effective.[32] Significantly in both elections local interests and family connections played less part than ever before. Charles's serious illness at the end of August 1679 helped the Whigs to focus the attention of the electorate on exclusion, and the Whigs' use of the press to disseminate pamphlet literature emphasizing the dangers of a Catholic monarch was unprecedented. In many 'provincial capitals', as well as in London, political dining clubs (like the London Green Ribbon Club) were set up to distribute Whig propaganda. Just how substantial Whig organization was in many constituencies can be seen in the election of 1681 when many MPs were presented apparently spontaneously with instructions purporting to be from their constituents and insisting that they grant no parliamentary supply unless the king conceded exclusion and a guarantee of frequent parliaments. So similar were the demands in these instructions that it is likely that they were copies of a model drafted by the Whig leadership in London.

Equally impressive were the Whig efforts to maintain the political tempo against exclusion during the long prorogation of parliament from May 1679 to October 1680, at a time when anti-Catholic hysteria associated with the 'Popish Plot' had dwindled. Using very similar tactics to those of the parliamentary leadership of the early 1640s the Whigs initiated a sustained campaign of bombarding the king with petitions for the early recall of parliament. Printed petition forms were distributed in London and the counties, where Whig supporters collected signatures. In January 1680 Charles was presented with two petitions from London and Wiltshire signed by a total of about 90,000 people. Less important were the mass pope-burning demonstrations organized on 5 and 17 November 1679 and 1680. Like other crowds in the seventeenth century the demonstrators of 1679–80 were not the violent rabble Tory propagandists at the time made them out to be. They showed a great respect for property, and at the end of the day they dispersed peacefully. But the demonstrators of 1679–80 illustrate the capacity of the Whigs to mobilize support outside as well as among the parliamentary classes.

The position of the Whigs, however, seemed stronger than it actually was. They were united on little apart from exclusion, and were most seriously divided on the question of who was to succeed Charles II. The two most obvious candidates had alarming drawbacks. James Scott, duke of Monmouth, might have been Charles II's son, but he was illegitimate. James's elder daughter, Mary, appeared to be a more suitable successor, but she was married to William of Orange, who it was feared (wrongly) was too dependent on his Stuart uncles, and (rightly) was likely to drag England into an expensive, continental war against France. It is not clear whether even Shaftesbury at the Oxford Parliament in 1681 ever publicly committed himself to Monmouth as Charles's successor. Consequently the Tories were able to exploit this basic weakness in the Whig position. The absence of an acceptable alternative successor to James partly explains why a substantial majority of the parliamentary classes still supported a policy of limitations, despite its obvious drawbacks. Many, however, were simply repelled by the revolutionary implications of exclusion. If the right of legitimate succession to the throne was overturned, might not this be but a preliminary to challenging the right of legitimate succession to property? If James was excluded, would not the country be torn again by civil war between the supporters of James and those of other claimants? 'Acts of Parliament', said Henry Coventry in 1680, 'have not kept the succession out of the right line but brought in blood and sword . . . show me one man excluded . . . that had right of descent but has come in again.'[33] Roger L'Estrange and other Tory propagandists were able to make great play with the fact that the Whigs' appeal to the people, like that of Pym in 1641–2, would end in the destruction of the Church and the monarchy.

The position of the crown and the Tories was much stronger than that of the Whigs. Although their electoral and parliamentary support was never so well organized as the Whigs, the Tories did have a rudimentary political organization. In 1679–80 there was a rash of Tory petitions 'abhorring' those of their rivals, and in 1680–1 pamphlets and sermons joined in a vociferous anti-exclusion chorus. Charles II too, unlike his father, responded cleverly to this conservative reaction. He remained firm in his insistence on his brother's right to succeed, but made many strategically timed concessions. In April 1679 he greatly enlarged his privy council to include many of his brother's opponents including the earl of Shaftesbury. Since Charles was not willing to concede the principle of exclusion the new privy council was an empty gesture. But for a time it disconcerted the opposition and it produced one notable permanent convert from the Whigs, the marquis of Halifax. The king's most notable political victory was the defeat of the second Exclusion Bill in the House of Lords in November 1680, which may have been achieved as much by Charles's presence in the House during the debate as by Halifax's speeches in favour of limitations.

Undoubtedly though, Charles would not have defeated exclusion if the political tide had not been running in his favour. The monarchy was much stronger than in 1641–2. Scotland and Ireland were subservient. The revolt of the Scottish Covenanters in June 1679 was easily suppressed by Monmouth at Bothwell Bridge, and James quickly reasserted royal control in Scotland. Although Shaftesbury had strong support in the City of London, he never controlled the City as Pym had done, nor was there in 1679–81 a radical revolution in the City; Charles II retained control of the London trained bands.[34] Indicative of his hold on the country is the ease with which from 1680–2 he purged leading Whigs, like the earls of Suffolk, Manchester, and Essex, from the lieutenancy and the commission of the peace, though not yet from the boroughs. The judiciary, too, was staunchly behind the king. Since 1660 Charles had filled the Bench with lawyers of authoritarian leanings, men like Lord Chief Justice Kelyng who in 1667 called Magna Carta 'magna farta'.[35] In great contrast to his father's position thirty years earlier, Charles's greatest asset was his financial strength which allowed him in 1681 to dispense with parliament. The contribution of French subsidies to the crown's new financial independence was slight; it was brought about much more by the work of the new treasury commissioners (especially Lawrence Hyde earl of Rochester) who took over after the fall of Danby in March 1679. It was they who at last persuaded Charles to curb his expenditure and allow the monarchy to benefit from the full effect of the improvement in crown revenue which had been underway for nearly a decade. The response of the Whigs to the King's dissolution of parliament in March 1681 typifies their inherent weakness. They dispersed to prepare for new elections which Charles never intended to authorize. The armed men they had brought with them to Oxford were not used. The Whigs were no more willing than the Tory magnates to plunge the country into another rebellion and civil war.

Notes

For abbreviations used throughout see p. xiv.
1. Robin Clifton, 'The fear of Catholicism during the English civil war', *P. & P.*, LII (1971); *idem.*, 'Fear of Popery', in Conrad Russell, ed., *The Origins of the English Civil War* (1973).
2. Quoted in Miller, *Popery and Politics*, p. 85. See Lamont, *Prynne*, for Prynne's obsession with Jesuit plots.
3. Quoted in Miller, *Popery and Politics*, p. 75.
4. *Ibid.*, pp. 9–10, 40.
5. Clifton, 'Fear of popery', pp. 146–7.
6. Quoted in Miller, *Popery and Politics*, p. 32.
7. Tanner, *Constitutional Documents*, p. 277.
8. *Ibid.*, p. 277.
9. Chandaman, *English Public Revenue*, p. 229.
10. *Ibid.*, p. 332.
11. *Ibid.*, p. 235.
12. A. Browning, 'Parties and party organisation in the reign of Charles II', *T.R.H.S.*, 4th ser., XXX (1948); Browning, *Danby*, I, pp. 167–72, 191–3, 201–7.
13. Many of these are printed in Browning, *Danby*, III, p. 33–151.
14. Quoted in Haley, *Shaftesbury*, p. 390.
15. Browning, *Danby*, III, pp. 65–6.
16. Quoted in Haley, *Shaftesbury*, p. 374.
17. Quoted in *ibid.*, p. 381.
18. Browning, *Danby*, I, p. 173. For a similar view see Ogg, *Reign of Charles II*, p. 535.
19. Quoted in Browning, *op. cit.*, I, p. 262 note.
20. *Ibid.*, II, pp. 69–71.
21. Ogg, *Reign of Charles II*, p. 547.
22. K. H. D. Haley, 'The Anglo-Dutch rapprochement of 1667', *E.H.R.*, LXXIII (1958), pp. 614–48.
23. Quoted in J. P. Kenyon, *The Popish Plot* (1974), p. 96; this is the most recent and authoritative account.
24. Quoted in *ibid.*, p. 80.
25. See *ibid.*, pp. 302–9, appendix A, 'The murder of Sir Edmund Berry Godfrey', for an historiographical survey.
26. G. N. Clark, *The Later Stuarts* (1955), pp. 94–5.
27. Quoted in Kenyon, *Popish Plot*, p. 103.
28. Miller, *Popery and Politics*, pp. 164–5.
29. J. R. Jones, 'Shaftesbury's "worthy men": a Whig view of the parliament of 1679', *B.I.H.R.*, XXX (1957), pp. 232–41.
30. Quoted in Haley, *Shaftesbury*, p. 423.

31. Quoted in *ibid.*, p. 395.
32. The best study of this is by J. R. Jones, *The First Whigs* (1971).
33. Quoted in J. R. Western, *Monarchy and Revolution: the English state in the 1680s* (1972), p. 40.
34. David Allen, 'The role of the London trained bands in the Exclusion Crisis, 1678–81', *E.H.R.*, LXXXVII (1972), pp. 287–303.
35. Quoted in Western, *Monarchy and Revolution*, p. 56.

Chapter 11

The trend towards absolutism, 1681–1688

After the dissolution of the Oxford Parliament in March 1681 the English monarchy was in a strong position, and during the early 1680s it grew even stronger. Like many other European states, in Germany, France, Sweden, and Denmark, England seemed set to become an absolutist state. Even the accession of a Catholic king in 1685 was accepted by a fiercely anti-Catholic country. But the next three years were to show that there were limits to what the king could achieve and that the country would not accept toleration for Catholics. The failure of James II's pro-Catholic policies was inevitable; but his downfall in 1688 was not. While there is no doubt that those policies united the great majority of Protestant Englishmen, Whig and Tory, against him, it is by no means certain that they made the 'Glorious Revolution' inevitable. Most propertied men were too fearful of the consequences to push their opposition to the crown to revolution and possible civil war. The key factors in bringing about the end of James's regime, therefore, must be sought elsewhere: in James's personal inadequacy in face of the crisis at the end of 1688, and, above all, in the role played by William of Orange.

The strengthening of royal authority, 1681–1685

Charles II in the declaration he ordered to be read from the pulpits of all churches after the dissolution of the Oxford Parliament recalled the horrors of the civil war when 'religion, liberty and property were all lost and gone, when the monarchy was shaken off, and could never be revived till that was restored'. So Charles and the Tories successfully smeared the Whigs with the taint of republicanism; moreover, the Whigs themselves by their extremist tactics lost the support of the propertied classes. In any case, with parliament dissolved the Whigs were stripped of their one chance of reviving support, by using their electoral organization, which had worked so efficiently in the elections of 1679 and 1681. All this partly accounts for the ease with which Charles crushed the Whigs after 1681. He was also helped by the criminal law which in the seventeenth century was weighted against defendants, especially those charged with treason and felony, who were allowed neither legal advice nor prior view of the charges and the list of witnesses against them. For opponents of the crown the situation was made even more threatening by the dismissal of judges who resisted royal wishes. The trials and executions in 1681 of Edward Fitzharris, an informer used and then abandoned by the court, and of Stephen College, a Whig supporter, illustrate the usefulness to the crown, as well as the intrinsic unfairness, of the late seventeenth-century legal process. The earl of Shaftesbury, who was imprisoned in the Tower early in July 1681 on a charge of treason, only escaped execution because the grand jury that considered the charges against him at the end of November 1681 was nominated by two Whig sheriffs.

It is a measure of Shaftesbury's desperation that he now seemed to pin his hopes totally on Monmouth, who in the autumn of 1682 toured Cheshire canvassing support among Whig magnates in a way that looked suspiciously like preparations for rebellion. Shaftesbury's flight to Holland in November 1682 was a recognition by him of the hopelessness of opposition to the regime in the face of the loyalist reaction. He died in exile two months later. In the next few months the government used its control of the judiciary to get rid of the remaining major Whig leaders, William lord Russell and Algernon Sidney, who were executed in 1683 for their alleged part in the so-called Rye House Plot to assassinate the king on his way to the races at Newmarket. A third Whig, the earl of Essex, committed suicide in the Tower before his trial. As in the case of the Popish Plot, it did not matter that the evidence for a conspiracy was so circumstantial, vague, and contradictory that one wonders whether there was a Rye House Plot at all.

In the early 1680s the crown not only harassed the Whigs but it intensified and extended its campaign to prevent the Whigs from ever again controlling parliamentary elections as they had done during the exclusion crisis. As has been seen, the crown had begun to purge county government in 1679. Like the Elizabethan efforts to purge the commission of the peace, the later effort to curb county independence was probably not completely effective. To claim as much would be to underestimate local resistance to central government in the seventeenth century. Yet by 1682–3 county government was as tractable as it had ever been. The early 1680s were punctuated by organized loyal addresses to the king containing thousands of signatures, on the dissolution of parliament in 1681, after the disclosure of the Rye House Plot in 1683, and on the accession of James II in 1685. Significantly there were no Whig counter-addresses. The government had even more success in purging its opponents from municipal government. There was a long previous history of intervention by the central government in municipal affairs, in Elizabeth I's reign, the 1620s, the 1640s, and immediately after the Corporation Act of 1661. Yet arguably the *quo warranto* campaign against municipal independence in the 1680s was more extensive than any of these.[1] *Quo warranto* writs compelled boroughs to substantiate the legality of their charters; since lawyers could easily find technical flaws in them, proceedings invariably resulted in the law courts declaring that borough charters were forfeit. This was the lesson other boroughs drew from London's unsuccessful defence of its charter. Although the crown's victory was hard-won – the *quo warranto* action against London was begun in December 1681 and not completed until June 1683 – the final judgement was for the crown. From now on the king's approval was required for the appointment of the lord mayor, sheriffs, and all London's other major office-holders. Many other boroughs took the hint from London's defeat and voluntarily surrendered their charters to the crown. Others fought the writs in the courts and lost. All were given new charters which enabled the crown's Tory supporters to entrench themselves in power. From 1681 until Charles's death fifty-one new charters were issued, fourteen before and thirty-seven after 1683. From James II's accession in February 1685 until parliament met in May 1685 another forty-seven new charters were granted.[2] Not only the law helped the crown to undermine municipal independence in this way: county landowning gentry, who since at least the sixteenth century had considered the towns to be within their legitimate spheres of influence and who often were the agents and beneficiaries of royal policy against the towns, gave the crown their enthusiastic support.

The financial 'sinews of monarchy' were also considerably strengthened in the 1680s. A combination of Charles's conversion to relatively restrained expenditure in his old age, increased revenue from the customs during a decade of commercial prosperity, and increased yields from both the hearth tax and the excise from 1683–4, when the crown began to collect these taxes directly and efficiently, enabled the crown's permanent ordinary revenue to soar beyond the £1,200,000 agreed in 1660–1. By 1684–5 it had risen to £1,370,750, and was still increasing.[3] The improving financial position of the crown was symptomatic of the development of adminstrative efficiency within central government that was to become a marked feature of England after 1689, as will be seen. But even before then the increase in size and efficiency of executive departments, especially the treasury under a succession of able heads, notably Danby and Rochester, was a significant addition to the power of the crown in the 1680s (see below, pp. 412–16).

Frequently during the course of his reign Charles II had abandoned the Church of England in his pursuit of religious toleration. But in the last years of his reign he at last harnessed the power of the crown with that of the Church of England. Albeit belatedly, Charles took the advice of Clarendon and Danby. From 1681–5, especially after the Rye House Plot, Tory magistrates persecuted Catholic and Protestant dissenters, spurred on by the privy council.[4] As Dr Robert South had pointed out in 1661, the alliance of monarchy and Church of England was potentially very powerful. With the addition of vastly improved royal financial resources it was the recipe for the establishment of authoritarian government in England in the 1680s. By exploiting the divisions among his Protestant subjects Charles bequeathed his brother an apparently strong political position. In 1684 there was no outcry when, despite the Triennial Act, Charles did not call parliament, James was restored to the privy council, and Danby was released from the Tower. Loyal addresses greeted James's accession in February 1685. It remains to be seen how James II transformed this situation. Within three and a half years he had forced Anglicans and Protestant dissenters to forget their differences temporarily, and to unite against him.

James II and protestant unity, February 1685–June 1688

Historians have now established that James II was not the villain described by Macaulay and later Whig historians.[5] His aim was not to establish Catholicism as the sole religion of the country, nor to eradicate Protestantism by force. Nor, though he had an authoritarian temperament, did he intend to rule without parliament or to govern unconstitutionally. He resisted many of the extremist plans projected by his Catholic advisers who urged him to compel his younger daughter, Anne, to become a Catholic and make her the heir to the throne, or to legitimize his bastard son, the duke of Berwick, and impose Catholicism with French help. James was especially sensitive to the charge that he was a client of Louis XIV, and he continually attempted to assert his independence of France. In reality, James's aims were much more moderate and limited than many contemporaries and later historians have thought. He simply wanted to establish the rights of English Catholics to worship without persecution and to take full part in the political life of the country. This could be done by repealing the penal laws, the Corporation Act of 1661 and the Test Acts of 1673 and 1678. Once this was done, he believed, Catholicism would triumph without any compulsion by the state. The conversion of most Englishmen to Catholicism would only be a matter of time. Historians may have rescued James II from the charge of extremism. What they have not done is to show that his aims were anything other than impracticable, foolish, and misguided. James was often unable to understand the views of those with whom he disagreed. He completely misunderstood the strength of the attachment of most of his contemporaries to anti-Catholicism, which made the defeat of his plans inevitable. He demonstrably failed to persuade the majority of Anglicans in the first phase of his reign (1685–6) and Protestant dissenters in the second (1687–8) to accept even limited toleration for Catholics.

The strength of the Anglican–Tory reaction following the exclusion crisis is reflected in the composition of the parliament which met in May 1685. Secretary of State Sunderland was very active during the elections; and of the 195 MPs returned by boroughs with remodelled charters only nine have been identified as Whigs.[6] 'Such a landed Parliament was never seen', wrote the earl of Ailesbury. It would be a mistake, though, to assume that this parliament, even in its first session (19 May to 2 July 1685), was totally submissive to the new king. Like the Cavalier Parliament elected in 1661, it was Anglican as well as royalist. Early in the session it passed resolutions in defence of the Church of England and in favour of executing the penal laws. Nor were all MPs happy about granting the crown its hereditary revenues for life; some were in favour of a temporary grant 'to be renewed from time to time that parliament might be consulted the oftener'.[7] However, these doubts were not reflected in the financial settlement of 1685. This 'landed parliament' was less anxious about granting taxes on trade than on land. As well as a life grant of the crown's hereditary revenues James was amply supplied by additional revenues from customs duties. Any doubts MPs might have had about the wisdom of generosity were overcome by their recognition of the crown's need for money to suppress the rebellions of Argyll and Monmouth in the summer of 1685. Monmouth drew most of his support from social groups outside the political nation. Con- temporaries reported thousands of farmers and clothworkers joining Monmouth as he marched through Dorset and Somerset in June to his final defeat at the battle of Sedgemoor on 5 July. Although there were more craftsmen and townsmen than farmers in the rank and file of Monmouth's army, Dr Peter Earl's systematic study of Monmouth's supporters largely bears out this conclusion about the types of people attracted by the duke. It may be that the area from which the rebels came – Somerset, west Dorset, and east Devon, where Protestant dissent flourished in cloth-working villages – was a natural recruiting ground for those in the middle ranks of society who feared the imposition of Catholicism and absolutism.[8] What is certain is that Monmouth, unlike William of Orange who landed in the south-west three years later, received little support from the gentry. Nor did his execution and the brutal suppression of his followers by Lord Chief Justice Jeffries during 'the Bloody Assizes' in the autumn arouse much sympathy among the properted classes.

Once the rebellions were over, however, the differences between the king and Tory–Anglican opinion became apparent. James brought the stormy second session of parliament to an end after less than two weeks (9–20 November). By this time he had made known his intention to secure the repeal of the Test and Corporation Acts. With characteristic lack of political guile he announced to parliament that the army raised to fight Monmouth would not be disbanded and that he had promoted Catholic officers in the army despite the Test Acts. Halifax had already been dismissed from the privy council when he opposed this, and significantly, the opposition to James's announcement in the Lords was led, not only by the Whig earl of Devonshire, but by two other privy councillors, the earls of Nottingham and Bridgewater, and by Henry Compton, bishop of London. It is possible that James's announcement by itself is sufficient explanation for the political storm. But what undoubtedly intensified Tory opposition was that the king's policies were identified with Louis XIV's cruel campaign against French Huguenots. The Revocation of the Edict of Nantes in October 1685 produced a new flood of French refugees to England, bringing with them another batch of horror stories about the sufferings of Protestants at the hands of Catholics. In these circumstances James's moderate Catholic aims were inevitably misunderstood. As with his father's Arminianism in the 1630s, what people *thought* James's plans were became more important than his actual intentions. His aim of securing limited toleration and political rights for Catholics was widely seen as the beginning of a policy of Catholic-inspired repression and *dragonnades*.

James's high hopes of mass conversions of Englishmen to Catholicism, which were crucial to the permanent success of his catholicization policies, were consequently doomed to disappointment. This was specially serious because it was not enough for him simply to rely on promoting Catholics in the army, privy council, and local government. The majority decision (by eleven judges out of twelve) in the *Godden* v. *Hales* case in June 1686 allowed him to do this by dispensing individuals from the Test Acts. But by 1688, despite a concentrated purge of the commission of the peace and lieutenancy, less than a quarter of JPs and deputy-lieutenants were Catholics.[9] Consequently James poured vast amounts of money and effort into a missionary campaign. Yet even the so-called 'closeting' tactic – James's programme of personal interviews with leading politicians – secured only one major conversion, that of the earl of Sunderland, and even that came very late, after the birth of James's son in June 1688. It is doubtful whether, given more time, James's missionary activity would have had more success. After Louis XIV's *dragonnades* anti-Catholicism was more than ever deeply entrenched in England.

Throughout 1686 there were many signs of James's failure to secure the support of Anglican opinion. The most important was his public confrontation with Henry Compton, bishop of London, which originated in March 1686 when James issued some Directions to Preachers, ordering the clergy to confine their sermons to doctrines to be found in the catechism and to steer clear of provocative topics, like attacks on Rome. When the rector of a London parish, John Sharp of St Giles in the Fields, disobeyed in May, James ordered Compton to suspend Sharp from preaching. Compton's refusal resulted in James's decision to establish the court of ecclesiastical commission in July 1686, and its first act in September was to suspend Compton from his bishopric. It is not clear exactly when James finally decided to commit himself to a political alliance with the Protestant dissenters against the Church of England, a line-up which had had such disastrous consequences for his brother in the 1670s. During 1686 James made several individual orders to dissenters, including the Quaker Penn family, dispensing them from the penal legislation, and in November 1686 he established a Licensing Office where dissenters could buy certificates of dispensation. What finally decided James to abandon the Anglican alliance was possibly the failure of William Penn's mission to Holland to get the support of William of Orange and Mary for the repeal of the Test and Corporation Acts. William, although sympathetic to the cause of religious toleration, saw how politically unpopular it was in England and refused to be identified with it. Penn's return was followed closely by the dismissal of James's two principal Anglican ministers, the Hyde brothers, the earls of Clarendon and Rochester. Later in April 1687, the king began a long campaign to force Magdalen College, Oxford, the symbol of the Anglican educational monopoly, to accept a Catholic as its president. By this stage there could be no doubt that a new phase in the reign had begun.

On 4 April 1687 James announced the cornerstone of his new policy of appealing for the support of the dissenters: a Declaration of Indulgence which suspended all the penal laws, the Test and Corporation Acts. In the next few months, during which the king announced the dissolution of the parliament which had stood prorogued since November 1685, it became clear that James expected, as a *quid pro quo* for the Declaration of Indulgence, dissenter support for an intensified campaign to secure a parliament that would repeal the Test and Corporation Acts. How feasible were James's twin policies of allying with the dissenters and the campaign to pack parliament, which occupied this last phase of his reign? There seems no more reason why the former should have been any more successful than his brother's similar policy earlier. Danby's ecclesiastical census of 1676, though quantitatively inexact, was probably a fair reflection of the relatively small numbers of dissenters on which both Charles II and James II placed such reliance. More serious was the fact that the reaction of Protestant dissenters to James's appeal was not unanimously enthusiastic. Most were prepared to take advantage of the grant of toleration, despite their scruples about the constitutional propriety of an arbitrary suspension of parliamentary legislation. What many dissenters could not do was to trust James's motives. Were they not being used to further James's long-term aim of imposing intolerant Catholicism? Were not Catholicism and toleration, in any case, incompatible? Both doubts were voiced by Halifax, whose *Letter to a Dissenter* was published in the summer of 1687. The dissenters, he argued, were 'to be hugged now, only that you may be the better squeezed at another time'. 'This alliance between liberty and infallibility is bringing together the two most contrary things that are in the world. The Church of Rome doth not only dislike the allowing liberty, but by its principles it cannot do it.'[10] In this respect, too, James's credibility with dissenters, as with Anglicans, suffered from the comparison many made with Louis XIV's Revocation policy in France.

It is less certain that James's campaign to pack parliament was bound to fail. From the autumn of 1687 James and his advisers, notably Sunderland and Jeffreys, began systematically to build up a powerful electoral organization in many constituencies. In October three standard questions were put to all JPs to assess their reaction to the projected repeal of the Test and Corporation Acts, and on the basis of their replies new commissions of the peace were issued early in 1688: those JPs who had given unsatisfactory replies were ejected and replaced largely by dissenters. The most intensive electoral preparations were made in the boroughs under the direction of Robert Brent and Sir Nicholas Butler. The *quo warranto* campaign was renewed against recalcitrant boroughs and unreliable municipal officers replaced. Ironically Brent and Butler consciously imitated the tactics used successfully by the Whig exclusionists in the elections of 1679 and 1681, relying on the support of merchants, traders and craftsmen in the towns. After an exhaustive review of their efforts Professor J. R. Jones concludes that the campaign to pack parliament may have been well conceived. James's alliance 'with the urban middle classes against the landowning aristocracy and gentry . . . with time . . . could have resulted in the emergence of a synthetic ruling class to replace the traditional associates of the crown in government'.[11] One wonders whether the interests of the landowning and trading classes were as opposed as this analysis supposes. Also, would the urban groups to whom James appealed have been any more willing than the landowning aristocracy and gentry to swallow their anti-Catholicism and approve the repeal of the Test and Corporation Acts?

Since James's packed parliament never met, these doubts will never be resolved. What is certain is that by the end of 1687 the traditional political nation – Whigs and Tories, Anglicans and Protestant dissenters – were very suspicious of James's intentions. Two events in the first half of 1688 cemented the alliance of all leading Protestants against James II. By issuing a second Declaration of Indulgence on 27 April 1688 James hoped to drive a wedge between Anglicans and dissenters, when the Anglican clergy refused to read the Declaration from the pulpits. However, Archbishop Sancroft and six bishops made it clear in a widely-distributed petition that they refused to publish the Declaration not 'from any want of due tenderness to Dissenters, in relation to whom they are willing to come to such a temper as shall be thought fit', but 'because that Declaration is founded upon such a dispensing power as hath often been declared illegal in Parliament'.[12] Anglicans and dissenters came together on the common ground of hostility to the king's use of the dispensing power. On 10 June Protestants were given an even more powerful reason to unite, when Queen Mary gave birth to a son and so made possible an unlimited period of Catholic rule. Hatred of Rome proved to be a stronger force than the mutual dislike of Anglicans and dissenters. On 30 June the seven bishops who had signed the petition against the Declaration of Indulgence were acquitted of seditious libel; and seven leading Protestants, representing Whig and Tory opinion, Edward Russell, Henry Sidney, Lord Lumley, Bishop Compton, and the earls of Shrewsbury, Devonshire and Danby, wrote to William of

Orange, pledging their support if he brought a force to England against James.

By his Catholic policies James had stunted the loyalist reaction which had grown since the exclusion crisis and which had threatened to make England an absolutist state. Had he also brought the country to the verge of revolution? The evidence is against such a view. A detailed analysis of the answers of the country's governing classes to the three questions of October 1687 reveals the extent of hostility to James's policies; yet the vast majority were not willing to make an *open* declaration against his plans.[13] Even the famous letter of 30 June was extremely vague about the purpose of William's invasion, beyond restraining James. Certainly there was no mention of James's deposition or exclusion. Nor were all the political nation willing to go even as far as the seven signatories of that letter. The earl of Nottingham represented a large body of conservative opinion which considered the letter 'high treason, in violation of the laws . . . and that allegiance which I owed to the sovereign and which I had confirmed by my solemn oath'.[14] Many hoped that James's policies would fail without radical opposition being necessary. Was it not likely that the new baby would die? There is very little evidence that many members of the political nation were willing to rebel against a king who was in a strong financial position and who had begun to remodel the army and navy.[15] In any case most propertied Englishmen were too fearful of another civil war, too constrained by considerations of obedience and non-resistance to become rebels. There would have been no 'Glorious Revolution' without the intervention of William of Orange.

The intervention of William of Orange, 1688

Why did William of Orange invade England? The key to this question, and therefore to the question of why the 'Glorious Revolution' happened, is to be found in events that took place in Europe. The prime aim of William of Orange throughout his life was to oppose French expansion in Europe which continued even after the Peace of Nijmegen in 1678. During the next six years French troops occupied territories beyond the northern and eastern frontiers of France, which she claimed were French by right. Strasburg (October 1681) and Luxemburg (June 1684) were the most notable French conquests, which were ratified by the Truce of Ratisbon in August 1684. William's admiration for French culture was as great as his determination to halt and reverse these French gains. Yet for many years he was unable to organize an effective European coalition against France. Spain demonstrated her weakness in the brief war of 1683–4. The United Provinces was dominated by a republican peace party which saw William's plans as a threat to its desire for low taxes and trade with France. William was unable to prevent cuts being made in military expenditure in his own country. The emperor was distracted by a serious Turkish invasion, which in 1683 brought the Turks to the gates of Vienna. Though the siege was defeated the Turks, encouraged secretly by Louis XIV, continued to occupy Emperor Leopold's troops in the Balkans. The England of Charles II was, of course, tied to France and incapable of an independent foreign policy.

After the Truce of Ratisbon events in Europe began to change slowly in favour of William's plan to organize European cooperation against France. William's first success was in his own country where events again illustrate the crucial impact made by the Revocation of the Edict of Nantes outside France. Since the connections between many Dutch merchants and French Huguenots were very close – some Dutch merchants had even become naturalized Frenchmen to further their trade – French atrocities against the Huguenots hit the business and family interests of many Amsterdam merchants. The Revocation had more effect than anything else in enabling William to obtain the support of the States of Holland and the City of Amsterdam and to secure the backing of the States General for war against France. Furthermore, in 1686 William organized the German states into the League of Augsburg, an anti-French coalition. Of more importance, in May 1687 the emperor's army won a crucial victory over the Turks at Mohacs, which ended the immediate threat of Turkish invasion and enabled the emperor to become an effective member of a grand coalition against France. The one power still necessary to strengthen the coalition was England. William never made clear his motives for invading England, but it is highly likely that his primary aim was to bring England out of her isolation and into the impending war against France. This is not to say that he was not also concerned to protect his wife's right of succession to the throne, which was threatened by the birth of James's son. But it is possible that this was subordinate to his major aim of gaining control of English foreign policy.

When did William decide to invade England?[16] Some historians have argued that William had been planning an invasion since the early 1680s. Certainly he had long been in touch with opposition leaders in England and had kept himself well informed about English opinion. In 1687 he sent two emissaries, Everard van Weede van Dijkvelt in the spring and Willem Zuylestein in August, who established an even firmer relationship between William and major political figures in England. There is, however, no evidence that he seriously considered armed intervention in England before the end of 1687. Nor is it likely that he did so, because the European situation was not conducive to such a step. It was not until early in 1688 that events in Europe enabled William to feel secure enough to consider an English invasion as a practical option for later in the year; and it was not until April 1688 that he told Edward Russell that this was what he intended. In June Zuylestein was sent on a second mission to England, under the cover of bringing William's congratulations on the birth of James's son, to procure a letter of invitation from leading figures in England.

The final problem about William's intervention is to explain why the invasion was successful and why it culminated in the 'Glorious Revolution'. Neither of these was inevitable. The odds against the success of the invasion were great: in Europe William risked exposing the United Provinces to a French attack in his absence; the practical problems associated with launching an invasion across the Channel caused many earlier (and later) efforts to be abandoned; and William's reception in England was far from certain. The problem of Dutch security was removed when the French in September committed themselves to a full-scale attack on the Palatinate. William overcame the logistical problems of the actual invasion by taking advantage of the prevailing winds which kept the English navy helplessly at anchor and helped his fleet sail westwards through the English Channel to land at Torbay on 5 November. Four days later he entered Exeter.

In the following weeks William's moderate public declarations encouraged the defection to his side of Tory as well as Whig magnates in a remarkable illustration of the extent to which James's Catholic policies had united the Protestant nation against him. Sir Edward Seymour and his West Country rival, the marquis of Bath, openly declared for William soon after he landed, ensuring that his rear was secure as he began to march from Exeter on 21 November slowly towards London. As he did so a series of provincial risings and demonstrations in his support occurred. Already on 15 November lord Delamere had secured control in Cheshire; a week later, on 21 and 22 November, the earls of Devonshire and Danby seized Nottingham and York respectively, and other provincial towns made declarations in William's favour.[17]

It is important that the widespread disaffection among Whigs and Tories with James's policies should not be played down. But it is far from certain that at this stage William and most of his supporters aimed to depose James II. There is no doubt that this was not in the minds of many powerful Tories and their supporters, including the Hyde brothers, Halifax and the earl of Nottingham, and most bishops, who were not prepared to abandon the king. It is true that they did very little to help James, and they were almost certainly prepared to see him compelled by the invasion to change his policies. But they were far too deeply attached to their principles of passive obedience and non-resistance to want to see James lose his throne. James, however, left this 'loyal opposition'[18] without a cause. On 23 November at Salisbury he appears to have lost his nerve. Instead of marching with his army to resist William's forces in the south-west he ordered a retreat to London. At this point John Churchill (who became earl of Marlborough in 1689 and duke in 1702) defected to William. On 11 December, with William's army marching slowly through the southern counties towards the capital, James left London intending to go to France. He was captured and returned to London, but on 22 December he made his escape to the Continent. James's collapse of nerve ensured that when William reached London he had the support of all leading Whigs and Tories. His decision not to stay in England removed the final obstacle to the 'Glorious Revolution' and a change of monarch. It remains to be seen whether the 'Glorious Revolution' brought about any more fundamental changes in Church and state.

Notes

For abbreviations used throughout see p. xiv.

1. P. Clark and P. Slack, eds, *Crisis and Order in English towns* (1972) pp. 72–3; J. H. Sacret, 'The Restoration government and municipal corporations', *E.H.R.*, XLV (1930), pp. 232–59.
2. J. R. Jones, *The Revolution of 1688 in England* (1972), p. 46.
3. Chandaman, *English Public Revenue*, pp. 254–5.
4. Miller, *Popery and Politics*, pp. 191, 193–4.
5. M. Ashley, 'King James II and the Revolution of 1688: some reflection on the historiography', in H. E. Bell and R. L. Ollard, eds, *Historical Essays 1600–1750 presented to David Ogg* (1963), pp. 185–202; Miller, *Popery and Politics*, pp. 196–8; Jones, *Revolution of 1688*, especially pp. 65–6, 81ff; John Miller, *King James II*, pp. 124–8.
6. Jones, *Revolution of 1688*, p. 47.
7. Quoted in Chandaman, *English Public Revenue*, p. 256.
8. Peter Earle, *Monmouth's rebels: the road to Sedgemoor 1685* (1977), especially pp. 196–212 for an excellent analysis of the rebels.
9. Miller, *Popery and Politics*, p. 219 and appendix 3; this excludes five English counties for which lists of JPs and DLs do not exist.
10. Quoted in Western, *Monarchy and Revolution*, p. 227.
11. Jones, *The Revolution of 1688*, p. 11.
12. Browning, *English Historical Documents*, p. 84.
13. J. Carswell, *The Descent on England* (1969), pp. 238–43; Jones, *The Revolution of 1688*, pp. 166–7; Western, *Monarchy and Revolution*, pp. 211–12. See also Miller, *James II*, pp. 178–9.
14. Quoted in Western, *ibid.*, p. 237.
15. See *ibid.*, pp. 121–4, 124ff, for the army and navy.
16. The most convincing answers are those put forward by S. B. Baxter, *William III* (1966), pp. 224–5, 229–33, and J. R. Jones, *The Revolution of 1688*, pp. 250–5.
17. For the northern risings in 1688 see David H. Hosford, *Nottingham, Nobles and the North. Aspects of the Revolution of 1688* (Hamden, Connecticut, 1976).
18. Western, *Monarchy and Revolution*, p. 270.

Part five

The reigns of William III and Queen Anne, 1689–1714

The reigns of William III and Queen Anne are characterized by three important features: the development of party rivalries which cut deeply into English society in London and in the provinces, the establishment of parliament as a permanent part of the constitution, and the prevalence of extreme political instability. These features and the problems associated with them are the themes of Part V on Britain after the Glorious Revolution.

During the last twenty years the nature of political rivalries and the existence of political parties in this period have been hotly debated. There is now little doubt that conflict between Whig and Tory politicians and Whig and Tory principles played a large part in English politics from 1689 to 1714. However, much uncertainty still remains. To what extent was Whig–Tory rivalry after 1689 simply an extension of that which had developed during the exclusion crisis? In what ways did the Glorious Revolution affect the Whig and Tory parties and what they stood for? Given that the Whig–Tory division was an important one after 1689, was this the only, or most important, one in English politics, or were Court–Country political alignments important? If they were, to what extent did the latter cut across or obliterate completely divisions on Whig–Tory lines? Perhaps the most intriguing question of all about the political history of this period is why did the Tories, who (as will be seen) were the strongest and most popular political group in England after the Glorious Revolution, suddenly collapse in 1714 and leave the way clear for the Whigs to dominate English political life for much of the Hanoverian age?

By 1714, in contrast to 1688, parliament's place in the constitution was assured. By the death of Queen Anne the English constitution had developed irrevocably in a different way from that of many other continental European absolutist states. It is not only the timing and reasons for this development that are in doubt, though these problems are important: when and why were the powers of the monarchy limited during the reigns of William III and Queen Anne? Did the Glorious Revolution play a crucial role in this process or was the impact of the long wars against France more crucial than the ideas and foresight of the 'revolutionaries' of 1688–9 in moulding the English constitution? Given that parliament's powers were greatly enhanced, can one exaggerate the extent to which the personal prerogative powers of the monarchy had been eroded by 1714? Is the growth of 'the cabinet system' in this period an indication of the diminution of royal authority, as is sometimes implied? Were the limitations on their power that William and Anne were forced to accept as effective as they were intended to be? To what extent were attempts to tie the monarch's hands counterbalanced by the growth during the war years of a large and efficient executive controlled by and at the disposal of the crown? The major aim of this part is to point the way to possible answers to all these questions.

Arguably the greatest and most intractable problem about the last twenty-five years of Stuart England, though, is to explain why these were years of great political instability, in great contrast to the relative peace and calm of political life in early Hanoverian England. Specific reasons for this will be suggested later, but perhaps a general explanation for the political volatility of the period will not be out of place here. The Glorious Revolution was not a blueprint for political stability. The Bill of Rights, like a large list of its seventeenth-century predecessors, including the Propositions of Newcastle 1646, the Heads of the Proposals 1647, the various versions of the Agreement of the People 1647–9, the Instrument of Government 1653, the Humble Petition and Advice 1657, and the 'Restoration Settlement' in the early 1660s, did not prove to be the 'settlement' which had been sought since the collapse of the Elizabethan constitution in 1640. The most dramatic change brought about by William III's accession in 1689 was to effect a revolution in English foreign policy, in which the Francophile policy of Charles II and the isolationism of his brother gave way to active and full-scale intervention by England in Europe against the might of France. These expensive wars against France (1689–97, 1702–13) in turn sparked off a revolution in public finance, since the existing system of parliamentary taxation and the hereditary revenues of the crown were insufficient to meet the massive financial burden which ensued. These twin revolutions in foreign policy and public finance necessitated frequent sessions of parliament to underwrite large grants of parliamentary taxation and eventually to provide a parliamentary guarantee for the repayment of loans made to the government. The consequent annual sessions from 1689 onwards were a breeding ground in which political rivalries could develop.

Parliaments had, of course, met frequently in Restoration England. In the twenty-one years after 1660 parliament only failed to meet twice, in 1672 and 1676. Of more importance, after 1714 there continued to be annual parliamentary sessions without producing the political instability of 1689 to 1714. However, the most startling contrast in the nature of political life during the reigns of William III and Queen Anne, and one which sets it apart from both the preceding and succeeding periods, is the frequency of general elections. From 1660 to 1688 there were only five; from 1689 to 1715 there were eleven. The Triennial Act of 1694 limited the life of individual Parliaments to a maximum of three years. The drafters of the Septennial Act in 1716 rightly commented that this 'proved very grievous and burdensome, by occasioning . . . more violent and lasting heats and animosities among the subjects of the realm, than were ever known before the said clause was enacted'. Not only did the frequent general elections help to maintain the intense political excitement of the period, but they also ensured that the membership of the House of Commons constantly changed, so preventing the crown from building up a court party in the House. Just how important the Triennial Act was in contributing to the political instability of these years can be seen by the dramatic effect of its repeal and its substitution by the Septennial Act in 1716, which facilitated the growth of political stability during the age of Walpole.

The third vital ingredient making for political instability was the emergence of an electorate, growing both in numbers and in independence. This process had been in progress since at least the early seventeenth century, until by the reign of William III the electorate numbered at least 200,000 and by 1715 250,700. Dr W. A. Speck has recently shown that this was a proportion of the total population (just 4.3 per cent) that was only slightly exceeded by those (4.7 per cent) enfranchised by the first Reform Act of 1832.[1] Of course, as historians of nineteenth-century England have shown, the independence of the electorate in the days of open balloting can be exaggerated. Tenants often found it difficult to disobey the wishes of their landlords. Yet the fact that bribery was common in late seventeenth- and early eighteenth-century elections is by itself an indication that voters could be influenced in the way they voted.[2] It does suggest that electors might also be persuaded to use their vote on grounds of principle. Indeed there is every indication that the electorate from the 1690s onwards was not only growing in numbers but was also becoming much better informed than ever before. In 1695 the Licensing Act was allowed to lapse and this marked the formal end of the censorship of the press by the state and Church, which in any case was becoming increasingly difficult to enforce. Nevertheless in 1695 the main restraint on the development of newspapers and political literature of all kinds was removed. Political journalism flourished, and with it appeared a more volatile electorate than ever before.

Nevertheless, it is likely that the development after 1689 of annual parliaments, frequent parliamentary elections, and the growth in both numbers and independence of an electorate, merely provided the framework for political instability. Without the appearance of issues towards which the electorate, as well as its representatives, could have fundamentally different attitudes, it is hardly possible that political rivalries would have been as intense as they became. Significantly the only period in Restoration England which compares with England after 1689 in this respect is the exclusion crisis of 1679–81; then too there were issues which divided the political nation. As will be seen, many of the same issues – commitment to the Protestant Succession *against* a willingness to accept a Catholic monarch with limitations, a belief in the individual's right to resist a tyrannical monarch *against* an attachment to the divine right of kings and passive obedience, a willingness to extend religious toleration and political liberty to Protestant dissenters *against* total opposition to any infringement of the Anglican monopoly in Church and state – re-emerged after 1689. Moreover, events in England after the Glorious Revolution not only revived these old issues, but they also provided new areas of political controversy. Above all, the long wars against Louis XIV after 1689, in which so many changes in England after the Glorious Revolution originated, forced English people for the first time to consider urgently and seriously the role their country should play in European affairs. William's determination to drag his new kingdom into the European struggle against Louis XIV eventually drove a great wedge into English society between those willing to participate with the European community to prevent Bourbon and Catholic hegemony of Europe and those who stood fast by their instinctive xenophobia and isolationism. The war, with questions such as how it should be conducted and when it should be ended, provided the flashpoint for political rivalries that, when they became entangled with issues like the Protestant Succession and Union with Scotland, threatened to plunge England again into a civil war. Only when these issues, as well as the conditions in which they could thrive, were removed would political stability be possible.

Notes

For abbreviations used throughout see p. xiv.
1.   J. H. Plumb, *The Growth of Political Stability 1675–1725* (1967), pp. 29, 34ff; W. A. Speck, *Tory and Whig: the struggle for the constituencies, 1701–15* (1970), pp. 16–17.
2.   See G. L. Cherry, 'Influence of irregularities in contested elections upon election policy during the reign of William III', *J.M.H.*, XXVII (1955), pp. 109–24.

Chapter 12

The reign of William III, 1689–1702

Politics in the reign of William III

In work published between 1940 and 1956 Professor Robert Walcott attempted to establish a new view of the structure of politics from 1689 to 1714, asserting that the political connections were held together less by adherence to a shared set of principles than by family relationships and ties of interest. In reaching this conclusion Professor Walcott was much influenced by the research of Louis Namier, whose similar analysis of the structure of politics in the middle of the eighteenth century had already gained the status of historical orthodoxy. In extending Namier's analysis backwards into the later seventeenth and early eighteenth centuries Walcott flew in the face of the accepted view of the politics of that period which had been arrived at and popularized between the two world wars, notably by Keith Feiling and G. M. Trevelyan. Feiling and Trevelyan believed that conflict between the Whig and Tory parties, though it was not the only one, was the prime feature of politics between 1689 and 1714. It was this belief that Walcott sought to prove wrong. 'The more one studies the party structure under William and Anne', he wrote in 1956, 'the less it resembles the two-party structure described by Trevelyan . . . and the more it seems to have in common with the structure of politics in the Age of Newcastle as explained to us by Namier.'[1] Walcott's version of politics after 1689 had a brief period of acceptance,[2] but in his Ford lectures in 1965 Professor J. H. Plumb launched a vitriolic attack on Walcott, followed two years later by Geoffrey Holmes who, in his *British Politics in the Age of Anne* also came out firmly against what Professor Plumb had called Walcott's 'basically very unsound' book, *English Politics in the Early Eighteenth Century*, which 'has led to appalling confusion'. Other historians in a long list of learned articles pressed home this attack, and with great vigour and skill – if with too much viciousness and too little humanity – Walcott's opinions were blasted out of sight and the importance of party political divisions after 1689 reasserted.[3]

As will be seen, however, Walcott's critics have been much more successful in proving the overwhelming importance of party strife as a consistent feature of the politics of Queen Anne's reign than they have been with those of the preceding reign. The confused picture of politics in William's reign that remains is partly a result of the lack of the types of primary sources, especially division lists, that have been used to prove the importance of parties in Anne's reign. Only eight division lists have been found for William's reign; all of them date from 1696 and after, and only two of them supply the names of MPs who voted on both sides of the division. Partly also, surviving contemporary comments sometimes add to the confusion. Since it was common for contemporaries to denigrate political parties as factious, many politicians were unwilling to claim that they were party politicians. It might be true that 'party activity in the late seventeenth century was like sin, universally condemned and widely indulged',[4] but this was an attitude which makes extremely difficult the task of the historian who wants to recreate the actual structure of politics. What is worse, contemporaries frequently used a bewildering array of names to describe political groups in William's reign, not only 'Whigs' and 'Tories', but the 'Court', 'Country' and 'Church' parties, 'Patriots', 'Jacobites', 'Trimmers', 'Republicans' and 'Commonwealthmen'. If all this were not bad enough, those politicians who with a fair degree of certainty can be classified as Whigs and Tories at the end of William's reign appear to hold different ideas and have different aims from those Whigs and Tories before and immediately after the Glorious Revolution. Looking at the political history of the 1690s the historian is in danger of suffering from attacks of double vision. With one eye he sees Whigs and Tories; with the other he sees court and country MPs. Is it possible to provide the student of this period with a guide – a pair of spectacles – that will bring definition to the otherwise blurred picture of politics in the 1690s?

In one sense it is not, because politics in the 1690s were confused. Though there are signs of its early development, there was as yet nothing resembling modern party political organization. There were no party whips, no means of disciplining MPs to prevent them from crossing party lines. Late seventeenth-century MPs were subject to the tugs of other loyalties than party – to the crown and the court or to their neighbours and constituents. As a result at times in the 1690s it is difficult to see any consistent party political alignment, and one begins to wonder if the word 'party' (like 'Puritanism') is a misleading term that ought to be abandoned in a seventeenth-century context. Certainly all comparisons with modern highly organized and permanent political parties ought to be rejected. With these qualifications three signposts can be suggested to guide the student through the confusion of politics in the 1690s. The first is that Whig and Tory political groups, separated by important differences of principles as well as by competition for office and power, did exist and were a fundamental part of the political structure of William's reign. It would be wrong to go on from there to assume that all MPs were Whigs or Tories or that all Whigs and Tories were consistent Whigs and Tories. Politics in William's reign were much too fluid for either of these assumptions to be correct. Yet one can identify typical Whig and Tory attitudes to three of the main political issues of the 1690s. Those who were unreservedly committed to the Protestant succession were invariably Whigs, while Tories were much less certain about the legality and morality of cutting their ties with James II and his son. On the other hand those who were staunch supporters of maintaining the monopoly of the Anglican Church were usually Tories, while Whigs were more willing to allow both religious toleration and political rights to Protestant dissenters. Commitment to the war against France, to an all-out war effort even if this meant an expensive land war in Europe, and to cooperation with fellow Europeans, were typical Whig responses to the war and foreign policy in the 1690s. Tories tended to view the war with much less enthusiasm, to demand a less expensive maritime strategy and an end to the war once English interests seemed to be no longer being served by it. As will be seen, there were three periods in William's reign when polarization along these Whig and Tory lines was specially marked, from 1689 to 1690, from 1694 to 1697, and from 1701 to 1702.

The second guideline to politics in William's reign is that conditions during the reign sometimes ensured that these Whig and Tory divisions, though never obliterated completely, were not as prominent as at other times. For one thing William III, like Queen Anne later, always used his influence to suppress party rivalry. As will be seen, he was determined to rule with ministers who were chosen regardless of party. Though he was not always successful (indeed in the mid-1690s he had to appoint many more Whig ministers than he wanted) he did have one major success in ensuring that the future of the Church was relatively dormant as a political issue for most of his reign. Anglican fears of the growth of dissent and heresy mounted, as will be seen, but when William appointed moderate churchmen as bishops and refused to allow Convocation to meet, militant Anglicanism was effectively suppressed as a political force. Nor for much of the 1690s was the royal succession the live political issue that it was to be after 1701. It is true that the Whigs were more content with a foreign, Calvinist king than the Tories, but the prospect of the succession on William's death of a firmly Anglican queen and then of her son, the duke of Gloucester, reconciled many Tories to the new regime. With the Church and the succession temporarily taken out of the political arena conditions were therefore ripe for the recrudescence of older 'country' grievances that had appealed to most MPs throughout the seventeenth century: a dislike of high taxes to finance wars, maladministration and corruption in central government, and lavish grants to royal favourites. As in the 1620s, the 1660s, and the 1670s, so in William's reign the House of Commons became the focus for country resentment and distrust at the growing power of royal government and its threatened incursions into provincial self-government. From 1690 to 1694 attempts to curb the power of the executive by means of treason, place and triennial legislation received the support of both 'country' Whigs and Tories. When the war was ended temporarily in 1697 the blurring of Whig–Tory party lines became even more marked, as MPs united to oppose the standing army which William III refused to demobilize. From 1697 to 1701, before the war against France was resumed, it is difficult to use Whig–Tory terminology to explain the great 'country' campaign to reduce the size of the standing army and to impose further limitations on the crown, which culminated in the Act of Settlement in 1701.

These alliances between 'country' Whigs and Tories, however, point to a third characteristic of politics in William III's reign: both Whigs and Tories were undergoing a major transformation, so that by the end of the reign both parties were in certain crucial respects different from their predecessors at the time of William's accession. The decisive political group that acted as a catalyst in this process was a small band of MPs associated with Paul Foley and Robert Harley. Despite having possibly as few as a dozen consistent supporters, Foley and Harley played a key role in the political configurations of the 1690s and indeed Harley continued to play a central and increasingly important role in politics right down to 1714. Immediately after the Glorious Revolution in 1689 and 1690 Foley, Harley, and their associates were indistinguishable from other Whigs. In January 1690 they voted for the Sacheverell Clause which the Whigs wanted to include in a new Corporation Act and which became the touchstone of post-Glorious Revolution Whiggery. In the early and mid-1690s it becomes less easy to identify the Foley–Harley group as Whigs, especially since both men took a leading part in pressing 'country' demands against the crown and its Whig ministers. Also Harley began to reiterate a non-party philosophy which remained a consistent principle throughout his subsequent career. Yet not all his followers shared his scruples about party government, and even Harley from the mid-1690s onwards was driven by his attacks on the king's Whig ministers into a close alliance with Tory MPs. By the late 1690s the new alignment of 'country' Whigs, led by Foley and Harley, and the Tories was very close, so that by this date it becomes possible to see the outlines of a 'new' Tory party: a party which through Foley and Harley had adopted the erstwhile Whig emphasis on distrust of the executive and on demands for limitations on the royal prerogative; a party which placed less emphasis than its pre-1689 predecessor on divine right and passive obedience; and a party which resented the heavy expense of the French War. Meanwhile the transition of the Foley–Harley group to the Tories allowed fundamental changes to be effected in the Whig party. The defection of the old 'country' Whigs paved the way for the prominence of a new generation of Whigs after 1690 (the Junto Whigs) whose views and attitudes were considerably different from those Whigs who had served their political apprenticeship before the Glorious Revolution. These 'new' Whigs were less fearful than their predecessors of a strong executive; men who sought to drop the traditional association of Whiggery with resistance and contractual monarchy (not completely successfully as will be seen), and men who were willing to support William III in effectively prosecuting the war. This transformation of the Whigs and Tories took a long time to complete (by itself it is another major reason for the confused political situation in the 1690s); but the process of creating a 'new Whig' and a 'new Tory' party had gone a long way by the last years of William's reign. As will be seen, conditions in those years, from 1700 to 1702, raised Whig and Tory party rivalry to a new pitch of tension, but it was a rivalry which undoubtedly had its antecedents in the 1690s. The character of the political parties which thrived during Queen Anne's war were moulded by the events which had taken place under the pressure of King William's war.

The Glorious Revolution, 1689–1690

The most striking feature of the Glorious Revolution was its failure to effect any fundamental changes in the English Church or constitution. Despite all the revolutionary claims that have been made for the legislation enacted after William and Mary's accession, the Declaration (later the Bill) of Rights was not a statement of sweeping, fundamental constitutional changes, the Mutiny Act did not guarantee annual sessions of parliament, and the Toleration Act must go down in history as one of the most misnamed pieces of legislation ever. The changes that came over the constitution between 1689 and 1714 did not originate directly in the legislation or pronouncements made in 1688–9, nor were they envisaged by the architects of the Glorious Revolution. They were instead the direct product of England's involvement in a major European war. Why was so little achieved by the Glorious Revolution?

Even if sweeping changes had been intended in 1689 it is extremely unlikely that William would have cooperated in bringing them about. He would have seen them as an unacceptable deviation from his major preoccupation with the European war and with his task of bringing England into it. However, it is clear that few people in 1689 envisaged making sweeping constitutional or ecclesiastical changes. Most prominent politicians had only limited aims; they were determined to restore old liberties, not enact new ones. Like the parliamentary leaders of the Long Parliament who regarded Charles I and the Arminians as the revolutionaries (as they were), so the political nation in 1688 had united to resist what it considered to be the revolutionary innovations of James II. But there the parallel with 1640 ends; as indeed the revolutionaries of 1688 were determined it should. The civil war and its aftermath still roused deep feelings, and the events of the 1640s and 1650s were commonly used as ammunition in the political propaganda warfare of the 1690s. But conservative propertied Englishmen were united in their aim of preventing a recurrence of the violence and radicalism of the English Revolution. When the old republican and regicide, Edmund Ludlow, returned from exile in Switzerland in November 1689, no one in the House of Commons opposed a motion for his arrest or tried to prevent his return into exile. The prime instinct of most politicians and political groups in 1688–9 was to work for a restoration of political order as soon as possible. Nor were they, unlike 1640, under much popular pressure to bring about constitutional and ecclesiastical changes. The only echo of the earlier popular tumults was another brief, spontaneous outburst of anti-Catholic rioting in many parts of the country in December 1688. But the mobs received no encouragement from their social superiors and, without it, the few popular demonstrations of 1688 were completely ineffective.[5] Were mobs in seventeenth-century England capable of sustained political activism independent of upper-class leadership? One is inclined to conclude that they were not. The main effect of mob activity in 1688 was to focus the attention of the political nation on the practical problems of filling the vacuum in English government, so ensuring the speedy restoration of law and order, and not to waste time tackling theoretical, ideological questions. In any case, though united on the need to restore order, the political nation was deeply divided on many major questions. The winter of 1688–9 revealed that the protestant unity of 1687–8 had only been temporary. Any chance that might have seemed to exist for altering the character of the constitutional and ecclesiastical structure in England was lost as the Convention disintegrated amid wrangling, animosity, and bitterness that were rooted in the feuds of the past.

The succession

By far the most immediately important source of political division was the succession problem. In the winter of 1688–9 many different possible solutions were publicized and discussed in print as pamphlet after pamphlet streamed from the presses. Was the return of James a possibility if he would accept limitations on his power? Was the establishment of William as Regent for James an acceptable compromise? If James was no longer king should William or Mary rule alone or should they jointly be offered the crown? These questions presented the Tories with the greatest heart-searching. As the group most passionately wedded to divine right and passive obedience, they were faced with the problem of reconciling their beliefs with the acceptance of a new monarch while the divinely appointed king was still alive. It is this which accounts for the frantic efforts of the Tories to maintain James as king. Obviously their chances were greatest before James's flight. A meeting of twenty-nine peers at the Guildhall on 11 December 1688 revealed strong support for James among the High Tories, led by the Hyde brothers, the earls of Rochester and Clarendon, and by Archbishop Sancroft and Bishop Turner of Ely.[6] But James's flight, coincidentally on the same day, emphasized the impracticability of the tactic of these Tory 'loyalists' of relying on a king who was a man of straw. Even James's return after his capture on 16 December did not alter this fact. James showed that he was incapable of taking immediate control of the government and removing the threat of disorder and that he was only looking for another opportunity to escape, and this he found on 22 December. From now on even the High Tories were forced to support William as the only guarantor of public order. On 24 December a meeting of sixty peers agreed to ask William to run the country and make arrangements to hold parliamentary elections. An assembly of MPs and the lord mayor, aldermen, and common councilmen of London concurred, and circular letters ordering parliamentary elections to be held were sent out on 28 and 29 December.

Yet these decisions did not resolve the Tory dilemma. In fact, it was even more acute when the Convention met on 22 January 1689. If they were to remain faithful to their long-held principles, the only honourable course for Tories was to refuse to recognize any other monarch than James II. Yet only a handful of mainly clerical 'non-jurors' took that course: Archbishop Sancroft, five bishops, and about 400 clergy later refused to swear an oath of loyalty to William and Mary and thereby abandoned all chance of holding public offices. This was clearly not an appealing prospect, but the alternative – accepting the new regime while retaining their belief in the legitimate succession – forced the Tories to rely on highly ingenious casuistry. The Tory dilemma was presented in its clearest form at the end of the debates in the Convention on 28 January when it was agreed

That King James the Second, having endeavoured to subvert the constitution of the kingdom by breaking the original contract between king and people, and by the advice of Jesuits and other wicked persons having violated the fundamental laws and having withdrawn himself out of this kingdom, has abdicated the government and that the throne is thereby become vacant.

To a believer in the Tory political theory of hereditary right a 'vacant' throne was an impossibility, and on 29 January the Tories in the House of Lords voted that the word be struck out of the resolution. When Rochester's motion for a Regency was defeated in the Lords by fifty-one votes to forty-eight, some Tories, led by Danby, brought forward a new proposal which smacked of sheer desperation. Princess Mary was to be recognized as rightful queen on the grounds that James had 'deserted' the kingdom, that the baby son born in June 1688 was not James's son but had been smuggled into Queen Mary's bedchamber in a warming-pan, and that therefore Princess Mary was James's lawful hereditary heir.

The stream of Tory fairy tales was cut short temporarily by William of Orange. It was he who held the key to the immediate situation and who was able to dictate the course of events. On 3 February he made it clear that he would rule neither as a regent nor as a consort, and Mary, who was always the model of wifely subservience, agreed. Her sister, Anne, meanwhile disclaimed the right to succeed if Mary should die before William. English politicians, therefore, were faced with the stark choice of accepting William and Mary as king and queen with William as the dominant partner, or of taking the consequences of a prolonged interregnum and possible popular insurrection. On 6 February the

House of Lords accepted the Commons' motion including 'abdication' and 'vacancy' and parliament agreed to offer the throne jointly to William and Mary. Desperately the Tories tried to justify what was in fact a serious contravention of their principles. To the warming-pan myth they also added the claim that the Glorious Revolution had been divinely ordained and therefore could not have been resisted.[7] A prominent Tory political theorist, Edmund Bohun, tried to justify allegiance to William and Mary on the grounds that William had acquired the right to the throne in a 'just war'.[8] The most popular Tory theoretical justification for accepting the Glorious Revolution, however, was the one used to justify allegiance to the republican regime of the 1650s: that obedience was due to any government that ensured security and protection for society. As propounded by William Sherlock, Dean of St Paul's, many Tories gratefully accepted this notion and quietened their uneasy consciences by the tortuous argument that they obeyed William only as *de facto* king, but continued to recognize James as the *de iure* monarch.[9]

The Whigs, unlike the Tories, had no scruples of conscience about accepting William as king. Their views about the original contract between monarchs and their subjects and about the latters' right to resist tyrannical monarchs, which had been worked out during the exclusion crisis, were well suited to justify their role in 1688. On the face of it, therefore, the Whigs came out of the Revolution in better shape than the Tories. In fact, this is only partly true. The equivocal attitude of the Tories to the new regime was a great political burden to them in the next few years. The fact that they were instrumental in ensuring that the oath of loyalty to William and Mary drafted in February 1689 did not describe the new king and queen as 'rightful and lawful' heirs was hardly likely to endear them to the new monarchs. And when that phrase was at last inserted in a new oath of loyalty in 1696 many Tory office-holders refused to take the oath voluntarily. Moreover, much later, at the end of Anne's reign, the ambiguous attitude of many Tories to the Protestant succession was, as will be seen, a major cause of the collapse of the Tory party. Yet the Whigs, too, were in a vulnerable position after the Glorious Revolution. The Whig association with doctrines of contract and resistance could easily be smeared as extremist, republican notions, a fact which was to prove extremely embarrassing to the Whigs in the future. Desperately Whig politicians tried to play down the radical implications of their philosophy, but the Sacheverell case in 1710 showed the extent of their failure (see below pp. 387–92). Nor was the position of the Whigs immediately after the Glorious Revolution as good as many of them hoped it would be. William was aware of the need to conciliate prominent politicians with the new regime. His first list of ministers must have been a great disappointment to Whig hopes. The Whig earl of Shrewsbury was appointed one of the secretaries of state, but the earl of Nottingham, a Tory 'loyalist' of 1688 and a very late convert to William's cause, was the other. In addition, such hated enemies of the Whigs as Danby and Halifax were given signs of royal favour, even though their offices, lord president and lord privy seal respectively, were only posts of dignity. Moreover, William put the key offices of lord treasurer and lord chancellor into commission so that no one could dominate them. Nothing could have better reflected William's desire to show that he commanded wide political support in England and his determination to assert the independent power of the crown.

The Declaration of Rights

It was this aim of the king, however, which many MPs were equally determined to prevent in 1689. Clearly both Whig and Tory MPs were unwilling to let pass this chance to limit the crown's powers. 'Will you establish the crown and not secure yourselves?', asked the West Country Tory, Sir Edward Seymour, while the Whig William Sacheverell pointed out that 'all the world will laugh at us, if we make a half settlement'. Therefore on 29 January the House of Commons, agreeing with Lord Anthony Falkland's plea that 'before you fill the throne, I would have you resolve, what power you will give the king, and what not', set up a committee to formulate a list of the rights of the subject, both those existing and those to be brought about by legislation which William and Mary were to agree to before they accepted the throne.[10] The committee's report, which was ready by 2 February contained a sweeping programme of constitutional changes, consisting of twenty-eight 'heads', including guarantees for the continuance of parliament, religious liberty for Protestants, and proposals for the reform of chancery and treason trials, and for judges to be appointed 'during good behaviour' with fixed salaries and not 'during the king's pleasure'.[11]

That there was a consensus of agreement in the Convention on the desirability of limiting the power of the crown can also be seen in the debates on William's request for a permanent financial settlement. When it was first discussed on 26 and 27 February 1689 voices from all parts of the political spectrum warned against granting either a large permanent revenue or a permanent revenue at all. The Tory Sir Thomas Clarges believed that 'we ought to be cautious of the Revenue, which is the life of the government, and consider the last two reigns'. 'Our greatest misery was, our giving it [the Revenue] to king James for life, and not from three years to three years, and so you may have often kissed his hands there,' said Colonel John Birch.[12] With sentiments like these prevalent in the Convention, as in the early years of the Cavalier Parliament, progress towards a financial settlement was very slow. By 11 March all that was agreed, despite William's urgent requests, was that the crown's existing ordinary revenue could be collected until 24 June 1689, and on 20 March the old familiar figure of £1,200,000 was brought forward again as the crown's estimated ordinary expenditure. Apart from voting extraordinary parliamentary subsidies for the war, this was as far as the Convention went towards settling the king's permanent revenue. The completion of this task was left to William's second parliament, which in March 1690 granted the king the excise for life, but only allowed him the receipts from customs for four years. How serious a limitation on the independence of the crown this would have been in peacetime remains a matter of controversy[13] because its provisions were soon rendered out of date by the financial needs of war, which permanently ended the possibility of the financial independence of the English monarchy.

What is certain is that the members of the Convention failed to carry out the aims many of them had of putting severe limits on royal power by a Declaration of Rights. Only eleven of the twenty-eight 'heads' drawn up by the committee which reported on 2 February were included in the final version of the Declaration of Rights. It is typical of the conservative achievement of the Glorious Revolution that the Declaration retained only those 'heads' which were considered to reflect existing rights. Undoubtedly the most important of these were the declarations that the use of the suspending power, the maintenance of a standing army in peacetime, and the raising of money without the consent of parliament were illegal. Many other statements in the Declaration (for example, 'Election of Members of Parlyament ought to be free') were so vague as to be as ineffective as other similar statements of intent. Other clauses begged important questions of definition, e.g. what was meant by 'excessive', 'cruell and unusuall' in the famous declaration 'that excessive Baile ought not to be required nor excessive Fines imposed nor cruell and unusuall Punishments inflicted'? Although the power of suspending laws was declared illegal, the Declaration of Rights was more ambiguous on the question of the power of dispensing with laws in specific cases. This power was declared illegal, with the qualification 'as it hath been assumed and exercised of late', a reservation that has not prevented the crown and its ministers since 1689 from using the dispensing power.[14] Most important of all, those 'heads' in the report of 2 February that needed new legislation were rejected by the Convention.

The Declaration left untouched most of the personal powers of the monarchy to choose its own ministers, make its own policy (especially foreign policy) and influence opinion in parliament by means of elections, placemen and the general disposition of patronage. Nor, contrary to legend, was the offer of the throne to William and Mary made conditional on their accepting even the castrated version of the Declaration of Rights. Though the Declaration was read to them before they formally accepted the crown, neither William nor Mary gave any indication that they felt bound to adhere to its provisions.[15] There are many possible reasons for the limited nature of the constitutional settlement in 1689. Probably for some MPs William's known intention not to allow drastic inroads into the royal prerogative was important; and ambitious politicians took the hint. Certainly some Whigs in 1689 seemed less in favour of restricting the power of the crown than might have been expected, given the attitude of Whigs during the exclusion crisis, largely because they hoped that it would be Whig ministers that would dominate the new king's government. For most MPs, however, the most important consideration was the pressing need to fill the throne quickly and not to waste time in drafting and passing complicated constitutional legislation. Since the prevailing mood among MPs was conservative, the Declaration of Rights (enacted as the Bill of Rights in December 1689) was a disappointing and conservative document.[16] It brought about no fundamental alteration in the constitution.

The Church: comprehension or toleration?

The Glorious Revolution, like the Restoration, presented another opportunity to widen the membership of the Church of England and extend toleration to those Protestants outside the Church. As in 1660 the hopes of non-Anglicans were raised both by the expectation of some reward for their political role in the events of the immediate past and by the tolerationist views of the new king. Though a firm Calvinist William had always appointed men to his service regardless of their personal religious convictions, whether Catholics or Jews.[17] On his arrival in England he had talks with prominent dissenters in which he dropped broad hints of his support for a comprehensive Church settlement. To emphasize the similarity with 1660 Richard Baxter was still active among the Presbyterian leadership, which felt itself in a strong enough position to put forward a plan that bishops should act in consultation with presbyters in diocesan affairs. Among prominent Anglicans, also, including high churchmen like the suspended Archbishop Sancroft, there was a strong feeling that the Protestant unity of 1688 should be made the basis for a more comprehensive Church and so permanently strengthen it against the Catholic threat. The leading lay exponent of this view was Nottingham, who at the end of February and early in March 1689 introduced a Comprehension Bill and a Toleration Bill into the House of Lords. These Bills were very similar to those which had been projected in 1680. It was hoped that the terms of the Comprehension Bill would be flexible enough to enable most Protestant dissenters to enter the Anglican Church; and for the tiny minority who could not, the Toleration Bill granted a limited freedom of worship. However, during the next few months, despite the apparently favourable climate, the plans for a comprehensive Church collapsed, and of the two measures only the Toleration Bill became law (on 24 May 1689).

Why was yet another chance missed either to establish a more comprehensive Anglican Church or to extend religious toleration to Protestant dissenters? Few MPs were working for toleration in 1689; the major political thrust of those pressing for religious reform was directed towards achieving comprehension. Many Anglicans had opposed this in the past, because they feared that it would mean the beginning of the end of the Anglican monopoly in Church and state. Unfortunately, events early in 1689 seemed to confirm these fears. William played a big part in this. As a Calvinist, not only was he the object of Anglican suspicion about his intentions, but on 16 March he made an ill-advised speech in the House of Lords in favour of throwing open public offices to 'all protestants that are willing and able to serve'.[18] Ironically within a few weeks of his accession William, in effect, was proposing the very thing – the repeal of the Test and Corporation Acts – that had united the political nation against his predecessor. Not surprisingly, Anglicans, whose consciences were already very tender because of the traumatic events of the last few months, reacted quickly to oppose the plan. On the evening of the king's speech over 150 MPs met at the Devil's Tavern in Fleet Street to condemn William's overt attack on the Anglican monopoly. Events in Scotland may also have contributed to Anglican militancy in England, as the Scottish Presbyterians in the succeeding weeks seized power and abolished episcopacy north of the Border yet again (see below, pp. 374–5). Moreover, early in April Richard Hampden, by introducing a Comprehension Bill which granted more generous concessions to dissenters, appeared to confirm that non-Anglicans would not be satisfied with Nottingham's proposals.

It is arguable that by this stage comprehension was already a lost cause. The deep repugnance felt for it by rank-and-file Anglican clergy and their provincial lay patrons would soon become apparent. But for the moment this was delayed, and for the rest of the year William and Nottingham kept the hopes of comprehension alive. William appears to have regretted his blunder of 16 March, and on 9 April, using a Whig privy councillor, William Harbord, as his spokesman, the king tried to make amends by stressing that he 'was altogether of the judgement of the Church of England', and indicating that he would listen favourably to a request for the summoning of Convocation to discuss the plans for comprehension.[19] For the next few months William attempted to conciliate churchmen by further pro-Anglican public statements and by encouraging Nottingham to secure the support of suspended non-juring bishops for comprehension. Nottingham also was authorized to draft detailed plans for comprehension to be submitted to Convocation. Just how useless these political preparations were, was seen when Convocation met on 21 November. Convocation allowed the fanatical fears of the mass of the lower Anglican clergy to be unleashed. During its short session of three weeks the lower house of Convocation would have no truck with any move that appeared to be a compromise with Protestant dissenters. Now that the threat of popery had diminished the fragile Protestant unity of 1688 crumbled.

As a result only the Toleration Bill became law in 1689. It is difficult to imagine a less satisfactory outcome. The Toleration Act became something it had never been intended by its drafters to be; what had been meant to be applied to only a minority who would not join the Anglican Church had to be enforced against all Protestant dissenters. It is not surprising, therefore, that it gave little satisfaction to the latter who had hoped for so much change from the Glorious Revolution. It is true that the Toleration Act allowed to worship all those who took the oaths of supremacy and allegiance and made a declaration against transubstantiation. But it also reimposed restrictions on all dissenters. Some of these were minor, but no less irritating in denoting the dissenters' continued status as second-class citizens; for example, dissenter meeting-houses had to be registered with a bishop or at the Quarter Sessions, and dissenting services had to be conducted with the doors of the meeting-house wide open. More seriously, the Test Acts enforcing acceptance of the Anglican sacraments on all office-holders were maintained. Moreover certain classes of Protestant, most notably those who denied the doctrine of the Trinity, were especially exempted from even the limited toleration allowed other Protestant dissenters. What is perhaps more surprising than the dissatisfaction with which dissenters viewed the Toleration Act is the fact that many Anglicans were unenthusiastic about it. Although on the face of it the religious settlement had left Anglican monopoly of public offices intact, the minimal encroachment on the Anglican monopoly of the Church allowed in 1689 was met with great alarm in many Anglican circles, especially outside the narrow episcopal group patronized by Nottingham and William. As will be seen, the next few years seemed to many rank-and-file Anglicans, clerical and lay, to justify their belief that dissent was a growing threat to the privileged position of the Church and this was to make 'the Church in danger' a potent political slogan (see pp. 348–51).

The only way William could smother the religious wrangling was to adjourn Convocation, which he did on 14 December 1689, and he did not allow it to meet again until 1697. A little over a month later, on 27 January 1690, William was driven to adjourn the Convention, and to dissolve it on 6 February. Perhaps if he had been more familiar with the history of English politics since the mid-seventeenth century the new king might have found the bitterness of politics during the Convention, if not less irritating, more intelligible. Much of the political passion of the 1690s derived its strength from the past. One sign of this is the blossoming interest in the mid-century Revolution. Clarendon's *History of the Rebellion*, completed by the 1670s, was not published until 1702–4. Clarendon's son, Rochester, emphasized in the preface that his purpose in printing it now was to buttress Tory propaganda, 'rather as an instruction to the present age than a reproach upon the Last'.[20] Rochester's opponents were not slow to use ammunition drawn from the past. A Whig edition of Edmund Ludlow's *Memoirs*, drastically bowdlerized to remove offending passages (probably by John Toland), first appeared in 1696.[21] Obviously the Whig and Tory caricatures presented by their opponents' propaganda – the Whigs as collaborators with and defenders of the regicide regimes of the 1650s, and the Tories as proponents of the type of absolutist pretensions Laud and Charles I were alleged to have held – were false. But the English Revolution and its aftermath contributed greatly to the bitterness of politics after the Glorious Revolution. Both Whigs and Tories felt that they had old scores to settle: the Tories for the sufferings of Anglicans and royalists from the effects of sequestrations and punitive taxation at the hands of the parliamentary and Cromwellian regimes in the 1640s and 1650s; the Whigs for the expulsion both of Puritan clergy from their livings in the 1660s and of Whigs and dissenters from municipal corporations in the 1680s.

In these circumstances William's initiative in pressing for an Act of Indemnity was bound to fail. His message to the Convention on 25 March 1689, calling for an end to 'all controversies' over the 'disorders in the late times' fell on deaf ears.[22] Instead many Whigs seized every opportunity to take revenge on their Tory opponents. The Idemnity Bill was lost, some Whig hotheads even pressed for two of James II's judges to be hanged, and those who had served in Charles II's and James II's governments were attacked. Halifax especially was singled out for his role in defeating Exclusion in 1681 and early in 1690 he was driven from office. The Whig offensive culminated in January 1690 in the debates on the Corporation Bill, which was designed to restore the franchises forfeited or surrendered by boroughs in the previous two reigns. Some Whigs, including William Sacheverell, determined to make this an even severer anti-Tory measure by proposing that a clause be added making anyone who had helped in the forfeiture of a charter ineligible for office for seven years. The Sacheverell clause split the lower House and it was defeated on 10 January, after long and bitter debate, by ten votes.

William's subsequent decision to dissolve the Convention was the result of a deep disillusionment with English politics, especially with the Whigs. It is possible that he even considered abdicating – though surely never seriously? The time he was having to spend on domestic affairs negated the primary reason he had come to England: to expedite the war against France. To this was also now added the need to reconquer Ireland which needed his personal attention. But, if William thought that dissolution of the Convention would end the bitterness of English politics, he was disappointed. The subsequent elections during February and March 1690 were characterized by severe partisan rivalry. Both Whigs and Tories circulated 'black lists' to persuade the electorate not to support the 150 MPs ('Jacobites') who had voted on 5 February 1689 against 'abdication' and 'vacancy', or for the 146 MPs ('Commonwealthmen') who had voted for the Sacheverell clause.[23] It is clear that by the spring of 1690 the Glorious Revolution had made no greater impact on the pattern of politics than it had on the constitution.

A country at war, 1690–1697

King William's War

The fact that England was involved in a large-scale European war against France for much of the period from 1689 to the death of Queen

Anne is the key to many developments in England (and, from 1707, Britain) during the last twenty years of the Stuart age. The most important effect of the Glorious Revolution was that it brought to the English throne a man whose prime aims were centred, not in England, but in Europe. William III was first and foremost a European, interested in establishing the peace of the continent by maintaining a balance of power between the two major European dynasties, the Habsburgs and the Bourbons. Since Louis XIV's France was the major threat to European peace William was committed to curbing French power. Therefore, a major effect on England of William's accession was to force a radical realignment in her foreign policy away from the puppet-like dependence on France of Charles II and the isolationist pose adopted by James II.[24] William dragged England into Europe against France, and in the process transformed his new kingdom into a major world power. The resulting pro-Habsburg, anti-Bourbon direction of British foreign policy was to last until the mid-eighteenth century; Britain's status as a great power endured even longer, until the mid-twentieth century.

Louis XIV's aims in Europe after 1688 are less easy to discern than William III's. The succession to the Spanish throne certainly was a principal concern of the French king at this time. Charles II, the Spanish king, was childless, had been an invalid since birth, and was likely to die at any time. Indeed in 1688 Louis's agents at Madrid reported that Charles II's health was deteriorating rapidly. Louis XIV's claim to determine the Spanish succession on Charles's death was very strong. Louis was married to Charles II's elder sister Maria Theresa and therefore their son, the Dauphin, was one of the chief claimants to the throne. The legality of this claim, however, was weakened by the fact that Maria Theresa had formally renounced her claims to the Spanish throne, so strengthening the case of two other claimants, Joseph Ferdinand the Electoral Prince of Bavaria, and Emperor Leopold. The Electoral Prince of Bavaria's claim lay through his mother, Maria Antonia, the daughter of Charles II's younger sister, Margaret Theresa, and Emperor Leopold. Maria Antonia, however, also had renounced her claims to the Spanish throne. The Emperor Leopold therefore traced his claim to the Spanish throne through his mother, the younger sister of Philip IV.

Confusing though the competing claims are, the simple point is that each of the three claimants felt his case was the strongest and each employed lawyers who supported this conviction. In all probability, therefore, Louis's invasion of the Palatinate in the autumn of 1688 was intended as a preliminary to the determination of the Spanish succession. By a show of military strength, not a long war, Louis perhaps hoped to break up the German opposition to France which had resulted in the League of Augsburg, and thus to persuade the German states and the Emperor to negotiate a settlement of the Spanish succession in the French interests.[25] If this was the case, Louis's aims backfired badly. Not only did the French invasion of the Palatinate allow William to invade England without the threat of French

Claimants to the Spanish succession

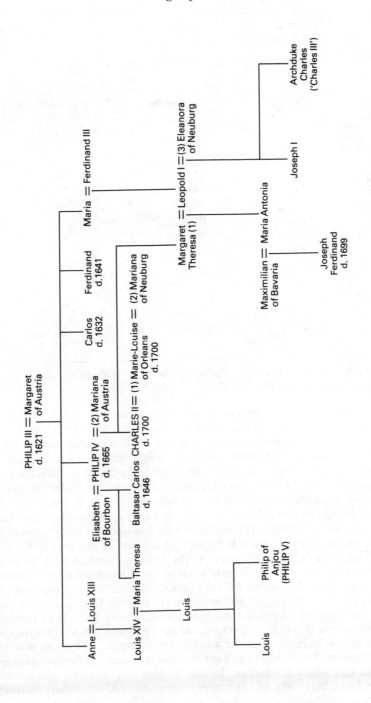

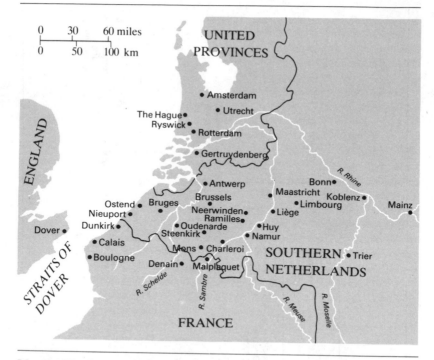

Map 3   The Low Countries during the wars of William III and Queen Anne, 1689–97 and 1702–13

occupation of his homeland (as has been seen), but Charles II did not die, indeed he lived for another twelve years. Moreover the French encountered unexpected resistance from the German states, which meant that Louis's planned short campaign escalated into a nine-year major war. In February 1689 the Dutch formally declared war on France and in May the States General and Emperor Leopold signed the Grand Alliance against France, which was joined in the succeeding months by England, Spain, Savoy, and many of the German states. France was diplomatically and militarily isolated. William's dream of a European coalition to curb French power was at last a reality.

Unfortunately for William, at the very moment of his diplomatic triumph he was distracted from what he considered to be his major task of organizing the Grand Alliance against France on the continent, not only by the wrangling of politicians in the English Convention, but also by the threat of a French-supported invasion from Ireland. In February 1689 James II left St Germain, and on 12 March landed at Kinsale in south-west Ireland, where he was met by the earl of Tyrconnel who held the country for him. James's arrival was the occasion for an upsurge of Irish Catholic nationalism. In the 'Patriot Parliament', which met in Dublin in May 1689, in a House of Commons of 224 members there were

only six Protestants, and it proceeded to pass a stream of anti-English
legislation, asserting Irish legislative and jurisdictional independence of
England. Moreover, the Patriot Parliament repealed the Act of
Settlement, restoring many of the estates confiscated from Catholic
landowners since 1641. 'It boldly announced our national independence', wrote Wolfe Tone of the Patriot Parliament, 'in words which
Molyneux shouted on to Swift, and Swift to Lucas, and Lucas to Flood,
and Flood to Grattan redoubling the cry, Dungannon church rang and
Ireland was again a nation.'

In the face of this Catholic nationalist explosion Ulster Presbyterians
had to arm themselves and many of them fled to Londonderry and
Enniskillen, where they appealed to William for support. It was an
appeal William could not afford to ignore, since Ireland was an easy
launching pad for a French invasion of England. In May he sent Colonel

Map 4   Western Europe during the wars of William III and Queen
Anne, 1689–97 and 1702–13

Percy Kirke with a force to relieve Londonderry, which had been under siege since 19 April 1689. This Kirke successfully did on 30 July, though amid accusations of his unwarranted delay from the besieged as thousands of them died from starvation and disease; and on the same day a Protestant detachment from Enniskillen won a skirmish with James's forces at Newton Butler.

These victories brought only temporary relief and in August William sent to Ireland a larger force of 10,000 men under General Schomberg. Though a veteran of many European campaigns Schomberg suffered the fate of many other generals sent to Ireland, though the subsequent disaster which hit his army was made more certain by the timing of the expedition and the lack of supplies. Heavy and persistent autumn rain, inadequate food and shelter, and proximity to the Irish bogs were the right conditions for the rapid spread of infectious diseases like typhus, which were common among seventeenth-century armies. Schomberg lost about half his army without firing a shot in battle. In retrospect the turning point in the English reconquest of Ireland was William's personal intervention and his victory at the battle of the Boyne on 1 July 1690, which was made possible, in part at least, by the best asset possessed by all prudent generals, numerical superiority over the enemy, though William's personal bravery during the battle is not to be denied. It was a turning point in retrospect only, however. William left Ireland in September, but it took over a year for his subordinates, Ginkel and Marlborough, to complete the conquest of Ireland.

On 3 October 1691 Limerick surrendered, and at Limerick the lords justices of Ireland signed the treaty negotiated by Ginkel and Patrick Sarsfield, James's general. Sarsfield and his Catholic colleagues won for their Irish co-religionists a fairly generous settlement: limited religious toleration (a return to the conditions of Charles II's reign), protection for the property of Catholic landowners, and freedom for the Irish army to go to France, all to be ratified by an Irish parliament. The Treaty of Limerick, though, was a worthless piece of paper. In 1690 and 1691 the English parliament overthrew it by repealing all the legislation of the Patriot Parliament and imposing an Anglican test on all office-holders and MPs. Catholics were driven from their estates and from politics. The Dublin Parliament which met in October 1692 was a Protestant one. As in England, Protestant unity crumbled once the immediate danger of Catholicism receded, and the Presbyterians, who had been crucial in securing the Glorious Revolution in Ireland, were abandoned to become second-class citizens. Williamite Ireland was ruled by a narrowly based Anglo-Irish landed class, supported by an established Church to which very few Irish people belonged. Ireland again was reduced to a colonial subservience, which was reinforced by subsequent enactments of the English parliament aimed at preventing Irish economic competition with English agriculture and industry.

If, as is likely, William considered the Irish campaign an irksome distraction from the major arena of the struggle against France, it did help him convince many of his subjects that the war was in England's interests. A responsible section of English opinion came to recognize that the war was necessary to preserve the Glorious Revolution, to prevent the invasion of Ireland, Scotland, and England, and the return of James II as a French puppet king. The Irish campaign pressed home the point that the war against France was necessary for English security, which was imperilled until Louis XIV recognized William's title as king of England. However, this fact did not always remain uppermost in the mind of some English MPs in the 1690s. As has been seen, the horizons of English country gentlemen in the seventeenth century were often bounded by their own county boundaries. They were sceptical of government demands for money to spend on wars beyond those boundaries. Consequently this scepticism grew stronger as the European war dragged on with very little evidence of allied successes.

The war at sea got off to a disastrous start. On 30 June 1690 off Beachy Head an allied Dutch–English fleet of fifty-eight ships commanded by Admiral Torrington fought a French fleet of seventy-five ships. When so many sailing ships meet each other clearcut results are unlikely, but in this case all reports agreed that the allied fleet was dispersed in a decisive French victory. The order to engage the enemy, despite being outnumbered, came from Queen Mary and her advisers, notably Nottingham, in London (William was in Ireland), and Torrington was forced to obey against his better judgement. But it was the admiral who took the blame for the defeat. He was court-martialled at the end of the year, and though acquitted he was dismissed. With the army in Ireland the defeat left England temporarily defenceless, but the French failed to take advantage. Farcically, given the frantic panic and fear of full-scale invasion in England, all that resulted was the bombardment of Teignmouth on 26 July by the French admiral, Tourville. But the defeat did stimulate another bout of reorganization of the English navy, the building of new men of war, a new shipyard at Plymouth, and a dry dock at Portsmouth. The reorganization may have played some part in the allied navy's subsequent success in preventing the French navy from covering an invasion force across the Channel. In May 1692, with James II watching from the nearby cliffs, the French fleet was dispersed in the Bay of La Hogue by Admiral Russell, although one suspects that as in the case of the battle of Beachy Head, ill-advised civilian intervention had more influence on the outcome of the battle than the resources or naval organization of the two sides. This time it was Tourville who, vainly protesting, was ordered by Louis XIV to engage the enemy at all costs.

The allied conduct of the war at sea was no more immune from mammoth blunders. In 1693 a large convoy of around 400 Dutch and English merchant ships bound for the Levant was allowed to sail, grossly underprotected by only a handful of men of war, and Admiral Tourville's fleet had little trouble in destroying at least 100 of the convoy off the south coast of Portugal. This was perhaps the crucial event which forced William in 1694 to order Admiral Russell to take a fleet to the Mediterranean where it stayed, based at Cadiz, until 1696. As well as being significant in pointing the way to the future British naval presence in the Mediterranean in the eighteenth century, this was the most successful naval decision of William's war. Russell's fleet in the Mediterranean hampered the French war effort in Italy and Spain and blockaded half of the French fleet in Toulon, and prevented it from joining with Tourville's fleet based in Brest. In 1696, however, these advantages were lost, as Russell was withdrawn from the Mediterranean to forestall another invasion attempt across the Channel.

If anything, the land war appeared to go even worse for the allies than the war at sea, and to be more interminable. William's war in Flanders rivalled the English civil war in its lack of an overall strategic pattern, with both armies manoeuvring and counter-manoeuvring with little apparent long-term aims. When the armies did, infrequently, meet in full-scale battles William's army came off the worst. The battles of Steenkirk (August 1692) and Neerwinden (July 1693) were not decisive in the war, both sides suffered heavy casualties, but on both occasions William's losses were heavier than the French and his military reputation was adversely affected. The major difference between the English civil war and William's war was the latter's lengthy sieges. No English towns had the military fortifications to withstand a lengthy siege like the towns in the Spanish Netherlands which were the battleground for much of William's war. In siege warfare the French proved superior, notably the French general Vauban, who successfully took a series of garrisons along the river Meuse, Mons (April 1691), Namur (June 1692), Huy (July 1693), and Charleroi (1694). William's only major success in the war was to recapture Namur in August 1695.

Like the mutual exchanges of pieces in a drawn game of chess, however, each capture and recapture of these towns brought victory in the war no nearer for either side. Why was the war so long-drawn-out and inconclusive? Partly, the answer lies in the fact that, like all wartime coalitions, the Grand Alliance was weakened by mutual suspicions and distrust. Both the imperial and Spanish courts felt a natural uneasiness at allying with the Protestant states of northern Europe, especially since they were, in effect, supporting a Protestant usurper against the rightful Catholic king of England. Although reassured by his theologians that this course was not sinful, Emperor Leopold remained sceptical, and from 1692 to 1696 engaged in secret negotiations with Louis XIV, during which the possibility of the succession of James II's son in England after the deaths of William and Mary was discussed.[26] Even if these differences had not existed, it is hardly likely that the council of allied ministers, which sat throughout the war at The Hague, would have been any more effective than it was in agreeing on a sensible war strategy. Louis XIV, in contrast, reaped all the advantages of a unified command.

Opinions differ about the extent of William III's success in overcoming these difficulties.[27] Certainly his task was immense. Not only had he to keep a large coalition together, and act as principal general of the allied army, but he had to divide his time between London and the continent. Not least of his difficulties was that of commuting between London and The Hague in conditions of great hardship and personal danger. In January 1691 after a voyage of four days the royal yacht became fogbound and lost somewhere off the Dutch coast. William then got into an open rowing boat for a journey which lasted for sixteen hours in freezing fog with loose ice floating in a sea infested with French privateers.[28] It is difficult to escape the conclusion that his success in overcoming his difficulties was greater in the diplomatic than in the military sphere. The Grand Alliance was his creation and that it kept together for as long as it did was largely due to his work. As a soldier he allowed the French to dictate the tactical pattern of the war of constant manoeuvring and sieges, and of avoiding conclusive battles. Seen in the context of seventeenth- and eighteenth-century warfare, however, perhaps this is too harsh a judgement on William's military abilities. Even a soldier of outstanding genius like Marlborough in the next war failed to break the pattern of long-drawn-out wars which characterized the seventeenth and eighteen centuries in Europe. Like the Thirty Years War (1618–48), Anne's War (1702–13), the War of Austrian Succession (1742–8), and the Seven Years War (1756–63), William's was a long war of attrition.

Such a war, of course, was not only long-drawn-out, it was also expensive. Financial exhaustion on both sides contributed greatly to the conclusion of peace. In addition the overseas trade of Europe was disrupted by the war. The allies operated a partially successful naval blockade of French ports, and French attacks on English and Dutch shipping, of which the Smyrna convoy disaster was the biggest example, had a serious effect on the economy of both maritime powers. However, peace negotiations began long before the war made an impact on the European economy. Louis XIV had not wanted a long war, as has been seen, and almost from the start of the war he appeared anxious for peace: 1693, it has been said, 'witnessed what we should now call a peace offensive on the part of France'.[29] In the second half of that year secret negotiations began between representatives of Louis XIV and William III, which were maintained intermittently throughout the war. William soon abandoned his initial hopes of reducing France to her frontiers of 1648 and 1659. Louis, however, found it harder to overcome his objections to recognizing William as king of England. But during the negotiations he eventually did so. When peace was finally concluded at Ryswick in September 1697 William's greatest gains were Louis's recognition of him as king of England and the French king's promise not to aid any of his enemies. Moreover, Louis abandoned the conquests he had made in the Spanish Netherlands and the Empire, though with the exception of Strasbourg. The Peace of Ryswyck, however, was not the basis for permanent European peace, simply because it ignored the

Spanish succession problem. Immediately after the conclusion of the war both Louis and William began to try to settle this by diplomatic means. Their failure was to produce another long period of war, the War of the Spanish Succession.

King William's war and politics: the transformation of the Whig and Tory parties, 1690–4

The effect of King William's war on English politics was no less decisive than its impact on English foreign policy and on the constitution.[30] As has been seen, the adjournment of Convocation at the end of 1689 effectively withdrew the Church controversy from the political arena until Convocation met again in 1697. Moreover, Tory doubts about the legality of William's accession were partially satisfied in the 1690s by the ingenuity of political theorists and by the comforting prospect that the successors to the throne, if William and Mary died childless, were staunch Anglicans, James's elder daughter, Anne, and her son, the duke of Gloucester. The way was therefore cleared for the war in Europe to become the principal political issue in England during the 1690s. Although the misgivings of xenophobic Englishmen about the wisdom of continental involvement were never completely satisfied, opposition to William's war was never so strong as that which developed to Anne's war later. However, in the 1690s there was plenty of room for disagreement about the conduct and expense of the war. Controversy about the vast amounts of money that were poured into supporting a large army in Flanders, and allegations about corruption and maladministration in the running of the war were constant themes in the parliaments of wartime England.

It soon became clear that this controversy cut across the Whig-Tory political alignment that had persisted from the exclusion crisis to the dissolution of the Convention in 1690. Most notably in the meetings of the commission of public accounts, former Whig and Tory opponents discovered that they had a great deal in common. Paul Foley, Robert Harley and their Whig associates led the way in working with Tory MPs to attempt to curb the financial extravagance of the crown and to secure some parliamentary restraints on government expenditure. Moreover, as time went on country Whigs and Tories united on a wider programme of attempting to check the power of the crown by securing many of the constitutional demands which had been put forward in February 1689 but which had been omitted from the Declaration of Rights, including frequent parliaments that were free of royally appointed placemen, and an independent judiciary. It must be strongly emphasized that the emergence of this new political alignment of country Whigs and Tories was very gradual, and that it never developed the cohesion that later commentators have ascribed to it by describing it as 'the Country Party'. Nor is it strictly true that Robert Harley was the 'leader' of this political group. Certainly, until he first headed the ballot for membership of the commission of public accounts in 1694, he was a junior member of the commission, and even then he was only one of its leaders, along with the more experienced Foley and Sir Thomas Clarges.[31] These qualifications, however, should not be allowed to obscure the fact that under the pressure of war the old Whig and Tory parties disintegrated and a new pattern in English politics began to appear.

It would be wrong to exaggerate the sharpness of the break in the pattern of politics between the Convention Parliament and William's second parliament which assembled in March 1690. But after 1690 the clashes between Whigs and Tories, raking over the feuds of the exclusion crisis and its aftermath, which had characterized the Convention, are not so prominent. In May 1690 William succeeded in getting passed an Act of Grace, pardoning all but a handful for their activities before 1688, which he had failed to do in the Convention. The new political climate was not so much due to William's attempt to dampen party strife, as to the fact that the war had introduced into politics a completely new situation which produced new responses from politicians. At first, from the crown's point of view, these responses were favourable. In the first two parliamentary sessions (March to May 1690 and October 1690 to January 1691) grants expected to produce almost £4,600,000 were approved which only fell just short of what the government had asked for. It is possible that this can be accounted for the fact that Danby, now lord privy seal, was once again busy using his old techniques of persuasion among MPs. But Danby's influence in post-Revolution politics can be exaggerated. In the competition for the king's favour he was certainly overshadowed by Secretary Nottingham. Bishop Burnet was probably nearer the mark. 'The French fleet', he wrote, 'by lying so long on our coast . . . and the King's behaviour in Ireland, as well as King James's meanness, has made so wonderful a change in all men's minds with relation to them both.'[32] The battles of Beachy Head and the Boyne had made many people in England appreciate that the war in Europe was not simply one that concerned the Dutch.

William's satisfaction at the parliamentary generosity in the first two sessions was tempered by the passage in December 1690 of an Act establishing a commission of public accounts, whose members were chosen by parliament and which was given a general brief to examine the state of the public finances. Although William was forced by his financial needs to give his assent, he may have hoped that the commission would have split the opposition: instead it gave his critics an institutional focal point from which to snipe at the power of the court. On the face of it, though, the disparate membership of the first commission did not make this a likely outcome. Its six Whig members, notably Sir Robert Rich and Paul Foley, who had all voted for the Sacheverell clause in 1690 and came from families with strong sympathies for dissenters, contrasted oddly with their fellow commissioners, like Sir Thomas Clarges and Sir Benjamin Newland, who were staunch Anglicans. These differences did prevent the commission working effectively at first, but gradually they were overcome and the commission became a powerful political force. After working throughout the summer of 1691 the first fruit of the commission's work was seen early in November when it presented to parliament a report which was a sweeping indictment of waste in government expenditure. Cranfield and Weston in the early seventeenth century had come to similar conclusions, which were largely ignored by James I and Charles II. War, however, gave Foley and Clarges an advantage which early seventeenth-century lord treasurers had not possessed. The commissioners used their findings to persuade a Commons' select committee to recommend cuts in the official army and navy estimates for 1692, thereby initiating regular parliamentary scrutiny of proposed government wartime spending. From now on officials were frequently summoned by the commission or by select committees of the Commons to account for the way public money had been or was to be spent. Most important of all, from 1690 and 1691 onwards it became common practice for parliament to appropriate many grants of money to specific named uses. No longer was it possible for the king or his officials to sidetrack money voted for the war for any other purpose. The successive annual commissions which were appointed until 1697 played an important role in reducing considerably the financial independence of the crown and increasing parliament's control of public finance.

The maturing alliance between country Whigs and Tories, which developed in the commission of public accounts, also resulted in a revival of the 'country' programme, which had been pressed by many MPs in the reign of Charles II and which had been restated in the 'heads' of February 1689, the preliminary version of the Declaration of Rights. The third session of William's first parliament (October 1691 to February 1692) is notable for the strong support seen in the Commons for two 'country' measures aimed at limiting the crown's ability both to determine the outcome of treason trials and of removing judges at will. Bills to protect personal liberties in these ways passed the Commons in the winter of 1691-2 and the Judges' Bill, which would have brought about an independent and salaried judiciary, passed the House of Lords as well. It is an early indication of the profound change that was coming over post-Revolution Whiggery and Toryism that, apart from the Foley–Harley group, prominent Whigs opposed both measures. It was with Tory support that these measures aimed at reducing the royal prerogative made such progress. As yet, however, in both these cases the new opponents of executive power had no more permanent success than their Whig predecessors of the 1670s and early 1680s. The Treason Trial Bill was defeated in the House of Lords and in February 1692 William used his personal veto to kill the Bill restricting his power of dismissing judges. It has been suggested that the king opposed the latter Bill because he was not willing to accept judges' salaries as a permanent charge on the ordinary revenue of the crown. But surely there is more to it than this. Even though he had been appointing judges 'during good behaviour' as the Bill proposed, his autocratic philosophy would not let him lightly accept from parliament a statutory restriction on the royal prerogative. William never lost fully his personal control of policy-making either abroad or in England. But the prolongation of the war did force the king to accept more limitations on his prerogative power, in addition to his loss of financial independence. During the next two years William was forced to trade some of his independence in choosing his ministers and control over the summoning and dissolution of parliament in return for grants of wartime revenue.

When William's first parliament met for its fourth session in November 1692 criticism of the conduct and expense of the war was fuelled by the failure to follow up the naval victory at La Hogue and the sequence of military defeats in Flanders, culminating in the loss of Namur and the disaster at Steenkirk. That dissatisfaction did not extend to opposition to the war itself is underlined by the fact that early in this session parliament approved war expenditure of just over £4 million, cutting the official estimates of what was necessary by only a token 5 per cent. Moreover, after the Christmas recess parliament resolved to raise the bulk of the sum needed by a land tax of four shillings in the pound. This agreement to a massive 20 per cent tax on their rental income was an impressive affirmation by the landed classes of their support for the war. But it is equally clear that the majority of MPs did not want to see their money poured into the Flemish theatre of the war, or even (as Nottingham urged) into a military invasion of France, to take advantage of the disarray of the French fleet after La Hogue. On the contrary, in the parliamentary debates in the winter of 1692-3 an alternative popular war strategy emerged, in which the emphasis was primarily naval not military: a reduction of the army and withdrawal of many of the land forces from Europe, to be replaced by a series of naval attacks on the French coastline and French shipping. The principal proponent of this strategy was the high Tory Rochester, who had recently been appointed to the privy council, and he had behind him much grass-roots support from already heavily taxed and conservative landed MPs. Among the bulk of provincial country gentlemen by the end of seventeenth century it was a common (though arguably wrong) assumption that naval warfare was cheaper than expenditure on a large European army. Moreover, through a romantic haze many English MPs looked back to the naval victories of Elizabeth's day against the Spanish, and of Charles II's reign against the Dutch (conveniently forgetting the Medway debacle). As will be seen, this 'blue-water' strategy was to become a prominent part of Tory ideology throughout the wars against France (see below, pp. 367-72).

In the 1692-3 parliamentary session dissatisfaction with the war produced mounting attacks on Admiral Russell, who was forced to resign, and on Secretary Nottingham. It also gave impetus to the campaign to secure legislation designed to curb the power of the crown. At the end of December 1692 a Place Bill, which excluded from the

Commons all MPs who were elected after February 1693 and who were office-holders, passed the House of Commons and only failed in the Lords by a couple of votes. Significantly this was a measure which had been a favourite Whig one in the reign of Charles II, but which was now pressed by Tory MPs and their country Whig allies. This alliance had even more success when a Triennial Bill passed both Houses, forcing William III to use his veto to kill the Bill at the end of the parliamentary session on 14 March 1693.

By the spring of 1693 William's constant disillusionment with English politics reached a new nadir. His ministers, Nottingham and Danby, had so far secured for him adequate war supplies, but the previous parliamentary session must have caused the king to wonder how much longer MPs would continue to finance a war strategy of which they were becoming intensely suspicious without major royal concessions such as triennial and place legislation. It was at this time that William, therefore, began to consider appointing new ministers who might be able to devise new means of financing the war and to provide more able leadership in parliament. This was the course of action urged by the earl of Sunderland, whose career is remarkable even in an age not short of examples of men of abundant political agility. The earl of Shaftesbury's survival despite changing regimes has been commented on, though perhaps his career is not as atypical as it seems at first sight. Danby's political career is also remarkable for its length, which even three impeachments could not curtail, but his power after 1689 was but a pale shadow of that which he had exercised in the 1670s. Sunderland, on the contrary, despite having committed himself fully to James II in the 1680s, returned to a position of influence in the counsels of William III, arguably greater than that he had held during the previous reign.

Nevertheless Sunderland at first had little success in persuading William to abandon his present ministers and appoint new ones. Partly, this is to be explained by William's personal dislike of the principal Whig contenders for office, Sir John Somers, Thomas Wharton, Charles Montague, Admiral Edward Russell, and Sir John Trenchard. Wharton especially had a scandalous private life and a reputation for irreligion that was to alienate Anne perhaps even more than William. The king, too, found it difficult to overlook the connection of these ambitious young Whig politicians with republican ideas. 'He believed the Whigs loved him best,' William is reported to have said, 'but they did not love monarchy, and although the Tories did not like him so well as the others, yet as they were zealous for monarchy he thought they would serve his government best'.[33] Above all, William was reluctant to abandon both his resolve to appoint men regardless of party affiliations and his independence in choosing his own ministers. Early in 1693 he appointed Somers as lord keeper and Trenchard as secretary of state, but he adamantly refused to go further. Sunderland, however, schemed assiduously during the summer during William's usual absence on the continent. Late in August he convened a meeting at his house at Althorp in Northamptonshire attended by Russell, Wharton, Montague, and the earls of Shrewsbury and Devonshire, and when William returned to England late in October he was met by intensified pressure to accept Sunderland's advice. He reluctantly conceded that Nottingham's dismissal was the least that was necessary to secure parliamentary supply in the forthcoming session; Nottingham surrendered his seals of office to his fellow secretary, Trenchard, on 6 November, the day before parliament reassembled. The 1693–4 sesson, however, showed that more than this was needed to divert the parliamentary opposition from its programme of constitutional legislation. The Triennial, Treasons Trial, and Place Bills of previous sessions were all revived and the latter this time passed both Houses. In January 1694 William's veto was again used and this provoked the Commons to pass a motion that whoever had advised William to use the veto was 'an enemy to their Majesties and the kingdom'.

After these parliamentary setbacks William at last heeded Sunderland's advice by making a succession of Whig appointments, Shrewsbury as secretary of state instead of Nottingham, and Russell as sole admiral in March, and Montague as chancellor of the exchequer in April. Furthermore, four prominent Whig earls, Shrewsbury, Devonshire, Bedford, and Newcastle, were promoted to dukedoms. (The Tory earl Danby was promoted duke of Leeds at the same time.) When William left for his subsequent summer visit to the continent in May Sidney lord Godolphin was excluded from Queen Mary's inner cabinet which was dominated by Whigs, and the king gave his permission for Shrewsbury, Trenchard and Somers to purge the customs and excise commissions and fill the vacancies with their supporters.

In favouring this group of young Whig politicians in these ways William was strongly swayed by the fact that some of them had close links with the City and had proved to be extremely able in financial matters. With parliamentary grants for the war under increasing criticism on the grounds that it was being spent with Dutch rather than English interests in mind, William had every incentive to explore new means of financing the war.

Out of the resulting multitude of financial schemes two stand out and have become permanent features of British government finance ever since: the National Debt which had its origins in the Million Loan Act of January 1693 and the Bank of England which was created by the Tonnage Act of April 1694. The constitutional significance of these measures was lasting (see below, pp. 414–17); their importance in the politics of William's reign is that they were essentially Whig creations in which Montague played a leading (if not a sole) role. Tory opposition, led by Rochester, Halifax, and Nottingham (though not by Danby), condemned the new Bank as 'fit only for republics',[34] but was not able to prevent the beginnings of a 'financial revolution' that brought immediate advantages to William III. Certainly the king felt it was more than coincidental that these Whig financial measures were succeeded by an improvement in the military situation, culminating in the recapture of Namur in August 1695. Moreover, events in 1693 and 1694 may have led him to doubt his original assessment that the new Whigs 'did not love monarchy'. Lack of evidence such as full accounts of parliamentary debates and personal letters and papers precludes certainty on this point, but (with the exception of Shrewsbury) all the new Whig ministers appear to have adopted towards the proposed constitutional legislation of 1693–4 an attitude which was at best ambiguous. Shrewsbury is the exception without doubt. When he became secretary of state in March 1694 he did so only on the understanding that William would withdraw his objection to a Triennial Bill. In the debates on a Bill for annual parliaments in December 1693 Montague was unreservedly opposed, and he rejected all medieval precedents in its favour. 'That of annual parliaments,' said Montague, 'is as much an antiquated law as any – annual parliaments were never insisted upon – when perhaps it will not be in the king's power to dissolve. You are setting up a Senate of Venice.'[35] In the debates on the Triennial Bill a year later, when William, as he had promised, gave the Bill his assent, the voices of the new Whig ministers apart from Shrewsbury were curiously silent.

The year 1694 is significant in the history of Britain after the Glorious Revolution in more than one respect. In the development of the constitution it saw the introduction of the principle that parliament should in future underwrite government debts; consequently, annual parliaments were needed thereafter to maintain the monarchy's financial credit. If this was in any doubt the Triennial Act was a further reminder that the pressure of war was forcing William to concede more of the crown's constitutional powers than ideally he would have liked. Henceforth parliaments were to meet once in every three years at least, no parliament was to last longer than three years, and the gap between the dissolution of a parliament and the issuance of writs for a new one ought not to be greater than three years. But 1694 was also a significant year in the history of domestic politics as well as in the development of the constitution. The Triennial Act ensured that politics remained unstable until its repeal in 1716. It also saw 'the last stand made by any Whig leader [Shrewsbury] to secure major constitutional change on behalf of the independence of the legislature'.[36] As the 'new' Whigs dissociated themselves from their radical past, the alliance between Foley and Harley's 'old Whigs' and the Tories became increasingly close. The last years of William's war were to see this new pattern in English politics more evident than ever before.

War and politics: the rise of the Junto Whigs, 1695–7

During the last years of William's war political alignments at Westminster along Whig and Tory lines are much clearer than at any time since the Convention of 1689–90. Yet in one crucial respect the Whigs and Tories of the mid-1690s were different from their predecessors immediately before and after the Glorious Revolution. 'By an odd reverse' wrote Burnet, 'the Whigs, who were now employed, argued for the prerogative, while the Tories seemed zealous for public liberty.'[37] It would be a mistake to think that the Foley–Harley 'country' Whigs had been fully absorbed by the Tories and that their association with the 'new' Whigs was totally cut, but on many issues the 'country' Whigs had much in common with the Tories. The first few existing division lists for the reign of William III (for the 1695–6 and 1696–7 sessions of William's third parliament) suggest that by 1696 there had occurred 'the virtual completion of the process whereby a House of Commons divided into court and country parties, each with its Whig and Tory members, has been replaced by one in which Whig and Court on the one hand, and Tory and Country on the other, are synonymous terms'.[38]

Certainly the main characteristic of the leaders of the 'new' Whigs, Somers, Montague, Wharton, and Russell, whom contemporaries began from the spring of 1695 to label derogatorily the 'Junto', was their desire to control the patronage and government of the king. Their appetite for power was more apparent than their adherence to principle. It would be difficult to imagine any less likely inheritors of the Good Old Cause. By 1694 the Junto Whigs' unqualified support for the war and its rejection of anti-prerogative principles had been rewarded by appointment to government offices. The Junto Whigs, however, had not succeeded in their aim of totally dominating the king's government. They never did so: William was too determined to maintain his own control of his government to allow that to happen. However, during the next three years the combined value of the members of the Junto in providing money for the war forced William to allow them to increase their hold on his government. Unlike the 'Cabal' of Charles II's reign, the Junto of William III's reign was united enough (despite differences of personality and temperament) and organized enough to secure by 1697 'a qualified form of party government'.[39] Nevertheless, the years from 1695 to 1697, as well as revealing the reasons why the Junto were able to achieve this dominating position, also indicate why this dominance was never total and why, once the war ended, it was quickly lost.

The obstacles preventing the Junto Whigs from controlling the king's government in the mid-1690s were daunting. Not only was William's personal power still great, despite the development of a 'cabinet council' in the early years of the war, but the king also never overcame the repugnance and suspicion he felt for the members of the Junto. This partly accounts for Sunderland's close relationship with William at this time. In the king's eyes Sunderland's greatest asset was that he was independent of the Junto, and so in a position to use the parliamentary skill and financial expertise of the Junto without allowing them a dominating position. In this respect Sunderland's role, acting in close collaboration with the king and independent of political groups in parliament, was that developed in Anne's reign by later royal 'managers', especially Godolphin, Marlborough, and Harley (see below, pp. 361–2). Arguably an even greater obstacle faced by the Junto than Sunderland's influence at court was that their support in parliament and in the country was limited. It is a fact of supreme importance, for Anne's reign as well as William's, that until 1715 the 'new' Whigs were a minority party in English politics. Their main political stronghold was the House of Lords. In the lower House and in the country at large they were less popular. In the 1690s they had in Montague and Wharton two superb parliamentary managers, but both had to face growing popular opposition to the royal policies with which the Junto Whigs had associated themselves. In the Commons the influence of Montague and Wharton was rivalled by that of Foley and Harley, who voiced the growing indignation felt by the bulk of landed MPs at England's escalating involvement in a full-scale continental war, and its effects: soaring land taxes, the new power of the Bank of England and the 'monied interest', the persistent favour shown to William's Dutch favourites, and the growth of executive power.

In the last session of William's second parliament (January to May 1695) this popular opposition became more intense, partly because the danger of James II's return had apparently receded, but mainly because of the death of Queen Mary at the end of December 1694. Throughout their joint reigns Mary's influence on her husband had been slight, but her mere presence as queen had reconciled many doubters to the new monarchy. Mary's death effectively removed any inhibitions many Tory MPs had felt about attacking the new regime. In January 1695 Nottingham for the first time since his dismissal mounted a full-scale parliamentary attack on the government's war strategy and on the 'evils' of the Bank of England. It is a significant indication of the Junto's weakness in the House of Commons that they were only successful when they allied with this 'country' opposition. In the spring of 1695 the commission of public accounts made a series of allegations of corruption against Henry Guy, a treasury secretary, and Sir John Trevor, the speaker of the House of Commons, who were accused of receiving bribes from the City of London and the East India Company. With Wharton's and Montague's encouragement the attack widened to include Danby among its targets and in April, for the third time in his career, articles of impeachment were drawn up against him. William III, like Charles II twice before, adjourned parliament to save Danby.

There is little evidence that the general election of October 1695 significantly improved the Junto Whigs' parliamentary position. In the first session of the new parliament (November 1695 to April 1696) Harley's influence was greater than ever; he received the highest number of votes of those elected to the 1696 commission of public accounts. The Junto was not able to prevent the government from coming under attack on many fronts, forcing William to grant many concessions. In order to divert demands for a parliamentary-nominated council of trade, in December 1695 William established his own council by royal order.

After the Christmas recess the king gave way with ill grace to a Commons' request that the grants of Irish land to Portland be stopped. 'I will find some other way of showing my favour to him,' he said.[40] Also in January William at last gave his assent to a Treason Trials Act. Most serious of all, from the Junto Whigs' point of view, Foley and Harley piloted through parliament in the spring of 1696 an Act establishing a Land Bank, which was established as a direct competitor of the Bank of England. Indeed the promoters of the Land Bank, in promising to raise over £2.5 million by subscription, appealed directly to the landed interest, because those who had subscribed to the Bank of England were specifically excluded from participating in the Land Bank scheme.

Why, then, did the fortunes of the Junto Whigs revive in the last eighteen months of the war? There were three major reasons. First, although William never totally lost his repugnance for the Junto lords or for party government, he was forced to recognize that only the Junto had an effective solution to the financial needs of the war. The Land Bank scheme was a total failure. It raised only a fraction of its promised £2m subscription, and the Bank of England had to step in with a large loan, once more emphasizing the Whigs' financial value to William. Already during the winter of 1695–6 Montague had steered through parliament a scheme to introduce a reformed coinage. Furthermore, in the spring of 1697 the Bank of England again provided the solution to a severe liquidity crisis by another large loan. In return in April 1697 an Act was passed incorporating the Bank, allowing it to increase its capital stock by another £1m, and giving it a monopoly of joint-stock banking until 1710. Secondly, not only did the Junto Whigs improve their position at court by their achievement of a Whig Financial Revolution, but for a brief period they found themselves in 1696 in an unusually popular position in the House of Commons. In February 1696 the revelation of a plot to assassinate the king gave the Whigs (as in 1679) an opportunity to discredit their opponents. The Tories of 1696, however, were in a much more vulnerable position than those of 1679. When in response to the assassination plot the Commons adopted a motion that all MPs should take an oath of loyalty to William as 'the rightful and lawful king', all the Tory doubts of 1689 were revived in an extreme form. About ninety MPs refused to take the oath and in the Lords nineteen peers, including Nottingham, refused to make a similar declaration. In April 1696 it was made compulsory for all office-holders to take the 'association' oath, and William gave his support for a full-scale purge of all non-subscribers from the lieutenancy and commission of the peace, and their replacement with Whig nominees. That the Junto Whigs were able to exploit to the full this fortunate turn of events points to a third reason for their success in 1696–7: the effective organization of their supporters both at Westminster and in the localities. Much of this organization was informal – private meetings of ministers to discuss parliamentary strategy and drum up support among individual MPs – and therefore is ill documented. Undoubtedly though these did take place, as well as the more formal meetings of Whig supporters before crucial parliamentary occasions at the Rose Tavern, near Covent Garden, which were common from the autumn of 1696 onwards.

The parliamentary session of October 1696 to April 1697 is one of the few examples of Whig ascendancy from 1690 to 1714. In November 1696 the Junto's control of the Commons secured majorities in favour of an Attainder Bill against Sir John Fenwick, who had been arrested in connection with the assassination plot, and the rejection of Fenwick's counter-accusations against Shrewsbury and Russell. Significantly, in this session also the political power of the Junto's opponents was undermined when the commission of public accounts was not continued in 1697. At the end of the session William recognized the Whig ascendancy by promoting Somers to a barony and the lord chancellorship, Russell to the earldom of Orford, and Montague to be first lord of the treasury. The Junto held power and influence which they were not to attain again until another brief period in 1708–9. The end of the war was to show that they could not maintain their ascendancy in peacetime.

Peace and politics: the collapse of the Junto, 1697–1701

Even in the last phase of William's war the Junto's political position in parliament and at court had not been secure. Their influence in the lower House was weakened considerably by the promotion of Somers and Russell to the House of Lords, where they joined Wharton, who had succeeded to his father's barony in February 1696. Sunderland's emergence at the same time from 'behind the curtain' to become lord chamberlain emphasized the continued power of their rival at court. It was, however, the end of the war which brought about the downfall of the Junto Whigs, who had risen to power as the party of war and a strong executive. The Treaty of Ryswick released a popular conservative reaction of pacifism and provincialism: a demand to end England's military involvement in Europe and to return power to the traditional rulers of provincial England. Like the county committees fifty years before, the Junto Whigs were considered to be the symbols of centralization and arbitrary rule, and were thus swept away. The years of peace culminated in their impeachment and the Act of Settlement, a statement of provincial resentment at the growth of executive power brought about by the war.

Increasingly during the war William and his ministers had had to work hard to convince his English subjects that his European policy was in their interests, as well as those of the Dutch. On the whole these efforts had been successful; MPs complained but voted the necessary war supplies. In peacetime, however, after 1697 William's dual position seemed less advantageous to England. Peace made the king seem more alien and less necessary to English security and political stability. Unlike his English subjects William realized that the Treaty of Ryswick did not provide a framework for permanent European peace, since it made no attempt to solve the problem of who was to succeed the ailing Charles II of Spain. In an effort to avert a major European war William and Louis XIV in the three years after the Treaty of Ryswick tried to settle the claims of the three principal contenders for the Spanish throne by diplomatic means. Their efforts produced two secret Partition Treaties which 'to a twentieth-century student ... look rather like a combination of the Great Powers to enforce a rudimentary system of collective security'.[41] The first Partition Treaty signed in October 1698 arranged for the bulk of the Spanish kingdom and Empire to go to Joseph Ferdinand, the electoral prince of Bavaria, for Naples, Sicily and Guipuzcoa to go to the Dauphin and for Milan to go to Archduke Charles. Not surprisingly, Archduke Charles's father, Emperor Leopold, refused to have anything to do with this arrangement. In any case a new treaty became necessary a few months later when Joseph Ferdinand died. As a result William, again without consulting parliament, concluded with Louis XIV a second Partition Treaty in March 1700, which granted all the Spanish possessions to Archduke Charles, leaving only Naples, Sicily, Guipuzcoa and Milan to the French claimant. During the Partition negotiations William felt that it was necessary to keep a large part of his army mobilized in order to strengthen his hand in the diplomatic manoeuvres, as well as to be ready for the war that would inevitably follow if the negotiations failed.

When the Partition Treaties were made public in England in the summer of 1700 they roused a storm of opposition. Before then, however, all that was generally known about William's policies was his intention to maintain the army at its wartime strength. It was therefore on the question of the standing army that the great gulf between William's European outlook and the insular pacifism of most of his subjects first became clear. 'There is a deadness and want of spirit in the nation universally', wrote Somers in the summer of 1698, 'so as not at all to be disposed to the thought of entering into a new war and that they seem to be tired out with taxes.'[42] It was not just high taxation that accounted for the anti-war sentiments of many after 1697, although the land tax, especially in the highly assessed southern and eastern counties, was greatly resented. Many people felt that the Treaty of Ryswick had removed the principal cause of England's quarrel with France: Louis XIV had recognized William as king of England. Moreover, the peace was seen as a marvellous opportunity to minimize all connections with the hated Dutch. To memories of three Anglo-Dutch wars over the previous fifty years and a long history of commercial rivalry were now added William's frequent visits to the Dutch republic and his apparent reliance on Dutch advisers. Like James I's favourites at the beginning of the century, William's Dutch entourage became the focus for an outbreak of escalating national xenophobia. In these circumstances it is debatable whether a concerted effort by William to explain that English interests were inextricably bound up with his efforts to secure European agreement about a Spanish succession would have made any headway. His failure to do this, or at least to inform his ministers of his activities made harder than it might have been the Junto lords' task of defending in parliament his intention of keeping most of his army mobilized.

For all these reasons many Whigs who had supported the Junto in the latter stages of the war joined with Tories in the attack on William's standing army in the last session of William's third parliament (December 1687 to July 1698) and the first session of his fourth parliament (December 1698 to May 1699). To a large extent Whig and Tory divisions are difficult to see in these sessions as the vast majority of MPs united, not only to oppose standing armies but also to support the traditional 'country' programme of place legislation, enquiries into mismanagement of the war, and so on. Consequently, it has become fairly common for historians to write about this interwar period as being dominated by a 'New Country Party' led by Robert Harley. Again, as in the early 1690s, this is an analysis which implies too much party organization and gives too much credit to Harley's manipulation of opinion. It is true that Harley was now no longer overshadowed by his colleagues; Foley, for example, was an ill man and died in 1699. But it seems likely that Harley did not need to manipulate MPs. There was already in parliament a *spontaneous* groundswell of opinion in favour of reducing taxation, and against English entanglement on the continent and the interference of foreigners in English government. Harley's achievement was to recognize the strength of this opinion in the country and to marshall it behind him with the principal aim of removing the Junto lords from office. Beyond that, Harley's aims are less clearcut. Especially uncertain is the degree of his association with the high Tory leaders, Rochester, Nottingham, and Seymour.[43] There is little evidence that at this stage he wanted office for himself. In this respect he was still typical of most MPs in the seventeenth century, who were inherently distrustful of central government and who therefore favoured a negative programme of limiting the power of that government, with little attempt to recognize the practical problems of government, let alone produce constructive suggestions to overcome them. It was not until 1704 that Harley accepted the challenge of ministerial office.

Before parliament met in December 1697, for the first time after the conclusion of peace, the arguments against standing armies had been well rehearsed in pamphlet literature.[44] Standing armies were unnecessarily expensive. The navy was all that was needed for the security of an island nation. Above all, did not English experience from the time of Cromwell to the reign of James II teach that standing armies were the bulwark of absolutism? Significantly the co-authors of the most famous anti-army pamphlet, *An Argument, Showing a Standing Army is Inconsistent with a Free Government*, John Trenchard and Walter Moyle, were 'old' Whigs who were steeped in republican theories. Their republicanism, however, was clothed in the respectable guise of admiration for ancient Rome and proved no obstacle to their association with more conservatively minded MPs. Even Harley gave Trenchard information to include in his influential pamphlet, *A Short History of Standing Armies*, published in November 1698.[45] The arguments did not fall on deaf ears. On 10 December 1697 the Commons passed a resolution that all forces raised since September 1680 should be disbanded, which would have effectively cut the size of the army in England to 8,000 men. In addition, the opposition pressed home its attacks on William's advisers. As a result Sunderland resigned at the end of December, and five Bills for the resumption of all royal grants since 1660, introduced in the Commons in February 1698, were aimed directly at the king's Dutch favourites. The Junto, too, faced enormous political opposition. As yet, however, they survived. Although they had made no effort to protect Sunderland, they were too valuable to William to be sacrificed. This was emphasized in the way the Junto piloted the East India Bill through parliament in the last months of William's third parliament. The charter of the old East India Company was revoked and a new company established, which promised to lend the government £2 million at 8 per cent interest. This and the fact that the money was quickly raised reinforced William's natural inclination not to allow parliament to dictate who his ministers should be. It took two subsequent stormy sessions of a new parliament to force him to change his mind.

The general election of the summer of 1698 must have brought home to William the realization that the new parliament would not be any more amenable to Junto management than the old one. Many local elections were characterized by anti-court propaganda, and when parliament met in December 1698 William's renewed request for supply to maintain the army at its wartime level provoked a Commons' resolution that the army should be reduced to 7,000 men, and that these were to be not foreigners but 'natural born subjects of England'. Not surprisingly, William sank into another of his periodic depressions, caused by what he considered to be the unreasonable behaviour of English politicians. As in 1690 his letters home to his Dutch confidants imply that he was toying with thoughts of abdication. At least that is the obvious interpretation of his dark threats of taking 'resolutions of extremity' and 'steps that will amaze' parliament in December–January 1698-9. In January the Disbanding Bill, putting into effect the Commons' resolution to reduce the size of the army, passed both Houses. In the remainder of this parliamentary session (to 5 May 1699) and in the next (16 November 1699 to 11 April 1700) the Junto's position collapsed after a succession of ministerial defeats. The resignation of Orford (Russell) from the admiralty in May 1699 was preceded by the rapid parliamentary progress of a new Place Bill, a parliamentary enquiry into his administration of the navy, and by a successful move to tack an amendment appointing a commission to investigate William's grants in Ireland on to a land tax Bill. Before parliament met again in November Montague resigned from the treasury. Somers remained in office and even rode out a parliamentary storm in December over allegations that he was partly responsible for the activities of Captain William Kidd, who had turned pirate after being sent to the Indian Ocean to protect East India Company merchants. But it became clear that Somers would not survive long, as a Bill to resume all royal grants of Irish land since February 1688 made rapid progress in parliament, and the Commons, on 10 April 1700, resolved that the king should eject all foreigners from his councils. For William this was the last straw. He prorogued parliament on 11 April and later in the month Somers, who refused to resign, was dismissed from his office of lord chancellor.

Even now William delayed accepting the logic of the situation and appointing ministers from among those who commanded such wide support in parliament. What forced him to do so, however, was the uncertainty about the succession brought about by the death of the eleven-year-old duke of Gloucester at the end of July 1700. It therefore became very urgent that arrangements should be agreed for the succession in the likely eventuality that both William and Anne would die childless. When William returned from his usual summer visit to the continent in October he had meetings with Rochester, Godolphin, and Harley of which no formal record survives but at which there is little doubt that William agreed to dissolve the existing parliament, appoint Tories to office, and pass an Act establishing the succession and embodying further limitations on the power of the crown. Consequently in December parliament was dissolved, Nottingham's nominee, Sir Charles Hedges, became secretary of state, Rochester was appointed lord lieutenant of Ireland, and Godolphin promoted to first lord of the treasury.

When parliament met in February 1701 these new appointments were the only visible important changes from the last parliament. Harley's election to the speakership of the new House of Commons stressed that its preoccupations would be the same as that of its predecessor: peace and limitations on the power of the crown. The long-awaited death of King Charles II of Spain in November 1700, the publication of his will leaving his kingdoms and empire to Louis XIV's grandson, Philip of Anjou, and Louis XIV's public acceptance of the will in November, failed to change the prevailing mood of pacifism in England. Many, indeed, believed that the will provided a good guarantee of European peace and English security, since Charles II had left his throne to Philip of Anjou on the condition that the crowns of France and Spain would never be united. Moreover, the Partition Treaties had now been published and this served also to increase support in England for acceptance of Charles II's will. Not only did both Partition Treaties favour French traders in the Mediterranean by granting France Naples and Sicily, but the fact that they had been conducted in secrecy also precipitated a major parliamentary attack on the king's ministers, culminating in impeachment proceedings against Portland and the Junto lords, Somers, Orford, and Montague (who had been created

Baron Halifax in December 1700). The second major concern of the new parliament was to put into practice the agreement reached between William, Harley, and the Tories in the previous autumn. The result was the Act of Settlement, which received the royal assent on 12 June. By it the successors to the throne after the deaths of William, Anne, and any children they might have were to be Protestant and Hanoverian, in the shape of the progeny of James I's daughter, Elizabeth, the wife of the elector palatine, namely Sophia electress of Hanover and her heirs, who were required 'to joyn in Communion with the Church of England as by Law established'.

Apart from settling the Protestant succession the Act of Settlement settled very little. The Act failed to live up to its full title, 'An Act for the further limitation of the Crown and better securing the Rights and Liberties of the Subject'. Since it was not to come into effect until after the death of Queen Anne none of its provisions limited the power of the Stuarts. Moreover, few of them troubled the Hanoverians. The two most potentially serious limitations were the clause which prevented office-holders from sitting in parliament and the provision that 'all Matters and Things relating to the well governing of this Kingdom which are properly cognizable in the Privy Council . . . shall be transacted there . . . and all Resolutions taken thereupon shall be signed by such of the Privy Council as shall advise and consent to the same'. These were ringing declarations in favour of free and open government, but both clauses were repealed in 1706 (see below, p. 372). Of the remaining clauses that which laid down that judges should hold their offices during good behaviour and with fixed salaries and not at the will of the monarch only made obligatory what William had done voluntarily. The provision that monarchs after Anne's death should not leave the country without parliamentary consent was repealed in the first year of George I's reign. All of importance that remained were clauses which prevented an English monarch who was of foreign birth from taking England into 'any Warr for the defence of any Dominions and Territories which do not belong to the Crown of England', and which excluded any foreigner from the privy council, any office or place in parliament in England. All this considerably reduces the significance of the Act of Settlement in the long-term development of the English (later British) constitution. The Act is much more significant as a reflection of majority opinion among MPs and their constituents and their disenchantment with William's war and its effects on their country.

Party issues redefined, 1701–1702

The last twelve months of William's reign witnessed a remarkable transformation in English politics. After the end of William's war opinion in England had turned decisively and unanimously against the effects of war and involvement in Europe. The Whig and Tory alignment of English politics, which had existed during the latter stages of the war, became blurred and indistinct as the nation united in favour of peace and withdrawal from Europe. But during the course of 1701 this unanimity was shattered by the reappearance of controversies about the renewal of war, the succession to the throne, and the state of the Church; these formed the basis of Whig and Tory rivalries which were to last throughout the reign of Queen Anne.

War and the succession

The most important determinant of political change, as in the earlier part of the reign, was war. Dramatically in the spring and summer of 1701 public opinion in England swung in favour of a renewed war against France. The pacificism seen in the first weeks of William's fifth parliament evaporated and within five months of its first meeting it voted large grants of money to finance the war (2 June) and agreed to support any alliances which William might make (12 June). This conversion was brought about almost entirely by the provocative actions of Louis XIV; as in 1685 decisions Louis made in Europe had a decisive and unforeseen impact on English opinion. As has been seen, many in England believed that Louis's acceptance of Charles II's will would not endanger England's security. Louis effectively destroyed that belief by persuading the French courts to recognize the right of the new Spanish king, Philip of Anjou, to succeed to the French throne if his elder brother should die, by forcibly taking over key towns in the Spanish Netherlands, and by announcing a series of embargoes on English trade with France and Spain. Fortunately the difficult task of finding a convincing explanation for Louis's action is not one for students of English history.[46] What is certain is that they made clear, in a way William by himself could not do, that Louis's expansionist aims in Europe were a threat to English interests.

This point was hammered home in England by a sustained propaganda campaign outside parliament in favour of war, which culminated early in May in the presentation to parliament of the Kentish Petition and the *Legion Memorial*. The former was drafted at the Maidstone Quarter Sessions on 29 April; the latter, allegedly representing the views of 'many thousands of the good people of England', was the work of Daniel Defoe. At least two other counties, Warwickshire and Cheshire, also presented urgent demands that parliament support William against France. This campaign so suited the king that historians have been tempted to believe that William inspired it and that he employed Defoe's literary talents for the purpose. Unfortunately the evidence to support the latter view is weak, though the connection between Defoe and the Junto is better documented.[47] There is no reason to doubt that both the king and the Junto at least condoned, if they did not inititiate, the popular war movement. Perhaps, though, historians, like many Tories in the House of Commons at the time, have been too anxious to see these events in terms of the manipulation of public opinion. In May a majority in the Commons voted the Kentish petition 'scandalous insolent and seditious and tending to destroy the constitution of parliament', and condemned the petitioners as 'tools of the ministry'.[48] But perhaps this criticism misses the point. Provincial England, as well as the capital, was well provided with foreign news by the many newspapers which had appeared in the years after the lapse of the Licensing Act in 1695. 'By 1700 the reading of newspapers had become a settled habit in England', writes G. C. Gibbs, 'and . . . the habit was not confined to a ruling minority.'[49] It is possible that volatile public opinion responded as much to what was written in newspapers as to persuasion by the king or his Junto ministers. The same is possibly true of the majority of MPs. Although some Tories pressed ahead with the impeachment proceedings against the Junto lords, there was no strong parliamentary opposition to the war by the time parliament was prorogued in June 1701. Any who did still have doubts were silenced early in September when James II died, and Louis XIV made another, impolitic decision and publically recognized James III as king of England. Consequently the new MPs, elected in November, assembled at Westminster on the last day of the year temporarily united in favour of war. It was a Tory, Edward Seymour, who successfully moved that a clause be added to the Grand Alliance, which had been negotiated between England, the United Provinces, and the emperor at the end of August, that the allies should continue the war until Louis XIV recognised the Protestant succession in England. In addition the Grand Alliance sought to curtail French power first by securing the Spanish Netherlands as a barrier to protect the Dutch Republic, secondly by ejecting French troops from the Italian possessions of Spain and the Empire, and lastly by ensuring that the thrones of Spain and France remained permanently separate.

However, differences between Whigs and Tories about the war did not take long to develop, as Tory scepticism about continental wars soon reappeared. Significantly, William in the autumn of 1701 began to think in terms of a return to a Junto ministry which had proved so successful in obtaining finance for the war of the 1690s. This inclination must have been confirmed by new evidence of Tory uncertainty about the Protestant succession. Whereas the enthusiasm of Whigs for the war was based on their full commitment to a Protestant succession, many Tories at Westminster and in the provinces soon made it apparent that, despite all their protestations, their support of a Protestant succession, and therefore of a war designed to secure such a succession, was less than wholehearted. This became clear in the Tory reaction to the Abjuration Act, agreed on in February 1702, which obliged all office-holders, members of the Houses of Lords and Commons, clergymen, dissenting ministers, teachers, and lawyers to take an oath repudiating the Pretender. The oath caused the earl of Nottingham such an agony of indecision that he only took it after a delay of two months and not before he had been assured by the Archbishop of York that 'you are left as much at liberty after you have taken this oath'.[50] Other MPs took the oath in a similar pragmatic spirit. 'The Jacks . . . should never be able to do any thing if they . . . did not take all the oaths that could be imposed,' said a future MP for Southwark.[51] Among Tories outside the Westminster limelight there was even more resistance to the Abjuration oath, and this was reflected in an attempt in Anne's first parliament (1702–3) to provide a Bill to extend by a year the time limit for taking the oath. Clearly many Tories had still not cut their ties with theories of divine right monarchy. This fact was of supreme importance in explaining why the Tories failed in the next reign to capitalize on the widespread support they enjoyed in the country on other issues. It also helps to explain why before the end of William's reign the war and the succession were joint issues on which Whig and Tory opinions polarized at opposite extremes.

The Church

To some extent Tory uneasiness about the long-term succession to the throne in the last months of William's reign was overcome by the knowledge that the immediate successor, at least, was an Anglican Stuart princess. However, even this prospect did little to alleviate Tory fears about the future of the Church of England; indeed, as will be seen, Anne's accession gave a new lease of life to militant Anglicanism. Already throughout the 1690s Tory landowners and the mass of parish clergy were becoming increasingly anxious about the state of the Church. At the end of 1696 these submerged fears broke the political surface with the appearance of a pamphlet written by Francis Atterbury, *A Letter to A Convocation Man*. A young Oxford don, nurtured in the heady atmosphere of Anglicanism and Stuart loyalism of Christ Church college, Atterbury was a natural propagandist for the High Church cause. *A Letter to a Convocation Man* reflected all the frustration of Anglicans who, with Convocation adjourned since 1689, had no political forum in which to ventilate their grievances, and who saw the hierarchy of the Church dominated by moderate bishops intent on keeping the Church out of politics. *A Letter* demanded that Convocation ought to be recalled on the revolutionary ground that the summoning of Convocation was the clergy's legal right and not part of the royal prerogative. Despite being condemned by Archibishop Tenison and leading bishops, Atterbury's pamphlet was seized on avidly by parish clergy and by the high Tory Rochester. When Rochester became lord lieutenant of Ireland in December 1700 he made it a condition of his acceptance of office that William give in to the growing demands of the lower clergy and their secular High Church allies. Therefore in February 1701 Convocation met for the first time since 1689, religion again became a prime political issue, and Tories rallied to the political slogan, 'the Church in danger'.

Why did militant Anglicanism reappear with such force in the last part of William's reign? Although the vast majority of Anglicans had supported the Glorious Revolution they had done so with troubled consciences. For Anglicans, writes Dr Bennett, the clerical nonjurors 'were like a ghost of the past, confessors who stood in the ancient ways, devout, logical and insistent'.[52] Such consciences were, therefore, easily alarmed, especially when the Glorious Revolution seemed to have allowed the rapid growth of Protestant dissent. Although, as has been seen, the Toleration Act of 1689 hardly deserves its name, it did allow licensed worship to take place outside the Church of England. Between 1689 and 1710 what must have seemed in Anglican eyes an alarmingly high number (3,614) of meeting houses of various sorts were licensed. Dissenting academies were established.[53] Moreover, the Anglican monopoly of state offices as well as its predominant religious role seemed threatened by the growing practice of occasional conformity. The Test and Corporation Acts remained in being, but were evaded by nonconformists, who attended Anglican services infrequently simply to receive from the magistrate a certificate of attendance in order to qualify for public office. In November 1697 the lord mayor of London, Sir Humphrey Edwin, twice worshipped at an afternoon service at a conventicle in his full regalia of office after attending an Anglican church in the morning. Incidents like this not surprisingly provoked a bitter response from Anglicans. After decades of persecution since the Restoration, relieved only by shortlived royal experiments in toleration, Protestant dissenters apparently seemed to be flourishing.

However, it remains an open question whether dissent was a real threat to the Anglican dominance in Church and state. Was dissent ever able to withstand the competition of the Church of England for the favours of the powerful landed and mercantile classes? Since membership of the Church of England was the passport to social acceptability and a political career it is difficult to believe that it could. But again, as on many other occasions in history, what appeared to be the truth was more important than the truth itself. To many Anglicans the Church did appear to be in danger. High Church Tories felt worried and threatened as they contrasted the apparently flourishing condition of dissent with the material poverty of the Anglican Church, which had undergone no serious economic reform despite the urging of generations of Puritans from the 1560s to the 1650s, and which more recently had been heavily hit by wartime taxation. Moreover, the size of the Church's congregations as well as its income seemed to be threatened. During the 1690s the Church came under severe attack from novel theological doctrines. In chapter 14 it will be seen that in the later seventeenth century with the development of science and scientific methods there also emerged a rational attitude to religion (see below, pp. 421–3). One aspect of this was the appearance in the 1690s of the Deists, whose basic philosophy was that all beliefs, including the belief in God, should be the product of reason. This was the theme of John Locke's *The Reasonableness of Christianity* (1695), in which, although he recognized the importance of revelation, reason was put forward as the prime source of Christian belief. Just what this concept could mean in the hands of a less careful writer than Locke was seen when John Toland, published his *Christianity Not Mysterious* in 1696. 'Whereas Locke was content to show that Christianity is reasonable, Toland proved that nothing contrary to reason and nothing above it can be a part of Christian doctrine.' Toland's book, therefore, was an explicit attack on the teaching of divines in the past and on the leadership of the Church in the present. Church ministers, wrote Toland (echoing those radicals who had criticized all professional groups during the English Revolution), used 'scholastic jargon' 'to make plain things obscure'.[54] With the lapse of the Licensing Act in 1695 radical notions like these were now easier to publicize. Another major theological line of attack on the Anglican Church was directed against the doctrine of the Trinity. Unitarians and Socinians were able to spread their ideas with the collapse of press censorship. So too were a host of less sophisticated anticlerical authors. In vain the Blasphemy Act of 1697 tried to stem the tide of words which seemed to threaten to engulf the Church.

What made all this especially shocking to many ordinary clergymen and country gentlemen alike was that the upper ecclesiastical hierarchy, far from opposing some of these heterodox ideas, seemed to share them. In the years after the Restoration a group of Anglican divines developed a philosophy which appeared very similar to that of the Deists. These Latitudinarian divines (so-called by their critics) stressed the importance of reason in religion, and reacted sharply to the 'fanaticism' and 'enthusiasm' of the religious sects of the early and mid-seventeenth century. Both Archibishop Tillotson and his successor in 1695, Archibishop Tenison, adopted this view, and in addition they saw their prime purpose as being to make the Church more spiritually effective, its strength more dependent on a reformed inner vigour than on the support of the state. Tenison especially encouraged the foundation of voluntary societies like the Society for the Promotion of Christian Knowledge and the Society for the Propagation of the Gospel in the late 1690s. His view of the Church – a Low Church view – was clearly worlds apart from that of militant High Church Anglicans who harked back to an authoritarian alliance between Church and state.[55]

When Convocation met in February 1701 there was at last a platform for all these High Church fears to be publicized. So extraordinary and violent were the attacks directed against Archbishop Tenison and his episcopal colleagues that the session had to be adjourned. But the high Tory politicians took up Convocation's demands for action against heresy and for protection for the Church. Rochester and Nottingham had little difficulty in dragging religion into the political arena and using it as a party weapon against the Whigs. Sermon after sermon pressed home the myth of King Charles the Martyr, which enjoyed a resurgence in the 1690s. William Lancaster's sermon to the Commons on 30 January 1697 is typical of many:

I know not but there may be men in the world, thus left to themselves, who instead of repenting of a most horrid murder and of shedding innocent blood, have themselves and their posterity justified the doing it, and advanced from the blood of one king, to maintain the lawfulness of resisting all kings.[56]

So the identification of dissent with Whiggery and Whiggery with republicanism, which had been used so effectively by Clarendonians in the 1660s, was revived as a party weapon against the Whigs in the 1690s and early 1700s. This was a formula that was to be used by the Tories against the Whigs with explosive effect in Anne's reign. But already when William III died on 8 March 1702 (from complications which developed after he had suffered a simple collar-bone fracture in a riding accident two weeks before) English political life was torn apart by bitter party rivalry.

Notes

For abbreviations used throughout see p. xiv.

1. R. Walcott, *English Politics in the Early Eighteenth Century* (1956), p. 160.
2. See D. Rubini, *Court and Country 1688–1702* (1968), *passim*.
3. See the Bibliographical note, section 4, p. 471.
4. E. L. Ellis, 'William III and the politicians' in G. Holmes, ed., *Britain after the Glorious Revolution 1689–1714* (1969), p. 119.
5. W. L. Sachse, 'The mob and the Revolution of 1688', *J.B.S.*, IV (1964–5), pp. 23–40; John Miller, *Popery and Politics in England 1660–88* (1973), pp. 259–61.
6. R. A. Beddard, 'The Guildhall declaration of 11 December 1688 and the counter revolution of the loyalists', *H.J.*, XI (1968), pp. 403–20; *idem.*, 'The loyalist opposition in the Interregnum: a letter of Dr Francis Turner Bishop of Ely and the Restoration of 1688', *B.I.H.R.*, XL (1967).
7. G. Straka, 'The final phase of divine right theory in England, 1688–1702', *E.H.R.*, LXXVII (1962); J. P. Kenyon, *Revolution Principles: the politics of party, 1689–1720* (1977), p. 54.
8. M. Goldie, 'Edward Bohun and *Ius Gentium*: the Revolution debate 1689–93', *H.J.*, XX (1977), pp. 569–86.
9. C. F. Mullett, 'A case of allegiance: William Sherlock and the Revolution of 1688', *Huntingdon Library Quarterly*, X (1946–7).
10. R. J. Frankle, 'The formulation of the Declaration of Rights', *H.J.*, XVII (1974), pp. 266–7.
11. This report is printed in Henry Horwitz, *Parliament, Policy and Politics in the Reign of William III* (1977), pp. 367–8.
12. Quoted in E. A. Reitan, 'From revenue to civil list, 1689–1702: the Revolution Settlement and the "mixed and balanced" constitution', *H.J.*, XIII (1970), pp. 576–7; Clayton Roberts, 'Constitutional significance of the financial settlement of 1690', *H.H.*, XX (1977), p. 67.
13. See the contrasting views of Reitan and Roberts (see note 12).
14. I am grateful to Mr Graham Gibbs for pointing out to me that in the South Africa postal boycott case in January 1977 the Appeal Court judges ruled that the attorney general had discretionary powers to decide not to enforce the law.

15. Frankle, 'Formulation of the Declaration of Rights', p. 270.
16. The Bill of Rights is printed in W. C. Costin and J. F. Watson, eds, *The Law and Working of the Constitution: Documents 1660–1914* (2 vols, 2nd edn, 1961), I, pp. 67–76.
17. S. B. Baxter, *William III* (1966), p. 186.
18. William apparently made this speech on the advice of Richard Hampden, Horwitz, *Parliament, Policy and Politics*, p. 22.
19. Horwitz, *Parliament, Policy and Politics*, p. 25.
20. Quoted in R. C. Richardson, *The Debate on the English Revolution* (1977), p. 32.
21. Blair Worden, editorial introduction to *A Voyce from the Watch Tower*, Camden Soc., 4th ser., XXI (1978).
22. Horwitz, *Parliament, Policy and Politics*, p. 29.
23. The Tory 'blacklist' is printed in A. Browning, *Thomas Osborne Earl of Danby and Duke of Leeds* (3 vols, 1944–51), III, pp. 164–72.
24. G. C. Gibbs, 'The revolution in foreign policy', in Holmes, ed., *Britain after the Glorious Revolution*, pp. 59–79.
25. See J. R. Jones, *The Revolution of 1688 in England* (1972), pp. 267–80 for a good analysis of Louis's intentions.
26. M. A. Thomson, 'Louis XIV and William III, 1689–97', in R. Hatton and J. S. Bromley, eds, *William III and Louis XIV. Essays 1680–1720 by and for Mark A. Thomson* (Liverpool 1968), pp. 26–7.
27. Contrast D. Ogg, *England in the Reigns of James II and William III* (1955), pp. 374–5 and S. Baxter's more favourable view in *William III*, especially pp. 288–364.
28. Baxter, *ibid.*, pp. 292–3.
29. Thomson, 'Louis XIV and William III, 1689–97', pp. 27–8.
30. For the effects of the war on the constitution see pp. 410–18.
31. J. A. Downie, 'The commission of public accounts and the formation of the country party', *E.H.R.*, XCI (1976), pp. 33–51.
32. Quoted in Horwitz, *Parliament, Policy and Politics*, pp. 62–3.
33. Quoted in J. P. Kenyon, *The Stuarts* (Fontana paperback ed. 1966), p. 174.
34. Quoted in Horwitz, *Parliament, Politics and Policy*, p. 131.
35. Quoted in Kenyon, *Revolution Principles*, p. 43.
36. Plumb, *Growth of Political Stability*, p. 134.
37. Quoted in B. W. Hill, *The Growth of Parliamentary Parties 1689–1742* (1976), p. 68.
38. I. F. Burton, P. W. J. Riley, and E. Rowlands, *Political Parties in the Reigns of William III and Anne: The Evidence of Division Lists (Bulletin of the Institute of Historical Research*, Special Supplement, no. 7, 1968), p. 33.
39. Ellis, 'William III and the politicians', in Holmes, ed., *Britain After the Glorious Revolution*, p. 131.
40. Quoted in Horwitz, *Parliament, Politics and Policy*, p. 164.
41. M. A. Thomson, 'Self-determination and collective security as factors in English and French foreign policy, 1689–1718', in R. Hatton and J. S. Bromley, eds, *William III and Louis XIV*, p. 276.
42. Quoted in Horwitz, *Parliament, Politics and Policy*, p. 240.
43. It is doubtful if Harley ought at any stage in his career to be classified as a Tory, let alone as the Tories' leader. See below pp. 393–4. For a different view see Hill, *The Growth of Parliamentary Parties*, p. 85.
44. See L. G. Schwoerer, *'No Standing Armies!' The antiarmy ideology in seventeenth-century England* (Baltimore, 1974), especially ch. 8.

45. Kenyon, *Revolution Principles*, p. 54.
46. See G. C. Gibbs, 'The revolution in foreign policy', p. 71 for a suggested explanation.
47. Kenyon, *Revolution Principles*, p. 57.
48. Quoted in Horwitz, *Parliament, Politics and Policy*, p. 289.
49. Gibbs, 'The revolution in foreign policy', p. 73.
50. Quoted in Henry Horwitz, *Revolution, Politicks: The career of Daniel Finch, 2nd Earl of Nottingham 1647-1730* (1968), pp. 165-6.
51. Quoted in G. Holmes, *British Politics in the Age of Anne* (1967), p. 88.
52. G. V. Bennett, *The Tory Crisis in Church and State 1688-1730: the career of Francis Atterbury Bishop of Rochester* (1975), p. 10.
53. *Ibid.*, p. 13.
54. Quoted in G. R. Cragg, *From Puritanism to the Age of Reason* (1950), pp. 141, 148.
55. See pp. 419-23 for an analysis of opinion within the Church of England in this period.
56. Quoted in Kenyon, *Revolution Principles*, p. 72.

Chapter 13

The reign of Queen Anne, 1702–1714

Politics in the reign of Queen Anne

If Whigs and Tories were to cooperate, wrote Lord Stawell on 3 May 1711, 'I shall conclude the lamb will lye down with the leopard'. Changing the metaphor, Lord Halifax believed it would be like 'mixing Oyl and Vinegar (very truly)'.[1] Unlike the reign of William III there is no doubt about the continuing predominance of party rivalries during the reign of Queen Anne. The evidence of division lists, tellers' names in divisions recorded in the Commons' *Journals*, and the Proxy Book of peers, which lists the names of those colleagues who were entrusted with the proxy votes of absent peers, indicates that the vast majority of MPs from 1702 to 1714 followed a consistent Whig or Tory voting pattern. Nor did most MPs only follow Whig or Tory party lines on major issues of principle, but on minor tactical issues as well – on the choice of speaker and the amendment to a South Sea Company Bill, as well as on the future of the Church. Moreover, party rivalry extended beyond parliament. To a certain extent smart London society polarized into separate Whig and Tory social circles. For the upper élite the Whig Kit-Cat Club and the Tory Society of Brothers became mutually exclusive dining and drinking clubs. Less grand and more popular, many of the coffee and chocolate houses, which proliferated in London at the turn of the century, developed a reputation either as Whig or Tory establishments, the Whigs frequenting the Cocoa Tree in Pall Mall and the St James's Coffee House, the Tories Ouzinda's Chocolate House in St James's Street and the Smyrna in Pall Mall. This political apartheid was sometimes carried to comically absurd limits: in 1713 the earl of Sunderland, arriving at the house of his Whig colleague, Lord Halifax, for a dinner party went home when he realized that Robert Harley (now earl of Oxford), who was by now more closely identified with the Tory party than ever before, was also invited.[2]

Not surprisingly many of the increasing number of newspapers committed themselves to one of the two major political groups. Whig newspapers, like John Tutchin's *Observator* and *The Post Man*, and Tory papers, like *The Post Boy*, *Rehearsal*, and the more sophisticated *Examiner* for which Jonathan Swift wrote in 1710–11, were well versed in the techniques of party propaganda. Some of the political journalism of the day had a literary polish – Addison, Steele, and Defoe, as well as Swift, contributed regularly to newspapers and journals – but its satire could be scurrilous as well as subtle, sometimes provoking a violent reaction. John Tutchin was beaten up at least twice by a Tory mob, and in September 1707 he died after being viciously attacked in the street.[3] A few newspapers wrote only for a London audience; the best example is *The Daily Courant*, the first daily newspaper in Britain, which began publication on 11 March 1702. Many, however, circulated widely in the provinces. It was a manuscript newsletter, produced by an army of clerks under the direction of John Dyer, that was read most avidly both by metropolitan and provincial Tory squires and parsons. It is 'very common in these northern parts', wrote William Bowes from Durham in May 1705.[4] By 1712 an estimated 67,000 copies of all newspapers were sold each week, in addition to an unknown number that were given away. The size of the readership is difficult to calculate, because it is not known how many people read each individual newspaper, but if one assumes that every newspaper circulated among ten people the conclusion is that by the end of Anne's reign newspapers were read by nearly three times the number of electors.[5] Moreover, like the 1640s, the two decades after the lapse of the Licensing Act in 1695 were a golden age for printed material of all kinds published for a wide audience. The vast numbers of printed sermons, pamphlets, and ballads on political issues which were published in the early 1700s, in addition to newspapers and weekly journals, helped to carry party divisions beyond Westminster and London into provincial society and politics.

It is very difficult to discover how far ordinary people were affected by the 'rage of party' in the reign of Queen Anne. But there is little doubt that from 1701 to 1715 its impact on the traditional rulers of country society was very great. As in the early 1640s and during the exclusion crisis the unity of vested interests which bound the landowning classes together was shattered by ideological divisions. In the sixteenth and seventeenth centuries competition for places in the lieutenancy, on commissions of the peace and for lesser local government offices, was always intense. But now a political element was injected into this competition, as well as considerations of patronage and social prestige. Both political parties, as will be seen, aimed to use their influence over the central government to purge the lieutenancy and magistracy of their opponents. The consequent division in county society can be most clearly seen at election times. In most counties and boroughs, elections were fought on party lines: the 'Church' or 'Tory interest' *versus* the 'Whig interest'. If anything this kind of grass-roots party competition intensified during the early 1700s as election followed election; there were seven general elections between 1701 and 1715. In many counties the role of election manager was filled by powerful landed magnates, like the Whig Lord Wharton, whose sphere of influence extended from Wiltshire through Buckinghamshire and

Oxfordshire to Yorkshire and Cumberland and Westmorland, or Sir Edward Seymour, who helped to maintain the Tory dominance in the south-west. In many boroughs, where there was a longer, if intermittent, history of party organization which went back to the exclusion crisis, it is hardly an exaggeration to talk in terms of the development of party caucuses which endeavoured to maintain their supporters in a state of readiness for parliamentary elections. It is clear that at the local constituency level the organization of parties was much more sophisticated than at Westminster. Many of the signs of party politics similar to historians of the late nineteenth and twentieth centuries can be seen, including party agents, party propaganda literature, canvassing. Even party symbols appeared in various forms. In 1710 (for reasons which will become apparent) the portrait of Dr Henry Sacheverell was a popular Tory emblem, displayed on banners at party meetings and the hustings. This caused an enterprising entrepreneur to manufacture chamberpots with this Tory device inside on the bottom, without doubt to sell to anti-Sacheverell Whigs.[6] The serious point, of course, behind all this party swagger is that it presupposes that there was an electorate, which was not only growing in numbers, but which was open to the influence of party propaganda, whether serious or frivolous, and which could not be depended on to follow meekly and unthinkingly the lead given by its social superiors.

If the existence of political parties in the reign of Queen Anne is not in doubt, the historian of this period must nevertheless beware of taking much of contemporary party propaganda at its face value. As in more recent times, political propaganda created party 'images' that were mere caricatures of the real political parties. The early eighteenth century produced its equivalent of the modern stereotypes of the cloth-capped, working-class Labour party worker and the tweed-suited, floral-hatted, middle-class Conservative party stalwart. The typical Tory was seen as someone closely identified with the 'landed interest' and with the Church of England, who bemoaned his falling rental income and his excessive land tax demands, and who was therefore critical of England's involvement in expensive continental wars. The 'average' Tory was also an xenophobic English nationalist, with a dislike of all foreigners including the Hanoverians. So the Tory image included lingering loyalty to the Pretender and flirtation with Jacobitism. The typical Whig image created by contemporary propaganda, on the other hand, was identified with the 'monied interest', with City businessmen and merchants who were profiting from the revolution in public finance brought about by the war. The Bank of England became in Tory eyes the hated symbol of sharing Whig profits made from investment in government stock, war supplies, and joint stock companies. So the 'average' Whig was as fully committed to the continental war as he was to the Hanoverians and to the cause of Protestant dissent. As will be seen, these party images contain a great deal of truth; but, like their modern counterparts, they see caricatures that obscure important features of contemporary politics.

First, there were no clearcut religious and social-economic divisions between Whigs and Tories during the reign of Queen Anne. Although Whigs were more willing than Tories to allow concessions to Protestant dissenters, the vast majority of MPs of both parties were Anglicans. Similarly the 'landed interest *versus* monied interest' picture is a reflection only of the hatred and envy felt by many Tories of those City financiers whose enhanced power and profits had been stimulated by the war. Not all Tories were landowners, nor all Whigs businessmen. Landowning Whigs were as common as Anglican Whigs; otherwise it would be difficult to substantiate an hypothesis of a Whig–Tory split within the upper reaches of landed society. Nor is it difficult to find Tories who had connections with City finance and trade. Even the Bank of England had Tory directors. To assume that the interests of the landowning and mercantile classes were completely separate is to ignore the fact that for landowners in the late seventeenth and early eighteenth centuries, as for their predecessors a century earlier, there was no significant barrier of social prejudice preventing them from extensive entrepreneurial activities outside their estates.

Secondly, it would be wrong to draw the conclusion from contemporary party propaganda that the political nation was divided into two numerically equal groups. Although in Anne's reign the number of uncommitted, independent MPs was probably smaller than at any other time during the seventeenth and eighteenth centuries, the prevailing opinion whether at Westminster or in the constituencies was Tory not Whig. This is reflected in the parliamentary history of Anne's reign. Although the Whigs maintained a stronghold in the House of Lords, never (apart from a brief period after the 1708 general election) did they represent majority opinion in the House of Commons. As in William's reign, the Whigs secured support from the crown because of their commitment to the war, but it was temporary. The Whigs' overwhelming defeat at the general election of 1710 emphasized that the Tories were much more representative than the Whigs of the views of the rulers of provincial England. Tory ideology had deep roots in rich historical soil. The Tory alliance with the Anglican Church had been secured by the traumatic events of the English Revolution, which for many had smeared dissent irrevocably with republicanism. Arguably the Tory attitude to expensive wars and continental entanglements had even longer historical roots, stretching back beyond the Anglo–Dutch wars in the later seventeenth century to Buckingham's and Charles I's wars in the 1620s, and perhaps even to the Elizabethan wars in the 1580s and 1590s. For propertied country gentlemen these European wars had driven home a clear, unpalatable lesson: that war necessitated, not only high taxation, but a large extension of the tentacles of central government into their own local spheres of influence. This was one threat which was guaranteed to cause the provincial rulers of country society to join hands to resist. In this sense the Tory party of Queen Anne's reign was the inheritor of the 'country' tradition of the seventeenth century, and it attempted (only partially successfully) to prevent a massive increase in the fiscal and executive powers wielded by the later Stuart state. Moreover, not only did the Tories fail to establish completely their ideology of provincial autonomy, but on the death of Queen Anne they disappeared for generations as an effective political force. It will be a major aim of the following section to find an explanation for the stark contrast between, on the one hand, the apparently strong position of the Tory party during Anne's reign and, on the other hand, its practical ineffectiveness before 1714 and its rapid collapse thereafter.

Finally, the ballyhoo created by the parties in the early 1700s must not be allowed to hide the fact that an important minority of politicians did succeed in resisting the appeals of either party. This is true especially of Godolphin and Harley, and, to a more qualified extent, of Marlborough. They were queen's men, her 'managers' as contemporaries described them, not party politicians. All three had close personal ties with Queen Anne: Marlborough and Godolphin through Sarah Churchill, and Harley because of Abigail Masham's friendship with the queen. But, of more importance than the influence of these women at court in binding Godolphin, Marlborough, and Harley to the queen was their common hatred of party politics. All three men were forced during Anne's reign to ally closely with Whig or Tory politicians, Marlborough and Godolphin from 1705 to 1710 with the Whigs, and Harley from 1710 to 1714 with the Tories, but they did so only after they had found it impossible to carry on the Queen's government without reference to party. Even then neither Godolphin, Marlborough nor Harley allowed themselves to be identified fully with the ideology of either Whig or Tory party. In this they were not alone in English politics. Some MPs continued to resist the appeal of party propaganda and to remain loyal to what they considered to be a national interest that was above narrow party advantage. During the reign of Queen Anne party rivalries predominated in English politics, but the pattern of politics is inexplicable without reference also to the continuing personal influence of the monarch and to the role of the queen's managers and their supporters.

The failure of the 'managers', 1702–1708

Queen Anne and the 'managers'

It is a measure of the continuity in seventeenth-century life and institutions that the political world at the beginning of the eighteenth century, as it had done at the beginning of the seventeenth, revolved round the monarch. Queen Anne, like her predecessors, ruled as well as reigned. As has been seen, in certain important respects the powers of the monarchy had been curtailed largely under the pressure of wartime conditions, but these changes had not removed the crown from the centre point of politics and government. Therefore, in order to understand the political history of Anne's reign one ought to make an effort to assess what kind of woman the new queen was. Anne's personality and even her intimate personal relationships are the concern, not only of romantic novelists and playwrights, but of the historian. They had an important impact on the course of politics during her reign.

When Anne came to the throne she was thirty-seven. Since her marriage to Prince George of Denmark in 1683 she had been pregnant annually. As a result she had had twelve miscarriages and six babies, which had all died before she became queen. The psychological effects of such a terrifying maternal history were *perhaps* tempered by the normality of the pattern of regular child-bearing suffered by seventeenth-century women and contemporary high infant mortality. (There can, of course, be no certainty that the frequency with which babies died made infant mortality easier to bear than nowadays.) Certainly, physically it had made Anne an ill and prematurely old woman by the time she became queen. She was also fat and continually plagued by gout and other circulatory complaints, and consequently she could not walk far unaided. All this, hardly surprisingly, limited her ability and effectiveness as ruler of the country, perhaps even more so than her reputed limited intellectual powers. Her physical deficiencies are easier to assess than her mental limitations; both inevitably led her to rely more than she might otherwise have done on her advisers and her friends.

The famous friendship of Anne and Sarah Churchill was intense, intimate, and private, with its own language; Anne called Sarah and her husband John Churchill earl (later duke) of Marlborough, 'Mr and Mrs Freeman', the queen and Prince George were 'Mr and Mrs Morley'. G. M. Trevelyan explained the passion that underlay the friendship by the contrasting temperaments of the two women: it was 'rooted in genuine human affection. . . . Anne's mind was slow as a lowland river, Sarah's swift as a mountain torrent'.[7] Historians living in an age more influenced by the writings of Freud look for a more explicitly sexual element in the relationship, akin to that between James I and Carr and Villiers, and William III and Portland and Albemarle. Whatever its roots and its importance in Anne's private life, the public effects of Sarah's friendship with the queen were to facilitate Marlborough's promotion to captain-general of the English army, and to help Marlborough and Sidney, Lord Godolphin (whose son married Marlborough's eldest daughter) maintain the most powerful position in England under the queen during the first half of Anne's reign. That it was far from being the only or major explanation can be seen by the fact that Marlborough's and Godolphin's political power survived the breakdown of Sarah and Anne's friendship in 1707. Yet the two men clearly recognized that it was important to their career prospects, as they signified by their hatred of Abigail Hill, Lady Masham, who replaced Sarah as Anne's closest confidante. The result of Sarah and Anne's petty and bitchy quarrel was to allow Abigail Hill, the cousin of Robert Harley, to become the daily companion of the most powerful person in the country. Undoubtedly later Whig historians exaggerated the dominating influence of Abigail over the queen, but it is undeniable that she did act as Harley's spokesman at court and helped her cousin's political career. The importance of bedchamber politics in Anne's reign can be overestimated, but it ought not to be discounted altogether. This is most forcibly illustrated by the blighted careers of those politicians whom Anne personally disliked, whether Tory or Whig. Her Hyde uncles, Rochester and Clarendon, were never accepted as part of her intimate circle of friends, and, though Rochester was appointed lord lieutenant of Ireland soon after his accession, Anne had no compunction in forcing his resignation within a few months. The most outstanding effect on a Whig politician of the queen's disfavour is that of Lord Wharton. Anne hated and distrusted all the 'five tyrannizing lords' of the Whig Junto, but of these she abhorred Wharton most of all. It is difficult to know to what extent Wharton deserved his outrageous anticlerical and sexually permissive reputation. It was widely believed that in 1681, as Danby alleged in the House of Lords years later, Wharton 'had pissed against a Communion table [and] done his other occasions in a pulpit' in Barrington parish church in Somerset.[8] What is certain is that Wharton made no secret of his atheist views. That alone, apart from his sexual adventures, was enough to ensure that he found no personal favour with a moral and devoutly Anglican queen, and also explains Anne's political antipathy to Wharton and his Junto colleagues.

Portraying the new queen as a weak, ill woman, reliant on friends and advisers, one is in danger of assuming that Anne was a pawn in a male political world. However, though not by any means an Elizabeth I, Anne could stand up for herself in a man's world. Significantly, her husband, Prince George of Denmark, remained as subservient to her as had Queen Mary to William III. Perhaps this is not surprising: historians have had little good to say about Prince George's abilities – G. M. Trevelyan called him 'a kindly, negligible mortal', while, more recently, to Professor G. Holmes he was 'boneheaded'.[9] Anne, however, could subdue more domineering and able men than George; even Godolphin and Harley when at the peak of their political influence could never take Anne for granted. She could be as independent to the point of stubbornness, and as mean and petty as could Elizabeth I. The heartless ways in which she dismissed Godolphin and Marlborough after many faithful years in her service indicate the calculating, iron quality in Anne's make-up. Her ill-health did give royal ministers more scope to assume control over details of policies than they were allowed by William III, but neither the cabinet council nor her ministers ever took major policy decisions without Anne's consent. Given her physical condition her attention to the details of administration and her attendance at major meetings of the cabinet council and important debates in the House of Lords is remarkable. Without doubt the queen was the most important political character of the reign.

Anne was just as determined as her predecessor to maintain the independence of the crown and to stave off any more incursions into the royal prerogative. She was equally determined to appoint her ministers without reference to the demands of political parties. 'All I desire', she wrote to Godolphin in 1706,

is my liberty in encouraging and employing all those that concur faithfully in my service, whether they are called Whigs or Tories, not to be tied to one or the other. For if I should be so unfortunate as to fall into the hands of either, I shall not imagine myself, though I have the name of Queen, to be in reality but their slave, which, as it will be my personal ruin, so it will be the destroying of all government. For instead of putting an end to faction it will lay a lasting foundation of it.[10]

These were sentiments wholeheartedly shared by the three men who became Anne's closest political advisers during her reign, Godolphin, Marlborough, and Harley. From 1702 until 1710 Godolphin as lord treasurer and Marlborough as captain-general were her chief ministers, the 'duumvirs'. Of the two Godolphin was the more influential, not because he was more politically skilful (which is doubtful), but largely because Marlborough was frequently absent abroad on military campaigns. It was still as true as in the reign of Elizabeth I that the cardinal principle of political success was constant presence at court. Until 1710 Godolphin's predominant position among the queen's ministers was more secure and unchallenged than any royal minister since the Restoration, and perhaps only equalled by Robert Cecil and the duke of Buckingham in the earlier seventeenth century. In that sense he was the 'prime minister'. In the early years of the reign Godolphin's and Marlborough's ally in the House of Commons was Robert Harley, as speaker of the House from 1702 and then as secretary of state from 1704. As yet, however, Harley hardly played as important a part in the government as implied by those who described the three ministers as the 'triumvirate'. Indeed from 1705 Harley began to drift away from the other two ministers until early in 1708 he resigned as secretary of state. Only in 1710 did he succeed to Godolphin's position as unrivalled 'prime minister' of the crown. Neither Godolphin from 1702 to 1710 nor Harley from 1710 to 1714, however, held anything like the position analagous to a modern prime minister; neither was the leader of the majority party in the House of Commons; their principal power base was instead the royal closet.[11]

Unfortunately Godolphin lacked a politician's thick-skin, which made him sensitive to criticism, especially that of High Church clerics. After the general election of 1705 Archbishop Sharp of York found Godolphin 'in great concern and very near weeping' after reading an attack on him in a pamphlet by James Drake, *The Memorial of the Church of England.*[12] Godolphin's chief merits in Anne's eyes were his administrative ability and his financial expertise. His career in public finance was long and distinguished. Much of Marlborough's success in the war against France was based on the work of Godolphin at the treasury, ably assisted by Henry Boyle as chancellor of the exchequer. Both Godolphin and Marlborough supported Anne at her accession in her resolve not to become the captive of any party and to concentrate on the prosecution of the war. It is true that Anne inclined to the Tories on her accession. The hated Whig Junto lords were stripped of their offices; Wharton even lost the lord-lieutenancy of Buckinghamshire. The principal High Tory leaders replaced the Whigs in key offices: Nottingham as secretary of state, Rochester as lord-lieutenant of Ireland, Seymour as comptroller of the household and Jersey as lord chamberlain. During the first general election of her reign in July 1702 the electorate followed the royal lead as usual and voted a Tory majority of about 133 in the House of Commons. Yet significantly the non-party Godolphin was victorious in his tussle with Rochester for the lord-treasurership in the first weeks of the reign. Clearly the appointment of High Tory ministers did not signify a surrender to single party government. What was intended was an alliance with the Tories, but with the latter very definitely as the junior partners.

Yet in the first phase of the new reign from 1702 to 1708 Anne, Marlborough and Godolphin were forced to abandon their ideal of non-party rule: the queen and her 'managers' surrendered surprisingly, given their Tory associations in 1702, to the Whigs. Within a very short space of time the High Tory ministers were forced to resign: Rochester in February 1703 and Seymour, Jersey, and Nottingham in the spring of 1704. Godolphin was the first to realize the inevitability and the necessity of the appointment of Whig ministers for the sake of effective government and he began to press for this from 1705. Marlborough was converted to the same view slightly later, but it was not until 1708 that Anne's resistance, ably supported by Harley, to party rule by the Whigs was overcome and she allowed the Junto lords to be appointed to important offices. Why were the queen and her managers from 1702 to 1708 driven, reluctantly and temporarily, to abandon their earnest attachment to non-party rule, and why did they turn to the Whigs and not to the Tories? The answer will be found in the following sections on the Church, the war, the succession, and the Union with Scotland. On these issues the English political world was deeply split into Whig and Tory camps. It was not very long before Anne and her managers realized that the Tory point of view on all these issues did not correspond with what they considered to be the national interest. To Anne's discomfiture the hated, obnoxious Junto Whigs, not the Tories, came to be seen to be the patriots.

The Church: occasional conformity

It hardly seemed likely at the beginning of the reign that Tory efforts to protect the Church of England would be a major reason why the new Anglican queen and her principal ministers would lose patience with Tory politicians. Most High Churchmen saw Anne's accession as the cause for a great deal of rejoicing. They hoped that the Church of England under an English, Anglican, Stuart princess would receive the support and protection of the crown against the growing tide of dissent and irreligion, which they felt it had not had under a foreign, Calvinist king. As a result the High Church revival which had been gathering pace in the last years of William III's reign carried forward into the new reign with increased impetus. And Anne appeared in the early months of her reign to be willing to fill the role the High Tories expected of her. She appointed leading high Tories as her ministers, and she allowed Secretary of State Nottingham and Lord Keeper Sir Nathan Wright to purge Whigs from the central and local administration. In her speech at the end of the old parliament on 25 May 1702 she inserted a passage suggested by Nottingham, which further fuelled Anglican aspirations. Her 'own principles,' she said, 'must always keep her entirely firm to the interests of the Church of England and would incline her to countenance those who had the truest zeal to support it.'[13] To the delight of Anglicans Anne even revived the practice of touching to heal the skin disease, scrofula, 'the Queen's evil', which had lapsed under William III. With a Tory majority being secured in the July general election, and Atterbury putting the finishing touches to his plans for an all-out attack on 'moderate' bishops, all seemed ripe for a massive High Church assault when parliament and Convocation met in the winter of 1702–3.

As might be expected this High Church offensive focused on the issue of occasional conformity, whereby dissenters attended an Anglican church to qualify for public office and so evade the Test and Corporation Acts. To Anglicans occasional conformity epitomized their fears about the apparent growth of dissent and its threat to the church. It was denounced as 'a religious piece of hypocrisy as even no heathen government would have endured', 'the vizor mask of cozenage, knavery and hypocrisy; it is the spiritual tool to serve the turn of all wicked designs, mere party cant and fanatical jargon, the very sound whereof should be a warning piece to alarm every honest man to stand upon his guard, and look about him'.[14] These were the typically forthright and extravagant views of a Fellow of Magdalen College, Oxford, Dr Henry Sacheverell, who in the early years of Anne's reign began to replace Atterbury as the major mouthpiece of the High Church movement. As original thinkers there is really no comparison between Atterbury and Sacheverell. Prolific though he was as a writer and preacher there is very little evidence that Sacheverell had any profound intellectual ability. His gifts lay in the propounding of ideas not in their formulation; he was the most prominent of a crop of brilliant, if detestable, Anglican preachers produced by Oxford University in the early eighteenth century. Like most self-appointed spokesmen of 'the silent majority' Sacheverell not only voiced the fears of many, but also in the process exaggerated them and so inflamed public opinion, sometimes to the point of violence. Yet whatever one thinks of his methods they were certainly effective. His first major sermon was preached at Oxford in June 1702 and printed as *The Political Union: A Discourse Showing the Dependence of Government on Religion*. Its contents were commonplace Tory-Anglican pulpit propaganda, proclaiming the indivisibility of Church and state and the vile nature of dissenters. But its language was emotive and highly charged. 'Presbytery and republicanism go hand in hand', thundered Sacheverell. The dissenters are the enemies 'against whom every man that wishes (the Church's) welfare ought to hang out the bloody flag and banner of defiance'.[15] With this battle-cry backwoods Tory Cavaliers came to parliament in October 1702 determined to make occasional conformity the major issue of the session. If they needed any further prompting this was provided early in the new session when the Commons investigated a disputed election at Wilton in Wiltshire, revealing that the Whig mayor of Wilton had packed his corporation with nonconformist burgesses to secure the election of two Whig MPs. On 4 November William Bromley and Arthur Annesley, the MPs for the two universities, introduced in the Commons the first punitive Occasional Conformity Bill. Anyone who qualified for office by receiving the Anglican sacrament and then attended a dissenter meeting was to be fined £100 on conviction and £5 for each subsequent day he continued in office. The Tory campaign to secure a ban on occasional conformity was maintained at a high pitch for three parliamentary sessions from November 1702 to December 1704. Why, despite the popular support it received in the country, in the Commons and from the pulpits, did it fail?

Firstly, of course, the Whigs voted consistently against a measure which would have effectively deprived many of their supporters of the vote and of public office. Outvoted the Whigs might be in the Commons, but in the Upper House they were stronger, and there all three Occasional Conformity Bills were killed in January 1703, December 1703, and December 1704. However, Whig strength in the House of Lords does not by itself explain the defeat of the High Church cause. The Whigs in fact secured the powerful support of the queen's managers, of the majority of the bishops, and eventually of the queen herself. As far as Marlborough and Godolphin are concerned it seems clear that their opposition to the Occasional Conformity Bill was rooted in the practical consideration that wartime was not a suitable period for the airing of controversial legislation. Like Pym and the middle group in the early 1640s, Marlborough and Godolphin were intent on defusing a potentially divisive political issue and concentrating on financing and organizing the war effort. As yet, however, the queen was in favour of an Occasional Conformity Bill, and therefore the opposition of the 'duumvirs' had to be covert. Both ministers voted for the measure in the House of Lords, but they allowed Robert Harley to use all his considerable political talents against it. This must have been a task which Speaker Harley found congenial. Although he had long since cut his close ties with his family's dissenting–Puritan–Whig background, he had no sympathy with the high Tory extremists. In addition, Harley was a master of the art of political wheelerdealing and intrigue.

On 21 October 1702 Harley had his first secret meeting with Atterbury, which was followed by other clandestine conversations with other high Tories, including one in a rowing boat in the middle of the Thames with Dean George Hooper of Canterbury. Sometimes one feels that Harley revelled in secrecy for its own sake. At these meetings Atterbury got the impression that Harley was promising the backing of the queen and Godolphin for a complete programme of High Church reforms. Meanwhile, however, in the House of Lords amendments were added to the Commons' version of the Occasional Conformity Bill which limited its scope only to state officers not municipal officials. The mangled Bill was subsequently defeated. Not surprisingly Atterbury was angry at Harley's trickery, and spurned his overtures in the next session in the winter of 1703. Instead Harley was forced to rely on a press campaign against the High Church and in this to use the talents of Daniel Defoe, who had published a witty parody of High Church propaganda, *The Shortest Way with Dissenters*, for which he was imprisoned in Newgate. Here Harley visited him and bought Defoe's pen for the service of the government. In December 1703, however, the second Occasional Conformity Bill was defeated in the House of Lords by only twelve votes. Therefore Harley, especially after he became secretary of state in May 1704, when he replaced Nottingham (who resigned because of the failure of the Occasional Conformity legislation) renewed his attempt to get Atterbury's support. This time he was successful. By securing the Deanery of Carlisle for Atterbury and holding out the prospect of richer ecclesiastical prizes, Harley effectively undermined Atterbury's influence with the High Church rank and file.

Undoubtedly the Whig numerical supremacy in the House of Lords and the political machinations of Harley and his political superiors were largely responsible for the collapse of the anti-Occasional Conformity cause early in Anne's reign. Yet it is difficult to avoid the conclusion that the High Church leaders themselves contributed to their own defeat. Especially after the overthrow of the first two Bills and the loss of office by their two principal leaders, Rochester and Nottingham, the high Tories adopted extremist tactics which lost them the support of many moderate Tories and of the queen. Soon after the start of the 1704–5 parliamentary session a meeting of 150 Tories at the Fountain Tavern in the Strand, at the prompting of Bromley and Nottingham (though perhaps not of Rochester), adopted the irresponsible tactic of agreeing to tack an occasional conformity clause on to the Land Tax Bill for the coming year. In effect, they proclaimed that they were willing to refuse to grant money for the war if their demands regarding the Church were not met. This blatant disregard of the national interest in the pursuit of party political considerations was too much even for many Tories. Significantly Henry St John turned against the high Tories and from this date began his turbulent and important political relationship with Robert Harley. Queen Anne, too, now turned against the high Tory leaders. It is tempting to believe that it was not just the constitutional radicalism of the proposed 'tack' that persuaded her to take this course. Despite the impression she made in the early months of her reign, Anne was not a High Church bigot from the same mould as Bromley and Seymour, who harked back nostalgically to the old union of Church and divinely appointed monarchy. Although a devout Anglican and anxious to further the interests of the Church of England, the new queen was astute enough to realize that the monarchy after the Glorious Revolution could no longer claim to rule by divine right. In 1710 she irritably dismissed references in a loyal address from the City of London to the divinity of her crown. 'Having thought about it often,' she told the duke of Shrewsbury, 'she could by no means like it, and thought it unfit to be given to anybody that she wished it might be left out.' By the winter of 1704 she withdrew her support for the High Church cause. The war effort must come first. 'Our enemies have no encouragement left but what arises from their hopes of our divisions,' she told parliament at the opening of the new session. ''Tis therefore your concern not to give the least countenance to those hopes. I hope there will be no concentration among you but who shall most promote the public welfare.' [16] When the 'tack' was proposed in November 1704 the Tories split – 'tackers' and 'sneakers' were the labels coined by the newspapers – and the 'tack' was easily defeated. In the following month the third Occasional Conformity Bill was thrown out by the House of Lords.

By 1705 the High Church cause was in complete disarray, the high hopes of 1702 unfulfilled. In June the general election even produced Whig gains in the House of Commons (on one estimate net Whig gains of sixty).[17] Moreover, when in December Rochester moved in the Lords that the Church was in danger, he was comprehensively defeated, and a motion was passed that 'whoever goes about to suggest that the Church is in danger under Her Majesty's administration, is an enemy to the Queen, the Church and the Kingdom'. As Sacheverell was to show in 1710, High Church sentiment was still there to be exploited. But for the time being it was a spent political force. To the dismay of the Whig Junto, however, the defeat of the High Church Tories brought them little nearer their ultimate political prize. By 1705 Godolphin and Marlborough supported the Junto's clamourings for office, but Anne held out stubbornly. It was only after much reluctance that she allowed the appointment of the Whig William earl of Cowper as lord keeper of the great seal in October 1705 and of Sunderland as secretary of state in December 1706. In the summer of 1707 she delivered a slap to the face of the Junto by ignoring their demands for the appointment of two Whig divines to vacant bishoprics, Exeter and Chester, and instead offered them to Offspring Blackall and Sir William Dawes, Tory nominees of Archbishop Sharp.[18] The importance of the bishoprics crisis of 1707 is its indication of Anne's resistance to Whig rule. Yet the pressure from the Whigs for office was growing; it was not just on the Church issue that they were proving to be more useful to the queen and her ministers than the Tories.

The war and the succession

If the Tory attitude to the Church played a part in driving the court and the royal managers unwillingly into the arms of the Whigs in the early part of the reign, so too did the reaction of many Tories to the war and to the prospect of Hanoverian succession to the throne. Anne's war against Louis XIV was partly to prevent French domination of Spanish Mediterranean and American trade; it was at least as strongly a war to safeguard the Protestant succession in England. The dramatic way in which English public opinion had swung sharply in favour of war against Louis XIV in 1701 has already been seen. Despite Dutch apprehensions, Anne's accession made no difference to England's commitment to the Grand Alliance concluded by William III in August 1701. As far as Anne was concerned the lesson taught by her predecessor had been well learned: that English interests were inextricably involved in maintaining the balance of power in Europe against French domination. Anne's first act as queen was to declare to her privy council that her two principal aims were the reduction of the power of France and the maintenance of the Protestant succession. On the same day parliament voted addresses calling for a vigorous prosecution of the war. This appearance of national unity on the war and the succession, however, was misleading. Soon a rift in English political life, familiar to students of William's reign, reappeared. The Whigs had no doubts about the desirability of a Protestant succession; they were therefore strongly and consistently in favour of the war. The Tories, on the other hand, as their attitude to the Regency Bill in 1705–6 illustrated, were much less firmly committed to the Protestant succession and therefore easily lost their early enthusiasm for the war. Consequently, as on the Church issue, Anne and her ministers discovered that the Whig view of the war and the succession was more attractive than that of the Tories.

During the first half of the reign the court faced unpalatable Tory opposition to its war policy. At first this manifested itself in Tory criticism of the ministry's strategic concentration on full-scale war in the Netherlands. The debate on war strategy began even before the formal declaration of war on 4 May 1702. It is clear from accounts that survive of discussions in the cabinet and privy council on 1 and 2 May that Rochester and Marlborough were engaged in a furious quarrel, partly over the lord treasurership, which Rochester, not without good reason given his financial experience in Charles II's and James II's reigns, felt ought to be his and not Godolphin's. However, the two men were also at odds over the type of war England should be involved in. Against Marlborough's project of a full-scale military expeditionary force to the Low Countries Rochester developed all the arguments he had used in the 1690s against William III's similar war strategy: the stupidity of attacking the enemy at his strongest points in the fortress towns of the Low Countries, and the vast expense of continental warfare which was considered to be of little concern to this country. Instead Rochester tried to persuade his ministerial colleagues to adopt the 'blue-water' war strategy so popular in Tory country houses and with Tory backbench MPs. England, Rochester proposed, should act only as an auxiliary in the continental war and should concentrate her war effort against Spain's and France's colonies and shipping. As Rochester saw it the 'blue-water' war strategy had at least three advantages over a continental strategy: it would hit France and Spain at the weakest places in their defences; a maritime colonial war was much cheaper than pouring money into supplying armies in Europe; and English interests were much more clearly identifiable in the New World than on the continent of Europe.

That these were persuasive arguments to many MPs can be seen by the activities of the House of Commons in the first session of parliament in the winter of 1702–3. Instead of concentrating on the war some MPs tried to revive the impeachment of 1701 against the Junto, and St John and Bromley brought allegations of corruption in the commission of public accounts against Paymaster-General Ranelagh and Halifax. When it came to granting money for the war the Commons showed the strong feeling in favour of Rochester's 'blue-water' ideas by voting twice as much money for the navy as for the army, and early in January 1703 the Tories tacked an anti-Dutch amendment on to a vote to increase the number of troops in the Low Countries; the government was to 'insist upon it with the States General that there be an immediate stop of all ports, and all letters, bills . . . trade and commerce with France and Spain'.[19] But was the 'blue-water' strategy a sensible one? The first reason to think it was not is that English expenditure on the army in this period was only marginally more than on the navy.[20] Moreover, not only would a 'blue-water' strategy have been as expensive as a continental war, but also it was based on the false assumption that colonies and colonial trade were as important to France as they were to England. It seems clear that the only way that the France of Louis XIV could have been defeated was militarily in Europe. Perhaps for these reasons Rochester received less support from his fellow Tory leaders, Nottingham, Bromley, and Seymour, than he did from the Tory rank-and-file. He lost the cabinet tussle with Marlborough: Godolphin was appointed lord treasurer, England declared in favour of full scale military intervention in Europe, and Rochester resigned as lord-lieutenant of Ireland in February 1703.

In the early phase of Anne's war the strategy of England and the allies changed, but in a way envisaged by William III rather than by Rochester. Before his death William realized that the chances of success of a claimant to the Spanish throne would be vastly improved by the claimant's presence in Spain along with allied troops. In 1702 an allied expedition to Cadiz, though abortive, was mounted with the intention of forcing Cadiz to submit to the Viennese Habsburgs as rightful rulers of Spain. This strategy was confirmed by the Methuen Treaties with Portugal in 1703. Portugal broke with France, and the allies agreed to proclaim Archduke Charles as King of Spain and to send him to Spain with a large army. The limited war aims of 1701 – the partition of the Spanish Empire – were transformed into securing the kingdom of Spain for Archduke Charles. This was the policy of 'No Peace without Spain' which in the long run ensured that England would become a major Mediterranean power. More immediately it meant that the allies had committed themselves to a prolonged war south, as well as north, of the Pyrenees. The most notable feature of the War of the Spanish Succession is the contrast between Marlborough's and Eugene's victories north of the Pyrenees and the eventual failure of the allied forces in Spain.

At the outset the war in northern Europe was not particularly successful for the forces of the Grand Alliance. The old deadlocked pattern of William III's war of sieges, manoeuvres, and counter-manoeuvres round the fortress towns on the Meuse and the lower Rhine was resumed. It is true that in the first campaign of the war in the summer and autumn of 1702 Marlborough took all the major fortresses on the Meuse and lower Rhine except Bonn. But this threatened to be merely an episode in the familiar story of the capture and recapture of these towns by allied and French troops. Nor were the allies any more united in 1702 than they had been during William's war. Emperor Leopold was still distracted by domestic problems, a Hungarian rebellion, and the imminent prospect of invasion by the Turks. Moreover, in September 1702 Louis XIV persuaded the Elector of Bavaria to join the war against the allies. Yet perhaps by 1706 – certainly by 1708 – the French had been effectively defeated in Italy and in north and central Europe. How can one account for the allied victory north of the Pyrenees? Much of the explanation can be seen in the military campaign which culminated in the battle of Blenheim on 2 August 1704: a combination of the military genius of Marlborough and Prince Eugene of Savoy and the financial support they received from the English treasury. Like Cromwell, Marlborough's success as a soldier stemmed from the fact that he did not obey the rules of conventional contemporary warfare. His diplomatic and military advisers recommended that he keep his forces engaged in the Low Countries; not only was it considered impractical to move large armies quickly over long distances, but Marlborough faced strong opposition, especially from the Dutch, against an alternative military strategy. Early in 1703, for example, Marlborough determined on a full-scale invasion of France, but he was forced by Dutch and English opposition to abandon his plans and concentrate instead on dislodging the French from more fortress towns in the Netherlands and lower Rhine, which he did successfully, capturing Bonn, Huy, and Limbourg in the spring of 1703. When the French and Bavarians launched an offensive later in the year along the Danube, threatening to march on Vienna, Marlborough's plan to counter it could easily have suffered a similar fate. That it did not was partly due to Marlborough's daring military leadership. Under the cover of a limited campaign in the Moselle valley Marlborough marched his army to Koblenz, and then on his own initiative he began a rapid advance along the Rhine valley to Mainz and Heidelberg, and from there he led his army south-east across Germany to the Danube, linking up at Mundelsheim with the forces of Prince Eugene of Savoy and Prince Lewis of Baden. Their joint forces then captured the fortress of Schellenberg near Donauworth on the Danube on 21 June, and on 2 August comprehensively defeated the Franco-Bavarian army at the battle of Blenheim. The French general, Tallard, was captured and condemned to the qualified blessing of a life as prisoner of war in Nottingham. Military historians rightly concentrate on Marlborough's skill as a strategist and tactician. But it must not be forgotten that Marlborough's march deep into Europe with very long supply lines was not possible without massive financial support. A significant feature of the campaign, in fact, was that the allied troops were well supplied and paid: a tribute to the work of Lord Treasurer Godolphin and Chancellor of the Exchequer Boyle who improved on the financial machinery erected during William's war. 'England', wrote G. M. Trevelyan, 'beat France with the purse as much as with the sword.' However, Marlborough's military skill is not to be underrated. Blenheim was a crucial victory, but it did not win the war. France was still strong both in Italy and in the Netherlands and, with Marlborough's resurrected scheme for an allied invasion of France in 1705 blocked by the Dutch and Austrians, the war seemed doomed to revert to its deadlocked pattern of conflict in the Netherlands. In this context Marlborough's two major victories in the Low Countries – at Ramilles on 12 May 1706 and at Oudenarde on 11 July 1708 – were specially significant, and are in startling contrast to William III's dismal military record in the same theatre of war. Finally, in explaining the defeat of the French in Europe, it would be an unforgiveable example of blinkered Anglocentric history not to record the military contribution of Prince Eugene of Savoy. Even his latest biographer considers him the junior military partner of Marlborough, but his victory at Turin in September 1706 delivered Italy from French control.[21]

In the early stages of the war in Spain the allied forces also secured some major victories. The English fleets under Sir George Rooke and Sir Cloudesley Shovell, which had been sent to escort Archduke Charles to pursue his claim to be Charles III of Spain, captured Gibraltar on 23 July 1704, and on 13 August prevented the French Toulon fleet from retaking the base after a full-scale naval battle off Málaga. Moreover, the military invasion of Spain also began well. Charles and the English general, the earl of Peterborough, captured Barcelona on 3 October 1705, and subsequently many towns in eastern Spain, especially in Catalonia, rallied to support 'Charles III'. Just how much the allies owed these victories to their own military skill and how much to Catalan fervour against the hated Castilians is difficult to judge, but that Catalan nationalism was undoubtedly a major factor is illustrated by the fact that the allies were much more successful in eastern Spain than elsewhere. Allied forces under the earl of Galway invaded Spain from Portugal and on 27 June 1706 occupied Madrid, but they were not able to hold it for long and on 14 April 1707 they suffered a crushing defeat at the battle of Almanza. Just as Archduke Charles found himself unwittingly the leader of Catalan separatism, so Philip V became the focus of Castilian nationalism against the foreign invaders. Other defeats in Spain followed, including eventually the fall of Catalonia and its subjugation to Castilian Spain. Partly the explanation lies in the fact that the allied resources were dangerously overextended, in north-west Europe, in Italy, and in Spain. But perhaps of more importance is the fact that the allied cause in Spain was wrecked on the rock of Castilian nationalism.

With the war in Europe apparently won and the war in Spain going very badly it is not surprising that by the middle of the reign Tory disenchantment with England's involvement in a continental war increased. Certainly Tory country gentlemen joined, like everyone else, in the bouts of jingoistic fervour which greeted Marlborough's victories; Blenheim, it was said, 'being more for their 4*s* in the pound than ever yet they saw'. But sentiments like this were shortlived, and the crushing financial burden of the war, which was by now costing £4 million a year, especially the land tax of four shillings in the pound assessed on landed incomes, produced constant complaints and inspired a running parliamentary attack on the conduct of the war. By 1708 Whigs and Tories were moving further apart on the question of the war than ever before: it was now no longer differences over war strategy that divided the parties. Already by 1708 one can detect the beginning of the Tory desire for peace, which after 1708 became a major area of contention between the parties, as will be seen. Without much question the unresolved doubts about the Protestant Succession in the minds of many Tories contributed to their cooling enthusiasm for the war. In 1705–6 the debates on the Regency Bill forced Tories to confront this difficult problem again, and again it became clear that the attitude of many Tories to the major aim of the war, the maintenance of the Protestant Succession, was, at best, lukewarm.

Ironically given the way it rebounded against the Tories, the origin of the Regency Bill was a Tory party manoeuvre to discredit the Whigs. In November 1705 the major Tory party leaders, Nottingham, Rochester, Buckingham, Anglesey, and Jersey, put forward for debate in the House of Lords the proposition that Anne should invite the successor to the throne, Princess Sophia, to England, arguing that this was the only safeguard against a sudden Jacobite invasion. Although there was undoubtedly a need for provisions to be made for carrying on the government after Anne's death, since most of the initiators of this 'Hanover motion' (Nottingham alone excepted) were Jacobite sympathizers, their true aim must have been to put the Whigs in an impossible dilemma. If the Whigs were to support it, as they must have wanted to, they would alienate the queen, who was against the motion; if they opposed it, it would descredit them at the electoral court and among their own supporters. In order to avoid this embarrassing choice, the Junto leaders, especially Somers and Wharton, cleverly devised the Regency Bill, which laid down the form to be taken by the interim government which was to rule on Anne's death and before the arrival of the Hanoverian successor. There was to be a Regency Council of 'lords justices' consisting of seven principal officers of state and the nominees of Princess Sophia or her successor, and parliament was to meet immediately on Anne's death and to sit for six months. Since this was a measure of which Anne approved the Junto turned the tables on the Tories. In addition, the Junto determined to use the opportunity, not only to gain the queen's favour, but to repeal some of the limitations on the monarch's power established by the Act of Settlement in 1701, which were to come into effect on Anne's death. The clause which would have forced privy councillors to put their signatures to the device they gave the monarch was repealed. Moreover, despite a furious battle in which some 'whimsical' Whigs supported the Tories, the Junto succeeded in amending the place clause of 1701 so that MPs appointed to an old office could remain in the Commons if they were re-elected at by-elections. The most satisfying aspect of the Regency Bill for the Junto, though, was probably the open opposition to the main provisions of the Bill that came from many Tory MPs. The impression this left was that the Tories aimed, in the words of a contemporary, 'to destroy the succession'.[22]

All this by itself was enough to alienate the queen further from the Tories: it has been suggested that Nottingham's role in the affair permanently destroyed his chance of being reappointed to any office by Queen Anne.[23] However in the parliamentary session of 1707–8 the Tories compounded their offence in the queen's eyes by supporting openly for the first time an attack on the official war policy of 'No Peace without Spain'. On 19 December 1707 Somers carried a motion supporting the policy in the House of Lords, but in the Commons early in 1708 there was a sustained bombardment by the Tories on the conduct of the war in Spain. More than ever now Marlborough and Godolphin were driven to rely on Whig support. Anne continued her resistance to the Junto, but was finding it increasingly difficult to maintain it. Whig support for the royal policy regarding Scotland made it virtually impossible.

The union with Scotland

That the union of England and Scotland as one country, Great Britain, was accepted by both nations in 1707 is, on the face of it, very surprising. Whenever union had been mentioned in the previous century, whether by Englishmen or Scotsmen, there had been little support for it. As has been seen, James I's proposed scheme in 1606–7 to unite his two kingdoms was met with howls of derision in England. Like most military conquests the Cromwellian union of the 1650s was resented by the mass of the population in Scotland, and when the English Republic collapsed so too did the union. In the later seventeenth century at least three tentative proposals for union were raised, in 1667, 1670, and 1689, but they found little support. Indeed the racial antagonism and national animosity which had characterized the relations between England and Scotland during the Middle Ages appeared to have intensified during the seventeenth century. Englishmen do not appear to have changed the opinion of the Scots they had expressed in the debates on James I's plan for a union, that the Scots were a barbaric race of savages. Scots' hatred of the English exploded in 1637 into a nationalist revolt. It has been seen that the Anglo-Scots alliance made in September 1643 was rendered ineffective as a military force by mutual distrust and religious differences. The Solemn League and Covenant was no longer operative after the battle of Marston Moor in July 1644; it had collapsed altogether by 1646, and in 1648 and 1650 Scots' armies invaded England. In 1689 the attempts in the previous twenty years by Lauderdale and James II to impose autocratic rule from England provoked the Scots to assert their political and ecclesiastical independence from England. It is, therefore, an intriguing historical problem, as well as an important one, to try to explain, first, why the Act of Union came about in 1707, a century after the failure of James I's union project and only eighteen years after the Glorious Revolution; and secondly, why the Union survived, despite a recurrence of Anglo-Scottish mistrust and hatred after 1707. Like many of the questions asked in this book, it is easier to formulate than to answer. It has been frequently emphasized that there are no single 'correct' answers to most historical problems. This is certainly true of the reasons for the making and for the success of the Act of Union.

The events of 1689–90 in Scotland make the union with England seventeen or eighteen years later harder than ever to comprehend. Much more than in England do those events in Scotland deserve to be called a 'revolution'. In England William's royal authority was only slightly diminished; in Scotland he was forced to accept the demands of one group of politicians for Scottish ecclesiastical and constitutional independence. Some English historians have the unfortunate habit of referring to the inhabitants of Scotland by the blanket term 'the Scots'. Yet in 1689 the Scots were no more united in their attitude to King

James's downfall than they had been to events in England in the 1640s and 1650s. Whereas James had united the English against him, in Scotland he still had supporters, especially the Episcopalians and (of more importance) many Highland chiefs. A web of motives determined Highland antipathy to William III: hatred of lowland Scotland, Catholic sentiment, dislike of the Campbells who, in the person of Archibald Campbell tenth earl of Argyll, returned from exile on William's accession. William therefore had to rely, much more than in England, on one section, albeit the largest, of the Scottish political nation: the Presbyterian element, which was strongly entrenched in Lowland Scotland. Ominously for William, when the Scottish Convention met on 14 March 1689 it quickly became clear that Presbyterian opinion was highly organized. Presbyterian MPs began to organize their political tactics at pre-session meetings of what contemporaries called 'the Club' under the leadership of Sir James Montgomerie, who could count on the support of about 70 of the 125 Scottish MPs. Even historians of Scotland have been taken aback by the 'surprising degree of political sophistication which distinguished its (the Club's) aims, tactics and organization'.[24] The Club played a major part in the drafting of the Claim of Rights and the Articles of Grievances which the Scottish Convention sent south to be approved by William and Mary. These documents embodied much more sweeping demands than the English Declaration of Rights: the Act of Supremacy of 1669 was to be repealed, and episcopacy as well as the Lords of Articles, the royally appointed ministers who had controlled political affairs in Scotland before the Revolution, were to be abolished. Not surprisingly William resisted these extreme demands for an independent Scottish Presbyterian kirk and parliament, and in the first session of the Scottish Convention (March – August 1689) his commissioner, George earl of Melville blocked legislation designed to bring into effect the Club's programme. But events in 1689–90 indicated that William was not in a position to resist for long organized opposition in Scotland. He had come to England primarily to strengthen his armies in the war in Europe, not to divert troops to Scotland.

In the summer of 1689 a Highland uprising in support of King James emphasized just how reliant William was on Presbyterian support in Scotland. The clansmen won a notable victory at the battle of Killiecrankie on 27 July 1689 though their leader, John Graham of Claverhouse, Viscount Dundee, was killed. A month later the Highlanders were defeated at Dunkeld, and Fort William was founded as a means of trying to impose Lowland domination on the Highlands. Nothing could have made clearer the extent of William's dependence on Presbyterian support. Consequently, when the Scottish Convention reassembled on 15 April 1690 he soon accepted all the Club's political and religious demands: the Act of Supremacy of 1669 was repealed on 25 April, the Lords of the Articles and lay patronage in the Church were abolished on 8 May and 19 July respectively. Presbyterianism was re-established with a revived general assembly, and episcopalians were expelled from their livings. The Scottish Glorious Revolution established a kirk and a parliament in Scotland more independent than ever of England and of the crown.

Nor did the course of William III's reign appear to further the prospect of Anglo-Scottish union. On the contrary relations between the two countries deteriorated alarmingly, especially because of two incidents, the Glencoe Massacre and the establishment of the Company of Scotland. Perhaps the importance of the former in this respect has been exaggerated in the past. The Glencoe Massacre is perhaps more significant as an indication of Highland – Lowland hostility than as a source of Scottish hatred of the English. The massacre grew out of efforts to pacify the Highlands where Jacobite loyalty and anti-Campbell sentiment continued to be a major security threat. The king's adviser on Scottish affairs in London, Sir John Dalrymple of Stair,[25] initiated a scheme compelling all Highland chiefs to take an oath of allegiance to William by 1 January 1692. Although Alexander Macdonald of Glencoe took the oath only five days after the deadline, it was decided to punish him, and on 13 February MacDonald and nearly forty men, women, and children of his clan were slaughtered by the Campbell regiments from Fort William. The responsibility for the massacre has never been determined. Though William and Dalrymple authorized the massacre, it is probable that the information that MacDonald had taken the oath was deliberately withheld from them by the privy council and by MacDonald's enemies in Lowland Scotland. Dalrymple and his agent, John Campbell earl of Breadalbane, though, had no sympathy for or understanding of the Highlanders and saw MacDonald's reluctance to take the oath as a great opportunity to get rid of 'that set of thieves'. William, too, ensured that the affair contributed to rising tension between England and Scotland by his lenient treatment of those who had allowed the massacre to take place.

Much more important in producing friction between England and Scotland was the history of the Company of Scotland, which was established in 1695 to trade to Africa and the Indies and to found colonies in any part of those continents not under the sovereignty of a European ruler. Because it was founded with high hopes that it would contribute to Scotland's much-needed economic recovery, English opposition to the Company was resented especially deeply in Scotland. Though English mercantile opinion was not totally hostile – a large part of the Company's initial subscription came from London – the powerful East India Company immediately organized a campaign against this threat of Scottish competition. More seriously, from William's point of view, the Company of Scotland endangered his foreign policy, especially when the Company, frustrated by English opposition to its proposed trade to the East, adopted the scheme of a financial adventurer, William Patterson, to set up a colony on the Darien Isthmus in Central America, in the heart of the Spanish Empire. William took very seriously indeed the subsequent Spanish complaints at a time when he was anxious that Spain should be given no excuse for joining France in a war against England. He had no wish to begin a war with Spain in defence of a Scottish colony. He forbad English merchants from investing in the Company of Scotland and English colonists from supplying the Darien colony. He also persuaded merchants in Hamburg and Amsterdam against investing in the Company. Though the economic rationale behind the Darien colony was sound – the establishment of a trade entrepôt between the East and Europe – its failure was perhaps inevitable even without English opposition. The hostility of the Spanish Empire and of the central American climate had already proved too much for similar colonization schemes. Nevertheless it would have been difficult in the late 1690s to persuade any Scot that the collapse of the Darien scheme was not caused by anything other than English treachery.

The effect of all these events after 1689 on Scottish and on English opinion was noticeably different. In Scotland, coming as it did at a time of major economic crisis, when there had been five disastrous harvests of famine proportions from 1695 to 1699, when Scottish trade in Europe was disrupted by the effects of an English war, as well as by English navigation legislation which excluded Scotland from English colonial trade, the English attitude to the Darien scheme roused anti-English sentiment near to breaking point and encouraged open consideration of total political separation from England. In England, however, the effect of the growing hostility between the two countries was to convert at least one section of opinion, the crown and its ministers, to the idea of a closer union between England and Scotland. By the end of his reign William, who had long been in favour of the idea, persuaded Godolphin and Marlborough to support him in proposing in the English parliamentary sessions of 1699–1700 and 1702 a legislative union between England and Scotland. It is clear that it was just because Anglo–Scots relations were deteriorating that the English government wanted a union of the two countries. Its major considerations were strategic: not only did the English rely on Scottish troops for their European armies, but in time of war the prospect of a Jacobite invasion from Scotland, a revival of the Auld Alliance between France and Scotland, and civil war in Scotland was intolerable. These were considerations that inevitably appealed not only to the crown and the 'duumvirs', but also to those other consistent supporters of the war against France and of the Protestant Succession, the Whigs. Significantly it was the high Tories who sabotaged both the proposals for a legislative union in 1700 and the negotiations of 1702–3. Their economic arguments were very similar to those of 1606. Sir Edward Seymour said he was opposed to union 'for this reason: that a woman being proposed to a neighbour of his in ye country for a wife, he said he would never marry her, for she was a beggar, and whoever married a beggar cou'd only exspect a louse for a portion'.[26] To the economic disparity between the two countries was now added high Tory repugnance at the prospect of union with a Presbyterian country. For Anne and her ministers and also increasingly the Whigs, however, by 1702 the needs of security in wartime seemed a more compelling argument for union than any misgivings about its possible effects on the English economy and Anglican Church

In Scotland at the beginning of Anne's reign there was no sign of any pro-union sentiment. On the contrary, the new Scots parliament which was elected in 1703, free from the royal control of the Lords of the Articles, seemed set on a course of political separation from England. Though disunited on other things most Scots seemed united in their hostility to England: on this, for example, a republican, Andrew Fletcher of Saltoun, could find common ground with a Jacobite, James Douglas duke of Hamilton. In the 1703 session James Douglas earl of Queensberry, the Queen's commissioner, was powerless in the face of overwhelming support for a series of anti-English measures. The Act Anent Peace and War enacted that all foreign policy decisions after Anne's death would have to be approved by the Scottish parliament. The Wine Act and the Wool Act allowed trade from Scotland in these commodities with France despite the war embargoes in force in England, so making possible English trade with France via Scotland, in other words allowing merchants to break the trade sanctions against France. Most serious of all the Act of Security of the Kingdom threatened to bar the Hanoverians from the Scottish throne 'unless . . . there be such conditions for government settled and enacted as may secure the honour and sovereignty of this crown and kingdom, the freedom, frequency and power of Parliaments, the religion, liberty and trade of the nation from English or any foreign influence'.[27] Although Anne gave her assent to the former measures she cavilled at the latter, dismissed Queensberry, and appointed in his stead the marquis of Tweeddale, the leader of a political group nick-named the 'Squadrone Volante', the Flying Squad. Tweeddale, however, failed as badly as Queensberry in his attempt to get the Scottish parliament to guarantee its support for the Hanoverian Succession, although he was not helped by Queensberry's defection to the opposition in 1704. The Act of Security again passed the Scottish parliament in the summer of 1704, and this time Godolphin, days before the news of Blenheim reached London and therefore faced by a threatening situation in Europe and the prospect of a collapse of government in Scotland, advised Anne to give her assent, which she did on 5 April 1704. The anti-English attitude of the Scottish parliament in 1703 and 1704 confirmed what English ministers already felt and what more English politicians were coming to realize: that the only alternative to the threat of an independent, Jacobite, Francophile Scotland on Anne's death was union. Therefore, after the passage of the Act of Security the Whig Junto proposed to Godolphin that he support the Aliens Bill as an explicit threat to force the Scots to negotiate for a union. The Aliens Act, which became law in March 1705, threatened that, unless by 25 December 1705 the Scottish crown was settled as the English crown had been settled, the import of all Scottish staple products into England would be banned and all Scots would be treated in law as aliens and therefore all Scottish property in England would be endangered.

By early 1705, then, pressing considerations of national security had converted the English crown, its ministers and leading Whigs to the need for an immediate union with Scotland. At this late date, however, there was still no sign of any similar conversion of opinion in Scotland. Just as the Aliens Act was passed in England, the case of Captain Green in Scotland illustrated the depth of anti-English feeling there. Green's ship, the *Worcester*, had been impounded in Leith on a charge of piracy which was clearly false, as was appreciated by many at the time. Yet, under the pressure of anti-English hysteria in the wake of the Darien scheme, the charge was proceeded with, and Green and two of his crewmen were executed. Given this background the events in the Scottish parliament which began on 28 June 1705 are remarkable. Within two months the royal ministers in Scotland, Argyll, the new queen's commissioner, Queensberry, now back in her government as lord privy seal despite his defection to the opposition earlier, and Seafield, the lord chancellor, had persuaded the Scottish parliament to approve the appointment of commissioners to negotiate for a union with England; even the choice of the commissioners was left to the queen. As a result the Scottish commissioners, as well as those from England, were strongly in favour of union. The negotiations were therefore relatively brief, and a draft treaty was ready by 22 July. England and Scotland were to become one country, Great Britain; the Hanoverian succession was guaranteed; there was to be a common parliament in which the Scots would be represented by sixteen peers and forty-five MPs (this was not a direct reflection of the Scottish population figures, but it was better than Scotland's contribution to crown revenues warranted); there was to be an economic union, free trade between the two countries with the same customs duties; in addition the Scots secured the promise of a cash payment of £398,085 10s 0d – the 'Equivalent' – which was reckoned to be compensation for taking on a share of the English national debt and was to be partly used to compensate those who had lost in the Darien scheme. The proposed union, then, was an economic and a parliamentary one, in addition to the already existing regal union. It was not the legal or ecclesiastical union which James I had wanted a century earlier. In fact, in November 1706 the Scottish parliament passed an Act 'for securing the Protestant Religion and Presbyterian Church Government within the Kingdom of Scotland', and this was incorporated into the draft treaty.

Early in 1707 the draft treaty, though attacked fiercely by the Tories, passed the English parliament to come into effect on 1 May. More surprisingly, in stormy debates from 2 October 1706 to 2 January 1707 the Scottish parliament had already approved the draft treaty, almost unchanged, thereby agreeing to legislate itself out of existence. What converted many Scottish politicians to vote for the union? In recent years Professor W. Ferguson has produced an elaborate hypothesis which seeks to explain this in terms of bribery.[28] Only a large-scale programme of bribes to Scottish politicians by English ministers can explain, he argues, the apparent sudden *volte face* of the Scots in 1706–7. This charge has a long history, originating in Jacobite propaganda at the time and reflected in later popular ballads like Burns's

> We're bought and sold for English gold
> Such a parcel of rogue in a nation!

What Professor Ferguson has clearly shown is that Queen Anne and her ministers gave money to Scottish politicians. But he has not shown that payments were made on a systematic scale or that they were intended as anything other than rewards for services rendered in the past; nor has he proved that, even if they were intended as bribes, they influenced their recipients's political views. Earlier cases of attempted bribery in the seventeenth century (by Gondomar in the reign of James I and by Louis XIV in the 1670s) suggest that bribery was an ineffective way of doing this.

Perhaps asking the question of why many Scots supported the union in terms of a sudden conversion of Scots politicians in 1706–7 is taking too much for granted. How representative of Scots opinion were the popular demonstrations against the union from 1705 to 1707? Were those who voted for the anti-English legislation of 1703 and 1704 in favour of a political separation? These are questions to which there can be no definite answer. However, there are strong grounds for believing that not all Scots, politicians and non-politicians alike, were against union with England before 1706–7. There were strong arguments expressed at the time in favour of union which must have had some effect. The most compelling pro-union argument from the Scottish point of view was the economic one. As has been seen, most contemporary commentators believed that the Scottish economy was plunging into a severe crisis, for which it could be argued that union with England offered a practical remedy. Since Scottish agriculture was chronically underdeveloped, the only prospect of rapid economic progress seemed to be in foreign trade and in allied industries. The long-term development of Scottish foreign trade in the course of the seventeenth century seemed to suggest that the best way of stimulating it was by closer economic union with England. During the previous century Scottish foreign trade had shifted from a concentration on France, north-west Europe, and the Baltic to become more focused on England. Therefore, the removal of hostile English import tariffs would undoubtedly benefit the trans-Border trade in cattle, corn, and grain. Moreover, although Scottish merchants had not been totally excluded by the navigation legislation from trade with the English colonies (they had done so legally via Whitehaven as well as by illegal direct trade) the removal of all barriers to trading with the English empire, especially in North America, was obviously an appealing prospect to Glasgow merchants, for example. Of course, not all Scottish merchants would have agreed with these supposed advantages of union. (Merchants like everyone else do not often conform to common, stereotyped behaviour and attitudes.) Those merchants trading to France, for example, would gain no advantage from a union with France's greatest rival. But it is probable that the prospect of union with a more prosperous and economically advanced country did as much in Scotland to popularize the cause of union as the converse argument helped to dissuade many people in England against it.

Arguments in Scotland in favour of union were not confined to economic reasons. It was probable that the political outlook of Scotland as an independent country was as gloomy as its economic prospects. An independent Scotland would not necessarily have resulted in a Jacobite restoration, but it would have been highly likely. The most probable outcome of that would have been civil war – the Presbyterian Lowlands *versus* the Jacobite Highlands – accompanied by a Scottish commitment to invading England in support of 'James VIII's' claims to the English throne. Few who foresaw that could have looked forward with much enthusiasm to a recurrence of the insecurity of the mid-seventeenth century when Scotland had tied its fortunes to another pretender to the English crown. It could be argued (and indeed was by proponents of union like Defoe) that political stability as well as economic prosperity was more certain for Scotland if she was united with England. Moreover, the draft treaty gave ample protection, not only for the Scottish law, but also for the Scottish Kirk, and so the opposition of Scottish presbyterian ministers was partially quieted. (They could hardly be said to have been silenced altogether: Scottish Presbyterian ministers in the early eighteenth century were more vociferous than contemporary English Anglican clergy if that is possible.) Some Scots may have also been persuaded to support union by other considerations, like the 'Equivalent', or the wise English decision to repeal the Aliens Act once the union debate began in Scotland. In the last resort, though, it is impossible to say why most Scottish MPs voted for union. Given the fact that few Scots left a record of their personal reasons for the way they acted in 1706–7, the best conclusion is perhaps to say that they were influenced by a variety of motives, considering their individual interests as well as those of their country. In the last resort the majority of Scots people, especially supporters of the Presbyterian Kirk, probably thought that the Act of Union was the best bargain they could make.

As everyone knows the Act of Union was made, it survived, and, though under attack, is still in existence over 270 years later. Its permanence, however, was far from certain for a long time after 1707. At no time is this clearer than in the first years of the union when at times it seemed possible that the Act might be repealed. For the Scots, especially, the disadvantages of the union seemed to outweigh easily what they had gained from it. The loss of Scottish independence, the demise of the Scottish parliament, after its brief period of unrestricted power since 1689, had been hard enough to swallow in 1707. Moreover, the English in the last years of Anne's reign seemed intent on securing further concessions from Scotland. From 1708 to 1713 the British parliament embarked on a series of measures which seemed designed to undermine many of the advantages Scotland had gained. Their legal independence which the Scots had jealously guarded in 1706–7, was invaded in 1708, when parliament adopted a Treason Bill which established one law of treason for both England and Scotland. Even the independence of the Kirk seemed to be the target of English MPs who, cock-a-hoop after the Sacheverell case (see below, pp. 387–92), in 1711 supported a House of Lords' decision in favour of an Edinburgh episcopalian minister, James Greenshield, in March 1712 passed a Toleration Act allowing greater freedom to episcopalians in Scotland, and in May 1712 restored lay patronage in the Kirk. Moreover, the introduction of an export duty on linen in 1711, an increased tax on salt in 1712 and a malt tax in 1713 (the latter in direct contravention of the terms of the Act of Union) highlighted the fact that the union had not brought Scotland the advantages its proponents had promised. Indeed one economic historian considers that the major economic benefits of union for Scotland did not appear until the 1780s.[29] So strong was the feeling against union in Scotland by 1713 that in June there was a concerted effort at Westminster by Scottish MPs, supported by the Junto Whigs, to secure the repeal of the Act of Union.

It therefore becomes far from easy to explain the survival of the union. The continued English attachment to it is more explicable than the Scottish. Union meant the Protestant succession in Scotland and therefore protection for England against a French and Jacobite invasion from the north. It is difficult to believe that the Junto Whigs would have sacrificed that. Surely their support of the Scottish MPs in June 1713 was primarily a cynical political manoeuvre designed to embarrass Harley and the government. For the Scots the advantages of continuing the union were less obvious immediately after 1707. They still retained an independent Kirk and law and therefore a large measure of their national identity, but, as has been seen, the English seemed to be determined to whittle that away. Nor did many Scots see much sign of the promised economic advantages of union in the years immediately after 1707. It is likely that the union survived its difficult early years from the Scottish point of view for two major reasons. Firstly, union was the lesser of two evils. It is true that more Scots than English were Jacobites, but many Scots realized the horrible consequences of a Jacobite Scotland in terms of civil war and war against England. Both the strength and weakness of the Jacobite cause in Scotland is most clearly illustrated by the reaction to the Jacobite invasions of 1708 and 1715. On both occasions a majority of Scots, in effect, rejected a Jacobite restoration in favour of the Hanoverian succession. Above all, though, the union continued because many Scots discovered that it is harder to dissolve any union than it is to enter it.

Anne's capitulation to the Junto

The main achievements of Anne, Marlborough, and Godolphin in the first half of the reign were brought about in large measure with the support of the Whigs and in the face of the hostile attitude of the Tories. All three Occasional Conformity Bills were rejected by the Whig-dominated House of Lords, which helped temporarily to stifle High Church fanaticism. The Whigs and the monied interest contributed as much to Marlborough's victories as they had to William III's. Moreover, the two major pieces of legislation of the early part of the reign, the Regency Act and the Act of Union, were essentially Whig measures. Yet, despite this and much to their disgust, the Whigs had received little political reward by 1707 beyond the appointments of Cowper as lord keeper of the great seal in October 1705 and Sunderland as secretary of state in December 1706. 'If one looks round every part of the administration, the management of the fleet (etc.) . . .', wrote Sunderland with understandable, though only slight, exaggeration, 'they are all of a Piece, as much Tory, and as wrong, as if Ld. Rochester and Ld. Nottingham were at the head of every thing'.[30] Anne resisted the arguments of Godolphin and Marlborough and consistently blocked all attempts to force her to give offices to the Junto lords. Not without good reason the Junto blamed Robert Harley for Anne's obstinate stance. Harley's influence with the queen increased, especially as Abigail Masham replaced Sarah Churchill as Anne's closest confidante at court in 1707, and Harley frequently warned the queen of the dangers of single-party government. Therefore in the summer of 1707 the Junto planned a sweeping campaign for the coming winter parliamentary session to force Harley out of office, and to convince the queen that she could not govern without them.

In the first aim they were helped by the revelation in January 1708 that Harley's secretary, Gregg, had leaked secrets to the French, and, although Harley was cleared of complicity, his reputation undoubtedly suffered. What weakened his position more seriously than the Gregg affair, however, was his failure to provide convincing defence of the conduct of the war in parliament. Clearly by now Harley and St John were becoming less convinced of the need to continue the war and this was reflected in the Commons at the end of January 1708 when St John, who was supposedly presenting the ministry's defence of war, produced a document which showed that only a quarter of the troops voted for Spain had in fact been at the disastrous battle of Almanza. In the preceding weeks Harley (though one can rarely be certain with such a slippery character) appears to have been negotiating secretly with Tory politicians with a view to forming a ministry without Godolphin.[31] If this is true, then it is a political battle which Harley lost. Marlborough and Godolphin brought matters to a crisis by absenting themselves from a Cabinet meeting on 8 February and threatening to resign. At the Cabinet meeting the moderate Whig peers, the duke of Somerset and earl of Pembroke, supported the 'duumvirs' by refusing to serve if Harley was retained. Even so Harley need not have resigned; he still had the queen's support and could have resumed his negotiations with the Tories for a reconstructed ministry. Three days later, however, he resigned. Was the decisive factor in his decision the threat of impeachment that the Junto, using Gregg's evidence, was aiming to bring against him? Certainly, impeachment was not to be taken lightly, and Harley may have wisely chosen temporary political retirement instead of impeachment and the death penalty.

Harley and St John, who also resigned, were replaced by junior Whigs, Henry Boyle as secretary of state, and Robert Walpole as secretary of war. It is a further illustration of Anne's independence that she held out against the Junto Whigs for a further nine months, despite heavy Whig gains in the general election of May 1708. In the autumn she resisted a Junto ultimatum that Prince George be replaced as lord admiral by the earl of Pembroke, and that the earl's two posts of lord president and lord-lieutenant of Ireland should go to Somers and Wharton. Only when her beloved George died on 28 October did Anne's resolve finally weaken, and early in November the Junto lords at long last received their long-hoped-for political reward.

The failure of the Whigs and Tories, 1708–1714

Godolphin and the downfall of the Whigs, 1708–1710

In 1708 the political fortunes of the Junto Whigs were apparently on the crest of a wave. Even their enemies conceded that Somers, Wharton, Halifax, and Orford were a group of gifted individuals. Moreover, in the early years of Anne's reign they attracted the support of a rising generation of brilliant politicians. Unlike his father, the minister of James II and William III, Charles Spencer the third earl of Sunderland was a committed party politician, but he inherited some, if not all, of his father's political skill. More talented were Robert Walpole and Charles viscount Townshend, whose families dominated Norfolk politics in the early eighteenth century. Walpole owed his first step forward in his political career to the patronage of the earl of Orford, and this early help was repaid by Walpole's almost constant support of the Junto in Anne's reign. The circle of political friends established by Walpole in these years reads like a *Who's Who* of early Hanoverian politics, including William Cavendish, marquis of Hartington (later duke of Devonshire), James Stanhope, and William Pulteney. With this kind of support the Junto became an even more formidable political force than in the previous reign. They were held together by a high degree of loyalty to each other and to the principles of the new Whiggery, which in 1708 had at last brought them political power. Furthermore, in the 1708 general election the Whigs secured a rare majority in the House of Commons, largely due to an abortive Jacobite invasion of Scotland, which had an effect on English politics very similar to the assassination plot of 1696. Yet, as a decade earlier, the Junto Lords were not able to hang on to power for long. Within less than two years of attaining office all the members of the Junto and their allies, including Godolphin, had either been dismissed or had resigned, and the general election of 1710 was a crushing victory for the Tories. Why was the Junto's second period of ascendancy as brief as the first?

In 1708 the position of the Junto was not so strong or so secure as it seemed. The Whig majority in the House of Commons was an aberration from the normal pattern of English politics since the Glorious Revolution. Usually the only secure parliamentary base the Whigs could rely on was the House of Lords. Very quickly in the following months, as the Jacobite threat of 1708 receded, Whig support in the House of Commons began to be eroded. Especially it was undermined by the growing opposition in the country to two major aims which the Junto stressed after regaining office: to continue to pour men and money into the war until Louis XIV was totally defeated and demoralized, and to weaken the power of the Church of England. As will be seen, opposition to these intentions both inside and outside parliament was very strong. But it is likely that even more damaging to the Whig Lords was their failure to secure the unqualified support of Queen Anne. Undoubtedly, the ending of the passionate friendship of Anne and Sarah Churchill after 1707 played a part in this. From 1707 to 1710 the two women indulged in a series of semi-public bitchy quarrels, which ended in Sarah being dismissed from Anne's presence for ever and being stripped of her household offices. No longer was Sarah able to attempt to influence the queen in favour of the Whigs, and her replacement as Anne's confidante, Mrs Masham, allowed her cousin, Robert Harley, to have a base at court to scheme against the Junto. Yet these bedchamber intrigues were probably not the most important reason why the Junto never became part of Anne's intimate circle. As has been stressed before, Anne's independence can be underestimated. Already she had strong reasons not to like the Junto. She was irritated by the way that they had sniped at her during the bishoprics crisis in 1707, and had only given way reluctantly to their appointment to office. The very way that they had forced themselves into office made her dislike them even more. Moreover, to these reasons by 1709–10 was added the fact that Anne's enthusiasm for the war, like that of most of her subjects, was cooling rapidly. She also made it clear that she was sympathetic to the popular fury roused by the Whigs' attack on the Church of England. She therefore needed little persuasion to connive at Harley's machinations in 1710 to engineer the dismissal of Godolphin and his Junto allies.

'No Peace without Spain'

One of the principal features uniting the Whigs and the Junto Lords remained their commitment to the war against France. Despite the fact that Louis XIV appeared to be anxious to make peace the Junto made it clear that they were not willing to end the war. Louis made his first peace proposal in 1705, but it was not until the winter of 1708–9 that he began to offer concessions that met the main demands of the allies. In March and April 1709 at The Hague, Louis's diplomats, Pierre Rouillé and his foreign minister, Jean Baptiste Colbert, marquis de Torcy, volunteered to withdraw French claims in Spain, the Indies, the Low Countries and Italy. When Marlborough and Lord Townshend arrived at The Hague to negotiate for Britain, de Torcy even promised that Louis XIV would recognize the Protestant succession in Britain and take measures (falling short of direct expulsion) to persuade the Pretender to leave France. These generous concessions were repeated at peace negotiations at Gertruydenberg in March 1710.[32] However, for Townshend, acting on instructions from his Junto masters, even these sweeping promises by the French were not enough. He persuaded the Dutch to raise their demands, and the allied negotiators drew up forty preliminary articles which included the requirement that, not only should Louis agree to Philip's withdrawal from Spain in favour of Archduke Charles, but that if this was not done within two months, Louis should join the allies in a war to secure his grandson's deposition. Louis's refusal of the preliminaries in May 1709, given such stiff terms, is not surprising. Clearly the Whigs were not willing to make peace on any terms. This was further illustrated at the end of the year when Townshend concluded the Barrier Treaty with the Dutch. So anxious were the Whigs to keep the Dutch in the war to pursue their war aim of 'No Peace without Spain' that Townshend promised British help to secure many 'barrier towns' in the Spanish Netherlands for the Dutch, as well as allowing the Dutch commercial concessions in the trade to Spanish America after the war.

It is easier to explain why the Whigs were so insistent on continuing the war than it is to accept that they were wise to do so. Some of the arguments in favour of extending the war aims in 1703 still held good in 1708. If the French and Spanish thrones were both occupied by Bourbons, would not the peace of Europe, or at the very least the Protestant succession in Britain, be threatened by an over-mighty Bourbon super-power? Distrust of Louis's protestations that he had no intention of uniting the French and Spanish thrones, given the French king's past record, was perhaps natural. Also there were still powerful commercial arguments for protecting and extending Britain's influence in Spain and the Mediterranean. In 1708 Britain concluded a secret agreement with Archduke Charles to allow British merchants limited rights to trade with Spanish colonies. Moreover, in September 1708 the navy captured Port Mahon and so paved the way for a further extension of British naval and commercial presence in the Mediterranean. However, the difficulty arises of determining whether or not 'No Peace without Spain' was a wise policy after the allied victories in Europe and defeats in Spain from 1704 to 1708. At what point did it become clear that the growth of Spanish nationalist support for Philip ensured that it was unreasonable to expect Louis XIV to be able to persuade Philip to give up Spain and impossible to force Spain to abandon Philip? Even the crushing allied defeat in Spain at the battle of Brihuega in December 1710 failed to shake the resolve of the Whigs (at least in public) that the war in Spain could still be won. On that point, at least, it is easier to sympathize with the Tory view that the war in Spain was now irretrievably lost.

In their bellicose attitude to the war the Junto soon became increasingly isolated in British political life. However it is important that a distinction should be made between responsible opponents of the war and the irresponsible attitude adopted by many country Tories. With the war apparently already won some politicians, like Queen Anne and Robert Harley, sensibly were converted to the view that a serious diplomatic effort should be made to secure a satisfactory peace settlement. Harley's opinion was confirmed after his departure from office in February 1708 during his enforced retirement in Hertfordshire. There he came into close contact with the war-weariness prevalent among country Tories. Unlike Harley, however, country Tories appear to have thought very little about the terms of the proposed peace, but simply that a peace treaty should be secured as soon as possible. Many events in 1708 and 1709 confirmed a majority of Tories in the view that Britain should withdraw from the war without delay. The bad harvest of 1708 and the following severe winter of 1708–9 added for many landlords the prospect of falling rental income to the actual escalating taxation caused by the war. Not only this, rocketing grain prices brought the possibility of famine and mob violence. To Tories on their country estates the spectre of rural rebellion at their gates was more real than the diplomatic subtleties of peacemaking in Europe. Moreover, early in 1709 the endemic hatred of many Tories for all foreigners was fed by the xenophobic propaganda released by the Whig Bill to naturalize all foreign Protestants. Though rooted in the commercial rivalry of the seventeenth century, English dislike of their Dutch allies by 1709 had progressed to an irrational stage. The earl of Shaftesbury neatly captured the fanaticism of anti-Dutch hatred current in England in the reign of Queen Anne: 'If you would discover a concealed Tory, speak but of the Dutch and you find him out by his passionate railing.'[33] All foreigners and foreign influences were subject to the same vilification, and the debate on the Bill for the Naturalization of Foreign Protestants produced examples of extreme racial prejudice which have become all too familiar in late-twentieth-century Britain. If unrestricted immigration was allowed, wrote one pamphleteer in 1709, foreigners would 'have admission into places of trust and authority, which in process of time might endanger our ancient polity and government, and, by frequent intermarriages, go a great way to blot out and extinguish the English race'.[34] Bigoted sentiments like these were unaffected by the evidence of the technical expertise and commercial enterprise contributed by immigrants to the British economy in the late seventeenth and early eighteenth centuries (see below, pp. 431, 434, 437). Instead the immigration of about 8,000 foreign Protestants from the Palatinate in the two months after the Naturalization Bill became law was seen by many Tories as the fulfilment of their prophecy that this country was in the process of being swamped by the poor of foreign countries. English insularity reached a peak, which complemented the already strong feeling that a European war was no longer being fought in the interests of Britain. The Barrier Treaty of December 1709 was further confirmation to the Tories that they were correct. Moreover, not only did the Tories see themselves as pouring money into a needless war, but men as well. Early in September 1709 came news of Marlborough's battle at Malplaquet on the border between France and the Spanish Netherlands, in which 20,000 allied soldiers and 15,000 Frenchmen were killed. This was war mortality on an unprecedented scale and the needless carnage at Malplaquet was a great encouragement to the growing anti-war sentiment. In this climate there were even those who began to play on the submerged fears of a standing army which had been so potent at the end of William's war. If the war continued would not the probable outcome be the emergence of Marlborough as a second Oliver Cromwell? 'History', wrote a correspondent of Harley in 1708, 'furnishes many examples of men who from the command of less force have aspired to sovereignty. But I believe there is no instance that ever any man who had tasted of absolute power could ever retire to a private life and become a good subject.'[35] By 1710 all these sentiments coalesced into a great popular desire for peace. It is an axiom of British politics after 1689 that the Whigs were in the strongest position when war fever was at its height, and vice versa. Unfortunately for their political prospects, the Junto only succeeded in forcing themselves into office at a time when hostility to the war was overwhelming in the country, in parliament, and at Court.

The impeachment of Dr Sacheverell

Without doubt the national revulsion against the Junto's war policy combined with Queen Anne's loss of enthusiasm for the war, alone would have caused the downfall of the Junto. After the next general election, which was due in 1711, the Whigs would certainly have faced a hostile majority in the House of Commons, and would have found it very difficult to convince Anne to retain them in office. However, the downfall of the Junto came about even sooner than it might otherwise have done because of their decision to impeach Dr Henry Sacheverell. In so doing they brought the Church back into the political arena. Ironically it was the Junto who took the initiative in sparking off an explosion which within a few months destroyed their immediate political position and damaged the Whig party's long-term prospects of recovery. Politically defeated though the High Church cause had been in

1705, the grievances that fuelled that cause were still deeply felt in the country houses and rectories of provincial England. With the advent of the Junto to power it was naturally feared that the power of the Church of England would suffer even more. Nor were these fears unfounded. Soon after Wharton arrived in Ireland as the newly appointed lord-lieutenant he announced his intention of repealing the sacramental test for public office. Not for the first time English apprehensions were roused by the fact that Ireland was apparently being used as a testing ground for policies that were to be later extended to England. Rumours spread that the Junto intended to repeal the Test Act, and these were apparently substantiated by a clause in the Bill for the Naturalization of Foreign Protestants (1709), which legalized the acceptance of the sacrament in a nonconformist chapel as a condition of naturalization. Might this soon be made the only condition of entering public office?

Equally important, in 1708 and 1709 Tory High Churchmen found themselves and their most fundamental political theories under a sustained bombardment in the sermons and pamphlets of Whig clerics and propagandists. In Benjamin Hoadley the Whigs at last found a clergyman who was prepared to stand up against the ranks of voluble High Church priests, led by Atterbury and Sacheverell. In a series of sermons from 1705 to 1709 Hoadley launched an attack on one of the basic justifications for the doctrine of passive obedience, St Paul's assertion in Romans xiii:1 that 'the powers that be are ordained of God . . . therefore let every soul be subject to the higher powers'. According to Hoadley's interpretation, St Paul had advocated only obedience to those rulers who 'answer the good end of their institution'. Resistance to those rulers who acted tyrannically, on the contrary, was permitted, indeed encouraged. 'There is nothing in nature, or in the Christian religion,' said Hoadley, 'that can hinder people from redressing their grievances, and from answering the will of Almighty God, so far as to preserve and secure the happiness of public society.'[36] Without doubt the most influential lay exposition of Whig political philosophy was *Vox Populi Vox Dei: or True Maxims of Government;* it was published in 1709 and went through eight editions in its first twelve months. Its assertion that ultimate power lay with the people was worthy of Leveller pamphlets of the mid-seventeenth century, and it was suitably dismissive of assertions that the people had no right to resist rulers who ignore 'the eternal laws of God and Nature'.[37]

Given the character of early eighteenth-century Anglican clergy one would not expect them to remain silent in the face of these attacks. Godolphin once wryly commented that 'a discreet churchman is as rare as a black swan'. Yet clearly some were more discreet than others. In 1708 and 1709 both Offspring Blackall (now clearly a High Church divine) and Atterbury delivered important sermons in defence of the doctrine of passive obedience as a counterattack to Hoadley. However, these were calm and reasoned pieces of academic exposition when compared with the notorious sermon delivered by Dr Henry Sacheverell on 5 November 1709 in St Paul's cathedral before the Corporation of the City of London. Like Sacheverell's earlier sermons, *In Peril Among False Brethren*, which was printed in large numbers soon after it had been delivered, is not remarkable for its originality. A contemporary, William Fleetwood, said that it was generally considered to be 'a rhapsody of incoherent, ill-digested thoughts, dressed in the worst language that could be found',[38] a view echoed by many later historians. Dr Bennett condemns it as 'a mish-mash of other men's sermons and the preacher's own past performances'.[39] Many High Church clerics, including Sacheverell, had delivered sermons before denouncing the threat to the Church and state posed by the growth of dissent, and asserting the fundamental importance of 'the subject's obligation to an Absolute and Unconditional Obedience to the Supreme Power'. However, what set *In Peril* apart was the extreme and provocative language which Sacheverell used. Indeed, Atterbury, who knew from Sacheverell's past performances what to expect, had attempted to prevent his fellow Oxford divine from being invited to give the sermon. Offensive and inflammatory the sermon was, but this does not seem a compelling reason why the government should have decided to single out Sacheverell for impeachment. Wharton and Godolphin (though not, according to his later account, Somers) pressed their colleagues to prosecute Sacheverell. On 13 December 1709 the House of Commons voted at the instigation of the government that Sacheverell's sermon was a 'malicious, scandalous and seditious libel', and on the following day the fateful decision was taken to bring articles of impeachment against Sacheverell.

The fact that the trial of Dr Sacheverell eventually rebounded against the Whigs makes the problem of discovering why he was brought to trial even more important. Unfortunately, since those behind the impeachment left no records of their thoughts or private discussions, this cannot be resolved with any certainty. One possible solution is that Godolphin and the Junto were stung into retaliation by the vicious personal abuse directed against them by Sacheverell's sermon; Godolphin was sensitive to criticism and could not have missed the use of his nickname in the reference to the 'crafty insidiousness of such wily Volpones'. Nor could the lord treasurer and his Junto colleagues have relished Sacheverell's condemnation of them for allowing the growth of dissent and wilfully conniving at the destruction of the constitution. Yet it is clear that Sacheverell offended more than the personal honour of the Whig ministers; his sermon was also a scathing attack on their political principles. As part of his defence of the doctrine of passive obedience he had made a withering onslaught on the Whig belief that the Glorious Revolution had been brought about by resistance. Sacheverell, alleged the articles of impeachment against him, 'doth suggest and maintain that the necessary means used to bring about the said happy revolution were odious and unjustifiable . . . and that to impute resistance to the said revolution is to cast black and odious colours upon his late majesty [William III] and the said revolution'.[40] In short, Sacheverell was attacking not only the subject's right to resist a tyrannical ruler, but also the Glorious Revolution itself.

In impeaching Sacheverell, the Junto saw a golden opportunity to present their own view of the Revolution and of their 'Revolution Principles', and to do so publicly in a parliamentary trial rather than more quietly in a court of law. They also, at the same time, saw the impeachment as a speedy, expeditious way of getting rid of a demagogue, whose scriptural exhortations to put on 'the whole armour of God' and to wrestle 'not only against the flesh and blood, but against principalities, against powers, against the rulers of the darkness of this world, against spiritual wickedness in high places' came oddly from the lips of a devout exponent of the doctrine of non-resistance. Moreover, it is likely that the queen's ministers also hoped to use the trial of Dr Sacheverell as a party weapon against the Tories, and so halt their opponents' apparently inevitable political resurgence. The Whig managers of the trial intended to use Sacheverell's extreme defence of passive obedience and his attack on the Glorious Revolution to illustrate that the loyalty of Tories to the queen and to the Protestant Succession was suspect and that the logical conclusion of Sacheverell's argument was Jacobitism. Walpole, who played a major part in organizing the trial in 1710, proved very adept after Anne's death in insinuating that all Tories were secret Jacobites. Yet in 1710 this political stratagem flopped. The trial, which began on 27 February 1710 and was intended to wreck the Tory party, misfired and instead came very close to destroying permanently the Whig party's political fortunes.

Just how badly wrong the trial went for the Whigs can be seen by the massive popular demonstrations throughout the country, but especially in London, in favour of Sacheverell. These culminated on the night of 1–2 March in frightening mob violence in the capital, only surpassed in scale by the Gordon Riots in the later eighteenth century. In part this was allowed to happen because of a tactical error on the part of the managers of the trial. By giving way to the delaying tactics of Sacheverell's lawyers the trial was postponed until 27 February, giving ample time for the London clergy to whip up the passions of their congregations to fever pitch. This by itself, though, is not sufficient explanation why the Church of England should have become the focus of vehement popular support. The fact is that Sacheverell in his ravings against dissenters struck a rich vein of popular paranoia and prejudice which had already been exposed by the growing disenchantment with the continuing war against France. It was fairly easy in London to identify wealthy dissenters with the 'monied interest', which, according to Tory propaganda, was prospering from the war. To many the magnificent large meeting houses and chapels being built in London were an obvious confirmation of the truth of Tory charges that the war was simply being prolonged to line the pockets of the 'monied interest'. Moreover, Sacheverell also appealed to the xenophobia which was so pervasive in early eighteenth-century London. Were not many of those profiting from the war not only dissenters but also foreigners – Dutch-men, Jews, Huguenots? Was not the Bank of England dominated by immigrant families? Sacheverell brought together many current threads of anxiety: that the Church was in danger from the growth of dissent, and that traditional society was being undermined by the 'monied interest' and obnoxious foreign influences. Deeprooted though these feelings were, Professor G. Holmes has left little room for doubt that the Sacheverell riots were not spontaneous.[41] Many of the 'mobs' who took to the streets in 1710 were people with respectable occupations; they were not the very poor and unemployed. They attacked only selected targets, mainly the bigger dissenting meeting houses, and made every effort to prevent damage to surrounding property. Behind the Sacheverell rioters were Tory and Church leaders, who exploited the popular hysteria in order to embarrass the government, and in this aim they were totally successful.

Even more serious for the Whigs, though, than events on the streets of London was that at the trial itself, although Sacheverell was found guilty, the Whig managers found that there were difficulties in defining their justification of the Revolution, their 'Revolution Principles', which was one of the main purposes of the trial. They argued that the resistance in 1688 had not been treasonable, since it had been in defence of the fundamental law: James II had been threatening to subvert the constitution and his deposition was therefore lawful. Although they played down the fully-blown version of the arguments they had used in 1688–9 – that subjects had a right to resist rulers who broke the original contract between rulers and the people – they found themselves nevertheless open to the charge that they were advocating rebellion and democracy. Desperately, Walpole and the other prosecution speakers at the trial asserted that they were not advocating a wholesale freedom to resist, but only one limited to cases of exceptional emergency. However, many must have agreed with Bishop Hooper, who, while rejecting the doctrine of passive obedience, nevertheless denounced the Whigs in 1710. Although

he allowed, indeed, of the necessity and legality of Resistance in some extraordinary cases . . .[he] was of opinion that this ought to be kept from the knowledge of the people, who are naturally too apt to resist. That the Revolution was not to be boasted of and made a precedent, but we ought to throw a mantle over it, and rather call it Vacancy or Abdication. And that the original compact were two very dangerous words; not to be mentioned without a great deal of caution.[42]

It is a measure of the extent to which the trial of Dr Sacheverell rebounded against its promoters, that the Tory and Church mobs of 1710 came to be blamed on the Whigs' incitement to popular rebellion.

Sacheverell's conviction by a small majority of seventeen votes in the House of Lords (sixty-nine votes to fifty-two) and his mild punishment of three years' suspension from preaching was a hollow victory for Godolphin and the Junto. The downfall of their ministry was now certain, and the process began in April 1710 with the appointment as lord chamberlain of the duke of Shrewsbury, who stirred himself to one of his few, but dramatic, short bursts of political activity. During his long period of retirement in Italy ('I have often commented', he wrote excusing his stay in the heart of Catholic Europe, 'that there's nowhere in Europe a Protestant country favoured with a warm sun') he had cut his ties with the Whigs, and was now closely associated with Harley in an attempt to bring about a mixed ministry. Harley knew very well that Whig support was needed to sustain the public credit, but he had also never abandoned his ideal of non-party government. His negotiations with the Junto during the summer on these lines may account for the surprising fact that, when Sunderland was dismissed in June and replaced by the Tory earl of Dartmouth, his Junto colleagues, normally so loyal, did not resign. However, after Godolphin's dismissal and the appointment of Harley as chancellor of the exchequer in August, it rapidly became clear that Harley's hopes of forming a joint Whig–Tory ministry were impossible. The Tory leaders insisted on the dissolution of parliament being brought forward to the autumn, and in September, facing the certain prospect of a massive Tory electoral victory, the Junto resigned *en masse*. Rochester and St John were appointed as lord president and secretary of state. As expected the general election in October 1710 reflected the overwhelming support in the country for Sacheverell and for an immediate peace. In the new House of Commons the Tories had an estimated majority of 151. From now on Harley had no choice but to rely, to a much greater extent than he would have liked, on the Tory party.

Harley and the downfall of the Tories, 1710–14

During the last four years of Anne's reign the political climate undoubtedly favoured the Tories. The outcry against the war and in favour of low taxation in the general election in October 1710 confirmed that the Whig cause was in tatters. 'It is as vain to hope [of] restoring that decayed interest as for a man of sixty to talk of entering on a new scene of life that is only proper for youth and vigour', wrote Swift shortly afterwards.[43] The dominance of Tory opinion in the country was translated into massive majorities in the House of Commons after the elections of 1710 and 1713. Moreover, in 1712 the Whigs were even ousted from their usual controlling position in the Upper House, when Anne (for reasons which will be seen) created twelve Tory peers. Yet despite all this, the Tories never exercised the influence over royal government from 1710 to 1714 that the Junto Whigs did in the periods of their ascendancy, 1694–7 and 1708–10. Royal government during Anne's last years never became Tory government; nor did the Tories achieve the kind of legislative changes that their political support in the country and in parliament led them to expect. Fully-blown Tory statutes enacted in this period can literally be counted on one hand: the Land Property Qualification Act 1711, the Act to Build Fifty New Churches 1711, The Occasional Conformity Act 1711, the Repeal of the Protestant Naturalization Act 1712, and the Schism Act 1714. It is true that under Tory pressure the war against France was brought to an end, but it was not achieved as quickly as many Tories wanted, and one important element of the peace settlement – a Franco-British commercial treaty – was overthrown. Nor did the three ecclesiastical statutes amount to the fundamental reform and protection of the Church demanded by many High Tory clerics and laymen. If all this is surprising what is even more so is that soon after Anne's death the Tory party became insignificant as a political force and continued in eclipse for much of the remainder of the eighteenth century. Prominent among the problems facing the student of the last era of the Stuart age, then, is that of attempting to provide an explanation for the limited political potency of the Tories after 1710.

The key to understanding why the Tories failed to achieve many of their aims from 1710 to 1714 is the role played in this period by Robert Harley. It is necessary again to stress that, despite Harley's close association with Tory politicians since the end of William's reign, it is a great mistake to classify him as a Tory. Like Marlborough and Godolphin before him, he was a 'manager', independent of party. Moreover, he was more successful than Marlborough and Godolphin in maintaining his independent position. They had capitulated to the Whig Junto before 1710 in a way that Harley never did to the Tory cohorts after 1710. Harley retained his position as 'prime minister' from August 1710 until within six days of Anne's death, and during that period he successfully blocked many of the extreme Tory measures advocated by politicians like Henry St John. If anyone has a claim to be the leader of the Tory party after 1710 it is, not Harley, but St John. After his departure from office in 1708 he spent nearly three years in the political wilderness among the country gentlemen of Berkshire and this experience showed him the apparently strong support he could gain by becoming a thoroughgoing Tory. It is this, not the contrasting personalities of Harley and St John, that lies at the heart of their well-known quarrel, which dominated the politics of the last years of Anne's reign. It is true that it would be difficult to find two more contrasting individuals: Harley, the introvert who clothed his aims in secrecy and who revelled in political intrigue, and St John, the extrovert who disdained hard political graft and often acted on impulse. But, more importantly, both men represented fundamentally different approaches to contemporary politics. St John had no time for Harley's attempts to build bridges between the two political parties; given the chance he would have driven all Whigs from office and done his best to exterminate the Whig party. Both men, too, had different aims regarding the major political issues of the day. Their quarrel became an ideological conflict on the future of the Church, the making of the peace, and the settlement of the succession. Both men attracted Tory support and in the process Harley detached a significant body of moderate Tories from St John's leadership. Consequently, unlike the Whigs, the unity of the Tory party was shattered. From 1710 to 1714, therefore, the Tory party, apparently so powerful, was rendered musclebound.

The failure of the Anglican 'counter-revolution'

In 1710 it seemed that the hopes of High Church supporters, so often frustrated in the past, would at last soon be fulfilled. By the autumn of 1710 High Church leaders had secured for themselves key political positions. St John was secretary of state, Bromley was speaker of the House of Commons, and Atterbury, despite the opposition of Archbishop Tenison and many bishops, was prolocutor of Convocation. After Harley's refusal to lend his support Atterbury broke with him and planned an Anglican 'counter-revolution': a programme of Church reforms, the details of which would be worked out in Convocation and its committees, and which would be pushed in its final form through the House of Commons by Speaker Bromley.[44] Moreover, the High Church party proved adept at harnessing for their cause the High Church fervour roused by the trial of Dr Sacheverell. In the spring and summer of 1710 a flood of loyal Addresses to the Queen demanded protection for the Church of England against its enemies. In August 1710 an influential political periodical, the *Examiner*, was founded by St John and others, and it began to employ writers like Swift and Atterbury to spread the High Church message. Everything seemed set to make 1711 the great year of Church reform.

However, as in the earlier part of the reign, the High Churchmen were opposed by a powerful political combination, that included not only the Whigs and the moderate bishops, but also the queen and Robert Harley. Working behind the scenes Harley set about his congenial task of manipulating opinion against St John and Atterbury. Moreover, the queen's distrust of the High Church campaign, which she saw caused intense political bitterness, was increased by her dislike of St John. Indeed the new secretary's well-known deist views and scandalous private life hardly suited him as a leading spokesman of the High Church cause. Consequently, despite all the hard work of Atterbury during the winter of 1710–11 in producing many detailed proposals to revive the powers of the ecclesiastical courts, to increase the powers of bishops, and to establish new parishes, the achievement of the High Church campaign was slight. The Act of February 1711 to establish fifty new churches was meant to be the first of many statutes to promote the Church of England. Not only did this Act have a limited effect (only twelve new churches were built during the next twenty years) but Atterbury, Bromley, and St John found it difficult to use their undoubted political strength to force the queen and Harley to agree to support High Church measures. In the new few months they managed to secure precious few concessions from the Court. Only after St John threatened to resign in August 1711, when the peace negotiations were at a critical stage, did Anne agree to send an open letter to Archbishop Tenison pledging her general support for Atterbury's 'counter-revolution'. She also appointed Bishop Robinson of Bristol as lord privy seal. But, if the High Churchmen saw this as auguring a revival of the secular power of the clery as in the days of Archbishop Laud, they were to be disappointed. In the remaining part of Anne's reign only two more High Church measures became law: the Occasional Conformity Act of December 1711 and the Schism Act of 1714. The first was the successful culmination of a long campaign, but it was rarely enforced in practice. The second Act was as potentially disastrous for opponents of the Church of England; it aimed to suppress the many dissenting schools and colleges established in recent years by imposing severe penalties on those who taught without a licence from a bishop. Fortunately, however, for the cause of nonconformity, the Schism Act was made inoperative by Anne's death. Moreover, significantly, both the Occasional Conformity Act and the Schism Act were not a direct outcome of High Church pressure, but were brought about because of disputes over the two issues which came to overshadow that of the Church in the last four years of Anne's reign, the making of peace and the succession.

The Peace of Utrecht

The years from 1710 to 1714 were remarkable for another distasteful display of isolationism in England, reflecting a deep desire for the withdrawal of the country from European affairs and from all contact with 'harmful' foreign influences. As the reaction to the Sacheverell trial had shown, these sentiments were part and parcel of the High Church hatred of dissent. Heretics and dissenters were seen as 'the importers of foreign vices'. But not just dissenters, Whigs and the 'monied interest' too were commonly lumped together with foreigners as the butts of a campaign against un-English activities. 'I scarce ever know a foreigner settl'd in England', wrote Atterbury, 'but became a Whig in a little time after his mixing with us.' Sir John Packington's main reason for wanting to end the war was 'to prevent the beggaring of the nation, and to prevent moneyed and military men becoming lords of us who have lands'.[45]

So powerful were these sentiments that at the beginning of the new parliament in November 1710 there developed an influential Tory pressure group to agitate for an end to the war and for measures to protect the 'landed interest' and the Church of England. The October Club began as a kind of beer-drinking society of provincial squires, but it developed into a serious political organization with a large and growing membership. It had reached about 150 MPs by April 1711, with regular weekly meetings at the Bell Tavern in King Street, Westminster, and with the experienced leadership of Sir Thomas Hanmer and Sir

John Packington. Clearly this was a ginger group that the ministry could not ignore, and Harley threw his weight behind an October Club Bill, introduced in December 1710, imposing qualifications of incomes of £600 p.a. on all MPs for country seats and £300 p.a. on all borough MPs. Similar Bills had failed in 1696, 1697, and 1702, but with Harley's support the October Club Bill became law in February 1711. It is true that this Property Qualification Act was a watered-down version of the Act hoped for by extreme Tories, who would have liked to see it extended to the university and Scottish constituencies, with its property qualifications restricted much more explicitly to income from land. Most of those who voted for the Bill, however, intended that it should sweep Whig financiers, merchants, and lawyers – the 'monied interest' and its hangers-on – out of parliament. The October Club also succeeded in 1712 in securing the repeal of the hated Protestant Naturalization Act passed in 1709, and the Club conducted a vigorous campaign against the war. In the process in January 1712 it brought about the expulsion from the Commons and imprisonment in the Tower of Robert Walpole on charges of corruption when he was secretary of war. Its most eminent victim was Marlborough, who was dismissed as captain-general at the end of December 1711.

Tory xenophobia and anti-war feeling voiced by St John and the October Club was not a major embarrassment to Harley. On the contrary, as has been seen, Harley had been unenthusiastic about the war since 1708, and immediately after entering office in 1710 he and Shrewsbury sent the earl of Jersey to France to begin secret peace negotiations. Subsequent events had confirmed Harley in his desire to end the war and to take the peace negotiations more seriously. The final allied evacuation of Madrid in November and the defeat of Stanhope's army at Brihuega in December 1710 convinced Harley and others that the war in Spain was irretrievably lost. Four months later any lingering doubts Harley may have had about abandoning the policy of 'No Peace without Spain' must have vanished when Emperor Joseph died without a son, making it likely that his brother Charles would become, not only king of Spain and the Spanish Empire, but also Holy Roman Emperor. There was now no point in pursuing a war to defeat a Bourbon super-power only to erect a Habsburg super-power in its place. There was thus a great deal of common ground between Harley and St John in their pursuit of peace. The main difference between them was not on the need for a peace settlement, but on its timing and its terms.

Harley rightly considered St John's pressure for an immediate peace irresponsible, totally ignoring the opinion of Britain's allies and the government's creditors. As far as the allies were concerned it was only a few months since British ministers had been advocating all-out war and persuading them to turn down Louis XIV's generous peace terms. Clearly there was a need to try to persuade the allies to accept the sudden change of tack in British policy. This was difficult enough without St John openly displaying his willingness to make peace without any consideration of the interests of the Dutch. For this reason St John was excluded from the peace negotiations until April 1711 and even then Harley ensured that the energetic secretary did not dictate the course of Britain's diplomacy with the French. Furthermore Harley attempted to win support in the City by his South Sea Company scheme, which he announced on 1 May 1711. The City had been shaken by the Tory electoral victory in 1710, and the talk of an immediate peace brought the threat that the government's major creditors, the Bank of England and the East India Company, might withhold further loans. The prime purpose of the new South Sea Company was to act as an alternative source of extra government loans to deal with the problem of the floating debt. The South Sea Company was to trade in South and Central America, which after the peace, it was hoped, would be thrown wide open to British investment. These commercial expectations proved unfounded and the Company collapsed amid great scandal in 1720. But at the time the South Sea Company scheme fulfilled Harley's immediate purposes. Government creditors bought South Sea Company stock, and Tory support in the City was attracted by the prospect of supporting a rival of the Whig-dominated Bank of England.

Harley's approach to peace-making was too circuitous for the zealots of the October Club, who wanted the ministry to follow a direct route to a peace settlement. Consequently, relations between Harley and St John, which were anyway becoming strained by their different attitudes to the future of the Church, were also soured by Harley's circumspect approach to peace-making. St John, in any case, was already angry at Harley's hesitation before appointing him to office in September 1710, and early in 1711 there occured the first open quarrel between the two ministers over St John's proposal for an expedition to capture Quebec. Later in the year ill-feeling between them increased, when St John learned that he had been kept out of the early phase of the peace negotiations. He remained frustrated as Harley kept a firm grasp on the course of events. Even when Harley was absent from parliament for two months after he had been seriously wounded on 8 March 1711 by the knife of a French spy, Guiscard, whom he had been interrogating, St John was not able to usurp Harley's predominant position. Soon after Harley recovered his health, at the end of May 1711, he was created earl of Oxford, and promoted to lord treasurer, so receiving the public seal on his political supremacy. If any further sign was needed, it appeared in June 1712 when St John, to his chagrin, was created a mere viscount – viscount Bolingbroke.

Bolingbroke may have failed to influence the peace negotiations as he would have liked, but that made it no easier for the Whigs and Britain's allies to stomach the preliminary peace articles agreed on by the British and French in the summer of 1711. To the disgust of the Whigs Spain was to be abandoned to Philip V, and Britain broke her promise not to make a separate peace. It is true that the French accepted the principle of a Dutch barrier in the Netherlands, but this was not to be anything like as extensive as that agreed in 1709. Moreover, the allies fumed as they saw Britain secure for itself extensive concessions from the French: recognition of the Hanoverian succession, a thirty-year monopoly (the *asiento*) of British trade to Spanish America, trade rights in Spain, and British possession of Gibraltar and Minorca in the Mediterranean, St Kitts in the Caribbean, and Acadia (Nova Scotia), Newfoundland, and Hudson Bay in North America. When these articles were published in September 1711 they were denounced predictably and rightly by the Whigs and allies alike as a sell-out. In Britain the opinion of one ally especially was noted with some alarm. Elector George of Hanover, son of Princess Sophia, who had been nominated as Anne's successor by the Act of Settlement of 1701, made no secret of his anger at those in Britain who were responsible for the peace. As a result, at the end of 1711 one can detect the first signs among Tories of uneasiness about the wisdom of supporting the government's peace policy. A record of opposition to the war would hardly be a recommendation for political promotion under a Hanoverian monarch. But there was also a more disinterested consideration which led other people than the Whigs to wonder if peace was such a good idea: might not the end of the war allow France and Spain to support a Jacobite restoration?

One of the first Tory converts to opposition to the peace was Nottingham. In November 1711 he moved into an open alliance with the Whigs, who in return cynically agreed to support an Occasional Conformity Bill similar to those they had successfully fought against earlier in the reign. Their reward for this unprincipled behaviour was only a temporary one: on 7 December with Nottingham's support the Whigs secured a vote in the House of Lords by a majority of one condemning the peace 'without Spain'. In the long run however, although the Occasional Conformity Bill became law, the opposition to the peace failed. Harley persuaded Anne to create twelve Tory peers and their votes in the upper House reversed the Whig motion of 7 December. Moreover, in the winter of 1711–12 Harley and St John mounted an effective propaganda campaign designed to overcome British scruples about making a dishonourable peace. Foremost in their literary armoury was Swift's pamphlet, *The Conduct of the Allies*, which was a violent attack on the Dutch, developing the Tory legend that the war had been prolonged to safeguard the particular interests of the allies, not of Britain, and therefore arguing that Britain ought to have no compunction about doublecrossing their erstwhile allies. As a result Harley marshalled majority opinion in parliament behind him against the Whigs and a small band of 'Hanoverian Tories', who in the spring of 1712 organized themselves into the March Club. A series of votes in parliament from December 1711 to June 1712 condemned the Dutch and endorsed the government's peace policy. The House of Commons even approved the 'restraining orders', ordering Ormonde, Marlborough's successor, not to make contact with the enemy, a decision which denied Prince Eugene British military support and undoubtedly contributed to the Austrian army's defeat at Denain in July. The events of the spring and summer of 1712 showed that a majority in Britain were willing to sweep aside all considerations of national honour and Britain's international obligations in the pursuit of peace.

Given its discreditable preliminaries one of the most surprising things about the peace settlement agreed in March and April 1713 at Utrecht by Britain, France, and the Dutch (peace between France and the Empire was made a year later by the treaties of Rastadt and Baden) is that it proved to be 'one of the great European peaces',[46] establishing an international framework which lasted for a hundred years. That it did so was due to two general aspects of the peace settlement. First, the Utrecht treaties did not neglect the interests of Britain's allies. As William III had foreseen, a fundamental condition of European peace was the partition of the Spanish Empire. Britain took the concessions in the Mediterranean and South America already agreed by the preliminary articles, along with the ex-French possessions of St Kitts, Nova Scotia, Newfoundland, and territories in Hudson Bay. France also formally agreed to recognize the Protestant succession in Britain established by the Act of Settlement. The emperor, though not represented at Utrecht, received massive chunks of the Spanish Empire in the Netherlands and Italy (Milan, Naples, and Sardinia), and the duke of Savoy was given Sicily. The Dutch did take part in the negotiations: that they did so was partly a measure of Oxford's success in curbing Bolingbroke's anti-Dutch outbursts, but after the allied defeat at Denain the Dutch really had no other alternative. Reluctant peacemakers they may have been, but at Utrecht they gained many of the barrier towns in the Netherlands which had always been their principal goal. The second merit of the Utrecht peace was its recognition of the limitations of what a peace treaty could achieve. The war had shown that Phillip V could not be forced off the Spanish throne, and this was accepted in 1713. The Catalans were abandoned and Philip V's possession of the Spanish throne and Spanish possessions in South America recognized. Of course, the peace of Utrecht did not provide a solution to all outstanding international problems. Its provision to prevent the future union of the Spanish and French thrones was very insecure indeed. In 1711 and 1712 three of the principal heirs of Louis XIV to the French throne died, the dauphin, the dauphin's eldest son the duke of Burgundy, and Burgundy's eldest son the duke of Brittany. As a result only a sickly two-year-old infant, Burgundy's younger son Louis, stood between Philip V and succession to the French throne. The only guarantee the Utrecht peacemakers could devise against that probability was Philip's renunciation of the French succession. Since this was hardly a promise that Philip could be relied on to keep, the peace of Utrecht cannot be given the credit for preventing the union of France and Spain. That came about instead by the fortunate fact that Louis XIV's heir did not die, but ruled France as Louis XV for nearly sixty years (1715–74). As far as Britain was concerned, too, the peace of Utrecht still left her without the emperor's recognition of the Protestant succession. Unfortunately history does not provide tidy solutions. Much was settled in 1713, but much still remained to be decided by the diplomats who made the Quadruple Alliance in 1718.[47]

A Jacobite restoration or Hanoverian succession?

With peace concluded political life in Britain came to be dominated by the question of who would succeed to the throne on Anne's death. This became increasingly urgent as the queen's health rapidly and visibly deteriorated; and in December 1713 she became seriously ill. Although she later recovered, the succession question was now again at the centre of the political world. The Whigs were totally united behind the provisions of the Act of Settlement of 1701 and the succession of Princess Sophia and, after her, of her son, George Lewis, elector of Hanover. The Tories, in contrast, were in disarray: only a minority had firm views about the succession. It is impossible to know how many were Jacobites like Richard Cresswell, the Tory MP for Bridgnorth, who after the Tory electoral victory of 1710 openly drank the Pretender's health at Bath. Undoubtedly, however, Jacobites were few in number in England where (as in Scotland) the propensity of people to voice Jacobite sentiments depended very much on the amount of alcohol they had consumed. When sober there were more Hanoverian than Jacobite Tories. Indeed in 1713–14 it is likely that the supporters of the March Club increased in numbers. In June 1713 during the debates on the Anglo-French commercial treaty negotiated by Bolingbroke it became clear that some Tories opposed it because they distrusted Bolingbroke's motives in drawing closer to France. It is true that this was not the only reason for the defection of the eighty Tories who helped to destroy the treaty. Like Bolingbroke's commercial treaties with Spain in 1713 the French treaty was badly drafted and presented (this was the work of Matthew Prior). It also excepted woollen manufacturers from its reduction of mutual tariffs, and therefore brought on itself the wrath of clothier vested interests, Tory as well as Whig.[48] Yet the treaty became identified in the minds of some Tories with the one occasion, in August 1712, when Bolingbroke had escaped from Oxford's restraint and had allowed himself to be seen in Paris in public with the Pretender.

The debates on the French commercial treaty showed that the ranks of the October Club were split, and that Sir Thomas Hanmer had emerged as the influential spokesman of a group of Hanoverian Tories. In April 1714 nearly a quarter of the 340 Tory MPs voted in favour of a motion that the Protestant succession was in danger. By 1713–14, then, there were fewer Jacobite Tories than Hanoverian Tories, but it is likely that the biggest group of Tories by far were those who were still undecided about their attitude to the succession. The chronic inability of many Tories to commit themselves to the Protestant succession has already been seen. Their unwillingness to abandon the principle of hereditary succession had thrown many into long periods of tortuous indecision in 1701-2 when faced with the Abjuration Oath. To this was now added the more immediate consideration that the Hanoverians who were Lutherans, foreigners, and deeply involved in European affairs, were representative of everything most Tories hated deeply. Moreover, it did not take much imagination to forsee the plight of those Tories who had voted for the 'restraining order' after the arrival in England of Elector George, who had fought alongside Prince Eugene at Denain.

With the country teetering on the edge of civil war and with the Tories split and uncertain about the succession the crying need was for clear leadership. They needed someone at the centre to give them unequivocal guidance. The Tories were still very strongly represented in the country. The general election of August–September 1713 produced a House of Commons of about 363 Tory MPs and only 180 Whigs.[49] Yet this Tory majority never received the leadership it needed. Part of the explanation for this is that from the spring of 1713 onwards the quarrel between Oxford and Bolingbroke, which had smouldered fitfully since 1710, exploded into an open and bitter rivalry. With peace concluded all common ground between the two ministers was gone. After the end of Anne's fourth parliament in July 1713 Bolingbroke and his allies, especially lord Harcourt and Atterbury (now promoted to the bishopric of Rochester), tried to force Oxford to appoint Tory ministers and pursue Tory policies. As usual, Oxford emerged triumphantly from a prolonged bout of political in-fighting, and in August he appointed Bolingbroke's political enemies to key posts. Especially galling to Bolingbroke was the announcement that Bromley and Hanmer, both Hanoverian Tories, were to be respectively secretary of state and speaker of the new House of Commons. Oxford's victory, however, was not conclusive; on the contrary it intensified the bitterness of the struggle between the two men in the last twelve months of the reign. Unfortunately for the Tory party at this crucial time it was left adrift because the energies of Bolingbroke and Oxford were channelled into political rivalry, not leadership.

The attitudes to the succession problem of Bolingbroke and Oxford are very difficult to determine with any certainty. In the winter of 1713-14 both were in contact with the Pretender through a French agent, the Abbé Gaultier. However, this is by no means evidence that either of them was a committed Jacobite; this form of insurance against the possibility, however remote, of a change of regime was very common in the early eighteenth century, no less than in the fifteenth or sixteenth centuries. Not surprisingly, neither minister left a record of his private hopes regarding the succession, but all the indications are that Bolingbroke before March 1714 was much more prepared than Oxford to envisage the prospect of a Jacobite restoration. His visit to the Pretender in August 1712 in Paris has already been noted. He also maintained close connections with Jacobites in Britain, and made no attempt to curry favour with the Hanoverian court. In March 1714, however, he received the news (as did Oxford and Anne) that the

Pretender refused under any circumstances to change his religion. This caused Bolingbroke to abandon during Anne's lifetime the prospect of a Jacobite restoration, and, with a Hanoverian succession almost certain, he began to look for a political strategy that would protect himself and the Tory party against the disfavour of Queen Sophia or King George. This he found in the scheme of uniting the Tories behind his leadership on the one issue on which the Tories were at one, the Church. At the same time, he would continue to undermine Oxford's position at court. Having secured an unassailable supremacy in parliament and at court, he would then be able to purge his opponents (Harleyites, Hanoverian Tories, and Whigs alike) from every public office of note, so that when the Hanoverians arrived they would have no alternative but to accept the *fait accompli* of the Tory dominance of public life.

Put like that it can be seen that this was an ambitious strategy, and at first it went well. At court Bolingbroke's influence rose at Oxford's expense. Partly by assigning some of the projected profits from the trade to Central and South America to Mrs Masham, Bolingbroke weaned Anne's confidante from Oxford's patronage. In addition, Oxford's close relationship with the queen, which had survived his absence from office from 1708 to 1710, ended in the autumn of 1713. The cause seems slight; in September Oxford asked that his son Edward, newly married to Lady Harriet Holles, be made duke of Newcastle. The queen became convinced that Oxford was pursuing family ambition at the expense of all else, and Oxford's influence with her was gone. Moreover, Bolingbroke, with the cooperation of Atterbury, piloted the Schism Bill through parliament, and must have been satisfied with the support the Bill received from Hanoverian Tories like Hanmer and the earl of Anglesey (though not from Nottingham). Defoe concluded that the Schism Bill was 'the mine to blow up the white Staff'.[50] Not only were the Tories temporarily reunited against the hated dissenter schools, but Oxford's dislike of the measure put him in a very difficult position.

In the end, however, Bolingbroke's plans failed for three main reasons. First, he did not reunite the Tory party on any other issue than that of the Church. The Hanoverian Tories especially remained suspicious of him and not without good reason. Bolingbroke may not have been a Jacobite in the last months of Anne's reign, but he appeared to be one. Secondly, he was never accepted into the inner circle of Anne's court. Anne maintained her personal grudge against Bolingbroke, as against others, with great tenacity. Even when the queen dismissed Oxford, she refused to promote Bolingbroke to the lord treasurership. Finally, the major obstacle to Bolingbroke's scheme was Oxford's tenacity in hanging on to office. The lord treasurer held on until 27 July 1714, giving Bolingbroke too little time to profit by his dismissal before Anne died.

During the period from the autumn of 1713 until Anne's death Oxford was the major block to Bolingbroke's ambitions to unite the Tory party, but he failed himself to provide the guidance the leaderless

Tories needed. Judging by his actions he was never anything other than a committed Hanoverian; in the spring of 1714 he even supported a Whig move to announce a reward for the capture of the Pretender if he should land in Britain. Oxford could have been the man to persuade uncommitted Tories to swell the ranks of the Hanoverian Tories. Unfortunately, however, in the winter of 1713–14 Oxford appears to have undergone a traumatic personal crisis, perhaps brought on by the death of his daughter or by the loss of the queen's favour. Whatever the reasons, outwardly he appeared apathetic and unassertive. He began to drink heavily and this adversely affected his work and his political influence. In the spring of 1714 he recovered slightly, but clearly all his diminishing energy was concentrated on the one aim of keeping himself in and keeping his rival out of office. Oxford was even less fitted in 1714 than in 1710 to be a leader of the Tory party.

When Anne dismissed Oxford on 27 July, though she was very ill, she was still the key political figure she had been throughout her reign. It is as difficult to know what her hopes about the immediate future were as it is to ascertain those of Bolingbroke and Oxford. It is clear that she did not want Bolingbroke as her prime minister, and royal disfavour, as others had found before, was a deadly blight to a political career. What is less clear is whether or not Anne was in favour of a Jacobite restoration. It is true that she suffered bouts of conscience about usurping her half-brother's hereditary rights in 1702, and she disliked the Hanoverians as vehemently as any Tory. But, though suspicions remain, it is unlikely that after March 1714 she could contemplate a Jacobite restoration seriously.[51] On 30 July, in any case, she fell into a coma and matters at last were taken out of her hands. On the initiative of Lord Chancellor Harcourt and the privy council, Shrewsbury was appointed lord treasurer, making the Hanoverian succession certain. When Anne died on 1 August the Act of Settlement came into operation, and the Regency Council governed until the arrival of George I (his mother had died in June). So despite all the fears the Stuart age ended, as it had begun, with the peaceful succession of a new dynasty.

The eclipse of the Tory party

The Tory party faced the end of the Stuart age in disarray, and on the accession of George I all their fears were confirmed. The Junto Whigs and their acolytes were appointed by the new king to every key public office. Moreover, this was the beginning of a long Whig supremacy in eighteenth-century British politics. Why did the Tories not recover in 1714 from this temporary setback as they had done in 1689, 1697 and 1710, and as the Whigs had done in 1695 and in 1708? It is true that Bolingbroke and Oxford were under a cloud, and that the older generation of Tory leaders was either dead (Rochester died in 1711 and Danby in 1712) or no longer acceptable to the Tory rank-and-file (Nottingham had opposed the peace in 1711 and the Schism Act in 1714). But the Tories did not lack young and able leaders, like Hanmer and Bromley. They still had a natural majority in the country. What is more the arrival of a foreign king presented them with the possibility, as in 1689, of rebuilding Tory unity by emphasizing the danger to the Church of England from a dissenter monarch, and by appealing to the traditional Tory hostility to the undue influence of foreign favourites and to involvement in Europe in the interests of the Elector of Hanover but at British expense. Nevertheless the fortunes of the Tory party did not revive in the early years of George I's reign as they had in those of William III's reign. Why did 1714 mark the eclipse of the Tory party's influence for much of the eighteenth century?[52]

This is a difficult question and it is fortunate that part of the answer to it lies beyond the scope of this book. Some contributory factors derived wholly from the period after 1714, most notably the Septennial Act of 1716. Typically the new Whigs of the early eighteenth century do not seem to have had any compunction about introducing a measure designed to increase executive influence. By extending the life of individual parliaments to seven years the Septennial Act greatly increased the scope of government patronage, which the Whigs quickly used to their own advantage. Moreover the Whigs did not have to face a general election during a period of internal divisions in 1717 and 1720. The Tory party did not disappear, but the Septennial Act made it very difficult for it to present a serious challenge to Whig supremacy. Thus 1716 is a more fitting conclusion to the political history of the Stuart Age than 1714. Nevertheless some possible causes of the Tory eclipse are visible before 1714. One is the vastly superior leadership and organization of the Whig party, which since 1689 had enabled the Whigs to overcome the drawback of being a minority party. By 1714 the Whigs were arguably more united than they had ever been before in defence of the Protestant succession and of their 'Revolution Principles'. Moreover, in Stanhope, Townshend, Pulteney, and Walpole they had a group of high-flying leaders to replace the now ageing Junto (most of whom died in 1715–16). Because of developments before 1714 the Whigs were thus well placed and capable of taking advantage of their supremacy in 1714. In the first few months after Anne's death they carried out a ruthless purge of their political opponents from public office on a scale never before attempted. Moreover, the general election of 1715 followed the formula established in earlier elections: the Whigs, because they had the open backing of the crown, secured the electorate's majority support. The Whig political advance of 1714–15 was made easier by the fact that only Nottingham of the major Tory leaders could be persuaded to accept office. Hanmer and Bromley were offered government posts by George I, but turned them down. Did they do so because the history of politics in the previous reign had shown that party unity could be an effective way to secure office? It is possible that they hoped to emulate the Whig Junto in 1708 and, after another general election, force the king to offer them more important ministerial positions. Whatever the reasons, their decision helped the Whigs to secure a firm grip on royal government. Do the technical organizational limitations of the Tories, though, provide a complete explanation for their failure to recover? It had not prevented Tory revival before.

A more cogent reason for the Tory collapse after 1714 can also be seen before Anne's death: the ambiguous attitude of many Tories to the Protestant succession. As has been seen, the failure of many Tories to come to terms with their conscientious objections to the Glorious Revolution had caused them endless trouble before 1714. It was still their Achilles' heel on Anne's death: it laid them wide open to charges that they were disloyal to the new king. Moreover, Whig allegations that Tory fence-sitting on the question of the succession was merely a cover for Jacobite loyalties were made more plausible by Bolingbroke's flight at the end of March 1715 to the Pretender's court. As a result during the Jacobite rebellion of 1715, though the vast majority of Tories rallied to George I, Walpole was able to find enough evidence of Tory sympathy for the Pretender to make his smear campaign against all Tories an enormous success. He employed the same tactics again in 1717, 1718, 1719, and 1723, when Jacobite invasions were feared. Certainly this was a major factor in the Tories' downfall. 'Toryism and Jacobitism' became as powerful a political cliché in the early eighteenth century as was 'Dissent and Sedition' in the reign of Charles II.

Finally, one wonders if the collapse of the Tory party after 1714 was rooted in its intimate connection for decades before 1714 with the ideology of 'country' opinion. On many occasions in Stuart England – whether in the unrealistic estimates of the expenditure necessary for foreign wars in the parliamentary debates of the 1620s, or in the rejection of considerations of government credit and national obligations in the urgent pursuit of peace after 1710 – it had shown itself to be an ideology unsuited to responsible government. It was rooted in provincial, local concerns, not in the wider interests of the country. The Tory party, as it developed in the later seventeenth and early eighteenth centuries proved to be a party of backbench critics, not a party that could produce the responsible statesmen that Britain needed as a new major European power.

Notes

For abbreviations used throughout see p. xiv.

1. Quoted in Holmes, *British Politics*, p. 49.
2. *Ibid.*, p. 21.
3. Kenyon, *Revolution Principles*, p. 122.
4. Quoted in Speck, *Tory and Whig*, p. 92.
5. Holmes, *British Politics*, p. 30.
6. Speck, *Tory and Whig*, p. 42.
7. G. M. Trevelyan, *England in the Reign of Queen Anne* (3 vols, 1930–4), I, p. 167.
8. John Carswell, *The Old Cause: three biographical studies in Whiggism* (1954), p. 59.

9. Trevelyan, *Anne*, I, p. 178, and Holmes, *British Politics*, p. 212.
10. Quoted in Trevelyan, *Anne*, I, pp. 175–6.
11. See Holmes, *British Politics*, pp. 440–2 (Appendix c) on the use of the term 'Prime Minister' in this period.
12. Bennett, *Atterbury*, p. 81.
13. Quoted in Trevelyan, *Anne*, I, p. 210.
14. Quoted in Kenyon, *Revolution Principles*, pp. 92, 116.
15. Quoted in *ibid.*, p. 93.
16. Quoted in Trevelyan, *Anne*, II, p. 12.
17. H. L. Snyder, 'Party configurations in the early eighteenth-century House of Commons', *B.I.H.R.*, XLV (1972), p. 45.
18. G. V. Bennett, 'Robert Harley, the Godolphin ministry and the bishopric crisis of 1707', *E.H.R.*, LXXXII, 1967. Professor Kenyon wonders whether Offspring Blackall was a Tory divine before 1708, though he clearly was subsequently, Kenyon, *Revolution Principles*, pp. 119–20.
19. Quoted in Holmes, *British Politics*, p. 68.
20. G. Holmes, 'Post-Revolution Britain and the historian', in Holmes, ed., *Britain after the Glorious Revolution*, p. 21.
21. Derek McKay, *Prince Eugene of Savoy* (1977), pp. 246–7.
22. Quoted in Holmes, *British Politics*, p. 91.
23. Holmes, *ibid.*, p. 200, n.
24. James Halliday, 'The Club and the Revolution in Scotland 1689–90', *Scottish Historical Review*, XLV (1966), p. 147.
25. Dalrymple is sometimes referred to as Stair. The student needs to beware of the confusion caused by some historians of Scotland who call people by their surname, while others use their place of residence.
26. Quoted in Baxter, *William III*, p. 375.
27. Browning, *English Historical Documents*, p. 678.
28. W. Ferguson, 'The making of the Treaty of Union of 1707; *Scottish Historical Review*, XLIII, 1964, and *Scotland's relations with England: a survey to 1707* (Edinburgh, 1977). For a more moderate view of the Act of Union from the Scottish point of view see David Daiches, *Scotland and the Union* (1977), T. C. Smout, 'The road to Union', in Holmes, ed., *Britain after the Glorious Revolution*, and 'The Anglo-Scottish Union of 1707: I. The economic background', *Econ. H.R.*, 2nd ser., XVI (1963–4), pp. 455–67, and G. S. Pryde, *The Treaty of Union of Scotland and England 1707* (1950).
29. R. H. Campbell, 'The Anglo-Scottish Union of 1707. II. The economic consequences', *Econ. H.R.*, 2nd ser., XVI (1963–4), p. 468.
30. Quoted in Trevelyan, *Anne*, II, p. 385.
31. G. Holmes and W. A. Speck, 'The fall of Harley in 1708 reconsidered', *E.H.R.*, LXXXI (1965), pp. 673–98.
32. M. A. Thomson, 'Louis XIV and the Grand Alliance, 1705–10', Hatton and Bromley, eds, *William III and Louis XIV*, pp. 201–10.
33. Quoted in A. D. MacLachlan, 'The road to peace, 1710–13', in Holmes, ed., *Britain after the Glorious Revolution*, p. 199.
34. Quoted in Holmes, *British Politics*, p. 69.
35. Quoted in Trevelyan, *Anne*, II, p. 387.
36. Quoted in Kenyon, *Revolution Principles*, p. 117.
37. Professor Kenyon thinks this was written by Thomas Harrison, *ibid.*, pp. 123ff. See also J. P. Kenyon, 'The Revolution of 1688: resistance and

contract', in N. McKendrick, ed., *Historical Perspectives: studies in English thought and society* (1974), pp. 62–4.

38. Quoted in Kenyon, *Revolution Principles*, p. 130.
39. Bennett, *Atterbury*, p. 110.
40. Browning, *English Historical Documents*, p. 206.
41. G. Holmes, 'The Sacheverell riots', *P.&P.*, LXXII (1976), pp. 55–85.
42. Quoted in Trevelyan, *Anne*, III, p. 54.
43. Quoted in Kenyon, *Revolution Principles*, p. 155.
44. G. V. Bennett, 'The Convocation of 1710: an Anglican attempt at counter-revolution', in G. J. Cumings and D. Baker, eds, *Studies in Church History*, VII (1971).
45. Quoted in Holmes, *British Politics*, p. 67, and Trevelyan, *Anne*, III, p. 107.
46. M. A. Thomson, 'Self-determination and collective security as factors in English and French foreign policy, 1689–1718', in Hatton and Bromley, eds, *William III and Louis XIV*, p. 283.
47. For the Quadruple Alliance see G. C. Gibbs, 'Parliament and the treaty of Quadruple Alliance' in Hatton and Bromley, eds, *William III and Louis XIV*, pp. 287–305.
48. D. C. Coleman, 'Politics and economics in the age of Anne: the case of the Anglo-French trade treaty of 1713', in D. C. Coleman and A. H. John, eds, *Trade, Government and Economy in Pre-Industrial England* (1976).
49. E. G. Cruickshanks, 'The Tories and the succession to the Crown in the 1714 parliament', *B.I.H.R.*, XLVI (1973), p. 176.
50. Quoted in Bennett, *Atterbury*, p. 177.
51. Edward Gregg, 'Was Queen Anne a Jacobite?', *History*, LVII (1972), pp. 358–75.
52. Recent work on eighteenth-century politics emphasizes the fact that the Tory party, though eclipsed by the Whigs, did not disintegrate and disappear altogether soon after 1714 as was once thought. See e.g., Linda J. Colley, 'The loyal brotherhood and the Cocoa Tree: the London organization of the Tory party, 1727–60', *H.J.*, XX (1977), pp. 77–95.

Part six

Later Stuart England: change and continuity

Chapter 14
Change

War and constitutional changes

In 1640–1 the Elizabethan constitution collapsed. Subsequently, during the English Revolution and the reigns of the later Stuarts, there was a search for a new constitutional 'settlement'. In the early years of the eighteenth century many people believed that this search had been successful in 1688–9, when, it was thought, the architects of the Glorious Revolution had erected a constitution in which the three elements in it – king, Lords, and· Commons – balanced and limited each other, producing conditions of political stability and constitutional harmony. 'Herein indeed consists the true excellence of the English government', wrote Sir William Blackstone in the middle of the century,

that all parts of it form a mutual check upon each other. In the legislature, the people are a check upon the nobility, and the nobility a check upon the people; by the mutual privilege of rejecting what the other has resolved: while the king is a check upon both, which preserves the executive power from encroachments. And this very executive power is again checked and kept within due bounds by the two houses. . . . Thus every branch of our civil polity supports and is supported, regulates and is regulated, by the rest. . . . Like three distinct powers in mechanics, they jointly impel the machine of government in a direction different from what either, acting by itself, would have done; but at the same time in a direction partaking of each, and formed out of all; a direction which constitutes the true line of the liberty and happiness of the community.[1]

However, the constitutional changes of the late seventeenth and early eighteenth centuries were not so straightforward or so complete as Blackstone and 'a prolific school of constitutional mythologists' in the latter century maintained.[2] It has already been seen that the Glorious Revolution of 1688–9, like the English Revolution and the 'Restoration Settlement', effected few permanent changes in the constitution or in the crown's financial and administrative system. In 1689 the English government was as ill-equipped to finance a major war as all previous governments in the later sixteenth and early seventeenth centuries. All attempts before 1660 to remedy this had failed: as has been seen, in peacetime there was no general desire to reform the king's government, and in wartime (the 1590s, 1620s, 1640s, and 1650s) attempts to create an efficient central executive invariable produced intense local opposition (notably the Petition of Right in 1628 and the 'second civil war' in 1648) which ensured that such measures were not permanent.

Therefore, in 1689 one of the major constitutional problems of the Stuart age remained: to establish a reformed, strengthened central government without sparking off violent provincial resistance. If this was to be solved, there would have to be both a major readjustment and a clearer definition of the respective powers of the crown and of parliament. In many contemporary European countries the solution had been found in the establishment of strong, absolutist monarchies and a reduction in the powers of representative assemblies. As has been seen, the restoration of Charles II in 1660 made this a possible outcome in England also; that the English monarchy before 1688 did not become as strong as that in France was ensured mainly by the opposition roused by Charles II's and James II's quixotic decisions to follow Catholic policies. After 1689 the English crown perhaps could still have made itself politically independent of parliament; that it did not do so is to be explained only in the most indirect way by the effects of the Glorious Revolution. The immediate result of the invasion of William of Orange and his accession as king was to involve England in a long and expensive war against France, which lasted (apart from 1697 to 1701) from 1689 to 1713. Because of the unprecedented scale and cost of this war the familiar problem faced by Tudor and Stuart rulers emerged in a more pressing form than ever before: how to finance a war with an antiquated system of public finance and with the likelihood that excessive demands for money would be met with hostility by parliament and most influential opinion in the country.

The wars of William III and Queen Anne's reigns proved to be a major catalyst of constitutional change. They had as great an impact on the long-term development of the British constitution as it has been seen that they had on the short-term pattern of English politics. During the 1690s and early 1700s for the first time practical solutions were discovered for one of the major constitutional problems of the Stuart age. The development of a powerful central executive and the 'financial revolution', which took place as responses to the demands of the wars against France, aroused enormous mistrust in the country, but, unlike previous occasions, local opposition did not prevent such administrative and financial changes from becoming permanent. The explanation lies mainly in the fact that they were accompanied by a shift in the respective roles and powers of the crown and of parliament which helped to reconcile the political nation to them. These changes by no means represented a perfect constitutional settlement by 1714, as will be seen (see below, pp. 458–9). Nevertheless, by 1714 under the pressures of war the British constitution had diverged permanently from the prevailing pattern of European absolutism.

War and the king's government

All statutory attempts to curb the powers of the Stuarts had only limited or temporary success. The parliamentary leaders in the 1640s were themselves well aware that the legislation of 1641 was not an effective means of restricting Charles I. Moreover, the constitutional legislation passed in and after 1689 was more important in the context of contemporary politics than in that of the long-term development of the British constitution. The Bill of Rights (1689), the Triennial Act (1694), and the Act of Settlement (1701) enacted only partial limitations on the powers of the monarchy. The Bill of Rights declared that extra-parliamentary taxation was illegal and that standing armies in peace-time had to be approved by parliament; it also abolished the powers exercised by James II of suspending parliamentary statutes. The Triennial Act inhibited the monarch's freedom to summon and dissolve parliaments at will. The Act of Settlement did not come into effect until Queen Anne's death, and before then its most important restrictions had been repealed. But when the Act did become effective in 1714 it guaranteed the independence of the judiciary by making permanent the tenure of office by judges, as well as preventing George I both from declaring war in defence of Hanover without parliamentary approval and from granting his countrymen offices or places in the privy council. All these were important, but they represented meagre limitations on the powers of later Stuart and Hanoverian monarchs. Moreover, in certain respects these powers had grown since the days of James I and Charles I.

Firstly, the later Stuarts had a bureaucracy that was bigger and more efficient than that possessed by their predecessors. Partly this was a reflection of the intellectual interests of some of the servants of the later Stuarts, like Samuel Pepys and William Blathwayt, who were friends of William Petty, the exponent of 'political arithmetic'. An expanded civil service was necessary, in their view, to collect statistics on which rational government decisions could be based (see below, p. 429). However, far more important in causing the expansion of the king's government were the wars of the late seventeenth and early eighteenth centuries. Before 1689 this can be seen most clearly in the emergence of the treasury as a financial department, challenging (although not supplanting) the exchequer's role as the central institution of public finance. In this process the key date is 1667, significantly at the end of the second Dutch war, which had highlighted the need for financial reorganization. In May 1667 Charles II, with the Cromwellian practice of 'government by committees' in mind, appointed a treasury commission, which (under the influence of its secretary, Sir George Downing) began systematic record-keeping 'as part of a deliberate campaign to exercise closer control of revenue and expenditure'. By a series of privy council orders in 1668 the treasury secured its independence of the secretaries and of the privy council.[3] Later treasury officials, especially the earl of Rochester and the treasury commissioners of 1679 to 1684, ensured the permanence of these reforms, with the result that 'between 1660 and 1702 the Treasury office grew from something approaching the personal retinue of a magnate into a professional body of civil servants'.[4] Soon the treasury exercised control over the administration of the customs and excise and other revenues. Before 1689 also professional administrative methods were introduced into naval and military organization, most notably due to the work of Samuel Pepys as secretary to the admiralty from 1673 to 1679 and 1684 to 1688, and of William Blathwayt as secretary at war from 1683.[5]

However, the most rapid growth in the king's government took place after 1689. During the wars against France, although by no means all traditional royal administrative methods were changed (see below, pp. 458–9), there was arguably a 'revolution in government' that made more impact on the structure of government administration than anything that happened in the 1530s.[6] The major changes did not take place in the older parts of the king's government; indeed the number of offices at the royal court declined during the Stuart age, from 1,480 during the reign of Charles I to under 1,000 in the reign of George I. In 1713 the principal secretaries' office had only four under-secretaries and eight clerks. The parts of the royal administration that expanded most were those directly affected by the needs of war: financial, military, naval, and diplomatic departments, manned by professional administrators, like Blathwayt, who served all four later Stuart monarchs.[7] Because there are few detailed studies of the civil service of the later Stuarts on the scale of Professor Aylmer's books on the administration system from 1625 to 1642 and from 1649 to 1660,[8] it is not possible to quantify the expansion in all departments, but it is clear from the work that has been done that in some cases vast numbers of officials were employed, especially in the revenue departments – customs, excise, the salt office (established in 1702), and the leather office (established in 1711). By 1718 there were 561 full-time and about 1,000 part-time customs officials working in London alone. The diplomatic service, too, increased greatly, from 80 representatives in William III's reign to 136 in Queen Anne's. The expansion of the army and navy was paralleled by a bureaucratic explosion, although it is easier to quantify the scale of the former than the latter: the tonnage of ships in the navy increased from 101,892 in 1689 to 167,219 in 1714, and the size of the army jumped from 10,000 troops in 1689 to 70,000 in 1711.[9] Although the royal civil service in Britain did not expand to the same extent as that in contemporary France, the development of the government of William III and Queen Anne was similar in kind to that in Louis XIV's France, a point emphasized by the admiration felt by the new breed of English civil servants like Pepys and Blathwayt for the authority and efficiency of French central government.

The second great change that had taken place in the king's government since the early seventeenth century was an improvement in the crown's finances. This is strikingly illustrated by the contrast between the inability of Charles I to pay even for the limited wars of the 1620s and the achievement of the government of William III and Queen Anne in financing two full-scale European wars. They were enabled to do so because after 1689, using precedents established since the mid-seventeenth century, all three major sources of royal revenue – the crown's hereditary income, taxation, and borrowing – were transformed. By the Restoration the only major element left of the traditional hereditary revenues of the crown was that from customs duties. Income from crown estates was already small before 1640, and the crown's revenue from wardships and purveyance, abolished with feudal tenures in 1646, was not restored in 1660. However, from the early 1670s customs duties which reached the crown rose rapidly, as a result of the expansion of overseas trade in this period and the decision to revert (as in the 1640s and 1650s) to direct collection of the customs. Between 1688 and 1702 22.7 per cent of the crown's income came from customs duties.[10] Before 1640 the burden of taxation in England had been the least onerous in the whole of Europe. Underassessment for direct parliamentary taxation had reached ludicrous proportions, and, unlike France, there was little indirect taxation. Moreover, it was still theoretically considered that parliamentary taxation ought to be levied only on extraordinary occasions, when the king could not 'live of his own'. The parliamentary regimes of the 1640s, followed by the royalist council of war inaugurated, however, the first attempts at a new taxation system in England. Weekly and monthly assessments from 1643 onwards were much more effective direct taxes than traditional parliamentary subsidies, and the excise, also introduced in 1643, was the first comprehensive purchase tax in England, levied on a wide range of commodities. Both were retained by Restoration governments. Moreover, from 1683 excise duties were collected directly by government officials, not tax farmers; and in the 1690s the land tax was revised on the same principles as assessments, to become the main source of direct taxation in later Stuart England. As in the case of the assessment, the yield of each land tax was decided on before it was levied and the sum then apportioned among the counties. Between 1688 and 1702 23.2 per cent of the crown's revenue came from the excise and 32.5 per cent from land taxes. The traditional concept that the king should 'live of his own' was now abandoned, and for the first time taxation was accepted as a *normal* part of the crown's revenue.

Easily as dramatic as the massive increase in the scale and sophistication of direct and indirect taxation in the later seventeenth and early eighteenth centuries was 'the financial revolution' in public borrowing that accompanied it.[11] Like governments at any time the income of Stuart governments always fell short of their expenditure, and the gap had to be filled by short- and long-term borrowing. In the early seventeenth century this was done largely by James I and Charles I borrowing money in much the same way as private individuals, using their own assets as security. This is why the early Stuarts found investors increasingly unwilling to lend money to them and why they (and the parliamentarians in the 1640s) had to resort to forced loans. However, in the 1660s there emerged the beginnings of a new system of public credit. As has been seen, the additional aid levied by parliament in 1665 was devised by Sir George Downing and supported by Charles II. In order to persuade investors to advance money to the government the tax was appropriated to a specific use (the second Dutch war) and creditors were to be repaid in rotation: those who had lent first were to be repaid first. Moreover, they received treasury orders promising repayment, and these orders were legally negotiable. Although these innovations received a setback in 1672 when the crown defaulted on interest payments to its creditors, they 'were to become the standard devices of "the financial revolution"'.[12] After 1689 the crown's need for loans was greater than ever before: between 1688 and 1702 the gap between royal income and expenditure was about £11.3 million. Among the many projects devised to meet this unprecedented deficit two were ultimately successful. In January 1693 parliament authorized William III to borrow £1 million; the creditors were to be repaid by annuities and these were funded by new parliamentary excise duties. The second project, the foundation of the Bank of England, is more complicated, but the principles employed were similar to those used in 1693: the 8 per cent interest on a loan of £1,200,000 was to be repaid by specific duties allocated by parliament, and in return the subscribers were incorporated as a bank and given power to borrow more money on the security of parliamentary taxation. The effect of these measures of 1693 and 1694, as had been the intention of Downing in 1665, was to ensure that royal debts were underwritten not by the crown but by parliament. The king's debt became the National Debt. This system took a long time to become established; other projects like the Million Lottery of 1694, a national sweepstake, were tried but failed. Gradually parliamentary guarantees were established as the basis of public credit, with the result that investors were now more willing than ever before to lend money to the government. Consequently, as well as enjoying a predictable income from taxation, William III and Queen Anne were able to borrow money on a more extensive scale than any other monarch in English history.

By 1714 the implications of these changes in the royal government in the late seventeenth and early eighteenth centuries were far-reaching for the prestige of the British monarchy. English governments after 1559, wrote J. P. Cooper, were 'more than ever limited to a basically defensive [foreign] policy, however much their subjects hankered after past glories'.[13] This remained true until 1689: the only possible exception is the Cromwellian Protectorate, which carved out for itself a respectable international reputation, which Stuart monarchs before 1689 did not have. James I did not possess the financial resources to enable him to be the powerful figure in European diplomacy he would have liked to be; Charles I and James II (with the exception of the former's brief excursions into wars against France and Spain) followed isolationist policies; and Charles II seemed to many at the time to be little more than a puppet of Louis XIV. William III and Queen Anne, however, were able to take a leading role in European affairs. Moreover, by 1714 England and Scotland were united as Great Britain, and the country's overseas possessions were expanding rapidly. In great contrast to the period before 1689 (and certainly before 1640) the British monarch was the head of a country which was a major European and imperial power.

War, parliament, and the local communities

Growing local resentment and mistrust at the development of a strong central executive in the late seventeenth and early eighteenth centuries, leading to attacks on alleged maladministration and corruption in government and attempts to protect parliament from royal interference, were not unexpected. By the 1690s 'country' mistrust of central government had a long history stretching back for at least a century. In the reigns of the later Stuarts fears about the future of parliament were as strong among some MPs as they had been in the reigns of James I and Charles I. However, after 1689 they had less foundation than earlier. By 1714 royal government in Britain was as strong as many continental governments, but it was far less free to indulge in policies of centralization and absolutism. The assertion that the evolution of a new system of public credit was made possible by a new constitutional framework after 1689 ought to be reversed. It was 'the financial revolution' that contributed directly to the development of a new constitutional system, in which parliament's permanent place was assured.

This came about in two major ways. First, the crown's dependence on parliamentary taxation for wartime expenditure forced it to concede parliament's demands to exercise some control over the way that the money was spent. During the period before 1714 the principle of parliamentary appropriation of supply and parliamentary audit of the royal finances became established. Parliament in effect became responsible for the maintenance of the armed forces, and annual sessions were therefore necessary in order to grant the bulk of the money for this purpose. This provided more certainty of annual parliamentary sessions in wartime than in peacetime. A second constitutional effect of 'the financial revolution' was therefore more crucial. By perpetuating royal debts (now the National Debt) on a parliamentary basis, 'the financial revolution' ensured that, even in peacetime, annual sessions of parliament would be necessary to provide a constant guarantee of public creditworthiness. Parliaments were now indispensible to the financial viability of the king's government and annual sessions of parliament were assured. In 1698 this dependence was underlined when MPs felt that the grant to the monarch of a regular income of £700,000 p.a. for life (the civil list) would not undermine it.[14]

The king's government by the end of the Stuart age was financially stronger than ever before, but in a position that ensured that it was heavily dependent on parliament. Before 1714 this is most clearly shown in two constitutional developments other than those directly resulting from 'the financial revolution': the erosion of the royal prerogative and the restraint exercised by the central government in its relations with local communities. By 1714 the royal prerogative was limited in two main ways; neither was openly admitted by anyone, least of all by William III and Queen Anne, but both became practical limitations on royal power. The last two Stuarts were not as free as their predecessors to choose their own ministers or to determine their own foreign policies. As has been seen, William III and Queen Anne, in order to get their business through parliament, at times had to accept as ministers men whom they detested. Later Stuart parliaments gained some voice in the choice of royal ministers, a vital erosion of the crown's prerogative which Pym and the parliamentary leadership in the 1640s had completely failed to achieve. Moreover, William III and Queen Anne were also forced to consult parliament to a much greater extent than ever before in the making of foreign policy.

The transformation was highlighted in 1700–1. Until 1700 William III had conducted his own foreign policy without reference to opinion in England. The war against France in the 1690s is rightly known as 'William's war'. Even his English ministers were not told about the negotiations resulting in the Partition treaty of 1698; parliament did not learn of them until 1700. However, in order to persuade parliament to accept the need for renewed war against France, in 1701 William III entered into a close dialogue with parliament about foreign affairs. 'What William had been forced to concede, Anne was unable to refuse', writes G. C. Gibbs; it 'became usual for ministers and others to expound foreign policy in Parliament and to lay treaties and papers before Parliament, either at its request or upon the initiative of the Crown.'[15]

However, there were limits to the king's dependence on parliament, and most MPs were content that this should be the case. Like their predecessors in the early seventeenth century most MPs did not want to exercise complete control over the king's government. They wanted their opinions to be taken into account in the formulation of policy, but they did not want to *initiate* policy. Most people saw that as the proper function of the crown and its ministers. The main concerns of most MPs remained bounded by their county horizons, and by the end of the Stuart age there appears to have emerged a new relationship between central government and the local communities which did not infringe the autonomy of the latter. It is difficult to write about this with a great deal of certainty, because there are at present few county studies of later Stuart England like those for the earlier period. But there is no reason to doubt Professor M. A. Thomson's generalization that 'after 1688 the ordinary conduct of local government was exempt from central control'.[16] Although there was no longer any systematic interference with borough charters as in the reigns of Charles II and James II, it is true that ministerial purges of lords-lieutenant, deputy-lieutenants, and justices of the peace continued after 1689. However, in 1660 the crown permanently lost many of the weapons it had used before 1640 to try to combat localism, especially the courts of high commission and star chamber. Moreover, after 1689 there are no signs even of sporadic intervention by the privy council (as in the early 1630s) to persuade local magistrates to enforce economic and social legislation. Perhaps the best illustration of the new relationship between the crown and the local communities is the way in which the land tax was administered. The assessment and collection of the tax was done by men who lived in the localities, not by bureaucrats foisted on the country by the central government. 'Land Tax administration underlined local social patterns.'[17] There were no equivalents in England of the *Intendants* employed in Louis XIV's France. By 1714 local autonomy, like parliament's place in the constitution, was secure.

Religious and intellectual changes

The Stuart age witnessed a search for a religious 'settlement' that lasted as long and was as difficult as the quest for a new constitutional relationship between crown and parliament. After 1660 the problems involved in reaching a religious settlement were more numerous than in the early seventeenth century, when there had been a large measure of agreement among most Protestants both about the form the Church should take and its relation to the state: its theology should be Calvinist predestinarianism; it should be governed by bishops; it should work in close cooperation with the state; and it should be the only Church allowed to exist. Religious toleration, it was felt, would inevitably upset the traditional hierarchical political and social order. However, developments during the 1640s and 1650s shattered the Protestant unity which had prevailed before 1640. During the revolutionary decades many varied forms of Protestantism emerged – Presbyterians, Independents, Congregationalists, Ranters, Quakers – and, although attempts were made after the Restoration to suppress these as effectively as Elizabeth I had crushed Presbyterians and separatists in the 1580s and 1590s, many of the sects survived. From this point onwards only their common hatred of Catholicism could bring English Protestants together, as in 1688, and then only temporarily. Theological diversity now prevailed: Calvinist predestinarianism was no longer the common theology of English Protestants. Dissenters – those who refused to conform to the Church of England as it was established in the 1660s – became a permanent feature of English life. As a result, from 1660 onwards the search for a religious settlement became more difficult than ever before.

After 1660 the established Church was presented with two major, novel problems. First, if it was now only one among many other Protestant churches, ought the Church of England to maintain its close alliance with the state and to continue to play a major political role? Second, could the Church of England come to terms with Protestant dissenters, either by agreeing to accommodate them within a broad established Church or by granting them the right to exist outside the Church? Moreover, in addition to these intractable questions of Church–state relations, and of religious comprehension or toleration, the restored Church of England also faced a new set of problems which emerged from changes in the intellectual climate of the period. Many of these changes were brought about, in part, by the spread of the new experimental science, as will be seen. Despite the pleas of scientists to the contrary, the spread of the new science led some people to question traditional Christian beliefs. Not only was the Church of England now faced with the competition of Protestant dissent, but also many churchmen feared that the Church was in danger of being overwhelmed by a growing tide of irreligion and atheism, as society became more secularized.

This section outlines some of the major responses of intellectual and religious opinion to these new problems in later Stuart England. As might be expected, the responses were diverse. However, in the period from 1660 to 1714 there developed, though not without intense opposition, the view that the Anglican Church was not (and never had been) independent of the state and ought to be subordinate to it, and that its major function ought to be pastoral rather than political. Furthermore, there emerged, again slowly and fitfully and in the face of much hostility, a conviction that Protestant dissenters ought to be tolerated and given freedom to worship. Finally, both these views were part of the response of some enlightened churchmen to the fact that later Stuart England appeared to be a period of diminished religious fervour, and that the Church had to concentrate on its missionary role and religion had to be defended on rational grounds. In the late seventeenth and early eighteenth centuries the vogue for rationalism in religion was part of a new rational approach to all current problems, in government and society as well as in the Church. Certainties founded on faith or on the writings of the 'ancients' were called into question. It came to be believed that by the application of reason – by basing arguments on facts discovered by observation and by personal experience, a method successfully adopted in the new sciences – there were no limits to the improvements that could be brought about in society and its institutions. With hindsight, to the late Stuart period can be traced the beginnings of a modern intellectual outlook: religious toleration, modern experimental science, and a belief in mankind's capacity for infinite progress.

Anglicanism and dissent

Anglicanism

Since most English Protestants before 1640 were members of the Church of England, 'Anglican' is not a very helpful term to use in analysing religious opinion in that period. However after 1640 'Anglican' denotes a separate group within the broad spectrum of English Protestantism. 'Anglicans' during the 1640s and 1650s were those who, unlike many others, remained faithful to the old form of episcopal church which was abolished in the 1640s. R. S. Bosher has shown how Anglican clergy survived during this period, either in exile or in the country houses of sympathetic landowners, exercising the old forms of worship in private. The shared sufferings of Anglican clergy and Anglican landowners during the revolutionary decades were tremendously important for the future, because they served to re-establish the relationship between the Church of England and the landed classes which Archbishop Laud in the 1630s had done much to undermine.[18] In 1660, despite Cromwell's relatively tolerant regime during the 1650s, resentment at the dispossession of Anglican clergymen and at the treatment of royalist landowners during the 1640s and 1650s exploded in a vicious outburst of revenge against those who had collaborated with the revolutionary regimes. As has been seen, even before the ecclesiastical legislation of the early 1660s was passed, Anglican patrons ejected clergymen installed since 1640 from livings under their control and replaced them by their own nominees. The Church of England was restored on a wave of Anglican loyalism which neither Charles II or Clarendon could resist (see below, pp. 249–53).

From 1660 to 1688 there was a remarkable degree of unanimity among the ecclesiastical hierarchy (including both archbishops of Canterbury, Sheldon, from 1660 to 1671, and Sancroft, from 1671 to 1691), rank-and-file clergymen, and their lay supporters about what should be the role of the restored Church. Among the characteristics of mainstream Anglicanism during the reigns of Charles II and James II three features stand out. First, most Anglicans emphasized that the restored Church of England should play a major political role. The Church was believed to be independent of the state, but it should work in close alliance with it. Although, as has been seen, both Charles II (apart from brief periods especially from 1681 to 1685) and James II refused to accept this alliance, nevertheless churchmen continued to offer that, in return for the crown's support against its rivals, the Church of England would provide a major support for royal authority by proclaiming the ideology of non-resistance from its pulpits. Second, many Anglicans in Restoration England believed that the Church should be narrowly defined and that no concessions should be made to those Protestants who could not accept the Anglican sacraments and Prayer Book. They opposed both the comprehension of dissenters within the church and the toleration of dissenters outside the church. 'Indulgence to dissenting zealots', wrote an Anglican apologist in 1669, 'does but expose the state to the perpetual squabble and wars of religion.'[19] Third, a sustained effort was made in this period to reinforce the authority of the restored Church by the writings of the Fathers of the early Church. Restoration Anglican scholars, especially at Oxford University, continued the patristic studies of early seventeenth-century divines. The high level of ecclesiastical scholarship which was maintained in the seventeenth century was the product not only of the love of research for its own sake, but also of a concern to buttress the authority of the Church of England.[20]

Not all Anglicans after the Restoration shared these conservative, militant opinions of the majority. The origins of an alternative Anglican view of the Church can be traced to a group of scholars at Cambridge University, the so-called 'Cambridge Platonists', including Ralph Cudworth, Henry More, Benjamin Whichcote, and John Smith. These teachers were a major influence on a younger generation of men, many of whom began a career in the Church of England after the Restoration, and who became known by their enemies as 'Latitudinarians', including John Tillotson, the future archbishop of Canterbury, Isaac Barrow, and Simon Patrick.[21] Like Arminianism and other 'isms', 'Latitudinarianism' is a loose term that obscures differences as well as reveals similarities among individuals. Professor Sykes, for example, points to affinities between Sheldon's outlook and that of the Latitudinarians, who were staunch episcopalians, and men who before 1688 emphasized the importance of non-resistance as strongly as other Anglicans.[22] However, there were certain ideas which set the Latitudinarians apart from other Anglicans. Firstly, they reacted against the development and manifestations of Calvinist predestinarianism during the 1640s and 1650s. In their circles the 'enthusiasm' of the sects became a derogatory word. By 'enthusiasm' they meant the emphasis placed by many sects on the importance of individuals being guided by an 'inner light', a philosophy which had been carried to extremes by sects like the Quakers and Ranters in the 1650s. The Latitudinarians rejected 'enthusiasm' and Calvinist predestinarianism, and placed much less importance in their religious thought on theological questions and dogmas. This negative response to the English Revolution led the Latitudinarians to make a more constructive contribution to religious thought, since they went on to argue that revelation and faith were much less important as the basis of Christian belief than rational argument. Since many Latitudinarian divines were associated with scientists and were members of the Royal Society, it is tempting to see their emphasis on producing a rational defence of religion as a product of their interest in the new science.[23] Just as scientists in expounding their discoveries placed less emphasis on ancient authorities, so Latitudinarians (unlike other Anglicans) showed little respect for the authority of the Fathers. Instead they defended religion rationally and coolly; their sermons were not cluttered with references to ancient authorities, nor were they the rousing, passionate sermons delivered by High Church divines, like Atterbury and Sacheverell. Furthermore, unlike many Anglicans, Latitudinarians wanted to broaden the Church to include many Protestant dissenters. 'Certainly in our English Church', wrote Cudworth in 1674, 'just as in Noah's Ark were all sorts of animals (if I may so express it), are all kinds of Protestants: Calvinists, Remonstrants, and I believe even Socinians all dwelling here, united with no apparent discord in one and the same communion.'[24] In this spirit Latitudinarians like William Lloyd bishop of St Asaph associated with William Penn and other dissenters. Protestants, they believed, ought to form a united front against Catholicism, immorality, and disbelief, which it was felt were growing in strength. English ecumenical Protestantism would be the first step on the road to a reunification of European Protestantism in order to wage more effectively the continuing war against Antichrist.[25]

The Glorious Revolution of 1688–9 had two major effects on the division within the Church of England which appeared in Restoration England between the High Church majority and the dissenting Low Church Latitudinarians. Firstly, High Church Anglicanism lost the leadership of the Church it had held since 1660. Because Archbishop Sancroft and other Church leaders refused to accept the Revolution, they and other non-jurors were deprived of their posts in the Church. Latitudinarian divines were appointed to key offices in the Church hierarchy in their place: Tillotson as archbishop of Canterbury (1691–4), Thomas Tenison as archbishop of Canterbury (1695–1715), Edward Stillingfleet as bishop of Worcester (1689), Simon Patrick as bishop of Chichester (1689) and bishop of Ely (1691), William Lloyd as bishop of Worcester (1699), and Gilbert Burnet as bishop of Salisbury (1689). Therefore from now on High Anglicanism became a movement centred in the rank and file of the clergy and among their lay patrons. The second effect of the events of 1688–9 was to widen the gap between the two groups. After 1689 High Church Anglicans were more than ever determined to protect the Church of England against its rivals. The different attitudes of High and Low Church Anglicans to Protestant dissenters became increasingly obvious in the bitter political debates of the reigns of William III and Queen Anne (see below, pp. 318–21, 348–51, 363–7). Moreover, High Anglicans found it much more difficult than Low Churchmen to accept the Glorious Revolution. Despite their earlier attachment to the ideology of passive obedience Latitudinarians persuaded themselves that they could support William III, on the grounds that James's departure and William's accession were part of God's providential plan. Bishop Lloyd even preached a sermon before the queen on 30 January 1691 declaring that 'the marks of God's hand were so visible in it (the Glorious Revolution), at first, and are so daily more and more; that he is blind that doth not see them'.[26] Tenison undoubtedly would not have been so forthright in public as he was round the earl of Clarendon's dinner table early in 1691, but his off-the-cuff remark captures the attitude of many Latitudinarians to the Glorious Revolution: 'after dinner', noted Clarendon in his diary,

we fell upon the subject of the times, and concerning the Bishops who were to be deprived. Dr Tenison owned there had been irregularities in our settlement; that it was wished things had been otherwise, but we were now to make the best of it, and to join in the support of this government, as it was, for fear of worse.[27]

Clearly with such men in control a redefinition of the role of the Church in the years after 1689 was as inevitable as was the opposition it encountered from High Churchmen. Latitudinarian bishops continued to work for a comprehensive Church after 1689. They also wanted to strengthen the Church, not like the High Churchmen by seeking the support of the state, but by making the Church more spiritually effective. Only by stamping out pluralism and absenteeism and by missionary activity could the Church be made strong, believed bishops like Tenison. When he became archbishop of Canterbury he patronized societies to undertake this work, including the Society for the Promotion of Christian Knowledge and the Society for the Propagation of the Gospel. The Word too was to be spread to the colonies and all parts of the world. 'Others also,' said Samuel Bradford, a Boyle lecturer in 1699, 'especially the bodies and societies of men, which have commerce with the gentile world, might contrive methods for propagating their religion with their trade.'[28]

However, the Latitudinarian ideal of a comprehensive Church was never realized, as has been seen. As a result some Anglicans came to accept yet another view of the Church of England's place in society: as only one among other Protestant churches that were allowed to exist. Clearly this was a view, demoting the status of the Church, the authority of the bishops, and its functions that many High Church Anglicans would not accept, as the support for the Occasional Conformity Act (1711) and the Schism Act (1714) proved. But in 1714 the Latitudinarian supremacy in the Church was confirmed and the High Church party's eclipse made permanent. Only three years later Bishop Hoadley of Bangor delivered a sermon that took the Latitudinarian view of the Church to its extreme conclusion. Christ, he said, 'left behind him no visible human authority, no Vice-regents, who can be said properly to supply his place; no Interpreters upon whom his subjects are absolutely to depend; no Judges over the consciences or religion of his people.' Private religious beliefs were all important; there ought to be freedom 'in affairs of conscience and external salvation'.[29] As the storm roused by the sermon showed not everyone agreed with Hoadley's view of the limited role of the Church of England and of the necessity for religious toleration. But in 1717 Convocation, the voice of intolerant High Church Anglicanism, was suspended, and it did not meet again (apart from a brief session in 1741) until 1855. Moreover, in 1719 both the Occasional Conformity and Schism Acts were repealed.

Dissent

These kind of vermin swarm like caterpillars
And hold conventicles in barns and cellars,
Some preach (or prate) in woods, in fields, in stables,
In hollow trees, in tubs, on tops of tables.[30]

So wrote John Taylor, 'the water poet', in 1641, and in the next two decades, as has been seen, many different religious sects proliferated, especially under Cromwell's tolerant regime. After the Restoration, especially in the 1660s and early 1670s and from 1681 to 1686, a determined campaign was mounted to suppress those sects that would not conform to the restored Church of England. Quakers and Baptists suffered especially because of their refusal to take the oath of allegiance. Quakers also refused to compromise like some other sects by attending church occasionally or by hiding their beliefs: Quakers carried on the evangelical tradition of pre-civil war Puritanism and therefore made their nonconformity obvious. Above all, Quakers refused to acknowledge their social superiors by raising their hats or by respectful speech, subversive behaviour which made it difficult for many to forget their radical antecedents in the 1650s. All dissenting groups suffered after the Restoration, but the Quakers bore the brunt of the malice of militant intolerant Anglicanism; many more than 15,000 Quakers are estimated to have been fined, imprisoned, or transported between 1660 and 1685.[31]

How did Protestant dissent survive the 'period of the great persecution' from 1660 to 1688? As other authoritarian regimes have found before and since, dissident minority groups flourish under conditions of oppression. For some dissenting sects the 'period of great persecution' was one of great spiritual enrichment, producing classics like William Penn's *No Cross, No Cross*, and John Bunyan's *Pilgrim's Progress*, both of which were begun in prison. Some sects battled against persecution by missionary work; by the end of the Stuart age the greatest missionaries, the Quakers, were the only dissenting sect to have meetings in every English county.[32] Later nonconformity owed an incalculable debt to the spiritual strength and vigour of early dissenters. In some areas, however, dissent flourished primarily because of the failure of the Church of England to provide enough churches and vicars. Mostly these were areas where the Church had always been weakest, in forest, pastoral, and fenland areas, for example, where parishes were large and communities scattered, and where there was a long tradition of opposition or apathy to the Church. Although the Church had made some attempts to fill these gaps in large parishes by building 'chapels of ease', these were often poorly endowed and there were not enough of them. In these areas dissent grew by default. The Yorkshire parish of Halifax, for example, covered 124 square miles in which there was only one parish church and twelve chapels of ease. Clearly this was a situation to be relished by an energetic Presbyterian minister like Oliver Heywood, even though he had been ejected from his living in 1662; when he died in 1702 there were seven Presbyterian meetings in the parish, with congregations of over 2,000 members.[33] Perhaps, however, the major factor in the survival of dissent during the reigns of Charles II and James II was the failure of some magistrates to execute the penal laws in full measure. Some were dissenters themselves, especially in towns, but most were Anglicans. It is possible that some Anglican magistrates were swayed by the intellectual arguments for toleration that began to appear in print after the Restoration: persecution is bound to be ineffective, since people can only be forced into *outward* conformity not *inner* belief; religious toleration is compatible with political stability, as in the case of the United Provinces; religious intolerance has disastrous economic side-effects, since it discourages the immigration of skilled Protestant workers.[34] But probably many Anglican magistrates were inclined to turn a blind eye to dissenters (and juries to acquit them) because most of the dissenters they knew were clearly not the seditious subversives they were often portrayed as being. Some dissenters, especially Presbyterians, attended parish churches, as well as their own meetings. Most were sober, respectable members of society. Moreover, from the early 1670s onwards the political cliché that dissent equalled sedition lost its appeal. Catholics not Protestants came to be seen as the greatest danger and Anglican magistrates were consequently less inclined to bring dissenters before the courts.

Dissent, then, survived the 'great period of persecution' and, limited though it was, the Toleration Act ensured that dissent would be a permanent feature of English society. However, the failure either to make it possible for dissenters to become members of the Church of England or to repeal the Test and Corporation Acts ensured that dissenters were deprived of their civil and political rights and were second-class citizens. So the great apartheid in English society between 'church' and 'chapel' was perpetuated, and this came about largely because of Anglican fears, especially after 1689, that dissent was growing at such a pace that it threatened to overwhelm the Church of England. How accurate was this Anglican image of Protestant dissent in the late seventeenth and early eighteenth centuries? As in the case of the popular view of Catholicism, there was an alarming discrepancy between reality and what many people believed. Dissenters were never more than a tiny fraction of the total population. Quantification is difficult obviously; too much reliance cannot be placed on Danby's religious census of 1676, but it estimated that the total dissenting population was 4.39 per cent (see below, p. 253). Dr Watt's analysis of the survey of dissenters made between 1715 and 1718 by the Committee of Three Denominations (Presbyterians, Congregationalists, and Baptists) is the most complete available. It was estimated then that dissenters made up only 6.21 per cent of the total population of England and 5.74 per cent of the Welsh population. In England Presbyterians were the most numerous (3.3 per cent), followed by Independents (1.1 per cent), Particular Baptists (0.74 per cent), Quakers (0.73 per cent) and General Baptists (0.35 per cent). In Wales there were more Independents (2.47 per cent) than Presbyterians (1.96 per cent) and Particular Baptists (0.31 per cent).[35] In 1704 the Kent General Baptist Association lamented 'the great decay, sinking and languishing' of the churches there, an assessment confirmed for the whole country by visitation records.[36] Moreover, the social and political stigma of dissent contributed to the falling off in the support of the landowning classes. Gentry patronage, which had been so important to Puritanism before 1640 and, to a lesser extent, to dissent during the 'great period of persecution', all but disappeared after 1689. It is less easy to be certain that dissent also lost much of its earlier spiritual vigour. However, it is possible that, as many dissenters, excluded as they were from politics and polite society, channelled their energies into trade and industry, so their spiritual zeal was sapped. The later history of the Quakers suggests that concentration on banking, brewing, and iron production is incompatible with the maintenance of a thrusting, evangelical religion.

A more certain difference between reality and the Anglican image of rampant, organized dissent threatening the Church of England is the fact that dissenters were far from united. 'Dissent' can be as misleading a term as 'Puritanism' in that it encompasses individuals and groups of many varied beliefs. Efforts to unite dissenters, most notably Baxter's voluntary 'associations' in the 1650s and the Common Fund and 'Happy Union' between Congregationalists and Independents in 1690 and 1691, met with only limited success. The differences between the denominations are reflected most clearly in the theological diversity among dissenters. The pre–1640 dominance of Calvinist predestinarianism was gone, though Congregationalists and Particular Baptists remained faithful to it. The General Baptists were the first sect to reject it in favour of a free will theology, followed after 1660 by many Presbyterians. The diversity of dissent provides another dimension to the splintered nature of Protestantism in England after 1640 both inside and outside the Church of England, in great contrast to the situation in the early seventeenth century. All Protestants, however, were united in their common concern at an apparent loss of support. It was not just Anglicans who felt that their Church was 'in danger'. Increasingly in the late seventeenth and early eighteenth centuries irreligion came to be seen as constituting as great a threat to Protestantism as Catholicism.

Science and rationalism

Inevitably Isaac Newton towers over the history of science in late Stuart England. Newton's genius was recognized during his lifetime: in 1669 the Lucasian Professor of Mathematics at Cambridge, Isaac Barrow, resigned his chair to allow Newton, his student, to be appointed in his place. His reputation still stands high for his work on the composition of light, published in *Opticks* (1704), and above all for his discoveries in mathematics and astronomy, which he presented in 1687 in the *Principia*. 'With the work of Isaac Newton', writes Professor A. R. Hall, 'the scientific revolution reached its climax as far as the physical sciences are concerned'. While recognizing the validity of that generalization, some of Newton's contemporaries deserve being rescued from unwarranted obscurity. These include Robert Boyle and Robert Hooke, whose *Micrographia* (1665) illustrates his wide-ranging interests in astronomy, optics, microscopy and physiology, as well as John Ray and Nehemia Grew, whose systematic classification of animals and plants respectively laid the foundations of modern biology.[37]

In all these ways and more English scientists continued to make a major contribution to the European scientific movement as they had done before 1640. However, after 1640 several aspects of the new science are noticeably different from the previous period. For one thing the interest in science spread outside a narrow circle of scientists to a much greater extent than before. John Aubrey thought that 'the searching into Naturall knowledge began but since or about the death of King Charles the first'.[38] Although this minimizes the importance of sixteenth- and early seventeenth-century scientists, it points to the great importance of the 1640s and 1650s in the history of science and its acceptance by intellectual society which has been well documented by Dr Charles Webster.[39] He has shown that at both Oxford and Cambridge the initial disruption caused by the civil war was quickly overcome, and, although the university statutes reflecting the conventional preoccupation with scholastic studies remained unchanged, there was enormous academic interest in all aspects of experimental philosophy. The major difference between the universities was the emphasis by academics at Cambridge (where John Ray was especially influential) on the biological sciences, while scientists at Oxford concentrated on the physical sciences. During the 1650s in Oxford, Cambridge, and London scientific clubs developed, at which scientists met to discuss and disseminate new scientific ideas. The most famous of these is the Oxford Experimental Philosophy Club, which met in the lodgings of John Wilkins, warden of Wadham college. Other formal and informal meetings of scientists were also held in Oxford, Cambridge, and London. Because these meetings were not well recorded historians of science have found it difficult to establish the connection between them and the Royal Society. Clearly, though, there was a great deal of overlap between the membership of all these societies. The formal beginnings of the Royal Society can be traced to November 1660, when a group of scientists meeting at Gresham College resolved to institute regular weekly meetings with John Wilkins as chairman. One and a half years later the Society received a charter from Charles II.

The Society's royal charter in 1662 and its wide membership drawn from the landed and professional classes illustrate the new influential standing of science in fashionable society in Restoration England. One of the aims of the Royal Society's journal, *Philosophical Transactions*, begun in 1665 and edited by Henry Oldenburg, was to publicize scientific discoveries and to attract the support of the leisured classes. All this need not imply that the discoveries of Newton, Boyle, Hooke, and the rest were well understood by those 'virtuosi' who took a fashionable interest in science, nor that these virtuosi in their own activities followed the Baconian ideal any more closely than did those in the early seventeenth century. John Aubrey's scientific work was 'haphazard and unsystematic'. His *Naturall Historie of Wiltshire*, he wrote, was a collection of 'the Observations of my frequent Road between South and North Wilts; that is between Broad-Chalke and Eston-Piers. If I had had then leisure, I would willingly have searched the Naturals of the whole County.'[40] Such an approach was miles away from the rigorously systematic, descriptive science of Ray and Grew.

Yet if the virtuosi did not fully understand or contribute much to the new science, they and many of their literate contemporaries did grasp the general principles and methods practised by the natural philosophers and they absorbed them into the intellectual mainstream of post-Restoration England. Firstly, it came to be believed that the best way to approach a problem was to clear one's mind of presumptions based on what one had read in books; instead accepted 'truths' were to be treated with suspicion until they had been tested by personal observation and by collection of data. Secondly, in constructing explanations of observed phenomena emphasis ought to be placed on mechanical rather than on occult causes. As will be stressed later, there was no clear break between science and magic in later Stuart England, but scientists were beginning (at least) to doubt magical explanations, as magic gradually lost the intellectual respectability it had had in the sixteenth and early seventeenth centuries. Finally, it was believed that these techniques of rational enquiry opened up the possibility of infinite progress in all fields. These were principles which amounted to a significant change in the intellectual climate of England in the late seventeenth and early eighteenth centuries.

One of the manifestations of this change has already been seen: the growth of Latitudinarianism within the Church of England. Another was the willingness of a few thinkers to apply the principles of rationalism to religion much more severely than the Latitudinarian divines by extending them into attacks on the Church and even in some cases on Christianity itself. Most scientists were concerned to reconcile their philosophy with religion. Nehemiah Grew argued that the two did not conflict, even though

Philosophy teaches that to be done by Nature; which Religion, and the Sacred Scriptures, teach us to be done by God: no more than to say, That the Ballance of a Watch is moved by the next Wheel, is to deny that Wheel, and the rest, to be moved by the Spring; and that both the Spring, and all the other Parts, are caused to move together by the Maker of them. So God may be truly the Cause of This Effect, although a Thousand other Causes should be supposed to intervene: For all Nature is as one Great Engine, made by, and held in His Hand.[41]

In July 1691 Robert Boyle endowed a series of lectures to be given eight times a year 'for proving the Christian Religion against notorious infidels viz. Atheists, Theists, Pagans, Jews, and Mahometans'.[42] As Boyle realized, scientists were in a vulnerable position, since the intellectual methodology of the new science could be used to undermine the Church and Christianity. This is illustrated after the lapse of the

Licensing Act in 1695 by the appearance of works by writers, like John Toland (see below, p. 350), who mounted an attack on organized Christianity. Most had in common both a hatred of the clergy and a desire to discard (or at least demote in importance) anything in religion that could not be explained by reason, especially 'revelation' and miracles. However, these writers were probably not as united or as organized as the hysterical reaction of churchmen to them might imply. It is difficult to put them into categories: 'deists' and 'freethinkers' are perhaps the vaguest and therefore the best, since there were wide differences among them. Some, but not all, rejected the doctrine of the Trinity, and attacked the belief in the resurrection, for example. Perhaps orthodox divines exaggerated their importance, but 'the freethinkers', no less than the Latitudinarians were products of the new rationalist intellectual climate.

Perhaps it is not being unduly schematic to see in this light, finally, the philosophy of John Locke and the attitude to government of men like Sir William Petty, John Graunt, and Gregory King. Locke, wrote Dr J. W. Gough, 'did not attempt to carry conviction by multiplying quotations from authorities: he sought rather to demonstrate every point by considering it rationally, without reference to what his predecessors had said'.[43] On a different level Petty sought to apply the same principles to the problems of government. 'The method I take', he explained in his *Political Arithmetick*

is not very usual; for instead of using only comparative and superlative Words, and intellectual Argument, I have taken the course (as a Specimen of the Political Arithmetick I have longer aimed at) to express myself in Terms of *Number, Weight* or *Measure*; to use only Arguments of Sense, and to consider only such Causes, as have visible Foundations in Nature.[44]

Here is an early statement of the potent belief that statistics ('political arithmetic') is the key to understanding the problems of society and the economy. John Graunt's *Observations on the London Bills of Mortality* (1662) and Gregory King's *Natural and Political Observations* (completed in 1696), statistical analyses of the population and wealth of the country, were important products of this intellectual optimism. Petty, Graunt, and King are undoubtedly lesser figures than Newton and Locke, but they are equally representative of the transformation that was coming over English intellectual life in the late seventeenth and early eighteenth centuries.

Economic and social changes

Contemporaries had little doubt that political crisis and civil war during the 1640s were largely to blame for 'the decay of trade'. 'The first and principal reason of the decay of trade hath been the late intestine and unhappy wars of this nation', declared Thomas Violet unequivocally in 1650.

Before the breaking out thereof, the trade of England was both free and flourishing at home and abroad. But immediately after by reason of obstructions both at home and abroad it began to fall into a consumption, under which it hath languished ever since.[45]

More melodramatically, but to similar effect, some London petitioners in January 1648 bewailed the economic ill-effects of political developments:

Oh that the cravings of our Stomacks could be heard by the Parliament and the City! Oh that the Tears of our poor famishing Babes were botled. . . . Oh ye great men of England, will not (think you) the righteous God behold our Application, doth not he take notice that you devour us as if our Flesh were Bread? . . . Its your Taxes, Customs, and Excize, that compells the Countrey to raise the price of food, and to buy nothing from us but meer absolute necessaries.[46]

It is difficult to say what truth there is in these comments. The disruptive effects of the civil war and its aftermath on the English economy are only now beginning to be studied.[47] However, although dislocation appears to have been great, it was only temporary and the economy quickly recovered. The middle of the seventeenth century is a valid dividing line in the development of the English economy. It marks the end of a long period of population expansion and price inflation, and the beginning of an era of much greater economic growth than in the previous century. By the end of the Stuart age the economy of England was much more soundly and broadly-based than it had been at its start.

Economic changes

Agriculture
In the late seventeenth and early eighteenth centuries there was a marked increase in the output of English farms at a time when agriculture was possibly employing a declining share of the national workforce. It is a mistake to describe changes in agriculture in terms of rapid and sudden surges forward. Alterations in farming practice and techniques are by their very nature bound to be slow and gradual. Yet in the period after 1650 more farmers than ever took up many of the improvements pioneered in the late sixteenth and early seventeenth centuries. The cultivation of coleseed and turnips and the practice of floating watermeadows spread in many areas of the south and west of England, and everywhere more land was cleared, drained and brought into cultivation. Moreover, many new farming improvements were introduced in the late seventeenth century that for a long time were thought by historians to have been innovations of eighteenth-century 'pioneers', especially Thomas Coke of Holkham, Viscount 'Turnip' Townshend, Jethro Tull, Arthur Young, and Robert Bakewell. With the possible exception of the last named and his experiments in animal breeding, the roles of these five men in the history of English agriculture have been reduced from that of pioneers to popularizers. As has been

seen, turnips were grown as a field crop in the early seventeenth century, and by the reign of Queen Anne Defoe recorded that they were to be found 'over most of the east and south parts of England.'[48] Probably more important both as fodder crops and in influencing husbandry practice in arable areas, however, were new artificial grasses like clover, lucerne, and sainfoin, which came to England from the United Provinces (sometimes brought by Dutch merchants) in the late seventeenth century. The new grasses could be sown instead of a fallow year, they fixed nitrogen in the soil, and they made possible convertible ('alternate' or 'up-and-down') husbandry on most arable farms. They therefore allowed more animals to be kept, and consequently, by heavier manuring, increased grain yields. The most spectacular application of these principles was in the so-called 'Norfolk' crop rotation of turnips, barley, clover, and wheat, which was in use on the Norfolk estates of the Walpole family in 1673, well before Coke of Holkham popularized it in the eighteenth century.[49] It quickly spread to other light-soil areas in East Anglia and in western England, transforming once barren heaths into rich grain and sheep farmland.

Although the late seventeenth and early eighteenth centuries provided a period of fairly sustained farming progress in the adoption of new crops and techniques, it is not easy to explain why this should have been the case. It is true that the intellectual climate favoured innovation in all spheres of life. Soon after its foundation the Royal Society turned its attention to farming problems, and in 1664 it appointed a 'georgical' committee whose prime aim was 'the composing of a good history of agriculture and gardening in order to improve the practice thereof'. In the best Baconian tradition questionnaires were distributed to collect detailed information about regional farming practices, 'whereby it may be known what is practised already and every place be enriched with the aids that are found in any place'.[50] However, as in other cases, there proved to be a wide gap between the aspirations and achievements of Restoration scientists in pure science and the practical applications of these principles. The survey of the 'georgical' committee was limited to six counties, and the only farming improvement the committee can be credited with is the planting of potatoes as a field crop, especially in Lancashire, where, however, it may well in fact have developed because of the proximity to Ireland, already the home of extensive potato cultivation. But the influence of the Royal Society in turning the attentions of some great landowners to farming cannot be discounted. Nor can the farming treatises written in this period, like Sir Richard Weston's *Discourse of Husbandrie used in Brabant and Flanders* 1645, Walter Blith's *The English Improver* 1649, John Worlidge's *Systema Agriculturae* 1669 (which advocated a seed drill long before Jethro Tull took out a patent for one in 1701), and John Houghton's agricultural newsletter, *A Collection of Letters for the Improvement of Husbandry and Trade*, which appeared regularly from 1681 to 1683 and from 1691 to 1703. It is impossible to estimate with any certainty how many people read these and how influential they were, but there is little doubt that they had more impact on landlords than on farmers; as a result some great landowners began to take a more active interest in farming and to encourage their tenants to adopt the new husbandry by inserting improvement clauses in their leases and by giving them security of tenure. Few great landlords as yet, though, took up farming themselves as a fashionable hobby by developing model farms as some did in the eighteenth century.

Farmers were probably more responsive to market forces than anything else. There is a clear connection, for example, between the adoption of advanced farming practices in parts of Norfolk and Suffolk and the demand for food and industrial raw materials generated by the growing towns of Norwich and London and by the Dutch brewing and distilling industries. For most farmers, however, the food market appeared unattractive. Generalizations about price movements in this period must be treated with as much caution as those in the sixteenth and early seventeenth centuries, and short-term fluctuations and regional variations are less well-established than is the long-term trend in food prices, which in the late seventeenth and early eighteenth centuries levelled off after the 'price revolution' from the early sixteenth century onwards. Wool and grain prices especially appear to have been very sluggish; grain prices were low from 1675 to 1691, rose only slightly from 1691 to 1700 (a period of bad harvests), and then fell again.[51] Rising prices are so often associated with economic innovation and enterprise (whether in the thirteenth century or in the sixteenth) that it might seem logical to equate conditions of falling prices with economic stagnation and decline, but this is a false assumption. Falling or stagnant prices can be as powerful an incentive to farmers (or indeed manufacturers) to innovate, to seek to increase output and to cut costs, as rising prices. Falling food prices may have been the mainspring of the remarkable development of English agriculture in the period after 1650. Agricultural innovation was seen by many farmers as the only practical way to escape from the spiral of falling food prices and farm profits.

What were the effects of the adoption of new crops and techniques by English farmers in the late seventeenth and early eighteenth centuries? First, it accelerated the trend towards regional specialization that was already under way in the earlier period, producing great diversity of English farming practice even within relatively limited areas. A general farming pattern, however, can be seen emerging in the late seventeenth and early eighteenth centuries, based on the differences between the lighter soil and heavier soil areas. The light soil regions (sandy and heath lands, especially in Norfolk and Suffolk in the east, the chalklands of the Cotswolds in Oxfordshire and Wiltshire in the west, and the downlands of Kent and Sussex in the south) were well suited to growing the new fodder crops, and so developed mixed sheep–corn husbandry. The heavy soil areas (especially the cold, ill-drained clay vales of the midland counties), on the other hand, were not suited to the new husbandry.

Here grain farmers came to terms with the competition of the more favoured areas by gradually converting to pasture farming. Leicestershire, Northamptonshire, and parts of Lincolnshire were slowly transformed from grain to grazing counties, producing sheep for mutton and wool and cattle for fattening and for specialized dairying. Other farmers elsewhere, too, came to concentrate on specific crops that were suited to the soil, climatic, and marketing conditions of their areas, as the market gardeners of the Thames Valley already were doing by the mid-seventeenth century. In the later period originated the fame of the Vale of Evesham and Kent as apple and cherry producers, and of Kent, Sussex, Herefordshire, and Worcestershire as hop-growing counties.

A second result of the adoption of new husbandry practices was an increase in the output of English agriculture after 1650. This is impossible to prove quantitatively: farm records before 1714 are practically non-existent. One therefore has to rely on qualitative evidence. For the first time England in the late seventeenth century became a grain-exporter: rising from only 2,000 quarters in the 1660s, English grain exports reached over 300,000 quarters between 1675 and 1677, and continued to rise until about the mid-eighteenth century.[52] No doubt this was partly as a result of the government bounties on the export of grain begun in 1670 and 1672, but it was also a reflection of the improved performance of English farmers. Probate inventories provide evidence to support this view. Oxfordshire, Leicestershire, and Yorkshire farmers in the late seventeenth and early eighteenth centuries all possessed more animals when they died than their predecessors. There is more conclusive evidence from the surviving records of individual farmers for the period in the decades after 1714, but one can assume with reasonable certainty that the growth in agricultural output began well before the death of Queen Anne.

Mining, manufacturing, and inland trade
In contrast to the earlier period mining and manufacturing in England, like agriculture, underwent a period of expansion and growth. Lacking much quantitative proof for this assertion, again one has to rely on other kinds of evidence: the diversification of English textile manufacturing, the development of more coalfields and production of more bar iron, the proliferation and technological advance of other industries apart from textiles, and improvements that were made in the means of internal trade.

In the century before 1650 the English woollen cloth industry was in a state of chronic dislocation as woollen broadcloth manufacturing centred in Gloucestershire, Wiltshire, Essex, and Kent, declined because of a falling-off in European demand, and the worsted new draperies took time to become established. In the late seventeenth and early eighteenth centuries this painful period of readjustment was largely over. Many diverse branches of cloth manufacturing flourished. Moreover, the range of textiles produced was extended by the expansion of non-woollen textile industries. After 1650 the 'New Draperies' were dominant in the English woollen cloth industry; but, apart from all being organized under the domestic system of production and all using some long-staple wool, the term new draperies covers a wide range of products. Three types of new draperies especially expanded in the late seventeenth and early eighteenth centuries: the coloured 'medley' cloths produced in an area stretching from Frome to Bradford-on-Avon, Norfolk 'stuffs' largely marketed through Norwich, and Devon serges (a mixture of long wool from Ireland and short wool from Spain) exported from Exeter, which in 1700 sent out about one-quarter of England's total cloth exports. Almost as significant in this period was the rapid development of non-woollen textiles: silk largely produced in Spitalfield in London by French Huguenot refugees; linen manufactured mainly in Lancashire, with a wide range of sub-branches, 'cottons' and 'fustians', made from mixtures of cotton and linen, and ribbons and tapes made on the newly introduced Dutch looms; and stocking knitting, which developed rapidly after 1650 in Leicestershire and Northamptonshire using the stocking knitting frame, invented by William Lee in the 1590s and now belatedly taken up to replace hand-knitting. The national pattern of textile manufacturing itself is diverse, but local studies reveal an even greater detailed variety. In the parishes in and around Wigan in the early eighteenth century occupations were noted not simply as 'weavers' but 'linen weavers', 'fustian weavers', or 'plod weavers'.[53] This diversification and expansion of textile manufacturing did not proceed without obstacles, the greatest being the rising imports of Indian cotton and calico textiles; in 1684 those amounted to 1.74 million pieces.[54] Pressure from native woollen manufacturers succeeded in gaining high import tariffs on Indian textiles in 1701 and 1721, but these were probably not so effective as the measures taken in the English parliament to prevent the development of an Irish cloth industry. An Act passed in the parliamentary session of 1698–9 forbad the export of cloth from Ireland and encouraged instead the export of Irish wool, which was needed for the Devon serge industry.

By the end of the seventeenth century the cloth industry was probably becoming less important in relation to other manufactures in England than it had been at the beginning. In the early 1660s woollen cloth made up 74 per cent of the total value of the exports of all goods of English origin; by 1700 the percentage had fallen to 69 per cent, and the figure fell more rapidly thereafter.[55] This was largely a reflection of the rapid progress made in this period by mining, the primary metal industries (the smelting of tin, copper, lead, and iron), and by a wide range of secondary industries. Coal output figures are as notoriously difficult to calculate for this period as for the earlier period. There is, though, little doubt about the fact (if not the scale) of growing coal output after 1650. The major coalfield in the north-east expanded from the Tyne to the Wear and up the Northumberland coast. Moreover, from the mid-seventeenth century coal production was boosted by the introduction of railed wagonways from the coalfields to the coast. This period also saw the exploitation for the first time on a major scale of the Welsh and Cumberland coalfields, as well as the rapid development of the south-west Lancashire coalfield. In the early eighteenth century production was facilitated by the introduction of steam pumping engines which enabled deeper mines to be worked. These were the invention, not of pure scientists, but of practical men faced with the day-to-day problem of waterlogged mines. It was not solved easily. Thomas Savery's contraption, which he invented in 1698 to drain Cornish tin and copper mines, is more correctly called an atmospheric engine, because it used atmospheric pressure to raise the water out of the mines and steam pressure was then applied to force the water out. Early versions of it were Heath Robinson type machines which frequently blew up, causing many accidents. Thomas Newcomen's improved version introduced in 1708 was more successful. Although it was not until the later eighteenth century that the principle could be adapted to steam-powered machinery, in its limited form as a pumping machine Newcomen's invention was used in many large mines by 1730 with successful results.

Rising coal output was closely linked with the expansion of the smelting of lead, copper, and tin. Largely because of the introduction of an improved reverberatory furnace after 1650 coal was increasingly used to smelt non-ferrous metals. Since the furnaces used more coal fuel than metal ore, the logical development was to locate these industries on coalfields and so save transport costs. Although this was done to a limited extent before 1714 by shipping Cornish copper to South Wales, laying the basis for the development of metal industries (especially tinplate) there from the 1720s onwards, for the moment most smelting was done near the ore mines: lead in Derbyshire and north Wales, tin in Cornwall, and copper in Cornwall, Wales, and the Lake District. Since it proved difficult to use coal to smelt iron ore, the production of bar iron has a divergent history from that of the non-ferrous metals. However, it is now certain that the iron industry's reliance on charcoal fuel did not hold it back. The discovery that there was no national timber fuel shortage in this later period (as before 1650) has explained what was hitherto a major mystery of the industrial history of this period. In the early 1700s a Bristol ironmaster, Abraham Darby, invented a method of using coal (coke) to smelt iron ore, which he developed in 1709–10, when he established his famous ironworks at Coalbrookdale in Shropshire. The puzzle was that few other iron-masters adopted Darby's invention until fifty or sixty years later. Earlier historians explained this by maintaining both that Darby tried to keep the invention secret within his closed circle of Quaker friends, and that his method was not perfect. Both these explanations, even if true, must now be regarded as secondary. The primary reason for the minor contemporary impact of Darby's invention is that there was no compelling need in the iron industry for it. Although there were occasional local timber shortages, generally ironmasters practised a sensible policy of timber cropping and replacement of trees. The move of the centre of the industry from the Weald to Wales, the Forest of Dean, and south Yorkshire was caused, not by abundant supplies of fuel in the new areas, but by a better class of ore and proximity to the secondary metal industries of the west Midlands. Although the English industry never produced enough bar iron to allow the cessation of Swedish imports, the output of the native industry continued to expand.[56]

Turning away from textiles, mining, and the primary metal industries, the range of English manufacturing after 1650 defies a brief description. Three features of it stand out in contrast to the period before 1650. First, a much wider range of commodities was now produced, most notably refined sugar and tobacco, a result of the development of the colonial trades (see pp. 438–40). Old manufactures like brewing (especially in London) and pottery-making in north Staffordshire expanded. Second, more manufacturing industries came to be located on coalfields, like glass and salt on the Tyne. The best example of the integration of different manufactures in this period is on the west Midlands coalfield. Behind the industry of that region producing small hardwares, like nails, axes, and agricultural implements, lay a multitude of industrial processes located in or near the same area: coal mining to produce the fuel for the metalworkers' smithies, the production of bar iron, and the manufacture of narrow iron rods in water-powered slitting mills. Each part of this industrial chain was typically a small manufacturing unit, but the ultimate control of the industry often lay with the owners of the slitting mills who put out the rods of iron to the metalworkers. By the late seventeenth century industry was densely concentrated in the Wolverhampton–Birmingham areas, where between 1660 and 1710 34 per cent of all those people for whom probate inventories survive were metalworkers.[57] Third, there were not only improvements in the range and output of manufacturing after 1650, but also in the quality of goods produced, largely due to improved technology. Finer silk, paper, and glass, for example, were all produced in the late seventeenth century than ever before, and often the improved technology was brought by immigrants, enabling English industry to narrow the gap between it and hitherto more technologically advanced countries like the United Provinces.

The impression of manufacturing expansion after 1650 is confirmed by the mounting evidence of improvements in the means of internal trade even before the turnpike and canal revolutions of the eighteenth century: river and harbour improvements, the introduction of more frequent carrier services, stagecoaches, and newspaper advertising.[58] These developments, of course, were a cause as well as a reflection of the developing economy. What else contributed to the industrial progress made in the late seventeenth and early eighteenth centuries? Although banking originated in the second half of the seventeenth century, its commercial influence was as yet slight compared to its importance in supplying the needs of public finance. The few private banks that developed (mainly as offshoots of the work of goldsmiths and scriveners) were in London: in the 1690s there were about forty, but the numbers fell in the early years of the eighteenth century. There were no private banks outside London before 1714; the first one was established in Bristol in 1716, but there were only about twelve country banks in 1750.[59] Most businesses were small in this period and did not need sophisticated banking facilities. Manufacturers overcame short-term financial crises by borrowing money from members of their family and from friends, and they expanded their businesses by 'ploughing back' profits, rather than by relying on investment from outside sources. Banking (and also joint-stock organization) was only of peripheral importance in English industrial development before the late eighteenth century.

More important in the later seventeenth and early eighteenth centuries were the important roles played by dissenters and aliens. Some have sought to explain the economic success of dissenters in terms of 'the Protestant ethic' which allegedly encourages a capitalist outlook. However, a more simple explanation may be that dissenters were political and social outcasts. As such, few were able to follow a political career or were influenced by the conservative curricula of the universities. Schooled in dissenting academies they learned useful skills like mathematics, accountancy, and foreign languages, and found an outlet for their talents in trade and industry. Above all, because they were dissident, minority groups they stuck together, intermarried, lent money to each other in times of trouble, and passed business on to each other. Impressive networks of business relationships developed among dissenting families, but they did so because dissenters were victimized groups not because they were Protestants. The same is true to a certain extent in explaining the economic success of aliens in England. Especially important in this period were the Huguenots, whose technical skills made as great an impact on industries like silk, paper, and glass as did the earlier wave of religious immigrants from the Low Countries on the woollen cloth industry. Because of the unknown extent of evasion one cannot be as certain about the beneficial effects of government protection of industries, but the total ban on the import of French goods imposed in 1678 (which was later replaced by high import duties) probably was a help to infant industries like the manufacture of fine paper. Probably, however, the main determinant of economic progress in this period was the rising demand for manufactured goods in expanding overseas and domestic markets. This assertion is based on assumptions about the development of English colonies and colonial trade and about a general rise in the standard of living in and the growing urbanization of later Stuart society. These assumptions will be dealt with in the following sections.

Commerce and colonization

In the 1730s Viscount Bolingbroke coined the term 'commercial revolution' to describe the changes in Britain's overseas trade since the mid-seventeenth century, and this term has now become firmly established in the historiography of this period.[60] The importance of overseas trade has perhaps been exaggerated at the expense of internal trade and the domestic market, largely because the primary sources for studying the latter are sparser than overseas trade records. Nevertheless economic historians are more justified in using 'revolution' in connection with changes in late-seventeenth and early eighteenth-century overseas trade than they are in the context of many other economic and social developments. In the late seventeenth century the nature of English overseas trade was transformed: commodities that had been traded in only negligible amounts before 1650 leaped to importance; English trade to Europe was overshadowed by that to the Caribbean, North America, West Africa, and the Far East; English provincial ports grew to challenge (although not by any means to overthrow) London's grip on the country's overseas trade; the English mercantile marine increased in size; and there developed new associated credit and insurance services. In short, in this period England (after 1707, Britain) emerged as a major imperial and commercial power, supreme over the Dutch, and with France as its only serious competitor for the major share of world trade.

Before 1650 English overseas trade had largely consisted of the exchange of woollen cloth for other manufactures, wine, and foodstuffs, including grain. In 1714 cloth was still exported – in 1699–1701 it made up 47 per cent of England's total exports – but its importance was challenged by the re-export of commodities of American and Indian origin – in 1699–1701 tobacco, sugar, and Indian calicoes amounted to 30 per cent of England's total exports.[61] An increasing percentage of these goods was retained for sale in England, but not as much as was re-exported to Europe. The demand for sugar and tobacco (and later for tea, coffee, and chocolate) in Europe is explicable only by the transformation of the status of these commodities from luxuries to necessities in a very short space of time. Other changes in the type of goods traded in by 1714 were less dramatic than the meteoric rise of re-export goods; for example England became a grain exporter not importer, and there was an increase in the export of English manufactured goods.

The transformation of the commodity structure of England's overseas trade was brought about by the establishment and development of Atlantic colonies and by trading ventures to Africa and the Far East. Unlike the period before 1650 these now made a definite impact on the nature of English overseas trade. However, it must not be assumed that the volume of English trade to Europe proportionately decreased. The import of flax, hemp, iron, and timber from the Baltic, Scandinavia, and Russia to London and east coast ports grew very fast. So too did trade to southern Europe, importing wine (from Spain and Portugal), fine wool, iron, dyestuffs, and fruit, in exchange for cloth, grain, and fish (from Newfoundland). This branch of English foreign trade became even more lucrative after the conclusion of the Methuen treaties in 1703. Moreover most of the re-exports (two-thirds by the end of the seventeenth century) were sent to northern Europe. However, important as was the English trade to Europe it has rightly received less attention than the growth of the new Atlantic, African, and Far Eastern trades, by which English merchants at last freed themselves from the straitjacket of trade to Europe. The volume of the trade of the East India Company increased enormously in the late seventeenth century. Whereas between 1600 and 1640 the total value of East India Company exports only twice exceeded £100,000 p.a., in the 1680s it sometimes reached over £600,000 p.a. and in 1700–1 a peak of £703,497 was achieved.[62] East India Company imports of calicoes and (increasingly) tea emphasized that by the late seventeenth century English merchants in the Far East were concentrating on the Indian subcontinent and trade to China, not on the Indonesian islands. The Company secured Bombay as its major base as part of Charles II's marriage settlement in 1661, but as yet it was not forced (as it was later in the eighteenth century) to do more than establish trading posts in the East. Across the Atlantic the English empire developed much more quickly. Although between 1660 and 1714 only four new colonies were established – New York and New Jersey in 1664, the Carolinas in 1670, and Pennsylvania in 1681 – the populations of these and of the settlements already established after 1607 grew rapidly in this period. In 1640 the free population of English colonies in America and the Caribbean was about 48,000; by 1700 it had risen nearly tenfold to about 440,000.[63] This had come about by natural population increase and also by immigration from Britain and Europe. European immigrants were a mixed bunch with varied motives, but included three types of religious migrants, Quakers who went to Pennsylvania in the 1680s, Huguenots to South Carolina in the same period, and refugees from the Rhine Palatinate to New York in 1708–9.

In addition to their free inhabitants the American colonies included another new major element in the late seventeenth century: in 1640 there were no slaves in the English colonies, by 1700 there were about 118,000, mainly in the Caribbean colonies of Jamaica, Barbados and the islands of the lesser Antilles.[64] By about 1660 Barbados, Antigua, St Christopher, and Montserrat were already experiencing severe problems of labour shortage. The indentured labour system, which continued to attract British migrants to the mainland colonies which had ample supplies of land to offer, could not be operated any longer in the small island colonies. The trade in slaves from West Africa, carried on at first mainly by the Dutch and then increasingly by the English merchants of the Company of Royal Adventurers to Africa, became the solution to the Caribbean labour problem. Within about forty years, from 1660 to 1700, the sugar plantation economy developed in the West Indies based on black slave labour. Whether or not the slave trade was profitable remains controversial (the indications are that it was not), but there is little doubt that by 1714 it had become a major axis of England's new overseas trading pattern. The Atlantic colonies produced sugar and tobacco for import to England and for re-export, and they provided an expanding market for English manufactured goods.

Three other major aspects of the 'commercial revolution' need emphasizing. First, partly as a result of the 'revolution', London's relative importance declined in relation to that of the provincial ports. It is true that London remained far and away the biggest city in the country. Between 1650 and 1700 its population grew from 400,000 to 475,000, and especially after the Great Fire the westward expansion of the City continued in a period of furious property development. However, in this period London's rate of expansion (18.75 per cent) was much slower than in the previous fifty years when its growth rate was 100 per cent. Moreover, in the late seventeenth century some provincial ports probably grew at a faster rate. It is difficult to be certain because population statistics of provincial towns are notoriously inexact. Certainly Liverpool grew more rapidly: its population increased by over 50 per cent between 1700 (5,145) and 1710 (8,168). This is also probably true of Glasgow and Whitehaven, the latter developed by the Lowthers, who exported coal from the mines on their estates from Whitehaven and then subsequently branched out into the tobacco trade to Virginia. Sugar and tobacco and the associated refining industries were the basis of the new prosperity of these western ports. Bristol also shared in the Atlantic trades and also was an outlet for the products of the west Midlands metal industries brought down the Severn. Exeter also grew, mainly as an exporter of serges to Europe. Some east coast ports also expanded rapidly, especially Hull and Newcastle: the latter's population grew from about 12,000 in the 1600s to 16,000 in 1700.[65] Secondly, in the late seventeenth century the size of England's mercantile marine grew considerably. Professor R. Davis estimated that the total tonnage of English merchant shipping rose from 115,000 tons in 1629 to 340,000 tons in 1686 and then levelled off to 323,000 tons in 1702. The new trades were in bulky commodities of sugar and tobacco from the American and West Indian colonies and of timber from Norway and the Baltic. Partly the growing tonnage of ships was supplied by prizes captured in the three Anglo-Dutch wars of the seventeenth century. Professor Davis estimated that in these wars English seamen captured between 2,023 and 2,723 Dutch ships and only lost at the most 500 ships. But the growing demand for ships came increasingly to be supplied by English shipyards which slowly adopted the successful techniques of their Dutch rivals.[66] Thirdly, the growth of longer trade routes and a more diversified trading pattern stimulated the growth of marine insurance and credit facilities in London. Often these were merely adaptations of practices long used in Amsterdam, but increasingly London insurance underwriters, who met at Edward Lloyd's coffee house in the City, captured business from their Amsterdam rivals, as did London exchange brokers, who operated a sophisticated system of bills of exchange by which merchants settled their international debts.

Perhaps the biggest contrast of all between English overseas trade before and after 1650 is that in the later period one can be reasonably certain that the total value of English foreign trade grew in value. Quantitative estimates (again by Davis) are not totally reliable, especially those for the late seventeenth century, but even after 1697 when customs records became more abundant the figures are questionable because of the unknown extent of smuggling. Nevertheless Davis's estimates would have to be very wrong to undermine the validity of the trend of trade expansion:[67]

Period	Total imports	Total exports
1663–1669	£4,400,000	£4,100,000
1699–1701	£5,849,000	£6,419,000
1722–1724	£6,758,000	£7,756,000

It is also true that there are uncertainties other than the statistical one. Did government protective legislation (the Navigation Acts, 1650, 1651, and 1660, and the Staple Act, 1663) play a major part in the trade expansion? Did the wars of the late seventeenth and early eighteenth century have a disruptive effect on English trade or were they a boon in supplying captured enemy ships and by stimulating technical progress in English shipbuilding? Both questions have produced varying answers from historians.[68] What is certain is that the period of English neutrality from 1674 to 1689, when the Dutch remained at war with France, was a vital one in the progress of English overseas trade. This is probably the point at which English merchants overtook the Dutch in the colonial slave trade and the European carrying trade. Moreover, the English victory was a permanent one. By 1714, unlike 1650, London not Amsterdam was well on the way to becoming the centre of the commercial world.

Social changes

The difficulties of describing social structure have already been stressed in connection with early Stuart England. The student of late Stuart society also needs to consider two additional problems. The first is how much reliance can be placed on Gregory King's 'Scheme of the Income and Expense of the Several Families of England . . . for the Year 1688', which he calculated in 1695–6. King was one of the foremost 'political arithmeticians' of his day, and his table neatly categorizing social groups and calculating incomes and expenditures *seems* to be an ideal description of the social structure of the late Stuart England. (see over). Unfortunately, long-held doubts about the reliability of King's work on the social structure of contemporary England have now been systematically confirmed by Professor G. Holmes. He has shown that King did much less research on this aspect of his work than on demography and

A scheme of the income and expense of the several families of England calculated for the year 1688[69]

Number of families	Heads per family	Ranks, degrees, titles, and qualifications	Number of persons	Income per family (£ s)		Total of the estates or income (£)	Income per head (£ s)		Expense per head (£ s d)			Increase per head (£ s d)			Total increase per annum (£)
160	40	Temporal Lords	6,400	2800	0	448,000	70	0	60	0	0	10	0	0	64,000
26	20	Spiritual Lords	520	1300	0	33,800	65	0	55	0	0	10	0	0	5,200
800	16	Baronets	12,800	880	0	704,000	55	0	51	0	0	4	0	0	51,200
600	13	Knights	7,800	650	0	390,000	50	0	46	0	0	4	0	0	31,200
3,000	10	Esquires	30,000	450	0	1,200,000	45	0	42	0	0	3	0	0	90,000
12,000	8	Gentlemen	96,000	280	0	2,880,000	35	0	32	10	0	2	10	0	240,000
5,000	8	Persons in offices	40,000	240	0	1,200,000	30	0	27	0	0	3	0	0	120,000
5,000	6	Persons in offices	30,000	120	0	600,000	20	0	18	0	0	2	0	0	60,000
2,000	8	Merchants and traders by sea	16,000	400	0	800,000	50	0	40	0	0	10	0	0	160,000
8,000	6	Merchants and traders by sea	48,000	200	0	1,600,000	33	0	28	0	0	5	0	0	240,000
10,000	7	Persons in the law	70,000	140	0	1,400,000	20	0	17	0	0	3	0	0	210,000
2,000	6	Clergymen	12,000	60	0	120,000	10	0	9	0	0	1	0	0	12,000
8,000	5	Clergymen	40,000	45	0	360,000	9	0	8	0	0	1	0	0	40,000
40,000	7	Freeholders	280,000	84	0	3,360,000	12	0	11	0	0	1	0	0	280,000
140,000	5	Freeholders	700,000	50	0	7,000,000	10	0	9	10	0	0	10	0	350,000
150,000	5	Farmers	750,000	44	0	6,600,000	8	15	8	10	0	0	5	0	187,000
16,000	5	Persons in sciences and liberal arts	80,000	60	0	960,000	12	0	11	10	0	1	10	0	40,000
40,000	4½	Shopkeepers and tradesmen	180,000	45	0	1,800,000	10	0	9	10	0	0	10	0	90,000
60,000	4	Artisans and handicrafts	240,000	40	0	2,400,000	10	0	9	10	0	0	10	0	120,000

	Families	Persons	Heads per family	Income per head	Expense per head	Income per family	Total	Decrease per head	Total decrease per annum
Naval officers	5,000	20,000	4	20 0 0	18 0 0	80 0	400,000	2 0 0	40,000
Military officers	4,000	16,000	4	15 0 0	14 0 0	60 0	240,000	1 0 0	16,000
	511,586	2,675,520	5¼	12 18 0	12 0 0	67 0	34,495,800	18 0	2,447,100
Common seamen	50,000	150,000	3	7 0 0	7 10 0	20 0	1,000,000	10 0	75,000
Labouring people and outservants	364,000	1,275,000	3½	4 10 0	4 12 0	15 0	5,460,000	2 0	127,500
Cottagers and paupers	400,000	1,300,000	3¼	2 0 0	2 5 0	6 10	2,000,000	5 0	325,000
Common soldiers	35,000	70,000	2	7 0 0	7 10 0	14 0	490,000	10 0	35,000
	849,000	2,795,000	3¼	3 5 0	3 9 0	10 10	8,950,000	4 0	562,000
Vagrants		30,000		2 0 0			60,000	1 0 0	60,000
	849,000	2,825,000	3¼	3 3 0	3 7 6	10 10	9,010,000	4 6	622,000
So the General Account is									
511,586 Fam. increasing kingdom's wealth	511,586	2,675,520	5¼	12 18 0	12 0 0	67 0	34,495,800	18 0	2,447,100
849,000 Fam. decreasing kingdom's wealth	849,000	2,825,000	3¼	3 3 0	3 7 6	10 10	9,010,000	4 6	622,000
Neat totals	1,360,586	5,500,520	4¹⁄₂₀	7 18 0	7 11 3	32 0	43,505,800	6 9	1,825,100

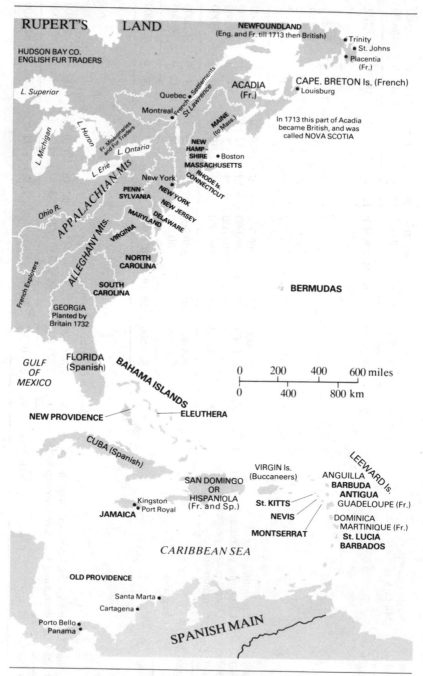

Map 5   English Colonies in America and the Caribbean in 1700

national income and wealth, which were more directly connected with his prime aim of providing the government with a statistical basis for levying taxation. Moreover, 'guesswork abounds in King's enumeration', especially of incomes which are gross under-estimates. Above all, King, by basing his estimates on the year 1688, ignored many of the important changes taking place in society at this time.[70] Not only is King's work now known not to be the reliable guide it was once thought to be, but recent work on the social history of later Stuart England has also called into question some long-held orthodox views about this period, without as yet producing any new ones to put in their place.[71] Perhaps this debate, which is still in its early stages, will eventually produce the kind of local studies that were stimulated by the 'storm over the gentry' about the earlier period. Only then will it be possible to put forward generalizations with more certainty than at present.

However, it is certain that the economic climate of late Stuart England was significantly different from that preceding it. The mid-seventeenth century marked the end of a fairly long period of price and population expansion throughout Europe. As with prices, lack of sources (in this case population censuses) makes it impossible to produce exact population figures. Yet, regional variations notwithstanding, it is likely that after about 1640–50 the population of England and Wales grew to about 5.2 million (based on King's figures)[72] from about 5 million in 1650. After 1700 it may have risen more quickly, but even in 1750 the population of England and Wales only reached about 6.25 million. Taken together these economic, price, and demographic trends represent a changed context in which to consider the standards of living of people in late Stuart England. The transition to an era of relatively stagnant prices and population has often been associated with the development of a more stable social structure than in early Stuart England. But it is likely that this assumption is as misguided as that which equates falling prices with a stagnant economy. In the late seventeenth and early eighteenth centuries the beginnings of three major changes in the social structure of England can be detected: the growth in the size of estates and of farms as large landowners and farmers proved more able than smaller ones to withstand the economic problems of the period; a rise in the numbers and standard of living of wage-earners; and an increase in the size of towns and therefore the growth in importance of urban social groups.

In the present state of knowledge the first of these generalizations must be considered to be the most tentative. This was not so until quite recently when there seemed little reason to doubt Professor H. J. Habakkuk's argument that 'the general drift of property in the sixty years after 1690 was in favour of the large estate and the great lord . . . the same period saw an appreciable diminution of the area owned by small squires and the landed gentry'.[73] This hypothesis has appealing arguments in its support, especially the development of two legal devices since the mid-seventeenth century which seemed to protect large estates from being broken up and to enable them to get even bigger. In the late sixteenth and early seventeenth centuries landlords found it difficult to ensure that on their deaths their estates would descend intact to their heirs. Estates disintegrated because deathbed settlements were not upheld in law. A legal solution was eventually found in the form of the strict settlement. This was an agreement made each generation between the head of the family and his heir, by which both agreed to become life tenants of the estates, therefore forgoing the right to alienate any portion of the estates for any period longer than their own lives. This agreement was guaranteed by the appointment of trustees whose duty was to look after the future interests of any unborn children (legally known as 'the contingent remainders'). Landlords also now seemed able to borrow money without the risk which was attached to mortgaging property in the early seventeenth century. With the development of the legal principle of equity of redemption in the late seventeenth century mortgagers who forfeited on mortgage repayments were given time by the law courts to redeem their property and creditors were prevented from foreclosing on their property as they had done in the early seventeenth century. Because these devices were thought to enable landlords to keep their estates together and to borrow money more easily and safely so that they could purchase more land, it was argued that they were in a good position to secure favourable marriages with wealthy heiresses, as well as to secure lucrative government offices. However, attractive as these explanations are, their validity is now doubtful. Professor Habakkuk may have exaggerated the extent to which the strict settlement was employed; it was not used by landlords in other areas as much as it was by those in Northamptonshire and Bedfordshire, the area he studied. Nor do many landlords appear to have used the improved mortgage facilities to purchase more land. Moreover, even an apparently good marriage could lead to financial difficulties, especially if the offspring were daughters who had to be provided with expensive dowries. Also opportunities to acquire government offices, even in the expanding civil service of the later Stuarts, were open only to a few.

Until there are more local studies uncertainty will remain and the Habakkuk model must be considered on trial. However, although legal explanations for the growth of large estates are dubious, there are reasons for thinking that in the century after 1640 economic conditions for landlords and for farmers were more difficult than in the preceding century, and that as a result many small landlords and farmers may have found themselves in difficulties from which they could only escape by selling out to their more wealthy neighbours. In what ways was the economic climate hostile to small landowners and farmers in late Stuart England? Undoubtedly the situation became worse in and after the 1690s but some of their difficulties originated earlier. This English Revolution brought about no large-scale redistribution of land in favour of 'new' men associated with the parliamentarian and republican regimes and drawn from outside the traditional ruling classes, as was once thought.[74] Yet rents fell throughout the civil war,[75] and taxation was maintained at a high level throughout the war and afterwards. For royalist landowners, of course, the situation was worse, since they had to borrow money to pay composition fines in order to recover their sequestered estates, and in 1651 and 1652 780 hard-line royalist 'delinquents' had their estates confiscated and sold by the Trustees of the Commonwealth. Although confiscated estates were restored in 1660 (along with crown and Church lands) no compensation was given to those who had sold lands to pay fines or who had incurred heavy debts in the process of repurchasing their lost estates. More seriously, after the Restoration many landlords apparently found it difficult to maintain their rental incomes. 'That rents decay every landlord feels, the reasons and remedies are not so well understood', wrote Sir William Coventry in 1670. Unfortunately, one is reliant on obviously biased views like this, but they were generally held during the reigns of Charles II and James II.[76] After 1690, however, the fall in rents is better demonstrated, and some landlords, especially in years of bad harvests, like 1693–1700 and 1709–10, even had to allow tenants to accumulate arrears of rents.[77] The rent problem facing landlords was a reflection of the difficulties of farmers in the period of generally sluggish prices for many agricultural products. Many landlords and farmers had to contend with stagnant or falling rents and prices in later Stuart England. In addition, landowners (whether landlords or farmers) from the 1690s onwards were burdened with an extra charge, the land tax. It is true that this tax was assessed at different rates throughout the country and that in some northern and western counties like Cumberland and Westmorland the rate was very light.[78] However, throughout most southern and eastern counties of England this was not the case, and it was levied at the full rate of four shillings in the pound throughout the war years. On the Coke estates in Norfolk between 1708 and 1710 over 17 per cent of the gross rental was paid in taxes.[79] Not surprisingly, many landowners resented their country's involvement in a war that hit them so severely.

The smaller the resources of the landlord or farmer the less able was he to cope with this situation of increasing expenditure and falling incomes. Small landlords could not afford to meet high tax bills, nor afford to allow their tenants' arrears of rent to accumulate for two or three years, as did some great landlords. Neither were they able to recoup their fortunes by other means – by borrowing or by investing in government stocks. Notwithstanding the possible drawbacks, it was large landlords who made the most advantageous marriages. By Sir Thomas Grosvenor's marriage in 1677 to a twelve-year-old bride, Mary Davies, the daughter of a London merchant, his family eventually inherited a large part of the present West End from Oxford Street to Vauxhall and Chelsea, including Grosvenor Square, Park Lane, and Victoria. Similarly, it was mainly larger farmers who had the capital to invest in farming improvements, which it has been seen was a way of

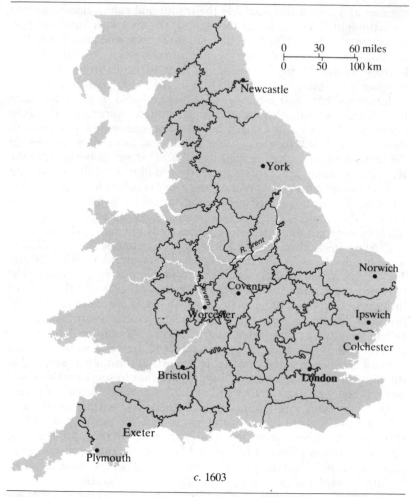

Scale:
```
0        30        60 miles
0        50        100 km
```

Newcastle

•York

Norwich

•Coventry

Ipswich

Worcester

Colchester

R. Trent

Severn

Bristol

London

Exeter

Plymouth

c. 1603

Map 6 England in 1603 and 1714: county boundaries and towns with over 5,000 inhabitants

escaping from the spiral of falling farm prices and profits. Many small farmers must have found it difficult to continue. Clearly, the decline of small farmers in England was a slow, gradual process. Some, like those in Chippenham in Cambridgeshire, disappeared in the early seventeenth century.[80] Others, especially those in market gardening, fruit growing, dairying, and meat production, survived into the late seventeenth and early eighteenth century. But for many, especially grain farmers, it is likely that the period from about 1640 to 1760 was critical and that the trend towards larger farms accelerated.

It is possible to come to a more optimistic conclusion about the standards of living of wage-earners in late Stuart England than in the

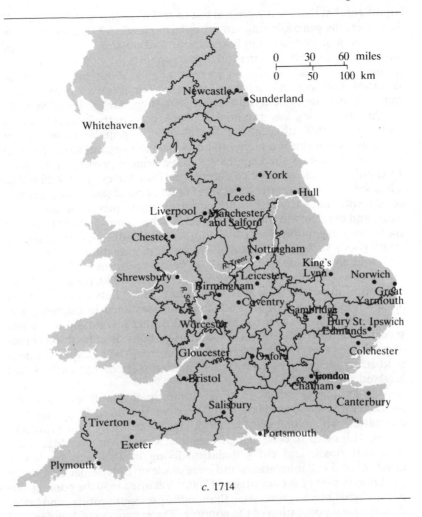

c. 1714

previous period. One must beware of overstating the argument. Gregory King's figures illustrate the extent of poverty in the lower levels of society. It is also true that wage rates in some areas of the country remained as depressed in this period as in the early seventeenth century. This was so in areas like Suffolk and Essex, where there were few alternative sources of employment other than farming and no alternative sources of income as waste and commonland rapidly disappeared. However, in those areas close to or in towns labourers could command higher wages, for example in London or in the industrial villages of the west Midlands small hardware industry or Sheffield cutlery trade. Unfortunately the statistical basis for the argument that there was a general rise in real wages after 1650 is shaky.[81] However, the generally stagnant population level in England probably produced a slackening supply of labour and possibly a rise in money wages. Moreover, the fall in food prices supports the view that there was a rise also in real wages. As in generalizing about the fortunes of landlords and farmers one has to litter one's remarks with 'perhaps' and 'maybe': one cannot be certain. There is, though, one final confirmatory indication of rising living standards of labourers in the late seventeenth and early eighteenth century: the change in popular consumption patterns. Again this is a highly tentative suggestion, but from the mid-seventeenth century there appears to have been, especially in southern England, a switch in cereal consumption from barley and rye bread to wheat bread, and a greater amount of meat being eaten. Also in the late seventeenth and early eighteenth centuries many people began to eat, wear, and use many of the new products of the colonial and Far Eastern trades and expanding English manufacturing industries. Increasingly many goods such as sugar, tobacco, and Indian textiles were retained and sold in this country instead of being re-exported. This is well documented for the mid-Hanoverian period: by 1750, for example, 90 per cent of imported sugar was sold in England.[82] Less is known about the amount of goods both produced and consumed in England, and perhaps it is too cavalier to talk of a 'consumer revolution' in the late seventeenth and early eighteenth centuries, but it is at least likely that many wage-earners were able to spend more of their income on non-food items in this period than their predecessors had in early Stuart England.

The hypothesis of a growing domestic demand for food and manufactured goods, whether imported or produced in England, is compatible with a final new feature of late Stuart society: the growth of towns. This needs to be seen in perspective. Most towns outside London were still small, and the population living in all towns (including London) of 5,000 inhabitants and over made up only 16 per cent of the total population of the country in 1700.[83] Yet after 1650 the populations of provincial towns grew faster than in the previous century, and faster than the total population of the country. The expansion of London and provincial ports, feeding on the growing trades to the colonies, the East and Europe has already been seen. The populations of others also grew, partly as a result of the industrial progress of the late seventeenth century, like Manchester and Salford (about 10–12,000 in 1700), Nottingham (about 7,000 in 1700), Leicester (about 6,000 in 1712), Birmingham (between 5,000 and 7,000 in 1700), and Leeds (about 5–6,000 in 1700). Others, like Chatham and Portsmouth (both with over 5,000 inhabitants in 1700) grew partly because of the demand for ships for war and peaceful uses. Finally, although their days of spectacular development lay in the future, by 1714 the growth of spa towns was noticeable: in 1660 the biggest, Bath, had a population of about 1,100.[84]

Dr Corfield believes that 'from about the 1670s onwards (or perhaps earlier) something of the configuration of modern urban England began to emerge at least in outline'.[85] Perhaps too the same can be said about the structure of modern landed society: a three-tiered structure composed of large landlords, big tenant farmers, and a mass of landless labourers, instead of the two-tiered rural society of landlord and small, independent farmers which persisted in Ireland, and in parts of Scotland and Europe.

Notes

For abbreviations used throughout see p. xiv.

1. Blackstone, *Commentaries on the Laws of England*, quoted in E. N. Williams, *The Eighteenth-Century Constitution 1688–1815* (1970), pp. 74–5.
2. Mark A. Thomson, *A Constitutional History of England, IV: 1642–1801* (1938), p. 353.
3. Henry Roseveare, *The Treasury 1660–1870: the foundations of control* (1973), pp. 20, 31.
4. S. Baxter, *The Development of the Treasury 1660–1702* (1957), p. 10.
5. For administrative development before 1689 see Howard Tomlinson, 'Financial and administrative developments in England, 1660–88', in J. R. Jones, ed., *The Restored Monarchy 1660–88* (1979), pp. 94–117.
6. J. H. Plumb, *The Growth of Political Stability 1675–1725* (1967), pp. 11–12. See G. R. Elton, *The Tudor Revolution in Government* (1953), for the 1530s.
7. Plumb, *Growth of Political Stability*, p. 108; G. Holmes, 'Post-Revolution Britain and the historian', in G. Holmes, ed., *Britain after the Glorious Revolution 1689–1714* (1969), p. 9.
8. G. E. Aylmer, *The King's Servants: the civil service of Charles I 1625–42* (1961), and *The State's Servants 1649–60* (1973).
9. Plumb, *Growth of Political Stability*, pp. 116, 123, 119–20.
10. The percentages in this paragraph are from the figures of Sir John Sinclair abstracted in Charles Wilson, *England's Apprenticeship 1603–1763* (1965), p. 217.
11. P. G. M. Dickson, *The Financial Revolution in England. A Study in the Development of Public Credit 1688–1756* (1967).
12. Roseveare, *The Treasury*, p. 25, see pp. 255–6.
13. J. P. Cooper, 'The fall of the Stuart monarchy' in J. P. Cooper, ed., *The New Cambridge Modern History, IV: 1609–1648/59* (1970), p. 531.
14. E. A. Reitan, 'The Civil List in eighteenth-century British politics: parliamentary supremacy versus the independence of the crown', *H.J.*, IX (1966), especially pp. 318, n. 2, and 319.
15. G. C. Gibbs, 'The revolution in foreign policy', in Holmes, ed., *Britain after the Glorious Revolution*, p. 72, see also Thomson, *Constitutional History*, pp. 231–3.
16. Thomson, *Constitutional History*, p. 455.
17. Colin Brooks, 'Public finance and political stability: the administration of the land tax, 1688–1720', *H.J.*, XVII (1974), p. 291.
18. R. S. Bosher, *The Making of the Restoration Settlement: the influence of the Laudians 1649–62* (1951).

19. S. Parker, *A Discourse of Ecclesiastical Polity*, quoted in G. R. Cragg, *From Puritanism to the Age of Reason* (1950), p. 202.
20. N. Sykes, *From Sheldon to Secker: aspects of English Church history 1660–1768* (1959), ch. 4.
21. The best introduction to the Cambridge Platonists and the Latitudinarians is Cragg, *From Puritanism to the Age of Reason*, pp. 37–86.
22. Sykes, *From Sheldon to Secker*, p. 146.
23. B. Schapiro, 'Science, politics and religion', *P.&P.*, LXVI (1975), pp. 133–8.
24. Quoted in Sykes, *From Sheldon to Secker*, p. 146.
25. See M. C. Jacob, *The Newtonians and the English Revolution 1689–1720* (Hassocks, Sussex, 1976), ch. 3 for the strand of millenarianism in Latitudinarian thought.
26. Quoted in Jacob, *The Newtonians*, p. 97.
27. Quoted in *ibid.*, pp. 92–3.
28. Quoted in *ibid.*, p. 167. See p. 428 for the Boyle lectures.
29. Quoted in Bennett, *The Tory Crisis in Church and State 1688–1730: the career of Francis Atterbury Bishop of Rochester* (1975), pp. 214–15.
30. Quoted in M. R. Watts, *The Dissenters from the Reformation to the French Revolution* (1978), p. 80.
31. W. C. Braithwate, *The Second Period of Quakerism* (2nd edn, 1961), p. 115.
32. Watts, *Dissenters*, p. 285.
33. *Ibid.*, p. 280.
34. For the intellectual case for toleration see Cragg, *From Puritanism to the Age of Reason*, pp. 190–224.
35. Watts, *Dissenters*, p. 270.
36. *Ibid.*, pp. 385–6.
37. A. R. Hall, *The Scientific Revolution 1500–1800* (2nd edn, 1962), p. 244. Newton's work on the composition of light was published in earlier papers in 1672 and 1675. The most recent assessment of Restoration science and scientists is by Michael Hunter. 'The debate over science' in Jones, ed., *The Restored Monarchy*, pp. 176–95. I am grateful to Dr Hunter for allowing me to read an early draft of this essay, from which I benefited greatly.
38. Quoted in Michael Hunter, *John Aubrey and the Realm of Learning* (1975), p. 42. .
39. Charles Webster, *The Great Instauration: science, medicine and reform 1626–60* (1975), especially pp. 129–78.
40. Quoted in Hunter, *Aubrey*, p. 132.
41. Quoted in Hall, *Scientific Revolution*, p. 291.
42. Quoted in Jacob, *The Newtonians*, p. 144. See *ibid.*, chs 4 and 5 for a discussion of the Boyle lectures.
43. J. W. Gough, ed., *The Second Treatise of Civil Government, and a Letter Concerning Toleration by John Locke* (1946), p. xi.
44. Quoted in C. Hull, ed., *The Economic Writings of Sir William Petty* (Baltimore, 2 vols, 1899), I, p. lxv.
45. Thirsk and Cooper, pp. 57–8.
46. D. Wolfe, ed., *Leveller Manifestos of the Puritan Revolution* (1967), pp. 275–6.
47. Ian Roy, 'England turned Germany? The aftermath of the civil war in its European context', *T.R.H.S.*, 5th ser., XXVIII (1978), pp. 127–44; J. Broad, 'Gentry finances and the civil war – the case of the Buckinghamshire Verneys', *Econ. H.R.*, 2nd ser., XXXII (1979), pp. 183–200.

48. Quoted in E. L. Jones, 'Agriculture and economic growth in England 1660–1750: agricultural change', in E. L. Jones, ed., *Agriculture and Economic Growth in England 1650–1815* (1967), p. 154.
49. J. H. Plumb, 'Sir Robert Walpole and Norfolk husbandry', *Econ. H.R.*, 2nd ser., V (1952), pp. 86–9; R. A. C. Parker, 'Coke of Norfolk and the agrarian revolution', *Econ. H.R.*, 2nd ser., VIII (1955–6), pp. 156–66.
50. Thirsk and Cooper, p. 150.
51. A. H. John, 'The course of agricultural change 1660–1760', in L. S. Pressnell, ed., *Studies in the Industrial Revolution* (1972), and *idem.*, 'Agricultural productivity and economic growth in England 1700–60', in Jones, ed., *Agriculture and Economic Growth*, pp. 172–93.
52. D. C. Coleman, *The Economy of England 1450–1750* (1977), p. 120.
53. J. Langton, 'Industry and Towns 1500–1730', in R. A. Dodgson and R. A. Butlin, eds, *An Historical Geography of England and Wales* (1978), p. 175.
54. Coleman, *Economy of England*, p. 162.
55. *Ibid.*, p. 139. These figures do not include re-exports, for which see pp. 438–40.
56. G. Hammersley, 'The charcoal iron industry and its fuel 1540–1750', *Econ. H.R.*, 2nd ser., XXVI (1973), pp. 593–613; M. W. Flinn, 'The growth of the English iron industry 1660–1760', *Econ. H. R.*, 2nd ser., XI (1958), pp. 144–53.
57. Langton, 'Industries and towns', p. 180.
58. J. A. Chartres, *Internal Trade in England 1500–1700* (1977).
59. D. M. Joslin, 'London private bankers 1720–86', *Econ. H.R.*, 2nd ser., VII (1954), repr. in E. M. Carus-Wilson, *Essays in Economic History* (1962), II, pp. 340–59; L. S. Pressnell, *Country Banking in the Industrial Revolution* (1956).
60. Plumb, *Growth of Political Stability*, p. 3; R. Davis, *A Commercial Revolution: English Overseas Trade in the Seventeenth and Eighteenth Centuries* (Historical Association pamphlet 1969); *idem.*, *English Overseas Trade 1500–1700* (1973).
61. R. Davis, 'English foreign trade 1660–1700', *Econ. H.R.*, 2nd ser., VII (1954), repr. in Carus-Wilson, *Essays*, p. 258.
62. K. N. Chaudhuri, 'Treasure and trade balancer: the East India Company's Export Trade, 1660–1720', *Econ. H.R.*, 2nd ser., XXI (1968), p. 482.
63. R. Davis, *The Rise of the Atlantic Economies* (1973), p. 126.
64. *Ibid.*
65. P. Corfield, 'Urban development in England and Wales in the sixteenth and seventeenth centuries', in D. C. Coleman and A. H. John, eds, *Trade, Government and Economy in Pre-Industrial England* (1976), pp. 240–1.
66. R. Davis, *The Rise of the English Shipping Industry in the Seventeenth and Eighteenth Centuries* (1962), especially pp. 15 and 51.
67. R. Davis, 'English foreign trade 1660–1700', p. 267; *idem.*, 'English foreign trade, 1700–74', *Econ. H.R.*, 2nd ser., XV (1962), pp. 300–3.
68. For a good brief guide to the first question see L. Clarkson, *The Pre-Industrial Economy in England 1500–1750* (1971), pp. 206–8; for the second see G. Holmes, 'Post-Revolution Britain and the historian', in Holmes, ed., *Britain after the Glorious Revolution*, pp. 26–34. The most important contribution to the latter debate is A. H. John, 'War and the English economy 1700–63', *Econ. H.R.*, 2nd ser., VII (1955).
69. Thirsk and Cooper, pp. 780–1.

70. G. Holmes, 'Gregory King and the social structure of pre-industrial England', *T.R.H.S.*, 5th ser., XXVII (1977), pp. 41–68.
71. Professors Habakkuk's and Mingay's view of the social structure of late seventeenth- and early eighteenth-century England in H. J. Habakkuk, 'English landownership 1680–1740', *Econ. H.R.*, 1st ser., X (1939–40) and G. E. Mingay, *English Landed Society in the Eighteenth Century* (1963) has been questioned especially by C. Clay, 'Marriage, inheritance and the rise of large estates in England 1660–1815', *Econ. H.R.*, 2nd ser., XXI (1968); B. A. Holderness, 'The English land market in the eighteenth century: the case of Lincolnshire', *Econ. H.R.*, 2nd ser., XXVII (1974), and J. V. Beckett, 'English landownership in the later seventeenth and eighteenth centuries: the debate and the problems', *Econ. H.R.*, 2nd ser., XXX (1977).
72. Corrected by Professor D. V. Glass, 'Gregory King's estimate of the population of England and Wales, 1695', *Population Studies*, III (1949).
73. Habakkuk, 'English landownership', pp. 2, 4.
74. Joan Thirsk, 'The sale of royalist lands during the Interregnum', *Econ. H.R.*, 2nd ser., V (1952–3), pp. 188–207; *idem.*, 'The Restoration land settlement', *J.M.H.*, XXVI (1954), pp. 315–28; H. J. Habakkuk, 'Landowners and the civil war', *Econ. H.R.*, 2nd ser., XVIII (1965), pp. 130–51; *idem.*, 'Public finance and the sale of confiscated lands during the Interregnum', *Econ. H.R.*, 2nd ser., XV (1962), pp. 71–87; *idem.*, 'The land settlement at the Restoration of Charles II', *T.R.H.S.*, 5th ser., XXVIII (1978), pp. 201–21.
75. Broad, 'Gentry finances in the civil war', pp. 183–200.
76. Thirsk and Cooper, p. 79. See *ibid.*, pp. 68–88 for other contemporary comments on this theme.
77. Mingay, *English Landed Society*, pp. 54–5.
78. Beckett, 'English landownership', pp. 573–4.
79. Mingay, *English Landed Society*, p. 82.
80. Margaret Spufford, *Contrasting Communities: English Villagers in the Sixteenth and Seventeenth Centuries* (1974), p. 91.
81. Professor Coleman's table estimating the rise in real wages is the best effort to make the most of the slight statistical evidence, *Economy of England*, p. 102.
82. *Ibid.*, p. 118.
83. Corfield, 'Urban development', p. 223.
84. C. W. Chalklin, *The Provincial Towns of Georgian England: a study of the building process 1740–1820* (1974), pp. 21–4.
85. Corfield, 'Urban development', p. 229.

Chapter 15

Continuity: 1714 – the end of the Middle Ages?

In describing and emphasizing historical change the historian can combine duty with pleasure. Not only are changes that happened in the past more exciting and dramatic than things that remained the same, but one of the major functions of the historian is to assess and describe ways in which society and its institutions have developed. However, concentration on historical change is not without its dangers. Not only do elements of continuity sometimes become obscured in the process, but also historians are tempted to highlight 'modern' developments that they know became influential later, but which were not all that significant at the time. It is undeniable that great changes took place in England during the reigns of the Stuarts, and one might be forgiven for taking these changes together as evidence that at some point during that period there occurred the 'beginnings of modern England' and 'the end of the Middle Ages'. Between 1603 and 1714 England made tremendous economic progress and fundamental changes took place in its social structure. Was not then the country poised in 1714 on the brink of transition from an agrarian to an industrialized society? Many religious and intellectual trends in the seventeenth and early eighteenth centuries seem 'modern' in line with a general secularization of European culture. Did 1714 not, then, mark the dawn of 'the Age of Reason'? Above all, the major constitutional changes that took place between 1603 and 1714 have sometimes been taken to mark a sharp break between medieval England and modern Britain, providing the basis for constitutional monarchy and political stability. However, it is likely that few people in 1714 would have been aware of any of these notions. The importance of the changes that took place during the Stuart age ought not to be minimized: but they need to be seen in their proper historical context. The essential continuity of life in Stuart England is often overlooked.

Britain's transformation in the late eighteenth and nineteenth centuries into a predominantly industrial, urban society is inexplicable without reference to the remarkable economic progress made in the seventeenth and early eighteenth centuries, especially in the latter part of that period. At least part of the answer to the hotly debated question of why Britain became the 'first industrial nation' lies in the achievement by the early eighteenth century by the British economy of more diverse and expanding manufacturing, trade, and agricultural sectors compared with its backward nature a century earlier.[1] The progress in overseas trade and in agriculture is especially significant in laying the foundation for Britain's later industrialization. The development of the colonies created a market and a source of raw materials for British industry. Moreover, some of the capital generated by overseas trade was invested in British manufacturing. Agricultural progress contributed to the expansion of Britain's industrial sector in at least three major ways. In increasing productivity agriculture enabled an expanding industrial and urban population to exist. Low prices for agricultural produce meant that the costs of many industrial raw materials (wool for cloth, barley for brewing, and so on) were kept low. Finally, low agricultural prices allowed people to spend more on non-food items, and so possibly helped to create an enlarged domestic market for the products of British industry.[2]

In 1714, however, Britain's transformation into an 'industrial nation' was a long way in the future. The basic social and economic framework of the country remained very much as it had been in 1603. Tarnished though Gregory King's reputation now is, no one has questioned his conclusions about the unequal distribution of wealth and the extensive nature of poverty in the England of his day. King believed that over half the total population in 1688 were 'decreasing the wealth of the kingdom', by which he meant that they spent each year more than they earned, and were dependent on charity or poor relief. Since poverty is not an easily definable concept, King's attempt to assess the scale of poverty in later Stuart England is bound to be arbitrary. However, whatever the statistical accuracy of King's conclusion, there is little doubt about the massive scale of poverty in the late seventeenth century or that it was a constant feature of English society during the Stuart age. Indeed many of the generalizations made in the first section of this book about English society in the early seventeenth century remained true down to 1714 and in some cases beyond: for example, geographical mobility was common and the average expectation of life remained in the lower thirties well into the eighteenth century. There is little evidence to sustain the idealized vision of life in pre-industrial England held by the romantic poets writing in the early stages of the country's industrialization.

A time there was 'ere England's grief began,
When every rood of ground maintained its man.
For him light labour spread her wholesome store,
Just gave what life required and gave no more.

So wrote Oliver Goldsmith in *The Deserted Village,* with scant historical justification. For most people life at the end of the Stuart age was a grim struggle for sustenance and survival. Prosperity still rose or fell with a good or bad harvest. England in 1714 still had a predominantly agrarian economy and therefore the state of the harvest affected the standards of living not only of landowners, farmers, and farm labourers, but also those not directly connected with agriculture. Industry in 1714 was still intimately linked with agriculture, both for its raw materials and its labour force. The Stuart age saw no great transformation in the organization of industrial production. Most industries remained labour-intensive and most were organized on the domestic system. Large-scale units of production with fixed capital plant, with the exception of a few shipyards and coalmines, were rare. In 1714 the factory age lay at least sixty years in the future. Despite the economic progress between 1603 and 1714 the English economy remained pre-industrialized.

The beginnings of religious toleration in England and 'modern' attitudes to science and progress are undeniably to be found in the period after 1640. More and more, explanations for phenomena were couched in natural rather than supernatural terms. Yet it would be the greatest exaggeration to suggest that these trends were the only ones apparent, let alone the dominant ones, in 1714. On the death of Queen Anne only a minority were reconciled to the fact that the search for a religious settlement which had gone on since 1640, should end in toleration for groups outside the Church of England. Most people probably realized that the cause of 'comprehension' was lost, but few were willing to accept 'toleration'. This is especially true of the general attitude of many to Protestant dissenters. The intolerant legislation passed in the last years of the reign of Queen Anne, the Occasional Conformity Act (1711) and the Schism Act (1714), was very popular among the bulk of the political nation. In another way, too, the search for a religious settlement was unresolved in 1714. Since at least the 1580s prominent Protestants, laymen and clerics, had been concerned to remedy 'the economic problems of the Church'. By 1714 their achievement was slight.[3] The last Stuart monarch, like the first, set an example of reform. Queen Anne assigned all the crown's revenue from the first fruits and tenths of ecclesiastical benefices to a fund, Queen Anne's Bounty, to augment the salaries of poorly endowed ministers. But little was done to follow the royal example. Few new churches were built in the areas where they were needed. The Church after 1660 was as riddled with poor livings and pluralism as its predecessor. All efforts during the Stuart age to remove the most obvious single cause of this state of affairs failed: tithes remained in the hands of laymen, who considered them part of their property and refused to abandon them.

The development of science and rationalism in the seventeenth and early eighteenth century was not a straightforward one of the inevitable and gradual victory of modern, rational ideas over medieval super-stition. The philosophy of the new science was by no means universally accepted in the late seventeenth and early eighteenth-century England.

Its reputation in the eyes of some was tarnished by its association with radicalism in the 1650s and the apparent growth of irreligion in Restoration England. Meric Casaubon in the 1660s led an attack on the new science for undermining ancient learning and paving the way for the growth of atheism.[4] The battle between the 'ancients and moderns' in intellectual circles was far from over. Moreover, opposition to science came not only from intellectuals. In popular circles science was criticized because most of the exaggerated claims made for the new experimental philosophy seemed to be empty ones. As has been seen, science made little contribution to technological advance and its general practical application was slight. This lay at the root of the sceptical attitude towards science which was reflected in Jonathan Swift's satirical description in *Gulliver's Travels* of the bizarre, useless experiments conducted by members of the Grand Academy of Lagado.

Not only did the new science not sweep all before it in the late seventeenth and early eighteenth centuries, but that period does not mark any clear break between science and magic. John Aubrey extended as much credibility to magical as to mechanical explanations. Moreover, occult interests were not confined to fellow travellers of the new science. The discovery that Isaac Newton's interest in alchemy and other occult notions co-existed with, and lasted longer than, his work on the *Principia* is a startling reminder that rationalism and mysticism were not yet seen to be incompatible by everyone, even by those deeply involved in the new science.[5] Moreover, even if some were beginning to express doubts about magic and alchemy in intellectual circles, at the popular level it may be that belief in magic was just as strong and prevalent as in the earlier period. Witchcraft prosecutions declined, but popular beliefs remained as distinct as ever from intellectual trends. There was still much about life in later Stuart England that was 'irrational' as well as intolerant.

The fact that the Stuart age was an important period of constitutional change can lead to two misleading assumptions: that the constitution inherited by the Hanoverians in 1714 was completely different from the ancient constitution, and that by 1714 the long search for a constitutional settlement had been successful. Late Stuart monarchs still ruled as well as reigned. Government in 1714 was still largely personal government by the monarch. William III and Queen Anne (and George I) retained a firm grasp on the process by which government decisions were made. The royal court remained the centre of politics. Ministers might have to secure support in parliament for their measures, but their main concern was to retain royal favour; when they lost that their political fortunes inevitably collapsed. The personal inclinations and friendships of the monarch were still of major political importance. Nor was the immense personal power of the monarch eroded by the appearance of the cabinet.[6] This body first appeared in the early 1690s to provide continuous day-to-day control of wartime administration during William III's frequent absences on the continent. From about

1695 the cabinet met regularly, even when the king was in England. During Anne's reign these weekly cabinet meetings continued with the queen present, and there were also twice-weekly meetings without her, known as meetings of the 'lords of the committee'. All this though did not necessarily mean a diminution of royal power and influence. Both William III and Queen Anne controlled the day-to-day business of government and all decisions of the cabinet had to be approved by them. Nor were all the important decisions of government made in cabinet, but continued to be made either in smaller committees or in informal consultations between monarch and ministers. Moreover, the changes in the royal administration, like those in the way policies were made, can also be exaggerated. The 'king's government' may have grown in size and efficiency under the last two Stuarts, but many aspects of it remained unreformed. Sinecures, outdated procedures, maladministration, and corruption persisted, especially in old departments like the exchequer. Here efforts both to introduce salaries for officials and to end the system of life tenures for office-holders had even less success than the pathetically limited achievement in some of the newer departments. Vested interests proved too strong and the importance of offices as a source of patronage too great to allow efforts at reform to succeed. Consequently, 'economical' reform of the administration was postponed until the eighteenth and nineteenth centuries.

When in the 1640s people had talked about 'settlement' they had meant a constitutional arrangement that would guarantee political stability, means by which the central government would rule in accordance with the wishes of the traditional rulers of the county communities. Clearly none of the regimes, parliamentary, republican, or royalist between 1640 and 1714 fully corresponded to that view of 'settlement'. Indeed the last twenty-five years of the Stuart period saw an intensification of political conflict as the nation split on many important issues. Differences about the Church, the war, and the succession were not the sole obstacles to political stability: when those issues cooled in the years after 1714 a fundamental constitutional problem still remained. As has been seen, both the royal government and parliament emerged in 1714 with enhanced powers, with the crown heavily dependent on parliament. But no system had been devised of establishing a working harmonious relationship between the two. As a result in 1714 the prospect of political stability seemed remote; there were few signs as yet of the way in which a practical solution to that problem would be found. That achievement was Walpole's in the 1720s, not that of the politicians of the Stuart age.

Notes

For abbreviations used throughout see p. xiv.
1. M. W. Flinn, *The Origins of the Industrial Revolution* (1966) and R. M.

Hartwell, ed., *The Causes of the Industrial Revolution in England* (1967) are good introductions to this controversy.

2. E. L. Jones, ed., *Agriculture and Economic Growth*, especially the editor's introduction.

3. See N. Sykes, *Church and State in England in the Eighteenth Century* (1934), ch. 8 for the state of the eighteenth-century Church.

4. R. F. Jones, *Ancients and Moderns: a study of the rise of the scientific movement in seventeenth-century England* (Gloucester, Mass., 2nd edn, 1961), pp. 241–4.

5. F. E. Manuel, *A Portrait of Isaac Newton* (1968).

6. J. Carter, 'Cabinet records for the reign of William III', *E.H.R.*, LXXVIII (1963); J. H. Plumb, 'The organisation of the cabinet in the reign of Queen Anne', *T.R.H.S.*, 5th ser., VII (1957).

Bibliographical note

Since I have included in my notes many books and articles on aspects mentioned in the text, the purpose of this note is to list mainly books which I think provide good introductions to particular topics. Guides to further reading can be found in the notes, the bibliographies in the following books, and standard bibliographies, especially Godfrey Davies and Mary F. Keeler, eds, *Bibliography of British History: Stuart Period 1603–1714* (1970); also useful are W. L. Sachse, ed., *Bibliographical Handbooks: Restoration England 1660–89* (1976), and G. R. Elton, *Modern Historians on British History 1485–1945* (1970).

1. General works covering the whole period 1603–1714

Excluding books which either end or begin in the middle of this period, the most useful brief introductory surveys are G. E. Aylmer, *The Struggle for the Constitution 1660–89* (1963) and J. P. Kenyon, *Stuart England* (1978). Christopher Hill, *The Century of Revolution* (Edinburgh 1961) is not a book for beginners: one needs to have read other books on the period before the value of this book and its controversial interpretations can be assessed. Alan Everitt's pamphlet, *Change in the Provinces: the seventeenth century* (University of Leicester Department of English Local History, Occasional Papers, 2nd series, no. 1, 1969) looks at the period from the fresh perspective of the local historian. Much more traditional is the constitutional approach of Clayton Roberts, *The Growth of Responsible Government in Stuart England* (1968).

The best brief introductions to foreign policy in Stuart England are G. M. D. Howat, *Stuart and Cromwellian Foreign Policy* (1974), J. R. Jones, *Britain and Europe in the Seventeenth Century* (1966), and D. B. Horn, *Great Britain and Europe in the Eighteenth Century* (1967).

Few books attempt the interesting task of combining seventeenth and early eighteenth-century English history and literature. For this reason both C. V. Wedgwood, *Poetry and Politics under the Stuarts* (1960) and William Lamont and Sybil Oldfield, eds, *Politics, Religion and Literature in the Seventeenth Century* (1975) are invaluable.

Much more numerous are general books on the economic and social history of Stuart England. Of the recent spate of such books my personal order of preference is D. C. Coleman, *The Economy of England 1450–1750* (1977), L. A. Clarkson, *The Pre-Industrial Economy in England 1500–1750* (1971) (this has a very useful bibliography), Charles Wilson, *England's Apprenticeship 1603–1763* (1965), B. A. Holderness, *Pre-Industrial England: economy and society 1500–1750* (1977), and C. M. Cipolla, ed., *The Fontana Economic History of Europe: the Sixteenth and Seventeenth Centuries* (1974), which is disappointing; I find Ralph Davis, *The Rise of the Atlantic Economies* (1973) much more helpful for understanding the European economic scene. Christopher Hill, *Reformation to Industrial Revolution. A social and economic history of Britain 1530–1780* (1967) offers an individual brand of brilliant, yet controversial, interpretation. Those who like to see the economic and social history of this period in its broad chronological context will find S. Pollard and D. Crossley, *The Wealth of Britain 1085–1966* (1968) an admirable work of synthesis. In the Macmillan Studies in Economic and Social History pamphlet series (commissioned by the Economic History Society) the student is well provided with excellent brief introductions, with annotated bibliographies, to some aspects of the economic history of Stuart England: Ralph Davis, *English Overseas Trade 1500–1700* (1973), D. C. Coleman, *Industry in Tudor and Stuart England* (1975), and J. A. Chartres, *Internal Trade in England 1500–1700* (1977). On the difficult problem of population history the best starting points are E. A. Wrigley, *Population and History* (1969) and E. A. Wrigley, ed., *An Introduction to Historical Demography* (1966). These may be superseded by R. S. Schofield and E. A. Wrigley, *The Population History of England 1541–1871* (forthcoming). On urban history Peter Clark and Paul Slack, eds, *English Towns in Transition 1500–1700* (1976) is a useful general survey, but contains no footnotes; much better in this respect is the volume of essays they edited in 1972, *Crisis and Order in English Towns 1500–1700*, and Penelope Corfield, 'Urban development in England and Wales in the sixteenth and seventeenth centuries', in A. H. John and D. C. Coleman. eds, *Trade, Government and Society* (1976).

There is no general survey of the Stuart Church. However, the major religious groups outside the Church of England are dealt with in excellent surveys: J. Bossy, *The English Catholic Community 1570–1850* (1975) and Michael R. Watts, *The Dissenters from the Reformation to the French Revolution* (1978). On the history of science see A. R. Hall, *The Scientific Revolution 1500–1800* (1954) and *From Galileo to Newton 1603–1720* (1962), and Hugh Kearney, *Science and Change 1500–1700* (1971). D. Cressy's introduction to *Education in Tudor and Stuart England* (1975) is disappointing as an introduction to the topic, but his choice of documents is excellent. Keith Thomas in *Religion and the Decline of Magic* (1971) succeeds in revealing many ideas held by ordinary people, as opposed to a tiny circle of intellectuals, a task which, before his book appeared, had seemed impossible.

There are many collections of essays on various aspects of the history of Stuart England including Christopher Hill, *Puritanism and Revolution* (1958), J. H. Hexter, *Reappraisals in History* (1960), W. A. Aiken and B. D. Henning, eds, *Conflict in Tudor and Stuart England* (1960), H. E. Bell and R. L. Ollard, eds, *Historical Essays 1600–1750* (1963), and Christopher Hill, *Change and Continuity in Seventeenth-Century England* (1974). The following collections contain mainly essays with an economic and social history bias: E. Carus-Wilson, ed., *Essays in Economic History* (3 vols, 1954, 1962), F. J. Fisher, ed., *Essays in the Economic and Social History of Tudor and Stuart England* (1961), C. W. Chalklin and M. A. Havinden, eds, *Rural Change and Urban Growth 1500–1800* (1974), and A. H. John and D. C. Coleman, eds, *Trade, Government and Economy in Pre-Industrial England* (1976).

For those who want to investigate the history of Ireland and Scotland much more thoroughly than I have been able to do here good starting points are T. W. Moody, F. X. Martin, F. J. Byrne, eds, *A New History of Ireland*, III: *Early Modern Ireland 1534–1691* (1976), G. Donaldson, ·*Scotland: James V to James VII* (Edinburgh 1965), and T. C. Smout, *A History of the Scottish People* (1967).

The best general collections of documents are the two volumes illustrating constitutional history in the Cambridge series, J. P. Kenyon, ed., *The Stuart Constitution 1603–88* (1966) and E. N. Williams, ed., *The Eighteenth Century Constitution 1688–1815* (1960); and a very comprehensive selection of economic and social history documents, J. Thirsk and J. P. Cooper, eds, *Seventeenth-century Economic Documents* (1972). W. B. Stephens, *Sources for Local History* (1973) and W. G. Hoskins, *Local History in England* (2nd edn, 1972) are good guides to the types of primary sources available and to their value and limitations.

2. Early Stuart England, 1603–40

S. R. Gardiner's massive *The History of England 1603–42* (10 vols, 1883–4) was the product of the 'Whig' school of historians, whose work was based on unfounded assumptions about the inevitability of English constitutional progress. That apart, however, Gardiner's classic account is the best full narrative of the political history of this period, based on an impressive array of primary sources. Beside it Godfrey Davies, *Oxford History of England: The Early Stuarts* (2nd edn, 1959) is a pale shadow, but it is an accessible source of factual information about early Stuart England. More recent general surveys of the political history of the same period, all containing many useful ideas, include J. P. Cooper, 'The fall of the Stuart Monarchy', in J. P. Cooper, ed., *The New Cambridge Modern History, IV: The Decline of Spain and the Thirty Years War, 1609–48/59* (1970), Conrad Russell, *The Crisis of Parliaments: English history 1509–1660* (1971), and D. M. Loades, *Politics and the Nation 1450–1660: obedience, resistance and public order* (1974).

Since this period is in the process of fundamental historical revision, it is fortunate that there are good guides to recent writing and to research conclusions on it. Of the two volumes in the Macmillan Problems in Focus series, A. G. R. Smith,ed., *The Reign of James VI and I* (1973) has a valuable introduction and good essays on the Catholic community, overseas trade, parliamentary history, the judicature, and local government; Conrad Russell, ed., *The Origins of the English Civil War* (1973) includes first-class contributions on parliamentary history, central and local government, political thought, Arminianism, cultural history, and economic issues from the 1620s to the early 1640s. Other collections of essays contain useful guides to current trends in historical writing on early seventeenth-century history, including E. W. Ives, ed., *The English Revolution 1600–60* (1968), D. H. Pennington and K. Thomas, eds, *Puritans and Revolutionaries. Essays in Seventeenth-History presented to Christopher Hill* (1978), and Peter Clark, Alan G. R. Smith and Nicholas Tyacke, eds, *The English Commonwealth 1547–1640: essays in politics and society presented to Joel Hurstfield* (1979); the latter unfortunately appeared too late for me to use in writing this book.

Stimulated by historians writing on earlier periods (especially J. S. Roskell, 'Perspectives in English parliamentary history', in E. B. Fryde and Edward Miller, eds, *Historical Studies of the English Parliament* (1971), II, pp. 269–323, and G. R. Elton, 'Tudor government: points of contact: parliament', *T.R.H.S.*, 5th ser., XXIV (1974), pp. 183–200), most recent spectacular progress on early seventeenth-century political history has been made in revising long-held ideas about parliament and the constitution. Three pieces of writing stand out in this respect: Derek Hirst, *The Representative of the People? Voters and voting in England under the Early Stuarts* (1975), Conrad Russell, 'Perspectives in parliamentary history, 1604–29', *History*, LXI (1976), pp. 1–27, and Conrad Russell, *Parliament and English Politics, 1621–29* (1979).

However, though increasingly important, this work on early seventeenth-century parliament has not yet overshadowed the mass of county studies which has been built up since the Second World War and especially since the 1960s: W. B. Willcox, *Gloucestershire: a study in local government, 1590–1640* (New Haven, 1940), J. Hurstfield, 'County government, 1530–1660', *Victoria County History of Wiltshire*, V (1957), T. G. Barnes, *Somerset 1625–40: a county government during the 'personal rule'* (1961), J. T. Cliffe, *The Yorkshire Gentry from the Reformation to the Civil War* (1969), Mervyn James, *Family, Lineage and Civil Society: a study of the society, politics, and mentality in the Durham region 1500–1640* (1974), Anthony Fletcher, *A County Community in Peace and War: Sussex 1600–1660* (1975), and Peter Clark, *English Provincial Society from the Reformation to the Revolution* (1977). Although it ends in 1603 A. Hassell Smith, *County and Court: government and politics in Norfolk 1558–1603* (1974) contains important conclusions that are still relevant about county society in the early seventeenth century. The political history of early Stuart London has not been as well studied as that of provincial England, but the early chapters of V. Pearl, *London and the Outbreak of the Puritan Revolution, 1625–43* (1961) and Robert Ashton, *The Crown and the Money Market* (1960) and *The City and the Court 1603–43* (1979) help to fill the gap.

There are few good biographies of early seventeenth-century political personalities. D. H. Willson's *James VI and I* (Cape paperback 1963) is in need of revision and there is no good study of Charles I. The best studies of their subjects are two complementary studies of Cranfield by R. H. Tawney, *Business and Politics under James I: Lionel Cranfield as merchant and minister* (1958) and M. Prestwich, *Cranfield: Politics and Profits under the Early Stuarts* (1976); H. R. Trevor-Roper's *Archbishop Laud* (2nd edn, 1962); C. V. Wedgwood's revised version of her 1935 study, *Thomas Wentworth, First Earl of Strafford* (1961); and Martin J. Havran's *Caroline Courtier: the life of Lord Cottington* (1973).

On the religious history of the period there are good recent collections of essays edited by F. Heal and R. O'Day, *Continuity and Change: personnel and administration of the Church of England 1500–1642* (1976) and *Church and Society in England: Henry VIII to James I* (1977), and a general survey by Claire Cross, *Church and People 1450–1660: the triumph of the laity in the English Church* (1976), which contains a good bibliography. Probably the best book on this topic (and I think the best book by Dr Hill) is Christopher Hill, *Economic Problems of the Church from Archbishop Whitgift to the Long Parliament* (1956). P. Collinson's *The Elizabethan Puritan Movement* (1967) ends with the Hampton Court conference (1604) but is invaluable for an understanding of the religious history of the early seventeenth century. Judging by the high standard of his article, 'Puritanism, Arminianism and counter-revolution' in Conrad Russell, ed., *The Origins of the English Civil War* (1973), Dr Nicholas Tyacke's long-awaited book on Arminianism will be a major contribution to a better understanding of the Church in this period.

Many of the best introductory books on aspects of the economic history of early seventeenth-century England have been mentioned already. Others which deal specifically with this period are R. B. Outhwaite *Inflation in Tudor and early Stuart England* (1969) and J. Thirsk, ed., *The Agrarian History of England and Wales*, IV: *1500–1640* (1967). One ought not to be put off by the size of the latter: it has many excellent essays on this topic and a good bibliography. Eric Kerridge, *The Agricultural Revolution* (1967) contains a mass of information about agrarian history, but its general thesis is suspect.

Since 1941 historical writing on the social history of England before 1640 has been dominated by the controversy over the economic fortunes of the landowning classes. Though the 'storm over the gentry' is now over, the contributions to it still make compelling reading. The original proposition about the fortunes of landowners between 1540 and 1640 was argued by R. H. Tawney, 'Harrington's interpetation of his age', *Proceedings of the British Academy*, XXVII (1941), pp. 199–223; R. H.

Tawney, 'The rise of the gentry, 1558–1640', *Econ. H.R.*, 1st ser., XI (1941), pp. 1–38, reprinted in Carus-Wilson, ed., *Essays*, I, pp. 173–206; L. Stone, 'The anatomy of the Elizabethan aristocracy', *Econ. H.R.*, 1st ser., XVIII (1948), pp. 1–53. The thesis and the historical methods employed by Tawney and Stone were vigorously condemned and a new thesis argued by H. R. Trevor-Roper in 'The Elizabethan aristocracy: an anatomy anatomized', *Econ. H.R.*, 2nd ser., III (1951), pp. 279–98, and 'The gentry, 1540–1640', *Econ. H.R. supplement*, 1953. Neither Tawney nor Stone took the attack lying down, L. Stone, 'The Elizabethan aristocracy: a restatement', *Econ. H.R.*, 2nd ser., IV (1952), pp. 302–21, and R. H. Tawney, 'The rise of the gentry: a postscript', *Econ. H.R.*, 2nd ser., VII (1954), pp. 91–7, reprinted in Carus-Wilson, ed., *Essays*, I, pp. 206–14. Christopher Hill also launched an attack on Trevor-Roper in 'Recent interpretations of the Civil War', in *Puritanism and Revolution* (1958), and J. P. Cooper revealed serious doubts about Tawney's and Stone's statistical methods in 'The counting of manors', *Econ. H.R.*, 2nd ser., VIII (1956), pp. 377–89. Academic in-fighting which was by now largely centred on Oxford, reached a climax in 1961 when the American J. H. Hexter joined the battle by publishing 'The storm over the entry' in *Reappraisals in History* (1961), in which Hexter usefully surveyed the controversy so far, pilloried all the participants, demolished their theses, and erected his own general explanation of landowning fortunes before 1640. One of the beneficial results of all this was to stimulate research on landowning families either individually or in regional groups: G. R. Batho, 'The finances of an Elizabethan nobleman; Henry Percy, 9th Earl of Northumberland', *Econ. H.R.*, 2nd ser., IX (1957), pp. 433–50; J. E. Mousley, 'The fortunes of some gentry families of Elizabethan Sussex', *Econ. H.R.*, 2nd ser., XI (1958), pp. 467–83; G. R. Batho, ed., *The Household Papers of Henry Percy, 9th Earl of Northumberland* Camden Soc., 3rd ser., XCIII (1962); Claire Cross, *The Puritan Earl: the third earl of Huntingdon 1536–95* (1966); M. E. Finch, *The Wealth of Five Northamptonshire Families* Northants Record Society, XIX (1955); Alan Simpson, *The Wealth of the Gentry 1540–1640: East Anglian studies* (1961), H. A. Lloyd, *The Gentry of South-West Wales 1540–1640* (1968), and J. T. Cliffe, *Yorkshire Gentry* (see above). In 1965 Lawrence Stone published another general explanation of the fortunes of one section of the landowning classes and an encyclopaedic survey of its life style and activities, *The Crisis of the Aristocracy 1559–1641*. The extensive comment the book excited (see for example the lengthy reviews by D. C. Coleman in *History*, LI (1966), pp. 165–78, by R. Ashton, in *Econ. H.R.*, 2nd ser., XXII (1969), pp. 308–22, by A. M. Everitt, *Agric. H.R.*, XVI (1968), pp. 60–7; by J. H. Hexter, *J.B.S.*, VIII (1968), pp. 22–78, and the debate, 'Stone and anti-Stone' by Conrad Russell, Christopher Thompson and Lawrence Stone in *Econ. H.R.*, 2nd ser., XXV (1972), pp. 114–36), indicates the book's importance as well as its major defects. L. Stone, ed., *Social Change and Revolution in England 1540–1640* (1965) and R. C. Richardson, *The Debate on the English Revolution* (1977) summarize the gentry controversy, but are not substitutes for reading some of the above books and articles.

An even better way of getting to understand the early seventeenth century is to read some contemporary material. Major constitutional collections specifically on the early seventeenth century are J. Tanner, ed., *Constitutional Documents of the reign of James I 1603–25* (1960) and S. R. Gardiner, ed., *Constitutional Documents of the Puritan Revolution, 1625–60* (3rd edn, 1906). See also Kenyon, *The Stuart Constitution* and Thirsk and Cooper listed in section 1 above. The following may stand as examples of the many available printed primary sources illustrating this period: W. Notestein, ed., *The House of Commons, 1604–10* (1971); S. R. Gardiner, ed., *Parliamentary Debates in 1610* Camden Soc., 1st ser., LXXXI (1862); S. R. Gardiner, ed., *Commons' Debates in 1625* Camden Soc., new series, VI (1873); F. J. Fisher, ed., *The State of England, 1600, by Thomas Wilson* Camden Miscellany, XVI (1936); J. P. Cooper, ed., *The Wentworth Papers 1597–1628* Camden Soc, 4th ser., XII (1973).

3. The English Revolution 1640–60

S. R. Gardiner again provides the best full narrative history of this period in his *The History of the Great Civil War* (4 vols, 1893) and *The History of the Commonwealth and Protectorate* (4 vols, 1903). Gardiner's work was completed after his death by C. H. Firth, *The Last Years of the Protectorate* (2 vols, 1910) and Godfrey Davies, *The Restoration of Charles II* (1955). In the same category of narrative history, but totally lacking any kind of thematic content or explanations of why events occurred, is C. V. Wedgwood's unfinished trilogy, *The King's Peace 1637–41* (1955) and *The King's War 1641–47* (1958). Ivan Roots, *The Great Rebellion 1640–60* (1966), which deliberately devotes more space to the Interregnum than to the 1640s, is the best brief narrative survey of this period and it has a good bibliography. This book may be supplemented by part two of Robert Ashton's *The English Civil War: conservatism and revolution 1603–49* (1978), which is a detailed account of the 1640s. J. S. Morrill, *The Revolt of the Provinces: conservatives and radicals in the English Civil War, 1630–50* (1976) is an admirable synthesis of recent work, with useful documents; although it lacks a bibliography the footnotes are a good guide to important books and articles on this period. Without any doubt the best general interpretation of the political history of this period is David Underdown, *Pride's Purge: politics in the Puritan revolution* (1971), which brilliantly reconstructs the interaction of events in the localities and at Westminster.

Good collections of essays on this period are Conrad Russell, ed., *The Origins* (listed in section 2) and its companion volume in the Macmillan Problems in Focus series, G. E. Aylmer, ed., *The Interregnum: the quest for settlement 1646–60* (1972), R. H. Parry, ed., *The English Civil War and After, 1642–58* (1970), and B. Manning, ed., *Politics, Religion and the English Civil War* (1973).

Many major and minor personalities who flourished in this period have attracted biographers. I have picked out the following, which I enjoyed and are valuable in illustrating aspects of the period. J. H. Hexter, *The Reign of King Pym* (1941) is not strictly a biography, but a valuable analysis of the structure of politics in the early 1640s. For insights into Pym's character see Conrad Russell, 'The parliamentary career of John Pym, 1621–29', in Peter Clark, Alan G. R. Smith and Nicholas Tyacke, eds, *The English Commonwealth 1547–1640: essays in politics and society presented to Joel Hurstfield* (1979); unfortunately it appeared too late for me to use in writing this book. Christopher Hill *God's Englishman: Oliver Cromwell and the English Revolution* (1970) is more useful as an excellent account of Dr Hill's view of the period than as an analysis of Cromwell's character. No one has really succeeded in doing that, but R. S. Paul, *The Lord Protector: religion and politics in the life of Oliver Cromwell* (1953) and Antonia Fraser, *Cromwell: our chief of men* (1973) – though the latter is far too long – are good attempts. John Gillingham, *Cromwell: portrait of a soldier* (1976) has an important explanation of Cromwell's success as a soldier. Perhaps the best way of reaching a conclusion about Cromwell is by studying his own writings (see Abbott below). Of biographies of lesser figures Peter Thomas, *Sir John Berkenhead 1617–79: a Royalist career in politics and polemics* (1969) is an important account of a royalist journalist and valuable for the study of propaganda and the early development of English newspapers; M. Ashley, *John Wildman: plotter and postmaster* (1947) and Pauline Gregg, *Free-born John: a biography of John Lilburne* (1961) are interesting studies of two Leveller leaders; and Ruth Spalding, *The Improbable Puritan: a life of Bulstrode Whitelock 1605–75* (1975) has important information about a political personality who survived all changes in regime in the 1640s and 1650s and whose memoirs are a major source of information about this period (see below).

A much more important development than the biographical approach in the historiography of the English Revolution has been the appearance of many county and regional studies. Local histories of this period are far from new. R. C. Richardson, *The Debate on the English Revolution* (1977), pp. 113–16, gives examples of many such studies written between the seventeenth century and the 1930s. However, Alan Everitt's writings in the 1960s marked a new departure in the local history approach to the English Revolution, especially his *Suffolk and the Great Rebellion* (Suffolk Record Society, III, 1961), *The Community of Kent and the Great Rebellion, 1640–60* (1966), 'The county community' in E. W. Ives, ed., *The English Revolution 1600–60* (1968), and *The Local Community and the Great Rebellion* (Historical Association pamphlet, 1969). With the conviction that England was divided into semi-autonomous counties Professor Everitt proceeded to recreate the political and social structure of the 'county communities' of

Suffolk, Kent, Leicestershire, and Northamptonshire. Under his influence others set about writing similar studies of other counties and towns. To those county studies mentioned in the previous section one might add the urban histories by A. M. Johnson, 'Politics in Chester during the civil wars and Interregnum', in P. Clark and P. Slack, eds, *Crisis and Order in English Towns, 1500–1700* (1972) and Roger Howell, *Newcastle-upon-Tyne and the Puritan Revolution* (1967). Recently there has been a significant deviation from the Everitt emphasis on a county community/Westminster dichotomy. Studies have appeared which stress the interaction between local and national politics. This is true of J. S. Morrill, *Cheshire 1630–60. County Government and Society during the 'English Revolution'* (1974), D. Underdown, *Somerset during the Civil War and Interregnum* (1973), and especially of Clive Holmes, *The Eastern Association in the English Civil War* (1975).

I have given a bibliographical guide to many specific aspects of the English Revolution in the footnotes to chapters 6 and 7. A good starting point for a study of the religious history of the period is Claire Cross, *Church and People 1450–1660* (1976), ch. 9, and her essay, 'The Church in England 1646–60', in G. E. Aylmer, ed., *The Interregnum* (1973), both of which include good bibliographies of primary and secondary source material. G. E. Aylmer, ed., *The Levellers and the English Revolution* (1975) provides excellent bibliographical help about that well-studied radical group. In contrast, the economic history of this period has been surprisingly neglected. M. James, *Social Problems and Policies during the Puritan Revolution, 1640–60* (1930) is the only study of economic developments and is badly in need of revision. A start has been made by Ian Roy 'The English civil war and English society' in Ian Roy and Brian Bond, eds, *War and Society: a yearbook of military history* (1975), Ian Roy, 'England turned Germany?', *T.R.H.S.*, 5th ser., XXVIII (1978), and John Broad, 'Gentry finances and the civil war – the case of the Buckinghamshire Verneys', *Econ. H.R.*, 2nd ser., XXXII (1979).

The political history of the 1640s has been characterized by a controversy about the use of the terms 'Presbyterians' and 'Independents' to describe the political groups of the period. The debate was begun by that inveterate American controversialist J. H. Hexter in 1938 in his 'The problem of the Presbyterian independent', *American Historical Review*, XLIV (1938), reprinted in his *Reappraisals in History* (1961). The major contributions to the ensuing discussion were G. Yule, *The Independents in the English Civil War* (1958); D. Underdown, 'The Independents reconsidered', *J.B.S.*, III (1964); L. Glow, 'Political affiliations in the House of Commons after Pym's death', *B.I.H.R.*, XXXVIII (1965); D. Underdown, 'The Independents again', *J.B.S.*, VIII (1968); V. Pearl, 'The "royal independents" in the English Civil War', *T.R.H.S.*, 5th ser., XVIII (1968); S. Forster, 'The Presbyterian Independents exorcised: a ghost story for historians', *P.&P.*, XLIV (1969); and J. H. Hexter, V. Pearl, David Underdown, Blair Worden, and George Yule, 'Presbyterians, Independents and Puritans', *P.&P.*, XLVII (1970).

Those tired of navigating through the morasse of conflicting views held by professional historians might find it refreshing to look at printed contemporary source material, which is abundant for this period. Here is a selection: S. R. Gardiner, ed., *Constitutional Documents of the Puritan Revolution 1625–60* (3rd ed, 1906); A. S. P. Woodhouse, ed., *Puritanism and Liberty, being the Army Debates 1647–9* (2nd edn, 1974); W. D. Macray, ed., *Clarendon's History of the Rebellion* (6 vols, 1888, repr. 1958); B. Whitelock, *Memorials of the English Affairs* (2 vols, 1853); W. Coates, ed., *The Journal of Sir Simonds D'Ewes* (1942); Lucy Hutchinson, *The Life of Colonel Hutchinson* (Oxford, 1973); Richard Baxter, *Autobiography* (ed. N. H. Keeble, 1974); D. H. Pennington and Ivan Roots, eds, *The Committee at Stafford 1643–5* (1957); D. Wolfe, ed., *Leveller Manifestos of the Puritan Revolution* (1967); W. Haller, ed., *Tracts on Liberty in the Puritan Revolution* (3 vols, 1934); W. Abbott, ed., *Writings and Speeches of Oliver Cromwell* (4 vols, 1937–47) and Christopher Hill, ed., *Winstanley: the Law of Freedom and other writings* (1973).

4. Later Stuart England 1660–1714

There is no classic history of the whole of this period to match Gardiner's multi-volume history of early seventeenth-century England. The nearest is T. B. Macaulay's account of England after 1685, *The History of England from the Accession of James II* (1849–61, ed., C. H. Firth, 1913–15). On this see C. H. Firth, *Commentary of Macaulay's History* (1938). David Ogg, *England in the reign of Charles II* (1955) and *England in the Reigns of James II and William III* (1953) are the best sources for the kind of factual information for which students of early seventeenth-century English history would turn to Gardiner's volumes. Alternatives for this purpose are G. M. Trevelyan, *England under Queen Anne* (3 vols, 1945–6) and G. N. Clark, *Oxford History of England: the later Stuarts* (1934; 2nd edn, 1955) which are old-fashioned in their interpretations of events but factually sound. For a recent survey see J. R. Jones, *Country and Court: England 1658–1714* (1978). Two volumes in the Macmillan Problems in Focus series, J. R. Jones, ed., *The Restored Monarchy 1660–88* (1979) and G. Holmes, ed., *Britain after the Glorious Revolution 1689–1714* (1969), contain invaluable bibliographical guidance and indications of recent trends in historical writing on this period.

This period has not yet been subjected to the same kind of intense historical revision as has early Stuart England and the English Revolution; this is true especially of Restoration England. Many of the books and articles on the political history of the reign of Charles II have a faintly old-fashioned air in comparison with those on the earlier periods. Apart from J. H. Sacret, 'The Restoration government and municipal corporations', *E.H.R.*, XLV (1930), D. H. Hosford, *Nottingham, Nobles and the North: aspects of the revolution of 1688* (Hamden, Connecticut 1976), and chapter 8 of J. R. Jones, *The Revolution of 1688 in England* (1972) there are no local studies on England between 1660 and 1689. There are, however, good studies of parliament, finance, early party political organization, and the importance of anti-Catholicism in politics before 1688: D. T. Whitcombe, *Charles II and the Cavalier House of Commons, 1663–74* (1966), C. D. Chandaman, *The English Public Revenue, 1660–88* (1975), J. R. Jones, *The First Whigs* (1970), and John Miller, *Popery and Politics in England 1660–88* (1973). More progress has been made in revising the political history of England after 1688 than during the reigns of Charles II and James II. J. R. Jones has taken a fresh look at *The Revolution of 1688 in England* (1972) which is now the best introductory book on this subject. The major stimulus to much of the historical revision that has taken place during the last twenty years about politics after the Glorious Revolution was the attempt by Robert Walcott in his *English Politics in the Early Eighteenth Century* (1956) to argue that political parties were not important and that the political structure of the period was like that outlined by Lewis Namier in his study of England in the middle of the eighteenth century. This provoked an opposition in the form of a legion of articles showing that political parties existed in this period (for a bibliography see H. Horwitz, 'Parties, connections and parliamentary politics, 1689–1714: review and revision', *J.B.S*, VI (1966–7). It also produced important books which are now the best introductions to political history of England in the reigns of William III and Queen Anne: J. H. Plumb, *The Growth of Political Stability in England, 1675–1725* (1967), G. Holmes, *British Politics in the Age of Anne* (1967), W. A. Speck, *Tory and Whig. The Struggle for the Constituencies, 1701–15* (1970), H. Horwitz, *Parliament, Policy and Politics in the Reign of William III* (1977), and B. W. Hill, *The Growth of Parliamentary Parties, 1689–1742* (1976). I also found J. P. Kenyon, *Revolution Principles. The Politics of Party, 1689–1720* (1977) a stimulating guide to the complicated politics of this period.

Students might like to study the history of later Stuart England by reading biographies of some major politicians. The briefest and best study of Charles II is K. H. D. Haley, *Charles II* (Historical Association Pamphlet, 1966). John Miller, *James II: a study in kingship* (1978) has many new insights into the history of England between 1660 and 1689. The standard biography of the last Stuart king is S. B. Baxter, *William III* (1966). The studies of the subjects of these later Stuart monarchs which I found most readable and useful are A. Browning, *Thomas Osborne, Earl of Danby* (3 vols, 1944–51), J. P. Kenyon, *Robert Spencer, Earl of Sunderland* (1958), K. H. D. Haley, *The First Earl of Shaftesbury* (1968), H. Horwitz, *Revolution Politics: the career of the Second Earl of Nottingham* (1968), and G. V. Bennett, *The Tory Crisis in Church and State 1688–1730: the career of Francis Atterbury Bishop of Rochester* (1975).

On foreign policy, the Church and dissent, and the economic history of later Stuart England there are useful introductory books listed in section 1. In addition K. Feiling, *British Foreign Policy, 1660–72* (1957) and especially the essays in J. S. Bromley and R. Hatton, eds, *William III and Louis XIV: essays by and for Mark A. Thomson* (1968) are invaluable. The standard works on the later Stuart Church are still the early chapters of N. Sykes, *Church and State in England in the Eighteenth Century* (1934) and *From Sheldon to Secker: aspects of English Church history 1660–1768* (1959); see also G. R. Cragg, *The Church and the Age of Reason, 1648–1789* (Pelican 1960); reading the same author's *Puritanism in the Period of the Great Persecution* (1957) is an excellent way into the history of dissent in this period, while his *From Puritanism to the Age of Reason* (1950) is unsurpassed as a general survey of theological trends and the history of ideas generally in this period. Most of the general books on economic aspects mentioned in section 1 also deal with this period, Ralph Davis, *A Commercial Revolution: English overseas trade in the seventeenth and eighteenth centuries* (Historical Association Pamphlet, 1969) deals mainly with the period after 1660, as does E. L. Jones, ed., *Agriculture and Economic Growth in England 1650–1815* (1967); the eagerly awaited *Agrarian History of England and Wales*, V will no doubt supersede this as the best single volume on this topic.

Unlike the two earlier periods there is a volume in the English Historical Documents series for this period. A. Browning, ed., *English Historical Documents, VIII: 1660–1714* (1953). Both this and W. C. Costin and J. Steven Watson, eds, *The Law and Working of the Constitution: Documents 1660–1914, I: 1660–1783* (2nd edn, 1961) are useful supplements to Kenyon, *The Stuart Constitution*, and Williams, *The Eighteenth Century Constitution* listed in section 1. Those who persevere will find that dipping into the following collections of parliamentary debates will enrich their view of the period: A. Grey, *Debates of the House of Commons from . . . 1667–1694* (10 vols, 1763); C. Robbins, ed., *The Diary of John Milward* (1938); B. D. Henning, ed., *The Parliamentary Diary of Sir Edward Dering 1670–73* (New Haven, 1940); and H. Horwitz, ed., *The Parliamentary Diary of Narcissus Luttrell, 1691–93* (1972). Easier to read and more obviously appealing are personal views of the period written by contemporaries, such as Samuel Pepys's *Diary* (ed. R. C. Latham and W. Matthews, 11 vols, 1970 – in progress), John Evelyn's *Diary* (ed. E. S. de Beer, 6 vols, 1955), the earl of Ailesbury's *Memoirs* (edited by W. E. Buckley for the Roxburgh Club, 2 vols, 1890), and Bishop G. Burnet's *History of My Own Time* (ed. J. Routh, 6 vols, 1833); on the last of these see H. C. Foxcroft, ed., *Supplement to the History of My Own Time* (1902).

Index